Intelligent Multidimensional Data and Image Processing

Sourav De
Cooch Behar Government Engineering College, India

Siddhartha Bhattacharyya
RCC Institute of Information Technology, India

Paramartha Dutta
Visva Bharati University, India

A volume in the Advances in Multimedia and
Interactive Technologies (AMIT) Book Series

Published in the United States of America by
IGI Global
Information Science Reference (an imprint of IGI Global)
701 E. Chocolate Avenue
Hershey PA, USA 17033
Tel: 717-533-8845
Fax: 717-533-8661
E-mail: cust@igi-global.com
Web site: http://www.igi-global.com

Library of Congress Cataloging-in-Publication Data

Names: De, Sourav, 1979- editor. | Bhattacharyya, Siddhartha, 1975- editor. |
   Dutta, Paramartha, editor.
Title: Intelligent multidimensional data and image processing / Sourav De,
   Siddhartha Bhattacharyya, and Paramartha Dutta, editors.
Description: Hershey, PA : Information Science Reference, [2018] | Includes
   bibliographical references.
Identifiers: LCCN 2017037447| ISBN 9781522552468 (hc) | ISBN 9781522552475
   (eISBN)
Subjects: LCSH: Three-dimensional imaging--Data processing. | Diagnostic
   imaging--Data processing. | Image processing--Digital techniques. |
   Artificial intelligence.
Classification: LCC TA1560 .I564 2018 | DDC 006.6/93--dc23 LC record available at https://lccn.loc.gov/2017037447

This book is published in the IGI Global book series Advances in Multimedia and Interactive Technologies (AMIT) (ISSN: 2327-929X; eISSN: 2327-9303)

British Cataloguing in Publication Data
A Cataloguing in Publication record for this book is available from the British Library.

All work contributed to this book is new, previously-unpublished material. The views expressed in this book are those of the authors, but not necessarily of the publisher.

For electronic access to this publication, please contact: eresources@igi-global.com.

Advances in Multimedia and Interactive Technologies (AMIT) Book Series

Joel J.P.C. Rodrigues

National Institute of Telecommunications (Inatel), Brazil &
Instituto de Telecomunicações, University of Beira Interior,
Portugal

ISSN:2327-929X
EISSN:2327-9303

MISSION

Traditional forms of media communications are continuously being challenged. The emergence of user-friendly web-based applications such as social media and Web 2.0 has expanded into everyday society, providing an interactive structure to media content such as images, audio, video, and text.

The **Advances in Multimedia and Interactive Technologies (AMIT) Book Series** investigates the relationship between multimedia technology and the usability of web applications. This series aims to highlight evolving research on interactive communication systems, tools, applications, and techniques to provide researchers, practitioners, and students of information technology, communication science, media studies, and many more with a comprehensive examination of these multimedia technology trends.

COVERAGE

- Multimedia Streaming
- Internet Technologies
- Audio Signals
- Mobile Learning
- Digital Images
- Digital Communications
- Gaming Media
- Digital Technology
- Social Networking
- Multimedia Services

IGI Global is currently accepting manuscripts for publication within this series. To submit a proposal for a volume in this series, please contact our Acquisition Editors at Acquisitions@igi-global.com or visit: http://www.igi-global.com/publish/.

Titles in this Series

For a list of additional titles in this series, please visit: www.igi-global.com/book-series

701 East Chocolate Avenue, Hershey, PA 17033, USA
Tel: 717-533-8845 x100 • Fax: 717-533-8661
E-Mail: cust@igi-global.com • www.igi-global.com

Editorial Advisory Board

Table of Contents

Detailed Table of Contents

Chapter 1
Mohamed Karam Gabr, German University in Cairo, Egypt
Rimon Elias, German University in Cairo, Egypt

Over the past years, 3D reconstruction has proved to be a challenge. With augmented reality and robotics attracting more attention, the demand for efficient 3D reconstruction algorithms has increased. 3D reconstruction presents a problem in computer vision and as a result, much work has been dedicated to solving it. Different design choices were made to consider different components of the process. Examples of these differences are how the scanning process is tackled, how the 3D reconstructed world is represented, among other aspects. Therefore, an evaluation of these algorithms is necessary. This chapter focuses on the properties that facilitate the evaluation of 3D reconstruction algorithms and provides an evaluation of the various algorithms.

Chapter 2
The Use of Written Descriptions and 2D Images as Cues for Tactile Information in Online
Flor Morton, Universidad de Monterrey, Mexico

Despite the steady growth in the use of online platforms for purchasing products in the past few years, e-commerce faces important challenges such as the inability of physically experiencing a product, specifically the inability to obtain tactile information. In this chapter, through a qualitative exploratory study approach, the author explores the possibility of conveying tactile characteristics of a product to consumers in an online shopping environment through product presentation formats such as written descriptions and 2D images. The author highlights the potential for sensory marketing through first reviewing literature on the subject with a special focus on touch and the inability to touch in online commercial channels. The methodology is presented along with the findings of the exploratory study. A concluding discussion of findings is presented and the potential for future research in the area of image processing to enhance 2D images ability to provide tactile information is discussed to conclude the chapter.

Chapter 3

Anass Nouri, University of Nantes, France
Christophe Charrier, University of Caen Normandy, France
Olivier Lezoray, University of Caen Normandy, France

This chapter concerns the visual saliency and the perceptual quality assessment of 3D meshes. Firstly, the chapter proposes a definition of visual saliency and describes the state-of-the-art methods for its detection on 3D mesh surfaces. A focus is made on a recent model of visual saliency detection for 3D colored and non-colored meshes whose results are compared with a ground-truth saliency as well as with the literature's methods. Since this model is able to estimate the visual saliency on 3D colored meshes, named colorimetric saliency, a description of the construction of a 3D colored mesh database that was used to assess its relevance is presented. The authors also describe three applications of the detailed model that respond to the problems of viewpoint selection, adaptive simplification and adaptive smoothing. Secondly, two perceptual quality assessment metrics for 3D non-colored meshes are described, analyzed, and compared with the state-of-the-art approaches.

Chapter 4

Sangita Roy, Narula Institute of Technology, India
Sheli Sinha Chaudhuri, Jadavpur University, India

Atmospheric particulate matter (APM) disturbs the biotic environment creating global warming, health hazards, and last but not the least, visibility reduction. Removing haze from degraded image is an extremely ill-posed inverse problem. Real time is another factor influencing the quality of resulting image. There is a trade-off between time and quality of resulting image. Single image makes the algorithms more challenging. In this work, the authors have developed fast, efficient, single gray or color image visibility improvement algorithms based on image formation optical model with minimum order statistics filter (MOSF) as the transmission model. The quantitative and qualitative evaluations of the proposed algorithms have been studied with other existing algorithms. The result shows improvements over existing state-of-the art algorithms with minimum time. Time has been evaluated by execution time along with time complexity Big (O). The resultant images are visibly clear satisfying the criteria for computer vision applications.

Chapter 5

Soumyadip Dhar, RCC Institute of Information Technology, India
Hiranmoy Roy, RCC Institute of Information Technology, India

In this chapter, a novel method is proposed for underwater image segmentation based on human psycho visual phenomenon (HVS). In the proposed method the texture property of an image is captured by decomposing it into frequency sub-bands using M-band wavelet packet transform. The sub-bands represent the image in different scales and orientations. The large numbers of sub-bands are pruned by an adaptive basis selection. The proper sub-bands for segmentation are selected depending on the HVS. The HVS imitates the original visual technique of a human being and it is used to divide each sub-band in Weber, De-Vries Rose, and saturation regions. A wavelet packet sub-band is selected for segmentation depending on those three regions. The performance of the proposed method is found to be superior to that of the state-of-the-art methods for underwater image segmentation on standard data set.

Chapter 6

Shashidhara H. R., JSS Academy of Technical Education, India
Siddesh G. K., JSS Academy of Technical Education, India

Authenticating the identity of an individual has become an important aspect of many organizations. The reasons being to secure authentication process, to perform automated attendance, or to provide bill payments. This need of providing automated authentication has led to concerns in the security and robustness of such biometric systems. Currently, many biometric systems that are organizations are unimodal, which means that use single physical trait to perform authentication. But, these unimodal systems suffer from many drawbacks. These drawbacks can be overcome by designing multimodal systems which use multiple physical traits to perform authentication. They increase reliability and robustness of the systems. In this chapter, analysis and comparison of multimodal biometric systems is proposed for three physical traits like iris, finger, and palm. All these traits are treated independently, and feature of these traits are extracted using two algorithms separately.

Chapter 7

Rajinikanth V., St. Joseph's College of Engineering, India
Suresh Chandra Satapathy, Kalinga Institute of Industrial Technology (Deemed), India
Nilanjan Dey, Techno India College of Technology, India
Hong Lin, University of Houston – Downtown, USA

An ischemic stroke (IS) naturally originates with rapid onset neurological shortfall, which can be verified by analyzing the internal regions of brain. Computed tomography (CT) and magnetic resonance image (MRI) are the commonly used non-invasive medical examination techniques used to record the brain abnormalities for clinical study. In order to have a pre-opinion regarding the brain abnormality in clinical level, it is essential to use a suitable image processing tool to appraise the digital CT/MR images. In this chapter, a hybrid image processing technique based on the social group optimization assisted Tsallis entropy and watershed segmentation (WS) is proposed to examine ischemic stroke region from digital CT/MR images. For the experimental study, the digital CT/MRI datasets like Radiopedia, BRATS-2013, and ISLES-2015 are considered. Experimental result of this study confirms that, proposed hybrid approach offers superior results on the considered image datasets.

Chapter 8

Priyank Saxena, Birla Institute of Technology, India
R. Sukesh Kumar, Birla Institute of Technology, India

The main aim of this chapter is to perform the restoration of computed tomography (CT) images acquired at the reduced level of radiation dose. Reduction in radiation dose affects the image quality as it increases noise and decreases low contrast resolution. In this chapter, an optimum decision-based filter (ODBF) is proposed as an image-space denoising technique, to detect and restore the low dose CT (LDCT) images corrupted with fixed valued impulse noise (salt and pepper) of unequal density. The detection stage employs k-means clustering to discriminate the noise-free pixels from the noisy-pixels by splitting the image data into three clusters of different intensities. The restoration stage employs mask else trimmed median (METM) estimation followed by an optional adaptive mask sizing for restoration of noisy pixels. The proposed method demonstrates noticeable improvement over other existing methods in restoration of LDCT images while maintaining the image contrast and edge details.

Chapter 9

Krishna Gopal Dhal, Midnapore College (Autonomous), India
Swarnajit Ray, J. B. Matrix Technology Pvt. Ltd., India
Mandira Sen, Tata Consultancy Services, India
Sanjoy Das, University of Kalyani, India

Proper enhancement and segmentation of the overexposed color skin cancer images is a great challenging task in medical image processing field. Computer-aided diagnosis (CAD) facilitates quantitative analysis of digital images with a high throughput processing rate. But, analysis of CAD purely depends on the input image quality. Therefore, in this study, overexposed and washed out skin cancer images are enhanced properly with the help of exact hue-saturation-intensity (eHSI) color model and contrast limited adaptive histogram equalization (CLAHE) method which is applied through this model. eHSI color model is hue preserving and gamut problem free. Any gray level image enhancement method can be easily employed for color image through this eHSI model. The segmentation of these enhanced color images has been done by employing one unsupervised clustering approach with the assistance of seven different gray level thresholding methods. Comparison of the segmentation efficiency of gray level thresholding methods has been done in the cases of overexposed as well as for enhanced images.

Chapter 10

Mohamed Fawzy Aly, Cairo University, Egypt
Mahmood A. Mahmood, Cairo University, Egypt

Medical images are digital representations of the body. Medical imaging technology has improved tremendously in the past few decades. The amount of diagnostic data produced in a medical image is vast and as a result could create problems when sending the medical data through a network. To overcome this, there is a great need for the compression of medical images for communication and storage purposes. This chapter contains an introduction to compression types, an overview of medical image modalities, and a survey on coding techniques that deal with 3D medical image compression.

Chapter 11

Deepika Dubey, SRCEM Gwalior, India
Uday Pratap Singh, Madhav Institute of Technology and Science, India

In this chapter, the authors present the technique of medical image segmentation which means to partition an image into non-overlapping regions based on intensity. The active contour is one of the most successful level set methods for segmentation and it is widely applicable in various image processing applications including medical image segmentation. Biomedical image segmentation and analysis plays an important role in medical science and healthcare. This chapter proposes a momentum term and resilient propagation-based gradient descent method which will remove the sensitivity of local minima of gradient descent. Proposed method is applicable in case of diseases like retinal, diabetic, and glaucoma, etc. Medical image segmentation via momentum and resilient propagation based gradient descent method can be optimized and effectively used. Extensive experiments have been performed over medical images to test the ability of the system. The proposed method is able to present the segmented medical image with clear and smooth boundary also it is simple to design and implementation.

The detection of cancer in the breast is done using mammograms (x-ray images). The authors propose a CAD framework for distinguishing little changes in mammogram which may demonstrate malignancies which are too little to be felt either by the lady herself or by a radiologist. In this chapter, they build up a framework for analysis, visualization, and prediction of cancer in breast tissue by utilizing Intelligent based wavelet classifier. Intelligent-based wavelet classifier is a new approach constructed using texture value and wavelet neural network. The proposed framework is applied to the genuine clinical database of 160 mammograms gathered from mammogram screening focuses. The execution of the CAD framework is examined utilizing ROC curve. This will help the specialists in determination of the breast tissues either cancerous or noncancerous in an accurate way.

To improve the classification accuracy of multidimensional overlapping objects, a new hybrid neuro-fuzzy FCNN-SOM-FMLP network, combining the fuzzy cell neural network of Kohonen (FCNN-SOM) and the fuzzy multilayer perceptron (FMLP), and the algorithms for its training are proposed. This combination allows for clustering of generalized intersecting patterns (the extensional approach) and training the classification network basing on the identification of integrated pattern characteristics in the isolated clusters (intentional approach). The new FCNN-SOM-FMLP architecture features a high degree of self-organization of neurons, an ability to manage selectively individual neuronal connections (to solve the problem of "dead" neurons), the high flexibility, and the ease of implementation. The experimental results show the temporal efficiency of algorithms of self-organization and training and the improvement of the separating properties of the network in the case of overlapping clusters. Calculated technological and economic generalized values of countries.

Advancements in technologies and increasing popularities of social media websites have enabled people to view, create, and share user-generated content (UGC) on the web. This results in a huge amount of UGC (e.g., photos, videos, and texts) on the web. Since such content depicts ideas, opinions, and interests of users, it requires analyzing the content efficiently to provide personalized services to users. Thus, it necessitates determining semantics and sentiments information from UGC. Such information help in decision making, learning, and recommendations. Since this chapter is based on the intuition that semantics and sentiment information are exhibited by different representations of data, the effectiveness of multimodal techniques is shown in semantics and affective computing. This chapter describes several significant multimedia analytics problems such as multimedia summarization, tag-relevance computation, multimedia recommendation, and facilitating e-learning and their solutions.

Preface

Images play a vital role as images are the most natural and convenient means of conveying or transmitting information. The information about positions, sizes and inter-relationships between objects can be obtained from an image.

The field of image processing has assumed paramount importance in the computer vision research community given the vast amount of uncertainty involved therein. Basically, proper processing of two-dimensional (2D) real life images play a key role in many real-life applications as well as in commercial developments. Due to the immense underlying data content and at the same time, the inadequacy of data description standards, three-dimensional (3D) object extraction is a challenging proposition for quality enhancement, segmentation and analysis. Basically, the application of the machine vision mostly runs by the three-dimensional image processing. 3D vision system can be categorized into four stages, i.e., data acquisition, low-level processing, object representation and matching. 3D image processing has also other application areas, like, geometric compression, volume visualization, object modeling, image registration, etc.

Due to less amount of data content and data variety, the 2D image processing is in limelight in research arena as well as in commercial arena. Due to unavailability of the 3D information about the subject, extraction of 3D volume images assumes greater complexity. Moreover, the integration of the 3D sensing capability with the human perception system may not be always successful in the implementation phases. The unavailability of well-known 3D image formats or data description standards is another setback for 3D image processing.

Basically, image processing techniques used to handle the noise removal, segmentation of the objects, object extraction, classification of the objects by a classifier to determine the nearest object classification and its associated confidence level. With the limitation and shortcoming of classical platforms of computation, particularly for handling uncertainty and imprecision prevalent in the challenging thoroughfare of image processing, Intelligence as an alternative and extended computation paradigm has been making its presence felt. Accordingly, a phenomenal growth of research initiative in this field is quite evident. Intelligence techniques include (1) the elements of fuzzy mathematics, primarily used for handling various real life problems engrossed with uncertainty, (2) the ingredients of artificial neural networks, usually applied for cognition, learning and subsequent recognition by machine inducing thereby the flavor of intelligence in a machine through the process of its learning and (3) components of evolutionary computation mainly used for search, exploration, efficient exploitation of contextual information and knowledge useful for optimization.

The proposed book would come to the benefits of several categories of students and researchers. At the students' level, this book can serve as a treatise/reference book for the special papers at the masters level aimed at inspiring possibly future researchers. Newly inducted PhD aspirants would also find the contents of this book useful as far as their compulsory course-works are concerned.

At the researchers' level, those interested in interdisciplinary research would also be benefited from the book. After all, the enriched interdisciplinary contents of the book would always be a subject of interest to the faculties, existing research communities and new research aspirants from diverse disciplines of the concerned departments of premier institutes across the globe. This is expected to bring different research backgrounds (due to its cross platform characteristics) close to one another to form effective research groups all over the world. Above all, availability of the book should be ensured to as much universities and research institutes as possible through whatever graceful means it may be.

The book comprises 14 well-versed chapters centered around the theme of the book.

Over the past years, 3D reconstruction has proved to be a challenging problem. Alongside that, with augmented reality and robotics attracting more attention, the demand for efficient 3D reconstruction algorithms has increased respectively. As 3D reconstruction presents an old problem in computer vision, much work is committed to it. Chapter 1 presents the properties which facilitate evaluating 3D reconstruction algorithms; afterwards, it demonstrates the evaluation of various algorithms.

Despite the steady growth in the use of online platforms for purchasing products in the past few years, e-commerce faces important challenges such as the inability of physically experiencing a product, specifically, the inability to obtain tactile information. In Chapter 2, through a qualitative exploratory study approach, the author explores the possibility of conveying tactile characteristics of a product to consumers in an online shopping environment through product presentation formats such as written descriptions and 2D images. The author highlights the potential for sensory marketing through first reviewing literature on the subject with a special focus on touch and the inability to touch in online commercial channels. The methodology is presented along with the findings of the exploratory study. A concluding discussion of findings is presented and the potential for future research in the area of image processing to enhance 2D images ability to provide tactile information is discussed to conclude the chapter.

Chapter 3 concerns the visual saliency and the perceptual quality assessment of 3D meshes. Firstly, the chapter proposes a definition of visual saliency and describes the state-of-the-art methods for its detection on 3D mesh surfaces. A focus is made on a recent model of visual saliency detection for 3D colored and non colored meshes whose results are compared with a ground-truth saliency as well as with the literature's methods. Since this model is able to estimate the visual saliency on 3D colored meshes, named colorimetric saliency, a description of the construction of a 3D colored mesh database that was used to assess its relevance is presented. The authors also describe three applications of the detailed model that respond to the problems of viewpoint selection, adaptive simplification and adaptive smoothing. Secondly, two perceptual quality assessment metrics for 3D non colored meshes are described, analyzed and compared with the state-of-the-art approaches.

Atmospheric Particulate Matter (APM) disturbs the biotic environment creating global warming, health hazards, and last but not the least visibility reduction. Removing haze from degraded image is extremely ill-posed Inverse problem. Real time is another factor influencing the quality of resulting image. There is a trade-off between time and quality of resulting image. Single image makes the algorithms more challenging. In Chapter 4, the authors have developed fast, efficient single gray or color image visibility improvement algorithms based on image formation optical model with minimum order statistics filter (MOSF) as the transmission model. The quantitative and qualitative evaluations of the proposed algorithms have been studied with other existing algorithms.

In this Chapter 5, a novel method is proposed for underwater image segmentation based on human psycho visual phenomenon (HVS). In the proposed method the texture property of an image is captured by decomposing it into frequency sub-bands using M-band wavelet packet transform. The sub-bands represent the image in different scales and orientations. The large numbers of sub-bands are pruned by an adaptive basis selection. The proper sub-bands for segmentation are selected depending on the HVS.

Authenticating the identity of an individual has become an important aspect of many organizations. The reasons are to secure authentication process, to perform automated attendance or to provide bill payments. This need of providing automated authentication has lead to concerns in the security and robustness of such biometric systems. Currently, many biometric systems that are organizations are unimodal, which means that use single physical trait to perform authentication. But, these unimodal systems suffer from many drawbacks. These drawbacks can be overcome by designing multimodal systems which use multiple physical traits to perform authentication. They increase reliability and robustness of the systems. In Chapter 6, an analysis and comparison of multimodal biometric systems is proposed for three physical traits like iris, finger and palm. All these traits are treated independently and feature of these traits are extracted using two algorithms separately.

An Ischemic Stroke (IS) naturally originates with rapid onset neurological shortfall, which can be verified by analyzing the internal regions of brain. Computed Tomography (CT) and Magnetic Resonance Image (MRI) are the commonly used non-invasive medical examination techniques used to record the brain abnormalities for clinical study. In order to have a pre-opinion regarding the brain abnormality in clinical level, it is essential to use a suitable image processing tool to appraise the digital CT/MR images. In Chapter 7, a hybrid image processing technique based on the Social group optimization assisted Tsallis entropy and Watershed Segmentation (WS) is proposed to examine ischemic stroke region from digital CT/MR images. For the experimental study, the digital CT/MRI datasets like Radiopedia, BRATS-2013, and ISLES-2015 are considered. Experimental result of this study confirms that, proposed hybrid approach offers superior results on the considered image datasets.

The main aim Chapter 8 is to perform the restoration of Computed Tomography (CT) images acquired at the reduced level of radiation dose. Reduction in radiation dose affects the image quality as it increases noise and decreases low contrast resolution. In this chapter, an Optimum Decision Based Filter (ODBF) is proposed as an image-space denoising technique, to detect and restore the low dose CT (LDCT) images corrupted with fixed valued impulse noise (salt & pepper) of unequal density. The detection stage employs k-means clustering to discriminate the noise-free pixels from the noisy-pixels by splitting the image data into three clusters of different intensities. The restoration stage employs Mask Else Trimmed Median (METM) estimation followed by an optional adaptive mask sizing for restoration of noisy pixels. The proposed method demonstrates noticeable improvement over other existing methods in restoration of LDCT images while maintaining the image contrast and edge details.

Proper enhancement and segmentation of the overexposed color skin cancer images is a great challenging task in medical image processing field. Computer-aided diagnosis (CAD) facilitates quantitative analysis of digital images with a high throughput processing rate. But, analysis of CAD is purely depends on the input image quality. Therefore, Chapter 9 presents a method for processing of overexposed and washed out skin cancer images with the help of Exact Hue-Saturation-Intensity (eHSI) color model and Contrast Limited Adaptive Histogram Equalization (CLAHE) method which is applied through this model.

Medical Images are the digital representation of the body images. The medical imaging technology has a tremendous growth in past few decades. The amount of diagnostic data produced in a medical image is vast and this could create several problems when sending the medical data through a network. To overcome this problem there is a great need for compression of medical images for communication and storage purposes. Chapter 10 provides an introduction on compression types, then overview on medical images modalities, and then a survey on coding techniques that deal with 3d medical images compression.

In Chapter 11, the authors present a technique of medical image segmentation which means to partition an image into non-overlapping regions based on intensity. The active contour is one of the most successful level set methods for segmentation and it is widely applicable in various image processing applications including medical image segmentation. Biomedical image segmentation and analysis plays an important role in medical science and health care. In this chapter, the authors propose a momentum term and resilient propagation based gradient descent method which will remove the sensitivity of local minima of gradient descent. The proposed method is applicable in case of diseases like retinal, diabetic and glaucoma etc. Medical image segmentation via momentum and resilient propagation based gradient descent method can be optimized and effectively used. Extensive experiments have been performed over medical images to test the ability of the system. The proposed method is able to present the segmented medical image with clear and smooth boundary also it is simple to design and implementation.

The detection of cancer in the breast is done using mammograms (X-ray images). Chapter 12 presents a CAD framework for distinguishing little changes in mammogram which may demonstrate malignancies which are too little to be felt either by the lady herself or by a radiologist. In this chapter, the authors build up a framework for analysis, visualization, and prediction of cancer in breast tissue by utilizing an intelligent based wavelet classifier.

To improve the classification accuracy of multidimensional overlapping objects, a new hybrid neuro-fuzzy FCNN-SOM-FMLP network, combining the fuzzy cell neural network of Kohonen (FCNN-SOM) and the fuzzy multilayer perceptron (FMLP), and the algorithms for its training, are proposed in Chapter 13. This combination allows for clustering of generalized intersecting patterns (the extensional approach) and training the classification network based on the identification of integrated pattern characteristics in the isolated clusters. The new FCNN-SOM-FMLP architecture features a high degree of self-organization of neurons, an ability to manage selectively individual neuronal connections (to solve the problem of "dead" neurons), the high flexibility and the ease of implementation.

Advancements in technologies and increasing popularities of social media websites have enabled people to view, create, and share user-generated content (UGC) on the web. This results in a huge amount of UGC (e.g., photos, videos, and texts) on the web. Since such content depicts ideas, opinions, and interests of users, it requires analyzing the content efficiently to provide personalized services to users. Thus, it necessitates determining semantics and sentiments information from UGC. Such information helps in decision-making, learning, and recommendations. Chapter 14 is based on the intuition that semantics and sentiment information are exhibited by different representations of data and that the effectiveness of multimodal techniques is shown in semantics and affective computing. This chapter describes several significant multimedia analytics problems such as multimedia summarization, tag-relevance computation, multimedia recommendation, and facilitating e-learning and their solutions.

The objective of this book is to bring a broad spectrum of artificial intelligence and its applications under the purview of 3D image processing so that it is able to trigger further inspiration among various research communities to contribute in their respective fields of applications thereby orienting these application fields towards 3D image processing and analysis.

Once the purpose, as stated above, is achieved a larger number of research communities may be brought under one umbrella to ventilate their ideas in a more structured manner. In that case, the present endeavor may be seen as the beginning of such an effort in bringing various research applications in the complementary fields of 3D image processing and analysis close to one another.

Sourav De
Cooch Behar Government Engineering College, India

Siddhartha Bhattacharyya
RCC Institute of Information Technology, India

Paramartha Dutta
Visva Bharati University, India

Chapter 1
3D Reconstruction Algorithms Survey

Mohamed Karam Gabr
German University in Cairo, Egypt

Rimon Elias
German University in Cairo, Egypt

ABSTRACT

Over the past years, 3D reconstruction has proved to be a challenge. With augmented reality and robotics attracting more attention, the demand for efficient 3D reconstruction algorithms has increased. 3D reconstruction presents a problem in computer vision and as a result, much work has been dedicated to solving it. Different design choices were made to consider different components of the process. Examples of these differences are how the scanning process is tackled, how the 3D reconstructed world is represented, among other aspects. Therefore, an evaluation of these algorithms is necessary. This chapter focuses on the properties that facilitate the evaluation of 3D reconstruction algorithms and provides an evaluation of the various algorithms.

INTRODUCTION

Three-dimensional reconstruction, the process of building 3D models out of multiple 2D scans representing different views of some objects, has presented a challenging problem that attracted much research attention for decades in computer vision. The hardness of the 3D reconstruction problem arises from the necessity of correlating the locations, alongside colors, of some features among different 2D scans in order to decide their locations in the 3D world. Due to the variance of applications, scanners setup alongside the algorithms in use varies as well. In other words, the nature of the application enforces the scanners setup and the algorithm in use. For example, 3D reconstructing an animated real life objects that we cannot control its motion pattern (an animal for example) demands the multiple 2D scans to be taken at once to capture the same pose in all views (as having multiple scanners in use at once). On the other hand, for 3D reconstruction of other objects, a turntable and a single 2D camera can be enough.

DOI: 10.4018/978-1-5225-5246-8.ch001

As mentioned above, the process of 3D reconstruction relies heavily upon the nature of the application, which directs (sometimes enforces) the scanning setup, changing the nature of the input provided by the scanning process. Thus, to fully evaluate 3D reconstruction algorithms, the nature of the scanning mechanism is to be taken into consideration. Three-dimensional scanning mechanisms (non-contact based to be more specific), can be divided into two categories: active and passive. *Active scanners* are those that use special light emitters as part of their setup. (Examples of active scanning methods are setups that use laser scanning.) Hence, these scanning setups demand specific components hardware, which caused these methods to attract less research attention.

Passive scanning, on the other hand, utilizes regular cameras. This approach has many advantages over the active one, which made it attract much more research interests over years. The main advantage of passive scanning over active scanning, is that no special hardware is needed, which makes it more applicable and useable. Another advantage is that cameras are easy to configure and calibrate in order to facilitate the process of correlating features among different views.

As per the provided discussion, defining a solid ground of comparison between various 3D reconstruction approaches is not straightforward. Alongside that, the aspects of improvement from one research view to another vary as well. Thus, over the past years, the process of 3D reconstruction has been subject of too many improvements. The aim of this work is to build a state-of-the-art survey on different 3D reconstruction techniques, with respect to the 3D scanning mechanisms in use, taking into consideration the range of applications of each. More specifically, this work will focus on the work committed in this field during the last decade, as older algorithms are reviewed in older surveys, as it will be presented in the background.

BACKGROUND

As mentioned above, this work will demonstrate various 3D reconstruction algorithms, and provide evaluations for them. Prior to this work, there are two surveys in this field, Slabaugh *et al.* (Slabaugh, Schafer, Malzbender, & Culbertson, 2001) that evaluated algorithms up to 2001, and Seitz *et al.* (Seitz, Curless, Diebel, Scharstein, & Szeliski, 2006) that evaluated algorithms up to 2006. Nevertheless, each of them had different perspective while evaluating the reviewed algorithms. In the rest of this section, each perspective is discussed.

Algorithms up to 2001

Slabaugh et al. (Slabaugh, Schafer, Malzbender, & Culbertson, 2001) demonstrated and reviewed work dated back to 1984 up to 2001. In their work, they presented two restrictions on the algorithms they reviewed; also they divided the algorithms into three categories. Restrictions, alongside categories are discussed in the sections below.

Restrictions

The first restriction they enforced is that they reviewed algorithms with sampled volumetric representations. Sampled volumetric representation refers to representing both real and reconstructed spaces as discrete colored points, known as pixels in 2D space and voxels in 3D space. Enforcing such restriction would result in avoiding some algorithms like (Pentland, 1990; Terzopoulos & Metaxas 1990). (Other representation techniques, like polygon meshes and depth maps are represented below in the work of Seitz et al.)

The second restriction is that the input to the reconstruction process is in the form of photographs. This restriction avoids algorithms that use active 3D scanning (laser scanning for example) as they require special hardware as mentioned in the introduction. Moreover, the input photographs should be provided by calibrated cameras. The advantage of having the photographs provided by calibrated cameras is that, given the location of a feature in 3D, its projection on different calibrated 2D views is calculable. This facilitates the reconstruction process as features correlation among different views is an important step in the process. However, this restriction requires having full control over the scene to be reconstructed, which in turn enforces some restrictions on the object to be reconstructed (size and portability for example).

Other restrictions are that objects are formed of Lambertian surfaces, and can be easily segmented from the background. Lambertian surfaces refer to surfaces that reflect light uniformly, unlike mirrors and transparent surfaces. Easy segmentation can be achieved by making the difference between the background and the foreground easy to detect. Ways of facilitating the segmentation process are, for example, make the background less detailed than the object to be scanned, or color the background in a color that does not exist in the object. This enforced more restrictions, however, they are assumed by most algorithms.

Categories

Slabaugh et al. categorized algorithms into three categories, namely: *Volumetric Visual Hull*, *Voxel Coloring Methods,* and *Volumetric Pairwise Feature Matching*, which are presented below.

Volumetric Visual Hull

Visual hulls, as defined in (Laurentini, 1994), are shapes that result from intersecting the volumes produced from all viewpoints. (Silhouettes of an object are its projections on different 2D views.) Producing a volume out of an object silhouette on a 2D image is performed by calculating the projection of the silhouette of the object back into the 3D world, given the calibrations of the camera creating this view. Thus, the overall process works as per the following steps:

Step 1: Segmenting silhouettes out of the given views
Step 2: Calculate the projected volume of each view
Step 3: Intersect these volumes creating a convex visual hull

Various improvements were made for each step, resulting in including many algorithms under this category (Worthy, Martin, & Aggarwal, 1983; Chien & Aggarwal, 1984, 1986; Shneier, Kent, & Mansbach, 1984; Massone, Morasso, & Zaccaria, 1985; Potmesil, 1985; Srivastava & Ahuja, 1990; Szeliski, 1993; Gortler, Grzeszczuk, Szeliski, & Cohen, 1996; García & Brunet, 1998; Luong & Faugeras, 1996; Saito & Kanade, 1999; Seitz & Dyer, 1995; Collins, 1996; Fromherz & Bichsel, 1994, 1995; Moezzi, Katkere, Kuramura, & Jain, 1996; Moezzi, Tai, & Gerard, 1997). The output shape of this process always encloses the real object. Moreover, the more input views the process gets, the smaller (and more accurate) the output shape; hence, the closer it is to the real object. Alongside that, this process produces what is called the convex hull of the object. Therefore, if the object is of a convex geometrical nature, given enough views, the 3D reconstructed object will be of a good quality. On the other hand, if the object contains many concavities, such an approach would fail in reconstructing it properly.

Voxel Coloring Methods

Algorithms under this category have a different perspective than visual hulls. The main procedure here is to loop over voxels one by one checking if it is consistent or not. Consistent voxels are those existing in each view, with the same color, where they should be. A consistent voxel gets colored, otherwise it is set to be transparent (or vacant). Checking voxel consistency starts by calculating its visibility, which is deciding in which images the voxel can be seen. Considering that this process is to be performed for every single voxel in the reconstruction space, this process presents a runtime bottleneck. Under this category, algorithms can be divided into three groups, space carving, generalized voxel coloring, and multi-hypothesis voxel coloring. Examples of space carving are (Kutulakos, 2000; Kutulakos & Seitz, 2000). Generalized voxel coloring is demonstrated in (Culbertson, Malzbender, & Slabaugh, 1999). Finally, (Eisert, Steinbach, & Girod, 1999) introduced multi-hypothesis voxel coloring technique.

Volumetric Pairwise Feature Matching

In this category, the main scope is objects scanned by a pair of cameras which are along epipolar lines that can be cross-correlated. These cameras produce pairs of images picturing the same side of the objects, and these objects (alongside their features) can be cross-correlated as well. The result of the cross-correlation process is what is called disparity vectors. Examples of work falling under this category are (Chen & Medioni, 1999; Faugeras & Keriven, 2002). This category is considered to be the most limited of the three. This is caused by the constraints enforced on the epipolar lines. Some of these constraints are that the cameras cannot be placed so far from each other, and the cameras are only viewing one side of the object (which is not a full 3D view).

Algorithms up to 2006

In the work of Seitz et al. (Seitz et al., 2006), they focused on algorithms developed between years 2001 and 2006. Out of this timeline, they limited the review for algorithms that produce dense models out of calibrated views. This limitation caused this review not to include any stereo methods that rely on having a baseline connecting cameras, binocular cameras for example, as they produce a single side depth map (as mentioned above). Also they share the same limitation that is assumed by most algorithms, that objects are formed of Lambertian surfaces.

Between years 2001 and 2006, 3D reconstruction algorithms development took the form of being application driven instead of solving the general form of the problem. Such a perspective resulted in making 3D reconstruction algorithms vary to the level of they are no longer comparable. Alongside that, some algorithms with very specific application would fail completely in reconstructing any other object other than those they are made for. For example, an algorithm that is built for reconstructing human faces would not be suitable for reconstructing a building. This would be caused by many assumptions made by the algorithm that does not apply to a building, like assuming the existence of specific features like eyes and nose for example. For this reason, to develop a ground of correlation among algorithms, the authors introduced six properties that classify these algorithms. Namely the properties are: *Scene*

Representation, Photo Consistency Measure, Visibility Model, Shape Prior, Reconstruction Algorithm, and Initialization Requirements. These properties are presented in more details in the following sections.

Scene Representation

Scene representation defines how the world and the scanned objects are modeled in different stages of the whole process. In this work, they discussed many representation techniques, which are demonstrated below.

Voxels

Voxels, or in other words the regularly sampled 3D grid (as mentioned above), are the most common in most algorithms (Broadhurst, Drummond, & Cipolla, 2001; Bhotika, Fleet, & Kutulakos, 2002; Yang, 2003; Bonfort & Sturm, 2003; Treuille, Hertzmann, & Seitz, 2004; Slabaugh, Culbertson, Malzbender, Stevens, & Schafer, 2004; Vogiatzis, Torr, & Cipolla, 2005). The main advantage of using voxels is that they are simple, uniform, and easy to use approximating any surface.

Polygon Meshes

Using polygon meshes as the representation method, surfaces are modeled as connected polygon patches (Zhang & Seitz, 2001; Isidoro & Sclaroff, 2003; Esteban & Schmitt, 2004; Yu, Xu, & Ahuja, 2004). There are many advantages for this representation method. First, it is efficient to store and render. Second, having the surface modeled as polygon patches facilitates visibility computations. Finally, this is the representation method many multi-view algorithms use as output format.

Depth Maps

Depth maps representation methods work by converting each 2D view into a depth map by segmenting different objects in the view, and deciding which is near and which is far (Kang, Szeliski, & Chai, 2001; Kolmogorov & Zabih, 2002; Zitnick, Kang, Uyttendaele, Winder, & Szeliski, 2004; Gargallo & Sturm, 2005; Drouin, Trudeau, & Roy, 2005; Vogiatzis, Torr, Seitz, & Cipolla, 2004; Zeng, Paris, Quan, & Sillion, 2005). This approach simplifies the geometrical nature of the 3D domain, and can make use of fewer 2D views.

Photo Consistency Measure

Photo consistency measure refers to how the correlation between different views with respect to a set of pixels representing the same object is built (Jin, 2003; Jin, Soatto, & Yezzi, 2003; Esteban & Schmitt, 2004; Slabaugh, Culbertson, Malzbender, Stevens, & Schafer, 2004). This is achievable by correlating the view directions of the multi-views with each other. Such correlation can be modeled with respect to the images space or the scene space. In both cases, the main procedure revolves around calculating the projection of the object into multi-views, given their calibration, and compares these calculated projections with the actual projections in the views. The difference between the calculated and the actual projections is called prediction error (Pons, Keriven, & Faugeras, 2005). Prediction error is used to better locate the object (or a specific feature) into the 3D reconstructed scene.

Visibility Model

Visibility model accounts for the possibility of the object (or a feature) not to be fully seen in one of the views in-hand. The occurrence of this problem depends on the way the viewpoints are distributed around the object, which is bound to happen in case full object coverage is sought. Thus, these views should be excluded from the photo consistency measure process. Thus, algorithms simply avoid this problem by limiting the positions the cameras can be in; however, this directly affects the full visibility of the object from all directions.

In the work conducted below, the authors divided the techniques for handling visibility to three types: geometric, quasi-geometric, and outlier-based approaches.

Geometric

In the case of geometric techniques, an estimate of the geometrical state in each view is made to predict the visibility of the point on the surface in these view (Kutulakos & Seitz, 2000; Kutulakos, 2000; Vogiatzis, Torr, & Cipolla, 2005; Zhang & Seitz, 2001; Isidoro & Sclaroff, 2003; Zeng, Paris, Quan, & Sillion, 2005). As an attempt of making the estimate conservative, it is favored to eliminate views where the points are visible rather than including views in which the points are not visible.

Quasi-Geometric

Quasi-geometric utilizes the geometric techniques and adds to them other reasoning component. The added reasoning component comes on the form of clustering cameras (Esteban & Schmitt, 2004), or estimating the shape of the surface (Vogiatzis, Torr, & Cipolla, 2005; Sinha & Pollefeys, 2005), in order to minimize the input set before processing.

Outlier-Based

Instead of considering the scene and the camera setup geometrically, outlier-based technique pays attention to occlusions. A heuristic function is used to avoid comparing far apart views with each other to increase the inlier chances (Kang, Szeliski, & Chai, 2001; Gargallo & Sturm, 2005; Drouin, Trudeau, & Roy, 2005).

Shape Prior

Building on the output provided by the photo consistency measure and visibility model steps (which are considered to be estimates about the visibility of surfaces and their geometrical aspects), shape prior adds the estimate about how smooth the surface should be. The choice of smoothness level depends on the algorithm procedure used in the reconstruction. For example, algorithms that use meshes in their reconstruction steps tend to smooth the object more (based on the size of the patches, the bigger the patch the smoother the output model), which is harmful for objects with high curvatures (Vogiatzis, Torr, & Cipolla, 2005; Sinha & Pollefeys, 2005; Zhang & Seitz, 2001; Esteban & Schmitt, 2004). On the other hand, algorithms that use voxels instead tend to smooth less, as the building unit is smaller, it has the capability to model smaller details (Bonfort & Sturm, 2003; Slabaugh, Culbertson, Malzbender, Stevens, & Schafer, 2004). This approach comes with the gain of representing highly curved and thin objects better; however, the cost is a much slower overall process. As a middle ground approach, the work (Kolmogorov & Zabih, 2002; Zitnick et al., 2004) applies local shape prior, which means that the smoothness factor may change along the surface.

Reconstruction Algorithm

The reconstruction algorithm is where all the previously analyzed data meet in order to produce the 3D model out of the scanned object. Reconstruction algorithms perform differently based on the available data, and the output format they produce. Based on the nature of the objects and environments, the task of reconstruction can become easier or harder. In other words, the more constrained the objects and the environments (objects of uniform geometrical shapes on blank backgrounds for example), the more efficient performance and accurate output can be achieved, and vice versa. In their work, Seitz *et al.* categorized reconstruction algorithm into four classes.

The first class operates by assigning scores to volumes, then reconstructing those with high scores (Treuille, Hertzmann, & Seitz, 2004; Vogiatzis, Torr, & Cipolla, 2005; Sinha & Pollefeys, 2005; Kolmogorov & Zabih, 2002). Voxel coloring is a member of this class. The second class starts by considering a surface, then iteratively improving it approaching more accurate models (Bhotika, Fleet, & Kutulakos, 2002; Slabaugh et al., 2004; Zeng, Paris, Quan, & Sillion, 2005; Zhang & Seitz, 2001; Isidoro & Sclaroff, 2003; Yu, Xu, & Ahuja, 2004). Space carving is one example of algorithms in this class. The third class algorithms utilize depth maps, either by merging them, or enforcing consistency constraints between them (Zitnick, Kang, Uyttendaele, Winder, & Szeliski, 2004; Gargallo & Sturm, 2005). Finally, the last class of algorithms locates features on objects (or consider them as input), then builds patches connecting them (Taylor, 2003).

Initialization Requirement

Initialization requirements consider, not only the constraints mentioned above, but also more geometrical aspects of the scenes and the cameras orientations. These requirements present the level of constraints that should exist for the whole process to produce the output desired. More importantly, these requirements define the capability of a certain scanning/reconstruction method to scan and reconstruct various objects. Consequently, such an aspect is the first to consider while deciding which scanning/reconstruction setup is suitable for which application. Many algorithms require the object to be scanned to fit in a specifically sized area (Bhotika, Fleet, & Kutulakos, 2002; Slabaugh, Culbertson, Malzbender, Stevens, & Schafer, 2004; Zeng, Paris, Quan, & Sillion, 2005). Some algorithms, as mentioned above, assume easy distinction between the foreground and the background in each view to facilitate the segmentation process (Vogiatzis, Torr, & Cipolla, 2005; Sinha & Pollefeys, 2005). Other algorithms assume some limitations in cameras placements with respect to the object location to limit the near and far values in the image space (Kolmogorov & Zabih, 2002; Zitnick et al., 2004; Gargallo & Sturm, 2005).

ALGORITHMS UP UNTIL NOW

In the following sections, modern 3D reconstruction approaches are presented. In recent years, machine learning was proved to provide useful assistance in solving various feature detection problems. Semantic

3D reconstruction, as presented below, utilizes the power of feature detection of machine learning in order to facilitate 3D reconstructing scenes with known object classes. Another group of approaches is making use of the Kinect sensor, as an RGBD camera (as discussed in RGBD scanning 3D reconstruction). Alongside these approaches, other approaches are presented, addressing different forms of the classical 3D reconstruction problem.

Semantic 3D Reconstruction

As a preprocessing step, several semantic classes are created for objects that can exist in the to-be-reconstructed scene. These classes are used afterwards in both segmentation and reconstruction processes (Russell, Kohli, & Torr, 2009; Ladický et al., 2012; Hane, Zach, Cohen, Angst, & Pollefeys, 2013; Zach, Hane, & Pollefeys, 2014; Savinov, Ladicky, Hane, & Pollefeys, 2015; Cherabier, Hane, Oswald, & Pollefeys, 2016; Hane, Zach, Cohen, & Pollefeys, 2017). In the application demonstrated in (Ladický et al., 2012), street-views presented the to-be-reconstructed scene. For that, seven classes were created, namely: *Building*, *Sky*, *Car*, *Road*, *Person*, *Bike* and *Sidewalk*, alongside an eighth class named *void*. The *void* class is used to refer to any object that cannot be referred to using any of the other seven classes.

Unlike the foreground/background segmentation mentioned above, the segmentation process in this work is addressed differently, resulting in a different output as well. The output of the semantic segmentation process is the input image with each pixel labeled with one of the eight classes. This process is performed using a machine learning engine, which was provided with a data set containing fully labeled images.

Alongside using the predefined classes in the segmentation process, they are utilized in the reconstruction process as well. The first benefit of having these classes of objects, utilizing the knowledge of the geometrical aspects of these objects in real life, transforming these geometrical aspects into the reconstructed world is more facilitated than treating objects as arbitral ones. Besides, some of the not-well-observed objects in the scene can be estimated.

As a clear initialization requirement for this 3D reconstruction technique, all objects subject for reconstruction need to be previously determined, learning data sets is created for these objects, and semantic classes are created for them. This is achievable by defining a semantic class for each, alongside providing a learning data set of fully labeled images containing them. In case such a requirement is not met, these objects would be labeled as void, resulting in complete exclusion of them from the reconstruction process.

RGBD Scanning 3D Reconstruction

RGBD scanning refers to having normal *red*, *green*, and *blue* imagery alongside a *depth* one. Moreover, it is commonly used to refer to Microsoft's Kinect sensor. Previously, as mentioned above, passive scanning was favored for the lack of need for specific hardware. More recently, with the release of Kinect on November 10, 2010, such constraint started to change. Beside its initial application as a tool for entertainment, Kinect attracted some researchers' attention. This is caused by its scanning capabilities, alongside its reasonable price and availability.

Distinguishable from all other passive scanning techniques discussed in this chapter, Kinect presents an active scanning one (Khoshelham, 2011). As part of the Kinect toolkit, it contains an infrared laser emitter, an infrared camera and an RGB camera. The scanning process is initiated by the laser emitter emitting a single beam. Using a specific diffraction grating, the emitted beam is split into multiple beams, generating a specific beams pattern, projected onto the scene. After capturing this projection using the infrared camera, the captured pattern is compared with a reference pattern. The reference pattern is created by projecting the beams on a plane at a specific distance from the device, then the projected pattern is captured and stored in the device memory (alongside the distance the plane is at afar from the device), during the manufacturing process. The variance between the captured and the reference patterns is calculated, and then used to calculate disparities among beams landing locations, which is used in creating a depth image of the scene. Finally, a step of transformation is performed in order to properly map the depth view with the RGB view, in order to attach texture to depth.

Kinect active scanning capability was utilized in different ways for different applications. The works of (Izadi et al., 2011; Newcombe et al., 2011; Endres et al., 2012; Choi, Zhou, & Koltun, 2015) present a moving sensor setup, which is suitable for scenes with static objects. The work of (Tong, Zhou, Liu, Pan, & Yan, 2012; Zeng, Zheng, Cheng, & Liu, 2013; Li et al., 2013) demonstrated scanning full human body using setups that contained a non-moving sensor, but the human subject of scanning rotates in front of the sensor, maintaining the same pose. Alongside these solutions, many techniques were proposed for objects that cannot maintain the same pose for too long (Dou, Taylor, Fuchs, Fitzgibbon, & Izadi, 2015; Slavcheva, Baust, Cremers, & Ilic, 2017; Innmann, Zollhöfer, Nießner, Theobalt, & Stamminger, 2016; Dou, Fuchs, & Frahm, 2013).

While building a scanning setup (especially with multiple Kinects), the range of the sensor detection is to be taken into consideration. The range of detection is this area between near and far planes that the sensor performs best in between. Given that the sensor unit is not customizable, this area is well defined. Such area defines a virtual bounding box which is to enclose the scene to be scanned. Therefore, there is a limitation presented on the size and placement of the object to be scanned. (Both limitations are with upper and lower bounds.) Thus, such limitation causes these setups to be better suited for human size objects, not much bigger or smaller.

Other Applications

The first group of applications falls under the human face reconstruction category (Roth, Tong, & Liu, 2015, 2016; Kemelmacher-Shlizerman, & Seitz, 2011; Zhu, Lei, Yan, Yi, & Li, 2015; Yang, Chen, Su, & Su, 2014; Peng, Xu, & Feng, 2016; Segundo, Silva, & Bellon, 2012). Other applications worked on reconstructed human faces from video streams (Beeler et al., 2011; Valgaerts, Wu, Bruhn, Seidel, & Theobalt, 2012; Garrido, Valgaerts, Wu, & Theobalt, 2013; Cao, Bradley, Zhou, & Beeler, 2015; Suwajanakorn, Kemelmacher-Shlizerman, & Seitz, 2014; Jeni, Cohn, & Kanade, 2015; Aissaoui, Martinet, & Djeraba, 2012). Another group of algorithms is built to work under the constraints enforced by the hardware limitations of smartphones (Muratov et al., 2016; Tanskanen et al, 2013; Ondrúška, Kohli, & Izadi, 2015; Prisacariu, Kahler, Murray, & Reid, 2013; Schöps, Sattler, Häne, & Pollefeys, 2015). The work of (Liu, Chen, & Yang, 2014; Herbort, Grumpe, & Wöhler, 2011; Liu, Hartley, & Salzmann, 2013; Han, Wong, & Liu, 2015; Zuo, Du, Wang, Zheng, & Yang, 2015) tackled the problem of reconstructing non-Lambertian objects.

CONCLUSION

In this chapter, 3D reconstruction algorithms were demonstrated. The main factor used in grouping algorithms adopted in this chapter was the date of publishing, as the challenge in the 3D reconstruction problem changed over time. Algorithms were divided into three groups, up till 2001, up till 2006, and up till now (2017). As discussed above, the behavior of some modern 3D reconstruction algorithms is affected by new techniques like machine learning, and new hardware like Kinect. Alongside that, some other algorithms tackled other challenging problems like reconstructing non-Lambertian objects and reconstruction under hardware limitations of smartphones, as classical approaches did not tackle these challenges.

REFERENCES

Aissaoui, A., Martinet, J., & Djeraba, C. (2012, September). 3D face reconstruction in a binocular passive stereoscopic system using face properties. In *Image Processing (ICIP), 2012 19th IEEE International Conference on* (pp. 1789-1792). IEEE.

Beeler, T., Hahn, F., Bradley, D., Bickel, B., Beardsley, P., Gotsman, C., ... Gross, M. (2011, August). High-quality passive facial performance capture using anchor frames. *ACM Transactions on Graphics*, *30*(4), 75. doi:10.1145/2010324.1964970

Bhotika, R., Fleet, D. J., & Kutulakos, K. N. (2002, May). A probabilistic theory of occupancy and emptiness. In *European conference on computer vision* (pp. 112-130). Springer. 10.1007/3-540-47977-5_8

Bonfort, T., & Sturm, P. (2003, October). Voxel carving for specular surfaces. In *9th IEEE International Conference on Computer Vision (ICCV'03)* (Vol. 1, pp. 691-696). IEEE Computer Society.

Broadhurst, A., Drummond, T. W., & Cipolla, R. (2001). A probabilistic framework for space carving. In *Computer Vision, 2001. ICCV 2001. Proceedings. Eighth IEEE International Conference on* (Vol. 1, pp. 388-393). IEEE. 10.1109/ICCV.2001.937544

Cao, C., Bradley, D., Zhou, K., & Beeler, T. (2015). Real-time high-fidelity facial performance capture. *ACM Transactions on Graphics*, *34*(4), 46. doi:10.1145/2766943

Chen, Q., & Medioni, G. (1999). A volumetric stereo matching method: Application to image-based modeling. In *Computer Vision and Pattern Recognition, 1999. IEEE Computer Society Conference on*. (Vol. 1, pp. 29-34). IEEE.

Cherabier, I., Hane, C., Oswald, M. R., & Pollefeys, M. (2016, October). Multi-label semantic 3d reconstruction using voxel blocks. In *3D Vision (3DV), 2016 Fourth International Conference on* (pp. 601-610). IEEE.

Chien, C. H., & Aggarwal, J. K. (1984). A volume/surface representation. In *Proceedings of the International Conference on Pattern Recognition* (pp. 817-820). Academic Press.

Chien, C. H., & Aggarwal, J. K. (1986). Volume/surface octrees for the representation of three-dimensional objects. *Computer Vision Graphics and Image Processing*, *36*(1), 100–113. doi:10.1016/S0734-189X(86)80031-7

Choi, S., Zhou, Q. Y., & Koltun, V. (2015). Robust reconstruction of indoor scenes. In *Proceedings of the IEEE Conference on Computer Vision and Pattern Recognition* (pp. 5556-5565). IEEE.

Collins, R. T. (1996, June). A space-sweep approach to true multi-image matching. In *Computer Vision and Pattern Recognition, 1996. Proceedings CVPR'96, 1996 IEEE Computer Society Conference* on (pp. 358-363). IEEE. 10.1109/CVPR.1996.517097

Culbertson, W. B., Malzbender, T., & Slabaugh, G. (1999, September). Generalized voxel coloring. In *International Workshop on Vision Algorithms* (pp. 100-115). Springer.

Dou, M., Fuchs, H., & Frahm, J. M. (2013, October). Scanning and tracking dynamic objects with commodity depth cameras. In *Mixed and Augmented Reality (ISMAR), 2013 IEEE International Symposium on* (pp. 99-106). IEEE.

Dou, M., Taylor, J., Fuchs, H., Fitzgibbon, A., & Izadi, S. (2015). 3d scanning deformable objects with a single rgbd sensor. In *Proceedings of the IEEE Conference on Computer Vision and Pattern Recognition* (pp. 493-501). IEEE. 10.1109/CVPR.2015.7298647

Drouin, M. A., Trudeau, M., & Roy, S. (2005, June). Geo-consistency for wide multi-camera stereo. In *Computer Vision and Pattern Recognition, 2005. CVPR 2005. IEEE Computer Society Conference* on (Vol. 1, pp. 351-358). IEEE. 10.1109/CVPR.2005.168

Eisert, P., Steinbach, E., & Girod, B. (1999, March). Multi-hypothesis, volumetric reconstruction of 3-D objects from multiple calibrated camera views. In *Acoustics, Speech, and Signal Processing, 1999. Proceedings., 1999 IEEE International Conference* on (Vol. 6, pp. 3509-3512). IEEE.

Endres, F., Hess, J., Engelhard, N., Sturm, J., Cremers, D., & Burgard, W. (2012, May). An evaluation of the RGB-D SLAM system. In *Robotics and Automation (ICRA), 2012 IEEE International Conference on* (pp. 1691-1696). IEEE. 10.1109/ICRA.2012.6225199

Esteban, C. H., & Schmitt, F. (2004). Silhouette and stereo fusion for 3D object modeling. *Computer Vision and Image Understanding*, 96(3), 367–392. doi:10.1016/j.cviu.2004.03.016

Faugeras, O., & Keriven, R. (2002). Variational principles, surface evolution, PDE's, level set methods and the stereo problem. IEEE.

Fromherz, T., & Bichsel, M. (1994, August). Shape from contours as initial step in shape from multiple cues. In *Proceedings-SPIE the International Society for Optical Engineering* (pp. 249–249). SPIE International Society for Optical.

Fromherz, T., & Bichsel, M. (1995). Shape from multiple cues: Integrating local brightness information. In *Proceedings of the Fourth International Conference for Young Computer Scientists, ICYCS* (*Vol. 95*, pp. 855-862). Academic Press.

García, B., & Brunet, P. (1998, January). 3D reconstruction with projective octrees and epipolar geometry. In *Computer Vision, 1998. Sixth International Conference* on (pp. 1067-1072). IEEE.

Gargallo, P., & Sturm, P. (2005, June). Bayesian 3D modeling from images using multiple depth maps. In *Computer Vision and Pattern Recognition, 2005. CVPR 2005. IEEE Computer Society Conference* on (Vol. 2, pp. 885-891). IEEE.

Garrido, P., Valgaerts, L., Wu, C., & Theobalt, C. (2013). Reconstructing detailed dynamic face geometry from monocular video. *ACM Transactions on Graphics*, 32(6), 158–1. doi:10.1145/2508363.2508380

Gortler, S. J., Grzeszczuk, R., Szeliski, R., & Cohen, M. F. (1996, August). The lumigraph. In *Proceedings of the 23rd annual conference on Computer graphics and interactive techniques* (pp. 43-54). ACM.

Han, K., Wong, K. Y. K., & Liu, M. (2015). A fixed viewpoint approach for dense reconstruction of transparent objects. In *Proceedings of the IEEE Conference on Computer Vision and Pattern Recognition* (pp. 4001-4008). IEEE. 10.1109/CVPR.2015.7299026

Hane, C., Zach, C., Cohen, A., Angst, R., & Pollefeys, M. (2013). Joint 3D scene reconstruction and class segmentation. In *Proceedings of the IEEE Conference on Computer Vision and Pattern Recognition* (pp. 97-104). IEEE. 10.1109/CVPR.2013.20

Hane, C., Zach, C., Cohen, A., & Pollefeys, M. (2017). Dense semantic 3d reconstruction. *IEEE Transactions on Pattern Analysis and Machine Intelligence, 39*(9), 1730–1743. doi:10.1109/TPAMI.2016.2613051 PMID:28113966

Herbort, S., Grumpe, A., & Wöhler, C. (2011, September). Reconstruction of non-Lambertian surfaces by fusion of shape from shading and active range scanning. In *Image Processing (ICIP), 2011 18th IEEE International Conference on* (pp. 17-20). IEEE. 10.1109/ICIP.2011.6115812

Innmann, M., Zollhöfer, M., Nießner, M., Theobalt, C., & Stamminger, M. (2016, October). VolumeDeform: Real-time volumetric non-rigid reconstruction. In *European Conference on Computer Vision* (pp. 362-379). Springer International Publishing.

Isidoro, J., & Sclaroff, S. (2003, October). *Stochastic Refinement of the Visual Hull to Satisfy Photometric and Silhouette Consistency Constraints* (Vol. 1335). ICCV. doi:10.1109/ICCV.2003.1238645

Izadi, S., Kim, D., Hilliges, O., Molyneaux, D., Newcombe, R., Kohli, P., ... Fitzgibbon, A. (2011, October). KinectFusion: real-time 3D reconstruction and interaction using a moving depth camera. In *Proceedings of the 24th annual ACM symposium on User interface software and technology* (pp. 559-568). ACM. 10.1145/2047196.2047270

Jeni, L. A., Cohn, J. F., & Kanade, T. (2015, May). Dense 3D face alignment from 2D videos in real-time. In *Automatic Face and Gesture Recognition (FG), 2015 11th IEEE International Conference and Workshops on* (Vol. 1, pp. 1-8). IEEE.

Jin, H. (2003, October). Tales of shape and radiance in multiview stereo. In *Computer Vision, 2003. Proceedings. Ninth IEEE International Conference on* (pp. 974-981). IEEE.

Jin, H., Soatto, S., & Yezzi, A. J. (2003, June). Multi-view stereo beyond lambert. In *Computer Vision and Pattern Recognition, 2003. Proceedings. 2003 IEEE Computer Society Conference on* (Vol. 1, pp. I-I). IEEE.

Kang, S. B., Szeliski, R., & Chai, J. (2001). Handling occlusions in dense multi-view stereo. *In Computer Vision and Pattern Recognition, 2001. CVPR 2001. Proceedings of the 2001 IEEE Computer Society Conference on* (Vol. 1, pp. I-I). IEEE.

Kemelmacher-Shlizerman, I., & Seitz, S. M. (2011, November). Face reconstruction in the wild. In *Computer Vision (ICCV), 2011 IEEE International Conference on* (pp. 1746-1753). IEEE. 10.1109/ICCV.2011.6126439

Khoshelham, K. (2011, August). Accuracy analysis of kinect depth data. In ISPRS workshop laser scanning (Vol. 38, No. 5, p. W12). Academic Press.

Kolmogorov, V., & Zabih, R. (2002). Multi-camera scene reconstruction via graph cuts. *Computer Vision—ECCV 2002*, 8-40.

Kutulakos, K. N. (2000, June). Approximate N-view stereo. In *European Conference on Computer Vision* (pp. 67-83). Springer.

Kutulakos, K. N., & Seitz, S. M. (2000). A theory of shape by space carving. *International Journal of Computer Vision*, *38*(3), 199–218. doi:10.1023/A:1008191222954

Ladický, L., Sturgess, P., Russell, C., Sengupta, S., Bastanlar, Y., Clocksin, W., & Torr, P. H. (2012). Joint optimization for object class segmentation and dense stereo reconstruction. *International Journal of Computer Vision*, 1–12.

Laurentini, A. (1994). The visual hull concept for silhouette-based image understanding. *IEEE Transactions on Pattern Analysis and Machine Intelligence*, *16*(2), 150–162. doi:10.1109/34.273735

Li, H., Vouga, E., Gudym, A., Luo, L., Barron, J. T., & Gusev, G. (2013). 3D self-portraits. *ACM Transactions on Graphics*, *32*(6), 187. doi:10.1145/2508363.2508407

Liu, D., Chen, X., & Yang, Y. H. (2014). Frequency-based 3d reconstruction of transparent and specular objects. In *Proceedings of the IEEE Conference on Computer Vision and Pattern Recognition* (pp. 660-667). IEEE. 10.1109/CVPR.2014.90

Liu, M., Hartley, R., & Salzmann, M. (2013). Mirror surface reconstruction from a single image. In *Proceedings of the IEEE Conference on Computer Vision and Pattern Recognition* (pp. 129-136). IEEE. 10.1109/CVPR.2013.24

Luong, Q. T., & Faugeras, O. D. (1996). The fundamental matrix: Theory, algorithms, and stability analysis. *International Journal of Computer Vision*, *17*(1), 43–75. doi:10.1007/BF00127818

Martin, W. N., & Aggarwal, J. K. (1983, February). Volumetric Descriptions of Objects from Multiple Views. *IEEE Transactions on Pattern Analysis and Machine Intelligence*, *5*(2), 150–158. doi:10.1109/TPAMI.1983.4767367 PMID:21869096

Massone, L., Morasso, P., & Zaccaria, R. (1985, January). Shape from occluding contours. In *1984 Cambridge Symposium* (pp. 114-120). International Society for Optics and Photonics. 10.1117/12.946170

Moezzi, S., Katkere, A., Kuramura, D. Y., & Jain, R. (1996). Reality modeling and visualization from multiple video sequences. *IEEE Computer Graphics and Applications*, *16*(6), 58–63. doi:10.1109/38.544073

Moezzi, S., Tai, L. C., & Gerard, P. (1997). Virtual view generation for 3D digital video. *IEEE MultiMedia*, *4*(1), 18–26. doi:10.1109/93.580392

Muratov, O., Slynko, Y., Chernov, V., Lyubimtseva, M., Shamsuarov, A., & Bucha, V. (2016). 3DCapture: 3D Reconstruction for a Smartphone. In *Proceedings of the IEEE Conference on Computer Vision and Pattern Recognition Workshops* (pp. 75-82). IEEE.

Newcombe, R. A., Izadi, S., Hilliges, O., Molyneaux, D., Kim, D., Davison, A. J., . . . Fitzgibbon, A. (2011, October). KinectFusion: Real-time dense surface mapping and tracking. In *Mixed and augmented reality (ISMAR), 2011 10th IEEE international symposium on* (pp. 127-136). IEEE.

Ondrúška, P., Kohli, P., & Izadi, S. (2015). Mobilefusion: Real-time volumetric surface reconstruction and dense tracking on mobile phones. *IEEE Transactions on Visualization and Computer Graphics*, *21*(11), 1251–1258. doi:10.1109/TVCG.2015.2459902 PMID:26439826

Peng, W., Xu, C., & Feng, Z. (2016). 3D face modeling based on structure optimization and surface reconstruction with B-Spline. *Neurocomputing*, *179*, 228–237. doi:10.1016/j.neucom.2015.11.090

Pentland, A. P. (1990). Automatic extraction of deformable part models. *International Journal of Computer Vision*, *4*(2), 107–126. doi:10.1007/BF00127812

Pons, J. P., Keriven, R., & Faugeras, O. (2005, June). Modelling dynamic scenes by registering multi-view image sequences. In *Computer Vision and Pattern Recognition, 2005. CVPR 2005. IEEE Computer Society Conference* on (Vol. 2, pp. 822-827). IEEE. 10.1109/CVPR.2005.227

Potmesil, M. (1987). Generating octree models of 3D objects from their silhouettes in a sequence of images. *Computer Vision Graphics and Image Processing*, *40*(1), 1–29. doi:10.1016/0734-189X(87)90053-3

Prisacariu, V. A., Kahler, O., Murray, D. W., & Reid, I. D. (2013, October). Simultaneous 3D tracking and reconstruction on a mobile phone. In *Mixed and Augmented Reality (ISMAR), 2013 IEEE International Symposium on* (pp. 89-98). IEEE.

Roth, J., Tong, Y., & Liu, X. (2015). Unconstrained 3D face reconstruction. In *Proceedings of the IEEE Conference on Computer Vision and Pattern Recognition* (pp. 2606-2615). Academic Press.

Roth, J., Tong, Y., & Liu, X. (2016). Adaptive 3D face reconstruction from unconstrained photo collections. In *Proceedings of the IEEE Conference on Computer Vision and Pattern Recognition* (pp. 4197-4206). IEEE. 10.1109/CVPR.2016.455

Russell, C., Kohli, P., & Torr, P. H. (2009, September). Associative hierarchical crfs for object class image segmentation. In *Computer Vision, 2009 IEEE 12th International Conference on* (pp. 739-746). IEEE.

Saito, H., & Kanade, T. (1999). Shape reconstruction in projective grid space from large number of images. In *Computer Vision and Pattern Recognition, 1999. IEEE Computer Society Conference* on. (Vol. 2, pp. 49-54). IEEE. 10.1109/CVPR.1999.784607

Savinov, N., Ladicky, L., Hane, C., & Pollefeys, M. (2015). Discrete optimization of ray potentials for semantic 3d reconstruction. In *Proceedings of the IEEE Conference on Computer Vision and Pattern Recognition* (pp. 5511-5518). IEEE. 10.1109/CVPR.2015.7299190

Schöps, T., Sattler, T., Häne, C., & Pollefeys, M. (2015, October). 3D modeling on the go: Interactive 3D reconstruction of large-scale scenes on mobile devices. In *3D Vision (3DV), 2015 International Conference on* (pp. 291-299). IEEE.

Segundo, M. P., Silva, L., & Bellon, O. R. P. (2012, September). Improving 3d face reconstruction from a single image using half-frontal face poses. In *Image Processing (ICIP), 2012 19th IEEE International Conference on* (pp. 1797-1800). IEEE.

Seitz, S. M., Curless, B., Diebel, J., Scharstein, D., & Szeliski, R. (2006, June). A comparison and evaluation of multi-view stereo reconstruction algorithms. In *Computer vision and pattern recognition, 2006 IEEE Computer Society Conference on* (Vol. 1, pp. 519-528). IEEE. 10.1109/CVPR.2006.19

Seitz, S. M., & Dyer, C. R. (1995, June). Complete scene structure from four point correspondences. In *Computer Vision, 1995. Proceedings., Fifth International Conference* on (pp. 330-337). IEEE. 10.1109/ICCV.1995.466921

Shneier, M. O., Kent, E., & Mansbach, P. (1984, July). Representing workspace and model knowledge for a robot with mobile sensors. *7th International Conference on Pattern Recognition.*

Sinha, S. N., & Pollefeys, M. (2005, October). Multi-view reconstruction using photo-consistency and exact silhouette constraints: A maximum-flow formulation. In *Computer Vision, 2005. ICCV 2005. Tenth IEEE International Conference on* (Vol. 1, pp. 349-356). IEEE. 10.1109/ICCV.2005.159

Slabaugh, G., Schafer, R., Malzbender, T., & Culbertson, B. (2001). A survey of methods for volumetric scene reconstruction from photographs. In *Volume Graphics 2001* (pp. 81–100). Vienna: Springer. doi:10.1007/978-3-7091-6756-4_6

Slabaugh, G. G., Culbertson, W. B., Malzbender, T., Stevens, M. R., & Schafer, R. W. (2004). Methods for volumetric reconstruction of visual scenes. *International Journal of Computer Vision, 57*(3), 179–199. doi:10.1023/B:VISI.0000013093.45070.3b

Slavcheva, M., Baust, M., Cremers, D., & Ilic, S. (2017). KillingFusion: Non-rigid 3D Reconstruction without Correspondences. In *IEEE Conference on Computer Vision and Pattern Recognition (CVPR)* (p. 19). IEEE.

Srivastava, S. K., & Ahuja, N. (1990). Octree generation from object silhouettes in perspective views. *Computer Vision Graphics and Image Processing, 49*(1), 68–84. doi:10.1016/0734-189X(90)90163-P

Suwajanakorn, S., Kemelmacher-Shlizerman, I., & Seitz, S. M. (2014, September). Total moving face reconstruction. In *European Conference on Computer Vision* (pp. 796-812). Springer.

Szeliski, R. (1993). Rapid octree construction from image sequences. *Computer Vision, Graphics, and Image Processing: Image Understanding, 58*(1), 23-32.

Tanskanen, P., Kolev, K., Meier, L., Camposeco, F., Saurer, O., & Pollefeys, M. (2013). Live metric 3d reconstruction on mobile phones. In *Proceedings of the IEEE International Conference on Computer Vision* (pp. 65-72). IEEE. 10.1109/ICCV.2013.15

Taylor, C. J. (2003, October). *Surface Reconstruction from Feature Based Stereo.* ICCV.

Terzopoulos, D., & Metaxas, D. (1990, December). Dynamic 3D models with local and global deformations: Deformable superquadrics. In *Computer Vision, 1990. Proceedings, Third International Conference* on (pp. 606-615). IEEE.

Tong, J., Zhou, J., Liu, L., Pan, Z., & Yan, H. (2012). Scanning 3d full human bodies using kinects. *IEEE Transactions on Visualization and Computer Graphics, 18*(4), 643–650. doi:10.1109/TVCG.2012.56 PMID:22402692

Treuille, A., Hertzmann, A., & Seitz, S. M. (2004, May). Example-based stereo with general BRDFs. In *European Conference on Computer Vision* (pp. 457-469). Springer.

Valgaerts, L., Wu, C., Bruhn, A., Seidel, H. P., & Theobalt, C. (2012). Lightweight binocular facial performance capture under uncontrolled lighting. *ACM Transactions on Graphics, 31*(6), 187–1. doi:10.1145/2366145.2366206

Vogiatzis, G., Torr, P., Seitz, S. M., & Cipolla, R. (2004). *Reconstructing relief surfaces.* BMVC. doi:10.5244/C.18.14

Vogiatzis, G., Torr, P. H., & Cipolla, R. (2005, June). Multi-view stereo via volumetric graph-cuts. In *Computer Vision and Pattern Recognition, 2005. CVPR 2005. IEEE Computer Society Conference on* (Vol. 2, pp. 391-398). IEEE. 10.1109/CVPR.2005.238

Yang, C., Chen, J., Su, N., & Su, G. (2014). Improving 3D face details based on normal map of hetero-source images. In *Proceedings of the IEEE Conference on Computer Vision and Pattern Recognition Workshops* (pp. 9-14). IEEE. 10.1109/CVPRW.2014.7

Yang, R. (2003, October). Dealing with textureless regions and specular highlights-a progressive space carving scheme using a novel photo-consistency measure. In *Computer Vision, 2003. Proceedings. Ninth IEEE International Conference on* (pp. 576-584). IEEE.

Yu, T., Xu, N., & Ahuja, N. (2004). Shape and view independent reflectance map from multiple views. *Computer Vision-ECCV, 2004*, 24–29.

Zach, C., Hane, C., & Pollefeys, M. (2014). What is optimized in convex relaxations for multilabel problems: Connecting discrete and continuously inspired map inference. *IEEE Transactions on Pattern Analysis and Machine Intelligence, 36*(1), 157–170. doi:10.1109/TPAMI.2013.105 PMID:24231873

Zeng, G., Paris, S., Quan, L., & Sillion, F. (2005, October). Progressive surface reconstruction from images using a local prior. In *Computer Vision, 2005. ICCV 2005. Tenth IEEE International Conference on* (Vol. 2, pp. 1230-1237). IEEE. 10.1109/ICCV.2005.196

Zeng, M., Zheng, J., Cheng, X., & Liu, X. (2013). Templateless quasi-rigid shape modeling with implicit loop-closure. In *Proceedings of the IEEE Conference on Computer Vision and Pattern Recognition* (pp. 145-152). IEEE. 10.1109/CVPR.2013.26

Zhang, L., & Seitz, S. (2001). Image-based multiresolution shape recovery by surface deformation. In *Proceedings-SPIE the International Society for Optical Engineering* (Vol. 4309, pp. 51–61). SPIE International Society for Optical.

Zhu, X., Lei, Z., Yan, J., Yi, D., & Li, S. Z. (2015). High-fidelity pose and expression normalization for face recognition in the wild. In *Proceedings of the IEEE Conference on Computer Vision and Pattern Recognition* (pp. 787-796). IEEE.

Zitnick, C. L., Kang, S. B., Uyttendaele, M., Winder, S., & Szeliski, R. (2004, August). High-quality video view interpolation using a layered representation. *ACM Transactions on Graphics*, *23*(3), 600–608. doi:10.1145/1015706.1015766

Zuo, X., Du, C., Wang, S., Zheng, J., & Yang, R. (2015). Interactive visual hull refinement for specular and transparent object surface reconstruction. In *Proceedings of the IEEE International Conference on Computer Vision* (pp. 2237-2245). IEEE. 10.1109/ICCV.2015.258

Chapter 2
The Use of Written Descriptions and 2D Images as Cues for Tactile Information in Online Shopping

Flor Morton
Universidad de Monterrey, Mexico

ABSTRACT

Despite the steady growth in the use of online platforms for purchasing products in the past few years, e-commerce faces important challenges such as the inability of physically experiencing a product, specifically the inability to obtain tactile information. In this chapter, through a qualitative exploratory study approach, the author explores the possibility of conveying tactile characteristics of a product to consumers in an online shopping environment through product presentation formats such as written descriptions and 2D images. The author highlights the potential for sensory marketing through first reviewing literature on the subject with a special focus on touch and the inability to touch in online commercial channels. The methodology is presented along with the findings of the exploratory study. A concluding discussion of findings is presented and the potential for future research in the area of image processing to enhance 2D images ability to provide tactile information is discussed to conclude the chapter.

INTRODUCTION

According to a study of the Pew Research Center (2016) roughly 79% of Americans say they purchase online, in 2015 they were spending around 350 billion dollars annually online. In Mexico, although at a lower rate, the use of e-commerce is constantly growing. For instance, from 2013 to 2015 the estimated number of sales through e-commerce raised from 9.2 billions of dollars to 16.2 billion dollars, respectively (AMIPCI, 2016). The principal product categories purchased online are fashion products, such as clothing and accessories, sought primarily by females under 35 years old, (Treviño & Morton, 2016).

DOI: 10.4018/978-1-5225-5246-8.ch002

Despite steady growth, e-commerce faces some challenges related to the forms available to consumers for evaluating products. For instance, marketing literature has found that touch is a direct form in examining products (Peck & Childers, 2003b). However, in today's online environment consumers are unable to physically experience the products and, for example, use their sense of touch for product evaluations and they must rely mainly on written descriptions and visual cues obtained through 2D images such as pictures and videos to obtain information of the products.

Despite the importance of the tactile information for consumers' evaluations and the effects of the information obtained through the haptic system on other consumer's variables such as perceptions and behaviors (Grohmann, Spangenberg, & Sprott, 2007; Guéguen & Jacob, 2006; Krishna & Morrin, 2008, Peck & Shu, 2009), almost no research on whether it is possible for consumers to obtain tactile information in an online shopping context through images, videos, or other types of stimuli has been conducted. Hence, the purpose of this work is to explore how consumers try to compensate for the missing sensory -specifically tactile- experience in an online shopping environment. That is, the characteristics of products can be discovered through the available sources of information that can provide effective somewhat equivalent information.

This book chapter contributes to the marketing literature which recognizes the importance of touch for consumers, but presents a research opportunity of exploring how to compensate touch in an online environment. Additionally, this chapter contributes to the image processing literature by exposing a relatively unexplored business application of the use of 2D images. Particularly, the chapter will explore the possibility of conveying tactile characteristics of a product to consumers in an online shopping environment through 2D images. Furthermore, practical implications of this research are also discussed.

This chapter is structured as follows: First, the chapter presents a literature review on sensory marketing with a special focus on touch and the inability to touch in online commercial channels. The research questions guiding the study are also presented. Second, the methodology of the exploratory study is described. Third, findings of the exploratory study are presented. Finally, conclusions and future research are discussed with a particular call for future research in the area of image processing and establishing the importance to develop techniques that enhance 2D images ability to provide tactile information.

BACKGROUND

Sensory Influences on Consumption

An increasing area of interest in the field of consumer behavior is the role that human senses play in the consumption context. Some of the research in this field of study has focused on the influences of vision on consumers' behavior and perceptions. For example, it has been found that the shape of the package or container can influence serving size and consumption (Wansink & Van Ittersum, 2003). Also, previous findings suggest that more attractive packages are perceived as larger in volume than less attractive packages with the same volume (Folkes & Matta, 2004). There is also evidence suggesting vision can bias product taste perceptions (Hoegg & Alba, 2007). Research focused on smell found this sense can influence information processing, store evaluations, memory of product information, consumption, and satisfaction. For example, researchers quantify that ambient scent influences consumer processing and decision making; specifically, consumers spend more time processing information and are more holistic in their processing (Mitchell, Kahn & Knasko, 1995). Likewise, other findings reveal evaluations of a store and its products as well as purchase intentions are positively influenced by pleasant or neutral ambient scents (Spanenberg, Crowley & Henderson, 1996). Other results suggest that evaluations of the store environment, impulse buying, and satisfaction are increased when scent and music are complimentary in their arousal characteristics (Mattila & Wirtz, 2001). Product scent is more effective than ambient scent in increasing long-term memory of product information according to another study (Krishna, Lwin & Morrin, 2009). Even more relevant to our study, researchers have looked at the congruence between scent and touch properties of a product, findings suggest that congruency between these two properties improves haptic perceptions and product evaluations (Krishna, Elder & Caldara, 2010).

Research focusing on the influence of the sense of touch on consumers has been gaining relevance among consumer researchers because of the importance that this sense has on the consumption process. As previously mentioned, this book chapter focuses on this particular human sense and how alternative channels for consumption such as e-commerce face a challenge of providing the tactile product information and characteristics that influence consumer's perceptions and behavior.

Marketing Literature on Touch

In this section, some of the studies that marketing scholars have made about touch are presented in order to provide an overview of what has already been studied on this topic. From this literature review three general studied variables in the touch and marketing research were found, including: individual differences, perception, and consumer's response/behavior.

Touch and Individual Differences

Previous researchers concentrated on the individual differences in haptic information processing. For example, Peck and Childers (2003b) identified differences among people in their level of preference to use the sense of touch, since these differences could explain why some people are more haptic oriented than others, and reveal the effects of this predisposition on consumer's behavior. The authors developed the concept of need for touch (NFT) and a scale to measure it. Specifically, NFT refers to "a preference for the extraction and utilization of information obtained through the haptic system" (p. 431). According to these authors, NFT has two dimensions: (1) autotelic, in which touch is hedonic oriented and an end of itself; and (2) instrumental, which refers to outcome-directed touch. Moreover, motivation to obtain haptic product information can be influenced by factors such as: product characteristics, individual differences, and situational characteristics (Peck & Childers, 2003a). For example, it has been found that tactile input has a positive influence on product evaluations; in particular, for products with characteristics best explored by touch, such as clothes (Grohman, Spangenberg, & Sprott, 2007).

Additionally, previous research indicates variables such as gender and fashion innovativeness can have an influence on NFT (Cho & Workman, 2011). Consistent with these findings, Citrin, Stem, Spanenberg and Clark (2003) found gender has a significant effect on the need for touch in product evaluation. Specifically, women were shown to have a higher need for touch than men.

Other studies confirm there are differences between consumers high in NFT compared to those with lower levels. For example, consumers with high levels of NFT prefer sales channels where product touch is available, such as physical stores (Cho & Workman, 2011). In particular, there has been found a negative relationship between need for touch and the use of Internet for product purchasing (Citrin, Stem,

Spangenberg & Clark, 2003). Suggesting that high need for touch individuals may not easily adapt to non-touch shopping scenarios, such as the Internet (Peck & Childers, 2003a).

Touch and Perception

The influence of touch on consumers' perceptions as also been addressed in marketing field literature. Interestingly, Peck and Shu (2009) observed when consumers touch a product, even if only in their imagination, perceived ownership of that product increases. As a result, product valuation also increases, especially if the product provides neutral or positive (pleasurable) sensory feedback. These findings provide important considerations with respect to touch and imagination, suggesting that touch can be imagined in a context where tactile input is not available such as the Internet.

Need for touch has also been studied in the area of fashion and clothes; studies in this area have surveyed the impact of visual and tactile attributes. Specifically, visual product aesthetics are considered to serve to make inferences about other sensory characteristics such as tactile attributes; a positive relationship between a person's NFT and the importance or centrality of visual aesthetics has been found (Workman & Caldwell, 2007). Interestingly, attitudes, product evaluations, and purchase intentions have been found to be significantly more impacted or influenced by tactile than by visual information, particularly for products salient on haptic properties (Balaji, Raghavan, & Jha, 2011). Therefore, it is not surprising the negative relationship between need for touch and the use of Internet for product purchasing (Citrin, Stem, Spangenberg & Clark, 2003). Nevertheless, it would be interesting to find ways to provide tactile cues on Internet stores that could diminish this negative association.

A promising and fairly recent concept of virtual touch has been developed by Demirci (2007). Virtual touch refers to the online sense of touch that consumers perceive in a virtual product experience when they are exposed to a 3-D format of a product through a computer screen. Findings from the same author suggest that there is a positive causal relationship between the interactivity of an object and virtual touch, and in creating such increases purchase intentions and product knowledge.

In spite of the multiple studies that find a positive effect of touch on consumer's perceptions, there are other researchers who have found that even though consumers like to touch products, they do not like the idea that a product has been touched by other consumers, and they may even respond in a negative way to such products (Argo, Dahl & Morales, 2006). Nevertheless, there is also evidence that positive contagion exists in certain situations, for example when the person who touches the product is attractive and from the opposite sex (Argo, Dahl, & Morales, 2008).

Touch and Consumer's Response/Behavior

Early studies of touch in the marketing area were interested in the effects of interpersonal touch on consumer's behavior. Previous findings from these studies suggest that interpersonal touch can ensure sampling, purchase of a product and increase the amount of shopping (Smith, Gier & Willis, 1982; Guéguen & Jacob, 2006). Also, interpersonal touch has been found to positively influence evaluations of the store, compliance with a request, shopping time, satisfaction, and tipping (Hornik, 1992a; Hornik, 1992b; Lynn, Le, and Sherwyn, 1998).

The influence of touch on affective response and persuasion has also been studied. Interestingly, the incorporation of touch into marketing messages has been found to create an affective response, which leads to a positive effect on persuasion, in particular for people who have high autotelic need for touch

(Peck & Wiggins, 2006). Concordantly, Peck and Wiggins (2011) found that individuals with high auto-telic need for touch are more persuaded when a haptic element is present, regardless of their involvement with the message. However, a haptic element increases persuasion for low autotelics under conditions of low versus high involvement with the message. Also, Peck and Childers (2006) found that people with a higher autotelic need for touch were more likely to purchase impulsively than lower autotelic individuals. Furthermore, consumers high in instrumental need for touch evaluate products in a more positive way and show stronger brand-self connection when a force feedback (haptic) stimulus is present than when no stimulus is present (Jin, 2011).

Consumers inability to touch products has been an ongoing challenge for those who use the Internet to commercialize products. Consumers often express unfavorable or frustrating feelings related to such inability to product touch (Peck & Childers, 2003a; Balaji, Raghavan, & Jha, 2011), in particular are those with high levels of NFT, which makes them reluctant to adapt or use online shopping channels (Citrin, Stem, Spangenberg & Clark, 2003). Although there is evidence that suggests touch can be perceived even if consumers cannot actually touch the product (Balaji, Raghavan, & Jha, 2011; Demirci, 2007), there is a lack of studies addressing this issue. Hence, the primary contribution of this research is establishing that touch could be compensated in a certain manner by non-touch commercial channels allowing for certain verbal and non-verbal stimuli.

E-Commerce

Inability to Touch Products as a Barrier for Online Shopping

Electronic commerce (e-commerce) can be defined as the purchase of products, services, or information through Internet platforms. Similar to traditional commerce, e-commerce consists of selling and buying from business-to-business, business-to-consumer, and consumer-to-consumer. One of the main differences between making a purchase through traditional commerce or through e-commerce is the opportunity that the buyer has to physically experience the product (Ashwini & Vincent, 2017). As previously mentioned, consumers evaluate products through touch and the lack of touch in e-commerce is a barrier for those consumers who are not confident to buy products when they cannot touch them making some consumers to avoid online shopping channels (Citrin, Stem, Spangenberg & Clark, 2003). However, despite consumer's inability to touch products in an online context, the use of e-commerce channels has increased steadily in the past years.

Use of Written Descriptions and 2D Images to Convey Information Online

Although consumers are not able to experience the product physically, online stores can provide visual information about products through written descriptions, and more importantly, through 2D images such as pictures and videos. In fact, until now most online stores employed these presentation formats to present and provide product information; specifically, written descriptions provide information such as product size, weight, warranty policies and 2D images are used to depict visual appeal of the product (Jiang & Benbasat, 2007). However, these product presentation formats lack of richness to provide information such as feel, try and touch of a product (Rose, Khoo, & Straub, 1999). But while research has recognized touch as an important aspect, there has been relatively few efforts to understand whether and how to compensate touch in an online context.

Integration of Intelligent Techniques for E-Commerce

The purpose of the artificial intelligence discipline is to understand human intelligence and construct computer programs that can imitate intelligent behavior. Intelligence techniques have been applied in several areas of science such as engineering, education, and business, among other areas. Particularly of interest for the present research, intelligent techniques have been applied for e-commerce platforms to correlate products and forecasting of sales, for user profiling in order to provide users appropriate recommendations, website ranking, etc. (Das, 2016; Prasad, 2003; Singh & Mehrota, 2016; Verma & Singh, 2017). There has been research on the use of artificial intelligence and machine learning techniques to predict consumer repurchase intentions, to analyze reviews in online retailing, and to model the relationships between sensory attributes and fabric properties (Chen et. al, 2014; Jeguirim et.al, 2012; Kumar, Kabra, Mussada, Dash, & Rana, 2017; Lin, Liaw, Chen, Pai & Chen, 2017). However, the present research identifies an opportunity to contribute to previous works on the area of intelligent techniques by adopting a consumer's perspective of the tactile attributes that consumers consider relevant for different types of products and how they cope to obtain this type of information online. Therefore, the following research questions are established.

Research Questions

This research focuses on the following question as its main guide through this study: How do consumers obtain tactile information in an online shopping context? Additionally, this research also addresses the following questions: Which product characteristics are evaluated through touch? Which products are considered important to touch before purchase? Which of the online product presentation formats are more effective in providing tactile information?

METHODOLOGY

As suggested by previous literature, qualitative methodology helps to understand a phenomenon in a specific context; generally, this type of research uses interviews, focus groups, case studies, and observation among other research methods (Bryman, 1984; Creswell, 2007; Eisenhardt, 1989; Smith, 1983; Spiggle, 1994). For the present research a qualitative approach was used to explore whether tactile information can be obtained from online stores. Specifically, data for this research consisted of eleven in-depth interviews. In the first part of the interview, participants were asked questions regarding the experience of buying in a traditional store. The second part of the interview was focused on online shopping. Finally, the third part consisted on questions about product presentation formats (written descriptions, photos, videos) used by online stores that could better provide tactile information about the products. Interviews were conducted at the participant's homes during a period of two weeks. Each interview was audiotaped and lasted between 30 and 45 minutes. After that, the categorization and analysis stage began, and then comparisons between the informant's responses were made to identify differences and commonalities.

Sample Profile

This research was conducted in Monterrey, Mexico, one of the three largest cities in the country with an estimated population of over five million in 2015 (Instituto Nacional de Estadística y Geografía- The National Institute of Statistics and Geography). The sample consisted of women from 18 to 27 years old, of the economic strata of A/B and C+. All of the participants were single and either college students or graduated professionals. See the Appendix for a complete list of names and descriptions of the participants. During the interviews it was noticed that six of the women participating in the study had never bought in an online store and the other five had purchased online at least one time.

FINDINGS

Consumers' Perceptions of Online Shopping

Participants in this study were asked for their perceptions on e-commerce. Perceived advantages of buying online were recognized and classified in this paper as: convenience, savings, variety and stock availability (see Table 1). Convenience refers to the type of access the store offers, i.e. every day and at any time (24/7), to its ease of use, and to the ability consumers have to find things they cannot find in their own city without the need to travel. Shopping online also comes with the advantage of saving time by not having to wait in a line or to wait to be attended by an employee; and, saving money because they can find products at lower prices. Additionally, variety refers to the advantage of being able to access different stores at the same time by simply opening a new window in the internet search engine which permits consumers to evaluate a greater amount of products. Finally, as mentioned by several participants, an additional advantage of e-commerce over going to a physical store is the stock availability, because the products shown in the online store are almost always available to buy.

It is more probable that you can find the size and there is more variety than in a store (physical). (Fabiola, age 18)

There are brands that you can buy at a lower price...there are products that you do not find here (in the city or country). (Tania, age 24)

I can do it (buy) whenever I want because the store (online) is also open at night... (Ana Rosa, age 25)

Despite the advantages previously mentioned, participants in this study also consider several disadvantages of purchasing online such as: uncertainty, delivery time, financial risks, and lack of physical experience with the product (see Table 1). As mentioned in the data collection, uncertainty comes from not knowing exactly what can be expected of the product quality and if the product will actually look as it is displayed on the store's web page. Delivery time is also perceived as a negative aspect of e-commerce

Table 1. Advantages and disadvantages of shopping online

Advantages	Disadvantages
• Convenience • Savings • Variety • Stock Availability	• Uncertainty • Delivery times • Financial risks • Lack of physical experience

when the waiting time is long (more than a week), but usually this disadvantage is compensated with the lower prices offered online and with the time saving in not having to wait in a line. Additionally, there are perceived financial risks to buying online, some of the participants actually mentioned that they do not buy online because they do not want to provide their credit card information. Finally, not being able to physically experience the product by touching or trying the product was also mentioned as a disadvantage of online shopping.

Precisely everything that you can not do, you can not touch it or try it on, you can not ask people (employees) which material is... (Isabel, age 27)

You do not know if the product is what you expected...also there is the risk that the package may not arrive. (Gaby, age 21)

The fact that you have to give a credit card...the time of delivery, that I do not have the product at that moment. (Sarai, age 22)

Shopping and Touch

Participants were asked about the experience of shopping in a physical store. All of the participants commented that when they were at a store they usually touched a great variety of products either for evaluation or just for hedonic purposes (pleasure), because they like the haptic feeling of certain products. Specifically, the majority of the participants who bought online said they touch products to obtain information. In contrast, the majority of the participants who had never purchased online answered that they touch products for pleasure.

To evaluate if is of good quality, to obtain information. (Isabel, age 27)

For both, for pleasure to know if it feels good or not and to obtain information. (Naila, age 24)

Additionally, participants were asked whether they imagine a sensation of a product prior to touching it and whether this perception is generally confirmed or disconfirmed after they actually touch it. The majority of participants mentioned that they do imagine how a product will feel when they look at it at a store. Most of those who had bought online commented that, generally, their perceptions about how the product feels does not change after touching it. In contrast, most of those who had never purchased online commented that generally their first perception of the product's sensation does change after touching it.

It (perception) can be confirmed or disconfirmed... because there are some fabrics that look very nice but when you touch them they do not feel nice. (Naila, age 24)

It changes only when they are materials that simulate to be another material...but generally it does not change. (Ana Rosa, age 25)

No, generally they feel how I imagined... (Tania, age 24)

One time I was looking at some dresses, they looked really nice, but then I went to touch them and it was not the fabric I imagined...it does change my perception when I touch the garments. (Pamela, age 25)

Participants in this study mentioned that touching products is important because they considered that by touching the product they could obtain information of certain characteristics that help them evaluate particular aspects of the product. Therefore, they were asked to mention products that they usually prefer to touch before purchasing them and the specific characteristics that they evaluate when touching that type of product. In particular, participants of this study mentioned nine product categories (see Table 2) that they like to touch before purchase and the tactile characteristics that they evaluate for these products. In general, these characteristics help them to determine product's durability, quality, and comfort.

Very, very important because then you can know if it really is of good quality. (Jessica, age 18)

Interestingly, all participants mentioned that they touch clothes and indicated they evaluated this product category by a greater list of characteristics than for the other product categories mentioned. Specifically, they mentioned that through touch they evaluate the texture of the garment to know if it is soft, smooth or itchy, in fact itchiness is an important characteristic that most of participants mentioned. If the product is evaluated as too itchy they avoid buying it. Through touch they also evaluate the weight of the garment, in general, the less weight the more comfortable they consider the product to be. Product thickness helps them to evaluate temperature insulation, for example if the garment is very thin they consider that it will be fresh, and if the fabric is thick, then they consider it to be warm. Thickness also

Table 2. Characteristics of products evaluated through touch

Product	Characteristics
Clothes	Texture (softness, smoothness, itchiness), Weight, Thickness (Temperature Insulation, Transparency), Stretchiness
Shoes	Material
Food	Firmness
Cosmetics	Greasiness, Moistness
Accessories	Weight
Quilts	Texture, Weight
Leather products	Texture, Thickness
Mobiles and accessories	Weight, Firmness

helps them to evaluate the transparency of the product; in fact they mentioned that it is important for them to be able to actually put their hands under the garment to assess transparency. Finally, through touch they also evaluate a fabric's stretchiness to obtain an idea of whether the product will fit them or not.

I like to feel the texture...I like a lot to feel the material, is one of the most important factors that I evaluate. (Elean, age 23)

That they are soft, that they do not itch, that they do not get damaged in the first wash...smoothness, fabric thickness. (Tania, age 24)

How hot it (fabric) can be, how heavy, or if it is of good quality or not. (Naila, age 24)

Fabric thickness, smoothness, if it is transparent. (Elean, age 23)

Participants who talked about shoes expressed that they need to touch them to evaluate the material. For instance, by touching the shoe they are able to know if the product is made out of leather or other material and whether they will feel comfortable or not wearing them. Participants who discussed food, specifically fruits and vegetables, mentioned that they evaluate freshness through touch, in general they noted that the firmer the fruit or vegetable is the more fresh they consider it to be. Cosmetics are also products that are considered by some participants as important to touch, because they want to evaluate characteristics such as greasiness and moistness, in general they dislike greasiness and look for moistness. Additionally, for accessories such as earrings, rings, and bracelets participants indicated they need to touch them to evaluate weight, some of them mentioned that the heavier the accessory the greater the perceived quality, but the less comfortable they consider it to be. Quilts are evaluated through touch for smoothness and weight to evaluate comfort, as participants pointed out, they prefer quilts that are warm but smooth and light weight. Moreover, as with shoes, texture and thickness are characteristics evaluated for other leather products; participants look for leather products that are thick and smooth to assess their quality. Finally, participants like to touch mobile phones and mobile accessories prior to purchase to evaluate the material's weight and firmness, their answers were mixed regarding the product's weight, but all of the participants who mentioned this product category agreed that they seek for firmness or hardness in this product to consider if they are of good quality.

Online Shopping and Touch

During the interviews, participants were explicitly asked to expound on their feelings to the inability to touch in an online shopping context. Participants in this study expressed that when they are not able to touch products – in particular clothes - before buying them they experience feelings of insecurity, uncertainty, doubt, frustration, fear, and risk. These feelings arise from: (1) uncertainty of whether or not the product will be what they expect to be because touch is principally their way to evaluate the quality of the garment; (2) if the product will not fit well because there is no uniformity in the sizes, even if they are buying from a brand they frequently purchase; (3) if it will be comfortable because, as they mentioned, through touch they evaluate if a garment is itchy or not and that is one basic characteristic to evaluate comfort.

Uncertainty...I do not like the idea of not touching or seeing physically what I am buying. (Elean, age 23)

Insecurity...sometimes they tell you the material but as I really do not know a lot about the types of materials or fabrics and I do not know what they are talking about. (Cynthia, age 25)

Despair...fear, distrust... (Sarai, age 22)

Furthermore, participants were asked whether or not touch could be simulated or compensated in an online environment. Although they recognize it is not the same experience, all of the participants answered affirmatively and the stimuli mentioned to provide them information of touch are classified in this paper as: written descriptions and two dimensional images (2D images). On one hand, written descriptions that provide tactile information to consumers include information about fabrics and texture of the product. This information can be provided either by the company or by online reviews of people who have already bought the product and provide written information about the product's tactile characteristics or sensation when touching it. In general, participants mentioned that written descriptions that include this type of information help them to get an idea of the texture and, consequently, to evaluate the possible comfort of the product. However, this was not true for all participants as it was noticed that those who buy online showed more knowledge about fabrics and most of them said that descriptions about fabrics do help them to imagine how the garment feels; yet, those who do not buy online expressed less knowledge about fabrics and how that type of fabric might feel.

On the other hand, it was observed that participants mentioned that 2D images such as photos, including pictures from different angles and zooms, along with videos can provide them with more information about tactile characteristics of the product than written descriptions. For example, 2D images can provide information such as weight, temperature insulation, type of material, itchiness, and softness/smoothness (see Table 3).

If they (written descriptions) describe the type of fabric and you have the experience of touching that type of fabric, then you can imagine how does it feels. (Naila, age 24)

I would like that for us that do not know much about fabrics...to have a description of how does it feels. (Cynthia, age 25)

Through sight... but it is not as effective as touch. (Gaby, age 21)

Table 3. Tactile information provided by characteristics of written descriptions and 2D images

Stimulus	Characteristics	Tactile Information
Written Descriptions	• Type of material • Description of sensation	• Texture
2D images	• Different angles • Movement • Zoom	• Weight • Thickness (Temperature insulation, Transparency) • Material • Texture (smoothness, softness, itchiness)

Through descriptions, pictures from different angles...and the video of how does it (garment) moves, but it is different the experience. (Naila, age 24)

Through images...I think that from all those years seeing types of fabric you can more or less recognize the type of material, it is more difficult but you can have an idea of the material's texture...now technology provides the capacity to see texture. (Elean, age 23)

According to participants, pictures from different angles with a model wearing the garment help them imagine how it could look on them and also to obtain an idea of the dimensions of the product and if it will fit them well, which helps to compensate for the fact that they are not able to try on the product. Additionally, participants mentioned that it is important for the 2D image to convey information about movement of the product, because that helps them to evaluate product's weight; interestingly, this information is not only obtained through videos, but also through pictures. For example, if the product looks somewhat folded simulating movement they perceive it to be lightweight.

Although, not all participants agreed, it was interesting that some of them suggest that a zoom in photo, showing a close up of the product's fabric, could provide information that otherwise would only be obtained by touching the product because of the way the seams looked in the photo. For example, open seams make some participants think that the product will make them feel fresh. Also, through 2D images participants can obtain information about the product's thickness, which also helps them to assess the product's temperature insulation and transparency. Other participants note that products with closed seams are soft and smooth and those with open seams -such as lace- might feel itchy.

I really like zooms...I can see better the material and it is like if I am actually feeling it. (Cynthia, age 25)

You can have an idea if the garment will be fresh or not depending on how close or open is the fabric. (Pamela, age 25)

Finally, there were comments that sometimes pictures can provide misleading information because of the manipulations they go through to make the product look better, these manipulations –according to some of the participants- make it difficult to obtain tactile information. On the other hand, almost all participants found videos more trustful than other techniques in providing tactile information because they perceive them as more realistic and difficult to modify than, for example, pictures.

It is more difficult for it (video) to be misleading, it is more realistic... (Ana Rosa, age 25)

DISCUSSION

There is a considerable amount of research concerning the influence of touch on consumers. As discussed earlier, the use of the Internet platforms for commercial purposes (e-commerce) has brought some challenges for companies that want to sell their products online. Specifically, the lack of opportunity for consumers to physically experience products through haptic explorations can make them become insecure and frustrated and forgo non-touch shopping environments (Peck & Childers, 2003b). This is supported in the findings from this research, which is also in line with the findings of previous studies, consumers experience feelings of insecurity and frustration when they are not able to touch products (Peck & Childers, 2003a). In particular, women in this study mentioned the lack of touch is an important disadvantage of e-commerce, and they also expressed feelings of frustration and uncertainty that makes them –in some cases- avoid purchasing online. However, the current research also revealed women will seek to obtain information about tactile characteristics of products in other ways when touch is not available.

Based on the results of this research, a new concept is introduced: tactile sensation confirmation. Tactile sensation confirmation is defined as when a person imagines an object's sensation (e.g. when the product is in the apparel or in a picture) and after touching that object the person corroborates that the object feels as he/she had previously imagined. As findings from this study suggest, some women tended not to have confidence in their perceptions of how a product feels when they cannot touch the product (e.g. online context). However, consumer's prior experiences of sensation confirmation could play an important role in the confidence of the evaluations of a product's tactile characteristics when touch is unavailable. For instance, due to the skills obtained from previous experiences of sensation confirmation, (i.e. if a person finds that his/her perceptions of how an object might feel are confirmed in most cases), a person could have a greater degree of confidence in the evaluations about tactile characteristics even when not touching the product. This could explain the fact that those who buy products online showed more confidence in their judgments than those who do not buy online. More specifically, those who purchased a garment online expressed that their prior-to-touch perceptions of the sensation of this product category generally remain the same after touching it. In contrast, perceptions of a garment's sensation were generally not confirmed after touching the product for those who had never purchased online. Therefore, previous experiences of sensation confirmation could influence the decision to use Internet platforms to make purchases.

Also, the majority of participants who had never bought online expressed that they touch products for pleasure, whereas the majority of those who buy online use touch just to obtain information. Knowledge of fabric sensation could explain why, as found in this research, people who buy online seem to have more knowledge about the fabrics than those who do not buy online. When touch is not available, those who bought online showed more confidence in tactile information obtained through sight than those who have never bought online.

Consistent with previous literature that suggests touch is a direct form of evaluation of a product and can influence purchase intentions (Peck & Childers, 2003a; Peck & Wiggins, 2006; Peck & Childers, 2006), findings from this research provide evidence of the importance of touch to evaluate products. In particular, this research found that the characteristics of products that are evaluated through touch are texture, thickness, weight, stretchiness, material, firmness, greasiness, and moistness. These characteristics help consumers to assess product's quality, comfort, and durability and influencing the purchase decision.

More importantly, consistent with the "visual preview model" (which states that vision can provide a quick glance of an object that may result in broad but coarse information about the haptic properties of that object) and with the attribution theory (which states that consumers make causal inferences about the quality and performance of a product based on intrinsic and extrinsic cues and that certain cues may influence the evaluation of others) (Klatzy, Lederman, & Matula, 1993; Folkes, 1988); findings from this research suggest that consumers base their evaluations on intrinsic cues such as appearance when evaluating another intrinsic cue such as texture. The women interviewed responded affirmatively to the question of whether or not it is possible to obtain information about the tactile characteristics of a product in an online shopping environment. Specifically, they get this information from written descriptions –either provided by the company or from reviews of other people who have already bought the garment- but also through 2D images.

On one hand, consumers obtain information about the haptic properties of products through written descriptions, especially those that include information about the type of material and description of sensation; this information helps people to imagine a product's texture. On the other hand, tactile information of products can be obtained through 2D images such as photos, including those that present the product from different angles or zoom in for a close up of product details, as well as videos. As found in this research, 2D images help to perceive product's weight, thickness, type of material, and texture, especially in clothing, through the appearance of movement and zooms to the product. Although, there is a concern regarding the manipulations that can be done to pictures and that could influence consumers to make wrong perceptions about the tactile characteristics of the products. In general, findings from this research suggest that the more realistic the 2D image looks like, the more trust they have in what they see and the tactile information the photos are able to convey. Finally, findings suggest that 2D images where considered as most effective to obtain tactile information than written descriptions.

CONCLUSIONS AND FUTURE RESEARCH DIRECTIONS

As found in this research, it is possible for consumers to obtain tactile information from 2D images and written descriptions. And while 2D images were found to be more helpful for this task, most online stores provide written descriptions with information regarding the type of material of the product, yet almost none include text describing the sensation of the product. Companies using e-commerce as a sales channel should consider describing in a deeper way the sensorial characteristics of a product to help consumers get a better idea of a product.

The concept introduced in this chapter -sensation confirmation- could be influenced by previous experience with similar products. It could be interesting to explore how some people become more skilled in perceiving and imagining the correct tactile sensation of an object than others, as previous sensation confirmation can affect confidence in evaluations. Also, future research could address the role of sensation confirmation in a person's decision to purchase online.

Researchers in the area of image processing and companies using e-commerce should consider finding ways to enhance the richness of 2D images in order to convey tactile information. Additionally, research regarding the use of 3D images and consumer's perceptions of tactile information through these images could contribute both to the literature and to practice. Perhaps more online stores could benefit from the integration of 3D images, as product presentation formats could somehow compensate for consumers' inability to touch in this environment.

Furthermore, the present research provides insights about the tactile characteristics evaluated by consumers for different product categories. Findings from this work could be used as a basis for future research in the area of intelligent techniques. Particularly, researchers could focus on the development of techniques (e.g. recommender) that can assist consumers on the evaluation of tactile characteristics of products when shopping online. For instance, a consumer shopping online could evaluate a product's tactile characteristics prior purchase based on the 2D images and written descriptions available for that product, later when the product is received they could evaluate it again based on real touch to determine whether their perceptions of tactile sensation where confirmed. An algorithm could learn from previous purchase experiences and develop accurate recommendations for new products being considered for purchase might feel.

Finally, because of the nature of this exploratory study, generalizations cannot be made. Future research could study this issue considering other types of product categories, using other methodologies, and including participants from different segments (e.g. men, older people). However, the findings of the present research contribute both theoretically and managerially, as previously discussed.

ACKNOWLEDGMENT

The author would like to thank Consejo Nacional de Ciencia y Tecnología (CONACYT) for the support in the development of this research, through the Grant No. 322346.

REFERENCES

AMIPCI. (2016). *Estudio Comercio Electrónico en México 2016*. Retrieved from: https://amipci.org.mx/images/Estudio_Ecommerce_AMIPCI_2016_by_comScore_Publica2.pdf

Argo, J. J., Dahl, D. W., & Morales, A. C. (2006). Consumer contamination: How consumers react to products touched by others. *Journal of Marketing*, *70*(2), 81–94. doi:10.1509/jmkg.70.2.81

Argo, J. J., Dahl, D. W., & Morales, A. C. (2008). Positive consumer contagion: Responses to attractive others in retail context. *JMR, Journal of Marketing Research*, *45*(6), 690–701. doi:10.1509/jmkr.45.6.690

Ashwini, K., & Vincent, D. R. (2017). Trust in e-commerce. *Imperial Journal of Interdisciplinary Research*, *3*(5), 1637–1639.

Balaji, M. S., Raghavan, S., & Jha, S. (2011). Role of tactile and visual inputs in product evaluation: A multisensory perspective. *Asia Pacific Journal of Marketing and Logistics*, *23*(4), 513–530. doi:10.1108/13555851111165066

Bryman, A. (1984). The debate about quantitative and qualitative research: A question of method or epistemology? *The British Journal of Sociology*, *35*(1), 75–92. doi:10.2307/590553

Chen, X., Zeng, X., Koehl, L., Tao, X., & Boulenguez-Phippen, J. (2014). Optimization of human perception on virtual garments by modeling the relation between fabric properties and sensory descriptors using intelligent techniques. In *International Conference on Information Processing and Management of Uncertainty in Knowledge-Based Systems* (pp. 606-615). Springer. 10.1007/978-3-319-08855-6_61

Cho, S. S., & Workman, J. J. (2011). Gender, fashion innovativeness and opinion leadership, and need for touch: Effects on multi-channel choice and touch/non-touch preference in clothing shopping. *Journal of Fashion Marketing and Management*, *15*(3), 363–382. doi:10.1108/13612021111151941

Citrin, A., Stem, D. E. Jr, Spangenberg, E. R., & Clark, M. J. (2003). Consumer need for tactile input: An internet retailing challenge. *Journal of Business Research*, *56*(11), 915–922. doi:10.1016/S0148-2963(01)00278-8

Creswell, J. W. (2007). *Qualitative inquiry & research design: Choosing among five approaches*. Thousand Oaks, CA: Sage.

Das, T. K. (2016). Intelligent techniques in decision making: A survey. *Indian Journal of Science and Technology*, *9*(12). doi:10.17485/ijst/2016/v9i12/86063

Demirci, S. (2007). *Virtual touch: An experimental study on the effects of online sense of touch on consumer behavior*. Maastricht University.

Eisenhardt, K. M. (1989). Building theories from case studies research. *Academy of Management Review*, *14*(4), 532–550.

Folkes, V., & Matta, S. (2004). The effect of package shape on consumers' judgments of product volume: Attention as a mental contaminant. *The Journal of Consumer Research*, *31*(2), 390–401. doi:10.1086/422117

Folkes, V. S. (1988). Recent attribution research in consumer behavior: A review and new directions. *The Journal of Consumer Research*, *14*(4), 548–565. doi:10.1086/209135

Grohmann, B., Spangenberg, E. R., & Sprott, D. E. (2007). The influence of tactile input on the evaluation of retail product offerings. *Journal of Retailing*, *83*(2), 237–245. doi:10.1016/j.jretai.2006.09.001

Guéguen, N., & Jacob, C. (2006). The effect of tactile stimulation on the purchasing behavior of consumers: An experimental study in a natural setting. *International Journal of Management*, *23*(1), 24–33.

Hoegg, J., & Alba, J. W. (2007). Taste perception: More than meets the tongue. *The Journal of Consumer Research*, *33*(4), 490–498. doi:10.1086/510222

Hornik, J. (1992a). Effects of physical contact on customers' shopping time and behavior. *Marketing Letters*, *3*(1), 49–55. doi:10.1007/BF00994080

Hornik, J. (1992b). Tactile stimulation and consumer response. *The Journal of Consumer Research*, *19*(3), 449–458. doi:10.1086/209314

Instituto Nacional de Estadística y Geografía (INEGI). (n.d.). Retrieved from: http://cuentame.inegi.org.mx/monografias/informacion/nl/poblacion/

Jeguirim, S. E. G., Adolphe, D. C., Sahnoun, M., Douib, A. B., Schacher, L. M., & Cheikhrouhou, M. (2012). Intelligent techniques for modeling the relationships between sensory attributes and instrumental measurements of knitted fabrics. *Journal of Engineered Fabrics & Fibers*, *7*(3), 88–97.

Jiang, Z., & Benbasat, I. (2007). The effects of presentation formats and task complexity on online consumers' product understanding. *Management Information Systems Quarterly*, *31*(3), 475–500. doi:10.2307/25148804

Jin, S. (2011). The impact of 3D virtual haptics in marketing. *Psychology and Marketing*, 28(3), 240–255. doi:10.1002/mar.20390

Klatzky, R. L., Lederman, S. J., & Matula, D. E. (1993). Haptic exploration in the presence of vision. *Journal of Experimental Psychology. Human Perception and Performance*, 19(4), 726–743. doi:10.1037/0096-1523.19.4.726 PMID:8409856

Krishna, A., Elder, R. S., & Caldara, C. (2010). Feminine to smell but masculine to touch? Multisensory congruence and its effect on the aesthetic experience. *Journal of Consumer Psychology*, 20(4), 410–418. doi:10.1016/j.jcps.2010.06.010

Krishna, A., Lwin, M. O., & Morrin, M. (2009). Product scent and memory. *The Journal of Consumer Research*, 37(1), 57–67. doi:10.1086/649909

Krishna, A., & Morrin, M. (2008). Does touch affect taste? The perceptual transfer of product container haptic cues. *The Journal of Consumer Research*, 34(6), 807–818. doi:10.1086/523286

Kumar, A., Kabra, G., Mussada, E. K., Dash, M. K., & Rana, P. S. (2017). Combined artificial bee colony algorithm and machine learning techniques for prediction of online consumer repurchase intention. *Neural Computing & Applications*, 1–14.

Lin, C. Y., Liaw, S. Y., Chen, C. C., Pai, M. Y., & Chen, Y. M. (2017). A computer-based approach for analyzing consumer demands in electronic word-of-mouth. *Electronic Markets*, 27(3), 225–242. doi:10.100712525-017-0262-5

Lynn, M., Le, J., & Sherwyn, D. S. (1998). Reach out and touch your customers. *Cornell Hospitality Quarterly*, 39(3), 60–65. doi:10.1177/001088049803900312

Mattila, A. S., & Wirtz, J. (2001). Congruency of scent and music as a driver of in-store evaluations and behavior. *Journal of Retailing*, 77(2), 273–289. doi:10.1016/S0022-4359(01)00042-2

Mitchell, D. J., Kahn, B. E., & Knasko, S. C. (1995). There's something in the air: Effects of congruent or incongruent ambient odor on consumer decision making. *The Journal of Consumer Research*, 22(2), 229–238. doi:10.1086/209447

Peck, J., & Childers, T. L. (2003a). To have and to hold: The influence of haptic information on product judgments. *Journal of Marketing*, 67(2), 35–48. doi:10.1509/jmkg.67.2.35.18612

Peck, J., & Childers, T. L. (2003b). Individual differences in haptic information processing: The 'need for touch' scale. *The Journal of Consumer Research*, 30(3), 430–442. doi:10.1086/378619

Peck, J., & Johnson, J. (2011). Autotelic need for touch, haptics, and persuasion: The role of involvement. *Psychology and Marketing*, 28(3), 222–239. doi:10.1002/mar.20389

Peck, J., & Shu, S. B. (2009). The effect of mere touch on perceived ownership. *The Journal of Consumer Research*, 36(3), 434–447. doi:10.1086/598614

Peck, J., & Wiggins, J. (2006). It just feels good: Customers' affective response to touch and its influence on persuasion. *Journal of Marketing, 70*(4), 56–69. doi:10.1509/jmkg.70.4.56

Prasad, B. (2003). Intelligent techniques for e-commerce. *Journal of Electronic Commerce Research, 4*(2), 65–71.

Rose, G., Khoo, H., & Straub, D. W. (1999). Current technological impediments to business-to-consumer electronic commerce. *Communications of the AIS, 1*(16), 1–74.

Singh, M., & Mehrotra, M. (2016). Bridging the Gap Between Users and Recommender Systems: A Change in Perspective to User Profiling. *International Journal of Intelligent Systems Technologies and Applications*, 379.

Smith, A., & Anderson, M. (2016). *Online shopping and e-commerce*. Pew Research Center. Retrieved from http://www.pewinternet.org/2016/12/19/online-shopping-and-purchasing-preferences/

Smith, D. E., Gier, J. A., & Willis, F. N. (1982). Interpersonal touch and compliance with a marketing request. *Basic and Applied Social Psychology, 3*(1), 35–38. doi:10.120715324834basp0301_3

Smith, J. K. (1983). Quantitative versus qualitative research: An attempt to clarify the issue. *Educational Researcher, 12*(6), 6–13. doi:10.3102/0013189X012003006

Spangenberg, E. R., Crowley, A. E., & Henderson, P. W. (1996). Improving the store environment: Do olfactory cues affect evaluations and behaviors? *Journal of Marketing, 60*(2), 67–80. doi:10.2307/1251931

Spiggle, S. (1994). Analysis and interpretation of qualitative data in consumer research. *The Journal of Consumer Research, 21*(3), 491–503. doi:10.1086/209413

Treviño, T., & Morton, F. (2016). Online shopping in Mexico: Exploring the promising and challenging panorama. In C. M. Coria-Sánchez & J. T. Hyatt (Eds.), *Essays on Mexican Business Culture* (pp. 166–182). McFarland.

Verma, N., & Singh, J. (2017). An Innovative Approach for E-Commerce Website Ranking. *International Journal of Advanced Research in Computer Science, 8*(4).

Wansink, B., & Van Ittersum, K. (2003). Bottoms up! The influence of elongation on pouring and consumption volume. *The Journal of Consumer Research, 30*(3), 455–463. doi:10.1086/378621

Workman, J. E., & Caldwell, L. F. (2007). Centrality of visual product aesthetics, tactile and uniqueness needs of fashion consumers. *International Journal of Consumer Studies, 31*(6), 589–596. doi:10.1111/j.1470-6431.2007.00613.x

KEY TERMS AND DEFINITIONS

E-Commerce: The exchange of information, products, and services through online platforms.
Haptics: Interaction through touch.
Need for Touch: A person's preference for information that is obtained through touching objects.
Product Evaluations: A person's perceptions of the characteristics of a product.

Product Presentation Format: Tool that can be either written descriptions or 2D images with the purpose of providing information of a product to consumers.

Tactile Sensation Confirmation: When a person imagines an object's sensation and this sensation is confirmed after touch.

Two Dimensional Images: Graphics, pictures, or videos that present objects in a flat manner (length and width).

Virtual Touch: Touch sensation that consumers perceive when exposed to a 3D format of a product through a computer.

APPENDIX

Table 4. Names and descriptions of participants in the study

Name	Age	Occupation
Elean	23	Graduated professional
Gabriela	21	College student
Sarai	22	Graduated professional
Pamela	25	College student
Cynthia	25	Graduated professional
Fabiola	18	College student
Naila	24	Ph.D. student
Isabel	27	Ph.D. student
Tania	24	Graduated professional
Jessica	18	College student
Ana Rosa	25	Ph.D. student

Chapter 3
Visual Saliency and Perceptual Quality Assessment of 3D Meshes

Anass Nouri
University of Nantes, France

Christophe Charrier
University of Caen Normandy, France

Olivier Lezoray
University of Caen Normandy, France

ABSTRACT

This chapter concerns the visual saliency and the perceptual quality assessment of 3D meshes. Firstly, the chapter proposes a definition of visual saliency and describes the state-of-the-art methods for its detection on 3D mesh surfaces. A focus is made on a recent model of visual saliency detection for 3D colored and non-colored meshes whose results are compared with a ground-truth saliency as well as with the literature's methods. Since this model is able to estimate the visual saliency on 3D colored meshes, named colorimetric saliency, a description of the construction of a 3D colored mesh database that was used to assess its relevance is presented. The authors also describe three applications of the detailed model that respond to the problems of viewpoint selection, adaptive simplification and adaptive smoothing. Secondly, two perceptual quality assessment metrics for 3D non-colored meshes are described, analyzed, and compared with the state-of-the-art approaches.

VISUAL SALIENCY OF 3D MESHES: INTRODUCTION

In every look thrown at a scene or an object, visual attention is fixed on particular regions distinct from their surrounding zones. These striking areas, essentially prominent in the field of 3D objects, are content dependent. However, they are not dependent of the behavior or the experience relative to the human observer (Itti and Koch, 1998). This faculty of fixation is known as visual attention. The saliency computation would allow detecting these perceptually important regions that guide the visual attention.

DOI: 10.4018/978-1-5225-5246-8.ch003

Visual saliency approaches proposed in the state-of-the-art are inspired from low level features of the Human Visual System (HVS). This permits to replace the geometric attributes used for the saliency computation by perceptual ones, and, as confirmed in Kim et al. (2010), these perceptual models succeed in modeling correctly the eye movements of the human observer.

Many applications in the field of 3D computer vision rely on the detection of visual saliency phenomena such as: 1) Automatic viewpoint selection (Lee et al., 2005) that aims at generating the most informative and attractive viewpoint. 2) Adaptive simplification (Shilane & Funkhouser, 2007) where the goal is to more simplify the non-salient areas for the visual quality preservation. Similarly, other applications such as Surface Matching (Gal and Cohen-or, 2006), automatic resizing (Jia, Zhang, and Zhou, 2014), facial recognition (Lee et al., 2004), etc. benefit from visual saliency.

In the following, a definition of visual saliency is proposed. Then, a description of the physiological elements that are involved in the sensitivity of the HVS to visual saliency is provided. Afterwards, different approaches proposed in the state-of-the-art that predict visual saliency are analyzed. This chapter focuses also on a recent approach proposed by Nouri et al. (2015a) that takes into account two characteristics of the Human Visual System (HVS) which are the sensitivity to strong fluctuations and high contrast. For this, a local vertex descriptor in the form of a local adaptive patch is introduced to characterize the 3D surface mesh. This descriptor is used as a basis for similarity measurement and integrated into a weighted multi-scale saliency computation allowing the enhancement of the quality measure and the robustness to the noise. Qualitative and quantitative comparisons with a pseudo ground truth as well as a comparison with the sate-of-the-art methods are achieved to assess its relevance. Finally, three applications guided by the detailed model of saliency are analyzed.

VISUAL SALIENCY: PHYSIOLOGICAL EXPLANATION

The colossal amount and the diversity of the visual information conveyed by the world around us is partially processed by the HVS because of its finite capability. For example, the number of photosensitive cells in the retina is limited and non-uniformly distributed. Thus, human beings can only perceive clearly and with a maximal visual acuity a small area of the visual field. This area is placed in the center of the gaze after several ocular movements. This restrained space of the human visual field, processed in detail by our HVS contrary to the rest, is selected using attentional mechanisms. Many complex processes are involved in visual attention. This chapter focuses only on the part of visual attention that concerns the saliency of a region. Visual saliency can be described as the perceptual information that permits to some objects or regions in the scene to stand out from their surrounding and thus captures the visual attention of the human observer. Therefore, the degree of saliency of a region depends on the distinction of the target region from its surrounding. In other words, this chapter is interested in attentional mechanisms linked to the visual signal or visual stimuli rather to those associated to human observers looking at the scene or to the tasks entrusted to them before the beginning of the visualization (see Bottom-up and Top-down processes below). Thus, a visual element of the scene is judged salient if it is easily remarkable without any prior provided to the observer or if it stands out first while looking to the scene. This element would tend to capture the attention more importantly than other elements in the scene and therefore further attract the observers gazes. Visual attention allows us to construct a perception that fits our needs and capacities. The power and the swiftness of this mechanism constitute a major feature for the selection of relevant information in the scene by moving the observer's eyes sequentially from a salient region to another salient region while focusing attention.

Attentional Process

There are two attentional processes in human vision influencing the orientation of the visual attention on a particular region of the scene:

1. **Bottom-Up Process:** Also called ascending process (from the retina to the brain), are exogenously mechanisms dependent of intrinsic properties of the visual stimuli such as contrast, texture, shape, etc. No willingness from the human observer occurs for placing his eyes on a particular region in the scene. Visual saliency in this context is involuntary and depends only on visual attributes of the region. (We would say that the region stands out from its surrounding or « jumps out » to the observer's eyes. This is called *Pop-out effect*.).

2. **Top-Down Process:** Top-down process, also called descending process (from the brain to ocu-lomotor muscles), are endogenous mechanisms dependent on the willingness of the observer and on what he's searching for in the scene. These are influenced by different factors such as the tasks entrusted to the human observer, its experience and the semantic of the stimuli.

Studies of these attentional processes have shown that the bottom-up process is faster and precedes the top-down process which is slower to enforce (Wolfe et al. 2000; Parkburst et al. 2002; Tatler et al. 2005).

This chapter is interested on the Bottom-up process which is induced by properties of the visual stimuli and that do not depend on the human observer. These will permit to detect perceptually salient regions that are able to guide visual attention of the human observer.

Theory of Visual Attention

It's important to present some elements of the visual attention theory in order to understand how are processed some visual attributes and how certain prevail over others. This chapter will present the Feature Integration Theory *(FIT)* proposed by Treisman and Gelade (1980) as well as the Guided Search Model (GS) which is a modification of the *FIT* proposed by Wolf et al. (1989).

Theory of Feature Integration

In order to represent the visual attention process, Treisman analyses the mechanisms involved in the processing of a visual stimuli to verify if its features are processed in parallel or in series. For this, he measures the reaction time to find among the distractors a target that is visually different from all the others and puts forward two suppositions: 1) If the analysis of a visual feature can be done simultaneously in the visual field, then, the detection of a target containing this feature will take a constant time regardless the number of distractors. 2) If the research of a target having a particular visual feature is sequential, then, the required time to find this target should increase linearly with the number of the distractors.

Consequently, Treisman defines two types of research associated to two experiments that will initi-ate the *FIT*:

- **The Disjunctive Research:** Takes place when the target is distinguished from the distractors by a visual feature. Figure 1 presents green distractors oriented vertically and a red target oriented similarly to the distractors. In this case, the reaction time (of the research) is constant regardless of the number of the distractors. The target strongly stands out from the distractors and guides the visual attention. This kind of research occurs in parallel and is qualified as pre-attentive. It can be associated to the Bottom-up mechanism.
- **The Conjunctive Research:** Takes place when the target and the distractors share many visual features. Figure 1 (b) presents a target represented by a red bar oriented vertically which has the same orientation of the green distractors and the same red color of the distractors oriented horizontally. In this case, the reaction time increases with the number of the distractors and becomes more important. This kind of research can be considered as sequential and calls in addition a voluntary attention. It can be associated to the Top-down mechanism.

Many experiments of Treisman conclude that the color, the orientation, the size, the shape, the intensity and the motion are part of the elementary attributes for which the research is disjunctive. These are called salient attributes.

The *FIT* theory states that visual information is decomposed into distinct elementary attributes in the visual cortex. These attributes are processed in parallel and are represented in specific maps of attributes (Figure 2). The different maps are then merged into a master card called *Master Saliency Map.* Regions that are highlighted on this map refer to salient regions.

The *Guided Research Model* follows the *FIT*'s principles (elementary attributes extraction into specific attributes maps then grouping into an activation global map (Figure 2)) while demonstrating that certain conjunctive researches take place faster than what is proposed in the sequential research of the *FIT* theory (Wolf et al. 1989). The *Guided Research Model* specifies that during a conjunctive

Figure 1. Examples of stimuli used in the research of a target (Wolfe et al. 2010): a) The target has a different color from the distractors. the research in this case is called disjunctive. b) The target shares two visual features with the distractors such as the red colors with the red distractors and the orientation with the green distractors. In this case, the research is called conjunctive.

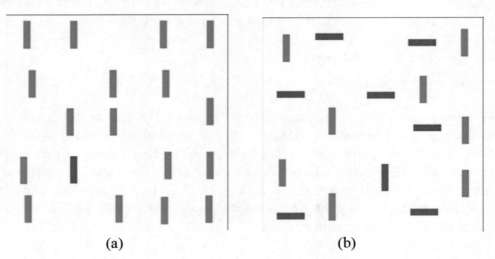

(a)   (b)

Figure 2. Color features map, orientation features map, size features map and their fusion into an attention map according to the Guided Search model in a conjunctive research (Wolfe et al. 1989)

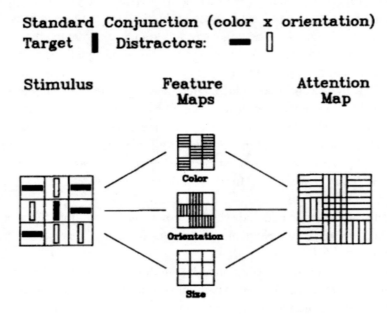

research, the stimuli are classified into distractors and potential targets and are processed in parallel. These targets are then analyzed sequentially which leads to a fast-sequential research in comparison to a random sequential research.

In another study, Wolfe and Horowitz (2004) inventory perceptual attributes that are able to guide the visual attention. Attributes such as color, motion, orientation have been judged capable of directing the attention.

Eye Movements

There are links between the visual attention and ocular movements. This chapter presents the different types of attention as well as the ocular movements which are associated.

Eye Movements and Visual Attention

There are two types of visual attention:

- **Covert Attention:** Studies have established that the attention isn't necessarily linked to eye movements and can move independently (Hederson, 2003) (Liversedge and Findlay 2000). This kind of attention occurs when a distinct region is putted forward without moving the eyes to it.
- **Overt Attention:** This kind of attention occurs when the observer moves its eyes toward a region on which the attention is focalized. Deubel et al. (1996), Hoffman and Subramaniam (1995), Kowler et al. (1995) show that the eye movements toward a region are preceded by a movement of the attention in the direction of that region.

Findlay (2004) suggests that the study of attention as Overt or Covert processes in a context that contains complex or ecologic stimuli is wrong. This is in accordance with the study of Rizzolatti et al. (1994) which shows that Overt and Covert attentions are controlled by extremely related mechanisms.

This chapter is interested on declared visual attention (Overt attention) which is followed (simultaneously) by ocular movements. With other terms, towards which regions the attention of the human observers is moved and then their glance? Visual saliency models answer this question and predict the phenomena of saliency associated to these regions.

A Better Acuity in the Center of the Glance

The HVS can be divided in two principal stages: the stage that relates the eye to the retina and the stage that processes the information coming from the couple eye-retina (Figure 3). The first stage captures and pre-treats the stimuli of the surrounding world then sends it to the second stage for decomposition and an analysis.

The Fovea, which constitutes the central area of the retina, contains a large number of the 130 million photoreceptors distributed non-uniformly on the retinal field. This difference in distribution plays a preponderant role in the human visual acuity. Regions that are fixed and placed in the center of the retina (center of the glance) are analyzed more in details and benefit from a better resolution than regions of the scene located in the periphery of the retina. This leads to the need of moving the gaze in order to place the target region we want to analyze minutely in the center of the retina.

The processing of the information by the primary visual cortex (V1) also confirms the necessity of placing the target regions in the center of the gaze. Indeed, the processing of the visual information coming from the Fovea occupies 50% of the area of the primary cortex (V1) while the 50% remaining treat the rest of the visual field.

Different Types of Ocular Movements

The ocular movements represent the eyes activity and can be measured by oculometry techniques. For this, different approaches exist, however the most used because of its non-invasive character consists

Figure 3. Human visual system: a) Retina (vision du futur). b) Cortex (Human-eye blog)

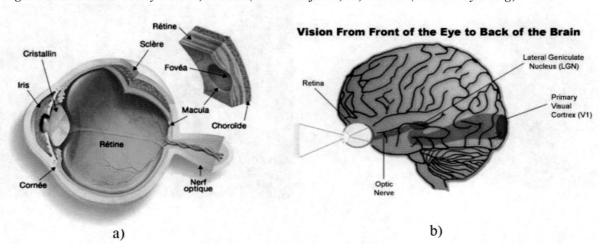

a)   b)

in filming the gaze of the observers using a camera placed on the screen. As a consequence, different ocular movements of the eye have been identified (Widdel, 1984):

- **Jerks:** Very fast movements of the eye (between 30 and 80ms) whose purpose is to place the target region of the scene in the center of the fovea. Between two jerks, the eye stops for a small period of time between 200 and 250ms on a specific point of the scene. This point is called fixation point. Figure 4 illustrates these fixation points. The net regions refer to the regions that have been fixed by the observers (Figure 4 (b)).
- **Continuous Movements of Pursuit:** Take place when the observer looks to an object in motion. At this moment, the SVH extracts a maximum of informations while placing the object in the center of the fovea. In contrary to jerks, these movements are continuous and are corrected continually.
- **Microjerks:** Movements carried out without any interruptions. Without these movements, the observed image will not be « refreshed » or « reloaded ». These jerks also avoid the exhaustion of the photoreceptors.

VISUAL SALIENCY DETECTION

The saliency prediction models of 2D images outnumber those of 3D meshes (Liu et al., 2014). However, one can notice an evident resemblance between all proposed models. Almost all the approaches are based on the FIT or GS of Wolfe. The reader can refer to two reference models of saliency detection in 2D images: (Itti et al., 1998) and (Achanta et al., 2009). Note that 3D volume data (or 3D stacks) are not considered in this chapter.

In the following, a state-of-the -art of saliency models related to 3D non-colored meshes is developed.

Figure 4. Fixations points and ocular path (Yarbus, 1967): a) Face observation with an eye-tracker and b) illustration of an ocular path

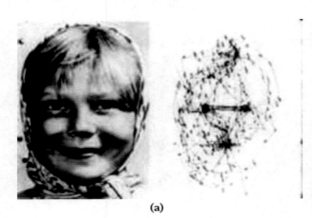

(a)

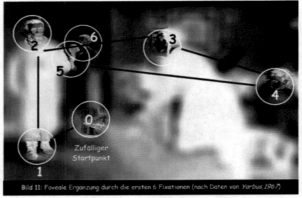

(b)

Visual Saliency of 3D Meshes

Some previous research works on the visual saliency of 3D non-colored meshes took back saliency models defined for 2D images and applied them to 2D projections of the target 3D meshes. This approach doesn't take into account sufficiently the relief of the 3D mesh which nevertheless constitutes an important feature in the perception of 3D multimedia contents (Howard, 2002).

This section presents model-based approaches that use the geometry of the 3D mesh for the saliency prediction. More details on the approaches that take back the 2D saliency models can be found in Guy and Mediouni (1997) and Yee et al. (2001). The models of Lee et al. (2005), Tal et al. (2012), and Song et al. (2001) will be presented in detail as they are used for the comparison with the approach of Nouri et al. (2015a).

Different Saliency Models of the State-of-the-Art

In Wu et al. (2013), Wu et al. detect salient regions using a descriptor based on the neighborhood's height field of each vertex; a squared map of projection heights is generated to represent its configuration (Maximo et al. 2011). Then, the Zernike moments are extracted from these maps to obtain a representation invariant to rotation. To obtain a multi-scale descriptor, the authors vary the size of the maps. The local saliency is first computed after a segmentation of the surface mesh. The saliency of a vertex is obtained using an interpolation of the saliency of the neighboring patches. Furthermore, the global saliency is computed after a gathering of similar vertices into patches. The global saliency of each vertex is then computed as the interpolation of the degrees of saliency of the closest patches. The final degree of saliency of a vertex is obtained by combining and normalizing values of global and local saliency.

Zhao et al. (2013) propose a sampling-based saliency detection method for the simplification of 3D non-colored meshes. The method begins by applying a Gaussian filter on vertices of the 3D mesh, then, features representing the curvature and its directions are computed on different scales. The obtained maps are filtered with a median filter before being combined to produce the final saliency map.

Acting on same principle, Zhao et al. (2012) propose a saliency model based on the diffusion of the surface index parameter by a non-local filter (Buades et al. 2005). This method was used for 3D mesh registration and 3D mesh simplification.

In Zhao and Liu (2012), Yitian and Lui detect salient region by transforming the 3D mesh into a 3D volume. The patch-based method begins by filtering the 3D mesh in order to suppress high frequencies, then, similarities between vertices are computer. Afterwards the mesh is transformed into 3D volumetric data on different scales. The dissimilarity between two patches localized into two sub-voxels provides the dissimilarity map. Finally, the saliency of a patch proportional to its dissimilarity is defined as the mean of its saliency degree over all considered scales.

With the integration of the CRF (Conditional Random Field) in a saliency detection model, Song et al., 2012 propose an approach generating firstly a multi-scale representation of the target 3D mesh by applying a set of Gaussian filters on neighborhoods delimited by a geodesic ray. The differences of Gaussians are computed into each scale and represent the displacement of a vertex after the filtering operation. Subsequently, these are projected on the normal vector of the target vertex to obtain the map of the considered scale. After the computation of the different maps, these are integrated into a CRF with a consistence constraint between the neighboring vertices in order to increase the robustness of the labeling process (labeling of salient regions and non-salient regions). Finally, each vertex is labeled in the CRF using the Belief Propagation algorithm.

Zhao et al. (2013) select points of interest using visual saliency. To obtain robust points of interest, noise on the surface mesh is suppressed by applying a bilateral filter on the vertices normals. Then, Retinex theory (Elad, 2005) is performed to strengthen local details and to estimate invariant properties of the the surface's points of views. After the surface segmentation, saliency is estimated according to the spatial distance between the obtained segments.

Tao et al. (2014), compute Zernike coefficients for patches obtained after an over-segmentation of the surface mesh. Then, after measuring the distinctness for each patch, its saliency is estimated based on its relevance to the most non-salient patches via manifold ranking.

Wang et al. (2015) detect salient regions using a multi-scale saliency model based on the low-rank and sparse analysis in a shape feature space. A new shape descriptor is designed to encode both local and global geometric features of the 3D surface. This leads to employ the low-rank and sparse analysis in the constructed feature space since low-rank components correspond to stronger patches similarities and the sparse components are associated to their differences.

Tass et al. (2015) propose a cluster-based approach to detect saliency on 3D point sets which lack topological information. Fuzzy clustering is used to segment 3D points into small clusters,then the cluster uniqueness and the spatial distribution of each small cluster are computed and combined into a cluster saliency function. Probabilities of points belonging to each cluster are used to assign a saliency value to each 3D point.

Limper et al. (2016) use the Shannon Entropy for saliency detection on 3D meshes. They show the usefulness of the proposed approach into a simplification application.

Liu et al. (2016) use the absorbing Markov chain into a 3D mesh saliency model. The target 3D mesh is segmented into a set of segments using the Ncuts algorithm. Afterwards, each segment is over segmented into patches using the Zernike coefficients. Background vertices are selected using feature variance. Afterwards, the absorbed time of each vertex is computed via absorbing Markov chain with the background patches as absorbing vertices. This gives rise to a preliminary saliency map. Afterwards, a refined saliency map is computed in a similar way but with foreground vertices extracted from the preliminary saliency map as absorbing vertices. Finally, a Laplacian based smoothing is used to spread the saliency patches to each vertex.

Reference Saliency Models of the State-of-the-Art

Model of Lee et al.

Lee et al. (2005) measure saliency using a center-surround operator on Gaussian curvatures in a *DoG* (Difference of Gaussian) scale space. The approach begins by computing a curvature map C and defines a neighborhood $N(v)$ around each vertex:

$$N(v,\sigma) = \left\{ x \mid \; \| \, x - v \, \| < \sigma \right\} \tag{1}$$

Where σ represents the Euclidean distance between the target vertex v and its neighboring vertices x. Then a Gaussian-weighted mean curvature $C(x)$ is computed for each vertex:

$$G(v, \sigma) = \frac{\sum\limits_{x \in N(v, 2\sigma)} C(x) exp[- \| x - v \|^2 / (2\sigma^2)]}{\sum\limits_{x \in N(v, 2\sigma)} exp[- \| x - v \|^2 / (2\sigma^2)]} \qquad (2)$$

The mono-scale saliency of a vertex is defined as the absolute differences of the Gaussian-weighted curvature at the fine and coarse scales:

$$S(v) = | G(v, \sigma) - G(v, 2\sigma) | \qquad (3)$$

Otherwise, the multi-scale saliency of a vertex v at the scale i is defined as:

$$S(v) = | G(v, \sigma_i) - G(v, 2\sigma_i) | \qquad (4)$$

Where σ_i represents the standard-deviation of the Gaussian filter at the scale i. Five scales are used $\sigma_i \in \{2\epsilon, 3\epsilon, 4\epsilon, 5\epsilon\}$ where $\epsilon = 0.3\%$ of the bounding-box's diagonal of the 3D mesh.

Once the saliency maps S_i are computed, a nonlinear suppression operator is applied in order to only consider the saliency maps with few pics of saliency. Each map is normalized and the maximal saliency values M_i as well as the mean of maxima $\bar{m}_i$ are computed. Finally, S_i is weighted by $(M_i - \bar{m}_i)^2$ and the final saliency map S_{final} is defined as the sum of the saliency maps over all the scales: $S_{final} = \sum\limits_i S$.

Figure 5 presents a synopsis of this method.

Figure 5. Synopsis (Lee et al., 2005)

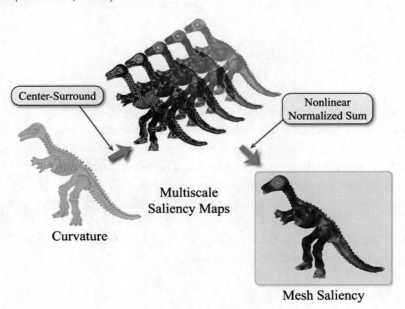

47

Model of Tal et al.

Tal et al. (2012) detect regions of interest of a 3D non-colored mesh by the use of the Spin Image descriptor (Johnson & Hebert, 1999) to encode the geometry of the surface mesh for local and global distinctness computation. The extremities of the 3D mesh are also taken into account in the pipeline of this method. The Spin Image descriptor provides a histogram that characterizes the local geometry of each vertex.

To compute the dissimilarity of two histograms $D(h_1, h_2)$, Tal et al., (2012) use the diffusion distance (Ling and Okada, 2006):

$$D(h_1, h_2) = \sum_{l=0}^{L} k(d_l)$$ (5)

where $d_0 = h_1 - h_2$ and $d_l = [d_{l-1} * \phi(\sigma)] \downarrow_2, l = 1, ..., L$ are the different levels of the Pyramidal Gaussian used for the discretization of the continuous diffusion process, L represents the number of levels of the pyramid, σ is the standard-deviation of the Gaussian filter ϕ, $k(.)$ represents the L_1 norm, and $\downarrow_2$ refers to a down-sampling by 2.

A vertex v_i is considered as distinct if its similar vertices v_j are close. Otherwise, a vertex is less distinct if its similar vertices are far. Consequently, the dissimilarity measure is inversely proportional to the geodesic distance between these vertices:

$$d(v_i, v_j) = \frac{D(h(v_i), h(v_j))}{1 + c.GeodDist(v_i, v_j)}$$ (6)

Where $GeodDist(v_i, v_j)$ represents the geodesic distance between vertices v_i and v_j and $c = 3$. The mono-scale distinction of the vertex v_i is then computed as:

$$D(v_i) = 1 - exp\left\{ -\frac{1}{K} \sum_{k=1}^{K} d(v_i, v_k) \right\}$$ (7)

Where K is the number of vertices similar to v_i over the surface mesh.

In order to reduce the distinctiveness of vertices located in a textured region (similar vertices constituting a large region), Tal et al. propose to compute vertices distinctions considering three scales $(F, F/2, F/4)$ with F representing the faces number. The multi-scale distinction D is defined as the mean of the distinction values over the three scales.

In regards to the detection of the 3D mesh's extremities, this is done in three steps:

1. Application of the MDS (Multi-Dimensional Scaling) transformation to the 3D mesh in order to equalize the Euclidean distance and the Geodesic distance.

2. The presence of an extremity on the surface mesh is defined by the ratio $\frac{V_{CH}}{V_o}$ where V_{CH} represents the volume of the convex envelope of the transformed 3D mesh and V_o is the volume of the original 3D mesh. If $\frac{V_{CH}}{V_o} > 1.5$, then the 3D mesh contains extremities. Indeed, the volume of a round object without extremities is equivalent to the volume of its convex envelope. Conversely, if the 3D mesh contains extremities, the volume of the convex envelope of its transformed version is different from its original volume.

3. 3. A vertex v is located at the extremity of a 3D mesh M if $\forall v_n \in N_v$, where N_v represents the neighborhood of v:

$$\sum_{v_j \in M} GeodDist(v, v_j) \geq \sum_{v_j \in M} GeodDist(v_n, v_j) \qquad (8)$$

Furthermore, this method considers vertices around which the shape of the 3D mesh is constructed named « centers of attention » (20% of distinct vertices of the mesh are considered). Regions that are close to the centers of attention are considered as regions of interest in comparison to the far ones. A vertex v_i is associated to its center of attention as the following:

$$A(v_i) = D_{foci}(v_i) exp\left\{ -\frac{GeodFoci^2(v_i)}{2\sigma^2} \right\} \qquad (9)$$

Where $GeodFoci(v_i)$ represents the geodesic distance between v_i and the closet center of attention, $D_{foci}(v_i)$ is the distinction value of this center of attention and $\sigma = 0.5$.

The vertices located at extremities of the 3D mesh are considered as centers of attention. Therefore, for each vertex, its geodesic distance to an extremity representing its degree of extremity is defined as:

$$E(v_i) = exp\left\{ -\frac{GeodExt^2(v_i)}{2\sigma^2} \right\} \qquad (10)$$

Finally, the degree of interest of a vertex on the surface mesh is defined as the maximum between its distinction and its degree of extremity:

$$I(v_i) = \max\left(\frac{D(v_i) + A(v_i)}{2}, E(v_i) \right) \qquad (11)$$

Figure 6 presents a synopsis of the method of (Tal et al. 2012).

Figure 6. Synopsis (Tal. et al, 2012)

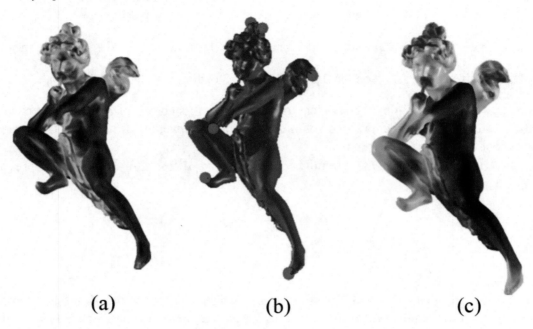

(a)   (b)   (c)

Model of Song et al.

Song et al. (2014) predict saliency in the spectral domain using the analysis of the Log-Laplacian spectrum. The underlying hypothesis is that the geometric Log-Laplacian spectrum of a 3D mesh comprises attributes exploitable for saliency estimation.

For a 3D mesh M with m vertices $\{p_1, ..., p_m\}$, the approach begins by computing a simplified version of the mesh $\hat{M}$ using the QSLIM algorithm (Garland & Heckbert, 1997). Then, a set of smoothed meshes are generated using Gaussian filters of different parameters t_s with s=1,2, . . . , 5

Where k is a constant, $p \in M(t_s)$ and F is a linear representation of the scale space defined by the following convolution:

$$F(., t_s) = U(.) \otimes g(., t_s) \tag{13}$$

Where U is a signal of dimension d and g is a Gaussian kernel with a standard deviation $\sigma = \sqrt{t_s}$ defined as:

$$g(p, t_s) = \frac{1}{(2\pi t)^{1/2}} exp(-p^T p / (2t_s)) \tag{14}$$

The neighborhood of the vertex p around which the Gaussian filter is applied contains all vertices located at a distance equal to $2.5\sqrt{(t_s)}$.

A second set of smoothed meshes $\hat{M}(k(i)t_s)$ is generated using a dynamic scale space:

$$D(p_i,t)=|F(p_i,k(i)t)-F(p_i,t)| \qquad (15)$$

Where the parameter k depends this time on the vertices density on the surface mesh:

$$k(i) = \frac{cn}{\sum\limits_{j\in N(i)} \| p_i - p_j \|} + 1 \qquad (16)$$

Where n represents the number of adjacent vertices to the vertex i, and c is a normalization constant equal to the mean of the distances between the vertices of the 3D mesh.

Similarly to the approach of (Lee et al., (2005)) for the multi-scale saliency detection, five scales are fixed $t \in \{e^2, 2e^2, 3e^2, 4e^2, 5e^2\}$ where e is equal to 0.2% of the bounding-box diagonal of the mesh.

Once the filter bank of the 3D mesh is constructed, the mono-scale saliency is performed as follows. First, the mesh Laplacian L is computed for a mesh of $\hat{M}(t_s)$:

$$L = A - D$$

where A represents the adjacency matrix between vertices:

$$A(i, j) = \begin{pmatrix} 1 & p_i \text{ and } p_j \text{ are adjacent vertices} \\ 0 & \text{Otherwise} \end{pmatrix} \qquad (17)$$

And D is a diagonal matrix in which D_{ii} represents the degree of the vertex p_i. In order to take into account the local geometric information, the adjacency matrix is weighted by the distance between the adjacent vertices:

$$W(i, j) = \frac{1}{\| p_i - p_j \|^2} A(i, j) \qquad (18)$$

The geometric Laplacian is then defined as:

$$L=W - D \qquad (19)$$

and the associated spectrum as:

$$H(f) = \{\lambda_f, 1 \le f \le m\} \qquad (20)$$

where λ_f represents the eigenvalues (frequencies) of the geometric Laplacian ordered increasingly.

It has been observed that the Laplacian spectrum of similar 3D meshes share strictly similar redundancy (Hou & Zhang, 2007) and that the detection of atypical information on the surface mesh represents saliency. To amplify local variations and global deviations at the level of low frequencies and discard the rest, a logarithmic transformation is applied to the spectrum:

$$\iota(f) = log(|H(f)|) \tag{21}$$

Once the transformation performed, the goal is to detect less common frequencies in the spectrum. Song et al. (2014) propose to locally average and smooth the spectrum. Then, significant frequencies that are different from the local mean are identified. For this, a local average filter $J_n(f)$ is used:

$$A(f) = J_n(f) * \iota(f) \tag{22}$$

Where $J_n(f) = \dfrac{1}{n}[11...1]$ is a vector of size $n \times 1$. The spectral deviation is defined by the irregularity R:

$$R(f) = |\iota(f) - A(f)| \tag{23}$$

The irregularity spectrum in the spatial domain is defined as:

$$S = BRB^T W \tag{24}$$

Where $R = Diag\{exp(R(F)) : 1 \leq f \leq m\}$ is a diagonal matrix where the values represents the exponentials of each line of the matrix S which is associated to a vertex of surface mesh, consequently, the saliency of a vertex $S(i)$ is defined as the sum of the values of S along each line. This process is used for computing a saliency map $\tilde{S}(i,t)$ at each scale t using the degrees of saliency of scales $k(i)t$ and t:

$$R(f) = |\iota(f) - A(f)| \tag{25}$$

The multi-scale saliency map of the simplified 3D mesh is computed by summing all the mono-scale saliency maps. A saliency mapping is performed toward the reference 3D mesh using *K-d-tree*. The final saliency map is finally smoothed to avoid discretization problems related to the simplification step.

Discussion

From the above state-of-the-art description, one can observe that a simplification step is integrated in the pipeline of some saliency models. Despite the swiftness provided by this simplification, the latter removes inevitably vertices of the mesh geometry that could have a high degree of saliency and therefore distorts the mesh surface by deleting initial fluctuations. This results in a saliency measure that does not take into account of all local irregularities and exiguous variations yet necessary for a precise estimation of saliency. Others steps such as smoothing and the segmentation lead to a measure of saliency of high complexity. One can also highlight from the defined state-of-the-art that only one method (Song et al., 2014) validates qualitatively its saliency detection results with a pseudo ground truth saliency.

Motivation

Nouri et al. (2015a) propose a new saliency model independent of any pre-treatment or post-treatment such as remeshing, simplification, smoothing or segmentation. This capability provides on the one hand a saliency model measuring precisely the initial degree of saliency and on the other hand a model the complexity of which is not important.

Many studies have shown that the visual saliency is associated to high contrast (Wolf, 1994) and strong discontinuities (Coren et al. 2003). For example, a flat surface would be visually less interesting than a surface with a unique fluctuation. Other studies conclude that the HVS is less sensible and suppress redundant patterns (Koch and Poggio, 1999). Figure 7 presents these two aspects in the context of 3D meshes. Figure 7 (a) and Figure 7 (b) respectively present a flat surface and a surface with strong discontinuities. The glance of a human observer will be mot attracted by the surface containing a high discontinuity than the flat surface.

Figure 7 (c) presents the paw of a 3D dinosaur mesh. The surface of this paw contains redundant bumps. In this case, the glance of a human observer would be more attracted by regions different from these redundant bumps.

Nouri et al. (2015a) propose a saliency model which integrates these SVH features and considers that a vertex on the surface mesh is salient if it stands out from it surrounding and if its local geometric configuration is different from the one of its adjacent vertices. Figure 8 presents a synopsis of this method.

Figure 7. Sensitivity of the HVS to high contrast and redundant patterns: a) Flat surface, b) surface with a strong discontinuity and c) surface with redundant patterns

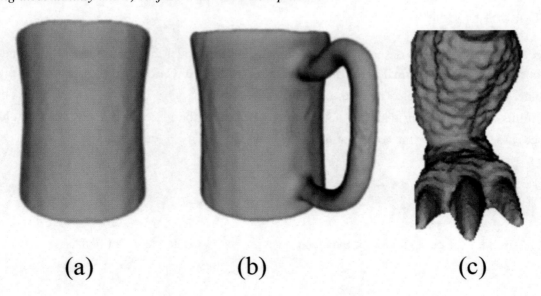

(a)   (b)   (c)

Figure 8. Synopsis of the approach proposed in (Nouri et al., 2015a)

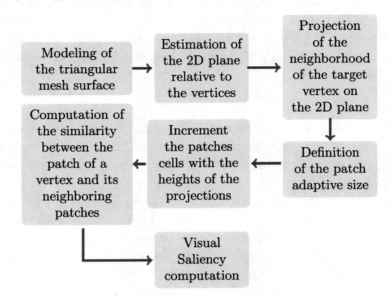

Concepts and Notations on Graphs

Nouri et al. (2015a) represent a 3D non colored mesh M by a non-oriented graph $G = \left(V, E, w\right)$ where $V = \left\{v_1, \ldots, v_N\right\}$ is a set of N vertices, $E \subset V \times V$ is the set of edges deduces from the triangular faces connecting the vertices and $w : E \to R$ represents a symmetric positive weighting function. The concerned graph is non-directed $\left(i.e., for \text{ each } x, y \in V, \left(x, y\right) \in E\right)$ if and only if $\left(y, x\right) \in E$. For each vertex of mesh surface are associated 3D coordinates $\vec{p}_i = (x_i, y_i, z_i)^T \in R^3$. The notation $v_i \sim v_j$ refers to two adjacent vertices in $G (i.e., (v_i, v_j) \in E)$.

3D Surface Modeling

In order to construct local descriptors, Nouri et al., (2005a) model the surface mesh by computing a vector representing the normal $z(v_i)$ on each vertex v_i and its directional vectors $x(v_i)$ and $y(v_i)$ for the tangent plane estimation. The method defines a sphere S_ε of ray ε centered in v_i. Vertices belonging to this sphere are considered as neighboring vertices of the target vertex v_i. These neighboring vertices are then used for the computation of the center of gravity v_i defined as:

$$\vec{\hat{v}}_i = \frac{1}{\mid S_\varepsilon(v_i) \mid} \sum_{j \in S_\varepsilon(v_i)} \vec{v}_j \tag{26}$$

And used for the computation of the covariance matrix associated to v_i defined as:

$$\text{cov}(v_i) = \sum_{j \in S_\varepsilon(v_i)} (\overrightarrow{v_j} - \overrightarrow{v_i})(\overrightarrow{v_j} - \overrightarrow{v_i})^T \in \mathbb{R}^{3\times 3} \tag{27}$$

Where $| S_\varepsilon(v_i) |$ is the cardinality of the spherical neighborhood S_ε. Eigenvectors of the covariance matrix are used to compute the vector representing the normal $z(v_i)$ and the two directional vectors x and y. A similar approach can be found in (Digne et al., 2012).

Hence the surface mesh is represented by vertices with their associated normal vectors and tangent planes. These normal vectors have different directions (outwards and inwards). In order to obtain vectors whose orientations are uniform, the orientation of a vector representing a normal which have been chosen arbitrary is propagated to the neighboring normal vectors. For this, the weight of the edge connecting two vertices v_i and v_j denoted $w(v_i, v_j)$ is defined as:

$$w(v_i, v_j) = 1 - | z_i^T z_j |, v_i \sim v_j \tag{28}$$

Where z_i and z_j represent the normal vectors respectively associated to the vertices v_i and v_j. Afterwards, a Minimum Spanning Tree is generated for the 3D mesh and the normal vectors are re-aligned by going through the MST with a depth first search (Hoppe et al., 1992).

Construction of the Local Descriptors: The Adaptive Local Patches

Once the 3D mesh modeled, the local adaptive patches are constructed. These can be considered as an extension of the works proposed in (Maximo et al, 2011)(Digne et al., 2012) with an adaptive size. For this, the vertices contained in a sphere centered at v_i $S_\varepsilon(v_i) = \left\{ v_j \mid \| \overrightarrow{v_j} - \overrightarrow{v_i} \|_2^2 \leq \varepsilon \right\}$ are projected on a 2D plane $\vec{P}(v_i)$ defined by the associated directional vectors. Therefore, 2D vectors are obtained $\overrightarrow{v'_j}$ defined as:

$$\overrightarrow{v'_j} = [(\overrightarrow{v_j} - \overrightarrow{v_i}) \cdot \vec{x}(v_i), (\overrightarrow{v_j} - \overrightarrow{v_i}) \cdot \vec{y}(v_i)]^T \tag{29}$$

To define the patch size, Nouri et al., (2015a) propose a dynamic configuration depending on the distance between the 2D coordinates of the projected vertices $\overrightarrow{v'_j}$. The patch dimensions are defined according to the horizontal and vertical axes (respectively denoted $T_x(.)$ and $T_y(.)$) as:

$$T_d(v_i) = \max_{(\overrightarrow{v'_j}, \overrightarrow{v'_k}) \in \vec{P}(v_i)} (\| \overrightarrow{v'^d_j} - \overrightarrow{v'^d_k} \|_2^2) \tag{30}$$

Where d represents the x or y coordinate, $\overrightarrow{v'^d_j}$ is the coordinate d of the vector $\vec{v'_j}$ and $\| . \|_2$ is the Euclidean norm. Hence, the patch at v_i is represented by a rectangle of size $T_x(v_i) \times T_y(v_i)$ (note that usually a patch is represented by a square of fixed size (Maximo et al., 2011)(Digne et al., 2012) and does not allow to get an adaptive local descriptor depending on the local geometry). The obtained patch is then divided into $l \times l$ cells in order to precise the index of the cell in which a neighboring vertex is projected:

$$indice^d = \left| \frac{\vec{v}_j'^d}{T_d(v_i) / l} \right| \quad \text{with } v_j \sim v_i \tag{31}$$

Where $\lfloor . \rceil$ denotes the integer rounded.

Finally each cell of the patch $P_i^k (k \in [1, l \times l])$ is filled with the absolute values of the sum of the projection heights:

$$\vec{H}(v_i) = \left(\sum_{\vec{v}_j' \in P_i^k} || (\vec{v}_j - \vec{v}_j') ||_2^2, \forall k \right)^T \tag{32}$$

Where $\vec{H}(v_i)$ represents the vector of accumulated heights in the patch cells.

Figure 9 illustrates the construction process of the local adaptive patches and Figure 10 presents three patches related to 3 vertices belonging to different regions: 1) Salient (finger of the 3D mesh) 2) Moderately salient (located at the neck or the shoulder of the 3D mesh) 3) Non-salient (the flat region situated on the tibia of the 3D mesh). The red pixels in the constructed patch refer to important projec-

Figure 9. Illustration of the local adaptive patches construction

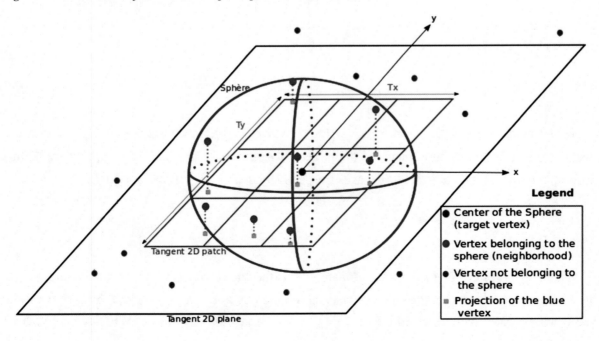

Figure 10. Constructed local patches associated to three vertices (red points) belonging to different regions on the surface of the 3D mesh: 1) salient region (finger of the 3D mesh). 2) Moderately salient (located at the neck or the shoulder of the 3D mesh). 3) Non-salient region (the flat region located on the tibia of the 3D mesh)

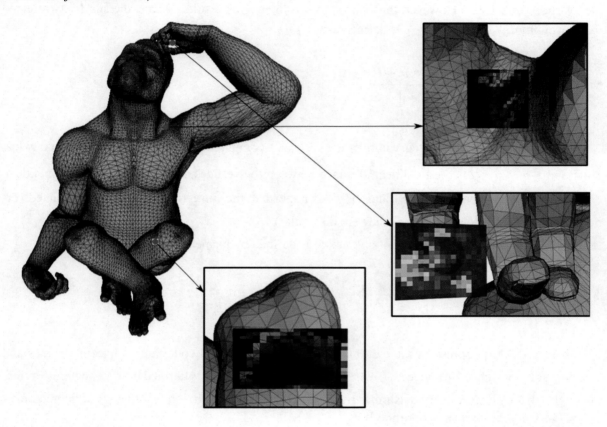

tions heights of the neighboring vertices associated to the target vertex. One can remark that the adaptive size of patches depends on the local configuration of the target vertex.

It's important to note that the adaptivity of the patches size isn't linked to the ray ε of the sphere, but rather to the maximal distance between 2D projections of the neighboring vertices along the x and y axes. This strengthens their adaptivity. This method also works for 3D point clouds instead of 3D meshes since the mesh topology isn't taken into account.

Mono-Scale Saliency

To compute the mono-scale saliency of a target vertex, Nouri et al. (2015a) define a similarity measure between the patch of a vertex and the patches associated to its neighboring vertices. A scale parameter (standard deviation of a Gaussian kernel measuring the dissimilarity) is computed locally. Indeed, the use of a specific scale parameter for each vertex permits to take into account the local distribution. The scale parameter is defined as:

$$\sigma(v_i) = \max_{v_k \sim v_i} (|| \vec{v}_i - \vec{v}_k ||_2) \tag{33}$$

Note that a scale parameter computed using the Euclidean norm between patches instead of coordinate vertices was tested. However, this has led to less interesting results. Hence, the similarity affected to the weight of the edge $e(v_i, v_j)$ is defined as:

$$w(v_i, v_j) = \exp\left[-\frac{\kappa(v_j)* || \vec{H}(v_i) - \vec{H}(v_j) ||_2^2}{\sigma(v_i) * \sigma(v_j)* || \vec{v_i - v_j} ||_2^2} \right] \text{ with } v_j \sim v_i \tag{34}$$

Where $\kappa(v_j)$ represents the curvature of the vertex v_j computed with the method of (Rusinkiewicz, 2004)and $|| \vec{v_i - v_j} ||_2^2$ is the Euclidean distance between the vertices v_i and v_j. When the Euclidean distance between the patches $\vec{H}(v_i)$ and $\vec{H}(v_j)$ is important, the similarity between the associated vertices v_i and v_j tends towards 0 (*i.e.*, they are dissimilar).

Finally, the mono-scale saliency of a vertex v_i is defined by its mean degree:

$$\text{Mono-scale-saliency}(v_i) = \left(\frac{1}{| v_j \sim v_i |} \right) \sum_{v_i \sim v_j} w(v_i, v_j) \tag{35}$$

Where $| v_j \sim v_i |$ represents the cardinality of the neighborhood containing adjacent vertices and $w(v_i, v_j)$ is the weight of the edge $e(v_i, v_j)$. This mono-scale saliency is defined in $[0 \ 1]$ where 0 refers to a high saliency degree (very dissimilar from its neighborhood) and 1 refers to a weak degree of saliency (very similar to its neighborhood).

The Contribution of the Curvature and the Distance-Coefficient Weights

Figure 11 presents the mono-scale saliency of the 3D mesh Gorilla with the method of Nouri et al.(2015a). One can remark that this method accurately highlights regions associated to the paws and toes and judge them as salient regions. Exiguous details such as the eyes, the nose, the mouth and the ears are well detected but with a certain imperfection at the level of the eyes. The saliency of the eyes is saturated. This will be corrected by the use of the multi-scale aspect.

It's interesting to analyze here the contribution of the curvature and the distance coefficient weights on the single-scale saliency rendering. Figure 12 presents a comparison between the detected saliency using the coefficient weights and the saliency without these. One can easily notice that the saliency estimated using the coefficient weights is widely finer than that one detected without. The surplus of saliency at the level of the ribs, the chest, the knees, the forearms and the paws has been corrected. Moreover, salient regions such as the nose, the eyes and the mouth have been preserved. Indeed, using vertex curvature (equation 9) permits to estimate the discontinuity between the target vertex and its adjacent vertices.

Figure 11. Mono-scale saliency (Nouri et al., 2015a). Red areas refer to very salient regions. Those in blue are not salient

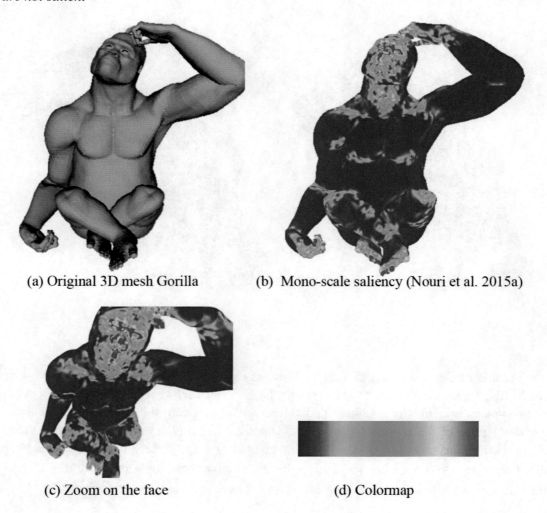

(a) Original 3D mesh Gorilla   (b) Mono-scale saliency (Nouri et al. 2015a)

(c) Zoom on the face   (d) Colormap

A strong discontinuity will more contribute to the saliency detection than a weak one. Therefore, this parameter helped to eliminate the surplus of saliency.

The distance coefficient in the denominator of the equation 9 reduces the contribution of the remote vertices in the computation of patch similarities which also explains the deletion of the surplus of saliency.

The Influence of the Number of Cells and the Neighborhood in the Saliency Detection

Two parameters affect the detection of saliency: the number of patch cells and the ray of the sphere S_ε. Table 1 presents the amplitude of the detected saliency according to the ε and l parameters. One can remark that saliency detection depends strongly on both the neighborhood delimited by the sphere S_ε

Figure 12. The contribution of the weighting parameters: (a) Saliency without the curvature and the distance coefficient weights ($\varepsilon = 2$ and $l = 17$) b) Saliency using the curvature and the distance weights ($\varepsilon = 2$ and $l = 17$)

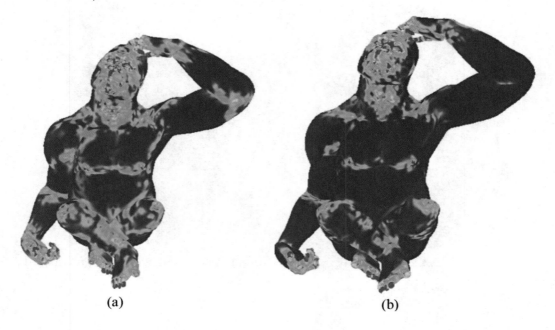

(a)   (b)

and the number of patch cells l . In Table 1, a radius equal to 1 provides the detection of very small salient details. Remark that in this case, increasing the number of cells doesn't affect the saliency estimation. In contrast, a sphere with a radius equal to three greatly expands the neighborhood, which lead to an over description of the surface mesh and thus detecting large salient regions. Note that the number of salient vertices increases proportionally to the number of cells. Hence, the neighborhood has to be specified according to the application using saliency. Finally, these three radii of the sphere S_ε will permit to design a multi-scale saliency detection model based on the local adaptive patches.

Multi-Scale Saliency Computation

In order to enhance the quality of their saliency measure, Nouri et al. (2005a) propose to compute saliency at different scales. Saliency at primary scales will detect finest and cramped details, while higher scales will highlight large regions (see Table 1). Another interest of the multi-scale aspect consists in the robustness of the approach to the noise since the latter is perceptible only on some scales. For this, three scales will highlight large regions (see Table 1).

Another interest of the multi-scale aspect consists in the robustness of the approach to the noise since the latter is perceptible only on some scales. For this, three rays are considered in the construction of the local adaptive patches. Three saliency maps are hence generated and merged taking into account their respective entropy. Indeed, the entropy weight permits to evaluate the disorder and the disparity of

Table 1. Influence of parameters

Raduis/Number of cells	Number of cells		
	7×7	17×17	27×27
$\varepsilon = 1$			
$\varepsilon = 2$			
$\varepsilon = 3$			

each generated map. For a defined scale k, histogram of saliency h_k is computed in order to obtain the probability of having a saliency value i:

$$Pr_{i,k} = h_k^i / \mid V \mid \tag{36}$$

Where h_i^k represents the number of vertices of degree of saliency equal to i at a scale k. Hence, the entropy at a scale k is defined as:

$$\text{Entropy}_k = -\sum Pr_{i,k} * log_2 Pr_{i,k} \tag{37}$$

By weighting the saliency degree of each vertex while merging the different scales with their respective entropy, a robust multi-scale saliency map is obtained which considers the saliency disparity on the different scales. The multi-scale saliency is defined as:

$$\text{Multi-scale-saliency}(v_i) = \frac{\sum_{k=1}^{3} \text{Mono-scale-saliency}_k(v_i) * Entropy_k}{\sum_{k=1}^{3} Entropy_k} \tag{38}$$

Where k is the scale index.

Figure 13(b) presents the multi-scale saliency of the 3D Gorilla mesh. One can remark that the proposed multi-scale saliency model brings out finely the salient regions on the 3D mesh surface. Figure 13(c) shows the saliency detected at the level of the face. In comparison with the saliency result presented in Figure 11, one can notice that the over estimation of saliency at the level of the eyes and nose has been corrected. Only the eyes are now judged as salient and not their peripheral zones (Figure 13 (d)). Note

Figure 13. Multi-scale saliency detected with approach of (Nouri et al., 2015a)

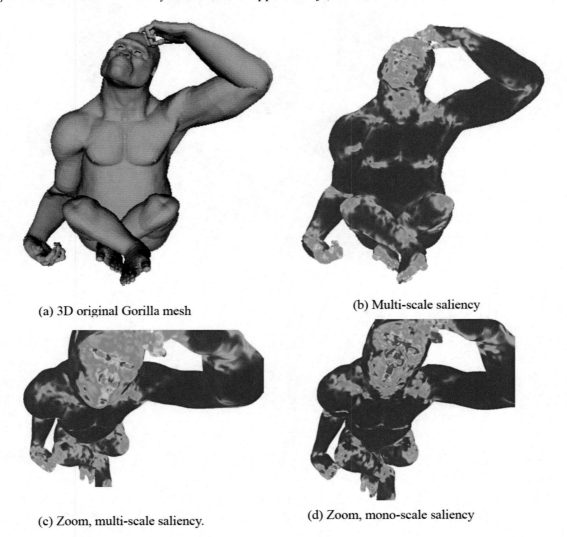

(a) 3D original Gorilla mesh

(b) Multi-scale saliency

(c) Zoom, multi-scale saliency.

(d) Zoom, mono-scale saliency

that a precise detection of the eyes in scenes containing faces is mandatory since the eyes are highly regarded parts (Henderson et al., 2005).

Model of Nouri et al. (2015b): Extension to Visual Saliency of 3D Colored Meshes

Recent studies on the contribution of color in the orientation of attention have shown that colorimetric information modifies the eye movements while visualizing a multimedia content (Shahrbabaki, 2015). Nouri et al. (2015b) have proposed to extend their multi-scale saliency model to 3D colored meshes whose saliency detection has never been studied before. Indeed, 3D colored meshes are of great interest for many applications such as video games, civil engineering, 3D impression, etc. With the recent development of 3D scanners, it is possible now to acquire simultaneously the geometry and colors of an object or a scene. A color $\vec{c}_i$ is provided for each vertex in the form of an RGB vector for the colorimetric description.

In their previous saliency model, Nouri et al. 2015a have only considered 3D coordinates $\vec{p}_i$ of vertices. In order to extend their multi-scale saliency model to 3D colored meshes, they proceed as follows: a local adaptive patch is constructed similarly to the one constructed for 3D non colored meshes, however, its cells $\mathcal{P}_i$ are filled with the mean RGB colors of the projected vertices $\dfrac{1}{|\vec{c'_j} \in \mathcal{P}|}\sum_{\vec{c'_j} \in \mathcal{P}_i} \vec{c'_j}$ thus defining a color vector $\vec{C}(v_i)$ representing the local patch on each vertex. Edges are then weighted by the following similarity:

$$w_C(v_i, v_j) = \exp\left[-\frac{\|\vec{C}(v_i) - \vec{C}(v_j)\|_2^2}{\sigma_C(v_i) * \sigma_C(v_j) * l^2}\right] \tag{39}$$

Where $\sigma_C(v_i) = \max_{v_k \sim v_i}(\|\vec{c}_i - \vec{c}_k\|_2)$. The mono-scale colorimetric saliency at a scale k is defined similarly to the mono-scale geometric saliency (mean degree of the target vertex):

$$\text{Mono-scale-colorimetric-saliency}_k(v_i) = \frac{1}{|v_j \sim v_i|}\sum_{v_i \sim v_j} w_C(v_i, v_j) \tag{40}$$

The multi-scale colorimetric saliency is defined as:

$$\text{Multi-scale-colorimetric-saliency}(v_i) = \frac{\sum_{k=1}^{3}\text{Mono-scale-colorimetric-saliency}_k(v_i) * \text{Entropy}_k}{\sum_{k=1}^{3}\text{Entropy}_k} \tag{41}$$

The results of the colorimetric saliency of 3D colored meshes are presented and analyzed.

Results and Validation of the Detected Visual Saliency of 3D Non-Colored Meshes

Comparison With a Pseudo Ground Truth

Figure 14 and Figure 15 present the saliency results of the approach of (Nouri et al., 2015a) as well as a subjective saliency (detected by human observers) of 3D non-colored meshes belonging to the 2007 SHREC Shape-based Retrieval Contest database (Chen et al., 2012) which constitutes a pseudo ground truth relative to visual saliency of non-colored meshes. These subjective results were acquired in an online experimentation where the observers were asked to select 3D vertices which are likely to be selected by other observers. From the collected information's, the authors perform a regression analysis to produce an analytical model that localizes salient vertices on the surface mesh. Figure 14 and Figure 15 show that the saliency detected by the approach of (Nouri et al., 2015a) corresponds well to the regions that have guided the visual attention of the human observes. The low values of the mean square errors (NMSE - Normalized Mean Square Error) confirm the accuracy of the proposed saliency model.

Note that the comparison with this pseudo ground truth can only be qualitative and not quantitative due to its nature (pseudo ground truth and not a real ground truth) (Liu et al., 2016). Indeed, there is no saliency prediction in the results of the proposed ground truth but only areas of interest. The computed NMSE values aren't strongly representative since the range values of the saliency degrees is different

Figure 14. Comparison of the predicted multi-scale saliency (Nouri et al., 2015) with a pseudo ground truth saliency (Chen et al., 2012). Images (a), (c), (e), (g), (i) and (k) represent the pseudo ground truth saliency for various non colored 3D meshes. Images. Images (b), (d), (f), (h), (j), (l) and (n) represent the predicted multi-scale saliency

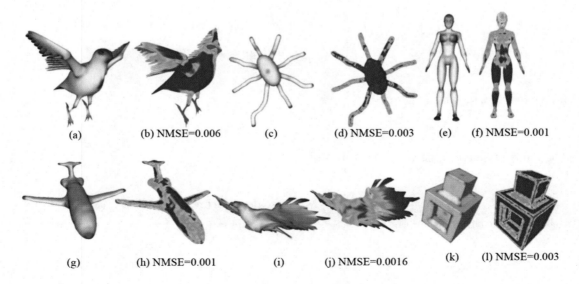

Figure 15. Comparison of the predicted multi-scale saliency (Nouri et al., 2015) with a pseudo ground truth saliency (Chen et al., 2012). Images (a), (c), (e), (g), (i) and (k) represent the pseudo ground truth saliency for various non colored 3D meshes. Images (b), (d), (f), (h), (j) and (l) represent the predicted multi-scale saliency

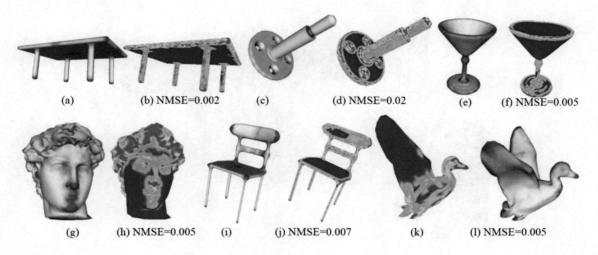

from the values of the produced analytical model provided by the pseudo ground truth. The design of a real ground truth saliency is mandatory for a deeper quantitative comparison. This constitutes a perspective of this work and is described in the Conclusion.

Despite this precision in the estimation of saliency, the approach of (Nouri et al., 2015a) doesn't perform well for some non « optimized » 3D meshes (Figure 16). The surface of a non-optimized 3D mesh is constituted from regular triangles (triangle with a constant area) and edges of the same length (Figure 17). Indeed, one can remark in Figure 17 (a) and Figure 17 (c) that all regions of the 3D mesh (regions with few details and regions containing lot of details) have similar number of triangles (for example the palm of the hand and the areas between the fingers). However, for an « optimized » 3D mesh (Figure 17 (b) and Figure 17 (d)), when some regions contain lot of details (for example the hollow at the top of the bird's back), the latter requires a high number of triangles. For regions with less details (the bottom of the bird's back), these need less number of triangles. Consequently, triangles on the surface of a 3D optimized mesh will have different areas and de facto edges with different lengths.

While computing similarities (equation 9), a weight representing the Euclidean distance between the target vertex and its neighbor is used. This coefficient allows reducing the influence of far vertices in

Figure 16. Inaccurate detection of saliency: a) - c) pseudo ground saliency and b) d) predicted multi-scale saliency

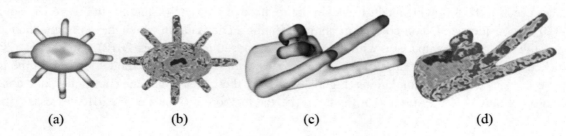

Figure 17. Non « optimized » and « optimized » 3D meshes: a) 3D non « optimized » mesh », b) 3D « optimized » mesh, c) zoom on (a). and d) zoom on (b). In optimized meshes, the number of triangles varies according to the amount of the details.

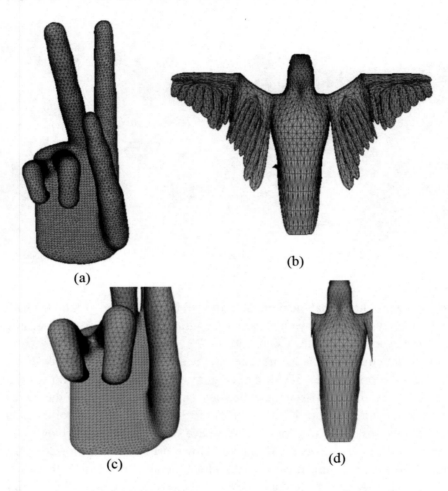

the computation of the saliency degree of a target vertex and vice versa. For non-optimized meshes, all neighboring vertices contribute with the same weight to the saliency degree of the target vertex since the distance weight is constant. This explains the surplus of red vertices on the saliency map (Figure 16).

Analysis and Comparison With the State-of-the-Art

As the source codes associated to the different approaches of the state-of-the-art are not available, the 3D meshes used for the following analysis are similar to those of the state-of-the-art. In Figure 18, Nouri et al., (2015) considers a 3D non-colored mesh representing a Dinosaur on which they compute the multi-scale saliency for the comparison with the methods proposed in (Tal et al., 2012), (Song et al., 2014) and (Lee et al., 2005). Tal et al., (2012) judge the ribs of the 3D Dinosaur model located on the back and the stomach as non-salient regions (Figure18(c)). Yet, these areas fluctuate enormously and contain high discontinuities in the surface. In Figure 18(b), the method of (Nouri et al., 2015) assesses ribs of

Figure 18. Comparison with the state-of-the-art: a) Original 3D mesh Dinosaur, b) Multi-scale saliency detected by (Nouri et al., 2015a), c) Saliency detected by (Tal et al., 2002), d) Saliency detected by the (Song et al., 2014) and e) Saliency detected by (Lee et al., 2005)

(a)   (b)   (c)

(d)   (e)

the mesh Dinosaur as salient regions given their high discontinuities, and contrary to the approach of (Tal et al., 2012) (see Figure18(c)), the relative area of skull (except the eye and some curvatures) is not considered as a completely salient region. This also means that at the first glance in the direction of the mesh Dinosaur, visual attention will be placed firstly on a part of the fluctuating ribs or the neck, rather than on the surface of its skull. In Figure 18 (d), one can notice that the method of (Lee et al., 2005) weakly detect the ribs of the mesh Dinosaur (colored in light green). Locally finest details are not taken into account, contrary to the approach of (Nouri et al., 2015a). However, in Figure 18(d), the approach of Song et al., 2014 provide a saliency map similar to one of (Nouri et al., 2015a). It can differentiate between areas with high discontinuities and flat ones.

Figure 19 shows a comparison of the estimated saliency on the 3D mesh Angel with the approaches of Nouri et al. (2015a), Tal et al. (2012) and Song et al. (2014). The 3D mesh Angel's surface is complex as it contains many extremities. It has also both rough and smooth surfaces. One can see that the extremity of the scarf presents lots of fluctuations. This one is considered as salient by the approach of (Song et al., 2014) and the approach of (Nouri et al., 2015a) while the approach of (Tal et al., 2012) considers it as non-salient. The discontinuities on the eyes, the arms, the hip and the stomach are represented as salient by the approaches of (Song et al., 2014) and (Nouri et al., 2015a) contrary to the method of (Tal et al., 2012).

Figure 20 shows a comparison between the saliency maps of the 3D mesh Horse. One can notice that the methods of (Song et al., 2014) and (Nouri et al., 2015a) are able to detect the eyes, highly regarded

Figure 19. Comparison with the state-of-the-art: a) Original 3D mesh Angel, b) Multi-scale saliency detected by (Nouri et al., 2015a), c) Saliency detected by (Tal et al., 2002) and d) Saliency detected by (Song et al., 2014)

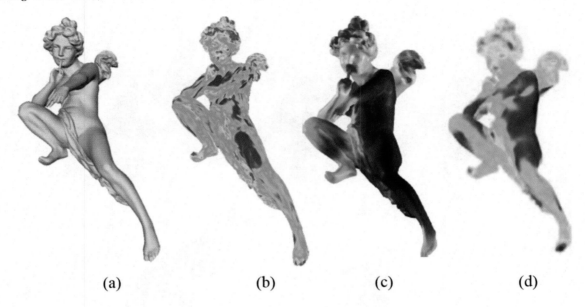

(a) (b) (c) (d)

Figure 20. Comparison with the state-of-the-art: a) Original 3D mesh Horse, b) Multi-scale saliency detected by (Nouri et al., 2015a), c) Saliency detected by (Tal et al., 2002) and d) Saliency detected by (Song et al., 2014)

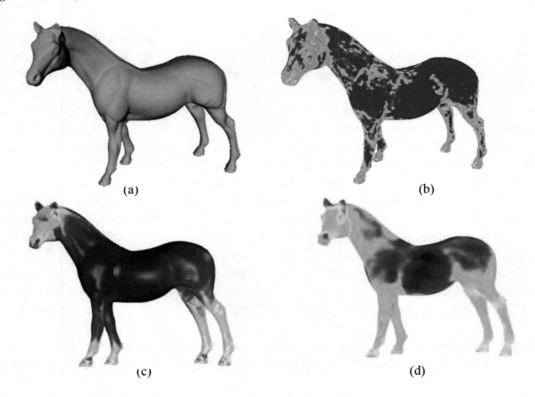

(a) (b)

(c) (d)

parts in scenes or meshes containing faces, and judge them as very salient regions while the method of (Tal et al., 2012) fails in this regard. Also, the horse's back has muscled parts. These areas are also assessed as salient regions with the methods of Song et al. (2014) and Nouri et al. (2015a) contrary to the method of Tal et al., 2012).

Note that the saliency map provided by the approach of Nouri et al., 2015a) isn't smoothed in contrary to other approaches. This aspect allows the detection of exiguous salient details which are of great interest for applications such as adaptive compression and smoothing.

Figure 21 shows the multi-scale saliency maps of various3D non-colored meshes provided by the approach of Nouri et al. (2015).

Figure 21. The multi-scale saliency maps of various 3D non-colored meshes provided by the approach of (Nouri et al., 2015a)

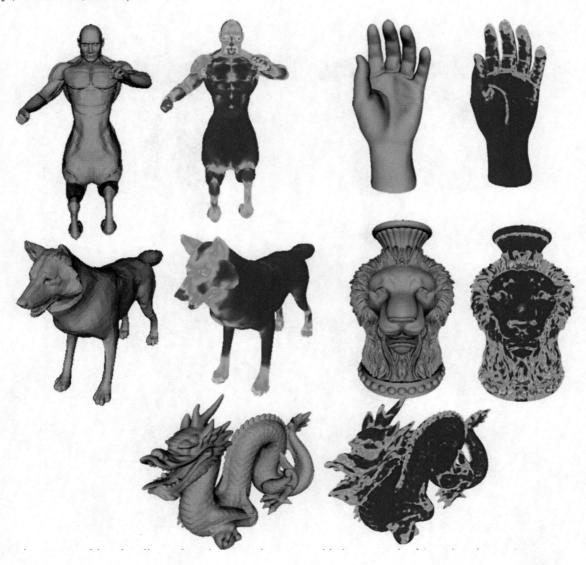

Robustness and Stability

To attest the robustness of their approach, Nouri et al. (2015a) distort a target 3D mesh (a 3D mesh representing a Centaur is used in this case) with noise by randomly displacing the positions of its vertices according to two levels of noise. Then, they apply their multi-scale saliency model for saliency estimation. Figure 22 shows this experimentation. One can see that the method of (Nouri et al., 2015a) always

Figure 22. Robustness to noise: a) Original 3D mesh Centaur noised (displacement= -0.1%), b) Original 3D mesh Centaur noised (displacement=-0.2%), c) Multi-scale saliency of (a) (Nouri et al., 2015a) and d) Multi-scale saliency of (b) (Nouri et al., 2015a). Note how the original salient regions still remain salient despite the sever noise

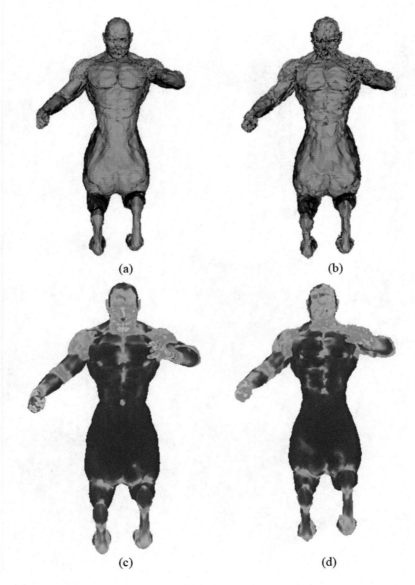

succeeds to detect the same salient regions despite the noise affected to the mesh surface. Areas like the eyes, the mouth, the nose, the paws still are considered salient and can be differentiated from the other flat regions. Also, the NMSE was computed between the saliency associated to the original mesh and the saliency on its noisy version. The low value of the NMSE confirms that their approach is robust to noise.

Another experiment that demonstrates the stability consists in measuring saliency on simplified meshes. Simplification was operated using the algorithm proposed in (Garland et al., 1997). Figure 23 shows the behavior of the method of (Nouri et al., 2015a) on simplified meshes. Firstly, the mesh was simplified to 25% (in Figure 23(a), 25% of vertices were deleted). One can notice that the initially salient

Figure 23. Robustness to simplification: a) 3D mesh Centaur simplified to 25%, b) 3D mesh Centaur simplified to 50%, c) Multi-scale saliency of (a) (Nouri et al., 2015a) and d) Multi-scale saliency of (b) (Nouri et al., 2015a). Note how the original salient regions still remain salient despite the sever noise

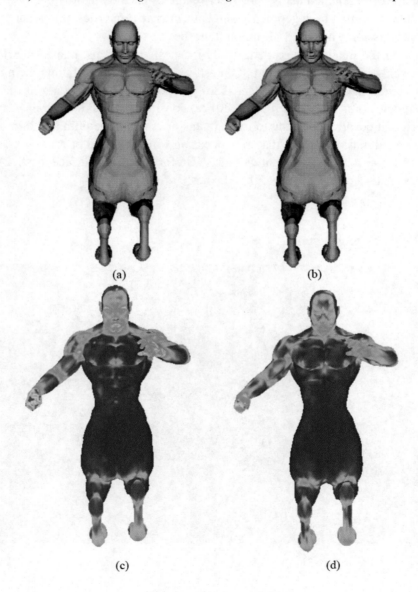

(a) (b)

(c) (d)

regions are always detected (see Figure 23(c)). In Figure 23(b), the mesh is simplified to 50%. The same regions remain salient (Figure 23 (d)) but with less intensity. This is due to the strong simplification that tends to delete discontinuities and therefore flattens the vertices. Flat surfaces present naturally a low visual saliency.

Results of the Detected Visual Saliency of 3D Colored Meshes

Construction of a 3D Colored Mesh Database

Currently, there's no 3D colored mesh database in the state-of-the-art which allows the evaluation of saliency models or quality assessment algorithms. Consequently, a 3D colored mesh database has been designed by (Nouri et al., 2017a) to evaluate their colorimetric saliency model (Nouri et al., 2015b). 15 real 3D objects have been scanned using a 3D laser scanner *NextEngine* provided with a rotating plate. This scanner is able to acquire both geometric and colorimetric properties of a target 3D object (Figure 24). Figure 25 presents some acquired 3D colored meshes.

In a context of visual quality assessment of 3D meshes, algorithms, named metrics, are designed for scoring the visual quality of a distorted 3D mesh in a similar way to human beings. The distorted versions of the acquired meshes have to reflect as fully as possible the degradations that may occur during common treatments. For this, (Nouri et al., 2017a) consider several distortions (Table 2) which are applied to the original corpus according to three intensities: weak, medium and high. In order to take into account the visual masking effect that may occur on some textured or rough regions, the selected distortions are applied according to four situations: 1) Uniformly on the surface mesh, 2) on rough areas, 3) on smooth areas and 4) on the colors of the 3D mesh.

Figure 24. A 3D object being acquired

Figure 25. Some 3D colored meshes of the constructed database

Table 2. Distortions of the proposed 3D colored mesh databases

Type of degradation
Gaussian noise on 3D coordinates
Simplification
Gaussian noise on RGB colors
Smoothing on 3D coordinates
Smoothing on RGB colors

In order to distinguish between rough and smooth regions, Nouri et al., (2017a) have implemented the method of (Wang et al., 2012) to generate a roughness map which associates a roughness value to each vertex in [0 1]. To distort a rough or smooth region of the surface mesh, it's necessary to modify the vertex coordinates belonging to this region:

$$\left\{\begin{array}{ll} \vec{p}_i = \vec{p}_i + \text{noise} \times \text{roughness}(v_i) & \text{distorsions on rough regions} \\ \vec{p}_i = \vec{p}_i + \text{noise} \times (1 - \text{roughness}(v_i)) & \text{distorsions on smooth regions} \end{array}\right\} \qquad (42)$$

The same process is used to distort the colors of the 3D mesh. Therefore the constructed colored mesh database contains 425 colored 3D meshes (17 reference meshes + 17x3x8 distorted meshes). Figure 26 presents examples of distorted 3D meshes from the proposed database.

Figure 26. Some distorted 3D colored meshes of the constructed 3D mesh database

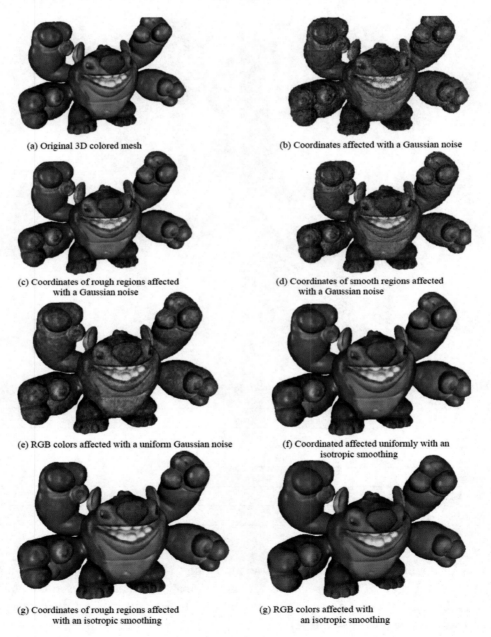

(a) Original 3D colored mesh

(b) Coordinates affected with a Gaussian noise

(c) Coordinates of rough regions affected with a Gaussian noise

(d) Coordinates of smooth regions affected with a Gaussian noise

(e) RGB colors affected with a uniform Gaussian noise

(f) Coordinated affected uniformly with an isotropic smoothing

(g) Coordinates of rough regions affected with an isotropic smoothing

(g) RGB colors affected with an isotropic smoothing

Results and Analysis

In order to illustrate the difference between the colorimetric saliency and the geometric saliency of 3D meshes, Figure 27(a) presents a 3D scan of a human being. Figure 27 (b) shows the geometric saliency which takes into account only coordinated of vertices during the construction of the local adaptive patches. One can remark that the flat regions are judged as non-salient while fluctuating regions not redundant are considered as salient. Furthermore, Figure 27 (c) presents the colorimetric saliency based only on the RGB colors of vertices. This result is very different from the geometric saliency map. Indeed, regions with important color variations such as the eyes and eyebrows are now considered as salient. White areas on the shirt that were considered non salient on the geometric saliency map are putted forward on the colorimetric saliency map. Likewise, the varying colors of the skin are well detected in the colorimetric saliency map while they were not in the geometric saliency map.

The same contribution of colors in the detection of saliency can be observed in Figure 28. The white collar of the duck is very contrasted due to the colors delimiting it (red and white colors). The latter is

Figure 27. Multi-scale saliency of a 3D colored mesh representing head of a human being: a) 3D colored mesh, b) Multi-scale geometric saliency (Nouri et al., 2015a) and c) Multi-scale colorimetric saliency (Nouri et al, 2015b)

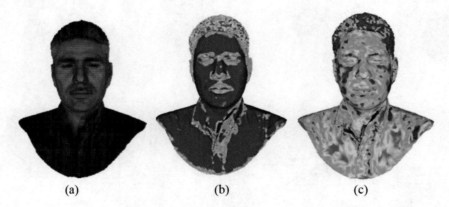

(a)   (b)   (c)

Figure 28. Multi-scale colorimetric saliency of a scanned 3D colored mesh representing a stuffed duck: a) 3D colored mesh, b) Multi-scale geometric saliency (Nouri et al., 2015a) and c) Multi-scale colori-metric saliency (Nouri et al, 2015b)

(a)   (b)   (c)

judged very salient in the colorimetric saliency map whereas it was considered to be moderately salient in the geometric saliency map.

Figure 29 presents the colorimetric saliency of various 3D meshes belonging to the constructed 3D colored mesh database. One can remark that the colorimetric saliency model proposed in (Nouri et al., 2015b) predicts saliency precisely. Note that all the colorimetric saliency results were computed in the RGB color-space. Figure 30 presents the colorimetric saliency of the 3D meshes representing a duck and a human being head in different color-spaces.

Currently, there is no pseudo ground truth or ground truth saliency available for 3D colored meshes allowing quantitative comparisons. The design of such ground truth for 3D colored meshes is of great interest for the research field and constitutes one of our perspectives.

Figure 29. Multi-scale colorimetric saliency of the 3D colored meshes presented in Figure 25

Figure 30. Multi-scale colorimetric saliency computed in LAB, YCbCr and XYZ colorspaces

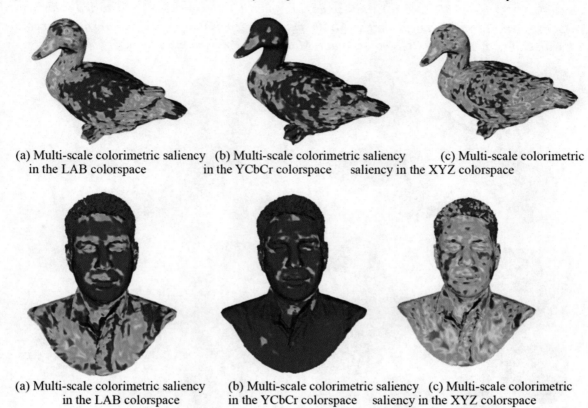

(a) Multi-scale colorimetric saliency in the LAB colorspace   (b) Multi-scale colorimetric saliency in the YCbCr colorspace   (c) Multi-scale colorimetric saliency in the XYZ colorspace

(a) Multi-scale colorimetric saliency in the LAB colorspace   (b) Multi-scale colorimetric saliency in the YCbCr colorspace   (c) Multi-scale colorimetric saliency in the XYZ colorspace

Robustness to Noise on Geometry and Colors

Nouri et al., (2015b) assesses the robustness of they colorimetric saliency models on distorted colored meshes from the constructed colored mesh database. Two distortions have been selected for this test: 1) Uniform Gaussian on the coordinates and 2) Gaussian noise on RGB colors. Figure 31 presents the results of the detected saliency on the distorted colored meshes. One can remark that despite the distortions affected to the coordinates or colors, the initial detected salient regions (Figure 31 (b)) are still considered as salient (Figure 31 (d) and (f)). This attests that the extended colorimetric saliency model (Nouri et al., 2015b) is as stable as the geometric saliency model (Nouri et al., 2015a).

FIELDS OF APPLICATIONS OF VISUAL SALIENCY

In this chapter, three saliency-guided applications are presented. The developed applications concern the automatic viewpoint selection of 3D non colored meshes, the adaptive simplification of 3D non colored meshes and the adaptive smoothing of 3D colored meshes. The saliency models of Nouri et al., (2015a, 2015b) are used to guide these applications.

Figure 31. Robustness of the multi-scale colorimetric model to Gaussian noise on 3D coordinates and RGB colors: a) Original 3D mesh, b) Multi-scale colorimetric saliency of (a), c) Distorted colored mesh with Gaussian noise on 3D coordinates, d) Multi-scale colorimetric saliency of (c), e) Distorted colored mesh with Gaussian noise on RGB colors and f) Multi-scale colorimetric saliency of (e)

For optimization and execution time purposes, the technologic advances associated to applications interacting with human beings and particularly with their vision are increasingly taken into account the capacities and limitations of the HVS.

Selective visual attention represents a major mechanism in the human perception. The latter significantly saves time when viewing the surrounding environment by selecting the visual information potentially interesting while ignoring the rest. Sections below explain how a saliency map allows to distinguish regions that can orient the visual attention of a human observer. We can denote applications such as the optimal viewpoint selection (Tal et al., 2012) (Nouri et al., 2015a) where the goal is to select the most informative and attractive viewpoint and the adaptive simplification (Shilane and Funkhouser, 2007) which aims to simplify the 3D mesh while preserving the most important features for quality purposes. Similarly, others application take advantage from the intake of visual saliency such as the Surface Matching (Gal and Cohen-or, 2006), the automatic resizing (Jia et al., 2014), the facial recognition (Jinho et al., 2004), the icon generation (Shilane and Funkhouser, 2007), mesh demonizing (Mao et al., 2006), etc.

In order to evaluate the intake of their saliency model, Nouri et al., (2015a) have proposed to select the optimal viewpoint selection of a 3D non colored mesh based on its visual saliency. Another application of this model is described in this section and is related to the adaptive simplification of 3D non colored meshes (Nouri et al., 2016a).

To validate the colorimetric saliency extension proposed in (Nouri et al., 2015b), Nouri et al., (2016a) propose to smooth and denoize 3D colored meshes adaptively.

Application to the Automatic Optimal Viewpoint Selection of 3D Non-Colored Meshes

Nouri et al., (2015a) propose to select automatically the optimal viewpoint with perceptually important regions to the human observer. The principal criterion of the proposed approach is to distinguish regions with high visual saliency degree. For this, a saliency map is computed, then, a viewpoint maximizing saliency is selected on the abscissa axis. This is done by uniformly sampling a sphere that bounds the 3D mesh. Let vp the viewpoint selection along the abscissa axis and $surface(vp)$ the visible vertices from this point of view. The total saliency of this surface is defined as:

$$\text{Total-saliency}_{axe_x}(vp) = \sum_{v \in surface(vp)} \text{Multi-scale-saliency}(v) \tag{43}$$

Hence the optimal viewpoint along the abscissa axis is defined as:

$$vp_x = \max(\text{Total-saliency}_{axe_x}(vp_i)) \tag{44}$$

Where vp_i represents the different viewpoints along the x-axis. From this viewpoint, the same processing is performed to select the optimal viewpoint maximizing saliency along the ordinate axis vp_y (see Figure 32). Once this viewpoint selected, a gradient descent is executed to search for the optimal viewpoint along the three axes at the same time. Figure 33 presents the most informative viewpoints of some 3D non colored meshes. One can remark that the generated viewpoints correspond well to the criterion of the proposed approach selecting the optimal viewpoints, and also, these viewpoints correspond to the most likely views of the associated 3D objects. .

It is interesting to note that the proposed approach of viewpoint selection can be used in a heritage valorization context. Indeed, to more attract the glance of a future visitor, it would be relevant to present the most informative and attractive viewpoint. Figure 34 shows an example of selected optimal viewpoints in a patrimonial context.

Figure 32. Illustration of the sampling of a sphere bounding a 3D non-colored mesh along the abscissa and ordinate axes: red and green dots around the 3D mesh refer to positions from which the viewpoints are generated. A selection of the viewpoint maximizing saliency is then performed. Note that the 3D mesh is a non-colored mesh. Colors in the Figure refer to saliency degrees.

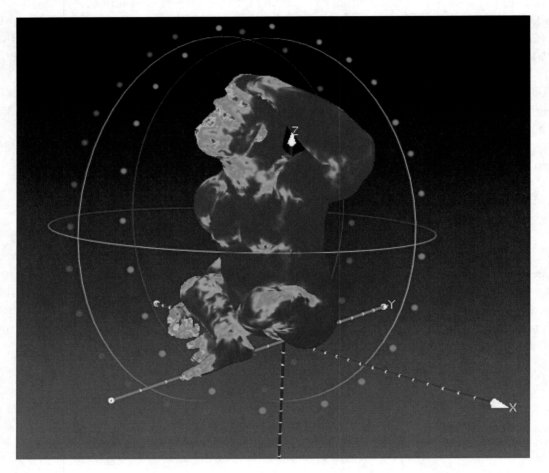

Figure 35 presents a comparison between the selected optimal viewpoints by the approach of (Nouri et al., 2015a) and the ones obtained by the approach of (Tal et al., 2012). One can remark that the method of (Nouri et al., 2015a) is very competitive with the method of (Tal et al., 2012). However, some limitations exist and are presented on Figure 35 (g) and Figure 35 (i).

To select the most informative viewpoints, the method of (Tal etal., 2012) begins by generating the candidates viewpoints by uniformly sampling a sphere that bounds the 3D mesh .From the viewpoint maximizing saliency, a gradient-descent optimization is applied to define the most informative viewpoint. On the contrary, to make the processing faster, the method of (Nouri et al., 2015a) generates first the candidates viewpoints by sampling the sphere bounding the 3D mesh along the x-axis and the y-axis, which leads to a fewer viewpoints candidates. Second, similarly to the method of (Ta let al., 2012), a gradient-descent optimization is applied.

Figure 33. Optimal viewpoints generated by the approach of (Nouri et al., 2015a). Images (a), (c), (e) and (g) present the initial viewpoints. Images (b), (d), (f) and (h) present the most informative viewpoints selected automatically

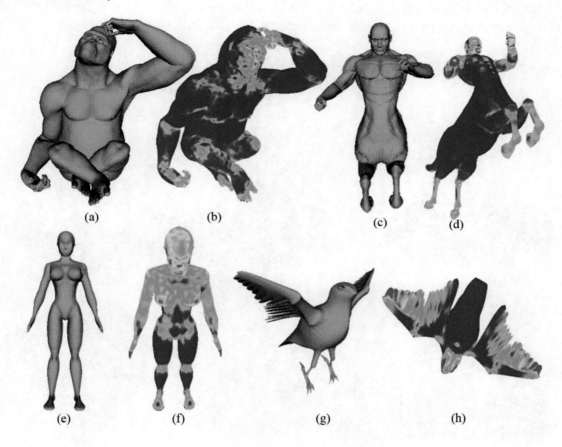

The observed limitations on the 3D meshes representing the Piano and the Car are due to the nature of the used 3D meshes that contain a small number of vertices (one can see the large faces on the surface of these). Indeed, the approach of (Nouri et al., 2015a) is based on the construction of adaptive patches that are filled with a local height-field of the mesh vertices. Thereby, if the number of vertices is low, this will lead to using mostly empty adaptive patches while computing the saliency. Besides, the viewpoints generated for the Car and the Piano seem to be logic insofar that the method of (Nouri et al. 2015a) selects the regions that are highly salient according to the used saliency model (i.e., the underside of the Piano contains much more discontinuities than its topside).

Application to Adaptive Simplification of 3D Non-Colored Meshes

In order to more evaluate the effectiveness of the saliency model, Nouri et al., (2016a) modify the quadric-based simplification approach of (Garland & Heckbert, 1997) by integrating weights obtained from the multi-scale saliency map. The goal is to preserve (less simplify) salient regions of a non-colored 3D mesh while the simplification process.

Figure 34. Results of the optimal viewpoints selection of two architectural heritages: (a) Initial viewpoint of a 3D mesh representing the statue « Le triomphe de la république » located at Place De La Nation in Paris-France. The scan was obtained with a Photogrammetry process from 500 high definition pictures. b) Multi-scale saliency of (a). c) Selected Optimal viewpoint. d) Initial viewpoint of a 3D mesh representing an Russian city. e) Multi-scale saliency of (d). f) Selected optimal viewpoint

Garland and Heckbert, (1997) simplify a 3D mesh by contracting vertices ranked in an ascending order according to their quadric error. Let p a plane belonging to the set of planes P associated to the triangles incident to the vertex v. The latter is defined by the equations $ax + by + cz + d = 0$, $a^2 + b^2 + c^2 = 1$ and is represented by the vector $(abcd)^T$. The quadric of the plan p is defined as $Q_p = pp^T$. Garland and Heckbert, (1997) define the error of a vertex v according to the plane p as $v^T Q_p v$. The quadric Q of the vertex v is computed by the sum of all the quadrics related to the neighboring planes: $Q = \sum_{p \in P} Q_p$. Once the quadrics have been computed for all vertices, the method computes the position of the vertex $\overline{v}$ related to the optimal contraction of each pair (v_i, v_j) in order to minimize the quadric error $\overline{v}^T (Q_i + Q_j) \overline{v}$ where Q_i and Q_j represent respectively the quadrics of v_i and v_j.

Figure 35. Most informative viewpoints selected by the approach of (Nouri et al., 2015a) and by the approach of (Tal et al., 2012): images (a), (c), (e), (g) and (i) show the most salient viewpoints. Images (b), (d), (f), (h) and (j) show the most salient viewpoints. Images (b), (d), (f), (h) and (j) show the most salient viewpoints selected by the approach of (Tal et al., 2012).

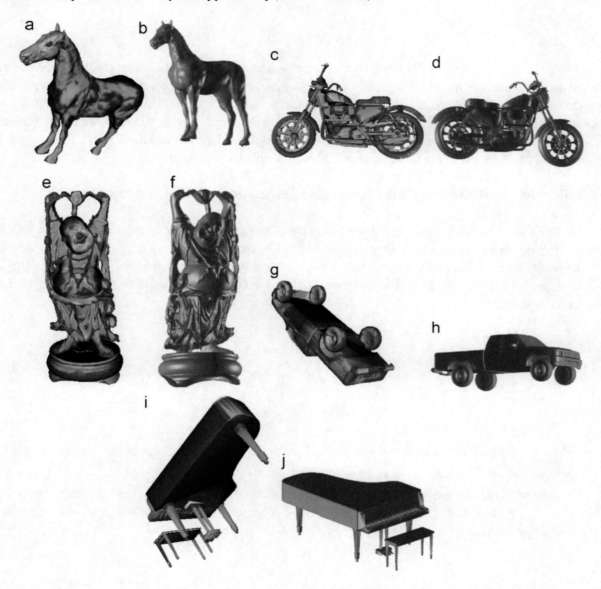

Afterwards, the method contracts iteratively all pairs of vertices having a minimal contraction costs $\bar{v}^T(Q_i + Q_j)\bar{v}$. After a contraction of a pair of vertices (v_i, v_j), the quadric of the resulting vertex $\bar{v}$ is defined as $Q_i + Q_j$.

Nouri et al., (2016a) modify the simplification process of Garland and Heckbert, (1997) by integrating weights from the multi-scale saliency map MS. Each quadric Q associated to each vertex v is multiplied by the weight $MS(v)$. In the same way, after a contraction of a pair of vertices (v_i, v_j), the weight of the quadric associated to the resulting vertex $\bar{v}$ is obtained by summing the degrees of saliency of the contracted vertices:

$$MS(v_i) + MS(v_j) \tag{45}$$

Figure 36 presents the contribution of the saliency weighting in the simplification results of a 3D mesh representing a head of a human being. One can remark that the proposed adaptive simplification approach based on visual saliency preserves salient regions such as the eyes, the forehead, the eyebrows and the mouth in the case of a strong simplification (Figure 35 (d)). Indeed, further triangles are maintained at the level of these regions in comparison with the method of (Garland & Heckbert, 1997). Figure 35 (e) and Figure 35 (f) respectively show these results in a wireframe representation.

Application to Adaptive Smoothing and Denoising of 3D Colored Meshes

In 3D mesh processing, smoothing and denoising are of major importance for noise suppression which may affect geometric or colorimetric properties of a 3D mesh. However, the smoothing process induces undoubtedly a loss of details on the surface mesh which may distort its visual rendering. Nouri et al., (2016a) propose to modify the diffusion process defined in (Elmoataz et al., 2008) which performs an isotropic smoothing:

$$\begin{cases} f^{(0)} = f \\ f^{(t+1)}(u) = \dfrac{\sum\limits_{v \sim u} w(u,v) f^{(t)}(v)}{\sum\limits_{v \sim u} w(u,v)} \quad \forall u \in V \end{cases} \tag{46}$$

Where f is a function associating a set of RGB color vectors $\vec{c}_i$ to vertices of the colored mesh M $f : G \rightarrow c \subset \mathbb{R}^3$ and $w(u,v)$ is the edge weight between the two vertices v_i and v_j.

In order to preserve details and salient features of the surface mesh while the smoothing process, Nouri et al., (2016a) propose to modify the diffusion process of (Elmoataz et al., 2008) with a multi-scale saliency weight:

$$\begin{cases} f^{(0)} = f^0 \\ f^{(t+1)}(u) = \dfrac{\sum\limits_{v \sim u} w(u,v) f^{(t)}(v) MS(u) MS(v)}{\sum\limits_{v \sim u} w(u,v)} \quad \forall u \in V \end{cases} \tag{47}$$

Where $MS(u)$, $MS(v)$ represent the multi-scale colorimetric saliency of vertices u and v, and $w(u,v)$ is the colorimetric similarity defined as:

Figure 36. Simplification results of a 3D mesh representing head of a human being with and without the use of a saliency map: a) Original 3D mesh (276402 faces), b) geometric saliency map of (a), c) 3D mesh simplified with the method of (Garland & Heckbert, 1997) (5000 faces), d) 3D mesh simplified with the proposed saliency-based method of (Nouri et al., 2016a) (5000faces), e) wireframe representation of (c), and f) wireframe representation of (d)

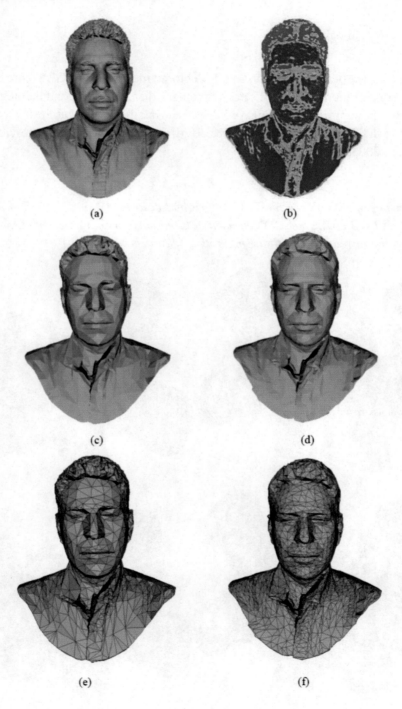

$$w(u,v) = exp\left(\frac{|| \vec{c}(v) - \vec{c}(u) ||_2^2}{\sigma_{\vec{c}}(u)\sigma_{\vec{c}}(v)}\right) \qquad (48)$$

Where

$$\sigma_{\vec{c}}(v) = \max_{v \sim u}(|| \vec{c}_u - \vec{c}_v ||_2) \qquad (49)$$

Figure 37 presents the denoising results of a 3D colored mesh whose RGB colors have been affected with a Gaussian noise (Figure 36 (b)). It's easy to remark that saliency weights integrated in the diffusion process allows the suppression of noise while preserving the contrast at the level of eyes, the mouth and the stomach of the 3D colored mesh (Figure 36 (d)) contrary to the result provided by the method of (Elmoataz et al., 2008) (Figure 36 (c)).

Figure 37. Denoising of 3D colored meshes: a) Original colored 3D mesh, b) 3D noised colored mesh (Gaussian noise on RGB colors), c) 3D denoised colored mesh with method of (Elmoataz et al., 2008) and d) 3D denoised colored mesh with the method of (Nouri et al., 2016a)

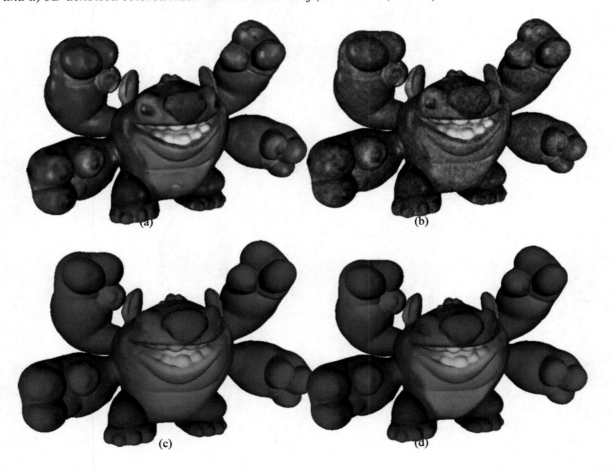

PERSPECTIVES

In this chapter, a complete and detailed state-of-the-art related to the visual saliency o 3D meshes has been presented. Limits of the state-of-the-art approaches have been identified and analyzed. Afterwards, a recent saliency model for non-colored meshes as well as a pioneering approach for 3D colored meshes have been presented and analyzed. These recent approaches associated to the works of (Nouri et al., 2015a, Nouri et al., 2015b) provide respectively a geometric and colorimetric saliency maps which point out regions with high potential of saliency. Local descriptors, in the form of patches of adaptive size filled with a local height field depending on the heights of the spherical neighborhood's projection associated to a target vertex or on its mean RGB values, are constructed in order to characterize the surface of a 3D mesh. The analysis of the model of (Nouri et al., 2015a) have shown that a spherical neighborhood with an important ε ray allows a more accounted detection of saliency (detection of large salient regions on the surface mesh), while a restraint ε ray leads to detect only finest salient areas related to small details. The generated saliency maps presented in the above sections depend of a ray ε specified empirically for each 3D mesh. For applications requiring a saliency map corresponding to a local analysis of the surface mesh, these should choose a reduced spherical neighborhood (small ε). Otherwise, applications requiring a saliency map associated to a less local analysis of the surface mesh will consider a larger ε. However, for applications whose need is a multi-scale saliency map computed in real time, an automatic ε has to be computed automatically. The analysis of this model has shown that the ε ray is inversely proportional to the number of vertices. Therefore, a first solution was to consider a coefficient of proportionality depending of the number of vertices of the 3D mesh. The associated results have not been very satisfying. Another solution would consist of taking into account the areas of the mesh faces in order to precise ε automatically.

In the above sections, results of the detected geometric and colorimetric saliency have allowed to distinguish the difference between them. These multi-scale saliency maps (geometric and colorimetric) can be merged in order to produce a final saliency map which take into account both the geometric and colorimetric saliency (HVS is sensitive to both the shape and colors). Figure 32 presents the fusion result of the two saliency maps obtained from a simple multiplication. The final saliency map (Figure 32 (e) and Figure 32 (j)) appears more informative than the previous saliency maps (geometric and colorimetric). Obviously, the two saliency maps could be merged in a more effective way. The aim of the proposed fusion is to show the intake of the colorimetric saliency to the geometric saliency map.

Currently, there's no ground truth related to the colorimetric saliency of 3D meshes. Future works will aim to lead various experimentations with an eye tracker in order to produce a ground truth associated to the constructed colored mesh database. This ground truth will permit to validate the colorimetric saliency model proposed in (Nouri et al., 2015b).

Also, a novel ground truth associated to the saliency of non-colored meshes will be of great interest. Indeed, the pseudo ground truth saliency (Chen et al., 2012) used in the work of (Nouri et al., 2015a) and another one proposed in (Dutgaci et al., 2011) are not fully related to the *Bottom-up* attentional process. In online experimentations associated to (chen et al., 2012), observers were asked to choose 3D points that might be selected by others observers. In the second ground truth (Dutgaci et al., 2011), observers were manipulating the 3D meshes while selecting 3D points which seemed interesting to them. This takes the form of a task provided to an observer which influences the orientation of his visual attention and therefore the detection of saliency (Yarbus, 1967). In addition, no eye-tracker was used to track the ocular movements that are sensitive to the intrinsic features of the visual stimuli. Consequently, a new ground truth related to the visual saliency of 3D non colored meshes associated to the bottom process is mandatory. This constitutes one goal of our future works.

The first publicly available 3D colored mesh database in the state-of-the-art has been described in details in this chapter. Examples of acquired meshes, as well as the characteristics of this database such as the size, the distortions selected and the process of acquisition have been analyzed.

This chapter has also presented three applications of the saliency models proposed in (Nouri et al., 2015a) and (Nouri et al., 2015b) in the processing of 3D non colored and colored meshes. The contribution of the saliency information is notable in all presented applications. However, some improvements can be developed:

- **Application to the Optimal Viewpoint Selection:** A first improvement would be to perform a local search around the generated optimal viewpoint. This will permit to refine the viewpoint maximizing saliency.
- **Application to the Adaptive Simplification:** In the process of the adaptive simplification, salient vertices are preserved according to their degree of saliency. One improvement would be to more preserve these salient vertices by amplifying their saliency degree if the latter is superior to a defined threshold.

PERCEPTUAL QUALITY ASSESSMENT OF NON-COLORED 3D MESHES

We live in a digital world where 3D data are ever more present. With the development of 3D acquisition techniques large quantities of 3D objects are represented mostly in the form of triangular 3D meshes and are used in several human centered applications like compression, watermarking, medical imaging, content enhancement and so forth. This progress, coupled with the fact that the decisions of human beings are strongly based on their vision, requires that the3D meshes representing the targets to analyze are of high quality.

A 3D mesh may be subject to various processing before being presented to a human observer. This can induce distortions that may affect its visual rendering. The first distortion that may affect a 3D mesh while its acquisition is the sensor noise. Then, for an optimal transmission, the 3D mesh can be compressed for the purpose of reducing size and lightening bandwidth. Also, for copyrights and intellectual property protection, a watermarking process may be performed to the 3D mesh. This process can also distort the surface mesh if it's not well performed. Thenceforth, assuming that one or more distortions previously listed are applied, a perceptual quality assessment processing becomes necessary in order to quantify the visual impact of these distortions on the geometry of the 3D mesh presented to the final consumer and which is generally a human observer.

In the following, we begin by briefly describing a feature of the HVS influencing the human perception and which is often used in the objective quality assessment of 2D images and 3D meshes. Afterwards, we present the two approaches for the quality assessment: Subjective and Objective quality assessment. While the first calls on human observers to evaluate and provide a quality score to a 3D mesh, the second aims at designing automatic quality assessment algorithms of the perceived quality called also *metrics*. These must provide a quality score that is correlated to the quality score provided by the human observers.

THE HUMAN VISUAL SYSTEM AND THE PERCEPTION OF QUALITY

Visual Masking Effect

Visual masking is one of the principal features of the HVS which have been strongly used in the quality assessment of 2D images and 3D meshes. The latter can be defined as the visibility reduction of a stimuli (masked signal) due to the simultaneous presence of another signal (masking signal). The degree of the visual masking effect is measured by the variation of the visibility of the masked signal while the presence or the absence of the masking signal. Generally, the visual masking effect is important when the spatial localization, the frequency content and the orientation of the masking and masked signals are similar. In the context of 3D meshes, the visual masking effect can occur when a rough region is able de hide a distortion.

The Perception of 3D Meshes Quality

Whereas the objective quality assessment of 2D images has experienced notable progress (Wang & Bovic, 2006, 2011), that of 3D meshes still is in its infancy (Corsini et al., 2013; Guo et al., 2016). Several authors have chosen to use 2D images metrics with a good comprehension of psychovisual and physiological factors in the quality assessment of 3D meshes (Qu & Meyer, 2008; Bolin & Meyer, 1998; Zhu et al., 2010). Generally, 2D views of the target 3D mesh are taken, then, a metric specific for 2D images is applied in order to assess the quality of these views. However, this type of metrics does not appear to be adequate to assess the quality of 3D meshes as confirmed in (Rogowitz et al., 2001). In this study, authors show that the depth, the animation and the orientation of illumination of 3D meshes affect the perception of quality. For example, the simplification distortion is less visible when a 3D mesh is animated and illuminated from face. The study concludes that model-based metrics operating on the geometry of a 3D mesh predict better the quality of 3D meshes.

Recently, the study of (Lavoué et al., 2016) compares performances of six based-image metrics with four model-based metrics. The results of this study show that 2D image metrics assess quality of 3D meshes with precision when only one distortion is considered in the corpus. In other complex cases where different types of distortions are present, the model-based metrics outperform 2D image metrics in term of correlation with human score quality. Therefore, all the metrics considered in the following are model-based metrics operating directly on mesh geometry.

Subjective Quality Assessment

Despite the proliferation of 2D image quality assessment algorithms and the advances currently being made in quality assessment approaches of 3D meshes, human beings remain the only reliable judges of any multimedia content. As a consequence, objective quality score which are provided by quality assessment metrics must correlate with human scores of quality obtained in the psychovisual experiments. However, this method of evaluation of quality remains inappropriate due to the huge amount of data obtained while psychovisual experiments and the time consuming associated (ITU-T Recommendation P.910, 2008). Nevertheless, this method allows to compute mean score of quality denoted *MOS (Mean Opinion Score)* for each considered 3D mesh. Therefore, the *MOS* values represent the ground truth that any measure must reproduce as rigorously as possible.

In contrary to 2D images (ITU-R BT.500-11, 2002) (ITU-T Recommendation P.910, 2008), there is no standard for the subjective quality assessment of 3D meshes. Notwithstanding such deficiency, researchers have been inspired from 2D images standards in order to design psychovisual campaigns for the quality assessment of 3D meshes and hence generate ground truths available for the scientific community (Lavoué et al., 2006, 2009; Silva et al., 2009).

Objective Quality Assessment

In addition to the disadvantage of the subjective quality assessment approach described above, is added the impossibility of integrating this latter into 3D mesh processing algorithms for purposes of optimization and visual rendering. These algorithms need a high execution speed as well as an optimal complexity, conditions that are not covered by the subjective quality assessment approach. The alternative approach to these problems consists in assessing the quality objectively using algorithms (or metrics) that predict the perceived quality. The objectives to be achieved while designing a quality assessment metric can be summarized as:

1. **Reliability of Predicted Scores:** Predicted *MOS* values of quality scores provided by the metric must correlate with the quality scores provided by human observers.
2. **Reproducibility:** The source code of a proposed metric must be stable and able to provide identical results on the same data regardless of the used CPU.

In the state-of-the-art, quality assessment metrics are classified into three categories:

1. **Full Reference Metrics (FR-Full Reference):** This type of metrics necessitates that the reference version (renowned perfect, without distortions) of the 3D mesh is present in its entirety. This reference version will be used to quantify the degree of distortion associated to the degraded version. Note that in this context, it is more convenient to use the term « fidelity measure or similarity measure » instead of quality measure or quality metric since the goal is to measure the degree of conformity of the distorted mesh to the reference mesh. This category of metrics is used in the comparison of compression or enhancement algorithms of 3D meshes. Another goal of these metrics correlated to human perception is to replace geometric metrics such as the Haussdorf distance or the mean squared error (MSE) which don't take into account of any feature of the SVH nor a visual correlated attribute. These geometric metrics fails to assess the quality similarly to the human visual perception as showed in (Lavoué & Corsini, 2010) (Bulbul et al., 2011). See Figure 38.
2. **Reduced Reference Metrics (RR-Reduced Reference):** Reduced reference quality assessment algorithms aims at assessing the visual quality of a 3D distorted mesh by having only partial information about the reference 3D mesh. The visual quality score is predicted using features extracted from both the reference and the distorted meshes.
3. **No Reference Metrics (NR-No Reference):** No reference quality assessment metrics are considered as the most interesting insofar as the availability of the reference 3D mesh isn't necessary to assess the quality of a 3D distorted mesh. Hence, this type of metrics can be integrated in all processing algorithms of 3D meshes.

Figure 38. Geometric metric and correlation with the human perception: a) Venus reference 3D mesh, b) Venus 3D mesh watermarked with the method of (Wang et al., 2011) and c) Venus 3D mesh watermarked with the method of (Cho et al., 2007)

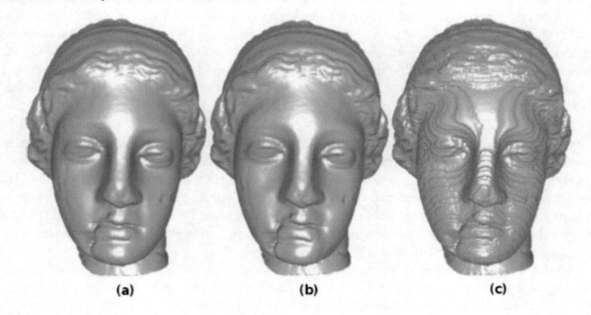

(a)　　　　　　　　(b)　　　　　　　　(c)

The two 3D meshes obtain a similar quality score computed with the MRMSE (Maximum Root Mean Squared Error) distance despite their different visual rendering (Wang et al., 2012).

The application fields of no reference metrics is very wide; they can be used in systems of acquisition, compression and communication, visualization, rendering, watermarking, etc.

RELATED WORKS

Research area of perceptual quality assessment metrics of 3D meshes has raised the interest of many researchers especially for its considerable use in various applications, but also because of its lack of maturity. Primary quality assessment metrics were purely geometric due to their simplicity and fast execution time. We can cite the Hausdorff distance (Aspert et al., 2002), the Root Mean Squared error (RMS) (Cignoni et al., 1998) and the Maximal Root Mean Squared error (MRMS). These metrics provide quality score not correlated to the human visual perception. To fix this problem, researchers have integrated some HVS features. In the following a brief state-of-the-art of model-based quality assessment metrics (also called viewpoint independent metrics) is described.

Karni and Gotsman, (2000) proposed a metric that combines the RMS geometric distance between corresponding vertices with the Laplacian coordinate error in order to evaluate their compression method. In the same context, Sorkine et al., (2000) improve this metric by increasing the weights associated to the Laplacian coordinate error. Gelasca et al., (2005) proposed a metric based on the variation of the global roughness measure. The roughness is computed as the difference between the 3D mesh and its smoothed version. Acting on the same principle, Corsini et al., (2007) proposed a metric based on the variation of the global roughness measure. The roughness is computed through the variance of the dihedral angles. Lavoué et al.,(2011) proposed an extension of the SSIM index developed for 2D images to the quality assessment of 3D meshes (called Mesh Structural Distortion Measure: MSDM). Differences of statistics are computed on the curvature maps of the two meshes being compared. Brian et al., (2009) measure the quality of a 3D mesh using the concept of strain energy. Strain energy refers to the energy that causes the deformation of the mesh geometry. Lavoué (2011) proposed an improvement of MSDM called MSDM2. This metric takes into account the multi-scale aspect and can perform on 3D meshes with different connectivities. Vása & Rus (2012) suggest to evaluate the quality of a 3D mesh by measuring the local changes of oriented dihedral angles. Wang et al., (2012) proposed a metric based on the variation of local roughness that is derived from the Laplacian of the discrete Gaussian curvature. Torkhani et al.,(2014) proposed a metric based on the comparison of the curvature tensors and the roughness character of the geometry. One can remark that the presented metrics model principally one feature of the human visual system: visual masking. Another major aspect of human perception is related to visual saliency. This feature is necessary to the human perception insofar that the human glance is attracted by distinctive regions having high saliency potential belonging to the surrounding environment. Nouri et al., (2016b) propose the first full-reference metric using both visual saliency and visual masking properties for the objective quality assessment of 3D meshes.

Another remark can be made from the state-of-the-art description. No approach using visual saliency was proposed to assess the quality of a 3D distorted mesh without the availability of its reference version. Indeed, blind assessment of the quality of a 3D distorted mesh is a new challenging problem since no information of the original 3D version is available. To address this problem, Nouri et al., (2017) propose a no-reference algorithm which permits to assess the perceptual quality of a 3D mesh without any reference to its reference version neither to the type of distortion.

FULL-REFERENCE SALIENCY-BASED 3D MESH QUALITY ASSESSMENT INDEX (NOURI ET AL., 2016b)

Synopsis

Nouri et al., (2016b) propose a novel metric named SMQI (Saliency Mesh Quality Index) for the full-reference quality assessment of 3D non colored meshes. The proposed metric is inspired from the approach of (Wang et al., 2004) named SSIM related to the quality assessment of 2D images and the approach of (Lavoué et al., 2006) named MSDM related to the quality assessment of 3D meshes. However, instead of computing local statistics reflecting structural information using a curvature map as MSDM, Nouri et al., 2016(b) propose to generate a saliency map that is used as a basis for computing local statistics over corresponding neighborhoods on the two compared 3D meshes. Indeed, the authors make the assumption that the perceived quality of a mesh is strongly related to the modification of local and global saliency of the mesh surface. That is to say, if a specified region on the reference mesh is attractive in a certain degree and if the latter on the distorted mesh is no longer attractive (or is more attractive), therefore, this region will have been distorted. Additionally, for the two compared 3D meshes, Nouri et al., (2016b) use a roughness map on which they compute the differences of mean local roughness of each node. This allows us to capture the visual masking effect that may occur while a rough region is able to hide a geometric distortion. This roughness information is combined with the statistics computed from the saliency map in order to provide a quality score of the target 3D mesh. Figure 39 presents a synopsis of the approach of (Nouri et al., 2016b).

Motivation: Visual Quality Assessment and Visual Saliency

Selective visual attention is a crucial characteristic in the HVS. We are constantly swallowed into a huge amount of information which cannot be neither processed in sum nor in details. Therefore, the natural solution is the real time selection of fractions of the available informations for detailed processing while the rest is discarded. Given a 3D objet, the human visual attention is attracted by particular regions on the surface object that are distinct from their surrounding zones. These striking areas, essentially prominent in the field of 3D objects, are content dependent. However, they are not dependent of the behavior or the experience relative to the human observer (Itti & Koch, 1998). Therefore, a saliency map can point out where the human visual attention is maximal or minimal. As said above, a distortion is much more perceived when it is located in a perceptually salient region (high scalar value on the saliency map) where the human visual attention is maximal and vice-versa. This has been proved by a series of subjective experiments where the outcome confirmed that a perceived degradation is the highest when a distortion affects a salient region in the content (Boulos et al., 2009) (Engelke et al., 2010). The same result can be seen in Figure 40. Figure 40 (a) and Figure 40 (b) respectively represent the reference 3D mesh and

Figure 39. Block diagram illustrating the pipeline of the approach of (Nouri et al., 2016b)

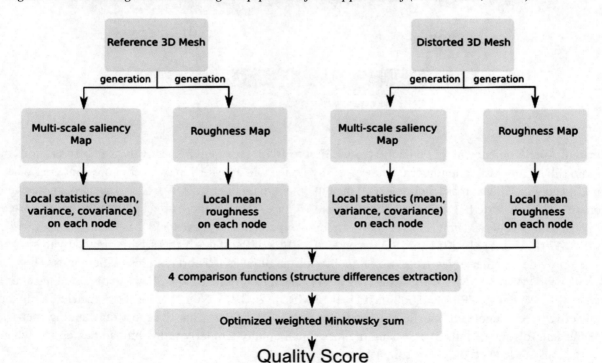

Figure 40. Comparison of 3D meshes with different perceptual qualities. (a) Original Gorilla 3D mesh. (b) Saliency map of (a) with the method of (Nouri et al., 2015a). (c) Gorilla 3Dmesh noised in more visual attention areas. (d) Gorilla 3D mesh noised in less visual attention areas. (e) color-map

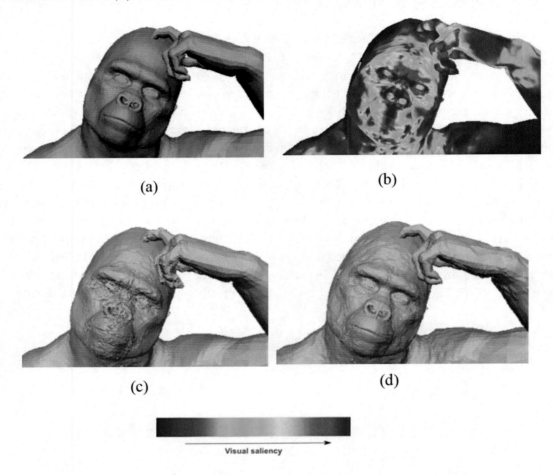

its multi-scale saliency map. Figure 40 (c) and Figure 40 (d) represent respectively the noisy versions in more salient and less salient areas. One can easily notice that a distortion is much more annoying when it is located in salient areas (Figure 40 (c)) than in other areas (Figure 40 (d)). Also, the global perceived quality of the distorted 3D mesh in salient regions (Figure 40 (c)) is more affected than the one distorted in less salient regions (Figure 40 (d)). The reference perceptual metrics TPDM (Fakhri et al., 2014), MSDM2 (Lavoué et al., 2011) FMPD (wang et al., 2012) of the state-of-the-art are limited by this case. They provide a higher objective score of quality for the 3D mesh distorted in less salient areas (Figure 40 (d)) TPDM=0.14 FMPD=0.54 MSDM2=0.41) and a lower one for the 3D mesh distorted in salient areas (Figure 40 (c)) TPDM=0.008 FMPD=0.15 MSDM2=0.36). Note that for those metrics, a higher objective score denotes a poor quality and vice versa. This shows that the most outstanding metrics of the state-of-the-art fails in assessing the perceptual quality similarly to the human perception when distortions are located on visual salient regions.

The Visual Saliency Map for Structural Information Extraction

To compute the local statistics (mean, standard-deviation and covariance) which reflect the structural information of a 3D mesh, Nouri et al., (2016b) use the multi-scale saliency map as a basis. For a local neighborhood $N(v_i)$ representing the adjacent vertices of v_i on the mesh surface, they define the local mean saliency and the standard deviation respectively denoted $\mu_{N(v_i)}$ and $\sigma_{N(v_i)}$ as:

$$\mu_{N(v_i)} = \frac{1}{|N(v_i)|} \sum_{v_j \in N(v_i)} MS(v_j) \tag{50}$$

Where $MS(v_j)$ represents the multi-scale saliency of the vertex v_j and $N(v_i)$ is the cardinality of the neighborhood of v_i.

For two corresponding local neighborhoods of the two compared meshes (the reference mesh M_1 and the distorted mesh M_2) $N_1(v_i) = N_{M_1}(v_i)$ and $N_2(v_i) = N_{M_2}(v_i)$, Nouri et al., (2016b) define the covariance $\sigma_{N_1(v_i)N_2(v_i)}$ as:

$$\sigma_{N_1(v_i)N_2(v_i)} = \frac{1}{|N_1(v_i)|} \sum_{v_j \in N_1(v_i), N_2(v_i)} (MS_{M_1}(v_j) - \mu_{N_1(v_i)})(MS_{M_2}(v_j) - \mu_{N_2(v_i)}) \tag{51}$$

Where MS_{M_1} and MS_{M_2} represent respectively the multi-scale saliency maps of the two compared meshes M_1 and M_2. Afterwards, Nouri et al., (2016b) define three comparison functions between two corresponding neighborhoods $N_1(v_i)$ and $N_2(v_i)$ in order to quantify the deformations that have affected the structural informations of the distorted 3D mesh:

$$L(N_1(v_i), N_2(v_i)) = \frac{\|\mu_{N_1(v_i)} - \mu_{N_2(v_i)}\|_2}{\max(\mu_{N_1(v_i)}, \mu_{N_2(v_i)})} \tag{52}$$

$$C(N_1(v_i), N_2(v_i)) = \frac{\|\sigma_{N_1(v_i)} - \sigma_{N_2(v_i)}\|_2}{\max(\sigma_{N_1(v_i)}, \sigma_{N_2(v_i)})} \tag{53}$$

$$S(N_1(v_i), N_2(v_i)) = \frac{\|\sigma_{N_1(v_i)}\sigma_{N_2(v_i)} - \sigma_{N_1(v_i)N_2(v_i)}\|_2}{\sigma_{N_1(v_i)}\sigma_{N_2(v_i)}} \tag{54}$$

Where L, C and S refer respectively to the saliency comparison, the contrast comparison and the structure comparison.

The Roughness Map for Taking Into Account the Visual Masking Effect

Once the saliency comparison functions defined, Nouri et al., (2016b) noticed that the visual masking effect on the 3D meshes isn't captured well by these functions when a rough region is present on the reference surface mesh. Indeed, given a rough and a smooth region, a distortion will be much more visible on the smooth region than on the rough one. To deal with this problem, they implemented the work of (Wang et al., 2012) that provides a roughness map of a 3D mesh based on the Laplacian of the Gaussian curvature. Consequently, Nouri et al., (2016b) introduced a fourth function based on the comparison of the mean local roughness. The aim of this function is to induce a large difference when a smooth region becomes a rough region and is defined as follows:

$$R(N_1(v_i), N_2(v_i)) = \frac{\| \delta_{N_1(v_i)} - \delta_{N_2(v_i)} \|_2}{\max(\delta_{N_1(v_i)}, \delta_{N_2(v_i)})} \tag{55}$$

Where $\delta_{N_1(v_i)} = \frac{1}{| N_1(v_i) |} \sum_{v_j \in N_1(v_i)} LRF(v_j)$ and $LRF(v_j)$ represents the roughness value of the vertex v_j. It's important to note that a roughness map is different from a saliency map since only novel non-redundant informations are putted forward in a saliency map in contrary to a roughness map. See Figure 41.

The Roughness Map for Taking Into Account the Visual Masking Effect

Once the four functions are defined, the extracted features from saliency and roughness maps are combined. Nouri et al., (2016b) have chosen one of the most used combinations in the field of quality assessment: the Minkowski sum. Hence, the quality measure SMQI between two 3D meshes M_1 and M_2 is defined as the weighted Minkowski sum of their local distances:

$$SMQI(M_1, M_2) =$$
$$\left(\frac{1}{|V|} \sum_i^{|V|} L(N_1(v_i), N_2(v_i)) \right)^{\alpha} + \left(\frac{1}{|V|} \sum_i^{|V|} C(N_1(v_i), N_2(v_i)) \right)^{\beta} + \tag{52}$$
$$\left(\frac{1}{|V|} \sum_i^{|V|} S(N_1(v_i), N_2(v_i)) \right)^{\gamma} + \left(\frac{1}{|V|} \sum_i^{|V|} R(N_1(v_i), N_2(v_i)) \right)^{\delta}$$

Where the coefficients α, β and δ are weights obtained from an optimization based on genetic algorithms. Indeed, the proposed perceptual distance depends of four independent parameters of which the manual tuning will be difficult and probably ineffective. It's important to note that the number of 3D meshes contained in the two datasets described in the next sections is small in comparison with available datasets of 2D images. Consequently, to deal with this weakness, Nouri et al., (2016b) opted for a Leave-One-Out training on a corpus constructed from the two considered databases. The goal of

Figure 41. Difference between a multi-scale visual saliency map and a roughness map: (a) The original 3D mesh Armadillo, (b) its multi-scale saliency map with the method of (Nouri et al., 2015a) and (c) its roughness map with the method of (Wang et al., 2012)

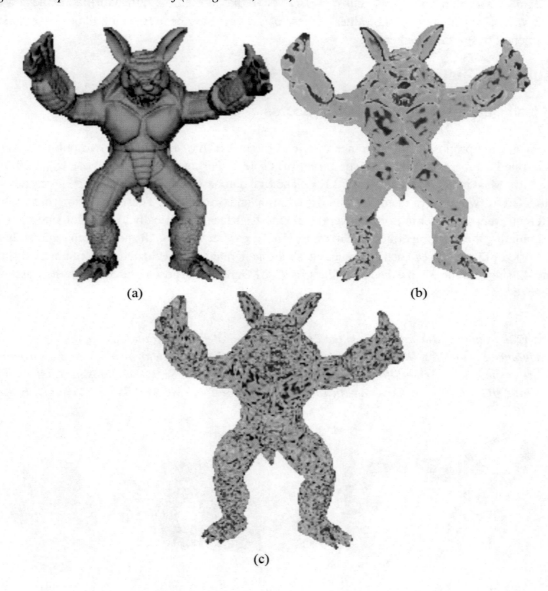

(a)

(b)

(c)

this approach is to perform the learning of the model on $k - 1$ observations and to validate it on the kth one. This process is repeated $k \times 999$ times. In this case, an observation refers to the MOS values of a reference 3D mesh and its distorted versions. The fitness function used to perform the genetic optimization is defined as:

$$f(\alpha, \beta, \gamma, \delta) = \sqrt{\sum_{i=0}^{k-1} (MOS_i - SMQI_i(M_1, M_2))^2} \tag{53}$$

Where MOS_i represents the vector of MOS values of the observation i and $SMQI(M_1, M_2)$ is the perceptual distance computed with equation (52). After genetic optimization, the parameters values are: $\alpha = 23.63$, $\beta = 3.26$, $\gamma = 5.04$ and $\delta = 0.77$. Note that in Figure 39, the Gorilla 3D mesh was assessed with these parameters. The values of these parameters have been fixed for all quality assessment experimentations in this chapter.

Results and Analysis

3D Mesh Databases and Subjective Scores of Quality

To compare the proposed full reference metric with state-of-the-art methods, two publicly available subject-rated databases are used: 1) The Liris/Epfl General-Purpose database (Lavoué et al., 2011) and 2) the Liris-Masking database (Lavoué, 2011). The first database contains 4 reference 3D meshes. They are affected by two types of distortions: Noise addition and Smoothing. These distortions are applied in 3 different strengths either uniformly over the 3D mesh surface, specifically to rough or smooth regions (for simulating the masking effect) and to transitional areas between rough and smooth regions. In total, 22 distorted 3D meshes of each reference mesh are generated and evaluated by 12 human observers. Figure 42 shows some 3D meshes from the Liris/Epfl General-Purpose database with their associated normalized MOS values.

Figure 42. Example of 3D meshes from the Liris/Epfl General-Purpose database. In the top row are the four reference 3D meshes. In the bottom row are four examples of the deformed 3D meshes, from left to right are respectively: Armadillo with noise on rough regions (MOS=0.84), Dinosaur after a uniform smoothing (MOS=0.43), RockerArm with noise on smooth regions (MOS=0.75) and Venus with uniform noise (MOS=1).

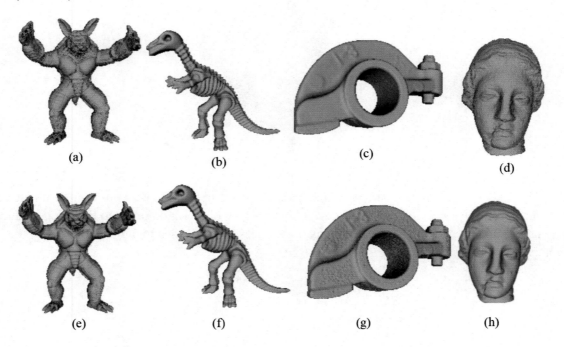

The Liris Masking Database consists of 4 reference 3D meshes which are distorted by adding noise of three different strengths in either rough and smooth areas to generate 6 degraded versions of each 3D mesh. 12 human observers have evaluated the database. Figure 43 presents some 3D meshes of this database.

Results and Comparison With the State-of-the-Art

To evaluate the performance of their proposed full-reference metric, Nouri et al., (2016b) use the Spearman correlation coefficient (SROOC: Spearman Rank Ordered cOrrelation Coefficient) between the subjective scores of quality provided by the human observers and the objective scores of quality pro-

Figure 43. Example of 3D meshes from the Liris Masking database. In the top row are two reference 3D meshes. In the bottom row are two examples of their distorted versions. From left to right: Lion 3D mesh with noise on rough regions (MOS=0.20), Bimba 3D mesh with noise in smooth regions (MOS=1.0)

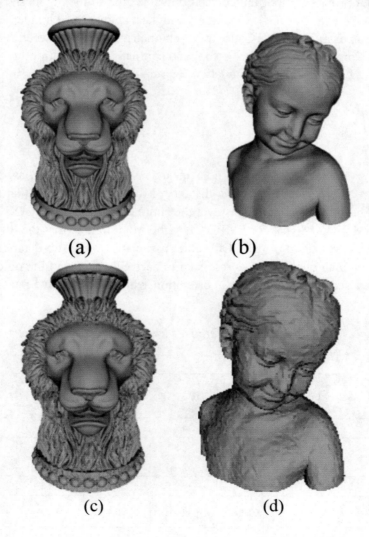

(a)   (b)

(c)   (d)

vided by the proposed metric. Commonly used, this term of correlation is used to define a link between two variables. In the field of statistics, the term « correlation » allows to quantify the link between two quantitative variables. This junction could be either symmetric (possibility to switch the quantitative variables x and y) or asymmetric (one of the two variables depends of the other and hence, the two variables x and y cannot be switched). This measure of correlation is characterized by the fact that the only ranks of the observations values are used instead of their real values. The Spearman correlation is defined between 1 and -1:

1: strong positive correlation.
0: no correlation.
-1: strong negative correlation.

Table 3 presents the performance of the proposed metric and the state-of-the-art metrics in term of the Spearman correlation with the subjective scores provided by the Liris/Epfl General-Purpose. One can notice that SMQI provides important correlation values for all the 3D meshes and particularly for the Venus 3D mesh where the SROOC values are the highest among the reminder values. The result of a psychometric fitting using a cumulative Gaussian psychometric function between the objective scores and the subjective ones is presented in Figure 44 (top) and confirms this result for the Venus 3D mesh. This fitting was performed by choosing the cumulative Gaussian psychometric function (Engeldrum, 2000):

$$g(m, n, R) = \frac{1}{\sqrt{2\pi}} \int_{m+nR}^{\infty} e^{-t^2} dt \qquad (54)$$

Where m and n are estimated with a non-linear least squares fitting based on the Levenberg-Marquardt algorithm and R is the objective distance. Moreover, it appears that the proposed metric SMQI is the second best metric after TPDM over the entire database (the SROOC values are 89.6% for TPDM, 84.6% for SMQI and 80.4% for FMPD). It's important to note that the SROOC value over the entire database isn't an average of the SROOC values associated to the sub-databases but it's a correlation between all the human quality scores referring to each 3D mesh and the objective quality scores provided by the proposed metric. This high correlation with the subjective rates in the LIRIS/EPFL

Table 3. SROOC values (%) of different full-reference viewpoint-independent metrics on the LIRIS/EPFL General Purpose database

Liris/Epfl General-Purpose	HD	RMS	3DWPM1	3DPWPM2	MSDM2	FMPD	TPDM	SMQI
Armadillo	69.5	62.7	65.8	74.1	81.6	75.4	**84.9**	77.5
Venus	1.6	90.1	71.6	34.8	89.3	87.5	90.6	**91.6**
Dinosaur	30.9	0.3	62.7	52.4	85.9	89.6	92.2	84.8
RockerArm	18.1	7.3	87.5	37.8	89.6	88.8	**92.2**	91.8
Entire database	13.8	26.8	69.3	49.0	80.4	81.9	**89.6**	84.6

Figure 44. Psychometric curve fitting between SMQI and MOS values: (top) the fitting performed using SMQI and MOS values from the Venus 3D mesh; (bottom) the psychometric curve plotted with the SMQI-MOS pairs from the whole LIRIS/EPFL General-Purpose database

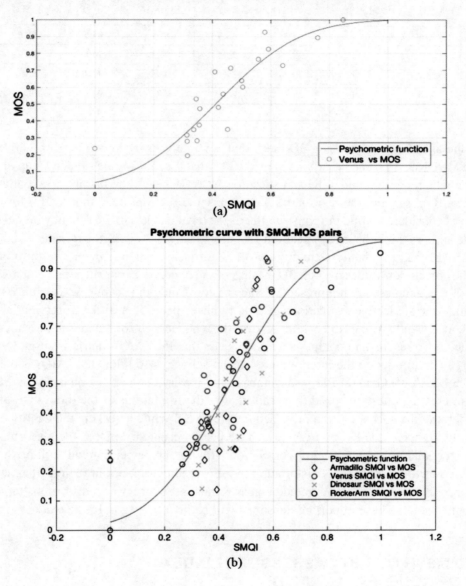

General-Purpose database demonstrates the capacity of the generalization over all the 3D meshes and can be confirmed by the curve fitting presented in Figure 44 (bottom) where the SMQI-MOS points are very close to the psychometric curve.

SMQI was also tested and compared with the state-of-the-art metrics on the Liris-Masking database. Table 4 provides the Spearman correlation values of the different metrics on this database. From these results, three main observations can be made. The first one is that SMQI is very competitive with TPDM and MSDM2 and succeed in capturing the masking effect. The second observation deals with the cor-

Table 4. SROOC values (%) of different full-reference viewpoint-independent metrics on the LIRIS-Masking database

Liris-Masking	HD	RMS	3DWPM1	3DPWPM2	MSDM2	FMPD	TPDM	SMQI
Armadillo	48.6	65.7	58.0	48.6	**88.6**	**88.6**	**88.6**	**88.6**
Lion-vase	71.4	71.4	20.0	34.3	**94.3**	**94.3**	82.9	83.00
Bimba	25.7	71.4	20.0	37.1	**100.0**	**100.0**	**100.0**	**100.0**
Dinosaur	48.6	71.4	66.7	71.4	**100.0**	94.3	**100.0**	**100.0**

relation value associated to the Lion 3D mesh that is slightly lower in comparison with the values of TPDM and MSDM2. This can be explained by the fact that the multi-scale saliency map of the distorted 3D mesh on which are computed the statistics doesn't reflect well the distorted salient areas. Indeed, the reference 3D mesh and the distorted 3D use the same ray (defined empirically) for the spherical neighborhood considered while the construction of the local patches in the saliency model (Nouri et al., 2015a). The authors think that a ray specified properly to each 3D mesh (the reference and the distorted 3D meshes) will lead to a better estimation of the multi-scale saliency map. The third observation is related to the correlation values over all 3D meshes of the database Liris-Masking database. Correlation rates over all this database are not presented since as confirmed in (Lavoué & Corsini, 2010), the used protocol while the subjective evaluations of quality have specified a different referential for each 3D mesh, and consequently, values of correlation over the whole corpus of 3D meshes are not significative.

From the above results and comparisons, it appears that the SMQI metric is strongly correlated to the human perception due to the integration of visual saliency. Additionally, SMQI is the second best metric in the Liris/Epfl General-Purpose Database and is very competitive on the Liris-Masking database. Two interesting questions need to be raised after the limitations of the three state-of-the-art best metrics so far and the success of the proposed metric SMQI while assessing the quality of a 3D mesh distorted in more perceptually important area have been presented: 1) Does the performance of state-of-the-art perceptual metrics in term of correlation with human perception will still be the same when they perform on a 3D mesh corpus distorted in more perceptual important regions than less important ones ? 2) Does the design of subject rated databases must account for new distortions targeting further visual salient regions? These important questions will be investigated in future works.

3D BLIND MESH QUALITY ASSESSMENT INDEX (MODEL OF NOURI ET AL., 2017B)

In most of applications that manipulate 3D meshes, the reference version of the 3D mesh isn't available which makes the quality assessment of the target 3D mesh more difficult. This capacity of assessing objects without their reference version is an easy task for humans but this is far from being the case for machines and algorithms. Many quality assessment metrics for 3D meshes were proposed in the state-of-the-art, however they are still limited due to their dependence to the reference version of the 3D mesh. To solve this problem, Nouri et al. (2017b) investigate the use of saliency and visual masking properties for the blind quality assessment of 3D non colored meshes and propose a novel no-reference metric named BMQI (Blind Mesh Quality assessment Index). Given a distorted non colored 3D mesh, the proposed metric is able to assess its perceived quality without referring to its reference version similarly to the human perception. No assumption on the degradation to evaluate is required for this metric, which makes it powerful and usable in any context requiring quality assessment of 3D meshes.

Proposed Approach

Visual Saliency, Roughness, and Quality Assessment

The principal challenge met while designing this quality assessment metric was to select visual features that have the capability to quantify the structural deformation that the 3D mesh undergo and that are correlated with human perception. To do this, a multi-scale visual saliency and a roughness map are used. Visual saliency is an important characteristic for human visual attention. Its use in computer graphics applications like mesh quality assessment (Nouri et al., 2016b), optimal view point selection (Nouri et al., 2015a) (Tal et al., 2012) and simplification (Lee et al., 2005) has proven beyond any doubt its correlation with the human visual perception. Nouri et al., (2017b) suppose as in their previous work (Nouri et al., 2016b) that visual quality of a 3D mesh is more affected when salient regions are affected rather than less or not salient regions.

Likewise, variations of 3D mesh roughness appear to be correlated with the human perception (Wang et al., 2012). Indeed, a roughness map points regions that expose a strong visual masking effect. Regions with high roughness magnitude expose an important degree of visual masking effect since distortions are less visible on these ones. Nouri et al., (2017b) show that local variations of saliency and roughness combined together succeed in assessing the visual quality of a distorted 3D mesh without the need of its reference version.

Method

Given a 3D distorted mesh, the method of (Nouri et al., 2017b) begins by computing a multi-scale saliency map MS and a roughness map R respectively with the methods of (Nouri et al., 2015a) and (Wang et al., 2012). Then, the method of (Simari et al., 2014) is adapted to segment the 3D mesh into a number of Superfacets N_{SF}. In this context, these Superfacets will play the role of local patches since the HVS locally processes information. Once the segmentation is performed, values of saliency $MS(v_i)$ and roughness $R(v_i)$ associated to each vertex v_i of a Superfacet SF_j are assigned to it. Afterwards, a feature vector of four attributes for each Superfacet SF_j is constructed:

$$\phi_j = \left[\mu_{SF_j}, \sigma_{SF_j}, \delta_{SF_j}, \gamma_{SF_j} \right] \text{ with } j \in \left[1, N_{SF} \right] \tag{55}$$

Where μ_{SF_j} and σ_{SF_j} represent respectively the local mean saliency and local standard deviation saliency of the Superfacet SF_j and are defined as:

$$\mu_{SF_j} = \frac{1}{|SF_j|} \sum_{v_i \in SF_j} MS(v_i) \tag{56}$$

$$\sigma_{SF_j} = \sqrt{\frac{1}{|SF_j|} \sum_{v_i \in SF_j} (MS(v_i) - \mu_{SF_j})^2} \tag{57}$$

where $|\text{SF}_j|$ represents the cardinality (*i.e,* the number of vertices) of the Superfacet SF_j.

δ_{SF_j} and γ_{SF_j} denote respectively the local mean roughness and the local standard deviation roughness and are defined as:

$$\delta_{SF_j} = \frac{1}{|SF_j|} \sum_{v_i \in SF_j} LRF(v_i) \tag{58}$$

$$\gamma_{SF_j} = \sqrt{\frac{1}{|SF_j|} \sum_{v_i \in SF_j} (LRF(v_i) - \delta_{SF_j})^2} \tag{59}$$

Finally a learning step using the constructed feature vector is performed. This is done using the Support Vector Regression (SVR) (Vapnik, 1995) which is also used for scoring the visual quality of the3D mesh. Figure 45 presents the block-diagram of the proposed approach.

Segmentation, Learning, and Regression

Segmentation Into Superfacets

One of the novelties of the proposed approach falls within the use of the Superfacets - the result of an over-segmentation of the mesh surface into regions whose borders fit well the semantic entities of the mesh - into the pipeline of a mesh quality assessment metric. To segment a 3D mesh mesh, Nouri et al., (2017b) modified the approach of (Simari et al., 2014) which, for a 3D mesh and a number of desired Superfacets, executes the following steps based on *the farthest point* principle:

- **Initialization:** The method begins by associating the center of the first Superfacet to the triangle of which the centroid is the nearest to the global centroid of the mesh. Then, each center of a new Superfacet is affected to the triangle with the euclidean distance to the latest considered triangle is the highest.
- **Update of the Centers:** Once the triangles have been affected to different Superfacets, it's necessary to compute the new center of each Superfacet. For this, the method computes the mean area of all triangles belonging to a Superfacet and associates the new center to the triangle of which the

Figure 45. Block diagram of BMQI (Nouri et al., 2017b)

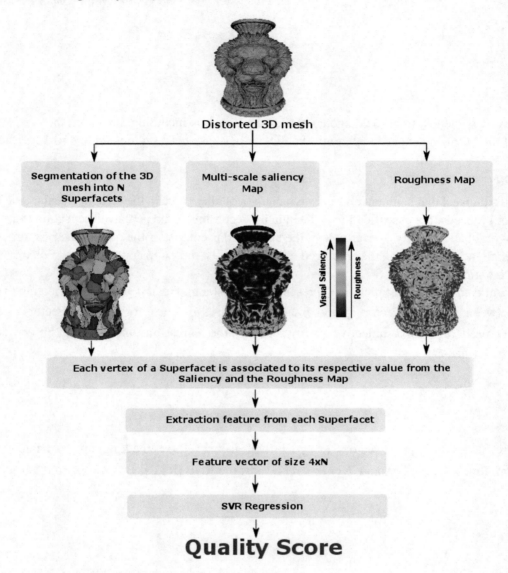

area is the nearest to the computed mean area. If the new center is different from the prior one, the algorithm stops. Otherwise, the classification step is computed.

- **Classification:** For each triangle, the method computes, using the Dijkstra Algorithm, the shortests paths between the centers of the defined superfacets and the triangles of the mesh. When a triangle is considered while computing the shortest path from a Superfacet center and if the current computed distance is less than the prior stored one (obtained from the initialization step or from an expansion that started from a different center) then both the distance and the label associated to the considered triangle are updated (the Superfacet that contains the triangle is fixed).
- **Geodesic Weight:** Given two adjacent faces f_i and f_j sharing an edge $e(i, j)$ with a median point $m_{i,j}$ and two respective centroids c_i and c_j, the geodesic weight is defined as

$geo\left(f_i, f_j\right) = \parallel c_i - m_{i,j} \parallel + \parallel m_{i,j} - c_j \parallel$. This latter is affected to the weight $w(f_i, f_j)$ of the edge $e(i, j)$ as follows:

$$w(f_i, f_j) = \frac{geo(f_i, f_j)}{d} \qquad (60)$$

Where d is the length of the diagonal of the bounding box including the 3D mesh.

In all the following experimentations, the 3D meshes have been segmented to 450 Superfacets.

Learning and Regression

Even if it's unusual that a human observer associates a quality score in the form of a scalar to a 3D mesh but rather proceeds to a classification of the quality according to the perceived sensation (for example: « good » or « bad » quality), nevertheless, the applications context of the quality metrics forces to provide a single scalar reflecting the perceived quality. For this, the extension of Support Vector Machines (SVM) to regression, named SVR, is used.

The aim is to estimate a function f presenting at most a maximal deviation e reflecting the dependence between a features vector x_i and an affiliation class y_i. Thus, for a feature vector x_i of a distorted 3D mesh M_i with a subjective quality score y_i, the regression function of an observation x to classify is defined as:

$$f_{SVR} = \sum_{x_i \in V_S} \alpha_i y_i K(x_i, x) + b \qquad (61)$$

Where V_S are the support vectors, (x_i, y_i) is the learning set, α is the Lagrange coefficient obtained from a minimization process and $K(x_i, x)$ represents the RBF (Radial Basis Function) kernel defined as:

$$K(x_i, x_j) = exp(\gamma \parallel x_i - x_j \parallel^2) \qquad (62)$$

Indeed, the RBF function is often used as a kernel function due to its resemblance to a similarity measure between two examples to classify. Also, the motivations related to the use of the SVR are as follows:

1. The regression solution includes a small number of examples x_i (rapidity and efficiency).
2. Results of the regression depend of the used kernel. The test of different kernels is beneficial in so far as the correlation rate between the objective scores and subjective ones may depend on the chosen kernel.

In order to compare the proposed no-reference metric BMQI with the state-of-the-art approaches, Nouri et al., (2017b) use the same publicly available subject-rated mesh databases as for their proposed full reference metric SMQI (Nouri et al., 2016b): 1) Liris/EpflGeneral-Purpose database (Lavoué et al.,

2006) and 2) Liris-Masking database(Lavoué et al., 2009). A learning step is carried onto the Liris-Masking database in order to determine the optimal RBF kernel's parameters (γ and C which represents the error penalty coefficient) with a 4 parts cross-validation. Each of these parts represents the distorted versions of one of the four reference meshes associated to their subjective quality score. The SVR regression was performed using the LIBSVM (Chang & Lin, 2001) library. The selected parameters of the RBF kernel for the Liris-Masking database are: $\gamma = 0.002$ and $C = 32$. For the Liris-Epfl General Purpose database, the selected parameters are: $\gamma = 0.005$ and $C = 2$.

Results and Analysis

Performance and Comparison With the State-of-the-Art

Table 5 presents the SROOC correlation values of the proposed no-reference metric and the correlation values of 7 full-reference metrics from the state-of-the-art associated to the Liris-Masking database. One can notice that the metric BMQI produces important correlation values for all the 3D meshes without the need of their reference version on the contrary of the full-reference metrics. These results confirm that the metric of (Nouri et al., 2017b) succeeds very well in taking into account the visual masking effect.

Table 6 shows the correlation values of BMQI associated to the Liris/Epfl General Purpose database. One can notice that the performances of BMQI on this database are not as good as those on the Liris-Masking database. Indeed, distortions on the Liris-Epfl General Purpose database (noise addition and smoothing) are applied on four distinct regions of the surface mesh (uniform regions, rough regions, smooth regions, and transitional regions).

This aims at reflecting the distortions associated to common mesh processing methods like simplification, compression and watermarking (Lavoué et al., 2006) which makes the quality assessment more difficult. From the results presented in Table 6, it seems that BMQI assesses the visual quality in a multi-distortion context with less precision than in a mono-distortion context even if the correlation values of the three groups of meshes (Dinosaur, Venus and RockerArm) are important. This is mainly due to the correlation value of the sub-corpus Armadillo which is lower in comparison to the other correlation values. This can be explained by the generated multi-scale saliency map that may not reflect well the distorted salient regions. Thus, the objective quality scores aren't consistent with the quality

Table 5. SROOC values (%) of different viewpoint-independent metrics on the LIRIS-Masking database

Mesh database	Full-reference								No-reference
Liris-Masking	HD	RMS	3DWPM1	3DPWPM2	MSDM2	FMPD	TPDM	SMQI	*BMQI*
Armadillo	48.6	65.7	58.0	48.6	88.6	88.6	88.6	88.6	**94.3**
Lion-vase	71.4	71.4	20.0	34.3	**94.3**	**94.3**	82.9	83.00	**94.3**
Bimba	25.7	71.4	20.0	37.1	**100.0**	**100.0**	**100.0**	100.0	**100.0**
Dinosaur	48.6	71.4	66.7	71.4	**100.0**	94.3	**100.0**	100.0	83.0

Table 6. SROOC values (%) of different viewpoint-independent metrics on the LIRIS/EPFL General Purpose database

Mesh database	Full-reference								No-reference
Liris/Epfl G. Purpose	HD	RMS	3DWPM1	3DPWPM2	MSDM2	FMPD	TPDM	SMQI	*BMQI*
Armadillo	69.5	62.7	65.8	74.1	81.6	75.4	84.9	77.5	20.1
Venus	1.6	90.1	71.6	34.8	89.3	87.5	**90.6**	91.6	88.9
Dinosaur	30.9	0.3	62.7	52.4	85.9	89.6	**92.2**	84.4	83.5
RockerArm	18.1	7.3	87.5	37.8	89.6	88.8	92.2	91.8	**92.7**
Entire database	13.8	26.8	69.3	49.0	80.4	81.9	**89.6**	84.6	78.1

scores of the human observers. The number of Superfacets and their size are two parameters that could influence the performance of the proposed metric. A precise definition of these parameters may improve the results. Finally, when the whole corpus of the Liris-Epfl General Purpose database is considered, the metric BMQI provides a correlation value relatively low in comparison to the full-reference metrics of the state-of-the-art. This is related on one hand to the low correlation value of the Armadillo sub-corpus and on the other hand to the number of 3D meshes considered in the learning step that is very small. Indeed, a corpus consisting in 88 meshes with their associated MOS wouldn't allow the design of an effective quality metric in a multi-distortion context.

In the light of these results, and given the capacity of the proposed approach to assess the perceived quality of a distorted mesh without the need of its reference version, BMQI seems nevertheless competitive with the full-reference methods. For example,

BMQI obtains better correlation rates associated to the Liris-Masking database in comparison to the full-reference metric SMQI proposed in (Nouri et al., 2016b). This could be explained by the contribution of the segmentation of the 3D mesh into Superfacets.

Performance on Indépendant 3D Meshes

Nouri et al., (2017b) have also tested the proposed no-reference metric BMQI for the quality assessment of 3D meshes not belonging to any database. This permits to analyze the behavior of this metric when assessing the visual quality of any 3D mesh. Figure 46 presents two reference 3D meshes with their distorted versions. The distortions considered are: additive noise and simplification. It's important to note that the simplification distortion wasn't considered in the learning process for selecting the parameters of the RBF kernel since both subject rated databases doesn't include this type of distortion. In these experimentations, the selected parameters associated to the Liris/Epfl General Purpose are used. From the top row of Figure 46, one can notice that BMQI provides coherent scores of quality in accordance with the human perception. The reference 3D mesh (Figure 46(a)) obtains a perceived quality score equal to 6.13. Its noised version obtains a quality score equal to 6.25 and its simplified version (more visually distorted) obtains a quality score equal to 6.74 (note that a low score signifies a good quality score and vice versa). The same remarks could be made to the second row of Figure 46.

Figure 46. Results of BMQI on independent 3D meshes not belonging to any database used in the learning or the regression step: a) Reference 3D mesh (276402 faces) BMQI=6.13, b) 3D mesh simplified adaptively with saliency information (Nouri et al., 2016a) (5000 faces) BMQI=6.25 and c) 3D mesh simplified with the method of (Garland & Heckbert, 1997) (5000faces) BMQI=6.75

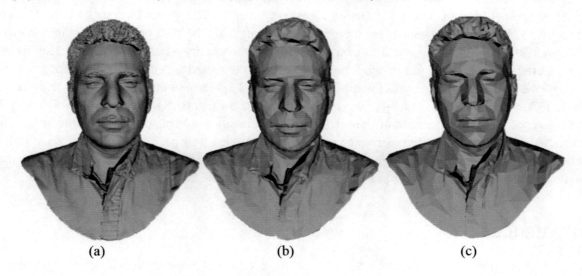

(a)   (b)   (c)

CONCLUSION AND PERSPECTIVES

In this second section (Perceptual quality assessment of non-colored 3D meshes), a full-reference perceptual quality assessment metric SMQI proposed in (Nouri et al., 2016b) was described. The latter compares structural informations of a reference 3D mesh with the ones of its distorted version. For this, a multi-scale saliency map is used from which local statistics reflecting the structures of the 3D mesh are computed. In order to take into account the visual masking effect, a roughness map is computed to measure means of roughness. Four comparisons functions are combined using a weighted Minkowski sum in order to provide an objective quality score which quantifies the visual similarity between the reference 3D mesh and its distorted version. Experimental results as well as well a comparison with the state-of-the-art approaches show the strong correlation of the full-reference metric SMQI with scores of quality provided by the human observers. This has attested its effectiveness.

However, as explained in the results analysis, an automatic ray - which serves to consider a spherical neighborhood while the construction of local adaptive patches for the saliency map generation - proper to the geometry of the target meshes can lead to better correlation results.

SMQI don't allow assessing the fidelity of a distorted 3D mesh having a different connectivity from its reference version (the case of a simplified mesh). An improvement would be to add a matching step from vertices of the distorted mesh towards vertices of the reference 3D mesh.

Sensitivity to the modifications of mesh frequencies can be taken into account since distortions are much more visible on high frequencies than lower frequencies. A first initiative proposed by (Corsini et al., 2013) suggests to obtain frequencies of the 3D mesh from the eigenvectors associated to its Laplacian matrix and to link these eigenvectors to perceptible frequencies of the HVS. Therefore, the modification of 3D mesh components will be linked to the sensitivity of the frequencies of the HVS.

The size of the considered subject rated databases plays an important role in the performance of the quality assessment metrics having a learning step in their pipeline. Existing 3D mesh databases have a small size. This would not allow designing a perceptual metric which is able to assess any type of distortion (Lavoué et al., 2006) (Lavoué, 2009) (Silva et al, 2009).

Also, another kind of perceptual quality assessment metrics was studied in this section. This one concerns the blind quality assessment metrics. Nouri et al., (2017b) have proposed to combine visual saliency and visual masking effect to design a no-reference quality assessment metric. This metric, BMQI, uses simple features (mean and standard deviation) computed on a multi-scale saliency map and a roughness map in order to assess the quality of a distorted 3D mesh without the need of its reference version. Correlation rates with subjective scores of quality show that BMQI is very competitive with the full-reference metrics of the state-of-the-art. Two improvements would be to ameliorate the multi-scale saliency map as well as the used regression process. Indeed, a learning performed on a corpus of important size would lead to a better prediction of quality in a multi-distortion context. Another amelioration would be to considerate the multi-scale aspect from the size of the Superfacets.

REFERENCES

Achanta, R., Hemami, S. S., Estrada, F. J., & Süsstrunk, S. (2009). Frequency-tuned salient region detection. In CVPR (pp. 1597-1604). IEEE Computer Society. doi:10.1109/CVPR.2009.5206596

Aspert, N., Cruz, D. S., & Ebrahimi, T. (2002). MESH: measuring errors between surfaces using the Hausdorff distance. In ICME (pp. 705-708). IEEE Computer Society.

Bian, Z., & Tong, R. (2011). Feature-preserving mesh denoising based on vertices classification. *Computer Aided Geometric Design*, *28*(1), 50–64. doi:10.1016/j.cagd.2010.10.001

Boulos, F., Parrein, B., Le Callet, P., & Hands, D. (2009). Perceptual effects of packet loss on H.264/AVC encoded videos. VPQM workshop.

Buades, A., Coll, B., & Morel, J.-M. (2005). A Non-Local Algorithm for Image Denoising. *Proceedings of the 2005 IEEE Computer Society Conference on Computer Vision and Pattern Recognition (CVPR'05)*, *2*, 60–65. 10.1109/CVPR.2005.38

Engelke, U., Pepion, R., Le Callet, P., & Zepernick, H. (2010). Linkingdistortion perception and visual saliency in h.264/AVC codedvideo containing packet loss. *Proc. SPIE*.

Bulbul, A., Çapin, T. K., Lavoué, G., & Preda, M. (2011). Assessing Visual Quality of 3-D Polygonal Models. *IEEE Signal Processing Magazine*, *28*(6), 80–90. doi:10.1109/MSP.2011.942466

Cignoni, P., Rocchini, C., & Scopigno, R. (1998). Metro: Measuring Error on Simplified Surfaces. *Computer Graphics Forum*, *17*(2), 167–174. doi:10.1111/1467-8659.00236

Coren, S., Ward, L. M., & Enns, J. T. (2003). *Sensation and Perception*. Wiley & Son.

Corsini, M., Larabi, C., Lavoué, G., Petrík, O., Vása, L., & Wang, K. (2012). Perceptual Metrics for Static and Dynamic Triangle Meshes. In M.-P. Cani & F. Ganovelli (Eds.), Eurographics (STARs) (pp. 135-157). Eurographics Association.

Cho, J.-W., Prost, R., & Jung, H.-Y. (2007). An Oblivious Watermarking for 3-D Polygonal Meshes Using Distribution of Vertex Norms. *IEEE Transactions on Signal Processing*, *55*(1), 142–155. doi:10.1109/TSP.2006.882111

Bolin, M. R., & Meyer, G. W. (1998). A Perceptually Based Adaptive Sampling Algorithm. In S. Cunningham, W. Bransford & M. F. Cohen (Eds.), SIGGRAPH (pp. 299-309). ACM. doi:10.1145/280814.280924

Corsini, M., Gelasca, E. D., Ebrahimi, T., & Barni, M. (2007). Watermarked 3-D Mesh Quality Assessment. *IEEE Transactions on Multimedia*, *9*(2), 247–256. doi:10.1109/TMM.2006.886261

Deubel, H., Schneider, W. X., & Bridgeman, B. (1996). Postsaccadic target blanking prevents saccadic suppression of image displacement. *Vision Research*, *36*(7), 985–996. doi:10.1016/0042-6989(95)00203-0 PMID:8736258

Digne, J., Chaine, R., & Valette, S. (2014). Self-similarity for accurate compression of point sampled surfaces. *Computer Graphics Forum*, *33*(2), 155–164. doi:10.1111/cgf.12305

Dutagaci, H., Cheung, C. P., & Godil, A. (2011). Evaluation of 3D Interest Point Detection Techniques. In H. Laga, T. Schreck, A. Ferreira, A. Godil, I. Pratikakis & R. C. Veltkamp (Eds.), 3DOR (pp. 57-64). Eurographics Association.

Findlay, J. M. (2004). Eye scanning in visual search. In J. Henderson & F. Ferreira (Eds.), *The interface of language, vision and action: eye movements and the visual world* (pp. 135–159). Psychology press.

Gal, R., & Cohen-or, D. (2006). Salient geometric features for partial shape matching and similarity. *ACM Transactions on Graphics*, *25*(1), 130–150. doi:10.1145/1122501.1122507

Garland, M., & Heckbert, P. S. (1997). Surface simplification using quadric error metrics. In G. S. Owen, T. Whitted & B. Mones-Hattal (Eds.), SIGGRAPH (pp. 209-216). ACM. doi:10.1145/258734.258849

Gelasca, E. D., Ebrahimi, T., Corsini, M., & Barni, M. (2005). Objective evaluation of the perceptual quality of 3D watermarking. *IEEE International Conference On Image Processing*, 241-244.

Guo, J., Vidal, V., Cheng, I., Basu, A., Baskurt, A. & Lavoué, G. (2017). Subjective and Objective Visual Quality Assessment of Textured 3D Meshes. *TAP, 14*, 11:1-11:20.

Hou, X., & Zhang, L. (2007). *Saliency Detection: A Spectral Residual Approach. CVPR*. IEEE Computer Society.

Guy, G., & Medioni, G. G. (1997). Inference of Surfaces, 3D Curves, and Junctions From Sparse, Noisy, 3D Data. *IEEE Transactions on Pattern Analysis and Machine Intelligence*, *19*(11), 1265–1277. doi:10.1109/34.632985

Henderson, J. M. (2003). Human gaze control during real-world scene perception. *Trends in Cognitive Sciences*, *7*(11), 498–504. doi:10.1016/j.tics.2003.09.006 PMID:14585447

Henderson, J., Williams, C., & Falk, R. (2005). Eye movements are functional during face learning. *Memory & Cognition*, *133*(1), 98–106. doi:10.3758/BF03195300 PMID:15915796

Hoffman, J. E., & Subramaniam, B. (1995). The role of visual attention in saccadic eye movements. *Perception & Psychophysics*, *57*(6), 787–795. doi:10.3758/BF03206794 PMID:7651803

Howard, J. (2002). *Seeing in depth*. Toronto: University of Toronto Press.

Human-eye blog. (n.d.). *Eye colour*. Retrieved from http://the--human-eye.blogspot.com/

Itti, L., Koch, E. N., & Niebur, E. (1998). A model of saliency-based visual attention for rapid science analysis. *IEEE Transactions on Pattern Analysis and Machine Intelligence, 20*(11), 1254–1259. doi:10.1109/34.730558

ITU-RBT.500-11. (2002). *Méthodologie d'évaluation subjective de la qualité des images de télévision*. Technical Report. International Telecommunication Union.

ITU-T Recommendation P.910. (2008). *Subjective video quality assessment methods for multimedia applications*. International Telecommunication Union.

Jia, S., Zhang, C., Li, X., & Zhou, Y. (2014). Mesh resizing based on hierarchical saliency detection. *Graphical Models, 76*(5), 355–362. doi:10.1016/j.gmod.2014.03.012

Johnson, A. E., & Hebert, M. (1999). Using Spin Images for Efficient Object Recognition in Cluttered 3DScenes. IEEE Transactions on Pattern Analysis and Machine Intelligence, 433-449.

Karni, Z., & Gotsman, C. (2000). *Spectral Compression of Mesh Geometry*. EuroCG, 27-30. doi:10.1145/344779.344924

Koch, C., & Poggio, T. (1999). Predicting the visual world: Silence is golden. *Nature Neuroscience, 2*(1), 9–10. doi:10.1038/4511 PMID:10195172

Kowler, E., Anderson, E., Dosher, B., & Blaser, E. (1995). The role of visual attention in the programming of saccades. *Vision Research, 35*(13), 1897–1916. doi:10.1016/0042-6989(94)00279-U PMID:7660596

Kim, Y., Varshney, A., Jacobs, D. W., & Guimbretière, F. (2010). Mesh saliency and human eye fixations. *Transactions on Applied Perception, 7*(2), 1–13. doi:10.1145/1670671.1670676

Lavoué, G., & Corsini, M. (2010). A Comparison of Perceptually-Based Metrics for Objective Evaluation of Geometry Processing. *IEEE Transactions on Multimedia, 12*(7), 636–649. doi:10.1109/TMM.2010.2060475

Lavoué, G., Drelie Gelasca, E., Dupont, F., Baskurt, A., & Ebrahimi, T. (2006).Perceptually driven 3D distance metrics with application to watermarking. *Proceedings of SPIE, Applications of Digital Image Processing, 6312,* 63120L-63120L12.

Lavoué, G. (2009). A local roughness measure for 3D meshes and its application to visual masking. *ACM Transactions on Applied Perception, 21,* 1-23.

Lavoué, G. (2011). A Multiscale Metric for 3D Mesh Visual Quality Assessment. *Computer Graphics Forum, 30*(5), 1427–1437. doi:10.1111/j.1467-8659.2011.02017.x

Lee, J., Moghaddam, B., Pfister, H., & Machiraju, R. (2004). Finding Optimal Views for 3D Face Shape Modeling. In FGR (pp. 31-36). IEEE Computer Society.

Lee, C. H., Varshney, A., & Jacobs, D. W. (2005). Mesh saliency. *ACM Transactions on Graphics, 24*(3), 659–666. doi:10.1145/1073204.1073244

Liu, Z. (2014). A Novel Saliency Detection Framework. *IEEE Transactions on Image Processing*, *23*(5), 1937–1952. doi:10.1109/TIP.2014.2307434 PMID:24710397

Ling, H., & Okada, K. (2006). Diffusion Distance for Histogram Comparison. In IEEE CVPR (pp. 246--253). IEEE.

Liversedge, S. P., & Findlay, J. M. (2000). Saccadic eyemovements and cognition. *Trends in Cognitive Sciences*, *4*(1), 6–14. doi:10.1016/S1364-6613(99)01418-7 PMID:10637617

Maximo, A., Patro, R., Varshney, A., & Farias, R. C. (2011). A robust and rotationally invariant local surface descriptor with applications to non-local mesh processing. *Graphical Models*, *73*(5), 231–242. doi:10.1016/j.gmod.2011.05.002

Nouri, A., Charrier, C., & Lézoray, O. (2015). Multi-scale mesh saliency with local adaptive patches for viewpoint selection. *Signal Processing Image Communication*, *38*, 151–166. doi:10.1016/j.image.2015.08.002

Nouri, A., Charrier, C., & Lézoray, O. (2015b). Multi-scale saliency of 3D colored meshes. *International Conference on Image Processing (IEEE)*, 2820-2824.

Nouri, A., Charrier, C., & Lézoray, O. (2016a). *Cartes de saillance et évaluation de la qualité des maillages 3D* (Doctoral dissertation). Retrieved from HAL ARCHIVES OUVERTES. (Accession No. tel-01418334)

Nouri, A., Charrier, C., & Lezoray, O. (2016b). Full-reference saliency-based 3D mesh quality assessment index. In ICIP (pp. 1007-1011). Academic Press.

Nouri, A., Charrier, C., & Lezoray, O. (2017a). *Greyc 3D colored Mesh Database*. Technical report. Retrieved from https://nouri.users.greyc.fr/ColoredMeshDatabase.html

Nouri, A., Charrier, C., & Lezoray, O. (2017b). 3D Blind mesh quality assessment index. *Proc. of IS&T Electronic Imaging. Three-Dimensional Image Processing, Measurement (3DIPM), and Applications*, 9-26.

Parkhurst, D., Law, K., & Niebur, E. (2002). Modeling the role of salience in the allocation of overt visual attention. *Vision Research*, *42*(1), 107–123. doi:10.1016/S0042-6989(01)00250-4 PMID:11804636

Rogowitz, B. E., & Rushmeier, H. E. (2001). Are image quality metrics adequate to evaluate the quality of geometric objects? In B. E. Rogowitz & T. N. Pappas (Eds.), Human Vision and Electronic Imaging (pp. 340-348). SPIE.

Rizzolatti, G., Riggio, L., & Sheliga, B. M. (1994). Space and selectiveattention. In C. Ulmità & M. Moscovitch (Eds.), *Attention and performance* (pp. 231–265). Cambridge, MA: MIT Press.

Rusinkiewicz, S. (2004). Estimating Curvatures and Their Derivatives on Triangle Meshes. In 3DPVT (pp. 486-493). IEEE Computer Society.

Song, R., Liu, Y., Martin, R. R. & Rosin, P. L. (2014). Mesh saliency via spectral processing. *ACM Trans. Graph.*, *33*, 6:1-6:17.

Sorkine, O., Cohen-Or, D., & Toledo, S. (2003). High-Pass Quantization for Mesh Encoding. In L. Kobbelt, P. Schröder & H. Hoppe (Eds.), *Symposium on Geometry Processing* (pp. 42-51). Eurographics Association.

Shahrbabaki, S. T. (2015). *Contribution de la couleur dans l'attention visuelle et un modèle de saillance visuelle* (Doctoral dissertation). Retrieved from HAL ARCHIVES OUVERTES. (Accession No. tel-01241487)

Shilane, P., & Funkhouser, T. (2007). Distinctive regions of 3D surfaces. *ACM Transactions on Graphics*, *26*, 7. Retrieved from http://doi.acm.org/10.1145/1243980.1243981

Silva, S., Santos, B. S., Ferreira, C., & Madeira, J. (2009). A perceptual data repository for polygonal meshes. *Second International Conference in Visualisation*, 207-212. 10.1109/VIZ.2009.41

Simari, P. D., Picciau, G., & Floriani, L. D. (2014). Fast and Scalable Mesh Superfacets. *Computer Graphics Forum*, *33*(7), 181–190. doi:10.1111/cgf.12486

Song, R., Liu, Y., Martin, R. R. & Rosin, P. L. (2014). Mesh saliency via spectral processing. *ACM Trans. Graph.*, *33*, 6:1-6:17.

Song, R., Liu, Y., Zhao, Y., Martin, R. R., & Rosin, P. L. (2012). Conditional random field-based mesh saliency. In ICIP (p./pp. 637-640). IEEE. doi:10.1109/ICIP.2012.6466940

Tal, A., Shtrom, E., & Leifman, G. (2012). Surface regions of interest for viewpoint selection. *IEEE Conference on Computer Vision and Pattern Recognition*, 414-421.

Tao, P., Cao, J., Li, S., Liu, X., & Liu, L. (2015). Mesh saliency via ranking unsalient patches in a descriptor space. *Computers & Graphics*, *46*, 264–274. doi:10.1016/j.cag.2014.09.023

Tatler, B.W, Baddeley, R.J&Glichrist, I.D. (2005). Visual correlates of fixation selection: effects of scale and time. *Vision Research, 45*, 643-659.

Fakhri, T., Kai, W. & Jean-Marc, C. (2014). A curvature-tensor-basedperceptual quality metric for 3d triangular meshes. *Machine Graphics and Vision*, 1-25.

Treisman, A. M., & Gelade, G. (1980). A Feature-Integration Theory of Attention. *Cognitive Psychology*, *12*(1), 97–136. doi:10.1016/0010-0285(80)90005-5 PMID:7351125

Vása, L., & Rus, J. (2012). Dihedral Angle Mesh Error: A fast perception correlated distortion measure for fixed connectivity triangle meshes. *Computer Graphics Forum*, *31*(5), 1715–1724. doi:10.1111/j.1467-8659.2012.03176.x

Vapnik, V. N. (1995). *The Nature of Statistical Learning Theory*. Springer. doi:10.1007/978-1-4757-2440-0

Vision du futur. La rétine. (n.d.). Retrieved from http://lavisiondufutur.e-monsite.com/pages/l-oeil/la-retine.html

Wang, K., Lavoué, G., Denis, F., & Baskurt, A. (2011). Robust and blind mesh watermarking based on volume moments. *Computers & Graphics*, *35*(1), 1–19. doi:10.1016/j.cag.2010.09.010

Wang, K., Torkhani, F., & Montanvert, A. (2012). A fast roughness-based approach to the assessment of 3D mesh visual quality. *Computers & Graphics*, *36*(7), 808–818. doi:10.1016/j.cag.2012.06.004

Wang, Z., & Bovik, A. C. (2011). Reduced- and No-Reference Image Quality Assessment. *IEEE Signal Processing Magazine*, *28*(6), 29–40. doi:10.1109/MSP.2011.942471

Wang, Z., & Bovik, A. C. (2006). *Modern Image Quality Assessment*. Morgan & Claypool Publishers.

Widdel, H. (1984). Operational problems in analyzing eye movements. *Theoretical and applied aspects of eye movement research, 22*, 21-29.

Wolfe, J. M., Alvarez, G. A., & Horowitz, T. S. (2000). Attention is fast but volition is slow. *Nature*, *406*(6797), 691. doi:10.1038/35021132 PMID:10963584

Wolfe, J. M., Cave, K. R., & Franzel, S. L. (1989). Guided research: An alternative to the feature integration model for visual research. *Journal of Experimental Psychology. Human Perception and Performance*, *15*(3), 419–433. doi:10.1037/0096-1523.15.3.419 PMID:2527952

Wolfe, J. M., Palmer, E. M., & Horowitz, T. S. (2010). Reaction time distributions constrain models of visual research. *Vision Research*, *50*(14), 1304–1311. doi:10.1016/j.visres.2009.11.002 PMID:19895828

Wu, J., Shen, X., Zhu, W., & Liu, L. (2013). Mesh saliency with global rarity. *Graphical Models*, *75*(5), 255–264. doi:10.1016/j.gmod.2013.05.002

Yarbus, A. L. (2002). *Eye movements and vision*. Plenum Press.

Yee, Y. H., Pattanaik, S. N., & Greenberg, D. P. (2001). Spatiotemporal sensitivity and visual attention for efficient rendering of dynamic environments. *ACM Transactions on Graphics*, *20*(1), 39–65. doi:10.1145/383745.383748

Zhao, Y., Liu, Y., Song, R., & Zhang, M. (2012). Extended non-local means filter for surface saliency detection. In ICIP (p./pp. 633-636). IEEE. doi:10.1109/ICIP.2012.6466939

Zhao, Y., & Liu, Y. (2012). Patch based saliency detection method for 3D surface simplification. In ICPR (p./pp. 845-848). IEEE Computer Society.

Zhao, Y., Liu, Y., & Zeng, Z. (2013). Using Region-Based Saliency for 3D Interest Points Detection. In R. C. Wilson, E. R. Hancock, A. G. Bors & W. A. P. Smith (Eds.), CAIP (vol. 2, pp. 108-116). Springer.

Zhu, Q., Zhao, J., Du, Z., & Zhang, Y. (2010). Quantitative analysis of discrete 3D geometrical detail levels based on perceptual metric. *Computers & Graphics*, *34*(1), 55–65. doi:10.1016/j.cag.2009.10.004

KEY TERMS AND DEFINITIONS

Colorimetric Saliency: Saliency detected from colors of the 3D colored mesh.
Geometric Saliency: Saliency detected from the geometry of the 3D non-colored mesh.
HVS: Human visual system.

Chapter 4
Low Complexity Single Color Image Dehazing Technique

Sangita Roy
Narula Institute of Technology, India

Sheli Sinha Chaudhuri
Jadavpur University, India

ABSTRACT

Atmospheric particulate matter (APM) disturbs the biotic environment creating global warming, health hazards, and last but not the least, visibility reduction. Removing haze from degraded image is an extremely ill-posed inverse problem. Real time is another factor influencing the quality of resulting image. There is a trade-off between time and quality of resulting image. Single image makes the algorithms more challenging. In this work, the authors have developed fast, efficient, single gray or color image visibility improvement algorithms based on image formation optical model with minimum order statistics filter (MOSF) as the transmission model. The quantitative and qualitative evaluations of the proposed algorithms have been studied with other existing algorithms. The result shows improvements over existing state-of-the art algorithms with minimum time. Time has been evaluated by execution time along with time complexity Big (O). The resultant images are visibly clear satisfying the criteria for computer vision applications.

INTRODUCTION

APM or aerosol is a real threat in our green world. Researchers are fighting against it. One of the reasons of APM is unplanned civilization and technological advancements. It has been observed from satellite images that Asian and African and very few parts of American countries are the most polluted places. Image sources from satellites show year wise degradation .APM are both natural and manmade. APM are a mixture of solid and liquid droplets. They are in variety of sizes. Coarse APM ranges PM10-PM2.5 (micrometre diameter), finer are below PM2.5 and ultrafine below PM0.1(Mao, 2015). Computer vision (CV) is a promising branch of technology which encompasses object tracking, object recognition, surveillance, image enhancement etc. Clear image is an essential requirement in CV. But APM degrades

DOI: 10.4018/978-1-5225-5246-8.ch004

visibility of the received image. Rain, fog, vog, mist, fume, smog, hail, snow etc. are the cause of visibility reduction in image. Outdoor image is a challenge in computer vision, especially in bad weather condition. Image formation at the viewer point (i.e. may be considered camera) is influenced by distance, airlight, transmission, and scattering coefficient [Koschmiede, 1924). There are some classical enhancement techniques, like, histogram equalization, imadjust, adaptive histogram equalization. These techniques work well in most of the cases. In some special cases (like, fog, haze, smoke, rain, vog etc.) these techniques fail. In those special cases of bad weather nothing can be seen from the image. The situation becomes worsen if no ground truth or reference image could be found. In these contexts special popular algorithms have to be selected. Those are working with no ground truth image or popularly called single image dehazing algorithms. The key observations found from outdoor haze free images are as i) image contrast of normal image is high, ii) airlight does not affect the richness of the image, iii) pixels intensity is well distributed in the intensity scale, and iv) pixel over-saturation and under saturation do not exist(Xhang, et al.,2004]. Contrary to that of hazy images are of low contrast and airlight makes images white. Most of the pixel intensities are very high i.e., under-saturated and flocked together. Degraded image pixels are over saturated in one of the channels. The cause may be due to the illuminant of strong colour cast or sensor/camera respond differently for different colour channels. Resultant of these artifacts makes image pixels achromatic. Visibility Improvement is under the category of Ill-Posed Inverse Problem. In this class best or optimum image has to be extracted from a series of attenuated received images. Sometimes it is extremely difficult to retrieve any information about the original image as the problem becomes Ill-Posed Inverse Problem (Roy, Chaudhuri, 2016). Paper is arranged as below. Section II consists of Literature survey. In section III Minimum OSF detail study has been presented. Proposed methods have been illustrated Section IV. Result is described in section V. Section VI explains qualitative and quantitative analysis. Section VII elaborates its applications and type of device used for the research. Finally section VIII is for Conclusion.

LITERATURE SURVEY

In some research work DCP (dark channel prior) has been used which is a statistical prior on haze free images. This prior indicates that in normal RGB image 75% pixels of any dark channel is zero where dark channel indicates the lowest intensities channel out of three RGB image channel. 90% pixels of that channel are below 25. However the scenario drifts radically in case of degraded weather. That corresponds to high intensity of dark channel. It is due to atmospheric airlight which shifts the pixels intensity to very high value producing almost white image. The method is efficient, but takes long time to reproduce. Therefore for real time application cannot be useful (He et al., 2009). The work of R Tan based on two observations, contrast of image is compromised in degraded image. Normal image has more contrast than that of hazy image. Degraded image has more airlight and it increases with distance. As a result distant part becomes smoother and invisible. The method is efficient as required single image, but not applicable for real time (Tan, 2008). The algorithm proposed by J P Tarel is fast and its complexity is linear function with the number of image pixels for both colour and gray image. The algorithm is tuned by only four parameters, atmospheric veil inference, image restoration, smoothing, and tone mapping (Tarel, et al., 2009). Research work of R Fattal based on haze estimation, scatter light estimation. From that information haze free image contrast has been recovered. It has been assumed that transmission and surface shading is locally uncorrelated. This simple statistical assumption reduces other complexity like surface albedo. The challenge of this method is to solve the pixels where no transmission is available. Implicit graphical model made it possible to extrapolate solution of those pixels(Fattal, 2008). It is not a patch based prior contrary to previous methods. It is non-local prior. D Berman et. al. emphasised that degradation is not uniform . It is different for different pixels of the image and is controlled by transmission coefficient. It has been proposed colours of haze free to be clustered and spread over the entire image. Whereas hazy image forms line of colours that was earlier clustered, called haze line. It recovers distance map. The algorithm is linear, faster, deterministic, no training required (Berman, et al., 2016). Authors are working on visibility improvements. Their earlier works were DCP based vision improvement where speed of the original algorithm was improved with reduced complexity and sky masking(Das, et al., 2016). In (Roy, et al., 2016) authors proposed three algorithms and revised DCP by gamma correction, contrast controller, sky masking and guided filtering. In [Datta, 2016; Datta, 2016; & Hore, 2016) authors emphasized on objective evaluation of DCP method and mathematical modeming of image formation. DCP is basically patch based or local prior. Patch size in (He, et al., 2009) was 15x15, omega was 0.95. These two parameters play a significant role. This has been shown (Roy, et al., 2016). DCP with sky masking is a useful algorithm. But the value of optimum value is difficult to find out. It is evaluated manually. In (Roy, et al., 2016) this difficulty has been recovered by using Cuckoo Search Algorithm. Resultant image using CSA removes the artifacts of sky reflection very well. Visibility Improvement is a classical Inverse problem. Haze is always associated with blurring. Here both have been treated and removed (Roy, et al., 2016).

MINIMUM ORDER STATISTICS FILTER (MOSF)

Images those are captured by sensors or camera have to be processed further. Therefore both haze as well as system noise is imposed on the scene radiance. Noise is forced on images during capture and transmission, etc. The resulting output images are under random noise effects. These random noise shift colour, brightness, sharpness, saturation, of the images contrast. These errors can be eliminated by filters those are mathematically modelled, either definite or statistical models. Noise deteriorates the fine details in images. Images are susceptible to stuck-pixel or impulse noise and other noises. Quality of image deteriorates during noise removal. Several noise removal filters, both linear and nonlinear are proposed and well-known. Linear filter are not suitable for removing impulse noise or non-Gaussian noise due to their inability to preserve edge details and they possess low-pass characteristics, as a result blurring occurs. Nonlinear filters maintain edge details. But it is difficult to design. Unifying all nonlinear filters are still a problem. There are broadly two types of nonlinear filters. They are classical and fuzzy technique. Classical filters are associated with blur, whereas fuzzy techniques smooth while preserving edges. Three common types of noises are i) impulse noise, ii) additive (Gaussian/amplifier) noise, and Multiplicative (Speckle) noise (Radhika, et al., 2010 & Mythili, et al., 2011). As the digital Image Processing gaining popularity the application of nonlinear filters are also increasing by lips and bound. Different types of nonlinear filters with their hybridization are coming up. OS are under this class.. It is very opulent. It is under the robust background of Estimation Theory by Tuckey for his time series analysis. It is popular for its simplicity and efficiency. Finally it can be said it works well under impulse noise or additive white Gaussian Noise with proper designing. It has good edge preserving properties. It is very important to remember that image characteristics vary from region to region. Whereas noise characteristics changes with time. These lead to constrain design of OSF, so that it must be adaptive both spatially and/ or temporally. Edge preservation and local contrast detection are two important issues regarding Human Visual System (HVS). Only adaptive systems can match this response. With advent of VLSI chips it has been used for hardware implementation of fast OSF design. Already it has been discussed that the OSF is robust as it is based on good estimation theory. It is efficiently reduces outliers. There are two robust measures, i) breakdown point, and ii) influence function. Most commonly used figure of merit performance for nonlinear filters are i) noise filtering characteristics under different types of noise, ii) edge preservation, iii) fine detail preservation, iv) un-biasedness, and v) computational complexity. One of the best OSF is median filer. Max/ Min filters are also under OSF. In case of median OSF median value from the mask or window is selected. Whereas in max OSF, maximum value is selected to reduce low pass noise or pepper type noise. In case of Min filter which is our concern salt noise or high pass or impulse noise are suppressed (Pitas, et al., 1992). In our proposed algorithms this min OSF has been used as the backbone for transmission map which is denoted as 't'. Therefore it is quite clear that our transmission map is free from impulse or high frequency noise or additive white Gaussian noise. It has already been stated that proposed methods are pixel based filter operation. But other methods those have been studied are path based. In pixel based methods all image pixels are taken into account. Whereas in patch based methods each path has same intensity vales. This phenomenon creates loss of edge and other detail of the image .Order statistics (OS) filter is a non-linear spatial digital filter. OSF is a rich and robust class of filter (Pitas, et al., 1992). Linear class of filter in image processing fails in some form of image degradation here noise is not additive, system non-linarites, non-Gaussian statistics encountered, maximum entropy criterion. Linear filters are unable to remove impulse noise and as a result blurs the edges in image processing where signal dependent noise present. This type of degradation arises at the time of image formation and transmission of image through non-linear channels. This has also been noticed that human visual perception mechanism to be non-linear. Nonlinear image processing emerged during 1958. Nonlinear digital image processing techniques can be classified as order statistics filter, homomorphic filters, polynomial filters, mathematical morphology, neural network, and nonlinear image restoration. Cross –fertilization among these classes can be proved encouraging. It is here to mention that image characteristics (logical statistics) vary from one area to the other. Apart from that noise characteristics is also time varying. Thus OSF must be adaptive temporally and /or spatially. Moreover human visual systems(edge preservation requirements, local contrast enhancement) follow spatially adaptive digital image filter structures. Some unique signal and noise characteristics can only be resolved by adaptive nature of OSF. Another important characteristic of OSF is its very less computational complexity. Their fastness depends on the nature of algorithms and hardware design. There are three types of OSF, namely median OSF, min OSF and max OSF (Pitas, et al., 1992). Response of the OSF pixels depends on the ordering or ranking of the pixels around the filter kernel. As an example in best popular median filter category a pixel value of an image is replaced by the median of the filter kernel used (Gonzalez, et al., 2008). MOSF has been used as base of transmission estimation pixel-wise rather patch wise in the algorithms to increase speed and efficiency without losing edge property. Pixel wise transmission estimation model picks more information contrary to path wise model (He, et al., 2009).

PROPOSED METHODOLOGY

In this paper two novel algorithms have been framed. First one is based on H Koschmieder and K He et. al. image formation Airlight principal (Koschmieder, 1924 He, 2009) and the second one is HSV corrected of the earlier one. They are elaborated below.

Algorithm I

Step-I: Input Hazy Image
Step-II: Minimum Order statistics filtered Image
Step-III: Average of highest 1% pixel intensity have been considered as Airlight of the image
Step-IV: Transmission Estimation from step-II
Step-V: Image formation equation used for recovery of image

Algorithm II

Step-I: Input Hazy Image
Step-II: Minimum Order statistics filtered Image
Step-III: Average of highest 1% pixel intensity have been considered as Airlight of the image
Step-IV: Transmission Estimation from step-I
Step-V: Image formation equation used for recovery of image
Step-VI: Intensity of the image is increased by HSV correction

H Koschmieder image formation equation is represented by

$$I(x) = J(x)t(x) + A(1 - t(x)) \qquad (1)$$

Here J(x) is the original scene radiance. t(x) and A are transmission and atmospheric airlight respectively. I(x) is the image at viewer point .Therefore scene radiance can be recovered only by

$$J(x) = \frac{I(x)}{t(x)} - A(1 - t(x)) \qquad (2)$$

Airlight can be calculated easily, as airlight is the highest intensity in each colour channel. In the original DCP airlight was considered 0.1% in the dark channel bright pixels. Transmission can be inferred from the above equation (1) and (2) as (3)

$$t(x) = 1 - \omega \left(\text{dark channel of the normalized hazy image} \right) \qquad (3)$$

The Dark channel is produced by normalised minimum transmission out of all channels. The output is computationally complex and time complexity is high. The faster optimum transmission can be found out by minimum ordered statistics filter . Therefore transmission has been extrapolated from the minimum of three channels with ordered statistics minimum filtered value and represented by

$$t(x) = 1 - \omega\left(\min_{c \in \{r,g,b\}} (\text{minimum ordered statistical filtered}\left(I^c(x)\right)\right) \tag{4}$$

Minimum OSF kernel is represented by

$$f(x,y) = \min_{(s,t) \in s_{xy}} \left\{ g(s,t) \right\} \tag{5}$$

g(s,t) is the pixel under the specified area sxy. f(x,y) is the filtered pixel. The 0th percentile filter is min filter. This filter is useful for darkest points in an image and reduces salt noise. This technique is computationally less complex. As a result time complexity reduces considerably. ω is an operational constant and kept 0.95, can be varied as per application ($0 < \omega \leq 1$). When it is zero, it indicates no haze at all and one indicates no vision. Practical consideration taking into account little amount of haze is essential for aerial perspective (He, 2009). Algorithm-I consists of above three equations. In algorithm-II, one extra step has been introduced as HSV correction. Here value channel, 'V' is adjusted to get bright output. The main purpose of this additional step is to increase brightness without shifting of colour properties and naturalness.

Figure 1. Flowchart of algorithm I

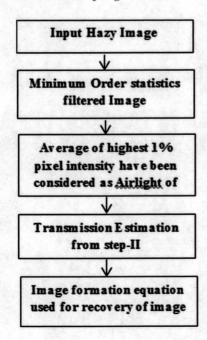

Figure 2. Flowchart of algorithm II

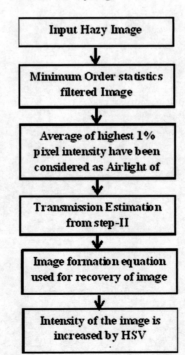

RESULT

Qualitative Analysis

In this section one outdoor long distance image with severe haze has been examined with different algorithms and their resulting images have been shown in figure 3. It has been observed that some of them are performing well and some are not. Performance of these algorithms with few robust parameters has between tabulated in table 1. Visual qualities of the output image of different algorithms are not the same. Our proposed algorithms are rich as well as natural looking, whereas He et. al. work is pleasing but dull.

In Figure 4 dark channel and transmission map of sample image have been shown. It is evident that both dark channel and transmission map of the proposed methods are better than that of the work of He et. al. Individual pixels are operated in our methods. Whereas patch based operation are applied on He et. al. method, and these patches are prominent in figure 4. This validates that the proposed methods are obviously extracting more information in comparison with other algorithms. Transmission map and dark channel of algorithm by He et. al. are unable to extract any original image layout. Whereas transmission map and dark channel of the proposed models produce the original image layout which is the major achievement of the proposed algorithms.

Figure 3. Sample Image of 525x600x3 size with different Algorithms and their output

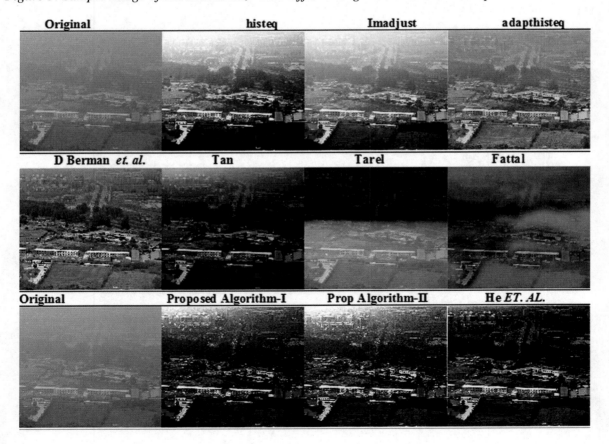

Table 1. Parametric evaluation

Sl. No.	PSNR in dB	CNR	Visible Edge in the original	Visible Edge in restored Image (VERI)	r	σ in %	e	Time CPU (T)
Histeq	13.1978	57.5534	25658	93689	3.1839	0.6927	2.6515	0.042s
imadjust	15.7788	58.0879	25658	77871	2.9118	0.35778	2.135	0.033s
adapthisteq	**22.0892**	61.2216	25658	87877	3.3127	**0**	2.4249	0.316s
He	8.7759	74.2366	25658	142850	5.4482	0.087619	4.5675	30minute
Tan	9.1426	50.7732	25658	18512	4.7412	0.0028571	0.27851	16.530mints
Tarel	10.2917	61.8767	25658	78045	2.3657	**0.0**	2.0417	26.76s
Fattal	11.7701	38.0591	25658	55301	4.7711	**0.0**	1.1553	16.167s
D Berman	15.1094	60.4885	25658	120981	4.9616	9.5238e-05	3.7151	3.471s
Proposed Method I	9.9767	70.7794	25658	**156462**	5.098	0.35524	**5.8146**	**0.383 sec.**
Proposed Method II	10.8262	**82.1917**	25658	**153281**	**6.7671**	0.33937	4.974	**0.498s**

Figure 4. Transmission map and dark channel of the sample image

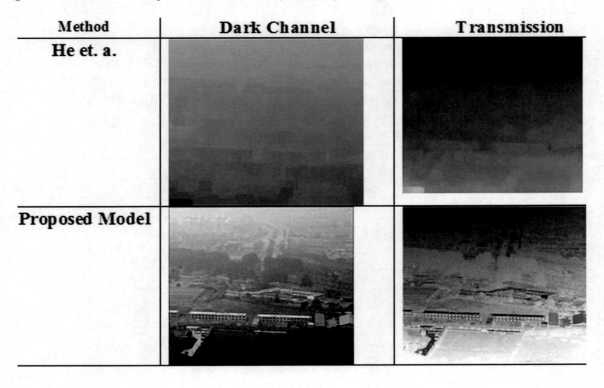

Quantitative/ Objective Evaluation

In Hautiere, et al. (2011) proposed three visibility parameter r, e, and σ referring as the geometric mean of VL, rate of newly visible edge, and normalised newly saturated pixels in the restored image respectively. High values of e and r are appreciated, whereas low value of σ is required. In the table 1 different images have been examined with our algorithms. It has been perceived that our algorithms performing equally well in different image conditions. Proposed algorithms are rich in colour and pleasing in appearance.

r= Geometric mean of VL (visibility level);
σ= normalised newly saturated pixels in the restored image ;
e= rate of new visible edge ;

Table 1 shows few important parameters for image evaluation. These parameters have been applied for evaluation of different well known algorithms performance. It has been found that PSNRs and 'σ' values of our proposed methods are not the best. Our algorithms show better performance in the parametric evaluation of CNR, VERI, r, e. Finally T (time) consumption of proposed methods outperform all other methods which is the requirement for any other real time application. Therefore this can be said that overall performance of the projected algorithms is satisfied. In this paper some of our previous works results have been shown. Figure 5 and figure 6 are derived from our earlier research works. In Figure 7 varied degree of haze with different outdoor atmospheric conditions are presented for the robustness and visual appearance of the presented algorithms. The Figure 7 shows algorithms' adaptability for different types of atmospheric conditioned images.

It is evident from Table 2 that time complexity of proposed algorithm is Big ($O(n^2)$) whereas that of He et. Al. is of the order of Big ($O(n^7)$). They are under P complexity class DTM (Deterministic Turing Machine) in polynomial time (Sipser, 2013). Time complexity is also dependent on filter kernel size. Hence it is validated that proposed algorithm is faster than that of the algorithm (He, 2009).

Table 2. Time Complexity in terms of Big(O)

Proposed Algorithm	Time Complexity	He et. al. Algorithm	Time Complexity
Get Input Hazy Image		Get Input Hazy Image	
Order statistics filtered Image	$O(n^2)$	Dark Channel prior	$O(n^2)$
Average of highest 1% pixel intensity have been considered as Airlight of the image	$O(n^2)$	Average of highest 1% pixel intensity have been considered as Airlight of the image	$O(n^2)$
Transmission Estimation from step-II	$O(n)$	Transmission Estimation from step-II	$O(n)$
recovery of image	$O(n)$	Scene Radiance recovery	$O(n)$
-	-	Soft Matting	$O(n^7)$
-	-	Scene Radiance recovery	$O(n)$
Total time	$O(n^2)$	**Total time**	$O(n^7)$

Potential Application

This algorithm can be used in surveillance, Military, under water, outdoor image post processing, on board moving vehicle. Intel core i3, 3110M CPU @ 2.40 GHz, 4.0 GB RAM, Intel HD Graphics 4000, 5 years old has been used for the research in MATLAB environment.

CONCLUSION

In this paper a low complexity, fast, robust visibility improvement for image is presented. The presented novel methods are qualitatively and quantitatively analysed. The outcome of the research shows that the proposed methods not only applicable for artefact free real time still as well as video, but also no ground truth image required. This approach is very simple applicable for colour and grey single image. The methods are equally adaptable for varied natural image conditions. All statistical parameters, those have been applied, are proved best in the proposed algorithms in comparison with other state-of-art work in this area. Time complexity reduced remarkably in comparison to the other existing techniques. PSNR is not the best but also not worst. Therefore PSNR can be improved in future. The recovered image is natural in look, as some of the other contemporary work output appears painted or dull. Visual appeal is rich in colour and contrast also reasonable than that of the other popular algorithms. The proposed algorithms are fit for any real time application. The minimum OSF is used for transmission map recovery is unique in this paper. Robust estimation theory is the heart of any nonlinear filtering. The essence of OSF which is under nonlinear filter class is its simplicity and robustness, edge preservation, no loss of details and last but not the least its speed. The OSF has been efficiently applied in the algorithms as the transmission estimator which is the main motivation for fast and good performance of the proposed methods. Dark channel is patch based technique which gives path information, whereas OSF gives detail pixel information. Another remarkable approach of this paper is its time complexity analysis This time complexity analysis also shows improvement along with execution time analysis. We are not claiming that it is the absolute outcome. More modification possibilities are there to improve the algorithms.

REFERENCES

Berman, D., Treibitz, & Avidan, S. (2016). Non-local Image Dehazing. *CVPR*, 27-30.

Das, D., Roy, S., & Chaudhuri, S. S. (2016). Dehazing Technique based on Dark Channel Prior model with Sky Masking and its quantitative analysis. *IEEE Explore*, 207-210.

Datta, S. K., Hore, M., & Roy, S. (2016a). Objective Evaluation of Dehazed Image by DCP. *NCEC-ERS2016-mainak*.

Datta, S. K., Hore, M., & Roy, S. (2016b). Mathematical Modelling of Image Formation through Atmosphere. *NSAMTM2016*.

Fattal, R. (2008). Single Image Dehazing. *ACM Transactions on Graphics*, *27*(72), 1–9. doi:10.1145/1360612.1360671

Gonzalez, R. C., & Woods, R. E. (2008). *Digital Image Processing* (3rd ed.). Pearson.

Hautiere, N., Tarel, J. P., Aubert, D., & Doumont, E. (2011). Blind contrast enhancement assessment by gradient rationing at visible edges. *Image Analysis & Stereology*, 1–9.

He, K., Sun, J., & Tang, X. (2009). Single image haze removal using dark channel prior. *IEEE Conference on Computer Vision and Pattern Recognition*, 1956- 1963.

Hore, M., Datta, S. K., & Roy, S. (2016). Subjective & Objective Evaluation of Dehazed Image by DCP. *IC2C2SE*.

Koschmieder, H. (1924). Theorie der horizontalensichtweite. *Beitr.Phys. Freien Atm.*, *12*, 171–181.

Mao, J. (2015). *Study of Image Dehazing with the self-adjustment of the Haze Degree* (Ph.D. Thesis). Division of Production and Information Systems Engineering, Muroran Institute of Technology.

Mythili, C., & Kavitha, V. (2011). Efficient technique for color image noise reduction. *The Research Bulletin of Jordan ACM*, *2*(3), 41–44.

Pitas, I., & Venetsanopoulos, A. N. (1992). Order Statistics in Digital Signal Processing. *Proceedings of the IEEE*, *80*(12), 1893–1921. doi:10.1109/5.192071

Radhika, V., & Padmavati, G. (2010). Performance of various order statistics filters in impulse and mixed noise removal for RS images. *Signal and Image Processing: An International Journal*, *1*(2), 13–20. doi:10.5121ipij.2010.1202

Roy, D., Banerjee, S., Roy, S.,& Chaudhuri, S. S. (2016). Removal of the Artifacts Present in the Existing Dehazing Techniques. *IC2C2SE*.

Roy, S., & Chaudhuri, S. S. (2016). Modeling of Ill-Posed Inverse Problem. *International Journal of Modern Education and Computer Science*, *12*, 46–55. doi:10.5815/ijmecs.2016.12.07

Roy, S., & Chaudhuri, S. S. (2016). Development of Real Time Visibility Enrichment Algorithms. *NCECERS*, 32.

Roy, S., & Chaudhuri, S. S. (2016). Modelling and control of sky pixels in visibility improvement through CSA. *IC2C2SE*.

Sipser, M. (2013). *Introduction to the theory of computation* (3rd ed.). Cengage Learning.

Tan, R. (2008). Visibility in Bad Weather from A Single Image. *IEEE Explore*, 1-8.

Tarel, J. P., & Hautiere, N. (2009). Fast visibility restoration from a single color or gray level image. *IEEE 12th International conference on Computer Vision*, 2201 – 2208.

Xhang, X., & Brainard, D. H. (2004). Estimation of Saturated Pixel Values in Digital Colour Imaging. *Optical Society of America*, *21*(12), 2301–2310. doi:10.1364/JOSAA.21.002301

APPENDIX

Figure 5. Results of previous method

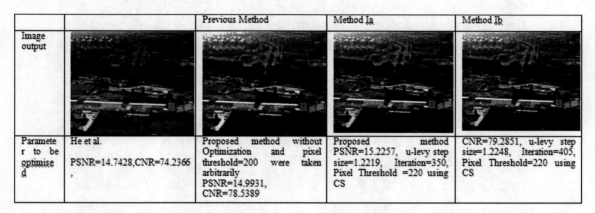

		Previous Method	Method Ia	Method Ib
Image output				
Parameter to be optimised	He et al. PSNR=14.7428,CNR=74.2366	Proposed method without Optimization and pixel threshold=200 were taken arbitrarily PSNR=14.9931, CNR=78.5389	Proposed method PSNR=15.2257, u-levy step size=1.2219, Iteration=350, Pixel Threshold =220 using CS	CNR=79.2851, u-levy step size=1.2248, Iteration=405, Pixel Threshold=220 using CS

Figure 6. Previous work results

Method I[5,6]	Gamma Correction	Method II	Method III	Method IV

Figure 7. Performance output of various image with proposed methods

Figure 8. Performance output of various image with proposed methods

Chapter 5
Underwater Image Segmentation Using Human Psycho Visual Phenomenon

Soumyadip Dhar
RCC Institute of Information Technology, India

Hiranmoy Roy
RCC Institute of Information Technology, India

ABSTRACT

In this chapter, a novel method is proposed for underwater image segmentation based on human psycho visual phenomenon (HVS). In the proposed method the texture property of an image is captured by decomposing it into frequency sub-bands using M-band wavelet packet transform. The sub-bands represent the image in different scales and orientations. The large numbers of sub-bands are pruned by an adaptive basis selection. The proper sub-bands for segmentation are selected depending on the HVS. The HVS imitates the original visual technique of a human being and it is used to divide each sub-band in Weber, De-Vries Rose, and saturation regions. A wavelet packet sub-band is selected for segmentation depending on those three regions. The performance of the proposed method is found to be superior to that of the state-of-the-art methods for underwater image segmentation on standard data set.

INTRODUCTION

The basic physics of the light propagation in the water medium is different than that of the air medium. (Schettini, 2010) . The properties of the water medium cause degradation of the underwater captured images, which is different from normal images taken in air. Deep inside the water the amount of light starts decreasing and the image gets darker. Water is approximately 800 times denser than air, and this density absorbs light quickly. As the amount of light is reduced when we go deeper, colors drop off one by one depending on their wavelengths. The blue color travels the longest in the water due to its shortest wavelength, making the underwater images to be dominated essentially by blue color.

DOI: 10.4018/978-1-5225-5246-8.ch005

Underwater images are basically characterized by their poor visibility due to dense water. The scenes deep inside the water is not clear rather hazy. The visibility is limited by light attenuation at about twenty meters in clear water and five meters or less in turbid water. The light attenuation is caused by absorption (which removes light energy) and scattering (which changes the direction of light path). The absorption causes the reduction of light energy and scattering results the change of pats of light. These two perturbations affect the image captured process at underwater. The underwater image is blurred due to the forward scattering which is generated by randomly deviated light from an object to the camera. On the other hand, backward scattering is caused by the fraction of the light reflected by the water towards the camera before it actually reaches the objects in the scene. Due to backward scattering is the reason behind the poor contrast of the underwater images.

The two perturbations, absorption and scattering also occur due to dissolved organic matter or small observable floating particles inside water. The floating particles increase absorption and scattering of light deep inside the water. The visibility range inside the deep water can be increased with artificial lighting. The artificial lighting also suffers from scattering and absorption. In addition, the artificial light illuminates the scene in a non-uniform fashion. This non-uniform illusion produces a bright spot in the center of the image with a poorly illuminated area surrounding it. Due the reasons mentioned above the underwater image segmentation is really a challenging task.

Segmentation is the first essential and important task in low level image processing. The segmentation is a generic term for those techniques which involves taking an image and extracting information relevant to specific picture 'segments', such as lines, regions and objects, and their inter-relationship. It is basically a process in which an image is segmented into subsets by assigning individual pixel to particular classes. The performance of segmentation of an image is affected by the different perturbations in an image. Due to different perturbations it is very difficult to detect the true boundaries between the regions. The underwater image suffers from different perturbations as described above. So, the segmentation of an underwater image is really a difficult task and it is a subject of attraction for the research community.

Related Work

In the literature, the methods for object background segmentations are quite rich. The conventional methods for object background segmentation includes region growth (Garcia, 2009), graph cut (Boykov, 2006) and image thresholding. Due to different perturbations in the underwater images these conventional methods fail to produce satisfactory results. Therefore, most of the methods used enhancement techniques before segmentation.

Several methods in the literature are proposed for segment the object from its background in an underwater image (Oliver, 2010) (Bazeille, 2012) (Rai, 2012). The CLAHE (contrast limited adaptive histogram equalization) based method is proposed in (Rai, 2012). The CLAHE is used to enhance the underwater gray images. Then, the image is segmented using a thresholding method where the threshold is generated from the histogram of the image. The limitation of the method is that the CLAHE operates on small data regions, rather than the entire image. Moreover, the computational complexity of the method is very high. Singh et al. (Singh, 2005) presented an underwater image segmentation method based on fuzzy c-means algorithm. In this method the same CLAHE enhancement technique was used to enhance the underwater images before segmentation. In this method, the fuzzy theoretic approach was used to reduce the uncertainties arise in an underwater due to different perturbations. Wang et al. (Wang, 2013) proposed a saliency based underwater image segmentation. In this method, at first, feature maps are generated by low-level vision features at different scales. The features are generated at different scales by dyadic Gaussian pyramid. The feature maps are combined to generate the saliency map. The limitation of the method is that the low-level features may be affected by the low contrast of the underwater image. Saliency based segmentation method was also proposed in (Liu X. a., 2016) . Liu et al. (Liu Z. a., 2005) proposed an underwater image segmentation is based on deformable template. Sang (Sang, 2005) also proposed a deformable template based underwater image segmentation. Fuzzy based technique with combination of OTSU was proposed by Yu (Yu, 2005). The authors in (Kabatek, 2009)proposed an efficient target detection system under deep water. Padmavathi et al. (Padmavathi, 2010) presented an underwater image segmentation method using fuzzy c-means. They used a thresholding technique to find out the final segmented regions. Zheng et al. (Zheng, 2015) proposed an efficient underwater image segmentation method. Before segmentation by thresholding they removed the haze in underwater image by dark channel method. Fractal theory based underwater image segmentation was proposed by Yang (Yang, 2007). Li (Li, 2013) proposed a segmentation method based on grayscale transformation. The method can enlarge the gray level difference between the object and background by changing the weights of three channels and reach the segmentation results by using adaptive thresholding method. More methods of underwater image segmentation can be found in the survey (Yan, 2010).

Most of the methods described above enhanced the underwater image or removed its haze prior to segmentation by filtering. But it may cause lose of finer information in the underwater images. As a result the performances of the methods are still below the expectation.

It is a fact that human visual system can recognize an object in an underwater image very efficiently in spite of the perturbations described. This is our motivation for finding a better solution better without losing the finer information. In this chapter we propose underwater image segmentation based on texture features. The texture features are selected using human psycho visual phenomenon.

Proposed Method

In the proposed method the underwater image segmentation is done mainly in two steps. In the first step the features to represent the object and background are generated. The features are generated based on multi resolution analysis of the underwater image. In the second step the features are selected based on human psycho visual phenomenon (HVS).

In the first step the underwater image is transformed into a number of sub bands by M-band wavelet packet transform. The motivation behind this transform is to produce a differentiable texture features for object and background in an underwater image. The M-band packet wavelet transform is rotation invariant and can capture the texture features at different angles. In the packet transform a large number of sub bands are generated. To reduce the number of sub bands and to select a set suitable sub bands for segmentation, the sub bands are pruned by an adaptive basis selection.

In the next steps finer sub bands or features are selected based on HVS. The sub bands represent the underwater image into different scale and orientations. But, the objects cannot be recognized in all scales and orientations by the human eye. The sub bands where the human eye can recognize and differentiate the object and background are the proper features for segmentation. This is the motivation to imitate the human visual system for selecting the proper features. The features thus selected are used for segmentation.

Novelty of the Proposed Method

The novelty or the major contributions of the proposed method are:

1. In the proposed method a novel texture based underwater image segmentation technique is presented. The method uses an effect M-band packet wavelet transform for segmentation. The transform helps to capture the texture property of underwater image efficiently. Thus it greatly improves the performance of underwater image segmentation over the conventional methods.
2. The human visual system model is used to select the sub band features for segmentation. The HVS is employed to select the proper sub band by decomposing it into De-Vries Rose, Weber and Saturation regions. The HVS imitates the human visual system and select M-band packet features under different perturbations.

The rest of the paper is organized as follows. The M-band wavelet packet transform and adaptive basis selection are described in section 2. Section 3 describes the human psycho visual phenomenon and sub-bands selection using HVS. The proposed methodology is described in section 4. Section 5 discuses the results.

M-BAND WAVELET PACKET TRANSFORM

The purpose of M-band packet wavelet transform (Steffen, 1993) is to transform the object and background of an underwater image into computable discontinuities. In the underwater image the object and background are in different frequency zone. The filter bank for M- band packet wavelet is fundamentally a set of band pass filters with selected frequency and orientation. In the filtering stage, we make use of orthogonal and linear phase M-band (M=4) wavelet. The motivation for M band wavelet transform arises from the need to have a more flexible representation of the time-frequency (scale-space) plane than that resulting from dyadic wavelet transform. It results some regions of uniform bandwidths instead of logarithmic spacing of the frequency division. Further the features sets derived from M-band wavelet transform are robust due to its invariance in rotation, noise and transformation. (Acharyya, 2008). Although the M-band wavelet decomposition results in a grouping of linear and logarithmic frequency (scale) resolution, a further recursive decomposition of the high frequency regions based on effective cost functions for basis selection would provide textures better. In M-band wavelet decomposition signal is decomposed in a set of independent, spatially oriented frequency bands. The discrete normalized scaling $\varphi_{j,k}$ and wavelet $\psi_{j,k,l}$ basis functions are defined in terms of their filter responses as

$$\varphi_{j,k}(x) = M^{j/2} h_j(M^j x - k) \tag{1}$$

and

$$\psi_{j,k,l}(x) = M^{j/2} g_{j,l}(M^j x - k), l = 1, 2 \ldots\ldots M - 1 \tag{2}$$

where j and k are the dilation and translation parameters and l is the number of wavelet functions. h_j and g_j are respectively the high-pass and low-pass filters of increasing width indexed by j, which satisfy the quadrature mirror condition (QMF). In standard wavelet decomposition method down sampling by a factor M at each scale is essential. But these decompositions are not translation invariant which is required for image analysis tasks. So here we make use of a over complete wavelet decomposition called a discrete wavelet frame (DWF) which is achieved without down sampling the transformed frequency bands. As a result we get a set of frequency bands as that of the same size of the input image. In the following we give a discrete M-band wavelet frame (DMbWF) decomposition (Acharyya M. a., 2007) which is identical as the discrete M-band wavelet transforms (DMbWT), except that no down sampling is done between levels of decomposition.

Let $I(x, y) \in l^2(R)$ be a 2D image. Its M-band wavelet frames can be represented as

$$c_j(x, y) = [h_{j,x} * [h_{j,y} * c_{j-1}]](x, y)$$
$$d_{j,l}^{s_l^1}(x, y) = [h_{j,x} * [g_{j,l,y} * c_{j-1}]](x, y)$$
$$d_{j,l}^{s_l^2}(x, y) = [g_{j,l,x} * [h_{i,y} * c_{i-1}]](x, y)$$
$$d_{j,l}^{s_l^3}(x, y) = [g_{j,l,x} * [g_{j,l,y} * c_{i-1}]](x, y)$$

(3)

where $c_0 = I(x, y)$ is the original image, * denotes the convolution operator, $h_{j,x}$ $(g_{j,l,x})$ and $h_{j,y}(g_{j,l,y})$ are the low-pass and band-pass filter coefficients along x and y direction respectively. The number of frequency channels resulting from the decomposition using the above equations is 16, 4 bands (M=4) along the x-direction and 4 bands (M=4) along the y-directions. $c_j(x, y)$ denotes low pass or approximate band whereas $d_{j,l}^{s_l^i}$ corresponds to detail frequency bands at scale j obtained by band-pass filtering along a specific direction. The sequence of low-pass and band-pass filters of increasing width corresponding to an increased level of decomposition is expanded by inserting an appropriate number of zeros between taps of filters. So, if the filter length becomes large, it is possible that it may bias the decomposition of the image. We have chosen an eight-tap filter for suitability of the size of the image that we have considered in this study. The frequency divisions of M-band wavelet decomposition are shown in Figure 1.

Figure 1. (a) Frequency bands corresponding to decomposition filters. (b): Frequency sector representations for filtering in horizontal (H), vertical (V) and diagonal (D) directions

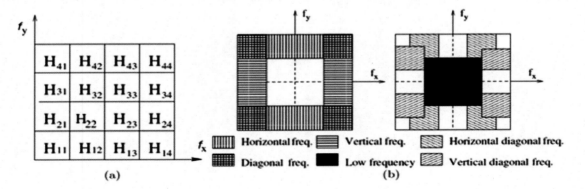

The M-band wavelet packet transform (DMbWPT) is a generalization of Discrete M-band wavelet transform (DMbWT). The DMbWPT recursively decomposes the higher frequency bands and results in tree structured multiband extension of wavelet transform. At scale $j = J$, the input image is first decomposed into $M \times M$ bands using all the filters h_j and $g_{j,l}$ with $l = 1, 2, 3\ldots\ldots$ and without down sampling. In our proposed method, in first level the image is decomposed into ($M \times M$) bands where M=4 corresponding to different directions and resolution. The process repeated recursively results a tree structure of frequency bands.

Adaptive Basis Selection

M-band wavelet packet decomposition gives rise to M^{2^J} number of sub bands for decomposition up to depth J. As a result the full tree decomposition produces too many wavelet coefficients having negligible information content. In order to avoid a full decomposition we used an adaptive decomposition algorithm (Acharyya M. a., 2001) (Acharyya M. a., 2001)using a maximum criteria of textual measure based on the statistics extracted from the each of the sub bands and identify the most significant sub bands. It is then decided whether further decomposition of the particular channel would generate more information or not. This search is computationally efficient and enables us to zoom any desired frequency channel for further decomposition. Energy is used as the textual measure of our work. Let B_j^i denotes the frequency band j at level i. A band B_j^i is selected for further decomposition if

$$\frac{\left[E(B_j^i) - E(B_{j'}^{i-1})\right]}{E(B_{j'}^{i-1})} \times 100 \geq \varepsilon_d \quad : i > 1, j > 0 \tag{4}$$

Where $E(B_j^i) = $ *Energy of band* B_j^i $j' = \left| \dfrac{j + (M-1)}{M} \right|$ ε_d = predefined +ve value which is the fraction of parent band. Further a band B_j^i is selected for feature vector generation if

$$\frac{\left[E(B_j^i)\right]}{\sum_{k=1}^{M^i} E(B_k^i)} \times 100 \geq \varepsilon_f \quad : i > 1, j > 0 \tag{5}$$

Where ε_f =predefined +ve value which is the fraction of total energy bands in the current level.

HUMAN PSYCHOVISUAL PHENOMENON (HVS)

The major problem in low intensity level image processing (Zudiema, 1983)like underwater image segmentation is that

1. Detection of changes occurring in a low steady but visible illumination i.e. minimum detectable changes and

2. Detection of mere presence of absence of light under a dark-adapted condition i.e. absolute visual threshold.

In the underwater image segmentation both the problems are present prominently due to light scattering and poor contrast of the underwater image. The two problems also affect the features which are the scale space representation of the image. So it is better to use the adaptive threshold or object detection by human visual system.

In human visual system the visual information is concentrated at points of large spatial point of light intensity in an image (Buchsbaum, 1980). The model to imitate the human visual system was proposed by Kundu et al. (Kundu M. a., 1986)as a human psycho visual phenomenon (HVS). The model was used successfully used for image edge thresholding by the authors.

In human visual system brightness is the sensation related with the amount of light stimulus. Due to adaptive visual capacity of the human eye, the absolute brightness cannot be measured by the human eye accurately. The relative grayness brightness is an observer's felling and it occurs due to the difference between the grayness of different objects. The term contrast is used to emphasize the difference in gray values of objects. The perceived grayness of a object depends on its local background. The perception about the gray values remain constant if the ratios of the contrasts between the object and the background remains constant (Hall, 1979).

The human eye scans the image and compares intensity of each portion with its immediate background. When the brightness value of an object is higher (or lower) than its surrounding or background or a reference intensity B by a threshold $\geq B_T$ the object can appear either brighter or darker. Depending on the behavior of B and B_T the image can be divided into three different regions; De-Vries Rose, Weber, and Saturation regions. The basis of the division in these regions is the change in threshold value with the increase in background intensity. If B is the background intensity and ΔB_T is the change in threshold value, then the characteristics response of the three regions is shown in $\log \Delta B_T - \log B$ plane in the Figure 2.

So, the relations between $\log B$ and $\log \Delta B_T$ in the Weber, De-Vries Rose and Saturation regions are given by Equation (6), Equation (7) and Equation (8) respectively.

$$\log \Delta B_T = \log K_1 + \log B \tag{6}$$

$$\log \Delta B_T = \log K_2 + \frac{1}{2}\log B \tag{7}$$

$$\log \Delta B_T = K_3 + 2\log B \tag{8}$$

Here K_1, K_2, K_3 are the constants of proportionality.

Figure 2. The incremental threshold ΔBT vs background intensity B

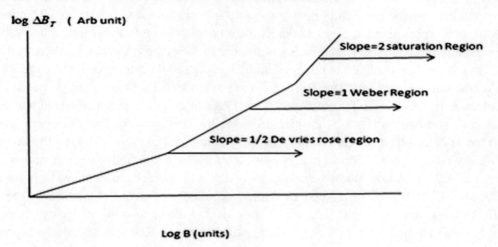

The three regions in an image is selected by the following three conditions

$$\frac{\Delta B}{\sqrt{B}} \geq K_2 \text{ when } \alpha_2' B_1 \geq B \geq \alpha_1' B_1 \tag{9a}$$

$$\frac{\Delta B}{B} \geq K_1 \text{ when } \alpha_3' B_1 \geq B \geq \alpha_2' B_1 \tag{9b}$$

$$\frac{\Delta B}{B} \geq K_3 \text{ when } B \geq \alpha_3' B_1 \tag{9c}$$

Here $\Delta B = | B_p - B |$ and B is calculated for each pixel by taking the weighted average of its 8 neighborhood pixels. Here B_1 represents the maximum value of B. In the above equations $\alpha_2' B_1 \geq B \geq \alpha_1' B_1$, $\alpha_3' B_1 \geq B \geq \alpha_2' B_1$ and $B \geq \alpha_3' B_1$ represent the background intensity B in the De-Vries Rose, Weber and Saturation region respectively for $0 < \alpha_1' < \alpha_2' < \alpha_3' < 1$. For the proposed method the value of for $\alpha_1', \alpha_2', \alpha_3'$ are taken as 0.10, 0.33 and 0.66 respectively. In the proposed method the HVS are used to select the proper sub bands from the sub bands selected by adaptive basis selection.

Selection of Sub Bands by HVS

In section 2 it is already stated that a set of sub bands are generated from the M-band wavelet packet transform. The appropriate bands are the selected based on the adaptive basis selection. The sub bands represent the underwater image into different scale and orientations. The size of each sub band is equal to the size of the original image. The sub bands where the edges can be detected clearly and where the object and background are clearly distinguishable are suitable for segmentation. That means if the human eye cannot recognize the edges or detect the object in the underwater image in a sub band, the band cannot be suitable for segmentation. So, it is better to select those sub bands where human eye can detect the low level features like the edges of an image. Again the detection of the edges in an image depends on the human visual system. To imitate the human visual system in the proposed method for feature selection the HVS model is employed. The HVS is used to select the sub band which represent the prominent edges and distinguish the object from background properly. The concept of feature selection based on HVS can be cleared from the following example. The Figure 4 shows the decomposition of a test image in Figure 3 by M-band packet wavelet transform and adaptive basis selection. Now from the above resultant sub bands, Human eye can easily detect the object and its edges from the sub bands 3, 4, 6, 7, 8, 9 10, 11, 12, 13, 14, 15 and 16. Moreover, the object can be recognized in the sub bands clearly. In the remaining sub bands (1, 2 and 5) the object in the underwater image cannot be detected. So, it can be said that the 3, 4, 6, 7, 8, 9 10, 11, 12, 13, 14, 15 and 16 sub bands are the appropriate sub bands or features for segmentation. From a careful observation of the proper sub bands it can be said that the variations among the wavelets coefficients are high. The remaining sub bands are not suitable for segmentation as the object cannot be detected in the sub bands. The reason for non detection of the object in the sub bands is due to the fact that our eye cannot differentiate the object from the background in those bands. To model the observations in the proposed method the HVS is used. That means, in the inappropriate sub bands no difference between the object and background is found in the Weber, De-Vries Rose and Saturation regions. On the other hand, in the appropriate sub bands the difference between the wavelet coefficients and its immediate background is prominent in any one of the three regions. So, the

Figure 3. A sample underwater test image

Figure 4. The M-band packet wavelet transforms of the image in Figure 3

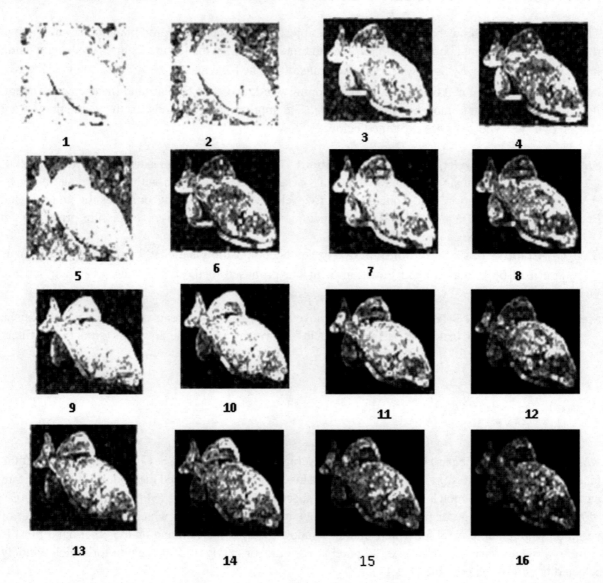

total variance between the object pixels (coefficients) and background pixels (coefficients) are high in the three regions of an appropriate sub band. The total variance is given by V where v is

$$V = Var(I_W) + Var(I_{DV}) + Var(I_{DS}) \tag{10}$$

Where $Var(I_W)$, $Var(I_{DV})$ and $Var(I_{DS})$ represent the variations of the wavelet coefficients in Weber, De-Vries Rose and Saturation regions respectively.

PROPOSED METHODOLOGY

The proposed algorithm is based on the fact that object and background region in an underwater image represents two different textures. With this idea in mind, we extract the texture features by decomposing it into sub-bands using M-band wavelet packet transform. The local energy $eng_{x,y}$ at (x,y) of each wavelet coefficient is computed using a small overlapping window of size 5×5 around the each coefficient. It is followed by noise removal in the sub bands. The appropriate sub bands for the segmentation are chosen by HVS. The steps are explained below.

Step 1 – M Band Wavelet Packet Decomposition: The underwater image is transformed into a set of frequency bands using M-band orthogonal packet wavelet transform without down sampling by Equation 1, Equation2 and Equation 3 up to level 3. M-band packet decomposes the image signal into constituted frequency band from which signature of different type of texture present in an underwater image can be extracted.

Step 2 – Adaptive Basis Selection: Full tree packet decomposition is guided by pruning algorithm as described by Equation 4and Equation 5. In our proposed methods the value of ε_d and ε_f are taken as $\varepsilon_d = 85\%$ & $\varepsilon_f = 5\% - 10\%$ respectively.

Step 3 – Smoothing of Selected Bands: To remove the low energy contents in the band which may be due to noise in the bands the basis selection is followed by a Gaussian low pass (smoothing) filters (Acharyya M. a., 2001) of the form

$$H_G(u,v) = \frac{1}{2\pi\sqrt{\sigma}} e^{\frac{1}{2\sigma}} \left(u^2 + v^2\right) \tag{11}$$

where σ determines the pass band width of the averaging window with $G \times G$ window centered at the pixel with the coordinates (x,y). The value of σ is taken as 1in our proposed method. G is an important parameter, the size of which is determined using a spectral flatness measure (SFM) (Kundu M. a., 2003). SFM has dynamic range of [0: 1]. SFM close to 1 means flatness high which is due to high rate of variation from pixel to pixel for which smaller window (3×3) is selected and on the other hand SFM is close to 0 means variation from pixel to pixel is very low or nearly uniform region for which window selected is as large as possible (15×15).

Step 4 – Selection of Sub Bands Using HVS: In this step the appropriate sub bands are selected based on HVS. For this in each of the sub bands the Weber, the De-Vries Rose and the Saturation regions are detected. One sub band is selected if the variation V_T is greater than some predefined positive quantity α.

Step 5 – Feature Vector Generation and Segmentation: After the selection, the feature vector is generated from the selected sub bands. This is followed by the segmentation by fuzzy c-means algorithm. The semantic diagram of the proposed method is shown in Figure 5.

Figure 5. Schematic diagram of the proposed method

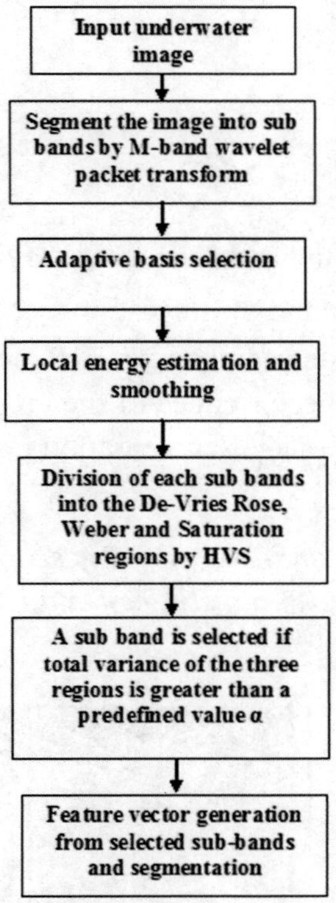

```
┌─────────────────────┐
│   Input underwater   │
│        image         │
└─────────────────────┘
           │
           ▼
┌─────────────────────┐
│ Segment the image into sub │
│ bands by M-band wavelet │
│   packet transform   │
└─────────────────────┘
           │
           ▼
┌─────────────────────┐
│ Adaptive basis selection │
└─────────────────────┘
           │
           ▼
┌─────────────────────┐
│ Local energy estimation and │
│       smoothing      │
└─────────────────────┘
           │
           ▼
┌─────────────────────┐
│ Division of each sub bands │
│ into the De-Vries Rose, │
│  Weber and Saturation │
│    regions by HVS    │
└─────────────────────┘
           │
           ▼
┌─────────────────────┐
│ A sub band is selected if │
│ total variance of the three │
│  regions is greater than a │
│  predefined value α  │
└─────────────────────┘
           │
           ▼
┌─────────────────────┐
│ Feature vector generation │
│ from selected sub-bands │
│   and segmentation   │
└─────────────────────┘
```

RESULTS AND DISCUSSION

In this section we tested the proposed method on the underwater images from Sun dataset (https://groups.csail.mit.edu/vision/SUN/.). From the dataset we used 100 images for segmentation. The image size varies from 200×200 to 500×500. The uncertainties in underwater images are more due to inherent noise in the image during capturing of the image and during analog to digital conversion. The proposed method was compared with Rai et al. (Rai, 2012), Liu et al. (Liu X. a., 2016) and (Wang, 2013) The quantitative performance of the proposed segmentation method and all the methods compared here are measured using widely used segmentation evaluation metric called segmentation accuracy (Li C. a., 2011) which is given by

$$SA = \sum_{i=1}^{c} \frac{A_i \cap C_i}{\sum_{j=1}^{c} C_j} \tag{12}$$

where c is the number of clusters, A_i is the set of pixels belonging to the i-th class which is found by the proposed method and C_i represents the set of pixels belonging to the i-th class of the ground truth of the test image. Another quantitative performance of the proposed thresholding method and all the methods compared here are measured using widely used segmentation evaluation metric called Misclassification error (M.E) which is given by

$$M.E = 1 - \frac{|T_o \cap T_t| + |G_o \cap G_t|}{|T_o| + |G_o|} \tag{13}$$

where B_o and F_o denotes the background and foreground of the original image(ground truth). B_T and F_T denotes the background and foreground of the test image. The $|.|$ is the cardinality of the set. M.E nearer to 1 means wrongly classified image and nearer to 0 means correct classification.

The Figure 6 shows the qualitative performance of the proposed method and all the other methods compared here. Additional underwater image segmentation results by the proposed method are shown

Figure 6. Segmentation results on the underwater images: (a) Original test image (b) Segmentation by Rai et al. (c) Segmentation by Wang et al. (d) Segmentation by Liu et al. (e) Segmentation by the proposed method

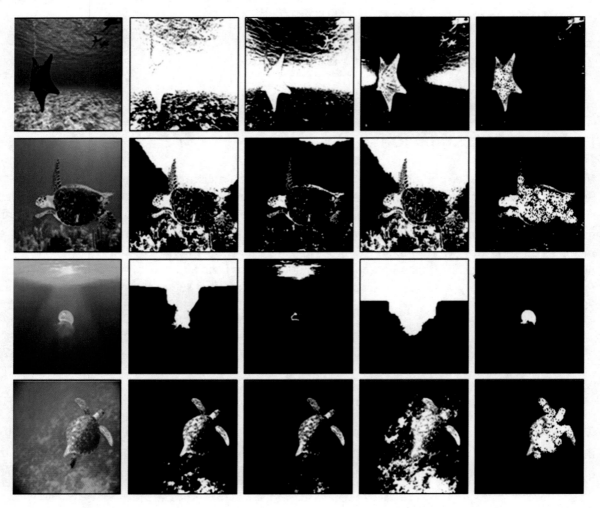

in Figure 7. From the visual inspection it can be said that the proposed method can perform better than that of the other methods compared here. The average quantitative performance on SUN dataset is shown in Table 1. The results indicate that on average the proposed method can segment the underwater image more accurately that the methods compared here. The method in (Wang, 2013) used color conspicuity map for object segmentation. Under the water due to scattering of light color of an object cannot be captured properly and hence the conspicuity map may not adequate to segment the object. The HVS based texture features used by the proposed method can segment the object and background more accurately. The method in (Rai, 2012)enhanced the image using CLAHE (contrast limited adaptive histogram equalization) method before segmentation by fuzzy c-means. But, the enhancement may not be effective due to high uncertainties in an underwater image. The method in (Liu X. a., 2016) used dark map to remove the haze in the image and then used saliency map for localization of the object locations. The preprocessing may increase the uncertainties in the image. On, the other hand the proposed method used the texture property of M-band wavelet transform for the segmentation. The M-band wavelet transform could efficiently capture the texture of the object in an underwater image with complex background. The appropriate sub bands were selected based on the three regions of the HVS. So, even if the constant of the underwater images are poor, the proper and optimal sub bands were selected. The different perturbations in the underwater image could affect few frequency bands, which were discarded by the HVS.

Figure 7. Segmentation results on the underwater images: (a) Original test image (b) Segmentation by the proposed method

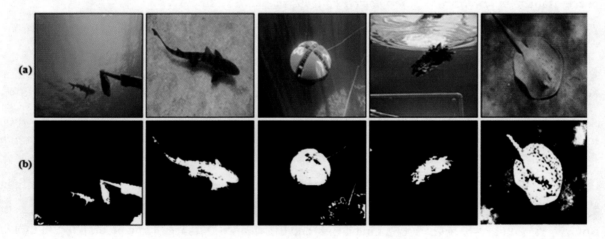

Table 1. Segmentation accuracy and misclassification error of different methods on the underwater image from the SUN dataset

Dataset	Methods			
SUN dataset	Rai (Rai, 2012)	Wang (Wang, 2013)	Liu (Liu X. a., 2016)	Proposed
Segmentation accuracy	0.7532	0.7934	0.8031	0.8342
Misclassification error	0.3000	0.2162	0.2001	0.1743

The proposed method imitates the human visual capability for selecting the feature i.e. the sub bands. The other methods compared here have no such provision of using human psycho visual phenomenon and the proposed method does not require any preprocessing.

CONCLUSION

In this paper we propose a method to segment an underwater image which has some inherent perturbations. The method uses the multi scale and multi directional M-band wavelet packet transform of the underwater images to capture the texture of the objects present in it. The proposed method judiciously chooses the appropriate sub band depending on the human psycho visual phenomenon. The method does not require any preprocessing steps to reduce the different perturbations in an underwater image. The method performed better than the state-of-the-art methods on the standard dataset of underwater images. The proposed method shows the efficiency of HVS for feature selection in multi resolution analysis of an image. So, it gives a new direction of research. With suitable modification in the current method, it can be extended for the recognition of the underwater images, which is being currently investigated.

REFERENCES

Acharyya, M. a. (2001). Adaptive Basis Selection for Multitexture Segmentation by M-band wavelet packet frames. *International Conference on Image Processing*, 2, 622-625.

Acharyya, M. a. (2007). Image Segmentation using Wavelet Packet Frames and Neuro Fuzzy Tools. Vol 5, no 4. *International Journal of Computational Cognition*, 5(4), 27–43.

Acharyya, M., & Kundu, M. K. (2001). An Adaptive Approach to Unsupervised Texture Segmentation Using M-Band Wavelet. *Signal Processing*, 81(7), 1337–1356. doi:10.1016/S0165-1684(00)00278-4

Acharyya, M., & Kundu, M. K. (2008). Extraction of noise Tolerant, Gray-scale Transform and Rotation Invariant Features for Texture Segmentation using Wavelet Frames. *Multiresolution and Information Processing.*, 6(3), 391–417. doi:10.1142/S0219691308002252

Bazeille, S., Quidu, I., & Jaulin, L. (2012). Color-based underwater object recognition using water light attenuation. *Intelligent Service Robotics*, 5(2), 109–118. doi:10.100711370-012-0105-3

Boykov, Y., & Funka-Lea, G. (2006). Graph Cuts and Efficient N-D Image Segmentation. *International Journal of Computer Vision*, 70(2), 109–131. doi:10.100711263-006-7934-5

Buchsbaum, G. (1980). An analytical derivation of visual nonlinearity. *IEEE Transactions on Biomedical Engineering*, 27(5), 237–242. doi:10.1109/TBME.1980.326628 PMID:7380439

Garcia, U. L. (2009). Automatic Image Segmentation by Dynamic Region Growth and Multiresolution Merging. *IEEE Transactions on Image Processing*, 18(10), 2275–2288. doi:10.1109/TIP.2009.2025555 PMID:19535323

Hall, E. (1979). *Computer Image Processing and Recognition*. New York: Academic Press.

Kabatek, M. a. (2009). An underwater target detection system for electro-optical imagery data. *OCEANS MTS/IEEE.*

Kundu, M. a. (1986). Thresholding for edge detection by human psychovisual phenomenon. *Pattern Recognition Letter*, 433-441.

Kundu, M., & Acharyya, M. (2003). M-band Wavelets:Application to Texture Segmentation for real Life Image Analysis. *International Journal of Wavelets, Multresolution, and Information Processing*, *1*(1), 115–119. doi:10.1142/S0219691303000074

Li, C. (2011). A level set method for image segmentation in the presence of intensity inhomogeneitics with application to MRI. *IEEE Transactions on Image Processing*, *20*(7), 2007–2016. doi:10.1109/TIP.2011.2146190 PMID:21518662

Li, X. (2013). *Research on the technologies of underwater image segmentation and object location based on monlcular vision* (Master's thesis). Harbin Engineering University.

Liu, X. a. (2016). Saliency segmentation and foreground extraction of underwater image based on localization. *Oceans.*

Liu, Z. a. (2005). Underwater acoustic image segmentation based on deformable template. *IEEE International Conference on Mechatronics and Automation*, 4, 1802-1806.

Oliver, K. a. (2010). Image feature detection and matching. *Progress in Biomedical Optics and Imaging*, *7*, 7678–7690.

Padmavathi, G. A. (2010). Non linear Image segmentation using fuzzy c means clustering method with thresholding for underwater images. *International Journal of Computer Science Issues*, *7*, 35–50.

Rai, R. A. (2012). Underwater Image Segmentation using CLAHE Enhancement and Thresholding. *International Journal of Emerging Technology and Advanced Engineering*, *2*, 118–123.

Sang, E. (2005.). Underwater acoustic image segmentation based on deformable template. *Chinese Journal of Acoustics*, 164–171.

Schettini, R., & Corchs, S. (2010). Underwater image Processing:state of the art of image restoration and image enhancement methods. *EURASIP Journal on Advances in Signal Processing*, *2010*(1), 1–14. doi:10.1155/2010/746052

Singh, S. A. (2005). Segmentation of underwater objects using CLAHE enhancement and thresholding with 3-class fuzzy cmeans clustering. *IEEE International Conference on Mechatronics and Automation*, 2, 1802-1806.

Steffen, P., Heller, P. N., Gopinath, R. A., & Burrus, C. S. (1993). Theory of regular m-band bases. *IEEE Transactions on Signal Processing*, *41*(12), 3497–3510. doi:10.1109/78.258088

Wang, H. a. (2013). Saliency-Based Adaptive Object Extraction for Color Underwater Images. *Proceedings of the 2nd International Conference on Computer Science and Electronics Engineering (ICCSEE 2013)*, 2651-2655. 10.2991/iccsee.2013.661

Yan, C. (2010). Study on underwater image segmentation technique. *International Conference on E-Health Networking*, 135-137.

Yang, G(2007*Study on segmentation and recognition algorithms for underwater images based on fractal theory* (Master's thesis). Huazhong.

Yu, X. (2005). *Study on segmentation and recognition algorithms for underwater images based on fuzzy theory* (Master's thesis). Huazhong University of Science and Technology.

Zheng, H. a. (2015). Underwater image segmentation via dark channel prior and multiscale hierarchical decomposition. *Oceans*.

Zudiema, P. (1983). A mechanistic approach to approach to threshold behaviour of visual system. *IEEE Transactions on Systems, Man, and Cybernetics*, *13*(5), 923–934. doi:10.1109/TSMC.1983.6313088

Chapter 6
Verification of Multimodal Biometric:
IRIS, Finger, and Palm Using Different Algorithms

Shashidhara H. R.
JSS Academy of Technical Education, India

Siddesh G. K.
JSS Academy of Technical Education, India

ABSTRACT

Authenticating the identity of an individual has become an important aspect of many organizations. The reasons being to secure authentication process, to perform automated attendance, or to provide bill payments. This need of providing automated authentication has led to concerns in the security and robustness of such biometric systems. Currently, many biometric systems that are organizations are unimodal, which means that use single physical trait to perform authentication. But, these unimodal systems suffer from many drawbacks. These drawbacks can be overcome by designing multimodal systems which use multiple physical traits to perform authentication. They increase reliability and robustness of the systems. In this chapter, analysis and comparison of multimodal biometric systems is proposed for three physical traits like iris, finger, and palm. All these traits are treated independently, and feature of these traits are extracted using two algorithms separately.

INTRODUCTION

Biometric authentication systems are those which used for identifying certain individuals and provide access control to the designated users to perform authentication the biometric systems rely on certain unique characteristics in an individual. These characteristics are provided by certain body parts such as finger, iris and palm etc.

DOI: 10.4018/978-1-5225-5246-8.ch006

Traditionally user authentication was performed through certain popular documents such as driving license or employee identity card, but these methods are prone to be duplicated. By using unique body characteristics of an individual robust, effective and efficient user authentication can be achieved.

The biometric systems are expected to provide the seven functionalities listed below:

1. The body parts that are chosen for performing authentication should be present in every individual.
2. The body characteristics which will be employed for designing the biometric systems should provide uniqueness property which means that no two individuals should have the same characteristics for the body part.
3. The designated characteristics of the body part remain free from deformities over a long period of time.
4. The characteristics must be easy to acquire and processed in order to come for authentication decision.
5. The authentication procedure always be robust and exhibit good efficiency.
6. The developed biometric systems should be acceptable to the community in-order to be effectively deployed in organizations.
7. The biometric systems should exhibit strict non-circumvention such that the body characteristics that will be used for authentication should not be duplicated by using another substitute.

There are number of performance metrics used to evaluate the efficiency and effectiveness of the biometric systems such as,

1. **False Match Rate (FMR):** It is the ratio of number of false authentication performed to the number of authentication attempted.
2. **False Non-Match Rate (FNMR):** It is the ratio of number of correct authentications which could not be established to the number of authentication attempted.
3. **Receiver Operating Characteristic:** It is the trade-off plot between False Match Rate and the False non-match rate.
4. **Equal Error Rate:** It is the rate in which the False Match Rate and False Non Match rate are equal.
5. **Failure to Enroll Rate:** It is the ratio of number of instances in which template creation was un-successful to the total number of template creation attempts.
6. **Failure to Capture Rate:** It is the ratio of number of instances in which the biometric system failed to capture the test image to the total number of biometric login attempted.
7. **Genuine Acceptance Rate (GAR):** It is the ratio of number of test image instances that needed to be authenticated and were authenticated to the total number of authentication instances.

The main issue in today's biometric system is of effectiveness and efficiency. Effectiveness means the authentication quality provided by the biometric system. The biometric systems need to provide high accuracy in above mentioned performance metrics. Currently many biometric systems have been unable to achieve the desired level of authentication accuracy. Efficiency refers to the response time of the biometric system to provide its decision on the user authentication status. Today large volume of user information is stored in the database. So has to provide good efficiency and still maintaining good effectiveness is an unresolved challenge in designing biometric systems.

Multi-modal biometric systems employ more than one physiological or behavioral characteristic to perform authentication. This system helps in reducing the False Acceptance Rate (FAR) and False Match Rate (FMR), also it overcomes the problem of unimodal biometric systems such as noisy data, class similarities and intra class variation. Even though many Multi-modal biometric systems have been proposed, they still suffer from ineffective performance due to lack of appropriate models, poor fusion performance and high redundancy in extracted features. The task is to design an efficient and effective Multi-modal biometric system Richard Saferstein (2007).

Multi-modal biometric systems employ more than one behavioral or physiological characteristic to perform biometric authentication. These systems provide significant advantages over unimodal systems such as reducing false matches, providing alternate mechanism to authenticate if some biometric characteristic provides insufficient information and protection against intruders who aim to hack the system.

There are several design variations for multi-modal biometric systems. But choosing suitable models, required fusion level and eliminating redundancy in extracted features are some of the existing challenges in designing efficient multi-modal biometric systems.

Depending on the fusion strategy multi-modal biometric systems are classified into three types:

1. Fusion at the Feature Extraction Level
2. Fusion at the Matching Score Level
3. Fusion at the Decision Level

This classification is based on the application of the fusion process in a specific stage of the authentication process. The entire biometric process flow chart is depicted in Figure 1. The features of biometric image data is extracted depending on the type of biometric image, these features vectors are used for template matching to determine the match score. Depending on the recognition threshold match score decision is obtained.

Fusion at the Feature Extraction Level

To achieve fusion at feature extraction level, feature vectors of different modalities are combined by using a combining function and then compared to every template stored in the database. The stored templates are also created through the same fusion process. This fusion mechanism is illustrated in Figure 2. Until now, not many multi-modal biometric systems have employed this fusion technique. The reasons being:

1. The numerical properties of different feature vectors might make it difficult to perform effective fusion. Sometimes, this issue can be resolved through careful design of feature vectors. Also some

Figure 1. Authentication process flow

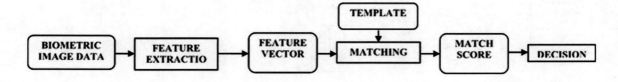

Figure 2. Fusion at the feature extraction level

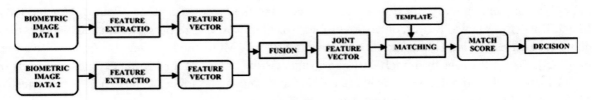

of the feature vectors of some modalities might not be available and this can drastically reduce the effectiveness of the system.

2. Generating effective matching scores is difficult when feature vectors have more components. This is largely due to the curse of dimensionality problem. Also combining multiple feature vectors can aggravate this problem.

Fusion at the Matching Score Level

In this fusion level test feature vectors that are created for every modality will be used to calculate the matching score by using the matching criteria defined for a particular modality. By using these individual scores of each test feature vectors, fusion is performed to obtain total score. The decision module uses this information to arrive at the biometric authentication decision. These matching score level fusion process is illustrated in Figure 3.

The advantage of this approach is that efficient models used for single modalities can be still retained and only individual modality scores are subjected to fusion.

There are multiple strategies to accomplish matching score fusion such as:

1. In the Sum Rule, weighted average of scores is used to obtain the fusion score.
2. In Decision tree strategy, decision is performed by using sequence of threshold comparisons. This comparison is achieved by using tree based machine learning techniques.

Figure 3. Fusion at the matching score level

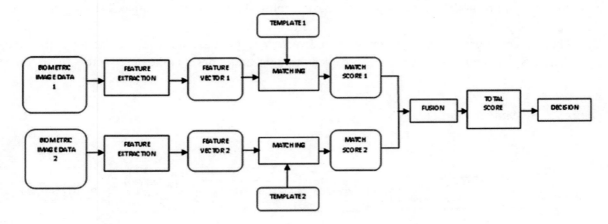

3. The Linear Discriminate Analysis method transforms the given score vectors into new vectors which belong to different subspace. This transformation ensures that, classes of impostor scores and genuine scores are separated with maximum inter-class distance. The parameters of this transformation need to be calculated by using training set. The output score is calculated by using the minimum distance between the centroids of two classes. The Mahalonobis distance metric is popularly used in this fusion mechanism.

Empirically sum rule has provided the best classification accuracy. Also, user specific weights can be provided to the sum rule to give preference to certain modality scores. This strategy has outperformed other matching score strategies.

Fusion at the Decision Level

In this fusion strategy a separate authentication decision is made for each biometric trait. These decisions are then combined into a final vote as shown in Figure 4.

This fusion mechanism requires each biometric trait to provide its decision. The final vote about the decision is made by combining each individual decision by the decision module.

This fusion architecture is a loosely coupled system and provides flexibility in coupling different biometric systems into a layered architecture hence; it has become quite popular among biometric vendors.

Many mechanisms have been presented to perform decision level fusion such as statistical methods, Boolean conjunctions etc. But the Boolean conjunction mechanism is quite popular due to its simplicity.

There is multiple combination strategies used in the fusion process such as:

1. AND rule applies the logical AND operator for the decision of all verification modules. The advantage is that, it reduces false authentication rates but increases false rejection rates.
2. OR rule applies the logical OR operator for verification modules decision. It is applied by giving single modality for verification. If the user fails, then next modality is presented. This mechanism trades low false rejection rate for high false acceptance rate.
3. RANDOM rule provides a biometric trait on random choice. This mechanism has security advantages against spoofing.

Figure 4. Fusion at the decision level

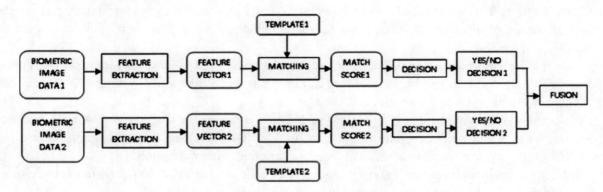

BACKGROUND

The initial overview of the biometric systems was first presented in Anil K Jain et al. (2004). In this work disadvantages, advantages, limitations, strengths and security concerns were briefly described. It stated that for any behavioral or philological characteristic to become a biometric input it has to satisfy these requirements

1. **Universality:** Every person should possess this characteristic.
2. **Distinctiveness:** This characteristic should be considerably different between any two persons.
3. **Permanence:** It should not undergo modification so that, matching cannot be done.
4. **Collectability:** Quantitative measurement of characteristic should be feasible.

For efficient deployment of biometric systems other desirable requirements are:

1. **Performance:** Practical biometric systems should exhibit attractive response time in providing the results of biometric systems.
2. **Acceptability:** The utilized biometric identifier/characteristic should be acceptable to most of the users.
3. **Circumvention:** Biometric systems should be robust against intruder hacking.

In Gamassi et al. (2004) high level system design framework to efficiently design multi-modal biometric systems was proposed. It proposes generic design framework which can be easily adapted in the design of multi-modal biometric systems. This generic design framework avoids most of the common design practice drawbacks.

In Anil Jain et al. (2005), design of multi-modal biometric system using fingerprint, face and hand modalities was proposed. The fusion was performed at matching score level. This task involved matching with different metrics such as z-score, min-max and tanh technique.

Analysis of different matching score techniques such as min-max, median-mad, Bayes-based normalization, double-sigmoid, z-score and piecewise linear method on various multi-modal biometric systems was performed in Slobodan Ribaric and Ivan Fratric (2006). This analytical study considered different modalities such as face, fingerprint and palm print.

Multi-modal biometric system using hybrid filtering technique that used both fast Fourier transform and Gabor filter was proposed in Aguilar (2007). Recognition module employed statistical parameters and local features. This system used fingerprint of both thumbs and each image was separately processed. The multi-modal results were obtained by the fusion of unimodal results. Empirical results demonstrate far=0.2% and frr=1.4%.

Fusion at matching score by using Support Vector Machine [SVM] and wavelet transform was proposed in F Yang and Baofeng M A. (2007) to design multi-modal biometric systems. The employed modalities were palm-print, fingerprint and hand geometry.

Feature level fusion implemented through Kernel Fisher Discriminant Analysis (KFDA) with product rule, average rule, and weighted-sum rule was proposed in Xiao-Na et. al. (2007). The proposed multi-modal biometric system employed fusion of face and ear biometric information.

Security issues in multi-modal biometric system were addressed in Yuko(2007). Different trade-offs were analyzed such as, security with respect to privacy, cost and convenience.

In Yang (2007), all the three modality information namely fingerprint, hand geometry and palm-print were extracted through the same image. But, matching score fusion was performed at different levels of the biometric process. Score matching was performed by fusing multi-modal system and the unimodal palm-geometry system. Empirical results were obtained on a dataset containing features of ninety-eight subjects.

Fusion between iris and fingerprint features was performed in Feten Besbes(2008) to create multi-modal biometric system. The unimodal decision was fused through an AND operator. Empirical results miss out on recognition performance.

Feature extraction in multi-modal biometric systems through Linear Discriminant Analysis [LDA], Principal Component Analysis [PCA] and Mel Frequency Cepstral Coefficients [MFCC] was proposed in Kartik (2008). Features were extracted from face, signature and speech. Score level matching was performed using sum rule to obtain decision.

In Aloysius George (2008), multi-modal biometric system using face and fingerprint images was proposed. The verification module employed MBP-ANN algorithm to provide the decision. Unimodal decision for face was obtained through linear discriminant analysis and for fingerprint, directional filter bank was employed.

Empirical analysis of unimodal biometric systems against multi-modal systems was presented in Subbarayudu V.C. And M.V.N.K. Prasad (2008). The unimodal systems used in the study are iris and palm-print systems. Matching score mechanism was used in biometric systems which included both palm-print and iris images to perform verification. Experiments were performed on Hong Kong polytechnic university to palm print database, which had hundred different subjects.

Advantages of performing fusion of biometric images at low level was exhibited in Kisku (2009). This system used face and palm modalities.

Another multi-modal biometric system using Daubechies wavelet technique for feature extraction was proposed in Anwesh a(2009). This system used speech and iris modalities. Fusion was performed at feature level.

In, Md Maruf Monwar And Marina L Gavrilova (2009) rank level fusion was performed by using logistic regression and highest rank. Principle Component Analysis [PCA] technique was used to aid the fusion process. This multi-modal biometric system used ear, face and signature modalities.

Multi-modal biometric system using two fingerprint images acquired from different acquisition process was proposed in Conti (2007). Fuzzy logic based matching score was used for fusion. Empirical results compared decision level fusion strategy with matching score fusion. It establishes that matching-score fusion strategy has 6.7% more accuracy.

Feature extraction through Mel Frequency Cepstral Coefficients (MFCC) and wavelet-based kernel PCA was employed to construct multi-modal biometric system in P K Mahesh And M N Shanmukha Swamy (2010). Fusion at matching score level was performed.

Another multi-modal biometric system was proposed in Hanmandlu (2008) where particle swarm optimization was employed to perform matching score level fusion.

Feature extraction through Gabor filtering technique for designing multi-modal biometric systems was proposed in Yazdanpanah (2010). The used modalities were gait, ear and face.

Rank level fusion through logistic regression approach was employed in Fernandez (2010), to design multi-modal biometric systems.

Multi-modal biometric systems built on 2d and 3d images was proposed in Cheraghian (2011). Feature extraction was performed through Gabor filtering technique and fusion was achieved at decision level.

Combination of 3d and 2d face images were used in Jahanbin (2011) to design a novel multi-modal biometric system. Feature extractions were performed through Gabor coefficients and fusion was achieved at decision level.

In Takao Murakami and Kenta Takahashi (2011), multi-modal biometric system was built by achieving fusion at decision level which employed Bayesian decision rule technique. The modalities used were face, iris and fingerprint and permutation based indexing technique was used to identify these modalities.

Design of multi-modal biometric system through multi-spectral face images was proposed in Y. Zheng and A. Elmaghraby (2011). four different fusion techniques were analyzed they are K-Nearest Neighbor [KNN] fusion, Hidden Markov Model [HMM] fusion, Linear Discriminant Analysis [LDA] fusion and mean fusion. HMM fusion was advocated because of its high accuracy.

Another multi-modal biometric system using face and fingerprint modalities were proposed in Gargouri (2011). It employed local binary pattern and Gabor wavelet techniques to achieve feature extraction. Finally, match score level fusion was performed through sum method.

In Shukla (2010), it was shown that performance of multi-modal biometric systems can be accelerated by using uncorrelated traits. Also, it was suggested that user specific parameters can also improve accuracy.

In S Hariprasath and T N Prabakar (2012), wavelet packet transform was used to extract features and score level fusion was employed to design multi-modal biometric systems. The utilized modalities were iris and palm-print.

Feature extraction through Haar wavelet and scale invariant feature transform was employed to design multi-modal biometric system in Kumar(2012). The used modalities were face and ear. Fusion was preformed through logistic regression method.

In Maleika Heenaye And Mamode Khan (2012), dorsal hand vein and palm hand vein was used in designing multi-modal biometric systems. The vein features are represented using ICA dimensionality reduction technique. Normalization of scores is performed prior to matching score fusion.

The important challenges faced in designing efficient and effective multi-modal biometric systems were discussed in Taruna Panchal and Dr. Ajit Singh (2013). It also details the contemporary applications of these systems in the field of security.

In P. S. Sanjekar And J. B. Patil (2013), the advantages of multi-modal biometric systems such as overcoming the problems of interclass similarities, intra class variation, noisy data, non universality and spoofing were listed. Important challenges in designing such as selection of appropriate models, fusion level choice and feature redundancy were highlighted.

Multi-modal biometric verification was achieved using neural networks in K Krishneswari and A Arumugam (2013). Palm and fingerprint modalities were used in this biometric system. Feature extraction was performed through Gabor filter. Classification accuracy of 96% was achieved.

MAIN FOCUS OF THE CHAPTER

The multi-modal biometric systems should provide functionalities such as Fast recognition rate (FAR and FRR), security for the stored data, simple and compact multi-modal architecture and high verification methodology for the large database.

The objective of the work is,

1. To design efficient and effective multi-modal biometric systems which help in reducing False Acceptance Rate and False Rejection Rate, which is built over three different physiological traits such as finger, palm and iris for authentication.
2. The features of unimodal system such as finger, palm and iris are extracted using two different algorithms and compared for False Acceptance Rate and False Rejection Rate.
3. These unimodal systems are fused and created as multimodal system verified for False Acceptance Rate and False Rejection Rate and compared.

Finger Recognition

Fingerprint is an image of the finger friction ridge. This Fingerprint has been extensively used for authentication of an individual. The physical structure of finger friction ridge remains largely unaltered during the lifetime of an individual. The most important aspect of finger friction ridge is that they are unique for every individual which make them an ideal case for individual authentication. Fingerprints can be classified into three classes based on characteristics of the ridges as arches, loops and whorls. Also they can be classified into multiple classes based upon the point from which the ridge structure changes as shown in Figure 5.

The complete ridge information can be used for creating codes to perform authentication. But, this is computationally expensive. Especially, when the authentication procedure has a constraint of providing its decision with low response time. Hence, some of the distinct features in the ridge are selected which are unique for every individual.

The design of finger identification system is illustrated in Figure 6. The stored image set and the scanned images are subjected for normalization and to detect the edges which are required for ridge analysis. The required features are extracted from both the stored image set and scanned image. Through linear scan of all the image features in the stored image set.

Figure 7 illustrates the algorithm of Fingerprint identification system. The original image is converted to binary format in-order to obtain the ridge information. In preprocessing step is performed to get the complete information of the ridges. Finally feature extraction is performed to achieve a decision for the identity of the person.

Figure 5. Finger print image

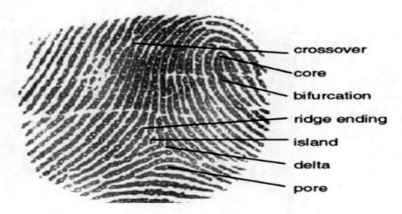

Figure 6. Finger identification system

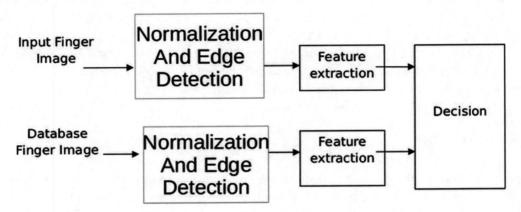

Figure 7. Flowchart of fingerprint recognition

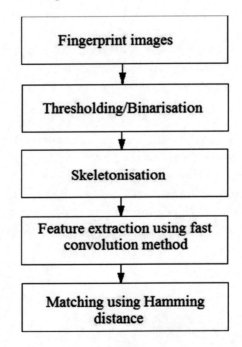

The fingerprint image usually has a white background which does not have any required information. This background region can be minimized through thresholding. The thresholding is done by splitting the image into blocks and then the mean value for each block is calculated by using Equation 1. Here $A_j((x,y)_i)$ is the pixel value of the pixel coordinate $(x,y)_i$ that belongs to the block j. This block has n pixels and $mean_j$ is the mean pixel value of block j. If the pixel coordinate has an pixel value which is less than the block's mean pixel value then, the pixel value of such an coordinate will be made into 0 otherwise, it will be made 1.

$$mean_j = \frac{\sum_{i=1}^{i=n} A_j\left(x, y\right)_i}{n} \qquad (1)$$

Thinning or Skeleton image creation is performed on binary image. The thinning process reduces all lines to the same thickness, so that the lines and the ridges are clearly visible. The connectivity of the lines is also maintained.

To delete a pixel, it should satisfy the following conditions:

1. The pixel should not be an endpoint.
2. The elimination of pixel does not break the connectedness of the skeleton.
3. The elimination should not cause dense erosion of the region.

This method will eliminate all the pixels of the image excluding those pixels that belong to the skeleton. This skeleton image is then used for performing feature extraction.

The first method of feature extraction is processed using overlap add method. Convolution is a mathematical process that multiplies the time invariant input signal with the impulse signal to get linear output as shown in Equation 2.

$$\sum y(t) = x(t) * h(t) \qquad (2)$$

Convolution is a major process in digital signal processing. It is extensively used in filtering, Denoising, edge detection, correlation, compression, and in many other applications. In convolution, the required signals are retained and the edge or unwanted signals are removed. The cost of fast convolution is $Nlog_2N$. For multi-dimensional or long input signals the best method to calculate the convolution is the fast convolution method. The fast convolution technique divides the input signal into samples and does parallel convolution for the large data samples and adds the output of each convoluted values. Due to this parallel operation, the computation is fast compared to the other convolution methods. The main advantage of this method is that there is no restriction for the length of the input signal. There are two methods in fast convolution:

Overlap Add Method

The overlap add method is a type of convolution for fixed coefficients and it is computationally efficient and requires more memory. This method can be applied to frequency domain and time domain. In basic convolution technique multiplication is performed first and then the output values are added. This procedure produces a long final output which is computationally expensive for evaluation. In overlap add method the output from rear end of the former block is overlapped with the front end of the present block for specified length. In this work, overlap-add method is used for feature extraction. The Figure 8 illustrates overlap add method. The input signal f is split into small signals f1(n), f2(n) and f3(n). Then it is convoluted with the kernel g. Each convoluted blocks are overlapped and then added. Finally the convoluted sequence is produced. The length of this sequence obtained is less than the basic convolution method. The Equation 3a to 3d describes the procedure.

Figure 8. Overlap add method

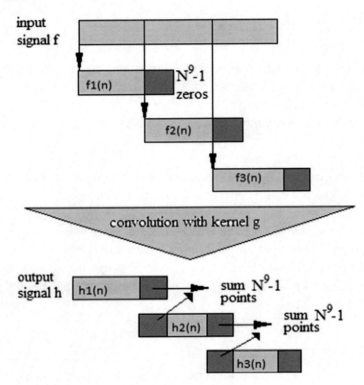

$$h(n)=f(n)*g(n) \tag{3a}$$

$$f(n)=f1(n)+f2(n)+f3(n)+\ldots\ldots \tag{3b}$$

$$f(n)*g(n)=(f1(n)+f2(n)+f3(n)\ldots\ldots)*g(n) \tag{3c}$$

$$h(n)=f1(n)*g(n)+f2(n)*g(n)+\ldots\ldots \tag{3d}$$

Overlap Save Method

A slightly different organization of the above approach is also often used for high-speed convolution. Rather than sectioning the input and then calculating the output from overlapped outputs from these individual input blocks, we will section the output and then use whatever part of the input contributes to that output block. In other words, to calculate the values in a particular output block, a section of length N + L -1 from the input will be needed. The strategy is to save the part of the first input block that contributes to the second output block and use it in that calculation. It turns out that exactly the same amount of arithmetic and storage are used by these two approaches. Because it is the input that is now overlapped and, therefore, must be saved, this second approach is called overlap-save. This method has also been called overlap-discard because, rather than adding the overlapping output blocks, the overlapping portion of the output blocks is discarded.

The second feature extraction algorithm is integer wavelet transform. The wavelet coefficients of DWT are real numbers, because of this efficient lossless coding through linear transforms is not possible. The lifting scheme (LS) allows an efficient implementation of the DWT. The LS structure ensures perfect reconstruction and the usage of new transformations such as Integer Wavelet Transform (IWT). In IWT output is rounded to the nearest integer, because the use of floating point numbers is expensive. There are several frameworks but, the most popular are S+P, Lifting scheme and overlapping rounding transform (ORT) frameworks. The S-transform is the most basic framework for Integer To Integer (ITI) transform.

The most popular framework of ITI transform is based on the lifting scheme. The lifting framework is a polyphase realization of UMD filter banks. It employs ladder networks for polyphase filtering. The 1-D two channel UMD filter bank contains lifting and scaling steps. In the lifting step, the filters A_k is constituted and in the scaling step, amplifiers are associated with the gains S_k which are shown in Figure 9.

The ladder network of lifting scheme has to maintain their invariability for quantization error (rounding error by finite precision arithmetic). The construction of lifting scheme based ITI transform, initially constricts the lifting scheme, eliminates the scaling function having a non-integer gain factor and then transforms each lifting step to rounding operation Q at the output of its corresponding filter as shown in Figure 9. The mathematical model of lifting framework is illustrated in Equations 4 and 5.

$$d[n] = d_0[n] + \frac{1}{16}\left(\left(s_0[n+2] + s_0[n-1]\right) - 9\left(s_0[n+1] + s_0[n]\right)\right) + \frac{1}{2} \tag{4}$$

$$s[n] = s_0[n] + \frac{1}{4}\left(d[n] + d[n-1]\right) + \frac{1}{2} \tag{5}$$

Figure 9. Lifting framework

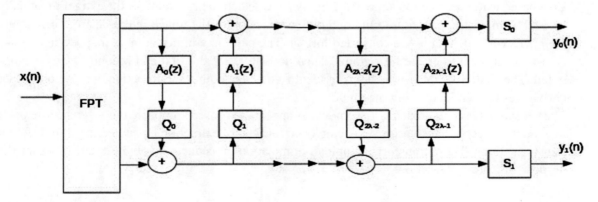

The matching is done through Hamming distance metric. The Hamming distance indicates the degree of similarity between two-bit patterns. Using Hamming distance metric, patterns that were generated from different patterns or from the same one can be identified. Equation 6 describes the Hamming distance metric, X_j and Y_j are the two-bit pattern having length N.

$$HD = \frac{1}{N} \sum_{j=1}^{N} X_j \left(xor\right) Y_j \tag{6}$$

Palm Recognition

The second physical trait used for multimodal biometric is palm print recognition. Palm based user authentication is gaining popularity as an alternative to fingerprint based biometric systems. It has significant advantages and also has uniqueness property. The Palm based biometric process involves scanning a palm image for feature extraction, and matching it with the features of palm images stored in database. There are two important categories of Palm image features:

1. Geometrical features
2. Palm-print features

The width length and area comprises the geometrical features. But these are coarse features and may repeat their values in many samples. Hence such features are avoided due to poor effectiveness.

The Palm print techniques include small wrinkles, delta points and principle lines Wu (2006) and Ajay Kumar and Cyril Kwong (2013). The minutiae that are extracted for fingerprints require images with high resolution. The palm print contains high amount of unique identification information. The palm identification features are secondary crease, ridges and flexion. The flexion is called as principle lines, and the secondary creases are denoted as wrinkles.

There are three procedures for extracting the features of palm image.

1. The texture based approaches employ distance metric the technique. These texture's are obtained through Gabor wavelets, Cosine transformation, Fourier transformation, wavelet transformation and standard deviation. Also it is difficult to align the palm image and subject it to cropping.
2. Line based feature extraction approach employ edge detection procedure for the extraction of palm lines. The matching procedure might employ conversion of the image into a desired format and then perform matching in the converted format. The palm line information is mapped in to a x-y coordinate system to create histograms. Then derivatives of the first and second order are computed. The first order derivative helps in identifying edge points and direction. The second order derivatives help in identifying magnitude.
3. The subspace-based approach is also known as appearance based approach. It converts entire palm image into a vector. This vector set is employed for feature extraction by subjecting it to different transformations. These transforms employ optimization procedures involving training set for the purpose of feature extraction.

Current approaches for palm print recognition suffer from transformation time. To overcome complexity issues, palm print recognition through 2-D SMDWT is proposed in this work. This technique uses single matrix for performing verification.

The proposed technique is shown in Figure 10. The scanned palm print image is subjected for edge detection. The edges are used for feature extraction. This is performed through Symmetric mask-based discrete wavelet transform. Matching is performed on images in database for authentication.

Thresholding is used for creation of binary images from gray scale images. Thresholding is a technique in which a gray scale image is converted into a binary format. Thresholding aids in extraction of required objects from the image. Since, a gray scale image pixel can have different pixel intensity values, binary image helps in properly identifying the foreground and background. Kernel based threshold technique estimates the density function of a continuous random variable in a non-parametric fashion. It helps in estimating the parameters of a population from a given sample.

The data set points X_1, X_2, ... X_n are divided into n partitions A_{n1}, A_{n2}, ..A_{nm}. The estimated density f(x) is given in Equation 7. Here, X_j is Column elements from 1 to j, A_i is Row elements from 1 to i and λ is Sum of all the elements in the matrix.

$$f(x) = \frac{1}{n} \sum_{j=1}^{n} \sum_{i=1}^{n} \frac{X_j A_{ij}}{\lambda} \tag{7}$$

Consider a gray scale image of 576x768. In gray scale digital images, the value of every pixel is considered as an independent sample. These images have black color at the weak intensity and white at strong. The column elements are compared with row elements. If same match occurs such pixel will be stored in the buffer. If match occurs with the next element then, this element is added with the element stored in buffer and this modified value is stored in-place. The final value present inside the buffer is considered as threshold value which is extracted through k-method. This will ultimately aid in detecting scanned palm image. The flow diagram is illustrated in Figure 11.

Figure 10. SMDWT block diagram

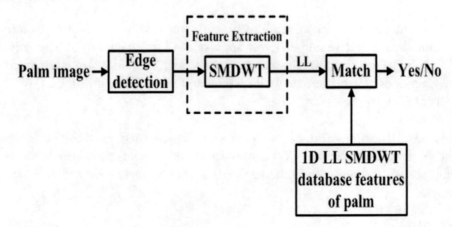

Figure 11. Edge detection

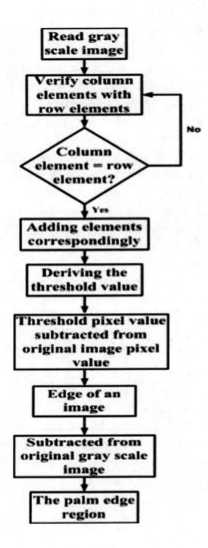

The LDWT technique is computationally efficient compared to classical convolution technique. The lifting scheme is an effective and efficient approach to implement DWT. The poly-phase matrix of DWT filter can be factorized through Euclidean approach. This results in a sequence of upper and lower triangular matrices which alternate with each other. Figure 12 exhibits the LDWT structure. The lifting scheme is of four stages:

1. **Splitting Phase:** The original signal is decomposed into two disjoint subsets as shown in Equation 8, X denotes set of even samples, X_o denotes set of odd samples. It is also called as lazy wavelet transform because it avoids de-correlating the data. It only creates odd and even samples from the input sample.

$$X_o[n]=X[2n+1], X_e[n]=X[2n] \qquad (8)$$

Figure 12. LDWT Structure

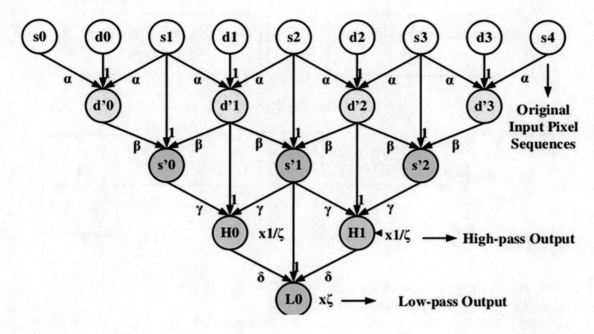

2. **Prediction Phase:** The prediction operator P denoted in Equation 9 is applied on the subset of odd values ($X_o[n]$) to obtain wavelet coefficients d[n].

$$d[n]=X_o[n]+PxX_e[n] \tag{9}$$

3. **Updating Phase:** The even values ($X_e[n]$) and predicted values (d[n]) are combined to obtain the scaling coefficients s[n] by using update operator U as shown in Equation 10.

$$s[n]=X_o[n]+Uxd[n] \tag{10}$$

4. **Scaling:** In final step, the normalization factor is operated on s[n] and d[n] to obtain Wavelet coefficients H[n] and L[n] as shown in Equations 11 and 12.

$$H\big[n\big] = \frac{1}{\varsigma} Xd\big[n\big] \tag{11}$$

$$L\big[n\big] = \varsigma Xd\big[n\big] \tag{12}$$

The 9/7 LDWT has property of perfect reconstruction. Also its each sub-band is subjected for preprocessing. But, 2D DWT suffers from high operation time, complex transpose memory and high complexity. The four sub-bands of 2D LDWT shown in Figure 13 are related with each other which make the task

Figure 13. 2D LDWT

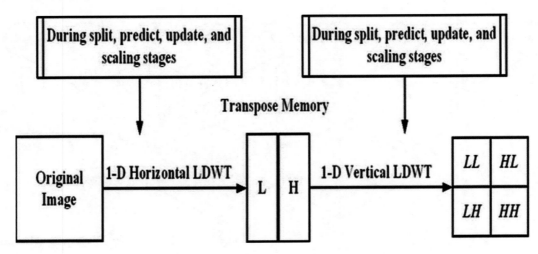

of obtaining target sub-band more difficult. Since, 2D DWT has the property of symmetry; this is used to reduce computational complexity of filtering process.

In this work, 2D 9/7 Symmetric Mask-Based DWT is employed. It uses a single matrix and the procedure has multiple advantages like independent sub-bands and low complexity. The four-matrix filters 7x7, 7x9, 9x7 and 9x9 which are obtained from 2D DWT of 9/7 floating point lifting based coefficients are used for substituting the original wavelet structure. The size of transpose memory N2 is large and this results in high computational complexity, 2D symmetric mask based discrete wavelet transform is proposed in this work to solve these problems, and is shown in Figure 14.

For Daubechies 9/9 filter, 9 original input pixels are required to obtain one low pass wavelet coefficient. These values are inserted into a matrix and 9x9 sub-matrices are used for producing lower sub-bands. The matrix should be tracing horizontal so that vertical elements can be traced. By this procedure 9 horizontal elements can be produced and through the usage of these elements vertical elements will be produced. The flow chart is shown in Figure 15.

Figure 14. 2D symmetric mask based DWT

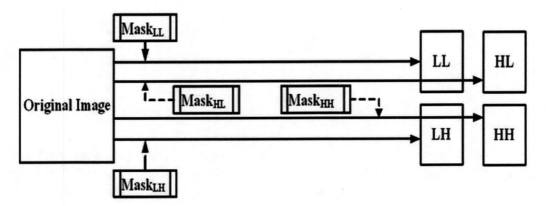

Figure 15. Flow chart of feature extraction

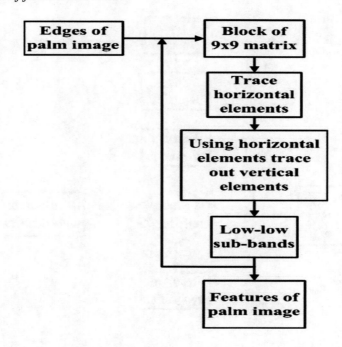

The main focus of image matching is to calculate the similarity distance between images. The Euclidean distance metric is most widely used image distance. Let x and y be the images that need to be matched. Both images are of MxN dimension, x=(x¹,x²,..x^MN) and y=(y¹,y²,..y^MN). Here x^{kN+l} and y^{kN+l} are the gray level values at the coordinate (k, l). The Euclidean distance is calculated using in Equation 13.

$$d_E^2\left(x,y\right) = \sum_{k=1}^{MN}\left(x^k - y^k\right)^2 \tag{13}$$

For the purpose of identification a test image needs to be generated. The required pixel values are extracted. These pixel values are used to extract the edges of test image by using K method. Then feature extraction is applied to extract the features. The feature vector is compared with database. If the Euclidean matching metric provides a matching distance within the acceptable limit then, it is considered a valid match otherwise, it is considered as a no match. The flow chart of the proposed technique is shown in Figure 16.

IRIS Recognition

Iris based authentication is a biometric system that employs pattern recognition technique by using iris of the individual for authentication.

Image processing techniques can be efficiently used for designing iris based authentication system. The iris image obtained is encoded in a biometric template and then stored in a database. The biometric template is a mathematical representation of the iris structure. A user who wishes to use the iris recog-

Figure 16. Proposed flow chart

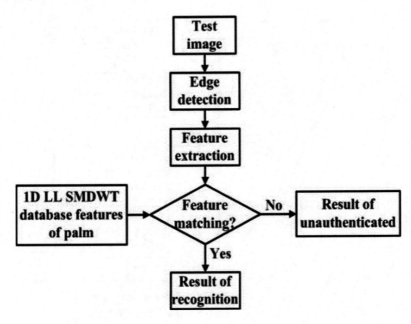

nition system, the image of user eye is obtained. For this image a template is created. This template is used for matching with other iris templates stored in the database. If the match occurs within specified threshold then, user authentication is successful otherwise, the user is rejected.

In this work iris image feature extraction is performed through two algorithms Neville's algorithm and Symmetric Frame-let. Block diagram of the iris recognition system is shown in Figure 17.

The iris based authentication system has three steps:

Figure 17. Block diagram of Iris recognition system

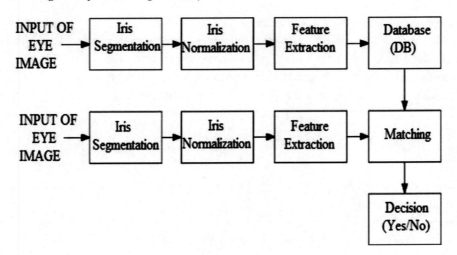

1. Segmentation and Normalization
2. Feature extraction
3. Matching

As seen in Figure 17, the iris region is extracted from the eye image through segmentation and normalization. The feature extraction module extracts the required important features. The matching module uses hamming distance metric. The matching is done by comparing with feature vector of database images with the test image feature vector.

Segmentation

Conversion of gray scale image into binary format is performed. Since the intensities of iris and the pupil differ considerably it helps in proper segmentation. The edge detection algorithm always provides a ring. The tangent for ring is calculated through horizontal scan. Also by performing vertical scan other tangents are calculated. In this way diameter and radius of the circle is calculated. The steps of segmentation module are detailed in below algorithm.

- Perform conversion of the RGB image into gray scale image.
- Convert this gray scale image into binary format through the calculated threshold value.
- Perform noise reduction by using Gaussian filter and smoothen the image.
- Perform edge detection through canny technique to compute the circle.
- Perform Vertical scan to obtain the tangent. Use the tangent information to calculate the center and radius of the circle.
- Similar technique is employed along with slightly higher threshold value for obtaining the outer circle.
- Perform vertical scan from the center pixel of the circle to obtain the radius and tangent.
- Reconstruction of Inner and outer circle is performed through the obtained values.

Normalization

Normalization is performed through rubber sheet model. The center of pupil is used to calculate the radial vectors. The data points on this radial line are selected. Then remapping formula is employed to transform circular coordinate to rectangular coordinates. This is shown in Equation 14.

$$r = \sqrt{\alpha\beta} \mp \sqrt{\alpha\beta^2 - \alpha - r_1^2} \tag{14}$$

$$Where, \alpha = \sigma_x^2 + \sigma_y^2 \ and \ \beta = \cos\left[\pi - \arctan\left(\frac{o_y}{o_x}\right) - \theta\right].$$

Feature Extraction

Neville's Algorithm

Interpolating subdivision algorithm is used to obtain the features of iris image. Neville's algorithm is one of the efficient and effective interpolating subdivision algorithms. It extracts all important and required features of the iris image. Every interpolating subdivision construct agrees to refinement relations. In Neville method, function f(x) is interpolated at the given point x=p. This task is achieved through higher order of Lagrange's interpolation polynomials.

Consider three distinct points x_0, x_1 and x_2 on which the function f(x) is applied. The task is to construct 0, 1st and 2nd order polynomials for the purpose of approximating the function f(p).

In Neville's procedure, 2D matrices are converted into row vectors. This row matrix is grouped together into a block of ten pixels. Polynomial root generation is employed for performing interpolation. Chebyshev polynomial is used for extracting polynomial roots. Equation 15 illustrates this process.

$$T_0(x)=1; T_{(n+1)}(x)=2T_n(x)-T_{(n-1)}(x) \tag{15}$$

Recurrence relation is an equation which has a recursive structure. To evaluate this relation, initial value of the relation is provided. Then by using the recursive structure higher order structure of the equation is calculated. The Equation 15 is computed for n^{th} iterations using the recursive structure. This provides the required nodes for the interpolation process. Then mean of the generated data set is calculated which is used in the Neville's algorithm for interpolation. In-order to obtain the nth order for the interpolation factor, n x n matrix is designed which uses Chebyshev nodes as the 1st row. It appends 0 for the left over n-1 rows.

P(f(p)) is the first order polynomial of x_i. It is shown in Equation 16.

$$f'(p) \approx P_0(p) = f(x_0); f(p) \approx P_2(p) = f(x_2) \tag{16}$$

The nth order polynomial used by the Neville's algorithm is shown in Equation 17.

$$f''(p) \approx P_{(0,1,2..n)}(p) = \left((p-x_n)P_{(0,1,2,..n)}(p) - (x-x_0)P_{(0,1,2,..n-1)}(p)\right) / (x_0 - x_n) \tag{17}$$

This n^{th} has the property of uniqueness which is not exhibited by other order polynomials. This provides higher accuracy in interpolating the values. In higher order polynomials, numbers of values are produced. But second order is used for computing the higher orders so, this decrease for every column.

Feature extraction is performed for large number of pixels as polynomials. There are two important considerations:

1. The two-dimensional matrix which is given as input is transformed into one dimensional matrix.
2. Clustering is performed on pixels which results in having order of polynomial equal to the number of pixels present in each cluster. Increased order of the polynomial provides higher number of samples. Then, matching is performed on these extracted features.

Symmetric Framelet

Iris region is decomposed into components which appear at different resolution by using wavelets. The main advantage of wavelets over Fourier transform is that, the localized information about data frequency can be obtained. This provides features at the same resolution and position. Iris region is subjected to different wavelet filtering process. Basis function is used to scale the resolution of each wavelet. Encoding is performed on the scaled wavelet to provide discriminating and compact representation of the image.

In even length low pass scaling filter, one wavelet is anti-symmetric and other is symmetric. By performing matching on the roots of polynomials, wavelet filters can be obtained. Both the wavelets are designed to have vanishing moments through the usage of low pass filter. For the scaling function the wavelet and dilation mechanism are illustrated in Equations 18 and 19.

$$\varnothing(t) = \sqrt{2} \sum_n h_0(n) \varnothing(2t - n) \tag{18}$$

$$\varphi(t) = \sqrt{2} \sum_n h_i(n) \varnothing(2t - n) \tag{19}$$

The poly-phase components are illustrated in Equation 20.

$$H_i(z) = H_{i0}(z^2) + z^{-1} H_{i1}(z^2) \, i = 0, 1, 2, \ldots \tag{20}$$

If $h_i(n)$ has to agree with the perfect reconstruction constraints and $h_i(t)$ shows its sufficient regularity. Then, the translations and dyadic dilations of $h_i(t)$ create a tight frame for $L^2(IR)$. The perfect reconstruction situation can be expressed in the matrix form shown in Equations 21 and 22.

$$H^t\left(\frac{1}{z}\right) H(z) = I \tag{21}$$

$$H(z) = \begin{matrix} H_{00}(z) & H_{01}(z) \\ H_{10}(z) & H_{11}(z) \\ H_{20}(z) & H_{21}(z) \end{matrix} \tag{22}$$

To achieve the perfect reconstruction constraints, a set of three filters will be designed such that, $h_0(n)$ which is a low pass filter will be symmetric, $h_1(n)$ and $h_2(n)$ will be either symmetric or anti-symmetric. The symmetry condition for $h_0(n)$ is shown in Equation 23.

$$h_0(n) = h_0(N - 1 - n) \tag{23}$$

There will be two cases, in case I, $h_2(n)$ will be anti-symmetric and $h_1(n)$ will be symmetric or vice-versa is illustrated in Equation 24 to26.

$$h_2(n) = h_1(N - 1 - n) \tag{24}$$

$$h_1^{new}(n) = \frac{1}{\sqrt{2}}(h_1(n) + h_2(n - 2d)) \tag{25}$$

$$h_2^{new}(n) = \frac{1}{\sqrt{2}}(h_1(n) + h_2(n - 2d)) \tag{26}$$

In case II, both $h_1(n)$ and $h_2(n)$ will be symmetric is discussed in Equation 27 to 29.

$$h_0(n) = h_0(N - 1 - n) \tag{27}$$

$$h_1(n) = -h_1(N - 1 - n) \tag{28}$$

$$h_2(n) = -h_2(N - 3 - n) \tag{29}$$

Unique features are extracted from the iris image to perform authentication. To perform feature matching, encoding of features is first accomplished. Currently, most of the iris biometric systems are designed though the usages of band pass decomposition. Matching

The hamming distance metric is used for matching encode features of iris image. This metric show the difference between two bit patterns in terms of distance. The hamming metric for comparing two irises encode features X and Y is shown in Equation 30.

$$HD = \left(\frac{1}{N}\sum_{k=1}^{N} X_{nk}(OR)Y_{nk}\right)\sum_{j=1}^{N} X_j(XOR)Y_j(AND)X'_{nj}(AND)Y'_{nj} \tag{30}$$

Here, X_j and Y_j are two bit-wise templates that need to be compared, X_{nj} and Y_{nj} are noise masks for X_j and Y_j, N is the number of bits in the template. The hamming distance metric is designed using a function which will use the encode features of two iris images. The decision to authenticate is described by the procedure shown below:

1. If HD<= 0.30 positively authenticate decide the person.
2. If HD>0.30 reject the authentication of the person.

High degrees of freedom can be seen in iris region. Due to this, each iris region generates independent bit pattern when compared to the other. Two iris codes from the same iris region are highly correlated. If the two-bit patterns are different then hamming distance will be more than 0.3. Similarly, for two same iris patterns, the hamming distance will be nearer to 0.

EXPERIMENTAL RESULTS AND DISCUSSIONS

The multimodal biometric system employs three biometric modalities namely fingerprint, palm and iris. The biometric techniques for all these three modalities that were developed in the previous sections are used in the design of multi-modal biometric systems. All the systems employ matching decision level fusion technique. The multi-modal techniques are compared with their unimodal counterparts.

All the unimodal systems are implemented for two algorithms as described above, so the probability combinations of these two algorithms are considered to implement the multi-modal using and rule are shown in Table 1.

As per Table 1, there will be eight combinations found for multi-modal systems and all the multi-modal system combination is implemented.

OA+LDWT+Neville's Multimodal Biometric System

Figure 18 illustrates the False Recognition Rate (FRR), Total Success Rate (TSR) and False Acceptance Rate (FAR) values for the proposed multi-modal biometric system using OA, LDWT and Neville's techniques. These values are obtained for different threshold parameter values. The graph shows the TSR will increases approximately at the threshold value of 6 and has a linear increase in the threshold

Table 1. Combinations of different unimodal to multi-modal systems

Sl. No.	Finger	Palm	Iris	Multimodal Fusion Combination
1.	Overlap-Add method (OA)	Lifting DWT (LDWT)	Neville's Algorithm (NV)	OA+LDWT+NV
2.	Overlap-Add method (OA)	Lifting DWT (LDWT)	Symmetric framelets (SF)	OA+LDWT+SF
3.	Overlap-Add method (OA)	Symmetric Mask DWT (SMDWT)	Neville's Algorithm (NV)	OA+SMDWT+NV
4.	Overlap-Add method (OA)	Symmetric Mask DWT (SMDWT)	Symmetric framelets (SF)	OA+SMDWT+SF
5.	Integer Wavelet Transform (IWT)	Lifting DWT (LDWT)	Neville's Algorithm (NV)	IWT+LDWT+NV
6.	Integer Wavelet Transform (IWT)	Lifting DWT (LDWT)	Symmetric framelets (SF)	IWT+LDWT+SF
7.	Integer Wavelet Transform (IWT)	Symmetric Mask DWT (SMDWT)	Neville's Algorithm (NV)	IWT+SMDWT+NV
8.	Integer Wavelet Transform (IWT)	Symmetric Mask DWT (SMDWT)	Symmetric framelets (SF)	IWT+SMDWT+SF

Figure 18. FRR, TSR and FAR values with threshold (OA+LDWT+Neville's)

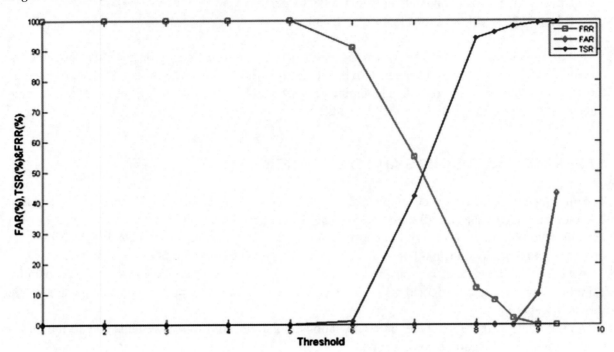

values from 6 to 8 and sudden increase in the TSR and reaches its maximum value at the threshold value of 9. It is evident that higher threshold values lead to higher FAR values and lower FRR values. The comparative FRR and FAR values for multi-modal system and unimodal systems is illustrated in Table 2, Figure 19 and 20. The Table 2 illustrates FRR and FAR values for Iris, Finger and Palm shows higher FRR and Lower FAR and in these multi-modal biometric systems is a clear winner in these experiments. The Figure 19 and 20 shows the FAR and FRR plotted between unimodal and multimodal biometric systems. The FRR reaches approximately zero around the threshold above 9 and FAR reaches maximum at threshold of 9. In the graphs it is observed that IRIS takes longer threshold values to settle but other unimodal biometrics are shorter threshold to settle. In the graph it is clear that Equal Error Rate (EER) is at 2.5 at the threshold of around 8.6.

Table 2. Unimodal vs. multimodal (OA+LDWT+Neville's)

Biometric System	%FRR	%FAR
Unimodal Iris(Neville's)	8	10
Unimodal Fingerprint (Overlap-Add)	14	0
Unimodal Palm-print (LDWT)	11	3
Multimodal(OA+LDWT+Neville's)	2	0

Figure 19. FRR vs. threshold of uni and multi modal (OA+LDWT+Neville's)

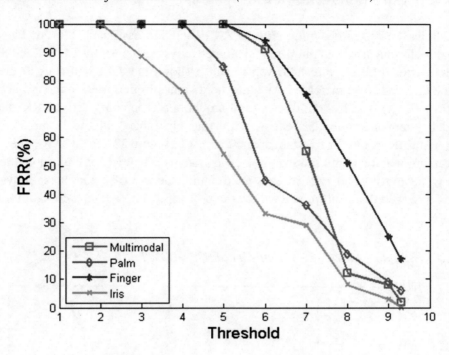

Figure 20. FAR vs. threshold of uni and multi modal (OA+LDWT+Neville's)

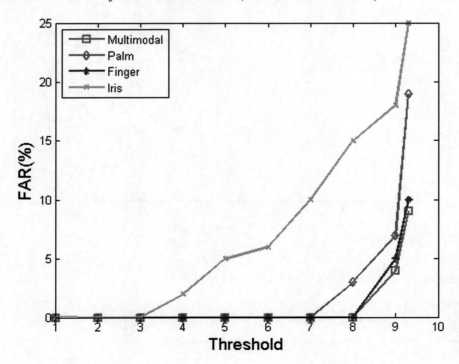

OA+LDWT+SF Multimodal Biometric System

Figure 21 illustrates the False Recognition Rate (FRR), Total Success Rate (TSR) and False Acceptance Rate (FAR) values for the proposed multi-modal biometric system using OA, LDWT and SF techniques. The graph plotted for different threshold values and it shows the TSR will start to increases at the threshold value of 6 and has a increase in the threshold values from 6 to 9. In the graph it is clear that Equal Error Rate (EER) is at 1 at the threshold of around 8.5. The comparative FRR and FAR values for multi-modal system and unimodal systems is illustrated in Table 3, Figure 22 and 23. The table 3 illustrates FRR and FAR values for Iris, Finger and Palm. The Figure 22 and 23 shows the FAR and FRR plotted between unimodal and multimodal biometric systems. The FRR of multimodal reaches zero at the threshold value above 9 and FAR reaches maximum value at 35% at the threshold value of 9.4. In the graphs it is observed that Multimodal will be the best approach as compared to unimodal systems.

Figure 21. FRR, TSR and FAR values with threshold (OA+LDWT+SF)

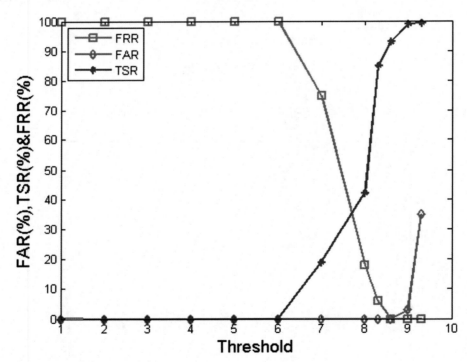

Table 3. Unimodal vs. multimodal (OA+LDWT+SF)

Biometric System	%FRR	%FAR
Unimodal Iris(SF)	12	5
Unimodal Fingerprint (Overlap-Add)	14	0
Unimodal Palm-print (LDWT)	11	3
Multimodal(OA+LDWT+SF)	3	0

Figure 22. FRR vs. threshold of uni and multi modal (OA+LDWT+SF)

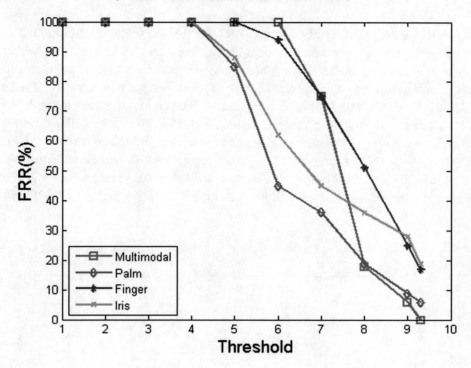

Figure 23. FAR vs. threshold of uni and multi modal (OA+LDWT+SF)

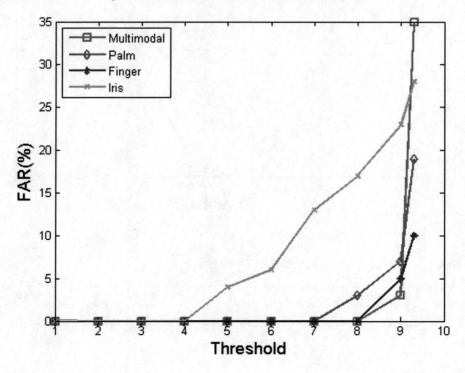

OA+SMDWT+Neville's Multimodal Biometric System

Figure 24 illustrates the False Recognition Rate (FRR), Total Success Rate (TSR) and False Acceptance Rate (FAR) values for the proposed multi-modal biometric system using OA, SMDWT and Neville's techniques. The graph shows the TSR which has maximum value of100% at the threshold value 9. In the graph it is clear that Equal Error Rate (EER) is at 0 at the threshold of around 8.4. The EER are plotted at the FRR and FAR of 1% and 1%. The comparative FRR and FAR values for multi-modal system and unimodal systems is illustrated in Table 4, Figure 25 and 26. The Table 4 illustrates FRR and FAR values for Iris, Finger and Palm. Due to loss in feature vectors in overlap add method, the FRR is to high as compared other unimodal systems and IRIS shows higher FAR due to large feature vector generation. In the multimodal system, FRR and FAR are to low due to higher feature vector generation. In the Figure 25 FRR of multimodal system is exactly zero at the threshold value of 9. The Figure 26 records

Figure 24. FRR, TSR and FAR values with threshold (OA+ SMDWT+Neville's)

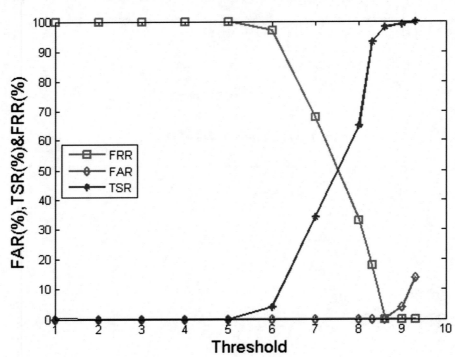

Table 4. Unimodal vs. multimodal (OA+SMDWT+Neville's)

Biometric System	%FRR	%FAR
Unimodal Iris(Neville's)	8	10
Unimodal Fingerprint (Overlap-Add)	14	0
Unimodal Palm-print (SMDWT)	10	1
Multimodal(OA+ SMDWT+Neville's	1.8	0

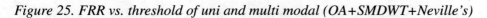

Figure 25. FRR vs. threshold of uni and multi modal (OA+SMDWT+Neville's)

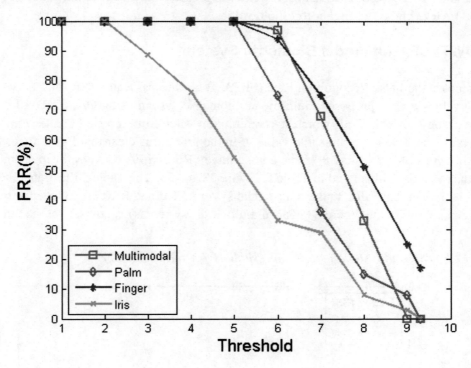

Figure 26. FAR vs. threshold of uni and multi modal (OA+SMDWT+Neville's)

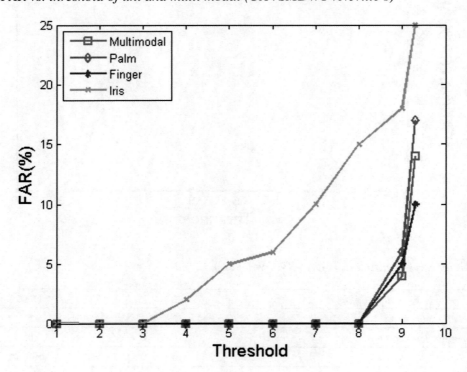

the higher and longer FAR for IRIS using Nevielle's approach due to large feature vectors but for other methods the FAR is higher for higher threshold values.

OA+SMDWT+SF Multimodal Biometric System

Figure 27 records the False Recognition Rate (FRR), Total Success Rate (TSR) and False Acceptance Rate (FAR) values for the proposed multi-modal biometric system using OA, SMDWT and SF techniques. The graph shows the TSR which starts minimum value from threshold value 7 and reaches its maximum value of100% at the threshold value 9. In the graph it is clear that Equal Error Rate (EER) is of 10 at the threshold of around 8.7. The comparative FRR and FAR values for multi-modal system and unimodal systems is illustrated in Table 5, Figure 28 and 29. The Table 5 illustrates FRR and FAR values for Iris, Finger and Palm. In the multimodal system, FRR and FAR are to low due to higher feature vector generation. In the Figure 28 FRR of multimodal system is exactly zero at the threshold value

Figure 27. FRR, TSR and FAR values with threshold (OA+ SMDWT+SF)

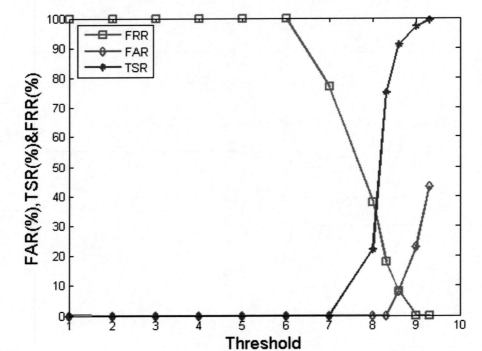

Table 5. Unimodal vs. multimodal (OA+SMDWT+SF)

Biometric System	%FRR	%FAR
Unimodal Iris(SF)	12	5
Unimodal Fingerprint (Overlap-Add)	14	0
Unimodal Palm-print (SMDWT)	10	1
Multimodal(OA+ SMDWT+SF)	2	0

Figure 28. FRR vs. threshold of uni and multi modal (OA+SMDWT+SF)

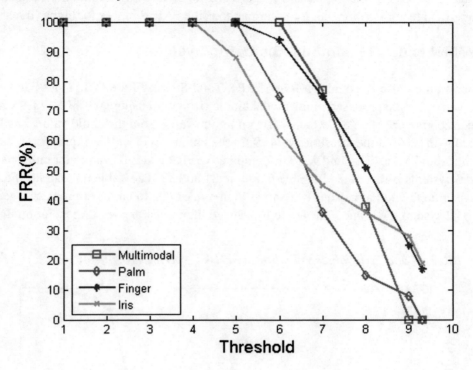

Figure 29. FAR vs threshold of uni and multi modal (OA+SMDWT+SF)

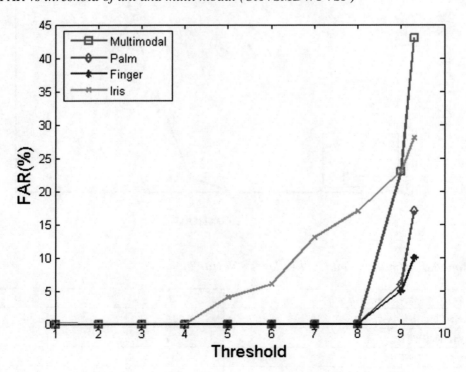

of 9. The Figure 29 records the higher and longer FAR for IRIS using Symmetric Framelet approach due to symmetrical feature vectors but for other methods the FAR is higher for higher threshold values.

IWT+LDWT+Neville's Multimodal Biometric System

Figure 30 shows the False Recognition Rate (FRR), Total Success Rate (TSR) and False Acceptance Rate (FAR) values for the proposed multi-modal biometric system using IWT+LDWT+Neville's techniques. The graph records the TSR which starts minimum value from threshold value 5 and reaches its maximum value of100% at the threshold value 9. In the graph it is clear that Equal Error Rate (EER) is of 13 at the threshold value of around 9.3. The comparative FRR and FAR values for multi-modal system and unimodal systems is illustrated in Table 6, Figure 31 and 32. The Table 6 illustrates FRR and FAR values for Iris, Finger and Palm. The IRIS shows higher FAR due to large feature vector generation. In the multimodal system, FRR and FAR are to low due to higher feature vector generation. In the Figure

Figure 30. FRR, TSR and FAR values with threshold (IWT+LDWT+Neville's)

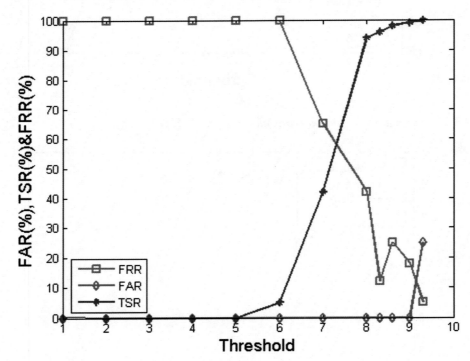

Table 6. Unimodal vs. multimodal (IWT+LDWT+Neville's)

Biometric System	%FRR	%FAR
Unimodal Iris(Neville's)	8	10
Unimodal Fingerprint (IWT)	9	0
Unimodal Palm-print (LDWT)	11	3
Multimodal(IWT+LDWT+Neville's)	1.5	0

Figure 31. FRR vs. threshold of uni and multi modal (IWT+LDWT+Neville's)

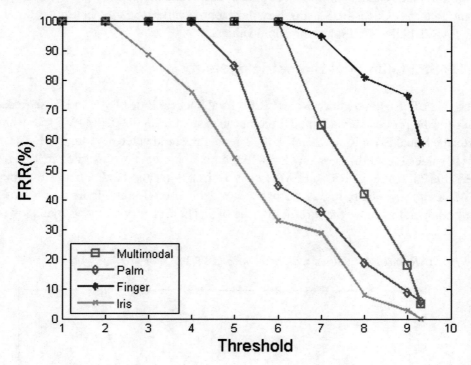

Figure 32. FAR vs. threshold of uni and multi modal (IWT+LDWT+Neville's)

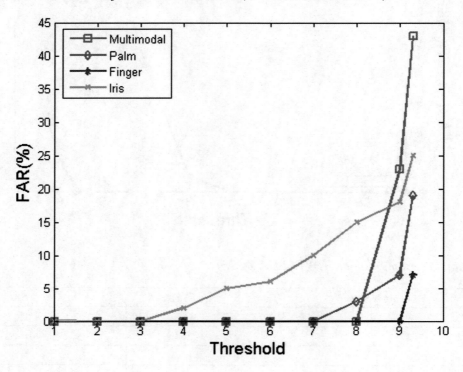

31 FRR of multimodal system is minimum at the above the threshold value of 9. The Figure 32 records the higher and longer FAR for IRIS using Neville's approach due to large feature vectors but for other methods the FAR is higher for higher threshold values.

IWT+LDWT+SF Multimodal Biometric System

Figure 33 shows the False Recognition Rate (FRR), Total Success Rate (TSR) and False Acceptance Rate (FAR) values for the proposed multi-modal biometric system using IWT+LDWT+SF techniques. The graph records the Equal Error Rate (EER) is of 12 at the threshold value of around 9.1. The comparative FRR and FAR values for multi-modal system and unimodal systems is illustrated in Table 7, Figure 34 and 35. The Table 7 illustrates FRR and FAR values for Iris, Finger and Palm. In the multimodal system, FRR and FAR are to low due to higher feature vector generation. In the Figure 34 FRR of multimodal system is minimum at the above the threshold value of 9. The finger print shows much lower value than

Figure 33. FRR, TSR and FAR values with threshold (IWT+LDWT+SF)

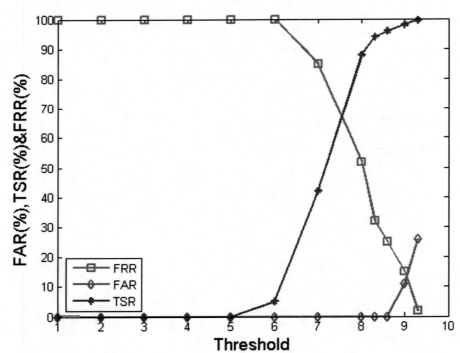

Table 7. Unimodal vs. multimodal (IWT+LDWT+SF)

Biometric System	%FRR	%FAR
Unimodal Iris(SF)	12	5
Unimodal Fingerprint (IWT)	9	0
Unimodal Palm-print (LDWT)	11	3
Multimodal(IWT+LDWT+SF)	1.4	0

Figure 34. FRR vs. threshold of uni and multi modal (IWT+LDWT+SF)

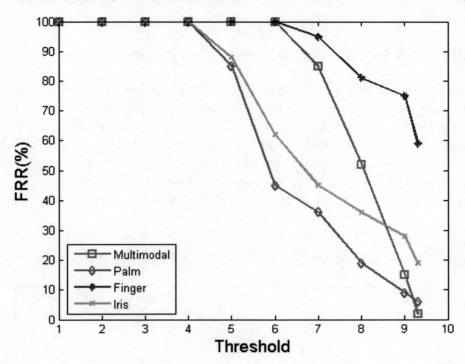

Figure 35. FAR vs. threshold of uni and multi modal (IWT+LDWT+SF)

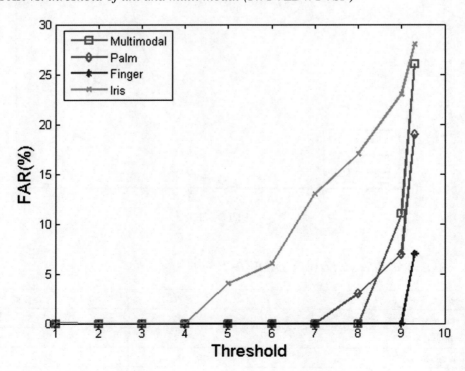

the higher threshold values due to integer conversion. The Figure 35 shows elongated FAR for IRIS from the threshold value of 4 to 9.

IWT+SMDWT+Neville's Multimodal Biometric System

Figure 36 shows the False Recognition Rate (FRR), Total Success Rate (TSR) and False Acceptance Rate (FAR) values for the proposed multi-modal biometric system using IWT, SMDWT and Neville's techniques. The graph records the Equal Error Rate (EER) is of 12 at the threshold value of around 9.1. The comparative FRR and FAR values for multi-modal system and unimodal systems is illustrated in Table 8, Figure 37 and 38. The Table 8 illustrates FRR and FAR values for Iris, Finger and Palm. In the multimodal system, FRR and FAR are to low due to higher feature vector generation. In the Figure 37 FRR of multimodal system is minimum at the above the threshold value of 9. The finger print shows

Figure 36. FRR, TSR and FAR values with threshold (IWT+SMDWT+Neville's)

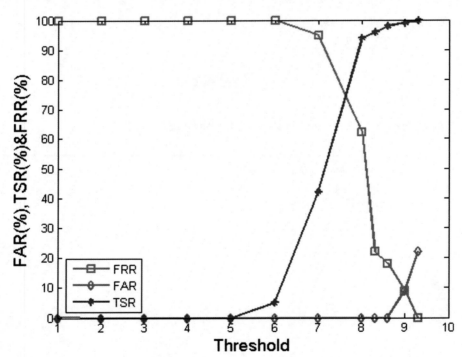

Table 8. Unimodal vs. multimodal (IWT+SMDWT+Neville's)

Biometric System	%FRR	%FAR
Unimodal Iris(Neville's)	12	5
Unimodal Fingerprint (IWT)	9	0
Unimodal Palm-print (SMDWT)	11	3
Multimodal(IWT+SMDWT+ Neville's)	1.4	0

Figure 37. FRR vs. threshold of uni and multi modal (IWT+ SMDWT+Neville's)

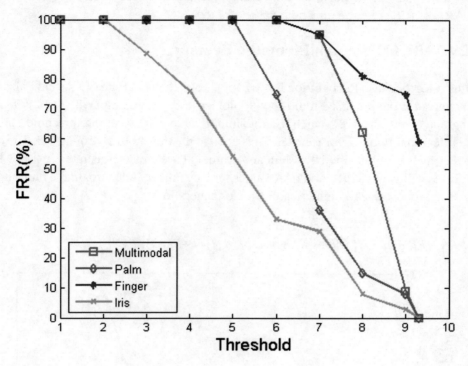

Figure 38. FAR vs. threshold of uni and multi modal (IWT+ SMDWT+Neville's)

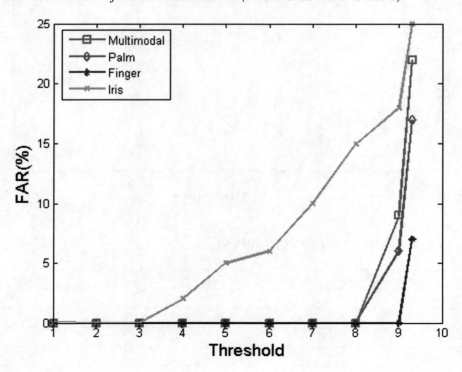

much lower value than the higher threshold values due to integer conversion. The Figure 38 shows elongated FAR for IRIS from the threshold value of 4 to 9.

IWT+SMDWT+SF Multimodal Biometric System

Figure 39 illustrates the False Recognition Rate (FRR), Total Success Rate (TSR) and False Acceptance Rate (FAR) values for the proposed multi-modal biometric system using IWT, SMDWT and SF techniques. The graph shows the TSR which has maximum value of100% at the threshold value 8 to 9. In the graph it is clear that Equal Error Rate (EER) is at 10 at the threshold of around 9.5. The comparative FRR and FAR values for multi-modal system and unimodal systems is illustrated in Table 9, Figure 40 and 41. The Table 9 illustrates FRR and FAR values for Iris, Finger and Palm. In the multimodal system, FRR and FAR are to low due to higher feature vector generation.

Figure 39. FRR, TSR and FAR values with threshold (IWT+SMDWT+SF)

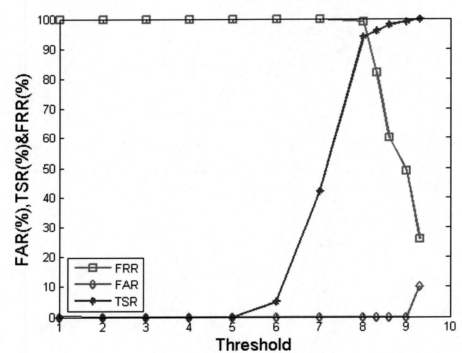

Table 9. Unimodal vs multimodal (IWT+SMDWT+SF)

Biometric System	%FRR	%FAR
Unimodal Iris(SF)	12	5
Unimodal Fingerprint (IWT)	9	0
Unimodal Palm-print (SMDWT)	11	3
Multimodal(IWT+SMDWT+ SF)	1.4	0

Figure 40. FRR vs. threshold of uni and multi modal (IWT+ SMDWT+SF)

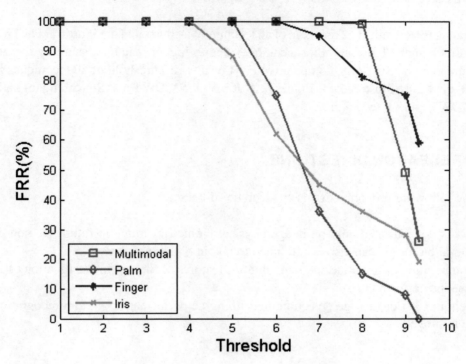

Figure 41. FAR vs. threshold of uni and multi modal (IWT+ SMDWT+SF)

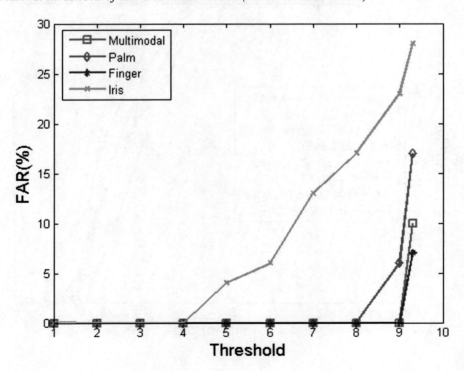

Comparative Results

The comparative FRR results vs Threshold of all techniques is illustrated in Figure 42. The IWT, SMDWT and SF records higher FRR than other techniques due to higher matching score by the generation of correct feature vectors. Similarly, comparative FAR results vs Threshold of all techniques is illustrated in Figure 43, the figure illustrates the higher FAR for IWT, SMDWT and SF techniques and lower FAR for OA, SMDWT and SF techniques.

FUTURE RESEARCH DIRECTIONS

In future, the following problems in this area can be addressed:

1. This work concentrated only on image physical biometrics traits; in future the non physical and behavioral biometric can also is combined to obtain higher uniqueness.
2. The combination of minutiae and non minutiae features of fingerprint verification can be tested to increase the performance.
3. By designing efficient edge detection algorithm, the performance of palm recognition technique can be improved.

Figure 42. Comparative FRR results

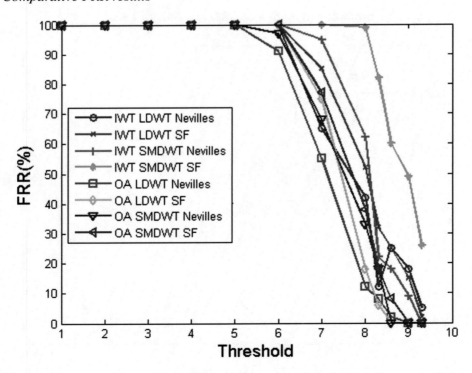

Figure 43. Comparative FAR results

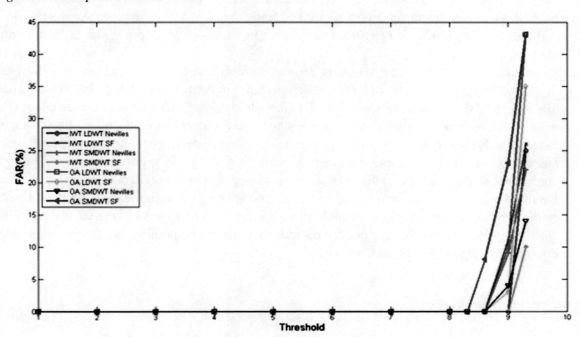

4. The iris recognition systems performance further increased by using other wavelet transforms.
5. The multimodal system can be tested using other fusion methods such as sensor level fusion or feature level fusion.

CONCLUSION

The chapter proposes efficient development for Multimodal Biometric systems, which takes advantage of three unimodal image biometric systems such as finger, palm and iris. These unimodal systems shows the reduced false recognition rate and more reliable in order to implement a fast authentication system.
In this chapter the following contributions were made:

- The Fingerprint recognition is designed and implemented, which shows the higher recognition rate and less resource utilization. The related work in this area has been discussed and listed the comparative results of the recognition rate. Two algorithms for feature extraction, over-lap add method and integer wavelet transform are introduced. The empirical results demonstrate the advantages of feature extraction algorithm. The IWT shows high recognition rate, low area and higher speed due to the non-reproduction of feature vectors. The over-lap add method generates large feature vectors and enquires large memory as compared to IWT with store previous vectors to add.
- The next unimodal system is palm recognition through Symmetric mask-based discrete wavelet transform and lifting scheme based DWT. These techniques were able to provide high recognition

rate and thus established its effectiveness in authentication process. The 2-D Symmetric mask-based discrete wavelet transform has performed better than 2-D Lifting discrete wavelet transform and former 2-D discrete wavelet transform. Also the proposed palm print system exhibits time efficiency.

- Biometric system through the iris image processing technique has been proposed as a third uni-modality. Two approaches for iris recognition through symmetric framelet and Neville's algorithm has been described. The symmetric framelet provides higher efficiency than other techniques due to its parallism and symetricity but the recognition rate is reduced as compared to Neville's technique. The Neville's technique creates large feature vectors compared with symmetric Framlets and utilizes lage area. Effective iris image segmentation technique has been proposed. Both, the algorithms have proved their effectiveness by providing high recognition rate.

- Finally the proposed multi-modal biometric system designed through iris, fingerprint and palm-print modules. Empirical study on multiple design configurations with respect to FAR, FRR and TSR parameter results was performed and compared by combining the different modalities through their feature extraction methods.

REFERENCES

Aguilar, G., Sanchez, G., Toscano, K., Nakano, M., & Perez, H. (2007). Multimodal biometric system using fingerprint. *Intellectuality Advancement System. International Conference on*, 145–150.

Alonso-Fernandez, F., Fierrez, J., Ramos, D., & Gonzalez-Rodriguez, J. (2010). Quality-based conditional processing in multibiometrics: Application to sensor interoperability. *IEEE Transactions on Systems, Man, and Cybernetics. Part A, Systems and Humans*, 40(6), 1168–1179. doi:10.1109/TSMCA.2010.2047498

Anil, K. (2004). An Introduction to Biometric Recognition. *IEEE Transactions on Circuits and Systems for Video Technology*, 14(1), 4–20. doi:10.1109/TCSVT.2003.818349

Besbes, F., Trichili, H., & Solaiman, B. (2008). Multimodal biometric system based on fingerprint identification and iris recognition. *Information and Communication Technologies: From Theory to Applications, 2008. ICTTA 2008. 3rd IEEE International Conference on*, 1–5. 10.1109/ICTTA.2008.4530129

Bhattacharjee, A., Saggi, M., Balasubramaniam, R., Tayal, A., & Kumar, A. (2009). Decison theory based multimodal biometric authentication system using wavelet transform. *Machine Learning and Cybernetics, 2009 IEEE International Conference on*, 4, 2336–2342. 10.1109/ICMLC.2009.5212174

Cheraghian, A., Faez, K., Dastmalchi, H., & Oskuie, F. B. (2011). An efficient multimodal face recognition method robust to pose variation. *Computers & Informatics (ISCI), 2011 IEEE Symposium on*, 431–435. 10.1109/ISCI.2011.5958954

Conti, V., Milici, G., Ribino, P., Sorbello, F., & Vitabile, S. (2007). Fuzzy fusion in multimodal biometric systems. *Springer International Conference on Knowledge-Based and Intelligent Information and Engineering Systems*, 108–115.

Gamassi, M., Piuri, V., Sana, D., & Scotti, F. (2004). A high-level optimum design methodology for multimodal biometric systems. *Computational Intelligence for Homeland Security and Personal Safety, 2004. CIHSPS 2004. Proceedings of the 2004 IEEE International Conference on*, 117–124. 10.1109/CIHSPS.2004.1360221

Gargouri, N., Ben Ayed, A. D. M., & Masmoudi, D. S. (2011). A new human identification based on fusion fingerprints and faces biometrics using lbp and gwn descriptors. Systems, Signals and Devices (SSD), 2011 8th International Multi-Conference on, 1–7.

George, A. (2008). Multi-modal biometrics human verification using LDA and DFB. *International Journal of Biometrics and Bioinformatics, 2*(4), 1–10.

Hanmandlu, M., Kumar, A., Madasu, V. K., & Yarlagadda, P. (2008). Fusion of hand based biometrics using particle swarm optimization. *Information Technology: New Generations, 2008. ITNG 2008. Fifth IEEE International Conference on*, 783–788. 10.1109/ITNG.2008.252

Hariprasath, S., & Prabakar, T. N. (2012). Multimodal biometric recognition using iris feature extraction and palmprint features. *Advances in Engineering, Scienceand Management (ICAESM), 2012 International Conference on*, 174–179.

Heenaye, M., & Khan, M. (2012). A multimodal hand vein biometric based on score level fusion. *Procedia Engineering, 41*, 897–903. doi:10.1016/j.proeng.2012.07.260

Jahanbin, S., Choi, H., & Bovik, A. C. (2011). Passive multimodal 2-d+ 3-d face recognition using gabor features and landmark distances. *IEEE Transactions on Information Forensics and Security, 6*(4), 1287–1304. doi:10.1109/TIFS.2011.2162585

Jain, A., Nandakumar, K., & Ross, A. (2005). Score normalization in multimodal biometric systems. *Pattern Recognition, 38*(12), 2270–2285. doi:10.1016/j.patcog.2005.01.012

Kartik, P., Vara Prasad, R. V. S. S., & Mahadeva Prasanna, S. R. (2008). Noise robust multimodal biometric person authentication system using face, speech and signature features. *India Conference, 2008. INDICON 2008. Annual IEEE, 1*, 23–27. 10.1109/INDCON.2008.4768795

Kisku, D. R., Rattani, A., Gupta, P., & Sing, J. K. (2009). Biometric sensor image fusion for identity verification: A case study with wavelet-based fusion rules graph matching. *Technologies for Homeland Security, 2009. HST'09. IEEE Conference on*, 433–439. 10.1109/THS.2009.5168069

Krishneswari, K., & Arumugam, A. (2013). An improved genetic optimized neural network of multimodal biometrics. *Journal of Scientific and Industrial Research, 73*(1), 23–30.

Kumar, A., Hanmandlu, M., & Vasikarla, S. (2012). Rank level integration of face based biometrics. *Information Technology: New Generations (ITNG), 2012 Ninth IEEE International Conference on*, 36–4. 10.1109/ITNG.2012.14

Kumar, A., & Kwong, C. (2013). Towards contactless, low-cost and accurate 3-D fingerprint identification. *Proceedings of the IEEE Conference on ComputerVision and Pattern Recognition*, 3438–3443. 10.1109/CVPR.2013.441

Mahesh, P. K., & Shanmukha Swamy, M. N. (2010). A biometric identification system based on the fusion of palmprint and speech signal. *Signal and Image Processing (ICSIP), 2010 IEEE International Conference on*, 186–190. 10.1109/ICSIP.2010.5697466

Monwar, M. M., & Gavrilova, M. L. (2009). Multimodal biometric system using rank-level fusion approach. *IEEE Transactions on Systems, Man, and Cybernetics. Part B, Cybernetics*, *39*(4), 867–878. doi:10.1109/TSMCB.2008.2009071 PMID:19336340

Murakami, T., & Takahashi, K. (2011). Fast and accurate biometric identification using score level indexing and fusion. *Biometrics (IJCB), 2011 IEEE International Joint Conference on*, 1–8. 10.1109/IJCB.2011.6117591

Panchal & Singh. (2013). Multimodal biometric system. *International Journal of Advanced Research in Computer Science and Software Engineering*, *3*(5), 1360–1363.

Pour Yazdanpanah, A., Faez, K., & Amirfattahi, R. (2010). Multimodal biometric system using face, ear and gait biometrics. *Information SciencesSignal Processing and their Applications (ISSPA), 2010 10th IEEE International Conference on*, 251–254. 10.1109/ISSPA.2010.5605477

Ribaric, S., & Fratric, I. (2006). Experimental evaluation of matching-score normalization techniques on different multimodal biometric systems. *Electrotechnical Conference, 2006. MELECON 2006. IEEE Mediterranean*, 498–501. 10.1109/MELCON.2006.1653147

Saferstein, R. (2007). *An Introduction to Forensic Science*. Pearson Education.

Shukla & Mishra. (2010). A hybrid model of multimodal biometrics system using fingerprint and face as traits. *IJCSES*, *1*(2).

Subbarayudu, V. C., & Prasad, M. V. N. K. (2008). Multimodal biometric system. *Emerging Trends in Engineering and Technology-2008 (ICETET '08)IEEE. International conference on*, 635–640. 10.1109/ICETET.2008.93

Wu, X., Zhang, D., & Wang, K. (2006). Palm line extraction and matching for personal authentication. *IEEE Transactions on Systems, Man, and Cybernetics. Part A, Systems and Humans*, *36*(5), 978–987. doi:10.1109/TSMCA.2006.871797

Xu, X.-N., Mu, Z.-C., & Yuan, L. (2007). Feature-level fusion method based on KFDA for multimodal recognition fusing ear and profile face. *Wavelet Analysis and Pattern Recognition, 2007. ICWAPR'07. International Conference on*, *3*, 1306–1310.

Yang, F., & Baofeng, M. A. (2007). Two models multimodal biometric fusion based on fingerprint, palm-print and hand-geometry. *Bioinformatics and Biomedical Engineering (ICBBE), Wuhan. 1st International Conference on*, 498–501. doi:10.1109/ICIAS.2007.4658364

Yang, F., & Ma, B. (2007). A new mixed-mode biometrics informationvfusion based-on fingerprint, hand-geometry and palmprint. *Image and Graphics, 2007. ICIG 2007. Fourth IEEE International Conference on*, 689–693.

Yuko, A., Nakanishi, J., & JeffreyWestern, B. (2007). Advancing the state of-the-art in transportation security identification and verification technologies: Biometric and multibiometric systems. In *Intelligent Transportation Systems Conference, 2007. ITSC 2007.* IEEE.

Zheng, Y., & Elmaghraby, A. (2011). A brief survey on multispectral face recognition and multimodal score fusion. *Signal Processing and Information Technology (ISSPIT), 2011 IEEE International Symposium on*, 543–550. 10.1109/ISSPIT.2011.6151622

Chapter 7

Evaluation of Ischemic Stroke Region From CT/MR Images Using Hybrid Image Processing Techniques

Rajinikanth V.
St. Joseph's College of Engineering, India

Suresh Chandra Satapathy
Kalinga Institute of Industrial Technology (Deemed), India

Nilanjan Dey
Techno India College of Technology, India

Hong Lin
University of Houston – Downtown, USA

ABSTRACT

An ischemic stroke (IS) naturally originates with rapid onset neurological shortfall, which can be verified by analyzing the internal regions of brain. Computed tomography (CT) and magnetic resonance image (MRI) are the commonly used non-invasive medical examination techniques used to record the brain abnormalities for clinical study. In order to have a pre-opinion regarding the brain abnormality in clinical level, it is essential to use a suitable image processing tool to appraise the digital CT/MR images. In this chapter, a hybrid image processing technique based on the social group optimization assisted Tsallis entropy and watershed segmentation (WS) is proposed to examine ischemic stroke region from digital CT/MR images. For the experimental study, the digital CT/MRI datasets like Radiopedia, BRATS-2013, and ISLES-2015 are considered. Experimental result of this study confirms that, proposed hybrid approach offers superior results on the considered image datasets.

DOI: 10.4018/978-1-5225-5246-8.ch007

INTRODUCTION

Brain is the most important internal organ, responsible to control the entire operation in human body. The major illness in the brain includes the stroke and the tumor. In order to plan for the proper treatment process, these sickness to be evaluated using an appropriate clinical level diagnose procedures. During the brain condition evaluation procedure a dedicated hardware systems are adopted to record the vital brain information based on the brain signals and brain images. From previous studies, it can be noted that, imaging procedures will provide clear information regarding the brain abnormality compared with the signal assisted evaluation (Palani & Parvathavarthini, 2017). The present chapter considers the evaluation of the brain images recorded using the Computed Tomography (CT) and Magnetic Resonance Imaging (MRI) approaches.

The brain strokes are the destructive illness in human community with enlarged morbidity and mortality rates. The current declaration by the World Stroke Organization (WSO) authenticates that; brain stroke is the second primary cause for disability in human community. The recent yearly statement of WSO also indicates that, each year 17 million persons suffer due to stroke worldwide, among them approximately 6 million die due to severe stroke and remaining 5 million persons experience everlasting disability. Due to its importance, brain stroke examination emerged as the significant research domain among the researchers.

Usually, a brain stroke is caused because of neurological deficit and also the interruption of blood supply due to malfunction in brain blood vessels which will lessen the oxygen and the nutrient supply to the brain tissue (Palani et al., 2016). In order to plan for the treatment process, it is essential to know the reason and location of the stroke. After getting the cause and region of stroke, the doctors can initiate and execute feasible treatment procedure to heal the patient.

An Ischemic Stroke (IS) naturally originates with rapid onset neurological shortfall, which can be verified by analyzing the internal regions of brain. CT and MRI are the commonly used non-invasive medical examination techniques widely considered to record the brain abnormality during the clinical study. In order to identify the disease severity and also to plan for the further treatment process, it is essential to analyze the brain images with the help of medical experts. In recent years, most of the imaging centers have the capability to record digital CT/MR images of the brain. In order to have a pre-opinion regarding the brain abnormality in clinical level, it is essential to use a suitable image processing tool to appraise the digital CT/MRI.

A considerable number of image processing approaches are adopted by the researchers to examine the CT and MRI (Bauer et al., 2013; Maksoud et al., 2015). In this chapter, a hybrid approach based on the Social Group Optimization (SGO) assisted Tsallis entropy function and Watershed (WS) algorithm is proposed to examine the considered test images. In which, the SGO + Tsallis entropy technique is chosen as the pre-processing practice, consider to enhance the brain image and the watershed segmentation approach is adopted as the post-processing procedure to extract the stroke lesion. In this chapter, a comparative examination is presented among Watershed (WS) algorithm, Active Contour (AC) segmentation and Markov Random Field (MRF) procedures existing in the literature (Rajinikanth et al., 2017). The experimental work is implemented using the Matlab software and the result of this study confirms that, WS based segmentation helps to achieve better values of image similarity and statistical measures compared with the AC and MRF based approaches.

The main motivation behind the proposed hybrid image processing approach is to develop a soft-computing assisted image processing tool to examine both the CT/MRI images with improved accuracy. In real time image processing applications, it is necessary to have a unique image processing tool; which can assist the doctors to examine the brain images recorded with CT and MRI.

BACKGROUND

Due to its significance, recently a number of semi-automated and automated procedures are developed and implemented by the researchers to locate and localise the brain stroke region. Usinskas and Gleizniene (2006) proposed a six-stage computer based examination procedure to detect the centre of Ischemic Stroke Lesion (ISL) using two dimensional Computed Tomography (CT) brain images. Kabir et al. (2007) proposed an approach to detect ISL using Magnetic Resonance Imaging (MRI) modalities, such as T2, Flair, and Diffusion-Weighted (DW) images. In the above said work, the segmentation of ISL is achieved using the Expectation Maximization (EM) algorithm and Markov Random Field (MRF). Tang et al. (2011) developed an automated tool based on Circular Adaptive Region of Interest (CARI) and obtained better detection of ISL with CT images. Rajini and Bhavani (2013) implemented k-means clustering technique to segment the ISL from CT brain images and also implemented an automated classification system to classify the considered image dataset based on the Gray Level Co-occurrence Matrix (GLCM) features. Their work also presented a detailed analysis with the well known classifiers and they reported an average classification accuracy of 95% on the CT brain dataset. Tyan et al. (2014) also developed an automated to detect the ISL region using the brain CT images. Recently, Yahiaoui and Bessaid (2016) discussed fuzzy C means based segmentation of ISL from CT brain images.

Maier et al. (2015) developed an image analysing technique based on extra tree forests in order to segment the sub-acute ischemic stroke lesion from MRI and attained a dice coefficient of 65% . *Mitra et al.* (2014) implemented a novel procedure to segment stroke lesion form MRI based on the Bayesian-MRF using the image modalities, such as Flair, T1 weighted and T2 weighted; and finally employed the random forest classifier to segregate the considered test images. The result of their study confirms that, Flair modality registered MRI offered better result with low False Positive Rate (FPR) compared with T1 weighted and T2 weighted MRI. The work by Kanchana and Menaka (2015) shows the existing computer assisted detection of ISL using the CT and MRI. This review also provides a detailed comparative analysis on the existing classifier units to segregate the CT and MRI based on the stroke volume. The recent work by Maier et al. (2015) proposes a study with nine well known classifier units to segregate the brain MRI dataset based on the ISL volume. Their work also reports that, due to the image abnormalities, such as the high, low, and hyper intensities inside the lesion area will affect the segmentation as well as the classification accuracies. The above work also provides the Ischemic Stroke Lesion Segmentation (ISLES 2015) challenge MRI dataset recently published in (Maier et al., 2017). From the above works, it can be observed that, a considerable number of image processing procedures are already implemented by the researchers to segment the stroke region from brain CT/MRI using traditional image processing techniques.

The recent literature confirms the involvement of heuristic algorithm based approaches to investigate the medical signals (Thanaraj et al., 2016) and images (Kamalanand & Jawahar, 2012; 2015; Balan et al., 2016; Lakshmi et al., 2016; Mostafa et al., 2017) to assess the severity of diseases. These works also confirms that, heuristic algorithm assisted image processing approach offers better accuracy compared with the classical approaches considered in early days. Hence, in the proposed work, a two-stage procedure combining the multi-level thresholding and segmentation is proposed to examine the abnormalities in brain CT/MRI. The initial pre-processing stage considers the Social Group Optimization assisted Tsalli's multi-level thresholding to enhance the abnormality by grouping the similar pixel values of the image based on a chosen threshold level. In the post-processing stage, a segmentation approach is considered to mine the abnormal region from the pre-processed brain images. In this study, a detailed comparative analysis also presented between well known segmentation procedures, such as WS, AC and MRF procedures. The performance of the considered segmentation approaches are analysed by computing the image similarity measures (Chaddad & Tanougast, 2016; Rajinikanth et al, 2017) and statistical measures (Lu et al., 2004; Moghaddam & Cheriet, 2010) with the help of a relative analysis with the Ground Truth (GT) image offered by the expert member.

MAIN FOCUS OF THIS CHAPTER

Recently, a significant amount of image examination techniques are proposed and implemented by the researchers to investigate the medical image datasets. The recent works by Palani et al. (2016) and Rajinikanth et al. (2017) reported that, a hybrid image processing approach will help to achieve better result compared with solitary technique. Hence, in this work, a hybrid image processing procedure by integrating the multi-level thresholding and the segmentation is proposed to examine the CT/MRI brain datasets. In which the multi-level thresholding will act as the pre-processing stage and the segmentation procedure will act as the post-processing stage. The details of the procedures considered in this chapter are presented below.

Social Group Optimization Algorithm

In recent years, a considerable number of heuristic algorithms are proposed in the literature to solve a variety of engineering optimization problems. Each algorithm has its own merits and demerits. Normally, a heuristic algorithm for a chosen problem can be considered based on: i) Number of initial algorithms to be assigned, ii) Complexity of the problem, iii) Optimization accuracy and iv) Run time of the algorithm. In this work, a recent heuristic approach known as the Social Group Optimization (SGO) is considered.

SGO is a newly invented heuristic approach by Satapathy and Naik (2016). Compared to other heuristic algorithms, the number of initial algorithm parameters to be assigned in SGO is small and the SGO is also confirmed its efficiency in obtaining the better optimal values compared with the recent heuristic algorithms considered in the work of Satapathy and Naik (2016). SGO is shaped by mimicking the performance in human group. SGO contain two main phases, namely i) improving phase to coordinate the positions of people based on the objective function and ii) acquiring phase that allows the agents to discover the best potential solution based on the chosen problem.

The mathematical model of SGO can be defined as:

$$Gbest_j = max \{ f(X_i) \, for \, i = 1, 2, \ldots N \} \tag{1}$$

where X_i is the initial knowledge of people in a group, $i = 1, 2, 3, \ldots, N$ indicate whole people in a group, and f_j is the fitness value.

The improving phase is used to renew the location of every person as in Eqn. (2):

$$Xnew_{i,j} = c * Xold_{i,j} + R * (Gbest_j - Xold_{i,j}) \tag{2}$$

where *Xnew* is the updated position, *Xold* is the early position, *Gbest* denotes universal top location, *R* is an arbitrary numeral [0,1] and *c* represents the self-introspection parameter [0,1]. The *c* is selected as 0.2 (Naik et al., 2016).

During the acquiring phase, the agents will find the global solution based on knowledge updating procedure as depicted in Eqn. (3).

$$Xnew_{i,j} = Xold_{i,j} + R_a * (X_{i,j} - X_{r,j}) + R_b * (Gbest_j - X_{i,j}) \tag{3}$$

where R_a and R_b are random numbers [0,1] and $X_{r,j}$ is the arbitrarily selected location of a person in group.

In this chapter, SGO algorithm is considered to choose the optimal threshold based on the Tsallis entropy.

The initial algorithm parameters are assigned as follows; number of people in human group is chosen as 25, the self-introspection parameter is chosen as 0.2, number of iteration is set to 2500 and the stopping criterion for the SGO search is allocated as the maximal Tsallis function '*f(T)*'.

Multi-Level Thresholding Using Tsallis Entropy

Thresholding procedure is normally considered to group identical pixels in an image based on user's requirement (Rajinikanth et al., 2014; Raja et al., 2014; Rajinikanth & Couceiro, 2015; Tuba, 2014). Recently, a multi-level thresholding scheme is considered to cluster the digital brain MR images into the background, normal brain region, and the tumor section (Palani et al., 2016, Rajinikanth et al., 2017). The multi-level thresholding will enhance the abnormality in brain CT/MRI, which can be mined by choosing a suitable segmentation procedure.

Normally, entropy is related with the measure of chaos within a system. Shannon primarily considered the entropy to compute the uncertainty regarding the information content of the system (Bhandari et al., 2015). Shannon also assured that, when a physical system is separated as two statistically free subsystems *A* and *B*, then the entropy value can be expressed as:

$$S(A + B) = S(A) + S(B) \tag{4}$$

Based on Shannon's theory, a non-extensive entropy concept was proposed by Tsallis and defined as:

$$S_q = \frac{1 - \sum_{i=1}^{T} (p_i)^q}{q - 1} \tag{5}$$

where, *T* is the system potentials and *q* is the entropic index (Agrawal et al., 2013; Sathya and Kayalvizhi, 2010).

Eq. (5) will meet the Shannon's entropy when $q \to 1$.

The entropy value can be expressed with a pseudo additivity rule as:

$$S_q(A + B) = S_q(A) + S_q(B) + (1 - q).S_q(A).S_q(B) \tag{6}$$

Tsallis entropy can be considered to find the optimal thresholds of an image. Consider a given image with L gray levels in the range $\{0, 1, ..., L\text{-}1\}$, with probability distributions $p_i = p_0, p_1, ..., p_{L\text{-}1}$.

Tsallis multi-level thresholding can then be expressed as:

$$f(T) = [T_1, T_2, ..., T_k] = argmax \left[S_q^A(T) + S_q^B(T) + ... + S_q^K(T) + (1 - q).S_q^A(T).S_q^B(T)...S_q^K(T) \right] \tag{7}$$

where

$$S_q^A(T) = \frac{1 - \sum_{i=0}^{t_1-1} \left(\frac{Pi}{P^A} \right)^q}{q - 1}, \quad P^A = \sum_{i=0}^{t_1-1} Pi$$

$$S_q^B(T) = \frac{1 - \sum_{i=t_1}^{t_2-1} \left(\frac{Pi}{P^B} \right)^q}{q - 1}, \quad P^B = \sum_{i=t_1}^{t_2-1} Pi$$

$$S_q^K(T) = \frac{1 - \sum_{i=t_k}^{L-1} \left(\frac{Pi}{P^K} \right)^q}{q - 1}, \quad P^K = \sum_{i=t_k}^{L_2-1} Pi$$

are subject to the following constraints:

$$\left| P^A + P^B \right| - 1 < S < 1 - \left| P^A - P^B \right|$$

$$\left| P^B + P^C \right| - 1 < S < 1 - \left| P^B - P^C \right| \tag{8}$$

$$\left| P^K + P^{L-1} \right| - 1 < S < 1 - \left| P^K - P^{L-1} \right|$$

During the multi-level thresholding process, the aim is to find the optimal threshold value T which maximizes the objective function $f(T)$. In the proposed work, the threshold value is chosen as $T = 2, 3$, and 4, thus the required probability values are P^A, P^B, P^C and P^D. In this work, the maximization of function $f(T)$, which deals with the segmentation of a given image, is carried using the heuristic algorithm. Finding the optimal threshold based on the manually selected threshold is a time consuming process, Hence, in this work, Social Group Optimization (SGO) algorithm is considered to discover the optimal thresholds based on the chosen T value. The thresholding operation enhances the test image by grouping the similar pixel values as described by Eqn. (8).

Image Quality Measures

The multi-thresholding (pre-processing) work is the key step in the proposed image processing tool. Hence, the final outcome of the segmentation process mainly depends on the quality of the thresholded image. The multi-thresholding result is assessed using well known image quality measures, such as the Root Mean Squared Error (RMSE), Normalized Absolute Error (NAE), Peak Signal to Noise Ratio (PSNR), Structural Similarity Index Matrix (SSIM), Normalized Cross Correlation (NCC) and Structural Content (SC) (Grgic et al., 2004; Wang et al., 2004).

Skull Stripping

Skull stripping is the initial step in the brain image segmentation process. Skull stripping is essential to eliminate the skull and the background area from MRI for quantitative analysis. Skull stripping is normally performed using an image filter which separated the skull and the rest of the image sections by masking the pixels having similar intensity levels. In MR image, generally the skull/bone will have the maximum threshold value (threshold > 200) compared to other brain regions. Hence, the image filter is used to separate the brain regions based on a chosen threshold value. Then by employing the solidity property, the skull is stripped from the brain MRI (Chaddad and Tanougast, 2016).

Segmentation

Watershed Algorithm

In this work, marker controlled watershed algorithm discussed in (Roerdink & Meijster, 2001) is considered to mine the enhanced tumor volume. This approach is the combination of the Sobel edge detection algorithm, marker controlled morphological operation and extraction. A detailed mathematical description of the watershed transform considered in this paper can be found in (Shanthakumar & Kumar, 2015).

Active Contour Segmentation

This section presents the details of Active Contour Segmentation (ACS) proposed in (Bresson et al., 2007; Houhou et al., 2009) to extract the abnormal region from pre-processed brain image. ACS has three essential steps such as, boundary detection, initial active contour, and final active contour which offer minimized energy. In this work, variable snake model is considered to track similar pixel groups existing in pre-processed image based on energy minimization concept (Qian et al., 2013; Chack & Sharma, 2015).

The energy function of the snake can be denoted as;

$$\frac{\min}{C} \left\{ \mathrm{E}_{\mathrm{GAC}}(\mathrm{C}) = \int_0^{\mathrm{L(C)}} \mathrm{g}(\left| \nabla \mathrm{I}_0 \mathrm{C}(\mathrm{s})) \right| \mathrm{ds} \right\} \qquad (9)$$

where ds is the Euclidean component of length and L(C) is the length of the curve C which satisfies $\mathrm{L(C)} = \int_0^{\mathrm{L(C)}} \mathrm{ds}$. The parameter g is an edge indicator, which will disappear based on the object boundary defined as;

$$\mathrm{g}(\left| \nabla \mathrm{I}_0 \right|) = \frac{1}{1 + \beta \left| \nabla \mathrm{I}_0 \right|^2} \qquad (10)$$

where I_0 represents original image and β is an arbitrary constant. The energy value rapidly decreases based on the edge value, based on gradient descent criterion.

This procedure is mathematically represented as;

$$\partial_t C = (kg - \left\langle \nabla_g, \mathrm{N} \right\rangle) \mathrm{N} \qquad (11)$$

where $\partial_t C = \partial C / \partial t$ represents the deformation in the snake model, t is the iteration time, and k, N are the curvature and normal for the snake 'C'. In this procedure, the snake silhouette is continuously corrected till minimal value of the energy; EGAC is achieved (Liu et al., 2014; Zhou et al., 2016).

Markov Random Field

Markov Random Field - Expectation Maximization (MRF-EM) is a widely considered methodology for gray scale image segmentation problems.

The MRF-EM can be expressed as follows;

Consider a gray scale test image $I = \{y(m.n) \mid 0 \leq y \leq L - 1$. Where y represents the intensity of the image at the pixel location (m, n) and L represents the number of threshold levels. During the segmentation process, MRF will approximate the formation of each pixel by mapping into a group of random labels defined as; $X = \{x_1, ... x_N) \mid x_i \in 1$. In this paper, number of labels is assigned as two, three, and four (since, during the multi-thresholding, T value is chosen as 2, 3, and 4). Hence, the MRF based segmentation will provide the labels such as white matter, gray matter and tumor based on the chosen threshold levels. More details regarding the MRF based brain image segmentation are available in (Zhang et al., 2001; Palani et al., 2016).

Implementation of MRF algorithm is defined below:

Step 1: Set the number of labels (l) based on number of threshold values (T)
Step 2: Formation of cluster classes based on the chosen l

$$k_1 = \{y(m.n) = x_1 \mid 0 \leq y \leq t_1$$

$$k_2 = \{y(m.n) = x_2 \mid t_1 \leq y \leq t_2$$

$$k_3 = \{y(m.n) = x_3 \mid t_2 \leq y \leq L - 1$$

Step 3: Determine the initial parameter set $\Theta^{(0)_1^l}$ and likelihood probability function $p^{(0)}(f_1 \mid x_1)$.

Step 4: Update the MRF model $x^{(t)}$ such that, the energy function U is minimised.

$$X^* = \arg\min_x \left\{ \sum_i \left[\frac{(y_i - \mu_{x_i})^2}{2\sigma^2_{x_i}} \ln \sigma_{x_i} \right] + \sum_{N_i} V_c(x) \right\} \tag{12}$$

where, N_i is a four pixel neighborhood and V_c is the clique potential.

Step 5: Execute the Expectation-Maximization algorithm to update the parameter set $\Theta^{(i)}$ constantly till the log likelihood of $p^{(t)}(f \mid x)$ is maximized.

Step 6: Display the labels such as white matter, gray matter and tumor.

Evaluation of MRI With Ground Truth

The major aim of this chapter is to extract the stroke/tumor region from the 2D brain MRI and to compute the features of stroke/tumor region for further analysis. In this paper, two types of data, such as brain MRI with and without the ground truth are considered. For both the cases, the tumor mass is analysed by extracting the key geometric features, such as spread area, major axis length, minor axis length, diameter, solidity and extent. For the image with the ground truth, the parameters, such as Jaccard index, Dice coefficient, False Positive Rate (FPR), and False Negative Rate (FNR) are computed (Chaddad and Tanougast, 2016 ; Rajinikanth et al., 2017). The mathematical expression is presented below;

The mathematical expression is presented below;

$$JSC(I_{gt}, \ I_t) = I_{gt} \cap I_t / I_{gt} \cup I_t \tag{13}$$

$$DSC(I_{gt}, \ I_t) = 2\left(I_{gt} \cap I_t\right) / \left|I_{gt}\right| \cup \left|I_t\right| \tag{14}$$

$$FPR(I_{gt}, \ I_t) = \left(I_{gt} / I_t\right) / \left(I_{gt} \cup I_t\right) \tag{15}$$

$$FNR(I_{gt}, \ I_t) = \left(I_t / I_{gt}\right) / \left(I_{gt} \cup I_t\right) \tag{16}$$

where, I_{gt} represents the GT and I_t symbolize mined region.

Further, the image statistical measures, such as sensitivity, specificity, accuracy, precision, Balanced Classification Rate (BCR), and Balanced Error Rate (BER) are also computed (Lu et al., 2004; Moghaddam, & Cheriet, 2010).

Mathematical expression for these parameters are given below:

$$Sensitvity = T_P / (T_P + F_N) \tag{17}$$

$$Specificity = T_N / (T_N + F_P) \tag{18}$$

$$Accuracy = (T_P + T_N) / (T_P + T_N + F_P + F_N) \tag{19}$$

$$Precision = T_P / (T_P + F_P) \tag{20}$$

$$BCR = 1/2 \ (T_P / (T_P + F_N) + T_N / (T_N + F_P)) \tag{21}$$

$$BER = 1 - BCR \tag{22}$$

where, I_{GT} is ground truth, I_S is mined region, T_N, T_P, F_N and F_P signifies true negative, true positive, false negative and false positive; correspondingly.

SOLUTIONS AND RECOMMENDATIONS

The proposed approach considers various classes of dataset obtained from Radiopaedia, BRATS 2013 and ISLES 2015 challenge. Initial investigation is implemented using haemorrhagic cerebral infarction images recorded with Diffused Weight (DW) modality and sub-acute middle cerebral artery infarct images recorded using the CT. Initially these test images are down scaled to 256 x 256 sizes from its original size of 630 x 630. Later the MRI of the BRATS 2013 and ISLES 2015 challenge is considered for investigation. These datasets consist of three-dimensional (3D) brain MRI recorded using various modalities. The 2D slices is then extracted using the ITK-SNAP version 3.6.0 (Yushkevich et al., 2006, ITK-SNAP), and the extracted image is then up scaled to 256 x 256 size from its original size of 77 x 77. Similar procedure is followed for the ground truth image existing in the database. The experimental work is implemented using a workstation of AMD C70 Dual Core 1 GHz CPU with 4 GB of RAM and equipped with Matlab software.

Figure 1 depicts the various stages existing in the proposed approach from the 3D input image to the examined abnormal brain region. Initially, the 3D images are sliced to attain 2D images which further considered for the pre-processing and post-processing tasks. Initially, after getting the result of the pre-processing process, the image quality measures are computed using the existing approaches and also the superiority of the post-processed image is examined using the similarity measures.

The proposed hybrid image evaluation procedure is initially tested on the Radiopaedia image database, in which the brain images are associated with the skull section. Before the assessment, skull region is eliminated using the skull stripping algorithm formerly discussed in this chapter. After stripping the skull, the pre-processing procedure (SGO + Tsallis multi-level thresholding) is applied on this image in order to enhance the abnormal region. Results obtained with the proposed pre-processing approach on the Radiopaedia dataset is shown in Figure 2. Here, Figure 2 (a) and (b) denotes the original test image and its skull stripped version. Figure 2 (c), (d) and (e) presents the outcomes of bi-level, tri-level and four-level respectively. From these images, it can be noted that, tri-level offers better image visibility compared with other threshold values.

Figure 2 presents the initial result obtained with the sample images (axial view) of the DW modality based MRI of Radiopaedia. Figure 2 (a) and (b) depicts the chosen test image and the skull stripped images. Fig. 2 (c), (d), and (e) represents the thresholded image for T = 2, 3, and 4 respectively. From this image, it can be noted that, the MRI offers approximately similar result for threshold levels T = 2, 3, and 4. But, the CT will provide better result only when T=4. For lower threshold images, it offers noisy images, which may fail to work during the post-processing operation. After implementing the pre-processing procedure, it is necessary to assess its performance using the well-known image similarity measures as depicted in Table 1. This table confirms that, irrespective of the threshold value, proposed approach is efficient in offering better values of the PSNR and SSIM for all the cases. Later than the thresholding process, the abnormal section of the brain image is then extracted using the marker controlled watershed algorithm with a chosen marker value of 12 based on a trial and error approach.

Figure 3 shows the various operations involved in the post-processing operation. Figure 3 (a) shows the Sobel based edge detection procedure, Figure 3 (b), (c), and (d) presents the result of the watershed procedure, morphological operation and the segmented section. From these results, is it confirmed that,

Figure 1. Block diagram of the proposed hybrid approach

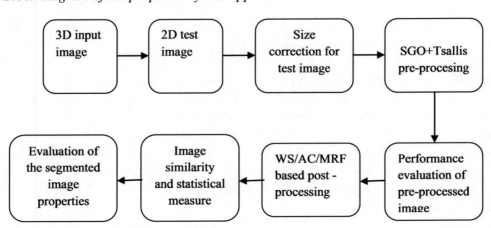

Figure 2. Results obtained with the proposed pre-processing approach on the Radiopaedia dataset. a. Test image, b. Skull stripped test image, c. Outcome of bi-level thresholding, d. Outcome of tri-level thresholding, e. Outcome of four-level thresholding

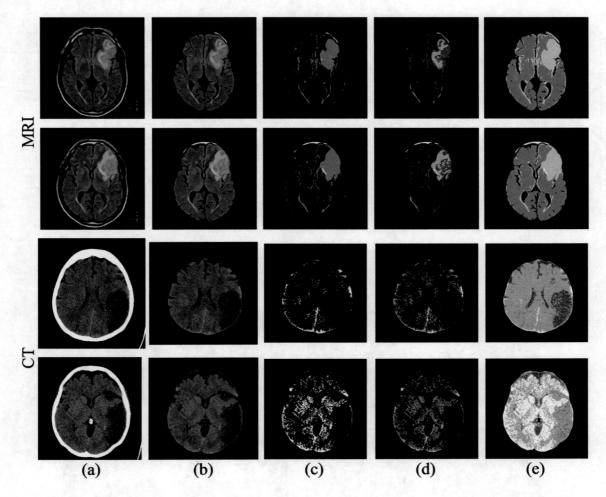

(a) (b) (c) (d) (e)

the proposed approach offers better result for the DW modality and CT brain images. Similar segmentation procedure is executed on the other views, such as coronal view and the sagittal view of the brain CT images, and the corresponding outcomes are shown in Figure 4. These results verify that, proposed approach is very efficient in extracting the abnormal sections from the CT brain images.

This approach is also tested on the Radiopaedia dataset recorded using T1, T2 and Flair modalities. These images are associated with the skull section and in order to have better assessment, skull stripping is carried before the pre-processing operation. Figure 5 shows the details of results obtained with the T1 sample image. Initially, the pre-processing is implemented based on the SGO + Tsallis multi-thresholding. Next stage involves in extraction of the infected section from the test image. The post processing is initially implemented using the watershed approach as discussed earlier. Later, other segmentation approaches like the Active Contour (AC) and the Otsu's + Markov Random Field approach discussed by Palani et al. (2016) is applied to extract the abnormal brain region.

Table 1. Image quality measures obtained for the Radiopaedia CT/MRI images

T	Test image	RMSE	PSNR	NCC	AD	SC	NAE	SSIM
2	MRI1	41.6071	15.7474	0.3770	20.6265	2.7006	0.7507	0.7264
	MRI2	48.6681	14.3859	0.2987	23.5117	3.1725	0.8225	0.7038
	CT1	53.0269	13.6409	0.3782	23.2136	1.2851	0.9982	0.6836
	CT2	61.4374	12.3622	0.8178	12.7179	0.5563	1.0579	0.6986
3	MRI1	41.4664	15.7769	0.3470	21.4477	3.2661	0.7644	0.7432
	MRI2	48.4582	14.4235	0.2745	24.3329	3.8368	0.8225	0.7538
	CT1	41.6981	15.7285	0.5470	18.1954	1.3777	0.7595	0.7366
	CT2	41.3246	15.8066	0.6484	16.9052	1.2158	0.6719	0.7417
4	MRI1	29.0521	18.8672	1.4980	15.6255	0.4354	0.5475	0.8163
	MRI2	37.0949	16.7445	1.2690	12.7402	0.5115	0.5864	0.7953
	CT1	51.0261	13.9750	1.9124	30.9142	0.2652	0.9779	0.7764
	CT2	77.9208	10.2977	2.3035	49.6459	0.1826	1.3939	0.7805

Figure 3. Segmentation results using watershed algorithm. a. Edge detection, b. Watershed, c. Morphological operation, d. Segmented region

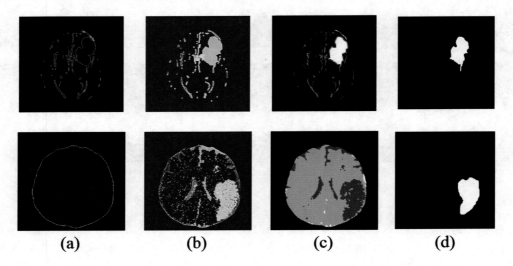

(a)　　　　(b)　　　　(c)　　　　(d)

The results depicted in Figure 6 confirms that, WS and AC approaches are efficient in extracting the stroke section from the MRI irrespective of its modality as shown in Figure 6 (d) and (e). But, the MRF approach fails to extract the required information from T2 modality based MRI as depicted in Figure 6 (f). This experimental approach also confirms that, the average CPU time taken by the WS approach is 58.61 sec, AC is 63.48 sec and MRF is 71.57 sec (computed using Matlab's Tic-Toc), these values confirms that, the WS approach is faster than AC and MRF techniques.

Efficiency of the proposed hybrid approach is further investigated using the benchmark brain tumor dataset knows as BRATS 2013. In this chapter, the T1C modality based brain tumor dataset along with

Figure 4. Results attained with CT images with different views. a. Image orientation, b. Test image, c. Extracted abnormality

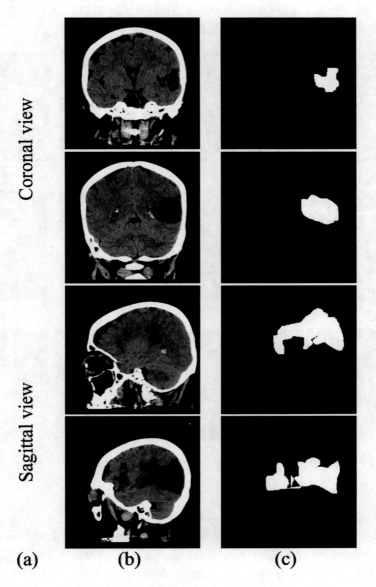

its ground truth is considered for the analysis and the sample 2D images are shown in Figure 7. Initially, a bi-level thresholding approach based on the SGO + Tsallis function and the watershed segmentation approach is implemented for the chosen images of the BRATS 2013. Figure 7 presents the experimental results obtained with the considered dataset. Figure 7 (a) and (c) presents the chosen 2D image slices and its related ground truth images correspondingly. The bi-level thresholded image and the extracted tumor core based on WS are presented in Figure 7 (b) and (d) respectively. This figure confirms that, implemented procedure is very efficient in extracting the tumor core from the T1C images.

Figure 5. Outcome of the proposed approach on the chosen test image. a. Test image, b. Skull stripped image, c. SGO+Tsallis thresholded image, d. Sobel edge detection, e. RGB colour space with water shed, f. Morphological operation, g. Outcome of WS, h. Tumor region by WS, i. Outcome of AC, j. Tumor region by AC, k. Outcome of MRF, and l. Tumor region by MRF

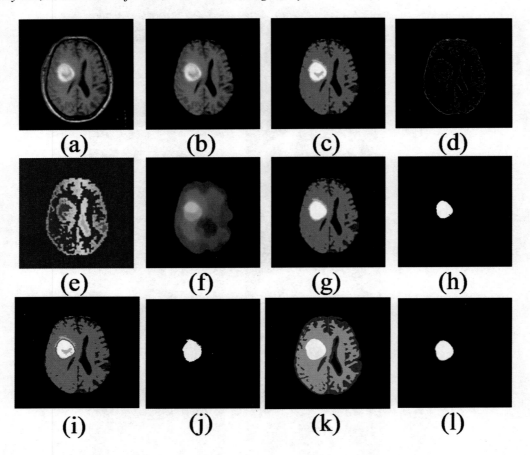

After extracting the tumor core, a relative examination between the tumor core and GT is performed to evaluate the superiority of the implemented hybrid approach. The comparative analysis presents the following average values of image similarity measures: Jaccard (86.18%), Dice (91.73%), FPR (6.36%), and FNR (1.94%). This approach also presents better values for the image statistical measures: sensitivity (98.27%), specificity (94.17%), accuracy (98.16%) precision (98.27%), BCR (97.53%) and BER (1.07%). These results confirm that, the proposed technique is efficient in extracting the abnormal brain region of the BRATS 2013 dataset. Hence, this approach can be considered to examine the real-time brain tumor images acquired from imaging clinics.

Efficiency of the proposed hybrid image processing is also verified using the test images of benchmark ISLES 2015 dataset. It is a three-dimensional (3D) dataset, in which the sample image slices are initially extracted by using the ITK-SNAP tool. Later, the original 77 x 77 pixel images are resized in to a 256 x 256 sized images in order to improve its appearance. This database consist the axial, coronal, and sagittal view of the images along with the respective ground truths. In this study, axial view of MR image is considered for the evaluation. Similar procedure is implemented for the ground truth (GT) image.

Figure 6. Outcome attained using various modality MR images. a. Modality, b. Test image, c. Skull stripped image. d outcome of WS, e. Outcome of AC, and f. Outcome of MRF

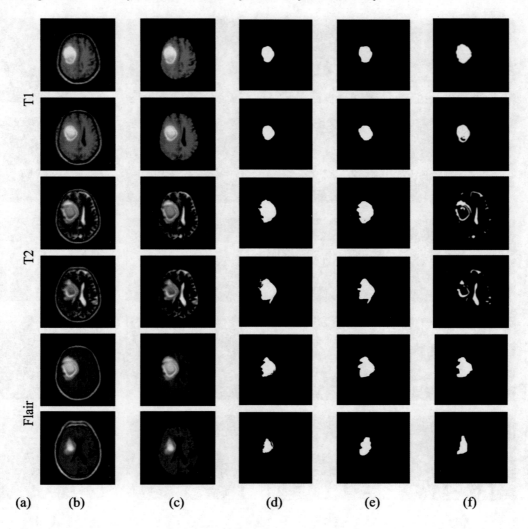

(a)　　(b)　　(c)　　(d)　　(e)　　(f)

Figure 7 depicts the results of the chosen slices of flair modality ISLES 2015 dataset image. Fig 8 (b) and (c) shows test image and GT. Fig 8 (d), (e), and (f) depicts the outcome of the WS, AC and MRF techniques. After extracting the stroke section, a comparative analysis is implemented between the extracted image section and the ground truth in order to compute the image similarity measures and the image quality measures.

The numerical results obtained with this study on the chosen ISLES 2015 dataset is clearly depicted in Table 2 and Table 3. Table 2 illustrates the image similarity measures obtained with the proposed pre-processing approach with watershed augmentation, active contour and the Markov random field. Pictorial representation in Fig 9 confirms that, WS offers better values of the Jaccard, Dice, FPR and FNR compared with ACS and MRF. Similarly, the results of Table 3 also confirm that, the average value

Figure 7. Result obtained for the BRATS 2013 dataset. a. Test images of T1C modality, b. Bi-level threshold image, c. Ground truth, d. Extracted tumor region

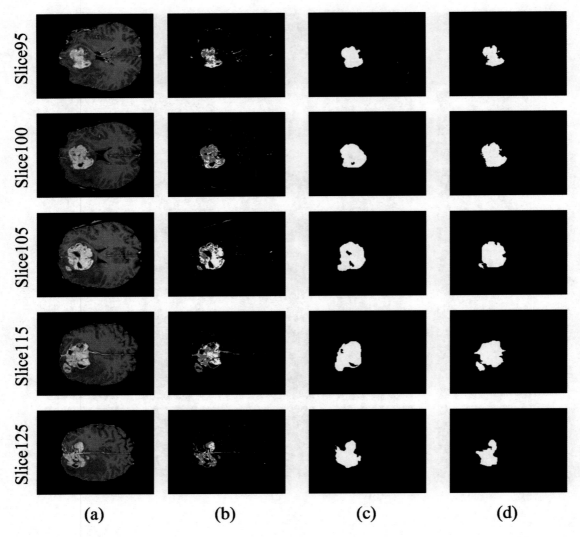

of the image statistical measure attained with the WS is superior to ACS and MRF. From these results, it can be confirmed that, proposed SGO + Tsallis entropy and WS approach can be considered to examine the CT/MRI brain images irrespective of its size, view and modalities.

FUTURE RESEARCH DIRECTIONS

In order to identify the disease severity and also to plan for the further treatment process, it is essential to analyze the brain images with the help of medical experts. In recent years, most of the imaging

Figure 8. Results obtained with flair modality ISLES 2015 dataset. a. Slice number, b. Test image, c. Ground truth, d. WS, e. ACS, and f. MRF

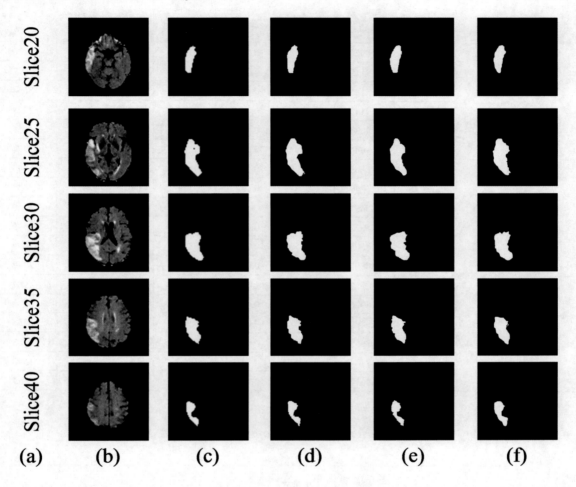

centers have the capability to record digital CT/MR images of the brain. In order to have a pre-opinion regarding the brain abnormality in clinical level, it is essential to use a suitable image processing tool to appraise the digital CT/MR images. The main aim of the research work presented in this chapter is to develop a heuristic algorithm assisted hybrid image processing procedure to examine the abnormal brain CT/MR images. In the proposed work, a hybrid image processing technique based on the Social group optimization assisted Tsallis entropy and Watershed Segmentation (WS) is proposed to examine ischemic stroke / tumor region from digital brain images. The proposed work focuses on extracting and analyzing the abnormal section of the brain image.

In future, the proposed work can be directed as follows: i) Implementation of recent heuristic algorithm to improve the pre-processing section, ii) Enhancing the results of the pre-processing by considering other thresholding procedures, such as Otsu's function, Kapur' entropy, Shannon entropy and Fuzzy-Tsallis entropy, iii) Implementing the well known segmentation approaches, like principal component analysis,

Table 2. Image similarity measures obtained for ISLES 2015 challenge database

Approach	Test image	Jaccard Index	Dice co-efficient	False positive rate	False negative rate	GT pixels	Image pixels	Common pixels
Watershed	Slice20	0.8925	0.9432	0.0846	0.0320	2092	2202	2025
	Slice25	0.9115	0.9537	0.0891	0.0073	4107	4443	4077
	Slice30	0.9106	0.9532	0.0593	0.0355	3695	3783	3564
	Slice35	0.9140	0.9551	0.0699	0.0221	2803	2937	2741
	Slice40	0.8883	0.9409	0.0858	0.0354	1608	1689	1551
	Average	**0.9034**	**0.9492**	**0.0777**	**0.0264**	**2861**	**3011**	**2792**
Active Contour	Slice20	0.8506	0.9193	0.1487	0.0229	2092	2355	2044
	Slice25	0.9049	0.9501	0.0321	0.0660	4107	3968	3836
	Slice30	0.8891	0.9413	0.0836	0.0365	3695	3869	3560
	Slice35	0.8972	0.9458	0.0517	0.0564	2803	2790	2645
	Slice40	0.8605	0.9250	0.0833	0.0678	1608	1633	1499
	Average	**0.8805**	**0.9363**	**0.0799**	**0.0499**	**2861**	**2923**	**2717**
Markov random field	Slice20	0.8373	0.9115	0.1343	0.0502	2092	2268	1987
	Slice25	0.8926	0.9433	0.0862	0.0304	4107	4336	3982
	Slice30	0.9104	0.9531	0.0517	0.9104	3695	3729	3538
	Slice35	0.8955	0.9449	0.0788	0.0339	2803	2929	2708
	Slice40	0.7704	0.8703	0.2432	0.0423	1608	1931	1540
	Average	**0.8612**	**0.9246**	**0.1188**	**0.2134**	**2861**	**3039**	**2751**

Figure 9. Assessment of image similarity measures obtained with WS, ACS, and MRF

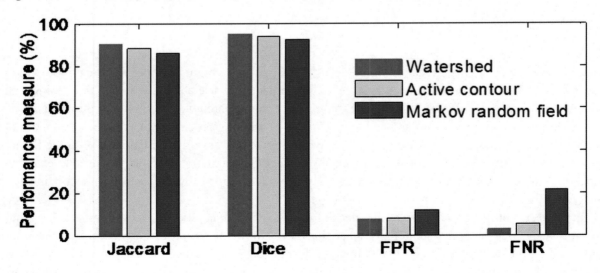

Table 3. Image statistical measures obtained for ISLES 2015 challenge database

Approach	Test image	Sensitivity	Specificity	Accuracy	Precision	BCR	%BER
Watershed	Slice20	0.9972	0.9679	0.9825	0.9989	0.9825	1.7408
	Slice25	0.9940	0.9927	0.9934	0.9995	0.9933	0.6631
	Slice30	0.9964	0.9645	0.9804	0.9979	0.9805	1.9497
	Slice35	0.9969	0.9779	0.9873	0.9990	0.9873	1.2621
	Slice40	0.9978	0.9645	0.9811	0.9991	0.9812	1.8803
	Average	**0.9965**	**0.9735**	**0.9849**	**0.9989**	**0.9849**	**1.4992**
Active Contour	Slice20	0.9951	0.9771	0.9860	0.9992	0.9861	1.3923
	Slice25	0.9978	0.9340	0.9654	0.9956	0.9659	3.4066
	Slice30	0.9950	0.9634	0.9791	0.9978	0.9792	2.0766
	Slice35	0.9976	0.9436	0.9703	0.9974	0.9706	2.9339
	Slice40	0.9979	0.9322	0.9645	0.9982	0.9650	3.4941
	Average	**0.9967**	**0.9501**	**0.9731**	**0.9976**	**0.9734**	**2.6607**
Markov random field	Slice20	0.9956	0.9498	0.9724	0.9983	0.9728	2.7310
	Slice25	0.9942	0.9695	0.9818	0.9979	0.9819	1.8099
	Slice30	0.9969	0.9575	0.9770	0.9974	0.9772	2.2789
	Slice35	0.9964	0.9661	0.9812	0.9984	0.9812	1.8707
	Slice40	0.9938	0.9577	0.9756	0.9989	0.9758	2.4202
	Average	**0.9954**	**0.9601**	**0.9776**	**0.9982**	**0.9778**	**2.2221**

seed based region growing, Chan-Vese active contour, and the level set approaches to enhance the image similarity measures and image statistical measures, iv) Extracting the features of the stroke/tumor region to implement the classifier units for the automated detection and diagnose of the brain abnormalities.

CONCLUSION

The proposed procedure implements an analyzing tool by integrating Tsallis function with Watershed (WS) extraction practice to enhance the performance of brain abnormality inspection. This work considers three well known brain image datasets, like Radiopaedia, BRATS and ISLES. Initially, the proposed procedure is tested on the CT/MR images of the Radiopaedia and its performance is evaluated using the well-known image quality measures existing in the literature. Later, the proposed approach is tested using the benchmark BRATS and ISLES dataset. The considered datasets are using various threshold levels (T= 2, 3, and 4) based on SGO + Tsallis. The outcome of the WS approach is validated against the ACS and MRF approaches considered in this work. The results confirm that, the CPU time taken by the WS is better compared with the SRG and MRF. A comparative examination between the segmented abnormal section of BRATS as well as ISLES and the ground truth image offered better values of image similarity measures and the image statistical measures compared with SRG and MRF. Hence, the proposed tool can be considered to examine the real time clinical MRI images.

REFERENCES

Abdel-Maksoud, E., Elmogy, M., & Al-Awadi, R. (2015). Brain tumor segmentation based on a hybrid clustering technique. *Egyptian Informatics Journal*, *16*(1), 71–81. doi:10.1016/j.eij.2015.01.003

Agrawal, S., Panda, R., Bhuyan, S., & Panigrahi, B. K. (2013). Tsallis entropy based optimal multilevel thresholding using cuckoo search algorithm. *Swarm and Evolutionary Computation*, *11*, 16–30. doi:10.1016/j.swevo.2013.02.001

Balan, N. S., Kumar, A. S., Raja, N. S. M., & Rajinikanth, V. (2016). Optimal multilevel image thresholding to improve the visibility of plasmodium sp. in blood smear images. *Advances in Intelligent Systems and Computing*, *397*, 563–571. doi:10.1007/978-81-322-2671-0_54

Bauer, S., Wiest, R., Nolte, L. P., & Reyes, M. (2013). A survey of MRI-based medical image analysis for brain tumor studies. *Physics in Medicine and Biology*, *58*(13), 97–129. doi:10.1088/0031-9155/58/13/R97 PMID:23743802

Bhandari, A. K., Kumar, A., & Singh, G. K. (2015). Modified artificial bee colony based computationally efficient multilevel thresholding for satellite image segmentation using Kapur's, Otsu and Tsallis functions. *Expert Systems with Applications*, *42*(3), 1573–1601. doi:10.1016/j.eswa.2014.09.049

Brain Tumor Database (BraTS-MICCAI). (n.d.). Retrieved from http://hal.inria.fr/hal-00935640

Bresson, X., Esedoğlu, S., Vandergheynst, P., Thiran, J. P., & Osher, S. (2007). Fast global minimization of the active contour/snake model. *Journal of Mathematical Imaging and Vision*, *28*(2), 151–167. doi:10.100710851-007-0002-0

Chack, S., & Sharma, P. (2015). An improved region based active contour model for medical image segmentation. *International Journal of Signal Processing. Image Processing and Pattern Recognition*, *8*(1), 115–124. doi:10.14257/ijsip.2015.8.1.12

Chaddad, A., & Tanougast, C. (2016). Quantitative evaluation of robust skull stripping and tumor detection applied to axial MR images. *Brain Informatics*, *3*(1), 53–61. doi:10.100740708-016-0033-7 PMID:27747598

Grgic, S., Grgic, M., & Mrak, M. (2004). Reliability of objective picture quality measures. *Journal of Electrical Engineering*, *55*(1-2), 3–10.

Houhou, N., Thiran, J.P. & Bresson, X. (2009). Fast texture segmentation based on semi-local region descriptor and active contour. *Numerical Mathematics: Theory, Methods and Applications*, *2*, 445-468.

ISLES. (2015). Retrieved from www.isles-challenge.org

ITK-SNAP. (n.d.). Retrieved from http://www.itksnap.org/pmwiki/pmwiki.php

Kabir, Y., Dojat, M., Scherrer, B., Forbes, F., & Garbay, C. (2007). Multimodal MRI segmentation of ischemic stroke lesions. *29th Ann Intern Conf IEEE Eng Med Biol Soc EMBC*. 10.1109/IEMBS.2007.4352610

Kamalanand, K., & Jawahar, P. M. (2012). Coupled jumping frogs/particle swarm optimization for estimating the parameters of three dimensional HIV model. *BMC Infectious Diseases*, *12*(1), 82. doi:10.1186/1471-2334-12-S1-P82 PMID:22471518

Kamalanand, K., & Jawahar, P. M. (2015). Prediction of Human Immunodeficiency Virus-1 Viral Load from CD4 Cell Count Using Artificial Neural Networks. *Journal of Medical Imaging and Health Informatics*, *5*(3), 641–646. doi:10.1166/jmihi.2015.1430

Kanchana, R., & Menaka, R. (2015). Computer reinforced analysis for ischemic stroke recognition: A review. *Indian Journal of Science and Technology*, *8*(35), 81006. doi:10.17485/ijst/2015/v8i35/81006

Lakshmi, V.S., Tebby, S.G., Shriranjani, D., & Rajinikanth, V. (2016). Chaotic cuckoo search and Kapur/Tsallis approach in segmentation of T.cruzi from blood smear images. *Int. J. Comp. Sci. Infor. Sec.*, *14*, 51-56.

Liu, T., Xu, H., Jin, W., Liu, Z., Zhao, Y. & Tian, W. (2014). Medical image segmentation based on a hybrid region-based active contour mode. *Computational and Mathematical Methods in Medicin*. doi:.10.1155/2014/890725

Lu, H., Kot, A. C., & Shi, Y. Q. (2004). Distance-reciprocal distortion measure for binary document images. *IEEE Signal Processing Letters*, *11*(2), 228–231. doi:10.1109/LSP.2003.821748

Maier, Menze, B. H., von der Gablentz, J., Häni, L., Heinrich, M. P., Liebrand, M., ... Reyes, M. (2017). ISLES 2015 - A public evaluation benchmark for ischemic stroke lesion segmentation from multispectral MRI. *Medical Image Analysis*, *35*, 250–269. doi:10.1016/j.media.2016.07.009 PMID:27475911

Maier, O., Schröder, C., Forkert, N. D., Martinetz, T., & Handels, H. (2015). Classifiers for ischemic stroke lesion segmentation: A comparison study. *PLoS One*, *10*(12), e0145118. doi:10.1371/journal.pone.0145118 PMID:26672989

Maier, O., Wilms, M., Von der Gablentz, J., Krämer, U. M., Münte, T. F., & Handels, H. (2015). Extra tree forests for sub-acute ischemic stroke lesion segmentation in MR sequences. *Journal of Neuroscience Methods*, *240*, 89–100. doi:10.1016/j.jneumeth.2014.11.011 PMID:25448384

Mitra, J., Bourgeat, P., Fripp, J., Ghose, S., Rose, S., Salvado, O., ... Carey, L. (2014). Lesion segmentation from multimodal MRI using random forest following ischemic stroke. *NeuroImage*, *98*, 324–335. doi:10.1016/j.neuroimage.2014.04.056 PMID:24793830

Moghaddam, R. F., & Cheriet, M. (2010). A multi-scale framework for adaptive binarization of degraded document images. *Pattern Recognition*, *43*(6), 2186–2198. doi:10.1016/j.patcog.2009.12.024

Mostafa, A., Hassanien, A. E., & Hefny, H. A. (2017). Grey wolf optimization-based segmentation approach for abdomen CT liver images. Handbook of Research on Machine Learning Innovations and Trends, 562-581. doi:10.4018/978-1-5225-2229-4.ch024

Naik, A., Satapathy, S. C., Ashour, A. S., & Dey, N. (2016). Social group optimization for global optimization of multimodal functions and data clustering problems. *Neural Computing & Applications*. doi:10.100700521-016-2686-9

Palani, T., & Parvathavarthini, B. (2017). Multichannel interictal spike activity detection using time–frequency entropy measure. *Australasian Physical & Engineering Sciences in Medicine*, *40*(2), 413–425. doi:10.100713246-017-0550-6 PMID:28409335

Palani, T. K., Parvathavarthini, B., & Chitra, K. (2016). Segmentation of brain regions by integrating meta heuristic multilevel threshold with Markov random field. *Current Medical Imaging Reviews*, *12*(1), 4–12. doi:10.2174/1573394711666150827203434

Qian, X., Wang, J., Guo, S., & Li, Q. (2013). An active contour model for medical image segmentation with application to brain CT image. *Medical Physics*, *40*(2), 021911. doi:10.1118/1.4774359 PMID:23387759

Raja, N. S. M., Rajinikanth, V., & Latha, K. (2014). Otsu based optimal multilevel image thresholding using firefly algorithm. Modelling and Simulation in Engineering.

Rajini, N. H., & Bhavani, R. (2013). Computer aided detection of ischemic stroke using segmentation and texture features. *Measurement*, *46*(6), 1865–1874. doi:10.1016/j.measurement.2013.01.010

Rajinikanth, V., & Couceiro, M. S. (2015). RGB histogram based color image segmentation using firefly algorithm. *Procedia Computer Science*, *46*, 1449–1457. doi:10.1016/j.procs.2015.02.064

Rajinikanth, V., Raja, N. S. M., & Latha, K. (2014). Optimal multilevel image thresholding: An analysis with PSO and BFO algorithms. *Australian Journal of Basic and Applied Sciences*, *8*, 443–454.

Rajinikanth, V., Satapathy, S. C., Fernandes, S. L., & Nachiappan, S. (2017). Entropy based segmentation of tumor from brain MR images–A study with teaching learning based optimization. *Pattern Recognition Letters*, *94*, 87–94. doi:10.1016/j.patrec.2017.05.028

Roerdink, J. B. T. M., & Meijster, A. (2001). The watershed transform: Definitions, algorithms and parallelization strategies. *Fundamenta Informaticae*, *41*, 187–228.

Satapathy, S., & Naik, A. (2016). Social group optimization (SGO): A new population evolutionary optimization technique. *Complex & Intelligent Systems*, *2*(3), 173–203. doi:10.100740747-016-0022-8

Sathya, P. D., & Kayalvizhi, R. (2010). Optimum multilevel image thresholding based on Tsallis Eetropy method with bacterial foraging algorithm. *International Journal of Computer Science Issues*, *7*(5), 336–343.

Shanthakumar, P., & Kumar, P. G. (2015). Computer aided brain tumor detection system using watershed segmentation techniques. *International Journal of Imaging Systems and Technology*, *25*(4), 297–301. doi:10.1002/ima.22147

Tang, F. H., Ng, D. K. S., & Chow, D. H. K. (2011). An image feature approach for computer-aided detection of ischemic stroke. *Computers in Biology and Medicine*, *41*(7), 529–536. doi:10.1016/j.compbiomed.2011.05.001 PMID:21605853

Thanaraj, P., Roshini, M., & Balasubramanian, P. (2016). Integration of multivariate empirical mode decomposition and independent component analysis for fetal ECG separation from abdominal signals. *Technology and Health Care*, *24*(6), 783–794. doi:10.3233/THC-161224 PMID:27315149

Tuba, M. (2014). Multilevel image thresholding by nature-inspired algorithms: A short review. *Computer Science Journal of Moldova*, *22*, 318–338.

Tyan, Y.S., Wu, M.C., Chin, C.L., Kuo, Y.L., Lee, M.S., & Chang, H.Y. (2014). Ischemic stroke detection system with a computer-aided diagnostic ability using an unsupervised feature perception enhancement method. *International Journal of Biomedical Imaging.* doi:.10.1155/2014/947539

Usinskas, A., & Gleizniene, R. (2006). Ischemic stroke region recognition based on ray tracing. *Proceedings of International Baltic Electronics Conference.* 10.1109/BEC.2006.311103

Wang, Z., Bovik, A. C., Sheikh, H. R., & Simoncelli, E. P. (2004). Image quality assessment: From error visibilitytostructural similarity. *IEEE Transactions on Image Processing, 13*(4), 600–612. doi:10.1109/TIP.2003.819861 PMID:15376593

WSO. (n.d.). Retrieved from http://www.world-stroke.org/

Yahiaoui, A. F. Z., & Bessaid, Y. (2016). Segmentation of ischemic stroke area from CT brain images. *International Symposium on Signal, Image, Video and Communications (ISIVC).* 10.1109/ISIVC.2016.7893954

Yushkevich, P. A., Piven, J., Hazlett, H. C., Smith, R. G., Ho, S., Gee, J. C., & Gerig, G. (2006). User-guided 3D active contour segmentation of anatomical structures: Significantly improved efficiency and reliability. *NeuroImage, 31*(3), 1116–1128. doi:10.1016/j.neuroimage.2006.01.015 PMID:16545965

Zhang, Y., Brady, M., & Smith, S. (2001). Segmentation of brain MR images through a hidden Markov random field model and the expectation maximization algorithm. *IEEE Transactions on Medical Imaging, 20*(1), 45–57. doi:10.1109/42.906424 PMID:11293691

Zhou, S., Wang, J., Zhang, S., Liang, Y., & Gong, Y. (2016). Active contour model based on local and global intensity information for medical image segmentation. *Neurocomputing, 186*, 107–118. doi:10.1016/j.neucom.2015.12.073

ADDITIONAL READING

Acharya, U. R., Ng, E. Y. K., Tan, J. H., & Sree, S. V. (2012). Thermography based breast cancer detection using texture features and support vector machine. *Journal of Medical Systems, 36*(3), 1503–1510. doi:10.100710916-010-9611-z PMID:20957511

Ahmed, S., Dey, N., Ashour, A. S., Sifaki-Pistolla, D., Bălas-Timar, D., Balas, V. E., & Tavares, J. M. R. S. (2017). Effect of fuzzy partitioning in Crohn's disease classification: A neuro-fuzzy-based approach. *Medical & Biological Engineering & Computing, 55*(1), 101–115. doi:10.100711517-016-1508-7 PMID:27106754

Das, S., & De, S. (2016). Multilevel color image segmentation using modified genetic algorithm (MfGA) inspired fuzzy c-means clustering. *Second International Conference on Research in Computational Intelligence and Communication Networks (ICRCICN)*, IEEE. 10.1109/ICRCICN.2016.7813635

Das, S., & De, S. (2017). A modified genetic algorithm based FCM clustering algorithm for magnetic resonance image segmentation. *Advances in Intelligent Systems and Computing, 515*, 435–443. doi:10.1007/978-981-10-3153-3_43

De, S., & Bhattacharyya, S. (2015). Color Magnetic Resonance Brain Image Segmentation by ParaOptiMUSIG activation Function: An Application. *Hybrid Soft Computing Approaches: Research and Applications, 611*, 185–214. doi:10.1007/978-81-322-2544-7_6

De, S., Bhattacharyya, S., & Chakraborty, S. (2012). Color image segmentation using parallel OptiMUSIG activation function. *Applied Soft Computing, 12*(10), 3228–3236. doi:10.1016/j.asoc.2012.05.011

De, S., Bhattacharyya, S., & Chakraborty, S. (2015). Multilevel and Color Image Segmentation by NSGA II Based OptiMUSIG Activation Function, Handbook of Research on Advanced Hybrid Intelligent Techniques and Applications, Chapter 11, 321-348. doi:10.4018/978-1-4666-9474-3.ch011

De, S., Bhattacharyya, S., Chakraborty, S., Sarkar, B. N., Prabhakar, P. K., & Bose, S. (2012). Gray scale image segmentation by NSGA II based OptiMUSIG activation function, *International Conference on Communication Systems and Network Technologies (CSNT 2012)*, IEEE, 104-108. 10.1109/CSNT.2012.32

De, S., Bhattacharyya, S., & Dutta, P. (2010). Efficient gray level image segmentation using an optimized MUSIG (OptiMUSIG) activation function. *International Journal of Parallel. Emergent and Distributed Systems, 26*(1), 1–39.

De, S., Bhattacharyya, S., & Dutta, P. (2016). Automatic magnetic resonance image segmentation by fuzzy intercluster hostility index based genetic algorithm: An application. *Applied Soft Computing, 47*, 669–683. doi:10.1016/j.asoc.2016.05.042

De, S., & Firoj, H. (2016). *Multilevel Image Segmentation Using Modified Particle Swarm Optimization*. Intelligent Analysis of Multimedia Information; doi:10.4018/978-1-5225-0498-6

Dey, N., Ashour, A. S., Beagum, S., Pistola, D. S., Gospodinov, M., Gospodinova, E. P., & Tavares, J. M. R. S. (2015). Parameter optimization for local polynomial approximation based intersection confidence interval filter using genetic algorithm: An application for brain MRI image de-noising. *Journal of Imaging, 1*(1), 60–84. doi:10.3390/jimaging1010060

Hore, S., Chakroborty, S., Ashour, A. S., Dey, N., Ashour, A. S., Sifaki-Pistolla, D., ... Chaudhuri, S. R. B. (2015). Finding contours of hippocampus brain cell using microscopic image analysis. *Journal of Advanced Microscopy Research, 10*(2), 93–103. doi:10.1166/jamr.2015.1245

Menze, B., Reyes, M., Leemput, K. V., & ... . (2015). The multimodal brain tumor image segmentation benchmark (BRATS). *IEEE Transactions on Medical Imaging, 34*(10), 1993–2024. doi:10.1109/TMI.2014.2377694 PMID:25494501

Moraru, L., Moldovanu, S., Dimitrievici, L. T., Ashour, A. S., & Dey, N. (2016). (2016). Texture anisotropy technique in brain degenerative diseases. *Neural Computing & Applications*. doi:10.100700521-016-2777-7

Raja, N. S. M., Rajinikanth, V., Fernandes, S. L., & Satapathy, S. C. (2017). Segmentation of breast thermal images using Kapur's entropy and hidden Markov random field. *Journal of Medical Imaging and Health Informatics, 7*(8), 1825–1829. doi:10.1166/jmihi.2017.2267

Rajinikanth, V., Raja, N. S. M., & Kamalanand, K. (2017). Firefly algorithm assisted segmentation of tumor from brain MRI using Tsallis function and Markov random field. *Journal of Control Engineering and Applied Informatics*, *19*(3), 97–106.

Rajinikanth, V., Raja, N. S. M., Satapathy, S. C., & Fernandes, S. L. (2017). Otsu's multi-thresholding and active contour snake model to segment dermoscopy images. *Journal of Medical Imaging and Health Informatics*, *7*(8), 1837–1840. doi:10.1166/jmihi.2017.2265

Rani, J., Kumar, R., & Talukdar, F. A. & Dey, N. (2017). The Brain tumor segmentation using Fuzzy C-Means technique: A study, Recent Advances in Applied Thermal Imaging for Industrial Applications, IGI global, 40-61.

Samanta, S., Ahmed, S., Salem, M. A.-M. M., Nath, S. S., Dey, N., & Chowdhury, S. S. (2014). Haralick features based automated glaucoma classification using back propagation neural network. *Advances in Intelligent Systems and Computing*, *327*, 351–358. doi:10.1007/978-3-319-11933-5_38

Suganthi, S., & Ramakrishnan, S. (2014). Semiautomatic segmentation of breast thermograms using variational level set method. *IFMBE Proceedings*, *43*, 231–234. doi:10.1007/978-3-319-02913-9_59

Vishnupriya, R., Raja, N. S. M., & Rajinikanth, V. (2017). An efficient clustering technique and analysis of infrared thermograms, In. *Third International Conference on Biosignals, Images and Instrumentation (ICBSII)*, IEEE, 1-5. 10.1109/ICBSII.2017.8082275

Wang, D., He, T., Li, Z., Cao, L., Dey, N., Ashour, A. S., ... Shi, F. (2016). Image feature-based affective retrieval employing improved parameter and structure identification of adaptive neuro-fuzzy inference system. *Neural Computing & Applications*, 1–16. doi:10.100700521-016-2512-4

Chapter 8

Restoration of CT Images Corrupted With Fixed Valued Impulse Noise Using an Optimum Decision-Based Filter

Priyank Saxena
Birla Institute of Technology, India

R. Sukesh Kumar
Birla Institute of Technology, India

ABSTRACT

The main aim of this chapter is to perform the restoration of computed tomography (CT) images acquired at the reduced level of radiation dose. Reduction in radiation dose affects the image quality as it increases noise and decreases low contrast resolution. In this chapter, an optimum decision-based filter (ODBF) is proposed as an image-space denoising technique, to detect and restore the low dose CT (LDCT) images corrupted with fixed valued impulse noise (salt and pepper) of unequal density. The detection stage employs k-means clustering to discriminate the noise-free pixels from the noisy-pixels by splitting the image data into three clusters of different intensities. The restoration stage employs mask else trimmed median (METM) estimation followed by an optional adaptive mask sizing for restoration of noisy pixels. The proposed method demonstrates noticeable improvement over other existing methods in restoration of LDCT images while maintaining the image contrast and edge details.

INTRODUCTION

Computed Tomography (CT) is the most widely used Medical Imaging Technique for medical diagnosis, which usually acquires noise, artefacts etc. during image acquisition. CT scan is well suited to detect the presence of lesions of very low contrast. As compared with other imaging modalities, there is a growing concern regarding the amount of radiation dose associated with CT. For medical examination, high amounts of radiation increases the risk of cancer during the examinee's whole lifetime (de González

DOI: 10.4018/978-1-5225-5246-8.ch008

et al., 2009). In CT, there is a trade-off between image quality and the amount of radiation exposure to patients. Reduction in radiation dose affects the image quality as it increases noise and decreases low contrast resolution. For instance, reduction in radiation exposure by a factor of 2 results in an increase in the noise approximately by a factor of $\sqrt{2}$ (Borsdorf et al., 2008). The image noise and non- stationary streak artefacts are highly apparent in Low Dose CT (LDCT) images. The image noise limits the visualization of low-contrast structures which in turn affects the diagnostic quality. Therefore, it is critically important to maintain diagnostically acceptable image quality in LDCT examinations. Now a days, LDCT examinations are useful in several clinical studies such as the annual repeat screening for lung cancer using shorter CT scan time (Oguchi et al., 2000).

CT Images are often corrupted with impulse noise which is mostly generated due to errors in image acquisition, recording, and transmission or by the use of low quality sensors (Lin et al. 2015). The Impulse noise can be of Fixed valued (salt & pepper) or Random valued. Fixed Valued Impulse Noise (FVIN) has the property that the pixel corrupted by this noise acquire either the highest (255) or lowest (0) intensity value present for an 8-bit gray scale image, consequently resulting in the degradation of the edge sharpness and textural information of the image.

In this chapter, the impulse noise model is considered to be of fixed valued with unequal probability distribution and the restoration of LDCT is performed by the proposed Optimum Decision Based Filter (ODBF). Detection of pixels corrupted with FVIN is performed by k-means clustering (Kanungo et al. 2014). The k-means clearly discriminates the noise-free pixels from the noisy-pixels by splitting the image into three clusters of high (salt), low (pepper) and medium (noise-free) intensities respectively from the corrupted LDCT image. Once the noise-free pixels are identified correctly, they remain unaltered. The proposed ODBF employs Mask Else Trimmed Median (METM) estimation technique followed by an optional Adaptive Mask Sizing for the restoration of the noisy-pixels for a wide range of Noise Density (ND). The option of adaptive mask sizing gets invoked in case of the failure of METM estimation to suppress noise of very high density. The proposed filter can be applied iteratively to remove the heavy noise.

The performance of the proposed method for FVIN removal from LDCT images is evaluated by comparing it with the other existing methods such as Standard Median Filter (SMF), Adaptive Median Filter (AMF), Decision Based Algorithm (DBA), Modified Decision Based Unsymmetric Trimmed Median Filter (MDBUTMF) and Decision Based Trimmed Median Filter (DBTMF). It is evident from the experimental results that the proposed ODBF method performs restoration of LDCT images significantly better than the other existing methods in terms of visual quality and the image quality assessment metrics such as Mean Square Error (MSE), Peak Signal to Noise Ratio (PSNR), and Structural Similarity Index Measurement (SSIM), Image Enhancement Factor (IEF).

The rest of this chapter is organised as follows. Background section reviews studies related to denoising of the LDCT images and their analysis results. The materials and method section gives explanation of the impulse noise model considered for the study and the detailed discussion on the proposed method followed by the results and discussion which makes the performance evaluation of the proposed method with other filtering methods. Finally, conclusion section highlights the major findings of this chapter.

BACKGROUND

Noise removal from clinical scans is not an easy task because of the complex nature of uncertainties present. Clinical scans consist of many artefacts and structures of different shape, size and contrast, hence, edge detection become more vital because inappropriate selection of edges may limit the possibility of correct diagnosis. The different strategies to improve the quality of LDCT images can be roughly divided into three domains: hardware, image reconstruction and by de-noising. The first domain deals with the improvement in hardware components such as Automatic Exposure Controls (AEC), which adapts the tube current according to the attenuation of the patient's body to achieve a remarkable improvement in image quality for LDCT images (Greess, 2000; Kalender, 1999).

The second domain deals with the image reconstruction which has a major effect on image quality of LDCT images. Image reconstruction methods are classified as analytical and iterative. The most commonly used analytical reconstruction method available on commercial CT scanners is Filtered Back Projection (FBP) method, which allows to apply different kernels or filters (smooth or sharp) to affect the image quality of different clinical procedures. Smooth kernels enhances the low contrast detectability and reduces noise in brain exams or liver tumour assessment. Sharp kernels are used for the requirement of better spatial resolution in exams of assessing bony structures. Slice thickness is another important reconstruction parameter to control the spatial resolution in the longitudinal direction. Based on the clinical applications, selection of an appropriate kernel with proper slice thickness influences the trade-offs among spatial resolution, image noise and radiation dose. As compared with typical analytical reconstruction, iterative reconstruction methods have shown potential benefit of reducing the noise in LDCT images. However, they require special software and are scanner specific (Hsieh, 2013; Lange, 1984; Le, 2007).

The third category of strategies deal with de-noising of LDCT images. De-noising can occur at various stages of the CT imaging process and can be applied in the projection space as a pre-reconstruction filtering step or in image space as a post-reconstruction filtering step. Other than the conventional reconstruction kernels, pre-reconstruction filtering step involves the use of noise removal techniques on the projection data. Non-linear filtering is adopted by most of the de-noising filters which perform especially well in suppressing structured noise in LDCT. Pre-reconstruction filtering step performs well to reduce the image noise in low dose scans while maintaining high contrast resolution. The application of pre-reconstruction filtering techniques are limited by the fact that they require large computations and are scanner specific (Ehman, 2012; Li, 2004; Riviere and Billmire, 2005; Wang, 2006; Zhu, 2012).

Post-reconstruction filtering step applied to CT images involves many techniques which can make them computationally fast and scanner independent. However, due to the unavailability of projection data, post-reconstruction filtering techniques have good practical applicability (Ehman, 2014; Luisier, 2011).

The noise removal techniques are broadly classified into spatial and frequency domain filtering methods. In this study, we mainly focus on the spatial domain filter. Spatial filtering is again classified in to linear and non-linear filtering techniques. Linear filters fail to remove noise effectively because the effect of filtering results in blurring of edges of an image. Among the many non-linear filtering methods, Standard Median Filtering (SMF) is the most common type of filtering for FVIN removal (Huang et al. 1979). SMF gives better results for the images corrupted with noise of low density but fails to preserve high frequency components and produces blurring in case of noise of high density. Modifications to SMF have been proposed by incorporating the concepts of Weighted Median Filter (WMF) (Hwang et al. 1979), Centre Weighted Median Filter (CWMF) (Chen, T et al. 2001; Ko et al. 1991; Lin 2007) and Adaptive Median Filter (AMF) (Hwang et al. 1979). In WMF and CWMF, selected pixels in a given window under operation are multiplied to the predefined weights. This results in altering the noise-free pixels as well, hence affects the de-noising performance as unsatisfactory at High Noise Density (HND). The main cause of failure for these filters is that they alter noise free pixels as well, when implemented on the entire image unconditionally. In AMF, adaptive window size is used but the computational time is extremely high for HND.

Decision based methods overcomes the above mentioned inadequacies. Decision based methods are based on the approach of detecting the corrupted pixels following a restoration step (Vijaykumar, 2014; Wang, 2010; Zhang, 2013). Some well-known methods with the switching scheme, such as Noise Adaptive Fuzzy Switching Median Filter (NAFSMF), Decision-Based Algorithm (DBA), Modified Decision Based Unsymmetrical Trimmed Median Filter (MDBUTM) and Decision Based Trimmed Median Filter (DBTMF). In NAFSMF, detection of the noisy pixels is performed from the histogram of the corrupted image and they are restored using a fuzzy reasoning concept (Toh et al. 2010). In DBA proposed by Srinivasan (2007), a pixel with a gray value of either 0 or 255 is identified as FVIN and is replaced by the median value as long as at least one noise free pixel is available in the selected window. In case of absence of noise free pixel, it will be replaced by its neighbourhood pixels. This repetitive replacement results in streaking artifacts at HND. Esakkirajan (2011) proposed a Modified Decision-Based Approach that utilises an Unsymmetrical Trimmed Median Filter (MDBUTM) as it replaces the central pixel with the mean value of the all noisy pixels in the filtering window in case of absence of noise free pixels. This results in artificial spots in the restored image. The strategy of DBTMF is that median of the pixels in the mask is calculated by considering pixels of other than 0 or 255. If all the pixels in the mask under operation are corrupted, then the proposed algorithm replaces noisy pixels by the midpoint of recently processed pixels (Vijay Kumar et al. 2014). DBTMF are capable of detecting noisy pixels with a high accuracy for highly corrupted images. To overcome the drawbacks of DBA and MDBUTMF, a Recursive approach employing an Adaptive Median Filter (RAMF) is proposed by Meher and Singhawat (2014). The impulse detection is simply performed by the histogram analysis of an image. The size of working window changes based on the presence of noise-free pixel(s). The noisy pixels are filtered through the replacement of their values using both noise-free pixels of the current working window and previously processed noisy pixels of that window. In a similar approach, another modification over DBA and MDBUTMF is proposed in Decision-Based Coupled Window Median Filter (DBCWMF) (Bhadouria et al., 2014).

A number of fuzzy reasoning based decision methods such as for FVIN removal have been proposed in the literature. To remove impulse noise from gray scale images, support vector machine (SVM) based fuzzy filter has been proposed by Roy (2016). Fuzzy Based Median Filter (FBMF) (Elaiyaraja and Kumaratharan, 2015), Rule Base Fuzzy Adaptive Median Filter (RBFAMF) by (Toprak et al. 2006) have been used for FVIN removal. Fuzzy Based Median Filter (FBMF) is a modification to the CMF and give good results but for a predefined thresholds. RBFAMF is a modification to the AMF and give good results. Fuzzy based methods indeed give a better image quality but space and energy complexity is bound to grow up when fuzzy logic method is leveraged.

MATERIALS AND METHODS

The main objective of this chapter is to detect and remove FVIN of high density from LDCT images without losing the clinically significant details. In the proposed ODBF model, the detection of the noisy-pixels is performed using k-means algorithm, while the restoration of the noisy pixels is performed by METM with an optional adaptive mask sizing.

Noise Model

The main difficulty lies in identifying the pixels of an image as impulses. In FVIN, corrupted pixels may take either minimum (0) or maximum gray level (255) for an 8-bit monochrome image. Let the probability of occurrence of noise as minimum gray level (0) and maximum gray level (255) be O_1 and O_2 respectively in any gray scale image I at any pixel location (i, j). Let $I_{i,j}$ be the gray level of the uncorrupted pixel and $I'_{i,j}$ be the gray level of current pixel at coordinate (i, j). In this chapter, the following noise model for FVIN is being considered.

$$I'_{i,j} = \begin{cases} I_{i,j} & \text{with probability } (1-P) \\ O_1 & \text{with probability } \dfrac{P_1}{2} \\ O_2 & \text{with probability } \dfrac{P_2}{2} \end{cases}$$

Where the noise density $P = P_1 + P_2$ and $P_1 \neq P_2$.

Fixed Valued Impulse Detection Using *k*-Means Clustering

The efficient removal of FVIN mainly depends on the detection phase. The detection method of the proposed algorithm employs *k*-means clustering to efficiently separate out the noisy-pixels from the noise-free pixels. The *k*-means is one of the most frequent method of clustering used in pattern recognition. The *k*-means clustering classifies a given set of data into *k* number of disjoint clusters by two distinct segments. In the first segment, *k* centroids are calculated and in the second segment, based on the minimum Euclidean distance, each data point is moved to the cluster having the nearest centroid from the respective data point (Dhanachandra et al., 2015).

Using a mask of size 15 × 15, the *k*-means algorithm divides the neighbourhood values of the centre pixel *p (i, j)* into three clusters of high intensity (salt), low intensity (pepper) and noise free pixels respectively. The central pixel *p (i, j)* is detected as noisy or noise-free, based on the cluster it belongs to as per the following assumption (Table 1).

The pixels belonging to either salt or pepper noise cluster will undergo the image restoration using an ODBF, while pixels belonging to the noise-free cluster will remain unaltered. *k*-means minimises the probability of blurring that may be caused due to the alteration of noise-free pixels.

Table 1.

p (i, j) =	Pepper noise cluster: low intensity pixels.
	Noise-free cluster : medium intensity pixels.
	Salt noise cluster : high intensity pixels.

Image Restoration Using a Mask elseTrimmed Median Estimation

Image restoration method while dealing with impulse noise most often results in blurring of the image details. LDCT images are of clinical importance and blurring may result in loss of clinically significant information. The proposed method for image restoration overcomes blurring effect, which results due to averaging of pixels. It employs METM estimation technique for noise removal followed by an optional adaptive mask sizing. For the restoration of a noisy sample, ODBF fist employs Mask Median (MM) estimation based on shear sort algorithm while Trimmed Median (TM) estimation (Esakkirajan et al., 2011) gets invoked at the failure of MM estimation. The option of adaptive mask sizing gets invoked in case of the failure of METM estimation either due to the availability of all noisy-pixels or even number of noise-free pixels present in the mask under operation. The pros and cons of each estimation technique in ODBF is discussed below separately.

Mask Median (MM) Estimation

The MM estimation uses an odd sized square mask of 3x3. The sorting algorithm consists of row and column sorting phases. After arranging the elements in rows/columns and then columns/rows of the mask in ascending/descending order, the mask median is obtained at the centre element of the mask. MM rules out the possibility of blurring due to averaging of noise-free pixels as compared to TM. MM estimation fails if more than 75% of the pixels in the given mask are noisy. An illustration of the failure of MM is given in Table 2.

Hence, MM fails as the centre pixel is still noisy. This failure is taken care by the second estimation technique TM.

Trimmed Median (TM) Estimation

TM estimation using mask of size 3 × 3 is performed for each noisy pixels. If the centre sample of the mask is noisy, the centre sample is changed by the median/average of the noise-free based on the number of odd/ even noise-free pixels available in the mask under operation. At high Noise Density (ND), if the count of noise-free pixels available in the given mask becomes minimum and probability of getting an even number of noise-free pixels increases, TM gives poor estimation by averaging of noise-free pixels. To rule out the possibility of blurring due to the averaging of pixels, the proposed OBDF method counts

Table 2.

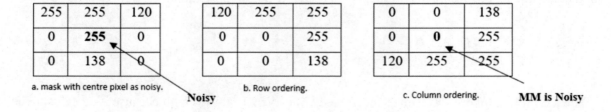

the noise-free pixels available in the mask under operation. In the proposed ODBF method, TM estimation replaces the centre sample by the median of the noise-free pixels only when the count of noise-free pixels available in the mask are odd. The other two following eventualities that may result during TM estimation are

1. If all the pixels in the mask under operation are found to be noisy, TM estimation fails.
2. If the count of noise-free pixels in the mask under operation are even, TM estimation results in blurring due to averaging of noise-free pixels.

The proposed ODBF method takes care of these eventualities by an optional adaptive mask sizing.

Adaptive Sizing of the Mask

At each location, the size of the mask K = 2n + 1 (n is a non-negative integer) is defined in terms of the coordinates symmetrically surrounding the input sample *P (i, j)*. In the beginning, a mask size of 3×3 (n=1) is used. The ODBF method employs adaptive sizing of the mask which gets invoked in case of any of the two eventualities mentioned above are met during TM estimation. To rule out the possibility of blurring and TM estimation failure, increasing the size of the mask automatically (n++ <K_{max}), includes more pixels in the mask under operation. This option increases the probability of getting more noise free pixels as compared to noisy pixels in the mask under operation. However, in case of non-availability of noise-free pixels even after maximum size ($K \leq K_m$) of the mask is exhausted, the noisy sample is replaced with the average value of the pixels present in the mask. The maximum mask size depends on the image size. After changing the size of the mask, the estimation process once again starts with MM estimation as shown in Figure 1. This process continues till all the noisy pixels in a LDCT image are restored. The flow diagram of the image restoration stage by the proposed ODBF is shown in Figure 1.

RESULTS AND DISCUSSION

The performance of the proposed ODBF method is evaluated based on the experiments performed on a number of LDCT images. The effectiveness of the proposed filtering method for reducing FVIN from LDCT images, has been evaluated by the following image quality assessment metrics (Wang et.al. 2004)

Mean-Square Error (MSE)

For a noise free m x n size monochrome image *P* and its noisy approximation *P'*, MSE is defined as

$$MSE = \frac{1}{mn} \sum_{i=0}^{m-1} \sum_{j=0}^{n-1} \left[P\left(i, j\right) - P'\left(i, j\right) \right]^2 \tag{1}$$

The MSE of an input LDCT image corrupted with FVIN is always high because it contains higher percentage of noise as compared to the standard LDCT image with less noise.

Figure 1. Flow diagram of the image restoration using ODBF

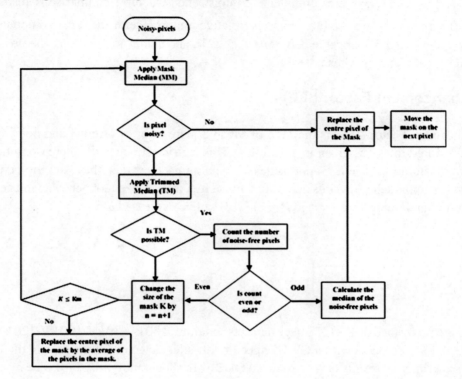

Peak Signal to Noise Ratio (PSNR)

PSNR is most easily defined by MSE. The PSNR (in dB) is defined as

$$PSNR = 10 \ \log_{10}(\frac{MAX_I^2}{MSE}) \qquad (2)$$

where, MAX_I is the maximum possible intensity of the image. PSNR of an input LDCT image corrupted with FVIN is always less because it contains higher percentage of noise as compared to the standard LDCT Image with less noise.

Structural Similarity Index (SSI)

SSI is a widely used quality metric for full reference image quality assessment i.e. measuring the quality based on the distortion free image as reference. It is a method of measuring similarity of the two images by comparing luminance, contrast and structure of the two spatial patches $i \, and \, j$ extracted from each image. Measurement of SSI between signals i and j is given by

$$SSIM\left(i, \ j\right) = \left[l\left(i,j\right)\right]^{\propto} \left[c\left(i,j\right)\right]^{\beta} \left[\ s\left(i,j\right)\right]^{\gamma} \qquad (3)$$

where, $l(i,j), c(i,j)$ and $s(i,j)$ are luminance, contrast and structural comparisons respectively and $\alpha > 0$, $\beta > 0$ and $\gamma > 0$ are used to adjust the relative importance of the three components. The resultant SSIM index is a decimal value between '0' and '1', and value '1' is only reachable in the case of two identical sets of signal patches i.e. $i = j$.

Image Enhancement Factor (IEF)

Image Enhancement Factor (IEF) is the ratio of Mean Square error of original and noisy image to the original and restored image as given in equation 4. This metric estimates the increase in the quality of the image after restoration. The IEF approaches its maximum value when the restoration quality is very good otherwise it approaches towards zero. For a noise free m × n size monochrome image P, its noisy approximation P' and the restored image P'', the IEF can be expressed as

$$IEF = \left| \frac{\sum_i \sum_j (P'(i,j) - P(i,j))^2}{\sum_i \sum_j (P''(i,j) - P(i,j))^2} \right| \tag{4}$$

Experiments are performed on the CT image datasets acquired at 80 kV/80 kV/100 kV/120 kV, 10 mA/40 mA/40 mA/360 mA protocols with a GE HI Speed multi-slice detector CT scanner in the DICOM file format. The experimental results of the proposed ODBF are shown in figures 2-10. The results obtained

Figure 2. (a) Test image 1 (10mA, 80kV), (b) Noisy image at 30% ND, (c) SMF output, (d) AMF output. (e) DBA output, (f) MDBUTM output, (g) DBTMF output, (h) proposed ODBF output

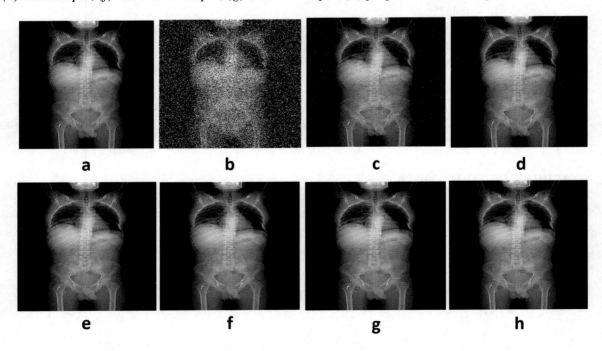

Figure 3. (a) Test image 1 (10mA, 80kV), (b) Noisy image at 60% ND, (c) SMF output, (d) AMF output. (e) DBA output, (f) MDBUTM output, (g) DBTMF output, (h) proposed ODBF output

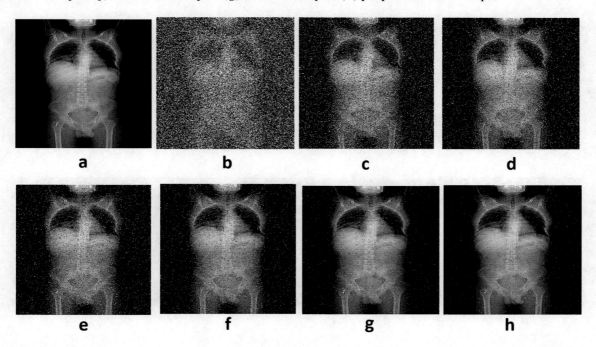

Figure 4. (a) Test image 1 (10mA, 80kV), (b) Noisy image at 90% ND, (c) SMF output, (d) AMF output. (e) DBA output, (f) MDBUTM output, (g) DBTMF output, (h) proposed ODBF output

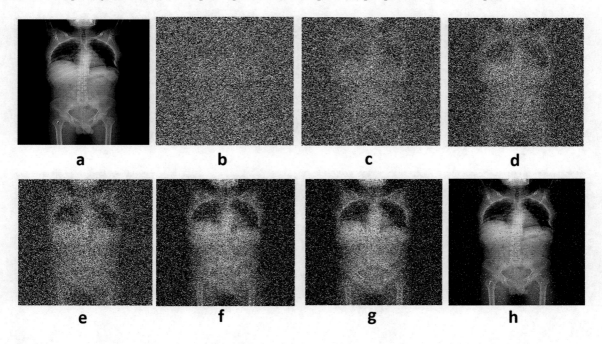

Figure 5. (a) Test image 2 (40mA, 80kV), (b) Noisy image at 30% ND, (c) SMF output, (d) AMF output. (e) DBA output, (f) MDBUTM output, (g) DBTMF output, (h) proposed ODBF output

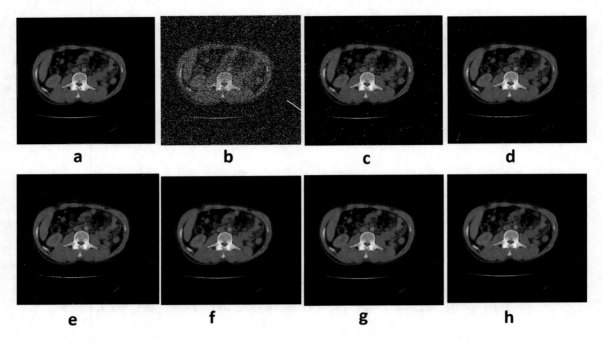

Figure 6. (a) Test image 2 (40mA, 80kV), (b) Noisy image at 60% ND, (c) SMF output, (d) AMF output. (e) DBA output, (f) MDBUTM output, (g) DBTMF output, (h) proposed ODBF output

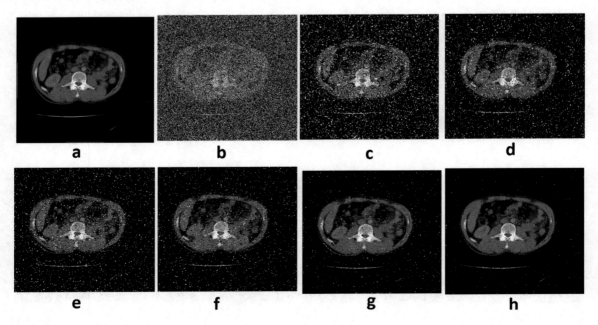

Figure 7. (a) Test image 2 (40mA, 80kV), (b) Noisy image at 90% ND, (c) SMF output, (d) AMF output. (e) DBA output, (f) MDBUTM output, (g) DBTMF output, (h) proposed ODBF output

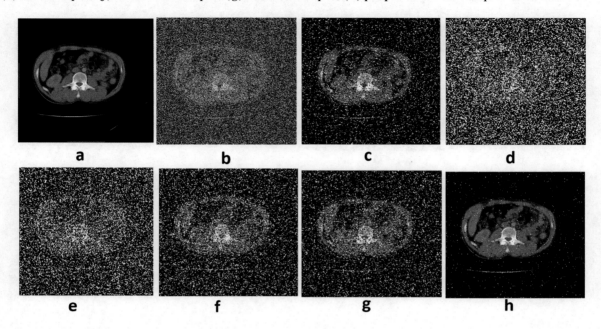

Figure 8. (a) Test image 3 (60mA, 120kV), (b) Noisy image at 30% ND, (c) SMF output, (d) AMF output. (e) DBA output, (f) MDBUTM output, (g) DBTMF output, (h) proposed ODBF output

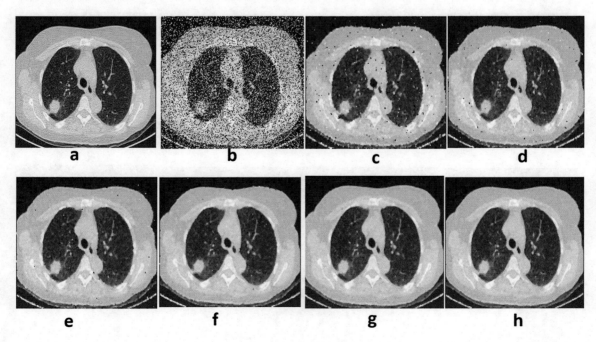

Figure 9. (a) Test image 3 (60mA, 120kV), (b) Noisy image at 60% ND, (c) SMF output, (d) AMF output. (e) DBA output, (f) MDBUTM output, (g) DBTMF output, (h) proposed ODBF output

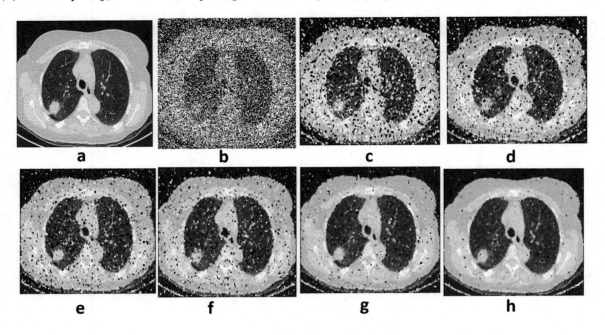

Figure 10. (a) Test image 3 (60mA, 120kV), (b) Noisy image at 90% ND, (c) SMF output, (d) AMF output. (e) DBA output, (f) MDBUTM output, (g) DBTMF output, (h) proposed ODBF output

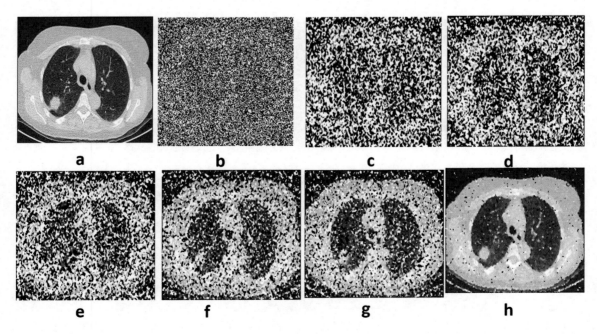

at three different levels of noise densities (30% to 90%) are included here for discussion. Figure 11 shows the performance comparison of the image quality assessment metrics for other existing filtering methods such as SMF, AMF, DBA, MDBUTM, and DBMF as defined in equations 1-4. The test images are contaminated with FVIN of unequal probability density in the range of 10% to 90% with an increment step of 10%. Tables 3-5 summarize the comparative measurements of the quality assessment metrics for different techniques tested on the given LDCT images. Figures 2-10 show the restoration results of the LDCT images 1-3 corrupted with noise density of 30-90% respectively.

Table 3. Comparative analysis of different filters at various noise density levels for the input test image 1

PSNR (in dB)									
Methods	**10%**	**20%**	**30%**	**40%**	**50%**	**60%**	**70%**	**80%**	**90%**
Noisy	14.11	11.10	9.34	8.09	7.12	6.33	5.66	5.08	4.57
SMF	35.09	29.26	23.13	18.09	14.13	11.13	8.73	6.86	5.32
AMF	36.78	33.97	28.30	24.09	19.52	16.97	13.41	10.23	8.01
DBA	37.24	34.22	32.12	29.45	26.71	23.12	20.24	14.73	10.26
MDBUTM	39.85	37.27	36.26	34.71	29.59	26.04	22.47	16.31	12.18
DBTMF	41.58	40.92	39.46	36.87	32.77	29.63	27.15	21.89	17.03
ODBF	44.62	43.71	42.05	40.68	37.91	34.98	32.16	29.48	24.11
MSE									
SMF	0.0003	0.0010	0.0049	0.0155	0.0386	0.0770	0.1338	0.2056	0.2933
AMF	0.0003	0.0006	0.0027	0.0116	0.0238	0.0573	0.0985	0.1674	0.2362
DBA	0.0003	0.0004	0.0024	0.0097	0.0187	0.0479	0.0862	0.1452	0.2202
MDBUTM	0.0003	0.0003	0.0020	0.0089	0.0149	0.0381	0.0796	0.1353	0.2111
DBTMF	0.0002	0.0002	0.0014	0.0056	0.0109	0.0257	0.0549	0.1141	0.1862
ODBF	0.0001	0.0002	0.0014	0.0052	0.0121	0.0265	0.0518	0.1059	0.1701
IEF									
SMF	141.4	75.0	23.9	10.0	5.0	3.0	2.0	1.5	1.2
AMF	184.2	124.3	106.2	67.8	45.0	27.1	14.9	7.0	6.4
DBA	228.5	168.0	139.2	104.0	71.1	42.6	31.3	24.8	10.0
MDBUTM	292.3	202.5	172.5	133.6	100.0	69.2	47.9	30.3	21.6
DBTMF	332.8	294.3	234.5	169.2	122.2	97.0	77.2	51.6	44.0
ODBF	406.2	387.6	312.9	256.8	211.4	191.8	143.8	105.8	80.3
SSIM									
SMF	92.7	87.5	72.4	47.2	22.3	8.5	2.9	1.1	0.5
AMF	94.7	92.9	86.9	76.8	54.0	40.1	29.7	23.1	20.3
DBA	95.6	94.1	92.5	86.1	68.6	54.8	41.7	32.8	27.9
MDBUTM	98.3	96.4	93.1	92.3	80.2	69.0	58.3	50.0	43.8
DBTMF	98.9	97.5	96.4	94.5	81.9	75.7	68.6	63.7	59.7
ODBF	99.4	98.8	97.3	96.1	90.6	86.1	81.4	78.2	74.5

Table 4. Comparative analysis of different filters at various noise density levels for the input test image 2

				PSNR (in dB)					
Methods	**10%**	**20%**	**30%**	**40%**	**50%**	**60%**	**70%**	**80%**	**90%**
Noisy	13.46	10.49	8.75	7.49	6.52	5.75	5.06	4.47	3.98
SMF	33.40	28.91	22.77	17.38	13.41	10.54	8.17	6.28	4.79
AMF	35.19	33.97	28.68	23.41	20.25	16.44	13.01	10.57	7.91
DBA	37. 04	35.90	30.45	27.51	24.23	21.02	18.42	14.41	11.02
MDBUTM	39.50	37.59	32.71	31.61	26.89	23.45	20.77	17.21	13.28
DBTMF	41.27	40.77	37.24	35.04	30.53	27.44	25.54	22.03	18.41
ODBF	44.11	43.23	41.71	38.11	34.81	32.01	30.96	27.11	23.87
				MSE					
SMF	0.0005	0.0013	0.0053	0.0183	0.0455	0.0882	0.1521	0.2351	0.3314
AMF	0.0003	0.0008	0.0037	0.0146	0.0338	0.0723	0.1385	0.2104	0.3162
DBA	0.0003	0.0007	0.0034	0.0127	0.0306	0.0648	0.1292	0.2081	0.3092
MDBUTM	0.0003	0.0007	0.0028	0.0119	0.0279	0.0596	0.1197	0.2049	0.3008
DBTMF	0.0002	0.0004	0.0018	0.0096	0.0228	0.0545	0.1106	0.1873	0.2852
ODBF	0.0002	0.0003	0.0018	0.0098	0.0234	0.0539	0.1074	0.1859	0.2813
				IEF					
SMF	97.4	68.8	25.2	9.7	4.9	3.0	2.0	1.5	1.2
AMF	146.54	135.26	120.54	98.54	77.4	67.1	32.05	20.6	10.4
DBA	174.2	154.6	144.5	126.3	91.4	80.2	61.8	40.3	25.6
MDBUTM	265.3	192.4	172.5	156.6	132.3	106.2	85.9	60.3	40.2
DBTMF	312.1	289.8	256.9	233.4	210.9	178.5	149.5	112.5	74.1
ODBF	395.4	363.6	332.7	305.7	271.4	222.9	182.4	145.2	94.5
				SSIM					
SMF	91.3	87.6	79.3	51.2	24.4	9.4	3.2	1.1	0.4
AMF	94.7	90.3	82.9	70.4	51.2	38.2	29.7	22.1	19.4
DBA	98.0	95.1	91.2	82.6	64.0	51.4	42.8	34.2	24.3
MDBUTM	98.0	96.8	93.9	90.7	82.2	78.0	66.3	58.1	51.2
DBTMF	98.2	97.0	95.4	93.5	91.0	87.7	82.1	78.5	66.0
ODBF	99.4	98.1	97.3	95.4	92.0	87.2	81.6	76.0	68.4

As far as the visual quality of the restored images for SMF, AMF, DBA and MDBUTM is concerned, the image details are preserved but noise removal is not completely successful at ND<50%. DBTMF and OBDF method remove noise completely without losing the image details at ND<50%. At ND>50%, SMF, AMF, DBA and MDBUTM completely fail in noise removal and image details are not preserved while DBTMF fails to remove noise completely and causes blurring in the restored images. The proposed OBDF method performs the restoration of LDCT images without blurring even at ND>90% successfully without losing the image details.

Table 5. Comparative analysis of different filters at various noise density levels for the input test image 3

PSNR (in dB)									
Methods	**10%**	**20%**	**30%**	**40%**	**50%**	**60%**	**70%**	**80%**	**90%**
Noisy	15.04	12.06	10.21	8.95	8.01	7.24	6.53	5.98	5.42
SMF	25.59	23.90	21.11	17.33	14.55	11.83	9.37	7.75	6.20
AMF	28.09	27.68	25.77	20.56	17.13	14.24	12.21	9.90	8.08
DBA	30.90	29.21	28.18	23.15	21.82	18.30	15.29	12.33	10.58
MDBUTM	34.84	31.97	30.39.	27.87	24.48	22.82	19.50	15.43	13.67
DBTMF	37.23	36.94	35.78	33.35	30.97	28.02	26.18	24.01	22.41
ODBF	41.62	40.84	40.09	38.73	35.97	32.74	30.11	28.43	25.65
MSE									
SMF	0.0028	0.0041	0.0077	0.0185	0.0350	0.0655	0.1155	0.1677	0.2398
AMF	0.0017	0.0031	0.0057	0.0145	0.0333	0.0613	0.1125	0.1624	0.2325
DBA	0.0018	0.0029	0.0054	0.0127	0.0301	0.0598	0.1092	0.1602	0.2317
MDBUTM	0.0016	0.0026	0.0048	0.0116	0.0289	0.0556	0.1079	0.1589	0.2298
DBTMF	0.0011	0.0019	0.0038	0.0097	0.0228	0.0497	0.1006	0.1515	0.2262
ODBF	0.0012	0.0021	0.0038	0.0099	0.0228	0.0500	0.0989	0.1489	0.2254
IEF									
SMF	20.74	15.66	12.12	6.88	4.48	2.89	1.93	1.50	1.18
AMF	94.4	87.8	75.4	64.2	53.3	39.7	28.0	17.2	10.5
DBA	128.3	124.8	115.1	107.0	91.2	78.6	62.3	39.1	26.4
MDBUTM	181.0	157.7	129.5	116.8	108.2	91.1	74.5	61.8	44.2
DBTMF	245.9	227.8	215.2	201.8	181.0	145.4	109.5	82.5	70.4
ODBF	297.6	276.3	243.4	227.8	197.1	157.7	130.5	98.2	86.4
SSIM									
SMF	66.29	62.54	53.59	38.24	25.44	15.79	7.92	4.86	2.43
AMF	94.7	90.3	82.9	70.4	51.2	38.2	29.7	22.1	19.4
DBA	98.0	95.1	91.2	82.6	64.0	51.4	42.8	34.2	24.3
MDBUTM	98.0	96.8	93.9	90.7	82.2	78.0	66.3	58.1	51.2
DBTMF	98.2	97.0	95.4	93.5	91.0	87.7	82.1	78.5	66.0
ODBF	99.4	98.1	97.3	95.4	92.0	87.2	81.6	76.0	68.4

Experimental results in terms of image quality assessment metrics summarized in Tables 3-5, clearly indicates that the proposed ODBF method gives better performance in comparison to the other filtering methods. As compared with DBTMF and ODBF methods for ND<50%, there is a marginal difference in image quality metrics for SMF, AMF, DBA and MDBUTMF while for ND>50%, there is a considerable difference.

It has been found experimentally that the maximum mask size of 21×21 gives optimum de-noising performance by ODBF method for an image of size 256×256in terms of visual quality and other image

Figure 11. Comparative analysis of image quality assessment metrics for different filtering techniques for the test image 1

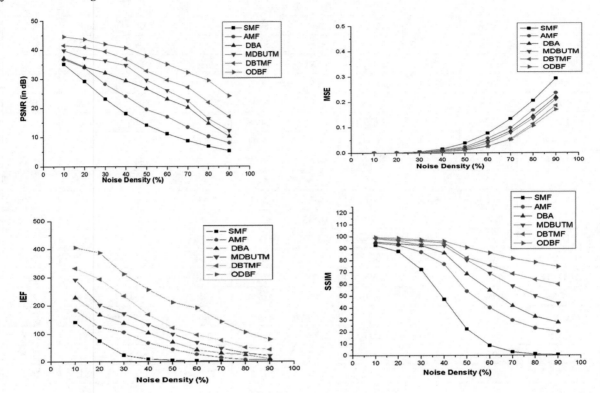

quality assessment parameters. The final de-noised image is constructed pixel by pixel using noise-free pixels and estimated noisy pixels.

The filtering algorithms has been developed using MATLAB 2015 installed in desktop with Intel Core i5-6400 CPU @ 2.70 GHz processor, 4 GB RAM running on Window 10 Pro operating system.

CONCLUSION

An image space decision based filtering method to restore LDCT images corrupted with FVIN of high density is proposed in this chapter. Accurate detection of noisy pixels using k-means clustering minimizes the possibility of blurring by avoiding the restoration of noise-free pixels. The restoration value of the corrupted pixel is estimated either by MM or TM estimation techniques based on the noise density. In the proposed ODBF method, an optimum decision is to be taken whether to proceed for adaptive mask sizing in order to overcome the eventualities of TM estimation failure and blurring of images in TM estimation technique. The visual quality of the restored images and image quality assessment metrics as defined in equation 1-4, clearly validate the effectiveness of the proposed ODBF method in restoration of LDCT images corrupted with FVIN of high-density without destroying finer details and coarser structures as compared with the other tested filtering methods. Restoration of LDCT images from random valued impulse noise can be studied in near future.

REFERENCES

Bhadouria, V. S., Ghoshal, D., & Siddiqi, A. H. (2014). A new approach for high density saturated impulse noise removal using decision-based coupled window median filter. *Signal, Image and Video Processing*, *8*(1), 71–84. doi:10.100711760-013-0487-5

Bhadouria, V. S., Ghoshal, D., & Siddiqi, A. H. (2014). A new approach for high density saturated impulse noise removal using decision-based coupled window median filter. *Signal, Image and Video Processing*, *8*(1), 71–84. doi:10.100711760-013-0487-5

Borsdorf, A., Raupach, R., Flohr, T., & Hornegger, J. (2008). Wavelet based noise reduction in CT-images using correlation analysis. *IEEE Transactions on Medical Imaging*, *27*(12), 1685–1703. doi:10.1109/TMI.2008.923983 PMID:19033085

Chen, T., & Wu, H. R. (2001). Adaptive impulse detection using center-weighted median filters. *IEEE Signal Processing Letters*, *8*(1), 1–3. doi:10.1109/97.889633

de González, A. B., Mahesh, M., Kim, K. P., Bhargavan, M., Lewis, R., Mettler, F., & Land, C. (2009). Projected cancer risks from computed tomographic scans performed in the United States in 2007. *Archives of Internal Medicine*, *169*(22), 2071–2077. doi:10.1001/archinternmed.2009.440 PMID:20008689

Dhanachandra, N., Manglem, K., & Chanu, Y. J. (2015). Image segmentation using *K-means* clustering algorithm and subtractive clustering algorithm. *Procedia Computer Science*, *54*, 764–771. doi:10.1016/j.procs.2015.06.090

Ehman, E. C., Guimarães, L. S., Fidler, J. L., Takahashi, N., Ramirez-Giraldo, J. C., Yu, L., & Harmsen, W. S. (2012). Noise reduction to decrease radiation dose and improve conspicuity of hepatic lesions at contrast-enhanced 80-kV hepatic CT using projection space denoising. *AJR. American Journal of Roentgenology*, *198*(2), 405–411. doi:10.2214/AJR.11.6987 PMID:22268185

Ehman, E. C., Yu, L., Manduca, A., Hara, A. K., Shiung, M. M., Jondal, D., & McCollough, C. H. (2014). Methods for clinical evaluation of noise reduction techniques in abdominopelvic CT. *Radiographics*, *34*(4), 849–862. doi:10.1148/rg.344135128 PMID:25019428

Elaiyaraja, G., & Kumaratharan, N. (2015). Enhancing Medical Images by New Fuzzy Membership Function Median Based Noise Detection and Filtering Technique. *Journal of Electrical Engineering & Technology*, *10*(5), 2197–2204. doi:10.5370/JEET.2015.10.5.2197

Esakkirajan, S., Veerakumar, T., Subramanyam, A. N., & PremChand, C. H. (2011). Removal of high density salt and pepper noise through modified decision based unsymmetric trimmed median filter. *IEEE Signal Processing Letters*, *18*(5), 287–290. doi:10.1109/LSP.2011.2122333

Greess, H., Wolf, H., Baum, U., Lell, M., Pirkl, M., Kalender, W., & Bautz, W. A. (2000). Dose reduction in computed tomography by attenuation-based on-line modulation of tube current: Evaluation of six anatomical regions. *European Radiology*, *10*(2), 391–394. doi:10.1007003300050062 PMID:10663775

Hsieh, J., Nett, B., Yu, Z., Sauer, K., Thibault, J. B., & Bouman, C. A. (2013). Recent advances in CT image reconstruction. *Current Radiology Reports*, *1*(1), 39–51. doi:10.100740134-012-0003-7

Huang, T., Yang, G. J. T. G. Y., & Tang, G. (1979). A fast two-dimensional median filtering algorithm. *IEEE Transactions on Acoustics, Speech, and Signal Processing, 27*(1), 13–18. doi:10.1109/TASSP.1979.1163188

Hwang, H., & Haddad, R. A. (1995). Adaptive median filters: New algorithms and results. *IEEE Transactions on Image Processing, 4*(4), 499–502. doi:10.1109/83.370679 PMID:18289998

Kalender, W. A., Wolf, H., Suess, C., Gies, M., Greess, H., & Bautz, W. A. (1999). Dose reduction in CT by on-line tube current control: Principles and validation on phantoms and cadavers. *European Radiology, 9*(2), 323–328. doi:10.1007003300050674 PMID:10101657

Kang, C. C., & Wang, W. J. (2009). Fuzzy reasoning-based directional median filter design. *Signal Processing, 89*(3), 344–351. doi:10.1016/j.sigpro.2008.09.003

Kanungo, T., Mount, D. M., Netanyahu, N. S., Piatko, C. D., Silverman, R., & Wu, A. Y. (2002). An efficient k-means clustering algorithm: Analysis and implementation. *IEEE Transactions on Pattern Analysis and Machine Intelligence, 24*(7), 881–892. doi:10.1109/TPAMI.2002.1017616

Ko, S. J., & Lee, Y. H. (1991). Center weighted median filters and their applications to image enhancement. *IEEE Transactions on Circuits and Systems, 38*(9), 984–993. doi:10.1109/31.83870

La Riviere, P. J., & Billmire, D. M. (2005). Reduction of noise-induced streak artifacts in X-ray computed tomography through spline-based penalized-likelihood sinogram smoothing. *IEEE Transactions on Medical Imaging, 24*(1), 105–111. doi:10.1109/TMI.2004.838324 PMID:15638189

Lange, K., & Carson, R. (1984). EM reconstruction algorithms for emission and transmission tomography. *Journal of Computer Assisted Tomography, 8*(2), 306–316. PMID:6608535

Le, T., Chartrand, R., & Asaki, T. J. (2007). A variational approach to reconstructing images corrupted by Poisson noise. *Journal of Mathematical Imaging and Vision, 27*(3), 257–263. doi:10.100710851-007-0652-y

Li, T., Li, X., Wang, J., Wen, J., Lu, H., Hsieh, J., & Liang, Z. (2004). Nonlinear sinogram smoothing for low-dose X-ray CT. *IEEE Transactions on Nuclear Science, 51*(5), 2505–2513. doi:10.1109/TNS.2004.834824

Lin, P. H., Chen, B. H., Cheng, F. C., & Huang, S. C. (2016). A Morphological Mean Filter for Impulse Noise Removal. *Journal of Display Technology, 12*(4), 344–350.

Lin, T. C. (2007). A new adaptive center weighted median filter for suppressing impulsive noise in images. *Information Sciences, 177*(4), 1073–1087. doi:10.1016/j.ins.2006.07.030

Luisier, F., Blu, T., & Unser, M. (2011). Image denoising in mixed Poisson–Gaussian noise. *IEEE Transactions on Image Processing, 20*(3), 696–708. doi:10.1109/TIP.2010.2073477 PMID:20840902

Meher, S. K., & Singhawat, B. (2014). An improved recursive and adaptive median filter for high density impulse noise. *AEÜ. International Journal of Electronics and Communications, 68*(12), 1173–11. doi:10.1016/j.aeue.2014.06.006

Oguchi, K., Sone, S., Kiyono, K., Takashima, S., Maruyama, Y., Hasegawa, M., & Feng, L. (2000). Optimal tube current for lung cancer screening with low-dose spiral CT. *Acta Radiologica*, *41*(4), 352–356. doi:10.1080/028418500127345451 PMID:10937757

Roy, A., Singha, J., Devi, S. S., & Laskar, R. H. (2016). Impulse noise removal using SVM classification based fuzzy filter from gray scale images. *Signal Processing*, *128*, 262–273. doi:10.1016/j.sigpro.2016.04.007

Saxena, P., & Kumar, R. S. (in press). A Locally Adaptive Edge Preserving Filter for Denoising of Low Dose CT using Multi-level Fuzzy Reasoning Concept. *International Journal of Biomedical Engineering and Technology*.

Srinivasan, K. S., & Ebenezer, D. (2007). A new fast and efficient decision-based algorithm for removal of high-density impulse noises. *IEEE Signal Processing Letters*, *14*(3), 189–192. doi:10.1109/LSP.2006.884018

Toh, K. K. V., & Isa, N. A. M. (2010). Noise adaptive fuzzy switching median filter for salt-and-pepper noise reduction. *IEEE Signal Processing Letters*, *17*(3), 281–284. doi:10.1109/LSP.2009.2038769

Toprak, A., & Güler, İ. (2006). Suppression of impulse noise in medical images with the use of fuzzy adaptive median filter. *Journal of Medical Systems*, *30*(6), 465–471. doi:10.100710916-006-9031-2 PMID:17233159

Vijaykumar, V. R., & Santhanamari, G. (2014). New decision-based trimmed median filter for high-density salt-and-pepper noise removal in images. *Journal of Electronic Imaging*, *23*(3), 033011–033011. doi:10.1117/1.JEI.23.3.033011

Wang, G., Li, D., Pan, W., & Zang, Z. (2010). Modified switching median filter for impulse noise removal. *Signal Processing*, *90*(12), 3213–3218. doi:10.1016/j.sigpro.2010.05.026

Wang, J., Li, T., Lu, H., & Liang, Z. (2006). Penalized weighted least-squares approach to sinogram noise reduction and image reconstruction for low-dose X-ray computed tomography. *IEEE Transactions on Medical Imaging*, *25*(10), 1272–1283. doi:10.1109/TMI.2006.882141 PMID:17024831

Wang, Z., Bovik, A. C., Sheikh, H. R., & Simoncelli, E. P. (2004). Image quality assessment: From error visibility to structural similarity. *IEEE Transactions on Image Processing*, *13*(4), 600–612. doi:10.1109/TIP.2003.819861 PMID:15376593

Zhang, X., Zhan, Y., Ding, M., Hou, W., & Yin, Z. (2013). Decision-based non-local means filter for removing impulse noise from digital images. *Signal Processing*, *93*(2), 517–524. doi:10.1016/j.sigpro.2012.08.022

Zhu, Y., Zhao, M., Zhao, Y., Li, H., & Zhang, P. (2012). Noise reduction with low dose CT data based on a modified ROF model. *Optics Express*, *20*(16), 17987–18004. doi:10.1364/OE.20.017987 PMID:23038347

Chapter 9
Proper Enhancement and Segmentation of the Overexposed Color Skin Cancer Image

Krishna Gopal Dhal
Midnapore College (Autonomous), India

Swarnajit Ray
J. B. Matrix Technology Pvt. Ltd., India

Mandira Sen
Tata Consultancy Services, India

Sanjoy Das
University of Kalyani, India

ABSTRACT

Proper enhancement and segmentation of the overexposed color skin cancer images is a great challenging task in medical image processing field. Computer-aided diagnosis (CAD) facilitates quantitative analysis of digital images with a high throughput processing rate. But, analysis of CAD purely depends on the input image quality. Therefore, in this study, overexposed and washed out skin cancer images are enhanced properly with the help of exact hue-saturation-intensity (eHSI) color model and contrast limited adaptive histogram equalization (CLAHE) method which is applied through this model. eHSI color model is hue preserving and gamut problem free. Any gray level image enhancement method can be easily employed for color image through this eHSI model. The segmentation of these enhanced color images has been done by employing one unsupervised clustering approach with the assistance of seven different gray level thresholding methods. Comparison of the segmentation efficiency of gray level thresholding methods has been done in the cases of overexposed as well as for enhanced images.

DOI: 10.4018/978-1-5225-5246-8.ch009

INTRODUCTION

Skin Cancer is of the most common type of cancer that affects human beings. It is a malignant tumour of the skin mainly caused by UV rays. Based on characteristics of skin cancer, they are grouped in two categories, namely Melanoma and Non-Melanoma (Wick, Sober, & Fitzpatrick, 1980). Basal cell carcinoma and squamous cell carcinoma are the most frequent types of Non-Melanoma and they form in the middle layer and upper layer of epidermis respectively (University of Michigan Health System, Kopf, Salopek, Slade, Marghoob, & Bart, 1994). The Non-Melanoma type cancer rarely spread to the other part of the body. On the other hand, Melanoma is the most vulnerable to all types of the Skin Cancer which affect the body rapidly. If it is detected at the first stage, then the survival rate is 100%. The rate of Melanoma skin cancer has increased especially in the USA. Globally the rate of Melanoma Skin Cancer is increasing from 6% to 15% (American Academy of Dermatology, Centers for Disease Control and Prevention, 2017; Elder, 1994; Xu, Jackowxki, Goshtasby, Roseman, Bines, Yu, Dhawan, & Huntley, 1999; Sober, Fitzpatrick, & Mihm, 1979; Xu et al., 1999; Salunke, 2014). To detect skin cancer in the early stage, various image processing based methods have been used. Cancer cell identification and segment the affected area is one of the critical steps of image processing. It becomes more difficult if the accrued image is low contrast. Image enhancement is a pre-prosing step in image processing which enhance the quality of an image depends upon the requirement (Ali, 2004; Hai, Li, & Gu, 2015). The tradition histogram equalization is one of the most widely use image enhancement technique, (Gonzalez & Woods, 2002) but it changes the mean brightness of the image middle of the gray level. So, it is not gives us good result for images like skin cancer. Therefore, in medical image enhancement field some local adaptive variants of the traditional HE like Adaptive HE (AHE), Contrast Limited Adaptive HE (CLAHE) (Hai, Li & Gu, 2015) have been used. Y Hai et. al. have proposed a CLAHE based method to enhance the colour stereoscopic endoscopy images (Hai, Li & Gu, 2015). Sasi et. al. (2013) applied CLAHE on Y component of the YCbCr space to enhance the myocardial Perfusion images. During pre 1980's input was taken through Gross feature method, but after 2000, it was taken through digital camera or digital microscope. The analyse or detection of cancerous region mainly consist of three stages:1) Proper Segmentation 2) Feature Extraction and 3) Lesions recognition. Image Segmentation is the first step in the detection of Skin Cancer Image. It plays a vital role to detect the cancerous region, but the proper segmentation is very difficult due to different parameters like the large variation of the lesion, shape, size and colour along with the different type of textures (Bhuiyan, Azad & Uddin, 2013; Ojala, Matti & Harwood, 1996). Otsu, GVF and colour based image segmentation methods had been used to segment out the cancerous region (Bhuiyan, Azad & Uddin, 2013). Feature extraction was done using ABCD (Nachbar et al., 1994; Ganster, Pinz, Rohrer, Wildling, Binder, & Kittler, 2001) (A=Asymmetry, B=Border, C=Colour, D=Diameter) rule over those segmented images. It had been found that the Otsu Method (Shannon & Weaver, 2001) shows the best result compared to the other methods proposed by Bhuiyan, Azad, and Uddin (2013). A pre-processing method has been used to remove undesired structures like hair from the image and also two segmentation techniques had been proposed which consider the lesion from the beginning using TDS value (Salunke, 2014). If the TDS value is 5.45 of the melanoma skin lesion, then this is the last stage of cancer. The TDS formula is based on the ABCD rule. For melanoma skin cancer the TDS value was said to be greater than 5.45. Xu et.al. proposed a thresholding based method to segment the gray level skin cancer images (Xu et al., 1999). A model of skin cancer lesion diagnosis system has been proposed by Saha et. al. (Saha & Gupta, 2014).

In this study, enhancement and segmentation of skin cancer images have been taken into consideration. CLAHE based colour image enhancement method has been successfully employed through Exact Hue-Saturation-Intensity (eHSI) model. Mainly entropy and relative entropy based methods have been employed to segment the skin cancer lesions. Entropy concept was proposed by Shannon et. al. (1948, Shannon & Weaver, 2001). Using the Shannon concept, maximum entropy based image segmentation method was first proposed by Pun et al. (1981). Later the method was corrected and improved by Kapur et al. (1985). Also using the Shannon concept Pal and Pal proposed the local entropy and joint entropy based methods (Pal & Pal, 1991, 1998). The relative entropy based concept was first proposed by Kullback-Leibler et. al. (1968). In this chapter, seven different types of image segmentation techniques have been used to segment the skin cancer lesions. The methods are local entropy (LE) and joint entropy (JE) (Pal & Pal, 1991, 1998), global entropy (GE), joint relative entropy (JRE), local relative entropy (LRE) (first proposed by Lee et. al. (2000), global relative entropy (GRE) (Joseph, 1997), Otsu method (Otsu, 1979). Relative entropy based methods i.e. local entropy and joint entropy based methods were used for segmentation of image and it was seen that the relative entropy based method gave better results than local and joint entropy based methods (Chang, Chen, Wang & Althouse, 1994). Unsupervised clustering algorithm based on intra-class and inter-class variance information has been proposed to segment the RGB colour images (Du, Chang, & Thouin, 2004). Chang et. al. did a comparative study among all the entropy based methods and used Histogram Compression and Translation (HCT) technique to increase the efficiency of relative entropy based methods as relative entropy based methods highly sensitive to the sparse histograms (Chang, Du, Wang, Guo, & Thouin, 2006). In the next section discuss about the image enhancement procedure.

IMAGE ENHANCEMENT

Proper enhancement of the colour image is a challenging job. Most of the enhancement methods are not gamut problem free i.e. the pixel values of output RGB image always lie within their respective intervals. Chien et.al. (2011) proposed exact Hue-Saturation-Intensity (eHSI) model to enhance the colour images. The advantage of this model is that any gray level contrast enhancement method can be successfully employed for colour image enhancement. eHSI model is a hue preserving and also gamut problem free. It is proved that eHSI model has significant ability to enhance the overexposed and washed out colour images in a proper way (Chien & Tseng, 2011). Traditional HE was applied by the author for enhancement purpose . But in this study CLAHE has been employed for enhancement purpose. The supremacy of CLAHE over HE clear from the Figures 2 and 3. The flowchart of the method is as follows and in next section discuss about the segmentation has been done.

SEGMENTATION

Thresholding is one of the most popular method for image segmentation. Seven different thresholding methods which are used in this study have been discussed below:

Figure 1. *Block diagram of the proposed scheme*

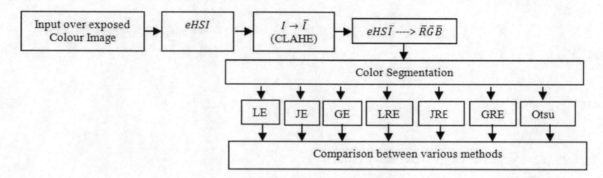

Otsu Method

In Otsu method, the optimal threshold has been calculated by maximizing the interclass variance. Here classes mean background and foreground of the image. It is automated cluster based thresholding. It divides the histogram into two classes and calculates optimum threshold value so that their intra class variance would be minimum. The probability of foreground and background t-thresholded binary image defined as:

$$P_B^t = \sum_{i=0}^{t} p_i \quad and \quad P_F^t = 1 - P_B^t \sum_{i=t+1}^{L-1} p_i \tag{1}$$

Where, P_B^t and P_F^t is the probability of background and foreground where t is the selected threshold value. An image can be described as 1-D histogram by a probability vector $\left(p_0, \ p_1 \ _{\ldots} \ p_{L-1}\right)$, where, $p_i = \dfrac{n_i}{n}$, ni is the total number of pixel of value in ith gray level and n is the total pixel in an image.

The mean of the background and foreground define as:

$$\mu_B^t = \frac{1}{P_B^t} \sum_{i=0}^{t} ip_i \quad and \quad \mu_F^t = \frac{1}{P_F^t} \sum_{i=t+1}^{L-1} ip_i \tag{2}$$

here μ_B^t and μ_F^t is the mean of foreground and background respectively.

The variance of foreground and background define as

$$var_B^t = \frac{1}{P_B^t} \sum_{i=0}^{t} \left(i - \mu_B^t\right)^2 p^i \text{ and } var_F^t = \frac{1}{P_F^t} \sum_{i=t+1}^{L-1} \left(i - \mu_F^t\right)^2 p^i \tag{3}$$

The interclass and intra class variance can be written as

$$\text{var}^t_{inter-class} = P^t_B \left(\mu^t_B - \mu \right)^2 + P^t_F \left(\mu^t_F - \mu \right)^2$$

$$= P^t_B P^t_F \left(\mu^t_B - \mu^t_F \right)^2$$

$$\text{var}^t_{intra-class} = P^t_B \text{var}^t_B + P^t_F \text{var}^t_F \tag{4}$$

Here $\mu = \sum_{i=1}^{L-1} i p_i$ is the global mean of the image.

So, in Otsu methods our aim is to maximize the inter class variance $\text{var}^t_{inter-class}$ and minimizes intra class variance $\text{var}^t_{intra-class}$. So it can be written as,

$$t_{Otsu} = \arg \left\{ \max_{1 \leq t \leq L} \{ \text{var}^t_{inter\_class} \} \right\}$$

$$= \arg \left\{ \min_{1 \leq t \leq L} \{ \text{var}^t_{intra\_class} \} \right\} \tag{5}$$

The Otsu method deals with 1-D histogram method.

Gray-Level Co-occurrence Matrix (GLCM)

An image can be described as 1-D histogram by a probability vector $(p_0, p_1 \dots p_{L-1})$, such 1-D histogram can't consider correlation among the gray level in the time of thresholding. But considering the correlation is crucial for proper image thresholding and segmentation. 2- D histogram with correlation improves the performance of thresholding. Co-occurrence matrix is one such approach and it is developed by Haralick et. al. (1973).

GLCM functions characterize the texture of an image by calculating how often pairs of the pixel with specific values and in a specified spatial relationship occur in an image. The number of gray levels in the image determines the size of the GLCM. Each element (i,j) in the resultant GLCM is simply the sum of the number of times that the pixel with value i occurred in the specified spatial relationship to a pixel with value j in the input image. The element of the (i, j)th entry of co-occurrence matrix is defined –

$$t(i, j) = \sum_{m=0}^{M-1} \sum_{n=0}^{N-1} \partial(m, n) \tag{6}$$

Where, M and N are the numbers of pixels in horizontal and vertical directions.

$$\partial\left(m,n\right) = \begin{cases} 1 & \begin{aligned} &\textit{if } f\left(m,n\right) = i \textit{ and } f\left(m,n+1\right) = j \textit{ or} \\ &f\left(m,n\right) = i \textit{ and } f\left(m+1,n\right) = j \end{aligned} \\ 0 & \textit{otherwise} \end{cases} \tag{7}$$

Co-occurrence matrix has been created depending on the two directions which are horizontal and vertical. In this paper normalized co-occurrence matrix has been used which can be defined as:

$$p\left(i,j\right) = \frac{t\left(i,j\right)}{\sum_{i=0}^{M-1}\sum_{j=0}^{N-1}t\left(i,j\right)} \tag{8}$$

Let t be the threshold value of an image. The co-occurrence matrix W is partitioned into four quadrants namely A, B, C, D. If we assume that in gray level the value of the pixels is above the threshold then assigned as foreground otherwise assigned as background, then A and C quadrants correspond to the local transition with foreground and background respectively. B and D quadrants are joint quadrants representing the joint transition across the boundaries of background and foreground respectively. The probability associated with each quadrant is as follows-

$$P_A^t = \sum_{i=0}^{t}\sum_{j=0}^{t}P_{ij}; \quad P_B^t = \sum_{i=0}^{t}\sum_{j=j+1}^{L-1}P_{ij}; \quad P_C^t = \sum_{i=i+1}^{L-1}\sum_{j=0}^{t}P_{ij}; \quad P_D^t = \sum_{i=i+1}^{L-1}\sum_{j=j+1}^{L-1}P_{ij} \tag{9}$$

$$P_{ij}^t\!\!\Big/_{\!\!A} = \frac{P_{ij}}{P_A^t}; \qquad P_{ij}^t\!\!\Big/_{\!\!B} = \frac{P_{ij}}{P_B^t}; \qquad P_{ij}^t\!\!\Big/_{\!\!C} = \frac{P_{ij}}{P_C^t}; \qquad P_{ij}^t\!\!\Big/_{\!\!D} = \frac{P_{ij}}{P_D^t}. \tag{10}$$

The Entropy of A i.e. $H_{BB}\left(t\right) = -\sum_{i=0}^{t}\sum_{j=0}^{t}P_{ij}^t\!\!\Big/_{\!\!A} \log P_{ij}^t\!\!\Big/_{\!\!A}$ \hfill (11)

The Entropy of D i.e. $H_{FB}\left(t\right) = -\sum_{i=t+1}^{L-1}\sum_{j=0}^{t}P_{ij}^t\!\!\Big/_{\!\!D} \log P_{ij}^t\!\!\Big/_{\!\!D}$ \hfill (12)

Box 1.

A (BB)	B (BF)
D (FB)	C (FF)

The Entropy of B i.e. $H_{BF}\left(t\right) = -\sum\limits_{i=0}^{t}\sum\limits_{j=t+1}^{L-1} P_{ij}^{t}/_{B} \, \log P_{ij}^{t}/_{B}$ $\qquad$ (13)

The entropy of C i.e. $H_{FF}\left(t\right) = -\sum\limits_{i=t+1}^{L-1}\sum\limits_{j=t+1}^{L-1} P_{ij}^{t}/_{C} \, \log P_{ij}^{t}/_{C}$ $\qquad$ (14)

Local Entropy (LE)

Here we consider A and C quadrants, where A is the local transitions from background to background (BB) and C is the local transition from foreground to foreground (FF).

Local Entropy is

$$H_{LE}\left(t\right) = H_{BB}\left(t\right) + H_{FF}\left(t\right) \qquad (15)$$

where $H_{BB}\left(t\right)$ and $H_{FF}\left(t\right)$ is the local transition entropy of BB and local transition entropy of FF respectively.

Threshold has been computed by the following rule (Chang, C.I., Du, Y., Wang J., Guo, S.M., Thouin, P.D. (2006))

$$t_{LE} = \arg\left\{\max_{t \in G\left(0,1............L-1\right)} H_{LE}\left(t\right)\right\} \qquad (16)$$

Joint Entropy (JE)

Here we consider B and D quadrants. It is joint transitions from background to fore ground (BF) and foreground to background (FB). The joint quadrants provide the edge information.

Joint Entropy is

$$H_{JE}\left(t\right) = H_{BF}\left(t\right) + H_{FB}\left(t\right) \qquad (17)$$

Threshold has been computed by the following rule (Chang, Du, Wang, Guo, & Thouin, 2006)

$$t_{JE} = \arg\left\{\max_{t \in G\left(0,1............L-1\right)} H_{JE}\left(t\right)\right\} \qquad (18)$$

Global Entropy (GE)

Global Entropy is the sum of local entropy $H_{LE}\left(t\right)$ and joint entropy $H_{JE}\left(t\right)$.

$$H_{GE}(t) = H_{BB}(t) + H_{FF}(t) + H_{BF}(t) + H_{FB}(t) \tag{19}$$

Threshold has been computed by the following rule:

$$t_{GE} = \arg\left\{ \max_{t \in G(0,1\ldots\ldots L-1)} H_{GE}(t) \right\} \tag{20}$$

Relative Entropy

It has been used to measure the information distance between two information sources. Let, M and N specified by the probability distribution p and h respectively. Then the relative entropy between p and h (or equivalently the entropy of p relative to h) is defined by Equation no. (21).

$$J(p;h) = \sum_{j=0}^{L-1} P_j \log \frac{p_j}{h_j} \tag{21}$$

It is also called the Kullback-Leiber's (1968): information discriminates measure and also known as Cross Entropy. Using this concept of relative entropy, Kittler and Illingworth (1986) proposed a new method called maximum entropy Thresholding (MET). In this case, the probability distribution p and h replaced by the gray-level transition $\{p_{ij}\}_{i=0,j=0}^{L-1,L-1}$ generated by the co-occurrence matrix of the original image and the gray-level transition probability $\{h_{ij}\}_{i=0,j=0}^{L-1,L-1}$ generated by the co-occurrence matrix of the threshold image. The transition probability defined by co-occurrence matrix contains the information of local gray-level transition in local quadrant A and C, and joint gray-level transition across the boundaries in joint quadrants B and D.

Using the gray-level transition probability $\{p_{ij}\}_{i=0,j=0}^{L-1,L-1}$ and $\{h_{ij}^t\}_{i=0,j=0}^{L-1,L-1}$ the second order relative entropy is define below-

$$J\left(\{p_{ij}\};\{h_{ij}^t\}\right) = \sum_{i=0}^{L-1}\sum_{j=0}^{L-1} p_{ij} \log \frac{p_{ij}}{h_{ij}^t} \tag{22}$$

Depending on this concept and LE, JE, GE, three relative entropies i.e. Local Relative Entropy (LRE), Joint Relative Entropy (JRE) and Global relative entropy have been employed in this paper.

Clustering Based Segmentation Method

Method of Du et. al. (2004) has been used here to segment the colour. As per the method, assume that the threshold values obtained for each of three colours, red (r), green (g) and blue (b) are specified by t_r, t_g and t_b respectively by using any thresholding method discussed. Let each pixel is denoted by

$p_{i,j} = \left(r_{i,j}, \ g_{i,j}, \ b_{i,j} \right)^T$ with $\left(i, j \right)$ being the spatial coordinate of the pixel. Using t_r, t_g, t_b as a preliminary threshold value in each colour domain, the pixel $p_{i,j} = \left(r_{i,j}, \ g_{i,j}, \ b_{i,j} \right)^T$ can be threshold as $\tilde{p}_{i,j} = \left(\tilde{r}_{i,j}, \ \tilde{g}_{i,j}, \ \tilde{b}_{i,j} \right)^T$ according to-

$$\tilde{r}_{i,j} = \begin{cases} 1, \ r_{i,j} > t_r \\ 0, \ r_{i,j} \leq t_r \end{cases}, \ \tilde{g}_{i,j} = \begin{cases} 1, \ g_{i,j} > t_r \\ 0, \ g_{i,j} \leq t_r \end{cases}, \ \tilde{b}_{i,j} = \begin{cases} 1, \ b_{i,j} > t_r \\ 0, \ b_{i,j} \leq t_r \end{cases}, \tag{23}$$

As a result, each $\left(r, g, b \right)$ colour pixel in a video image can be encoded by a 3-bit binary code word $\left(c_1, c_2, c_3 \right)$, where c_i for $1 \leq i \leq 3$ is a binary value taking either 0 or 1. Then we cluster all image pixel into eight classes $\left\{ C_k \right\}_{k-1}^8$ according to their associated codeword, where each codeword represents a clustered class. For example, all pixel encoded by (1, 0, 0) will be clustered into one class.

Next the mean of the each clustered class, say the kth class C_k, denoted by $p_{i,j} = \left(r_{i,j}, \ g_{i,j}, \ b_{i,j} \right)^T$ is calculated by

$$r_k = \sum_{r_{i,j} \in C_k} r_{i,j} \ / \sum_{r_{i,j} \in C_k} 1 ; g_k = \sum_{g_{i,j} \in C_k} g_{i,j} \ / \sum_{g_{i,j} \in C_k} 1 ;$$

$$b_k = \sum_{b_{i,j} \in C_k} b_{i,j} \ / \sum_{b_{i,j} \in C_k} 1 \tag{24}$$

Following the definitions of intra-class and inter-class variances given in Otsu method, we further calculated the intra-class variance σ_k for each class of $\left\{ C_k \right\}_{k-1}^8$ as

$$\sigma_k = \frac{1}{N_k} \left\{ \sum_{i,j \in C_k} \left[\left(r_{i,j} - r_k \right)^2 + \left(g_{i,j} - g_k \right)^2 + \left(b_{i,j} - b \right)^2 \right]^{1/2} \right\} \tag{25}$$

Where, N_k is the number of pixel in class C_k. The inter-class variance σ_{ck} between two classes C_k and C_j with $k \neq j$ can be calculated as,

$$\sigma_{ck} = \sqrt{ \left(\left(r_k + r_j \right)^2 + \left(g_k + g_j \right)^2 + \left(b_k + b_j \right)^2 \right)^{1/2}} \tag{26}$$

Where r_k, g_k, b_k and $(r_j, g_{j,} b_j)$ are the mean value of classes C_k and C_j respectively which is defined by Eq. no. (25)

Now we use the intra-class variance σ_k, σ_j and inter-class variance σ_{kj} acquired earlier as measures to rearrangement pixel to form a new set of the cluster. If two classes C_k and C_j for $k \neq j$ with either $\sigma_k \geq \sigma_{kj}$ or $\sigma_j \geq \sigma_{kj}$ then these two classes are combined into one class as the inter-class variance between two classes σ_{kj} must be greater than their individual intra-class variance σ_k and σ_j. This re-clustering process is repeated until all the inter-class variances and greater than their corresponding intra-class variance in which case no classes will be re-organized.

The procedure of the employed colour segmentation method has been discussed below:

Step 1: Apply one gray level thresholding method such as Otsu, LE, JE, GE, LRE, JRE or GRE to threshold colour skin cancer images in three coloured component i.e. R, G, B individually. Let t_r, t_g and t_b denote the resulting thresholding values respectively.

Step 2: By using Eq. no. (23) all the RGB-pixel vectors has been formulated into 3-bit binary code words. All pixels belong to same code word has been clustered into a single class.

Step 3: Using Eq. no. (24); mean for each class has been calculated, i.e. the gray level intensity average of pixel in each class along the R, G, B colour domains.

Step 4: Use Eq. no. (25) to calculate the intra-class variance and the inter-class variance for each class

Step 5: For any two class C_k and C_j with $k \neq j$ compare the intra-class variance σ_k and σ_j against the inter-class variance σ_{kj} to see if $\sigma_k \geq \sigma_{kj}$ or $\sigma_j \geq \sigma_{kj}$. If not, then terminate the re-clustering process. Go to step 7 otherwise continue.

Step 6: Merge the classes C_k and C_j into one class and go to step 3. If one of and C_j class is merged with a third class C_l then these three classes C_k, C_j and C_l must be merged into one class. Go to step 3.

Step 7: In this step no pixel vectors will be re-shuffled and the colour of the centroid of a class will be assigned to all the (RGB)- pixel vectors in that particular class.

EXPERIMENTAL RESULTS

This section depicts the experimental results of the enhancement and segmentation of the 15 overexposed colour skin cancer images. The dataset of 15 images has been made by us and also from "Google" image. All experiment are done on MatlabR2009b with Windows-7 OS, x32-based PC, Intel(R) Pentium (R)-CPU, 2.20 GHz with 2 GB RAM.

In Figure 2(a) and 3(a), red marks indicate the lesions. The segmented results of each method over the overexposed image i.e. Figure 2(a) are given as Figure 4.

The segmented results of each method over the enhanced image i.e. Figure 2(b) are given as Figure 5.

The segmented results of each method over the overexposed image i.e. Figure 3(a) are given as Figure 6.

The segmented results of each method over the enhanced image i.e. Figure 3(b) are given in Figure 7.

Quality Parameters

The description of the quality parameters is given below:

Figure 2. Original (b) result of CLAHE with eHSI (c) result of HE with eHSI

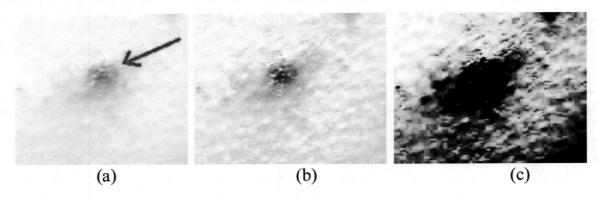

Figure 3. Original (b) result of CLAHE with eHSI (c) result of HE with eHSI

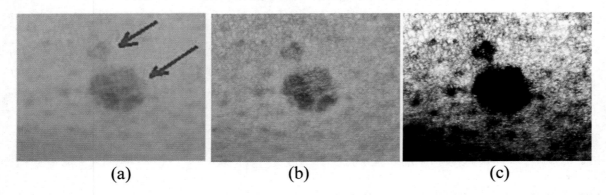

Figure 4. (a) Otsu (b) LE (c) GE (d) JE (e) LRE (f) JRE (g) GRE

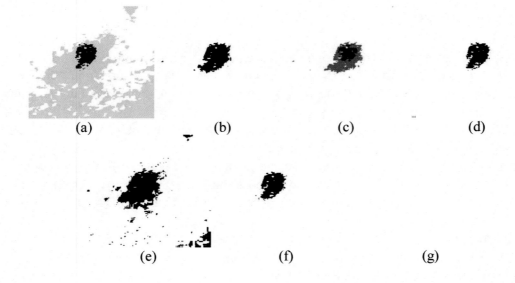

Figure 5. (a) Otsu (b) LE (c) GE (d) JE (e) LRE (f) JRE (g) GRE

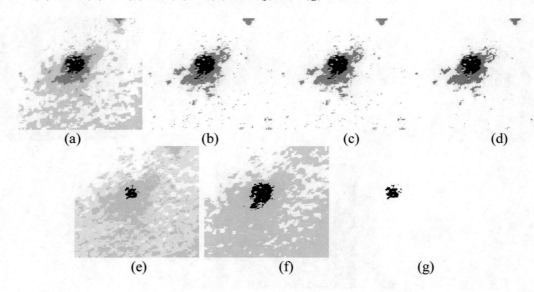

Figure 6. (a) Otsu (b) LE (c) GE (d) JE (e) LRE (f) JRE (g) GRE

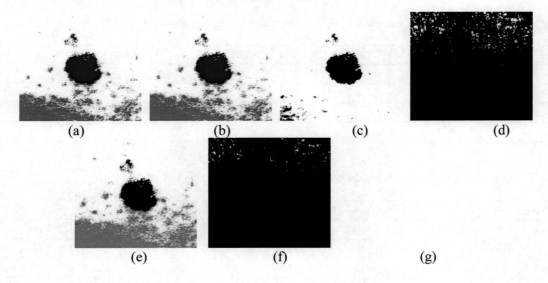

Quality Index Based on Local Variance (QILV)

QILV is used to measure the structural information of the image (Yim & Bovik, 2011). A great amount of the structural information of an image is coded in its local variance distribution. Local variances features of an image can help to compare two images properly. The local variance of an image I is defined as $\mathrm{Var}\left(\mathrm{I}_{i,j}\right) = \mathrm{E}\left(\left(\mathrm{I}_{i,j} - \overline{\mathrm{I}_{i,j}}\right)^2\right)$, being $\overline{\mathrm{I}_{i,j}} = \mathrm{E}\left(\mathrm{I}_{i,j}\right)$ the local mean of the image. It may be estimated using a weighted neighbor-hood $\eta_{i,j}$ pixel under analysis with respective weights ω_p as:

Figure 7. (a) Otsu (b) LE (c) GE (d) JE (e) LRE (f) JRE(g) GRE

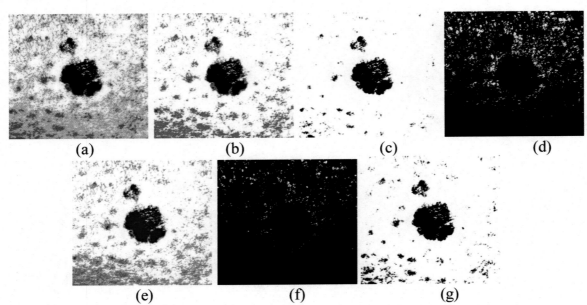

(a)   (b)   (c)   (d)

(e)   (f)   (g)

Table 1. Number of colour required for RGB colour thresholding methods

Img.	Otsu	LE	JE	GE	LRE	JRE	GRE
Figure 4	3	2	2	3	2	2	1
Figure 5	4	4	3	4	4	3	2
Figure 6	3	3	2	2	3	2	1
Figure 7	4	4	3	4	4	2	2

Table 2. Threshold values generated by RGB colour thresholding methods

Img.	Otsu	LE	JE	GE	LRE	JRE	GRE
Figure 4	(233,208,206)	(237,202,17)	(231,172,151)	(231,174,159)	(249,102,249)	(238,218,142)	(155,101,249)
Figure 5	(215,187,176)	(229,181,140)	(229,163,128)	(229,177,140)	(249,35,249)	(222,246,238)	(76,32,249)
Figure 6	(191,143,130)	(191,144,130)	(214,192,178)	(212,136,122)	(202,148,138)	(221,197,187)	(204,148,189)
Figure 7	(188,133,120)	(156,132,117)	(214,187,172)	(210,120,108)	(167,138,128)	(228,206,197)	(167,138,199)

Table 3. Values of the quality parameters of intensity component of the enhanced images

	Figure 2(b)	Figure 2(c)	Figure 3(b)	Figure 3(c)
QILV	0.9097	0.3028	0.8704	0.2917
PSNR	25.4524	6.4370	29.7198	10.5588
Entropy	5.9582	7.9782	5.7726	7.9835

$$\text{Var}\left(I_{i,j}\right) = \frac{\sum_{p \in \eta i, j} \omega_p \left(I_{i,j} - \overline{I_{i,j}}\right)^2}{\sum_{p \in \eta i, j} \omega_p} \quad \text{where,} \quad \overline{I_{i,j}} = \frac{\sum_{p \in \eta i, j} \omega_p I_p}{\sum_{p \in \eta i, j} \omega_p} \tag{27}$$

The estimated local-variance of the image will be used as a quality measure of the structural similarity between two images. The mean of the local variance μ_{V_I} is estimated as:

$$\mu_{V_I} = \frac{1}{MN} \sum_{i=1}^{M} \sum_{j=1}^{N} \text{Var}\left(I_{i,j}\right) \tag{28}$$

The (global) standard deviation of the local variance is defined as:

$$\sigma_{V_I} = \left(\frac{1}{MN-1} \sum_{i=1}^{M} \sum_{j=1}^{N} \left(\text{Var}\left(I_{i,j}\right) - \mu_{V_I}\right)^2\right)^{\frac{1}{2}} \tag{29}$$

Finally, the covariance between the variances of two images I and J is defined as:

$$\sigma_{V_I V_J} = \frac{1}{MN-1} \sum_{i=1}^{M} \sum_{j=1}^{N} \left(\text{Var}\left(I_{i,j}\right) - \mu_{V_I}\right)\left(\text{Var}\left(J_{i,j}\right) - \mu_{V_J}\right) \tag{30}$$

We defined the Quality Index based on Local Variance (QILV) between two images I and J as:

$$\text{QILV}\left(I, J\right) = \frac{2\mu_{V_I}\mu_{V_J}}{\mu_{V_I}^2 + \mu_{V_J}^2} \cdot \frac{2\sigma_{V_I}\sigma_{V_J}}{\sigma_{V_I}^2 + \sigma_{V_J}^2} \cdot \frac{\sigma_{V_I V_J}}{\sigma_{V_I}\sigma_{V_J}} \tag{31}$$

The first term of QILV equation carries out a comparison between the mean of the local variance distributions of both images. The second one compares the standard deviation of the local variances. The third term is the one to introduce spatial coherence. To avoid some computational problems with small values, some constants may be added to every term in the equation.

Peak-Signal to Noise Ratio (PSNR)

This statistical metric is also used to measure the performance of image enhancement methods. PSNR is the ratio between the maximum possible power of the signal and the power of the noise. It is actually distortion metric which crucially depends on Mean-Squared Error (MSE). MSE defined as:

$$\text{MSE}\left(f, G\right) = \frac{\sum_{i=0}^{N-1} \sum_{j=0}^{M-1} \left[f\left(i,j\right) - G\left(i,j\right)\right]^2}{M \times N} \tag{32}$$

Where f and G are the inputs and output image respectively. M, N are the number of rows and columns of the image.

The PSNR is calculated as follows:

$$PSNR\left(f, G\right) = 10 \ \log_{10}\left(\frac{\left(L - 1\right)^2}{MSE\left(f, G\right)}\right) \tag{33}$$

L is the number discrete gray level. For 8 bit image it is 256.

If the value of PSNR is increased then the contrast of the image is also enhanced and Absolute Mean Brightness Error (AMBE) is also reduced to some extent.

Analysis of the Results

In this study, overexposed skin cancer images have been properly enhanced with the help of eHSI colour model and CLAHE method. Figures 2 and 3 reveal that CLAHE has great contribution for enhancing these overexposed images. From the table no. 3, it is clear that for CLAHE based enhancement gives better values of QILV and PSNR. Values of Entropy unveil that entropy is not a good criterion for this kind of image enhancement.

Lesion segmentation of those overexposed images is the main aim of this paper. Unsupervised clustering based segmentation approach has been employed here. Figures 4, 5, 6 and 7 reveals that the colour segmentation efficiency significantly depends on two factors: 1. the proper enhancement of the overexposed images. 2. Usages of thresholding method like Otsu, LE, JE and so on. From Figures 4, 5, 6 and 7, it is clear that CLAHE based enhancement increases the efficiency of clustering based segmentation method. Specially, Figures 4(g), 5(g), 6(g) and 7(g) proves the effect of before and after enhancement segmentation efficiency where GRE gives better segmented result over enhanced image. Table 1 reveals that after enhancement number of colours required for representing the segmented colour images always increase. From the visual analysis, it can be easily verified that Otsu and LE based segmentation results always outperforms the other six thresholding methods. Among relative entropy based methods, LRE outperforms the other two i.e. JRE and GRE. Collectively, JRE and GRE based segmentation give worst result than other five thresholding based segmentation based methods. Table 2 represents the initial threshold values which have been found by applying any specific gray level thresholding method over R,G,B component respectively i.e. t_r, t_g and t_b.

CONCLUSION

From the experimental results, it can be easily concluded that CLAHE based enhancement significantly helps to increase the segmentation efficiency of the employed method. The enhanced images are free from out of gamut problem. The applied enhancement approach can be easily employed in colour medical image domain in future. Visual analysis clears that Otsu and LE outperforms the other five thresholding methods in the skin cancer image segmentation field. All relative entropy based methods fail to produce good results and LRE is best among them. In future, this combined enhancement and segmentation approach can be applied in other medical image processing field. The main demerits of the employed clustering based segmentation approach are that it significantly depends on the used gray level segmentation method and maximum number classes are eight which is very small. In future, overcome of these demerits are the main challenges. It is also vital to point that image represented in any colour space like YUV, CIE and so on can be easily processed by using the applied approach because the only overhead is a conversion between colour spaces.

REFERENCES

Aja-Fern'andez, S., Jos'eEst'epar, R.S., Alberola-L'opez, C., Westin, C. F. (2006). Image Quality Assessment based on Local Variance. *28th IEEE EMBS Annual International Conference*, 4815-4818. 10.1109/IEMBS.2006.259516

Ali, M. R. (2004). Realization of the Contrast Limited Adaptive Histogram Equalization (CLAHE) for Real-Time Image Enhancement. *Journal of VLSI Signal Processing Systems for Signal, Image and Video Technology, 38*, 35-44.

American Academy of Dermatology. (n.d.). Retrieved from https://www.aad.org/media/stats/conditions/skin-cancer

Bhuiyan, A. H., Azad, I., & Uddin, K. (2013). Image Processing for Skin Cancer Features Extraction. *International Journal of Scientific & Engineering Research, Vol, 4*, 1–6.

Centers for Disease Control and Prevention. (2017). Retrieved from http://www.cdc.gov/cancer/skin/statistics/race.htm

Chang, C. I., Chen, K., Wang, J., & Althouse, M. J. G. (1994). A Relative Entropy-Based approach to Image thresholding. *Pattern Recognition, Vol, 27*(9), 1275–1289. doi:10.1016/0031-3203(94)90011-6

Chang, C. I., Du, Y., Wang, J., Guo, S. M., & Thouin, P. D. (2006): Survey and comparative analysis of entropy and relative entropy thresholding techniques. *IEE Proceedings - Vision, Image and Signal Processing, 153*, 837-850. 10.1049/ip-vis:20050032

Chen, H. C., & Wang, S. J. Visible colour difference-based quantitative evaluation of colour segmentation. *IEE Proceedings - Vision, Image and Signal Processing, 153*, 598-609. 10.1049/ip-vis:20045221

Chien, C. L., & Tseng, D. C. (2011). Colour image enhancement with exact HIS colour model. Int. *J. of Innovative Computing, Information and Control, 7*, 6691–6710.

Du, Y., Chang, C. I., & Thouin, P. D. (2004). Unsupervised approach to colour video thresholding. *Optical Engineering, 43*(2), 282–289. doi:10.1117/1.1637364

Elder, D. E. (1994). Skin cancer Melanoma and other specific non melanoma skin cancers. *Cancer, 75*(1), 245-256.

Ganster, H., Pinz, A., Rohrer, R., Wildling, E., Binder, M., & Kittler, H. (2001). Automated Melanoma Recognition. *IEEE Transactions on Medical Imaging, 20*(3), 233–239. doi:10.1109/42.918473 PMID:11341712

Gonzalez, R. C., & Woods, R. E. (2002). *Digital Image Processing* (2nd ed.). New York: Prentice Hall.

Gotlieb, C. C., & Kreyszig, H. E. (1990). Texture descriptor Based on Co-occurrence Matrix. *Computer Vision, Graphics, and Image Processing, 51*, 71-86.

Hai, Y., Li, L., & Gu, J. (2015). Image Enhancement Based on Contrast Limited Adaptive Histogram Equalization for 3D Images of Stereoscopic Endoscopy. *2015 IEEE International Conference on Information and Automation*, 668-672 10.1109/ICInfA.2015.7279370

Haralick, R. M., Shanmugam, K., & Dinstein, I. (1973). Textural features for image classification. *Trans. on systems man and cybernetics, 3*, 610–621.

Joseph, C. E. (1997). Unifying the derivations for the Akaike and corrected Akaike information criteria. *Statistics and Probability Letters, 33*(2), 201–208. doi:10.1016/S0167-7152(96)00128-9

Kapur, J. N., Sahoo, P. K., & Wong, A. K. C. (1985). A New Method for Gray-Level Picture Thresholding Using the Entropy of the Histogram. *Computer Vision, Graphics and Image Processing, Vol, 29*(3), 273–285. doi:10.1016/0734-189X(85)90125-2

Kittler, J., & Illingworth, J. (1986). Minimum error thresholding. *Pattern Recognition, Vol, 19*(1), 41–47. doi:10.1016/0031-3203(86)90030-0

Kopf A.W., Salopek T.G., Slade J., Marghoob A.A., & Bart R.S. (1994). Techniques of cutaneous examination for the detection of skin cancer. *Cancer, 75*(2), 684–690.

Kullback, S. (1968). *Information theory and statics*. Dover.

Lee, S. K., Lo, C. S., Wang, C. M., Chung, P. C., Chang, C. I, Yang, C. W., Hsu, P. C. (2000). A computer-aided design mammography screening system for detection and classification of micro calcifications. *Int. J. Med Inform.,60*, 29-57.

Liu, G. H., & Yang, J. Y. (2008). Image retrieval based on the texton co-occurrence matrix. *Pattern Recognition, Vol, 41*(12), 3521–3527. doi:10.1016/j.patcog.2008.06.010

Nachbar, F., Stolz, W., Merkle, T., Cognetta A.B., Vogt T., Landthaler, M., Bilck, P., Braun-Falco, O., & Plewig, G. (1994). The ABCD rule of dermatoscopy: High Prospective value in the diagnosis of doubtful melanocytic skin lesion. *Journal of the American Academy of Dermatology, 30*, 551-559.

Naik, S. K., & Murthy, C.A. (n.d.). Hue Preserving Colour Image Enhancement without Gamut Problem. *IEEE Transactions on Image Processing, 12*, 1591-1598.

Ojala, T., Matti, P. A., & Harwood, D. (1996). A comparative study of texture measure with classification based on feature distribution. *Pattern Recognition, 29*(1), 51–59. doi:10.1016/0031-3203(95)00067-4

Otsu, N. (1979). A Threshold Selection Method from Gray-Level Histograms. *IEEE Transactions on Systems, Man, and Cybernetics, 9*(1), 62–66. doi:10.1109/TSMC.1979.4310076

Pal, N. R., & Pal, S. K. (1989). Entropic thresholding. *Signal Processing, 16*(2), 97–108. doi:10.1016/0165-1684(89)90090-X

Pal, N. R., & Pal, S. K. (1991). Entropy: A New Definition and its Applications. *IEEE Transactions on Systems, Man, and Cybernetics, 21*(5), 1260–1270. doi:10.1109/21.120079

Pal, S. K., & Pal, N. R. (1989). Object Background segmentation using a new definition Entropy. *IEEE Proceedings, 136*, 284-295. 10.1049/ip-e.1989.0039

Pun, T. (1981). Entropic Thresholding, A New Approach. *Computer Graphics and image processing, 16*, 201-239.

Saha, S., & Dr. Gupta, R. (2014). An Automated Skin Lesion Diagnosis by using Image Processing Techniques. *International Journal on Recent and Innovation Trends in Computing and Communication, 2*, 1081–1085.

Salunke, S. (2014). Survey on Skin lesion segmentation and classification. *International journal of image processing and data visualization, 1*, 1-5.

Sasi, N. M., Jayasree, V. K. (2013). Contrast Limited Adaptive Histogram Equalization for Qualitative Enhancement of Myocardial Perfusion Images. *Engineering, 5*, 326-331.

Shannon, C. E. (1948). A mathematical theory of communication. *The Bell System Technical Journal, 27*(3), 379–423. doi:10.1002/j.1538-7305.1948.tb01338.x

Shannon, C. E., & Weaver, W. (2001). The Mathematical Theory of Communication. *ACM SIGMOBILE Mobile Computing and Communications Review, 5*(1), 3–55. doi:10.1145/584091.584093

Shyu, M. S., & Leou, J. J. (1998). A genetic algorithm approach to colour image enhancements. *Pattern Recognition, 31*, 881–890.

Sober, A. J., Fitzpatrick, T. B., & Mihm, M. C. (1979). Early recognition of cutaneous melanoma. *JAMA, 242*(25), 2795–2799. doi:10.1001/jama.1979.03300250051033 PMID:501893

Strickland, R. N., Kim, C. S., & McDonnel, W. F. (1987). Digital colour image enhancement based on saturation component. *Optical Engineering (Redondo Beach, Calif.), 26*(7), 609–616. doi:10.1117/12.7974125

University of Michigan Health System. (n.d.). Retrieved from https://www.med.umich.edu/1libr/cancer/skin04.html

Wick, M. M., Sober, A. J., Fitzpatrick, T. B., Mihm, M. C., Kopf, A. W., Clark, W. H., & Blois, M. S. (1980). Clinical characteristics of early cutaneous melanoma Cancer. *Cancer, 45*(1), 2684–2706. doi:10.1002/1097-0142(19800515)45:10<2684::AID-CNCR2820451033>3.0.CO;2-2 PMID:7379001

Xu, C., & Prince, J. L. (1998). Snakes, shapes, and gradient vector flow. *IEEE Transactions on Image Processing, 7*(3), 359–369. doi:10.1109/83.661186 PMID:18276256

Xu, L., Jackowskia, M., Goshtasbya, A., Roseman, D., Binesb, S., Yu, C., Dhawand, A., & Huntley, A. (1999). Segmentation of skin cancer images. *Image and Vision Computing, 17*, 65-74.

Xu, L., Jackowxki, M., Goshtasby, A., Roseman, D., Bines, S., Yu, C., Dhawan, A., & Huntley, A. (1999). Skin Images Segmentation. *Vis. Comput., 17*, 65-74.

Yim, C., & Bovik, A. C. (2011). Quality Assessment of Deblocked Images. *IEEE Transactions on Image Processing*, *20*(1), 88–98. doi:10.1109/TIP.2010.2061859 PMID:20682474

Yousefi, S., Qin, J., Zhi, Z., & Wang, R. K. (2013). Uniform enhancement of optical micro-angiography images using Rayleigh contrast-limited adaptive histogram equalization. *Quant Imaging Med Surg, 3*, 5–17. PMID:23482880

KEY TERMS AND DEFINITIONS

Gamut Problem: The pixels values of the channels of the color space do not lie within their respective intervals.

Hue: Hue represents the kind of color (i.e., the dominant wavelength that exists in mixture of colors).

Image Enhancement: Image enhancement is the technique of transforming one image into a better-quality image according to the requirements.

Segmentation: Image segmentation is a process which sub-divides the image in the non-overlapping subset containing similar property, color, intensity, etc.

Chapter 10
3D Medical Images Compression

Mohamed Fawzy Aly
Cairo University, Egypt

Mahmood A. Mahmood
Cairo University, Egypt

ABSTRACT

Medical images are digital representations of the body. Medical imaging technology has improved tremendously in the past few decades. The amount of diagnostic data produced in a medical image is vast and as a result could create problems when sending the medical data through a network. To overcome this, there is a great need for the compression of medical images for communication and storage purposes. This chapter contains an introduction to compression types, an overview of medical image modalities, and a survey on coding techniques that deal with 3D medical image compression.

IMAGE COMPRESSION

Image compression is the appliance of data compression on digital images which are made up of large number of pixels. Compression is the reduction in the amount of image data (the number of bytes) while preserving information (image details) with the intention of optimizing and putting to maximum use the data storage and data transmission facilities. Images transmitted over the internet are an excellent example of why data compression is important. Suppose we need to download a digitized color photograph over a computer's 33.6 kbps modem. If the image is not compressed (a TIFF file, for example), it will contain about 600 kilo bytes of data. If it has been compressed using a lossless technique (such as used in the GIF format), it will be about one-half this size, or 300 Kbytes. If lossy compression has been used (a JPEG file), it will be about 50 Kbytes. The download time for these three equivalent files are 142 seconds, 71 seconds, and 12 seconds, respectively which is a huge difference.

DOI: 10.4018/978-1-5225-5246-8.ch010

The following table (Table 1) shows the qualitative transition from simple text to full-motion video data and the disk space transmission bandwidth, and transmission time needed to store and transmit such uncompressed data (Sachin Dhawan, 2011).

There are two major components of compression which are Redundancy and Irrelevancy Reduction. Redundancy Reduction aims to eliminate duplication from the image. Irrelevancy Reduction neglects parts of the signal that will not be noticed by the signal receiver, namely the Human Visual System (HVS). The mechanism of compression can be achieved by removing one or more of three basic data redundancies:

- **Coding Redundancy (Spectral Redundancy):** This is caused by correlation between different color levels or spectral bands.
- **Interpixel Redundancy (Spatial Redundancy):** This is caused by correlation or dependence between neighboring pixel values.
- **Psycovisual Redundancy (Temporal Redundancy):** This is caused by correlation between different frames in images.

Various techniques could be used to compress the images and could be classified into two ways; Lossless compression techniques and Lossy compression techniques.

Lossless compression techniques are where the reconstructed image after compression is numerically identical to the original image. No noise or any losses are found in the reconstructed image. Lossless compression includes: Run Length Coding, Dictionary Coding, Transform Coding, and Entropy Coding. Entropy Coding includes: Huffman Coding which is a simple Entropy Coding and commonly used as the final stage of compression, Arithmetic Coding, Golomb Coding which is a simple Entropy Coding for infinite input data with a geometric distribution and finally the Universal Coding which is also an Entropy Coding for infinite input data with an arbitrary distribution.

Lossy compression techniques are where the reconstructed image after compression is not identical to the original image; some losses are found in sense of noise, blurring etc. in reconstructed image. Lossy techniques cause image quality degradation in each compression or decompression step. Lossy techniques have greater compression ratio as compared to Lossless techniques.

Table 1. Multimedia data types and uncompressed storage space, transmission bandwidth, and transmission time required; the prefix kilo- denotes a factor of 1000 rather than 1024

Multimedia Data	Size / Duration	Bits/Pixel or Bits/ Sample	Uncompressed Size (B for Bytes)	Transmission Bandwidth (b for bits)	Transmission Time
A page of text	11" x 8.5 "	Varying resolution	4-8 KB	32 – 46 kb / page	1.1 – 2.2 sec
Telephone Quality Speech	10 sec	8 bps	80 KB	64 kb / sec	22.2 sec
Gray Scale Image	512 x 512	8 bpp	262 KB	2.1 Mb / image	1 min 13 sec
Color Image	512 x 512	24 bpp	786 KB	6.29 Mb / image	3 min 39 sec
Medical Image	2048 x 1680	12 bpp	5.16 MB	41.3 Mb / image	23 min 54 sec
SHD Image	2048 x 2048	24 bpp	12.58 MB	100 Mb / image	58 min 15 sec

MEDICAL IMAGE COMPRESSION

Compression methods are important in many medical applications to ensure fast interactivity through large sets of images (e.g. volumetric data sets, image databases), for searching context dependent images and for quantitative analysis of measured data. Medical data are represented in digital form. Medical imaging is the technique and process of creating visual representations of the interior of a body for clinical analysis and medical intervention, as well as visual representation of the function of some organs or tissues (physiology) (Ukrit et al., 2011; Sridevi et al., 2012). Medical imaging seeks to reveal internal structures hidden by the skin and bones, as well as to diagnose and treat disease. Medical imaging also establishes a database of normal anatomy and physiology to make it possible to identify abnormalities. Although imaging of removed organs and tissues can be performed for medical reasons, such procedures are usually considered part of pathology instead of medical imaging.

Traditional medical imaging systems provide 2D visual representations of human organs while more advanced digital medical imaging systems (e.g. X-ray CT) can create both 2D and in many cases 3D images of human organs. Systems capable of 3D digital medical imaging are currently only a small part of the overall medical imaging market. Current medical imaging systems are being provided with displays that can only visually represent the imaging data collected in 2D or at best in simulated 3D on 2D. As advances continue to be made in 3D displays, including glasses-free 3D volumetric displays, the potential applications are endless.

By increasing the demand of direct digital imaging systems for medical diagnostics, digital image processing becomes more crucial. Hence to make this process easy, National Electrical Manufacturers Association (NEMA) created the Digital Imaging and Communications in Medicine (DICOM) standard (Shreya, 2016), which assists the allocation and analysis of medical images such as MRI'S, CT scans and ultrasound. Digital image processing basically covers four major areas for medical image processing, as shown in Figure 1.

- **Image Formation:** It includes all the steps from capturing the image to outlining the digital image matrix. Acquisition and digitization comes under formation.
- **Image Enhancement**: It includes all the steps of transforming, registration and filtering the images.
- **Image Visualization**: It demotes all classes of manipulation for optimized output of the image of that matrix. It involves illumination, shading and display steps.
- **Image Analysis**: It includes all the steps for processing the image like feature extraction, segmentation and classification. These steps require prior knowledge on the content and nature of the system.
- **Image Management**: It summarizes all the techniques that offer the efficient storage space, transmission, archiving, and retrieval of image data.

MEDICAL IMAGING COMPRESSION MODALITIES

Medical Imaging applies different techniques to acquire human images for clinical purposes, including diagnosis, monitoring, and treatment guidance. As a multidisciplinary field, medical imaging requires the improvements in both science and engineering to implement and maintain its noninvasive feature.

Figure 1. Steps of medical image processing

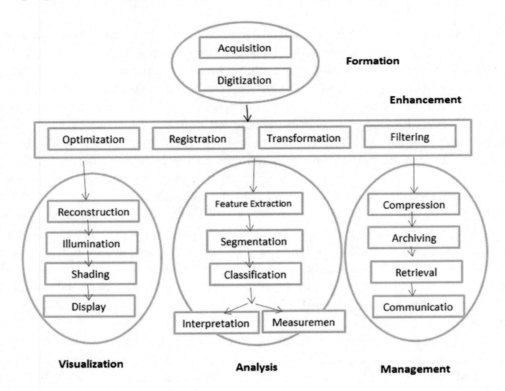

Computational and mathematical methods are involved with imaging theories, models, reconstruction algorithms, image processing, quantitative imaging techniques, acceleration techniques, and multimodal imaging in medical imaging. The main purpose of this issue is bridging the gap between mathematical methods and their applications in medical imaging.

Nowadays a huge volume of medical images are produced in both 2D and 3D through various advancement remedial imaging modalities, particularly, Magnetic Resonance Imaging (MRI), Ultrasound Imaging (US), Digital Flurography (DF), X-bar imaging (Radiography), Single Photon Emission Computed Tomography (SPECT), Positron Emission Tomography (PET), Nuclear Medicine(Scintigraphy), Computed Tomography (CT) pictures and Digital Subtraction Angiography (DSA). Table (2) shows typical sizes of some medical images.

Radiography uses electromagnetic radiation to take images of the inside of the body. The most well-known and common form of radiography is x-ray. For this procedure, an x-ray machine beams high-energy waves onto the body. The soft tissues, such as skin and organs, do not absorb these waves, whereas hard tissue like bones does absorb the waves. The machine transfers the results of the x-ray onto a film, showing the parts of the body that absorbed the waves (the bones) in white and leaving the unabsorbed materials in black. X-rays can depict a two-dimensional image of a body region, and only from a single angle (figure 2). In contrast, more recent medical imaging technologies produce data that is integrated and analyzed by computers to produce three-dimensional images or images that reveal aspects of body functioning.

Table 2. Typical matrix sizes for different types of digital diagnostic images

Digital Imaging Modality	Matrix Size	Typical Bit Depth
Nuclear Medicine	128 x 128	12
Magnetic Resonance Imaging	256 x 256	12
Computed Tomography	512 x 512	12
Digital Subtraction Angiography	1024 x 1024	10
Computed Radiography	2048 x 2048	12
Digital Radiography	2048 x 2048	12
Digital Mammography	4096 x 4096	12

Figure 2. X-Ray of a hand

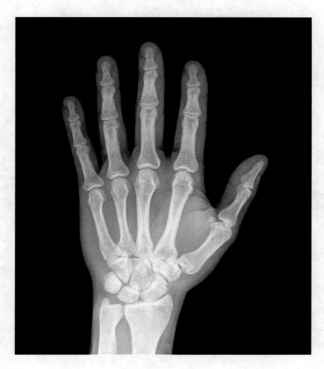

Computed tomography (CT) is a noninvasive imaging technique that uses computers to analyze several cross-sectional X-rays in order to reveal minute details about structures in the body. The technique was invented in the 1970s and is based on the principle that, as X-rays pass through the body, they are absorbed or reflected at different levels. In the technique, a patient lies on a motorized platform while a computerized axial tomography (CAT) scanner rotates 360 degrees around the patient, taking X-ray images (Brenner et al., 2007). A computer combines these images into a two-dimensional view of the scanned area, or "slice" (figure 3).

Magnetic Resonance Imaging (MRI) involves radio waves and magnetic fields to look at the organs and other structures in the body. The procedure requires an MRI scanner, which is, simply put, a large

Figure 3. The results of a CT scan of the head are shown as successive transverse sections

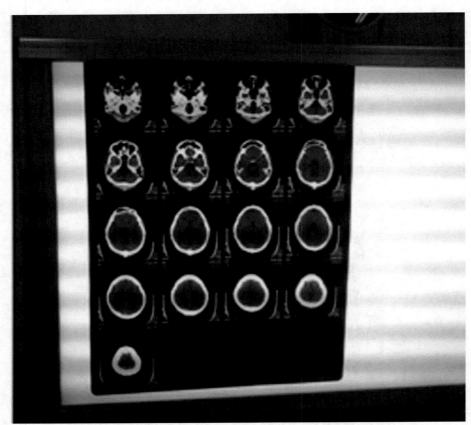

tube that contains a massive circular magnet. This magnet creates a powerful magnetic field that aligns the protons of hydrogen atoms in the body. Those protons are then exposed to radio waves, causing the protons to rotate. When the radio waves are turned off, the protons relax and realign themselves, emitting radio waves in the recovery process that can be detected by the machine to create an image (Sabbagh, 2016). The early MRI scanners were crude but advances in digital computing and electronics led to their advancement over any other technique for precise imaging, especially to discover tumors. MRI also has the major advantage of not exposing patients to radiation. Drawbacks of MRI scans include their much higher cost, and patient discomfort with the procedure (figure 4).

Positron emission tomography (PET) is a medical imaging technique involving the use of so-called radiopharmaceuticals, substances that emit radiation that is short-lived and therefore relatively safe to administer to the body. PET is widely used to diagnose a multitude of conditions, such as heart disease, the spread of cancer, certain forms of infection, brain abnormalities, bone disease, and thyroid disease, (figure 5).

Nuclear medicine is a rather general term that involves any medical use of radioactive materials. But in terms of imaging, it usually refers to the use of radioactive tracers, which are radioactive materials that are injected or swallowed so that they can travel through the digestive or circulatory system. The radiation produced by the material can then be detected to create an image of those systems.

Figure 4. An MRI machine generates a magnetic field around a patient

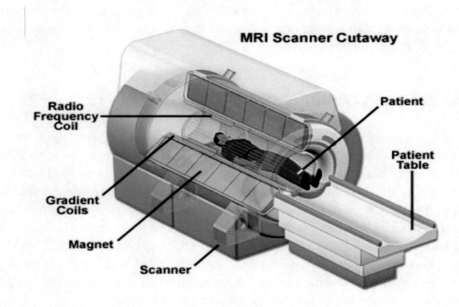

Figure 5. PET scans use radiopharmaceuticals to create images of active blood flow and physiologic activity of the organ or organs being targeted

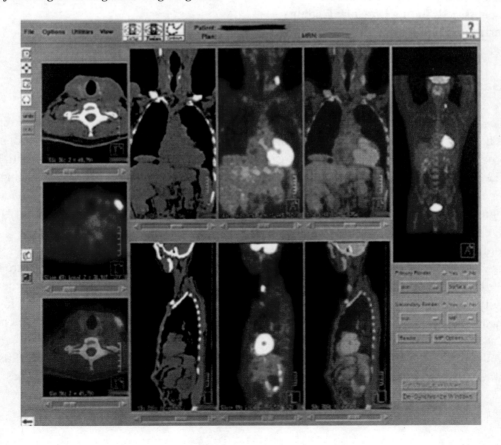

Ultrasound utilizes high-frequency sound waves which are reflected off tissue to create images of organs, muscles, joints, and other soft tissues. It's kind of like shining a light on the inside of the body, except that this light travel through the skin layers and can only be viewed using electronic sensors (Pramod et al., 2014; Gijsbertse et al., 2015).

3D MEDICAL IMAGES COMPRESSION CODING

3D image compression seems to be a simple extension of 2D image compression, there are many unique properties that are ignored in 2D, Scalability, scan order, overhead control, along with near-lossless quantization. Among the handful of volume compression methods, most are lossy, for example in researches by (Jeyanthi et al., 2016; Mohammad et al., 2016; Wang et al., 2016). Due to the probable loss of information in the many steps towards preparing a 3D medical image, lossless compression on the other hand is too strict and sometimes overkill. Near lossless seems to be a natural compromise. CT and MR image sets normally have different resolutions within a slice and between slices. The pixel distances within a slice are normally less than 1 mm and the distance between slices can vary from 1 mm to 10 mm. A slice is a graphical representation of a cross section of the part of the human body that is currently analyzed. The collection of all these slices composes a 3-D image.

3D medical image compression coding could be based on many types such as:

- Mesh Based Coding Scheme
- Object Based Coding (Wavelet Coding)
- Interframe Coding
- Region of Interest Based Coding

Mesh Based Coding Scheme

3D meshes may be considered to be the most popular discrete virtual surface and volume representation. The need for precision leads to the generation of meshes composed of a large number of elements, whose processing, visualization and storage is complex. 3D Mesh compression is a potential tool for solving the issues raised. First, it reduces data size, which is useful for storing and transmitting meshes. Then, some algorithms also embed several versions of the input model in the compressed data; this enables progressive transmission and interactive visualization of large meshes on low capability terminals (Srikanth et al., 2005; Maglo et al., 2013; Ahn et al., 2013).

Compressing meshes is different than compressing other types of multimedia data such as sound, images or videos. The common point between sound, images and videos is that their structure is known in advance by the encoder and the decoder. A mesh is, however, not necessarily regularly structured. Its connectivity is completely unknown to the encoder before the compression. So, besides having to code the geometry (vertex positions), as the pixel colors would be coded for an image, a mesh encoder must encode the structure, which is the connectivity.

Many algorithms have been proposed to compress 3D meshes efficiently since early 1990s Meshes can be either static or dynamic. Static mesh compression approaches classified in three types:

- Single-Rate Algorithms build a compact representation of an input mesh. The decompression algorithm generates a mesh that is either identical to the input model or only slightly different.
- Progressive Algorithms, during decompression, reconstruct successive levels of detail as more data are decoded. The user does not have to wait for all the data to be downloaded and decompressed to visualize the model, which is useful in a remote visualization context. These algorithms are also used to select the best level of detail to display according to device rendering capabilities, network constraints or the viewpoint.
- Random accessible algorithms are used to decompress only requested parts of the input mesh to save resources. They provide access to models that do not fit into the device main memory, but the user has no overview of the non-selected parts. Progressive random accessible approaches are used to decompress different parts of the input model at different levels of detail.

Progressive and random accessible algorithms can also be used for single-rate compression, although they are not as efficient as pure single-rate methods in general.

Single-rate compression is a typical mesh compression algorithm which encodes connectivity data and geometry data separately. Most early work focused on the connectivity coding. Then, the coding order of geometry data is determined by the underlying connectivity coding. However, since geometry data demand more bits than topology data, several methods have been proposed recently for efficient compression of geometry data without reference to topology data. The existing single-rate connectivity compression algorithms are classified into six classes namely, the Indexed Face Set, the Triangle Strip, the Spanning Tree, the Layered Decomposition, the Valence-Driven Approach, and the Triangle Conquest (Amjoun et al., 2009).

Most 3D mesh compression algorithms focus on triangular meshes. To handle polygonal meshes, they triangulate polygons before the compression task. However, there are several disadvantages in this approach. First, the triangulation process imposes an extra cost in computation and efficiency. Second, the original connectivity information may be lost. Third, attributes associated with vertices or faces may require duplicated encoding. To address these problems, several algorithms have been proposed to encode polygonal meshes directly without pre-triangulation.

The state-of-the-art connectivity coding schemes require only a few bits per vertex, and their performance is regarded as being very close to the optimal. In contrast, geometry coding received much less attention in the past. Since geometry data dominate the total compressed mesh data, more focus has been shifted to geometry coding recently. All the single-rate mesh compression schemes encode connectivity data losslessly, since connectivity is a discrete mesh property. However, geometry data are generally encoded in a lossy manner. To exploit high correlation between the positions of adjacent vertices, most single-rate geometry compression schemes follow a three-step procedure: pre-quantization of vertex positions, prediction of quantized positions, and entropy coding of prediction residuals. The valence (or degree) of a vertex is the number of edges incident on that vertex. It can be shown that the sum of valences is twice the number of edges Thus, in a typical triangular mesh, the average vertex valence is 6. When reporting the compression performance some papers employ the measure of bits per triangle (bpt) while others use bits per vertex (bpv).

With progressive algorithms, a coarse version of the mesh can be quickly displayed to the user. It is then progressively refined as more data is decompressed until the initial model has been restored.

Connectivity-preserving schemes restore during the decompression the connectivity of the input model while connectivity-oblivious schemes resort to remising to encode an input model with a higher compression performance.

The issue with single-rate and progressive mesh compression algorithms is that, when the user wants to access a specific part of a very large mesh, the full model must be downloaded and decompressed. Random accessible algorithms allow decompressing only the required parts. Some algorithms give access to only the original level of detail of the mesh but others allow decompressing different parts at different levels of detail.

Dynamic meshes constitute an emerging media content, which may carry large amounts of data (large meshes × large frame numbers). Like 2D videos, dynamic mesh compression requires specific features such as scalability and streaming capability (Corsini et al., 2013).

Object Based Coding

In object-based coding different objects that are present in a scene are assigned priorities in the encoding process, based on their importance in the framework of the considered application, and these applications discussed by many authors (Meganez & Thiran, 2002; Ranjan et al., 2016). A prior knowledge about the image contents makes such approaches particularly suitable for medical images. The object-based algorithms are also suitable for being combined with modeling techniques. Medical images usually consist of a region representing the part of a body under investigation (i.e. heart in a CT, MRI chest scan etc.,) on an often noisy background which is of no diagnostic interest. Hence it seems to be natural to process such data in object-based framework by assigning high priority to objects of interest to be retrieved losslessly and low priority to irrelevant object. Even though some authors have addressed the task of object-based coding for medical images, such an approach still deserves some investigation. A fully three-dimensional (3-D) object-based coding system exploiting the diagnostic relevance of the different regions of the volumetric data for bit rate allocation is addressed in where the data's are first decorrelated via a 3-D discrete wavelet transform and the implementation via the lifting steps scheme allows mapping integer-to-integer values, enabling lossless coding, facilitating the definition of the object-based inverse transform. The coding process assigns disjoint segments of the bit stream to the different objects, which can be independently accessed and reconstructed at any up-to-lossless quality.

Wavelet Coding

Wavelet coding is a form of data compression well suited for image compression and the goal is to store image data in as little space as possible in a file. Wavelet compression can be either lossless or lossy. Wavelet is originated from the French word Ondelettes. A wavelet is a small signal which does not have a regular shape. The shape of wavelet is to represent the different details or resolution and the location of wavelet represents the location of events in time. The basic idea behind the wavelets is that the function gives the time and frequency localization and can provide a high frequency resolution at low frequency and high time resolution at high frequency. Using single function called mother wavelet, the other functions are obtained by changing the size of function or scaling and translating. The scaling and translating parameters are related to each other because the scaling of basis function is narrow; the translation step is small and vice versa.

The term wavelet comes from the fact that they integrate to zero when wave up and down across the axis. A signal can be decomposed into many shifted and scaled representations of the original mother wavelet. A wavelet transform can be used to decompose a signal into component wavelets. Once this is done the coefficients of the wavelets can be decimated to remove some of the details. Wavelets have the great advantage of being able to separate the fine details in a signal. Very small wavelets can be used to isolate very fine details in a signal, while very large wavelets can identify coarse details.

In general, a wavelet image compression system consists of three blocks, namely, mapper, quantizer, and statistical coder. A mapper is a mathematical framework which converts and transforms the spatial domain image into an arrangement of wavelet coefficients in order to make the compression effectively and productively in the ensuing operations subsequently. Compression can be accomplished by quantizing the coefficients so that critical coefficients (low frequency coefficients) are transmitted and the rest of the coefficients are disposed of or discarded. A variable entropy coder is applied to make a bit stream of the given image. The reverse process is called as decompression in order to get back the original image from the compressed data.

A wavelet transform disintegrates and breaks down a signal into a series of smooth signals and their associated detailed signals at different resolution levels (singh & Sharma, 2012). At every level, the smooth signal and associated detailed signal have all the data important to remake the smooth signal at the next higher resolution level. Coding can be accomplished very easily in the wavelet framework on the grounds that the transformed signal has both spatial and frequency information from the original signal. These sub-images are obtained by utilizing low pass h (n) and high pass g (n) filters.

A 3-D wavelet decomposes a 3-D image set into a number of slices based on the X, Y and Z direction. Each slice contains the various frequency bands. A separable 3-D wavelet transform can be computed by extending the 1-D pyramidal algorithm. The decomposed or disintegrated image slice provides an excellent representation for further quantization and coding.

The complete subband structure of 1-level decomposition is shown in (Figures 6 and 7), where 'H 'and 'L' represent temporal highpass and lowpass subbands respectively. When the low pass filter h(n) and high pass filter g(n) is applied in X direction and Y direction, it generates four sub-bands, namely, horizontal highpass, horizontal lowpass, vertical highpass and vertical lowpass subbands in the spatial domain respectively. When the Z direction is used, it results a total of 8 subbands from the one-level Subband/wavelet decomposition (Ravichandran et al., 2016).

The scalar quantization is applied to wavelet coefficients to reduce information entropy by trading off the accuracy of the information. Decreasing entropy allows more compression. The quantization step maps a large number of input values into a smaller set of output values. The original information cannot be recuperated precisely after quantization. Thus, it gives the lossy compression. Therefore, it is very important to design a quantization methodology which specifically quantizes the wavelet coefficients and preserves the image quality. In the third step, run-length coding took after by Huffman coding is applied to the quantized data. Run-length coding is powerful and effective when there is more than one pixel with the same grey level in a sequence. Huffman coding is a minimum redundancy coding. It assigns fewer bits to the codeword with higher repeat of event and more bits to the code word with lesser repeat of occasion. Huffman coding will allow us to represent the data in less memory storage area than the original data size.

By many research works it has been proved that the Discrete Wavelet Transform (DWT) is a versatile signal processing tool for many applications. It is an important step of JPEG 2000 based image compression. Further enhancement in wavelet transform is achieved via the technique of lifting. Traditional

Figure 6. Analysis of filter bank

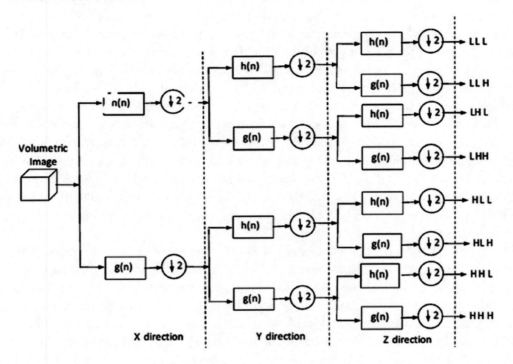

Figure 7. Synthesis of filter bank

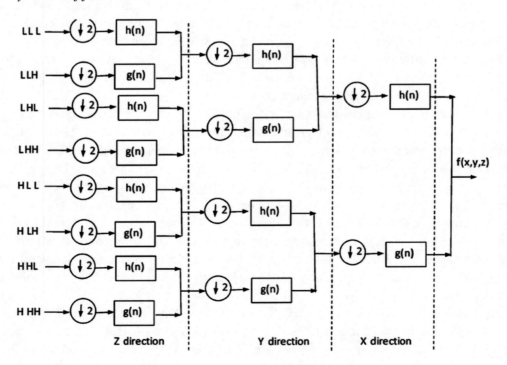

implementation of wavelet transforms was based on convolution, as compare to that, lifting scheme can be implemented in more efficient way. With the help of this scheme new types of nonlinear wavelet transforms may be implemented. The Integer Wavelet Transforms (IWT) maps integers to integers and allows for perfect invariability with finite precision arithmetic. Thus, Integer Wavelet Transform can be used for lossless compression of medical images, for that firstly the traditional DWT is reconstructed into a form of lifting steps. After that at each step rounding operation is performed.

AP Bradley, FWM Stentiford (2002) discussed JPEG 2000 compression engine as it consists of encoder and decoder. At the encoder, the discrete transform is first applied on the source image data. The transform coefficients are then quantized, and entropy coded before forming the output code stream (bit stream). The decoder is the reverse of the encoder. The code stream is first entropy decoded, de-quantized, and inverse discrete transformed, thus resulting in the reconstructed image data. Although this general block diagram looks like the one for the conventional JPEG, there are radical differences in all of the processes of each block of the diagram (figure 8).

For clarification, the whole compression engine is decomposed into three parts: the preprocessing, the core processing, and the bit-stream formation part, although there exists high interrelation between them. In the preprocessing part the image tiling, the dc-level shifting, and the component transformations are included. The core processing part consists of the discrete transform, the quantization and the entropy coding processes. Finally, the concepts of the precincts, code blocks, layers, and packets are included in the bit-stream formation part.

Figure 8. JPEG 2000 block diagram

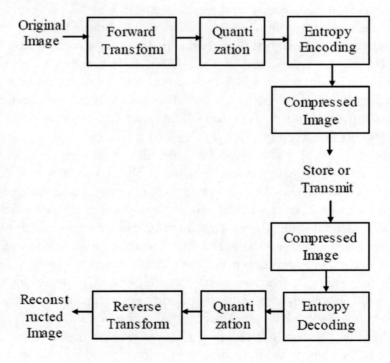

Interframe Coding

As far as MRI is concerned although a significant amount of redundancy exists between successive frames of MRI data, the structure of cross dependence is more complicated. MRI data contain a large quantity of noise which is uncorrelated from frame to frame. Until now, attempts in using inter frame redundancies for coding MR images have been unsuccessful. The authors believe that the main reason for this is twofold: unsuitable Inter Frame estimation models and the thermal noise inherent in Magnetic Resonance Imaging (MRI). In Inter Frame coding method for magnetic resonance (MR) images the inter frame model used a continuous affine mapping based on (and optimized by) deforming triangles. The inherent noise of MRI is dealt with by using a median filter within the estimation loop. The residue frames are quantized with a zerotree wavelet coder, which includes arithmetic entropy coding. The method of quantization allows for progressive transmission, which aside from avoiding buffer control problems is very attractive in medical imaging applications (Srikanth et al., 2005).

Region of Interest (ROI)

Region of Interest Based Coding techniques are more considerable in medical field for the sake of efficient compression and transmission. ROI is designed to owing to the boundaries of lossy and lossless compression techniques. Most of the lossless compression techniques, the compression ratio are near to 80% of original size, while for lossy coding method, the compression ratio is much higher (up to 5-30%), but there may be major loss in data. Thus, ROI is mainly introduced for medical images, as medical images do not afford any loss of information in highly diagnostic important parts. Hence there is need to apply lossless compression technique for preserving the quality of the diagnostic part (ROI), as well as provide high compression ratio. During the transmission of the image for telemedicine purposes, the ROI part is required to be transmitted first or at a higher priority, so the coefficients associated with ROI are transferred first before those associated with non-ROI part. In a medical image, a region of interest can be selected manually or else detected in a semi-automatic or automatic manner.

The medical image includes three parts in image. These are ROI (region of interest), non-ROI and background (figure 9). These parts have their own advantages. ROI is the most critical part of the image that located over very small regions of the image. Non-ROI is also included so that user can easily find out the most critical part from the whole image. Part other than image contents is known as background and most ignored part of the image. In medical field, these critical parts needed to be compressed with high quality compression without any loss than other parts of image. The critical parts from the image obliged to be transmitted first or at higher need amid the transmission for telemedicine purposes.

In ROI instead of transforming the whole image, the same transformation can be separately applied to the diagnostically important regions and background. In a medical image ROI is selected according to a predetermined characteristic or as per users need. The goal of such compression method is to maximize the overall CR i.e. compressing each region separately with its own CR, depending on its significance, so as to preserve the diagnostically important characteristics. Hence, such a strategy that exploits the feature of ROI is becoming beneficial and compact, providing better CRs and fast processing especially on a low bandwidth media. Further, ROI coding provides an excellent trade-off between image quality and CR. Most of the ROI coding methods are based on the wavelet coding techniques of JPEG2000 like EBCOT, Maxshift, general scaling, implicit and few other modified methods. Figure (10) shows Flow diagram for ROI compression (Gupta et al., 2014).

Figure 9. Different parts of an image

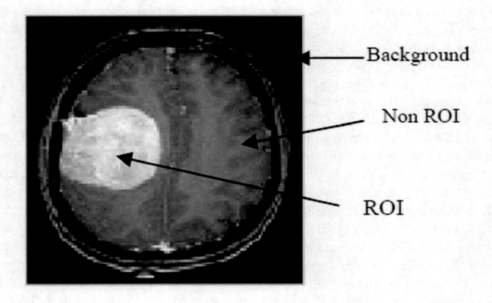

Figure 10. Flow diagram for ROI compression

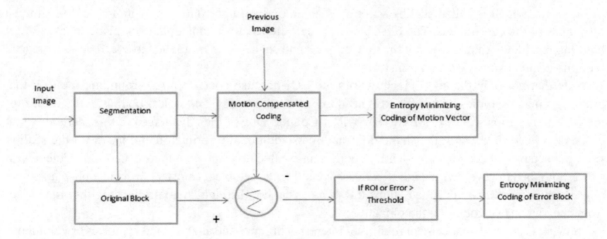

ROI Based Compression Scheme could be shown as:

- Once the ROI is segmented in each slice
- A hybrid compression scheme is used for coding the images.
- The first slice of the volume is compressed with a lossless coder.
- Each slice is then coded by motion compensated coding.
- The difference between the real image ROI block and the predicted ROI block is coded by entropy minimizing lossless coder (Huffman).

Region growing is a simplest region-based method. It is also known as pixel-based method. Region growing method examines the entire neighboring pixels of primary seed points and check whether these neighboring pixels are adding to the region or not. This procedure is same as data clustering method. Firstly, region growing choose a set of seeds. Selection of seed point depends on the user criteria such as it may depend on pixel intensity, gray level texture or color level. Primary region starts at the exact location of the seed point and seed point (selected pixel) select all the adjacent pixels to add in the region. The image information is also important in the region growing.

Doukas C. and Maglogiannis I. (2007) proposed a scaling-based ROI coding adopted in JPEG2000 which we call SB-ROI, an entire volumetric image is transformed, and the coefficients associated with the ROI (within and around the ROI) are scaled up by a certain number of bit-shifts. Then the bit-planes of coefficients are encoded plane by plane. The difference of image quality between the ROI and non-ROI can be controlled by specifying the scaling value. Although JPEG2000 specifies scaling-based ROI coding only for rectangular or elliptic areas of a two-dimensional image, the concept of scaling-based ROI coding can be easily extended to arbitrary-shape ROI coding for volumetric imagery. In the scaling-based ROI coding, shape information has to be transmitted to the decoder unlike the max-shift ROI coding. Therefore, in scaling-based ROI coding, the object can be exactly decoded by discarding all of the background, but looking at the background near the object, the additional coefficients still might cause unwanted effect at an early stage of progressive coding. The max-shift ROI coding adopted in JPEG2000, which we call MS-ROI, an entire volumetric image is transformed and only the coefficients associated with the ROI are scaled up through a given number of bit-shifts, where the number of bit-shifts, which is called scaling value s, is given by the largest number of non-empty magnitude bit-planes of the coefficients. The bit -planes of coefficients are encoded plane by plane to let the ROI have higher fidelity than the rest of the image. The same concept can be applied to coefficients produced with three-dimensional wavelet transform.

Note that not only the coefficients within the ROI but also coefficients surrounding the ROI that affect the image samples within the ROI need to be encoded to realize lossless coding of the ROI. Figure (11) shows Flow Chart of MAXSHIFT ROI Coding. One of the advantages of this method is that it does not need to transmit the shape information as additional information and just send the scaling value s, because the decoder can identify coefficients scaled up just by comparing each coefficient with a threshold 2s. However, with code stream associated with the object (most significant s bit-planes) the object cannot be exactly decoded, since the decoder cannot distinguish coefficients within the object from coefficients surrounding the object.

In 1994, Chen et al. made use of regions of interest using subband analysis and synthesis or volumetric datasets using wavelets. They followed up this work with (Chen et al., 1995) by using structure preserving adaptive quantization methods as a means of improving quality for compression rates in the regions of interest. But all of their effort was on lossy approaches. In the most relevant work developed a region-based coding approach. They discussed two approaches: one uses different compression methods in each region such as 'contour-texture' coding and subband decomposition coding, and the other uses the same compression method in each region such as the discrete cosine transform but with varying compression quality in each region such as by using different quantization tables. They used two multi-resolution coding schemes: wavelet zerotree coding and the S-transform and considered only 8-bit images. In their implementation, the regions of interest were selected manually.

Ueno I. and Pearlman W. (2003) proposed ROI coding technique combines shape-adaptive wavelet transform and scaling-based ROI, which we call SA-ROI. In this method, the samples within the object

Figure 11. Flow chart of MAXSHIFT ROI coding

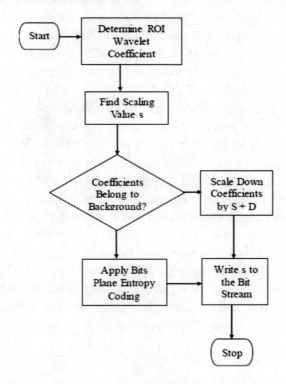

are transformed with shape-adaptive wavelet transform according to the shape-information. If necessary, the background is also transformed by shape-adaptive wavelet transform independently (figure 12).

Then the samples within the object are scaled up by a certain number of bit-shifts, and encoded plane by plane. In this case, the number of coefficients to be encoded does not change from the number of image samples within the object, and by scaling-up the coefficients of the object, the difference of image quality between the object and background can be controlled. If all of the samples (both of the object and

Figure 12. Block Diagram of shape adaptive wavelet transform

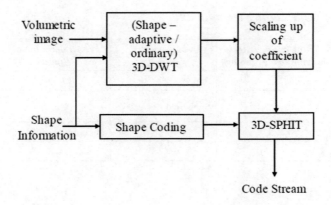

background) are transformed with shape-adaptive wavelet transform, an ROI can be specified independently of the object/background, and user-driven ROI coding can also be realized. But computational cost of shape-adaptive wavelet transform is generally higher than conventional transform, because the length of each segment is not constant. The scaling value of the VOI coefficients is empirically assigned and the shape information of the VOI must be encoded and transmitted, which may result in an increase in computational complexity as well as bit rate. Table (3) shows a comparison of arbitrary-shape ROI coding.

Liu Y. and Pearlman W. A. (2006) proposed another ROI coding technique, Subband Block Hierarchical Partitioning (SBHP) algorithm, which is modified and extended to three dimensions and applied to every code block independently. The resultant algorithm, 3D-SBHP, efficiently encodes 3D image data by the exploitation of the dependencies in all dimensions, while enabling progressive SNR and resolution decompression and Region-of-Interest (ROI) access from the same bit stream. The code-block selection method by which random access decoding can be achieved is outlined. The 2-D SBHP algorithm is a SPECK variant which was originally designed as a low complexity alternative to JPEG2000. 3-D SBHP is a modification and extension of 2-D SBHP to three-dimensions. In 3-D SBHP, each subband is partitioned into code-blocks. All code-blocks have the same size. 3-D SBHP is applied to every code-block independently and generates a highly scalable bit-stream for each code-block by using the same form of progressive bit-plane coding as in SPIHT. But in this scheme the background information is only decoded after the VOI is fully decoded, which prevents observing the position of the VOI within the original 3-D image. Table (4) shows a comparison of some coding techniques.

Table 3. Comparison of arbitrary-shape ROI coding

		MS – ROI	SB – ROI	SA – DWT	SA – ROI
Factors concerning compression performance	Number if coefficients needed to decode the object	More	More	Fewer	Fewer
	Number of coefficients needed to decode the entire image	Same	Same	--	Same
	Shape information transmission	Necessary	Necessary	Necessary	Necessary
ROI coding functionality	User driven ROI coding	Partly Possible	Possible	Difficult	Possible
	Decoding exactly the object	Not Possible	Possible	Possible	Possible

Table 4. Comparison of some coding techniques

Coding Techniques	Shape information incorporated in coding	Arbitrary ROI coding	Exact decoding of the object	PSNR in dB (bits Per pixel)
General Scaling Method	Required	Supported	-	44.91 (0.08 bpp)
MAX SHIFT	-	Supported	-	44.90 (0.08 bpp)
SA-DWT	-	-	Possible	52.5 (0.50 bpp)
3D-SPIHT	-	-	-	38.78 (0.52 bpp)

Image Compression Evaluation

The image quality is measured in terms of PSNR and MSE. For good quality image, PSNR value should be as high as possible & MSE value should be as low as possible. It has been observed that PSNR is not always an indicator of the subjective quality of the reconstructed image, so that we can used MSE (Mean Square Error), PSNR (Peak Signal to Noise Ratio), SSIM (Structural Similarity Index), compression ratio and Entropy as an objective quality measures.

PSNR is used to find out the ratio between the maximum power of a signal and the noise corrupted signal that affects the reliability of the signal representation it is a measurement to measure the quality of the image. The high PSNR value denotes the reconstructed image quality is high, and the low PSNR value denotes the reconstructed image quality is low (eq. 1–PSNR).

$$PSNR = 10 Log_{10} \frac{255 \times 255}{MSE} \tag{1}$$

MSE is the metric used to verify the mean square error of the image. The MSE is used to estimate the difference between two images in terms squared error value (eq. 2–MSE).

$$MSR = \frac{1}{M \times N} \sum_{x=0}^{M-1} \sum_{y=0}^{N-1} \left(i\left(x,y\right) - i\left(x,y\right) \right)^2 \tag{2}$$

Compression Ratio: Data redundancy is the centric release in digital image compression. If n1 and n2 denote the number of information carrying units in original and encoded image respectively, then the compression ratio, CR and saving space can be specified as shown in eq. 3 (Compression Ratio – Symbol format) eq. 4 (Compression Ratio) and eq. 5 (Space Savings).

$$CR = \frac{n1}{n2} \tag{3}$$

$$\text{Compression Ratio} = \frac{\text{Uncompressed Size}}{\text{Compressed Size}} \tag{4}$$

$$\text{Space Savings} = 1 - \frac{\text{Compressed Size}}{\text{Uncompressed Size}} \tag{5}$$

Basically, the desired compression ratio is at least 2:1. The computational needs of an algorithm is expressed, in terms of how many operations (additions/multiplications, etc.) are required to encode a pixel (byte). The third metric is the amount of memory or buffer required to carry out an algorithm.

REFERENCES

Al-Rababah & Al-Marghirani. (2016). Implementation of Novel Medical Image Compression Using Artificial Intelligence. IJACSA, 7(5).

Amjoun, R., & Straßer, W. (2009). Single-rate near lossless compression of animated geometry. *Computer Aided Design, 41*(10), 10. doi:10.1016/j.cad.2009.02.013

Bradley, A. P., & Stentiford, F. W. M. (2002). JPEG 2000 and region of interest coding. Digital Image Computing: Techniques and Applications (DICTA'02), 303-308

Brenner. (2007). Computed Tomography an Increasing Source of Radiation Exposure. *The New England Journal of Medicine.*

Chen. (1994). Subband analysis and synthesis of volumetric medical images using wavelet. *Visual Communication and Image Processing, 2306*(3), 1544–1555.

Corsini, M., Larabi, M. C., Lavoué, G., Petřík, O., Váša, L., & Wang, K. (2013, February). Perceptual Metrics for Static and Dynamic Triangle Meshes. *Computer Graphics Forum, 32*(1), 1. doi:10.1111/cgf.12001

Dhawan. (2011). A Review of Image Compression and Comparison of its Algorithms. *IJECT, 2*(1).

Doukas, C., & Maglogiannis, I. (2007). Region of interest coding techniques for medical image compression. *IEEE Engineering in Medicine and Biology Magazine, 25*(5). PMID:17941320

Gijsbertse. (2015). *Three-Dimensional Ultrasound Strain Imaging of Skeletal Muscles.* IEEE.

Govindan & Saniie. (2014). Processing algorithms for three-dimensional data compression of ultrasonic radio frequency signals. *IET Signal Processing.* doi:10.1049/iet-spr.2014.0186

Gupta. (2014). ROI Based Medical Image Compression for Telemedicine Using IWT & SPIHT. *International Journal of Advance Research in Computer Science and Management Studies, 2*(11).

Jae-kyun, A. (2013). Efficient Fine-Granular Scalable Coding of 3D Mesh Sequences. *IEEE Transactions on Multimedia, 15,* 3.

Jeyanthi & Suganyadevi. (2016). A Survey on medical images and compression techniques. *International Journal of Advances in Science Engineering and Technology, 4*(2).

Liu, Y., & Pearlman, W. A. (2006). Resolution Scalable Coding and Region of Interest Access with Three-Dimensional SBHP Algorithm. *Third International symposium on 3D Data Processing.* 10.1109/3DPVT.2006.120

Maglo, A. (2013). 3D mesh compression: survey, comparisons and emerging trends. ACM Computing Surveys, 9(4).

Meganez, G., & Thiran, J. P. (2002, September). Lossy to lossless object based coding of 3D MRI Data. *IEEE Transactions on Image Processing, 11*(9).

Ravichandran, D. (2016). *Performance Analysis of Three-Dimensional Medical Image Compression Based on Discrete Wavelet Transform.* IEEE doi:10.1109/VSMM.2016.7863176

Sabbagh, M. (2016). Accelerating Cardiac MRI Compressed Sensing Image Reconstruction using Graphics Processing Units. Northeastern University.

Senapati, R. K. (2016). Volumetric medical image compression using 3D listless embedded block partitioning. *SpringerPlus.* PMID:28053830

Shreya, A. (2016). A Survey on DICOM Image Compression and Decompression Techniques. *International Journal of Computer Engineering and Applications, ICCSTAR-2016*(Special Issue).

Singh & Sharma. (2012). Hybrid Image Compression Using DWT, DCT & Huffman Encoding Techniques. *International Journal of Emerging Technology and Advanced Engineering, 2*(10).

Sridevi. (2012). A Survey on Various Compression Methods for Medical Images. *I. J. Intelligent Systems and Applications, 3*, 13-19.

Srikanth, R., & Ramakrishnan, A. G. (2005). Contextual encoding in uniform and adaptive mesh-based lossless compression of MR images. IEEE Trans. Med. Imag., 24(9).

Srikanth, R., & Ramakrishnan, A. G. (2005). *Context based Interframe coding of MR Images. MILE labs.* Department of Electrical Engineering, Indian Institute of Science.

Ueno, I., & Pearlman, W. (2003). Region of interest coding in volumetric images with shape-adaptive wavelet transform. *Proceedings of the Society for Photo-Instrumentation Engineers, 5022*, 1048. doi:10.1117/12.476709

Ukrit. (2011). A Survey on Lossless Compression for Medical Images. *International Journal of Computer Applications, 31*(8).

Wang, Q., Chen, X., Wei, M., & Miao, Z. (2016). Simultaneous encryption and compression of medical images based on optimized tensor compressed sensing with 3D Lorenz. *Biomedical Engineering Online, 15*(1), 118. doi:10.118612938-016-0239-1 PMID:27814721

Chapter 11
Momentum- and Resilient-Based Level Set for Medical Image Segmentation

Deepika Dubey
SRCEM Gwalior, India

Uday Pratap Singh
Madhav Institute of Technology and Science, India

ABSTRACT

In this chapter, the authors present the technique of medical image segmentation which means to partition an image into non-overlapping regions based on intensity. The active contour is one of the most successful level set methods for segmentation and it is widely applicable in various image processing applications including medical image segmentation. Biomedical image segmentation and analysis plays an important role in medical science and healthcare. This chapter proposes a momentum term and resilient propagation-based gradient descent method which will remove the sensitivity of local minima of gradient descent. Proposed method is applicable in case of diseases like retinal, diabetic, and glaucoma, etc. Medical image segmentation via momentum and resilient propagation based gradient descent method can be optimized and effectively used. Extensive experiments have been performed over medical images to test the ability of the system. The proposed method is able to present the segmented medical image with clear and smooth boundary also it is simple to design and implementation.

INTRODUCTION

The active contour is one of the most successful level set methods for segmentation. Active contour based segmentation is based on energy functional and minimization of energy functional is known as segmentation (Kichenassamy, Kumar, Olver, Tannenbaum, & Yezzi, 1995; Cohen, 1991; Kass, Witkin, & Terzopoulos, 1988; Caselles, Kimmel, & Sapiro, 1995). The active contour model is a well-known image segmentation model which is widely applicable in various image processing applications such as in automated surveillance, graphics animation, robotics or medical image partition or segmentation

DOI: 10.4018/978-1-5225-5246-8.ch011

(Sundaramoorthi, Yezzi, & Mennucci, 2007; Charpiat, Keriven, Pons, & Faugeras, 2005). The contour motion equation is based on energy gradient depends upon Euler-Lagranges (Morse & Feshbach, 1993), it consists of evolving a contour in images toward the boundaries of objects or convergence. A parametric curve or contour are evolved according to minimization of cost functional up to convergence to an equilibrium state representing the segmentation. Medical image Segmentation is an important challenge in the field of image processing and computer vision. Steepest descent (gradient) is an important method for image segmentation. For, nonconvex functional various global optimization methods as Metropolis algorithm (Metropolis, Rosenbluth, Rosenbluth, Teller, & Teller, 1953), subdivision method (Kearfott, 1996), Monte-Carlo (Kirkpatrick, Gelatt, & Vecchi, 1983) techniques. Unfortunately these methods suffers from slow convergence. To improve the convergence method of evolving contours Mumford-Shah (Mumford & Shah 1989) Chen-Vese (Chan & Vese, 2001) and total variation (Chan, Esedoglu, & Nikolova, 2006; Bresson, Esedoglu, Vandergheynst, Thiran, & Osher, 2007) are used in order to fast convergence of boundary. Great efforts have been made to develop more advanced techniques in the field of segmentation in recent years. Image segmentation is the most essential and crucial process for facilitating the delineation, characterization, and visualization of regions of interest in any medical image. Automatic segmentation of medical images is a difficult task, since medical images are complex in nature and rarely have any simple linear feature. Enhancement of curvilinear object in medical images are obtained using matching filters, basic idea behind these filters is that locate the position of objects using some initial points. Therefore segmentation is based on selection of some initial points and spatial properties of objects. The backbone of any image segmentation is the heavily depends upon the feature extraction process using color or textures. Biomedical image retrieval using texture features superbly suited to the type of diseases present in the image (Quellec, Lamard, Cazuguel, Cochener & Roux, 2010; Traina, Castanon, & Traina, 2003, Zakeri, Behnam, & Ahmadinejad, 2012; Felipe, Traina, & Traina, 2003). A local diagonal pattern based on centre pixel and local diagonal neighbour are proposed (Dubey, Singh, and Singh, 2015) for CT images, a Directional binary wavelet patterns and local ternary co-occurrence matrix based texture are used for MRI and CT images (Murala, & Wu, 2013; Murala, Maheshwari, & Balasubramanian, 2012).

Segmentation is the process dividing an image into regions with similar properties such as gray level, color, texture, and shape. For medical image segmentation, mainly the aim is to:

- Study anatomical structure.
- Identify Region of Interest i.e. locate tumor, lesion, breakage of veins of retina and other abnormalities.
- Measure tissue volume to measure growth (for e.g, of tumor and also decrease in size of tumor with treatment).
- Help in treatment planning prior to radiation therapy.

Segmentation algorithms can be classified into two categories: low level and high level. The first category, which operates at the pixel level, includes five popular methods:

- Gray intensity or histogram analysis,
- Texture analysis,
- Edge enhancement and linking,

- Region growing
- Contour following

The second category, which is anatomical segmentation, needs some prior knowledge, which is usually supplied by an expert. One of such high-level segmentation is active contour models (Kass, Witkin, & Terzopoulos 1988) can be easily formulated under an energy minimization framework and allow incorporation of various prior knowledge, such as shape and intensity distribution, for robust image segmentation. Second, they can provide smooth and closed contours as segmentation results, which are necessary and can be easily used for further applications, such as shape analysis and recognition. Existing active contour models can be categorized into two major classes: edge based models and region based models. Edge based models utilizes an image gradient to construct an edge stopping function to stop the contour evolution at the desired object boundaries and region based models typically aim to identify each region of interest by using a certain region descriptor. Image segmentation supervised (Singh, Saxena, & Jain, 2011) or unsupervised (Singh, Saxena, and Jain, 2011) provides object representation ad description, feature measurement object classification, delineation, characterization, visualizations of regions of interest in any medical image (Patil & Deore, 2013; Heydarian, Michael, Kamath, Colm, & Poehlman, 2009). Doing the segmentation process manually is very tiresome job as it consumes a lot of time and effort, and in spite of that there is no surety to get the exact result. We have a number of active imaging systems which produces different kinds of images such as laser images, microscope images, which causes the manual measurement to fail sometimes. Image segmentation algorithms can also be classified as interactive and non-interactive algorithms (Singh, Saxena, & Jain, 2011; Nguyen, Nhat, Jianfei, Zhang, & Zheng, 2012). Interactive ones demand some contribution from user while deciding the initial contour. Here user inputs the regional information where user creates division of pixels into foreground or background pixels and algorithm completes the labelling of pixels into object or non-object region. Region based interactive segmentation algorithm include graph cut based methods (Yi, 2012), random walks (Grady, 2011), geodesic methods (Paragios & Deriche, 2000). Some basic image segmentations are discussed below.

Classification of Image Segmentation

Image Segmentation divides an image into its constituent regions or objects. Segmentation of images is a difficult task in image processing and is still under research. Segmentation allows extracting objects in images. Segmentation is based on supervised or unsupervised method, image segmentation is a difficult task mainly because of a big variability of object shapes, as well as different image quality. The techniques of image segmentation can be classified into two basic methods: edge based method and region based method. The two important categories of segmentation method are given as follows.

Edge Based Method

This method attempts to resolve image segmentation by detecting the edges or pixels between different regions that have rapid transition in intensity are extracted and linked to form closed object boundaries (Gonzalez, Woods, & Eddins, 2004). The result is a binary image. Based on theory there are two main edge based segmentation methods: (i) gray histogram and (ii) gradient based method. Edge detection is a well-developed field of image processing, region boundaries and edges are closely related, since there is often a sharp adjustment in intensity at the region boundaries. Edge detection techniques have therefore been used as the base of another segmentation technique. The edges identified by edge detection are often disconnected. To segment an object from an image however, one needs closed object contour or object boundaries. The desired edges are the boundaries between such objects, edge based methods i.e. frequent changes in intensity or contrast near edges. But these methods are error prone because of sensitivity to noise or blur, so care must be taken to remove the noise level acceptably.

Region Based Method

Region-based segmentation algorithms operate iteratively by grouping similar type of pixels using some similarity measures (Singh, Saxena, & Jain, 2011), which form relations among neighbouring pixels i.e. pixels which are neighbours of each other and have similar values and splitting groups of pixels which are dissimilar in value. Region based methods can be categorized into:

- Split regions
- Merge regions
- Split and merge regions

The region based algorithm groups pixels in whole image into sub regions or larger regions based on similarity measure criteria. There are four steps (i) Group of seed pixel in original image is selected (ii) Set of similarity criteria is selected and stopping rule is set (iii) Attaching similar pixels to seed pixels, their predefined properties should match (iv) Stop the procedure when no more pixel fulfils the criteria. Instead of choosing seed pixels, user can partition an image into set of arbitrary disjoint regions and merge them according to image segmentation standard rules.

Active Contour Model

Active contour is a level set based segmentation model and it is popular techniques. The solution contour is obtained by optimization problem where cost functional are minimized. Active contour is most important segmentation model for medical images. Deformable models became popular since their publishing in work (Kass, Witkin, & Terzopoulos, 1988; Andersson, Gunnar, Lenz, & Magnus, 2013) 'Snakes: Active contour models' which was published in 1987 and since then they have become active and successful research in area of image segmentation. Active contours are classified (Birgit & Stefan 2012) into snake and level set methods. Snakes explicitly represent a contour by a parametric curve, whereas level sets use an implicit representation as the zero level of an embedding function. Despite of the common ideas both techniques based on minimization of given energy or cost functional, they differ considerably with regard to the capacity to handle multiple objects, the ability to change or preserve topology, the optimization techniques including numerical stability, as well as computation time. Snake framework is formulated such that it approximates the locations and shapes of object boundaries in images based on the assumption that boundaries are piecewise continuous or smooth. On the other side, with the level set representation (Li, Huang, Ding, Chris, Dimitris, & John, 2011), the image segmentation problem can be formulated and solved in a principle way based on well-established mathematical theories, including calculus of variations and partial differential equations (PDE). An advantage of the

Figure 1. Basic form of active contour
(Marian, 2007)

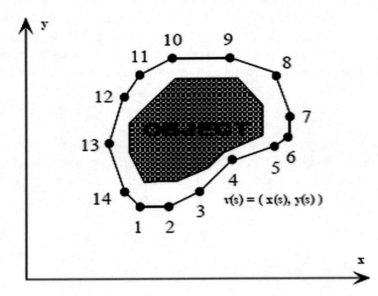

level set method is that numerical computations involving curves and surfaces can be performed on a fixed Cartesian grid without having to parameterize these objects.

To efficiently apply such techniques on medical images for segmentation problems from a specific domain it is fundamental to develop understanding and experience for the characteristics of different active contour approaches and their behaviours. Active contour are shown in Figure 1 and different approaches for active contour model (Marian, 2007) are described below:

Parametric Model

Representation of object curves and surfaces during deformation explicitly in parametric form. The parametric models can be described with help of some of the following formulations: formulation of energy minimizing or formulation of dynamic force (Huang, Ding, Chris, Dimitris & John, 2011; Marian, 2007). Most famous active contour method is introduced by Kass (Kass, Witkin, & Terzopoulos, 1988). Kass named his algorithm "snakes" because during the evolution, the contours motion toward the object resembles snakes' movement. Given an approximation of the boundary of an object in an image, called initial contour, snakes locate the "actual" boundary. Let us define a contour parameterized by arc length s as:

$$C(s) = \left\{ (x(s), y(s)) : 0 \leq s \leq L \right\} \tag{1}$$

Where L denotes the length of the contour C, and Γ denotes the entire domain of an image $I(x, y)$. This algorithm is based on energy minimization scheme, the basic idea of energy minimization the weighted sum of the internal energy, which depends on the shape of the contour i.e. smoothness of the contour, and the external energy which depends on image properties.

$$E_{snake}^* = \int_0^1 E_{snake}\left(v(s)\right)ds = \int_0^1 \left(E_{\mathrm{int}}\left(v(s)\right) + E_{image}\left(v(s)\right) + E_{con}\left(v(s)\right)\right)ds \tag{2}$$

where E_{int} represents the internal energy of the spline due to bending, E_{image} denotes image forces, and E_{con} external constraint forces. Usually, v(s) is approximated as a spline to ensure desirable properties of continuity. The internal spline energy can be written

$$E_{\mathrm{int}} = \alpha(s)\left|\frac{dv}{ds}\right|^2 + \beta(s)\left|\frac{d^2v}{ds^2}\right|^2 \tag{3}$$

where $\alpha(s), \beta(s)$ specify the elasticity and stiffness of the snake.

The second term of the energy integral is derived from the image data over which the snake lies. As an example, a weighted combination of three different functional is presented which attracts the snake to lines, edges, and terminations:

$$E_{image} = \omega_{line}E_{line} + \omega_{edge}E_{edge} + \omega_{term}E_{term} \tag{4}$$

The line-based functional may be very simple

$$E_{line} = f(x, y), \tag{5}$$

where $f(x, y)$ denotes image grey-levels at image location (x, y) . The sign of ω_{line} specifies whether the snake is attracted to light or dark lines. The edge-based functional

$$E_{edge} = -\left|\nabla f(x)\right|^2 \tag{6}$$

attracts the snake to contours with large image gradients that is, to locations of strong edges. Line terminations and corners may influence the snake using a weighted energy functional E term: Let $\psi(x, y)$ denote the gradient directions along the spline in the smoothed image g, and let

$$n(x, y) = (\cos \psi(x, y), \sin \psi(x, y)), \ n_R = (-\sin \psi 9x, y), \cos \psi(x, y))$$

be unit vectors along and perpendicular t o the gradient directions $\psi(x, y)$. Then the curvature of constant-gray-level contours in the smoothed image can be [35]. $E_{term} = \dfrac{\partial \psi}{\partial n_r} = \dfrac{\partial^2 g / \partial n_r^2}{\partial g / \partial n}$

$$= \frac{\left(\partial^2 g / \partial^2 y\right)\left(\partial\, g / \partial x\right)^2 - 2\left(\partial^2 g / \partial x \partial y\right)\left(\partial g / \partial x\right) / \left(\partial g / \partial y\right) + \left(\partial^2 g / \partial^2 x\right)\left(\partial g / \partial y\right)^2}{\left[\left(\partial\, g / \partial x\right)^2 + \left(\partial\, g / \partial y\right)^2\right]^{\frac{3}{2}}} \qquad (7)$$

The snake behaviour may be controlled by adjusting the weights ω_{line}, ω_{edge}, ω_{term}. A snake attracted to edges and a termination is shown in figure (2). Constraints imposed either by a user or some other higher-level process which may force the snake toward or away from particular features. If the snake is near to some desirable feature, the energy minimization will pull the snake the rest of the way. However, if the snake settles in a local energy minimum that a higher-level process determines as incorrect, an area of energy peak may be made at this location to force the snake away to a different local minimum. A contour is defined to lie in the position in which the snake reaches a local energy minimum, the functional to be minimized as

$$E^*_{snake} = \int_0^1 E_{snake}\left(v\left(s\right)\right) ds \qquad (8)$$

Then, from the calculus of variations, the Euler-Lagrange condition states that the spline v(s) which minimizes E^*_{snake} must satisfy

$$\frac{d}{ds} E_{v_s} - E_v = 0 \qquad (9)$$

Where E_{v_s} is the partial derivative of E with respect to dv / ds and E_v is the partial derivative of E with respect to v. denoting $E_{ext} = E_{image} + E_{con}$, the previous equation reduces to

$$\frac{d}{ds}\left(\alpha\left(s\right)\frac{dv}{ds}\right) + \frac{d^2}{ds2}\left(\beta\left(s\right)\frac{d^2v}{ds^2}\right) + \nabla E_{ext}\left(v\left(s\right)\right) = 0 \qquad (10)$$

To solve the Euler-Lagrange equation, suppose an initial estimate of the solution is available. An evolution equation is formed

$$\frac{\partial v\left(s,t\right)}{\partial t} - \frac{\partial}{\partial s}\left(\alpha\left(s\right)\frac{\partial v\left(s,t\right)}{\partial s}\right) + \frac{\partial^2}{\partial s^2}\left(\beta\left(s\right)\frac{\partial^2 v\left(s,t\right)}{\partial s^2}\right) + \nabla E_{ext}\left(v\left(s,t\right)\right) = 0 \qquad (11)$$

The solution is found if $\partial v\left(s,t\right) / \partial t = 0$. Nevertheless, minimization of the snake energy integral is still problematic; numerous parameters must be designed (weighting factors, iteration steps, etc.), a reasonable initialization must be available, and, moreover, the solution of the Euler-Lagrange equation

Figure 2. A snake attracted to edges and terminations: (a) Contour illusion. (b) A snake attracted to the subjective contour

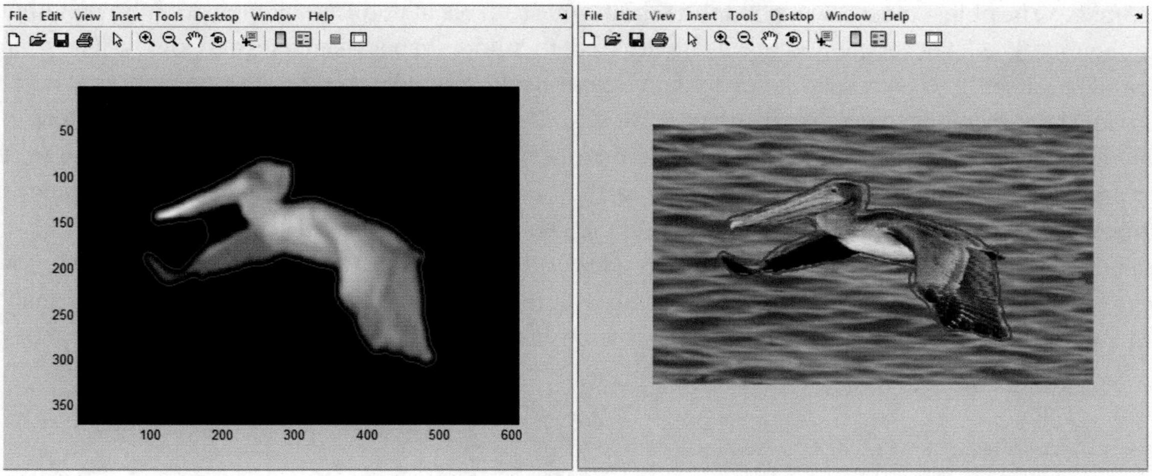

suffers from numerical instability. There are two important parameter active contour model formulation given below:

- **The Formulation of Minimizing Energy:** The base of deformable models on the basis of energy minimization is searching of parametric curve that minimizes weighted sum of internal energy and potential energy.
- **The Formulation of Dynamic Force:** These formulations facilitate the use of common external forces, even those which are note potential, e.g. forces which cannot be described as a negative gradient of potential energy function.

Geometric Active Contour

These models (Marian, 2007) are based on the evolution curve theory and the *level set* method. At curves and surfaces evolution, only geometric criteria are used that leads to the evolution independent from parameterization. These models may be implemented using level sets, and have been extensively employed in medical image computing. Geometric Active Contours are based on the theory of curve evolution implemented via level set techniques. Geometric deformable models provide an elegant solution to address the primary limitations of parametric deformable models. These models are based on curve evolution theory and the level set method. For capturing moving fronts in a wide range of problems, level set method has shown to be a robust numerical option. Some fields using level set techniques are image processing, computer vision and graphics.

Level Set Method

The level set method (Mohammadreza, Noseworthy, Kamath, Markad, Boylan, & Poehlman, 2009) is a geometric active contour model, can be used to isolate and build a coherent mathematical description of a particular shape. Unfortunately, there is no one set of parameters that works on all types of images. The level set method is a shape detection method, which isolates a particular shape of an object inside the image. The object must correspond to a region whose pixels have different intensity from neighbouring regions. The level set method makes it very easy to follow shapes that change topology. The central idea of level set is to represent the evolving contour using a signed pressure force function, where its zero level corresponds to the actual contour. Then, according to the motion equation of the contour, one can easily derive a similar flow for the implicit surface that when applied to the zero-level will reflect the propagation of the contour. The level set method encodes numerous advantages: it is implicit, parameter free, provides a direct way to estimate the geometric properties of the evolving structure, can change the topology and is intrinsic. The main idea of the level set method can be described as follows. In an open region Γ is a closed interface evolving with the velocity υ to the object. The goal is to analyze and compute the motion of the interface. Define an implicit smooth function $\phi(x, t)$ which represents the interface as the set where:

$$\phi(x,t) = 0 : if\ x \in \Gamma$$
$$\phi(x,t) < 0 : if\ x \in \Gamma_{in} \qquad\qquad (12)$$
$$\phi(x,t) > 0 : if\ x \in \Gamma_{out}$$

Where Γ_{in} shows the area inside the interface and Γ_{out} shows the area outside as shown in figure 3. The evolution could be described by convecting the ϕ with the velocity field υ on the interface:

$$\frac{\partial \phi}{\partial t} + v . \nabla \phi = 0 \qquad\qquad (13)$$

If the normal component of v is $v_N = v . \dfrac{\nabla \phi}{\left|\nabla \phi\right|}$, where $\left|\nabla \phi\right|$ represents modulus of gradient ϕ.

Equation (13) can be written as:

$$\frac{\partial \phi}{\partial t} + v_N . \left|\nabla \phi\right| = 0 . \qquad\qquad (14)$$

A useful property of this approach is that the level set function remains a valid function while the embedded curve can change its topology. Geometric active contours have many advantages over parametric active contours, such as computational simplicity and the ability to change curve topology. Unlike the snake can start far from the boundary and will converge to boundary concavities. Key terms and some key technological advances in level set methods are given below:

1.   The interface boundary $\Gamma(t)$ is defined by $\left\{x : \phi(x,t) = 0\right\}$. The region is bounded and its exterior is defined by $\left\{x : \phi(x,t) > 0\right\}$.

Figure 3. The construction of level set function

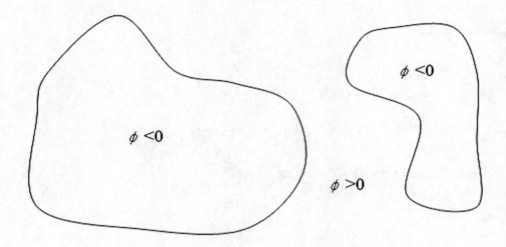

$\phi = 0$ defines Γ

2.   The unit normal N to $\Gamma(t)$ is defined by: N= $\dfrac{\nabla\phi}{|\nabla\phi|}$.

3.   The mean curvature κ of $\Gamma(t)$ is defined by

$$\kappa = -\nabla.\left(\frac{\nabla\phi}{|\nabla\phi|}\right)$$ (15)

where $\nabla\phi$ is the gradient defined as

$$\nabla\phi = \left(\frac{\partial\phi}{\partial x}, \frac{\partial\phi}{\partial y}\right)$$ (16)

4.   The Dirac delta function concentrated on interface is

$$\delta(\phi)|\nabla\phi|$$

where $\delta(\phi)$ is a one -dimensional delta function.

5.   The characteristic function χ of a region $\Gamma(t)$ is

$$\chi = H(-\phi) \tag{17}$$

where H is a one-dimensional Heaviside function and

$$H(x) \equiv 1 \; if \; x > 0 \; and \; H(x) \equiv 0 \; if \; x < 0. \tag{18}$$

6.   The surface (or line) integral of a function f over Γ is

$$\int_{Rn} f(x)\,\delta\,(\phi)\left|\nabla\,\phi\right| dx$$

$$= \int_{Rn} f(x)\,H\,(\phi)\;dx \tag{19}$$

7.   In many cases, ϕ will develop steep pr flat gradients which cause problem in numerical approximations. For preventing ϕ from becoming too flat or too steep near the interface as well as keeping the zero location unchanged, the distance re-initialization procedure reshapes a general level set function ϕ (x, t) by $d(x, t)$ which is the value of the distance from x to $\Gamma\left(t\right)$, positive outside, and negative inside. Let $d(x, t)$ be signed distance of x to the closed on Γ. The quantity $d(x, t)$ satisfies $\left|\nabla\,d\right|=1$, d is positive outside and negative inside and also is the steady state solution to

$$\phi_t + \operatorname{sgn}(\phi\circ)\left(\left|\nabla\,\phi\right|-1\right)=0 \quad and \quad \phi(x,t=0)=\phi\circ(x) \tag{20}$$

   Here ϕ_0 shows the level set function before the re-initialization. For most application, the re-initialization is only needed for a neighbourhood around the zero level set, and the diameter of this neighbourhood depends on the discretisation of the partial derivatives in the PDE. This implies that only a few time sets in t are needed.

8.   The basic level set method concerns a function ϕ which is defined all over space. Obviously this is wasteful unless one only cares about information near the zero set. The local level set method defines ϕ only near the zero level set. Some applications of image segmentation in different areas are given below.

Applications

Applications of image segmentation are given below:

- **Medical Imaging:** Image Segmentation techniques are playing very important role in medical field e.g. biomedical and health care. Medical imaging help the doctors with X-ray, MRI and CT scan images etc. Medical imaging provide excellent results in many areas like:
  - ○ Locate tumors and other pathologies
  - ○ Measure tissue volumes
  - ○ Computer guided surgery
  - ○ Diagnosis
  - ○ Treatment planning
  - ○ Study of anatomical structure
- **Locate Objects in Satellite Images:** With the help of image Segmentation techniques we can locate the objects in the Satellite images like roads, forests, buildings etc.
- **Face Recognition:** With the help of image Segmentation techniques we can recognize the face of the person and identify it once stored in database. It is used for the purpose of security.
- **Fingerprint Recognition:** With the help of image Segmentation techniques we can recognize the fingerprints of the person and identify it once stored in database. It is used for the purpose of security.
- **Army:** At the military level, image classification can be used in the analysis of satellite images or aerial mapping. Study and retrieve information about satellite images has a lot of application, for example where the river passes, where to establish industry, residential purpose etc.
- **Sports:** In professional sports (e.g. NBA or Football World Cup), the statistics, movements and tactics of a team or a game could be analyzed using techniques of image classification by its visual content.
- **Content-Based Image Retrieval**: Retrieval of the image as output using an image in the input based on some similarity features like texture, color, edge.

This section gives the basic ideas about the image segmentation methods and its applications. Some small details about active contour model and level set method are presented, so that we can develop an understanding of the work for proceeding further.

LITERATURE REVIEW

A number of research papers have been studied related to medical image processing. Research in medical informatics concentrates primarily on integrating computer technology to improve all areas of the field from education to diagnosis and treatment. Extensive study has been made and many techniques have been proposed among which the active contour model (ACM) (Xu, Ahuia, and Bansal, 2007) is one of the most successful methods. The basic idea in active contour models (or snakes) is to evolve a curve, subject to constraints from a given image, in order to detect objects in that image. They are classified as either parametric active contours or geometric active contours according to their representation and implementation. Geometric active contours have many advantages over parametric active contours. Parametric active contours have been reproduced in geometric active contours, the relationship between the two has not always been clear.

Active contours, also called snakes, are among the most important tools in computer vision. They were introduced in (Kass, Witkin, & Terzopoulos, 1988) and have been widely used for image analysis tasks such as object boundary detection. Despite its success, the original parametric active contour model has some noticeable drawbacks. First, it depends not only on the intrinsic properties of the contour but also on its parameterization; thus, it is a non-geometric model. Second, it cannot naturally handle changes in the topology of the evolving contour; significant progress towards topologically adaptable parametric snakes has been done only recently (McInerney, & Terzopoulos, 2000). These drawbacks of standard active contours were addressed by geometric active contours, introduced in (Malladi, Sethian, & Vemuri, 1995). An important development has been the introduction of geodesic active contours (Paragios, & Deriche, 2002). Augmenting the edge-based geodesic active contours with other region-based visual cues has led to many powerful geometric active contour models. Many region-based geometric active contours, have been inspired by the piecewise smooth Geodesic active contour model (Andersson, Gunnar, Reiner, & Magnus, 2013).

Modified Gradient Search for Level Set Based Image Segmentation (Osher, Fedkiw, 2002) is a level set methods used to solve the image segmentation problem. The solution contour is found by solving an optimization problem where a cost functional is minimized. Gradient descent methods are often used to solve this optimization problem since they are very easy to implement and applicable to general non-convex functional. In medical images edges are very thin and finer and optimizing the level set method for detecting object boundary in MR and CT images (Mohammadreza, Noseworthy, Kamath, Markad, Boylan, & Poehlman, 2009) Specifying the boundary of tissues or an organ is one of the most frequently required tasks for a radiologist. Four quantitative measures are used in calculating geometric differences between the object boundaries, as determined by the level set method. A semi-automated method is also developed to find the desired boundary for the object. Fast and robust level set method for image segmentation using fuzzy clustering and Lattice Boltzmann Method (LBM) (Souleymane, Gao, & Wang, 2013) which incorporates the bias field that accounts for the intensity in homogeneity of the medical or real-world image. LBM method is fast, robust against noise, independent to the position of the initial contour, effective in the presence of intensity in homogeneity, highly parallelizable and can detect objects with or without edges. Experiments on medical and real-world images demonstrate the performance of the proposed method in terms of speed and efficiency.

Some noise are often exist in the medical image, in such situation segmentation is very hard and cumbersome process. Active contour model for corrupted image are discussed in (Wang, Pan, Xu, Zhang, Liu, & Ding, 2011, Srivastava, & Singh, 2014) and constrained active contours for boundary refinement in supervised image segmentation (Zhao, Kang, & Irwin, 2013) can be used to improve the segmentation results of many existing region-based interactive segmentation algorithms. Takagi-Sugeno-Kang (TSK) fuzzy model (Zhao, Kang, & Irwin, 2013; Sakhre, Singh, & Jain, 2016) neural network models (Sakhre, Singh, & Jain, 2016; Singh, & Jain, 2016) are used learning approach considering both nonlinear parameters in the rule premises and linear parameters in the rule consequents is proposed. Thus, a new Jacobian matrix is proposed and efficiently computed to achieve a more accurate approximation of the cost function by using the second order Levenberg-Marquardt optimization method. On large datasets, the popular training approach has been stochastic gradient descent (SGD) that significantly improves the performance over the traditional gradient method (Sun, Kashima, Matsuzaki, & Naonori, 2010; Moorthi, Gambhir, Misra & Ramakrishnan, 2011). The only drawback of this models discussed above is the existence of local minima in the active contour formation of energy functional, which makes the initial guess are not correct and does not gives satisfactory results. We will prove results to determine the existence of a global minimum of cost functional. From a numerical point of view, we propose a new practical way to solve the cost functional minimization due to momentum and resilient propagation based gradient descent models.

PROPOSED MODEL

The robust and efficient enhancement, segmentation and modelling of structures using level set methods are depends on formation of contours. A popular level set method to solve the medical image segmentation problem is momentum and resilient based gradient descent approach. Momentum method has a lot of variation, showing large sensitivity to its parameters. A set of parameters that is robust to local optima and gives high segmentation velocity may not converge and oscillates around a solution. Resilient propagation is very sensitive to large changes in the direction of the gradient since it uses the signs of the gradient components. As far as the directions and the parameters sensitivity are concerned, momentum and resilient approach are to be better than others. It overcomes all such issues in the image segmentation problem. Curvilinear structure or solution contour is found by solving an optimization problem where a cost fitness function is minimized. Gradient descent methods are often used to solve such optimization problem. This chapter we propose a momentum term and resilient propagation based gradient descent method which will remove the sensitivity of local minima of gradient descent. Proposed method is applicable in case of diseases like retinal detachment, diabetic retinopathy, glaucoma; a standard eye examination is performed to detect changes. The detection of object boundary will be useful for the doctors to locate any object clearly, the doctor may required to observe the veins of the retina very closely to find out any crack in veins. The proposed model is helpful to remove the some drawback like local minima of medical image segmentation model based on its functional energy, which makes simple to obtain initial contour to extract meaningful objects lying in images. Proposed method helps in accurate locating the boundary and minutely outlines the fine and thin veins and side by side giving faster convergence. Extensive experiments have been performed over real and medical images like retina, leaver, brain etc. to test the true ability of the system. The proposed method is able to present the segmented medical image with clear and smooth boundary also it is simple and feasible to design and implementation. We have presented the flowchart of proposed model in Figure 4.

Steepest descent or Gradient optimization method are very common and easy to implement because it depends only on first derivative but it suffers from convergence to local minima and slow convergence rate. To overcome this problem various methods are introduced in recent years like conjugate gradient, Newton, and Quasi-Newton etc. (Nocedal & Wright, 2006). To improve the convergence rate and avoid local minima we introduce two term (i) momentum (Rumelhart, Hinton, & Williams, 1986) and (ii) resilient propagation (Rprop) (Riedmiller, & Braun, 1993) based gradient descent. Let us consider the following search optimization method

$$x_{k+1} = x_k + n_k \qquad (21)$$

Figure 4. Illustration of the flowchart for proposed method

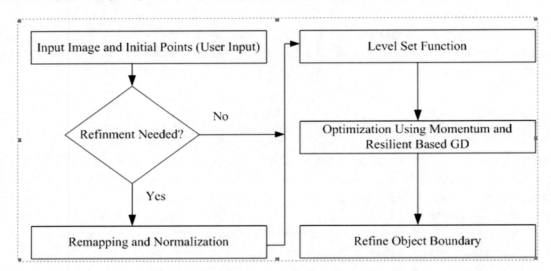

$$n_k = \alpha_k \overline{p}_k \tag{22}$$

where x_k is the current solution and n_k is the next step of length α_k in direction of $\overline{p}_k$. For the convergence it is required that $\overline{p}_k$ is right direction and $\alpha_k \geq 0$, gives the sufficient condition of decreasing cost function. The right direction $\overline{p}_k$ can be determine by the equation $\overline{p}_k = -\overline{\nabla} f_k$, where f is the energy or cost function. To introduce momentum term we consider a search vector

$$n_k = -\lambda(1 - \omega)\nabla f_k + \omega n_{k-1} \tag{23}$$

where λ is learning rate and $\omega \in [0, 1]$ such that if $\omega = 0$ then $n_k = -\lambda \nabla f_k$ and if $\omega = 1$ then $n_k = n_{k-1}$. In gradient descent search method value of α_k is constant and if α_k is to small the search method takes more iteration to converge and if α_k is too large the search method may oscillates. Thus the optimal value of α_k is not in hand but it depends upon cost functions.

The resilient propagation was introduced to control the step size Δ_k known as updated values and given as $\dim(\Delta_k) = \dim(x_k)$. For Rprop consider search vector

$$n_k = -sign(\nabla f) * \Delta_k \tag{24}$$

where *sign(.)* denote the sign function and Δ_k^i is the updated value in ith direction and kth step and calculated by equation (25)

$$\Delta_{k}^{i} = \begin{cases} \min(\Delta_{k-1}^{i}.\lambda, \Delta_{\max}), & \nabla^{i}f_{k}.\nabla^{i}f_{k-1} > 0 \\ \max(\Delta_{k-1}^{i}.\lambda, \Delta_{\min}), & \nabla^{i}f_{k}.\nabla^{i}f_{k-1} < 0 \\ \Delta_{k-1}^{i}, & \nabla^{i}f_{k}.\nabla^{i}f_{k-1} = 0 \end{cases} \qquad (25)$$

where $\nabla^{i}f_{k}$ denotes the partial derivative in i^{th} direction of cost function at k^{th} step.

For segmentation of medical images let us consider energy function as optimization function, a gradient descent method are used in region Ω_{C} bounded by closed contour *C*, gives the solution of segmentation problems. Let us consider functional

$$f(C) = \iint_{\Omega_{C}} \psi(x, y)\, dx\, dy \qquad (26)$$

where $\psi(x, y)$ is an scalar function defined in region Ω_{C} bounded by closed curve $C = \left\{ x : \phi(x, t) = 0 \right\}$. The contour *C* evolved in time represented by Partial Differential Equation (PDE) (Kimmel, 2003) of level set function.

$$\frac{\partial \phi}{\partial t} = -\psi(x, y)\left|\nabla \phi\right| \qquad (27)$$

where gradient of cost functional ∇f can be determine using equation (28)

$$\nabla f(t_{k}) \approx \frac{\phi(t_{k}) - \phi(t_{k-1})}{h} \qquad (28)$$

and $h = t_{k} - t_{k-1}$

Proposed Algorithm

Input: the image and selection of seed pixel at the stage of applying level set method
Output: desired refined boundary in image

Algorithm being used in the proposed approach:

Step 1: Load Image: Select an input image from dataset.
Step 2: Normalization: If the image needs any refinement then normalization is performed.
Step 3: Filtering and Transformation: Bilinear Transformation is applied on image for remapping.
  Here we can notice the difference between the stages at before mapping and after mapping.
Step 4: Level Set: Update level set using equation $n_{k} = -\lambda(1 - \omega)\nabla f_{k} + \omega n_{k-1}$ and
  $\nabla f(t_{k}) \approx \dfrac{\phi(t_{k}) - \phi(t_{k-1})}{h}$. momentum and Rprop term are used as follows:

1. For given level set function $\phi(x, t_{k-1})$ compute next time step of $\phi(x, t_k)$ using equation (27).

2. Compute approximate gradient using equation (28)

3. Compute $n(t_k) = -\lambda(1 - \omega)\left(\dfrac{\phi(t_k) - \phi(t_{k-1})}{h}\right) + \omega n_{k-1}$ and $\phi(t_k) = \phi(t_{k-1}) + n(t_k)$ for momentum term and $n_k = -sign\left(\dfrac{\phi(t_k) - \phi(t_{k-1})}{h}\right) * \Delta(t_k)$ for Rprop.

4. Compute the next time step $\phi(t_k) = \phi(t_{k-1}) + n(t_k)$ and go to (i).

Step 5: Optimization: In order to solve the optimization problem in level set segmentation methods, the momentum and Rprop based gradient descent method is used, our proposed method is applied which takes input from user, as the user knows which part of the image has more intensity.

EXPERIMENTAL RESULTS

In this section we will discuss some medical image segmentation problem using momentum and resilient propagation based gradient descent method. The main objective of proposed model is to design to obtain fast convergence rate and global optima. For experiment of segmentation we use MATLAB 7.12 software. Improved gradient descent using momentum and Rprop are used for medical image segmentation. Whereas the traditional gradient descent method suffers from slow convergence and local optima, proposed method remove these two drawbacks. The size of the test image is 250x250 to 512 x 512 pixels. For these size of input images proposed method, the evolution of the level set function converges in few iterations and takes less time, while for the traditional gradient descent model, the evolution converges in more iterations and more time. Proposed method accurately detects the exterior and interior boundaries of the objects, as well as the weak edge object, whereas the traditional gradient model fails to detect the interior boundary of the object and the weak edge object. Object extraction of some medical images are shown in Figure (5) to Figure (10).

In next experiment we consider retinal image of human eye shown in Figure 11(a). The image shows a veins of retina without clarity. A magnitude gradient from top to bottom has been calculated and effects may result in local optima in the solution space for certain parameter choices, and will help us test the

Figure 5. Demonstrates the global segmentation using proposed method. (a) Input image (liver) (b) Object contours (c) Extracted object

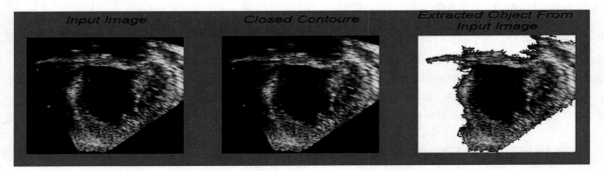

Figure 6. Demonstrates the global segmentation using proposed method. (a) Input image (brain) (b) Object contours (c) Extracted object

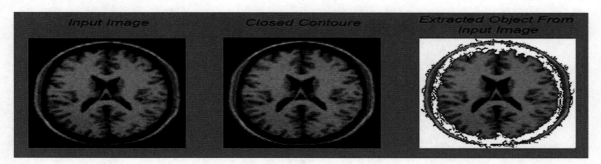

Figure 7. Demonstrates the global segmentation using proposed method. (a) Input image (b) Object contours (c) Extracted object

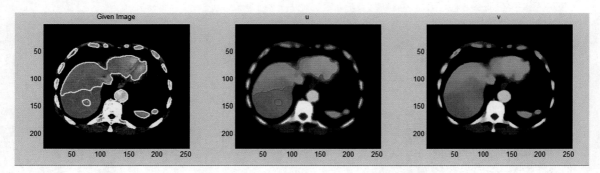

Figure 8. Demonstrates the global segmentation using proposed method. (a) Input image (b) Object contours (c) Extracted object

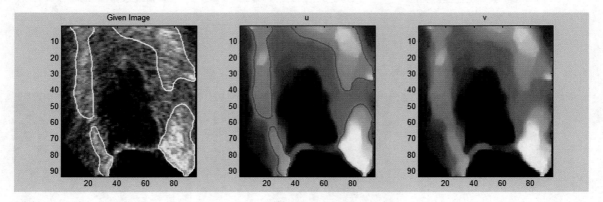

robustness. Figure 11(b) and Figure 11(c) shows the retina image before and after remapping. Whereas Figure 12 shows that selection of some seed pixels and segmentation of veins after some iterations.

In this chapter we present the experimental results based on proposed approach. Firstly we have selected the region of interest. Then with the help of level set parameters, we apply the momentum and

Figure 9. Demonstrates the global segmentation using proposed method. (a) Input image (b) Object contours (c) Extracted object

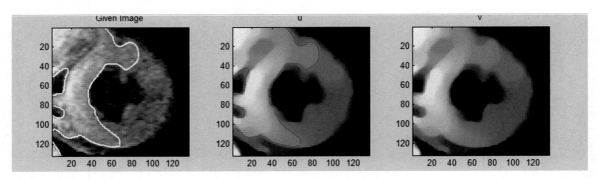

Figure 10. Demonstrates the global segmentation using proposed method. (a) Input image (b) Object contours (c) Extracted object

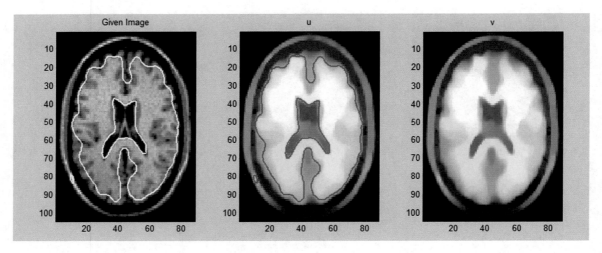

Figure 11. (a) Retina image of Human eye (b)before remapping(c) After Remapping

Figure 12. (a) Selection of seed pixels(b)segmentation after some iteration(c) complete segmentation

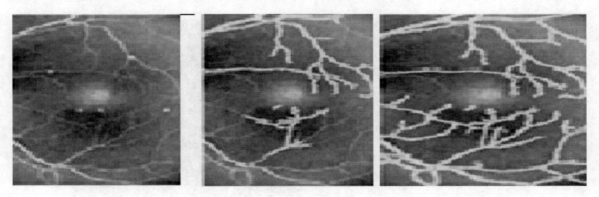

Rprop based gradient descent method. Input for level set will be the seed pixels that will be selected by the user. As much as the selection of the seed pixels will be accurate, the more accurate the result will be and the convergence rate will be faster. We have selected the images from various data sets and they are kept within same folder so as to access them directly. The work is focused for the retina of eyes so basically the dataset involved is DRIVE.

Comparison With Existing Methods

We compare our method modified SGD with the enhancements of gradient descent methods first being the gradient descent method with momentum term. This method low pass filters gradient against small local variations. Its importance depends upon parameter setting.

Second method being resilient propagation which is modified so as to take adaptive step size, it avoids local optima and uses sign of potential derivative. Now we are showing the resultant images that are obtained after the application of our approach.

Figure 13. Comparative Visualization of Retina image (a) input retina image (b) segmented image

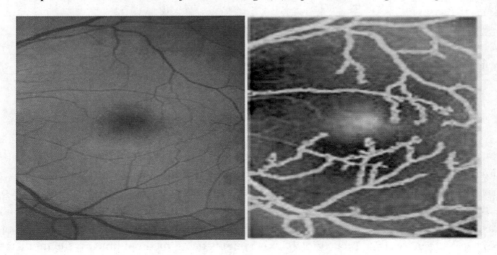

Figure 14. Comparative Visualization of Angio volume (a)input image, (b) output image of Angio

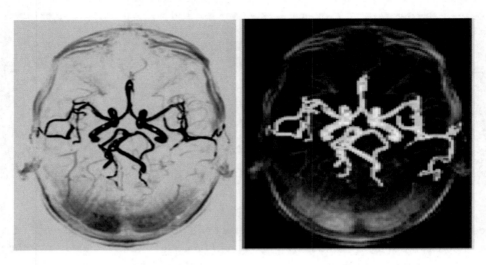

Table 1. Experimental results of the image Retina

Methods and Parameters	GD	SGD	Momentum	R-prop	Proposed
Conv. Ratio	19%	27%	30%	95%	97%
# weighted iter.	400	353	324.5	195	186
Clock time/iter.	0.4	0.4	0.5	0.5	0.42
Youdens Index, Y	0.79	.80	0.80	0.80	0.86

Table 2. Experimental results of the image Angio volume

Methods and Parameters	GD	SGD	Momentum	R-prop	Proposed
Conv. Ratio	50%	50%	56%	100%	98%
# weighted iter.	253	249	241	145	141%
Clock time/iter.	27	26	34.5	46	0.24
Youdens Index,Y	0.84	0.84	0.83	0.84	0.91

CONCLUSION

The author proposed momentum and resilient propagation based gradient descent methods. With help of momentum term it help to motion in solution space which simulates physical properties. This allows search to overstep local optima and take larger steps in favourable direction. Momentum method low pass filters gradient against small local variations. Another method called Resilient Propagation method uses sign of partial derivative, magnitude does not keep any importance. It is capable of using adaptive step size. It also avoids local optima. In a series of experiments using medical images, the modifications are shown to reduce the sensitivity for local optima and to increase the convergence rate. Momentum method has a lot of variation, showing large sensitivity to its parameters. A set of parameters that is robust to local optima and gives high segmentation velocity may not converge as it oscillates around a solution. R-prop, is very sensitive to large changes in the direction of the gradient since it uses the signs of the gradient components. As far as the directions and the parameters sensitivity are concerned, our approach proves to be better. The proposed method i.e. improved gradient descent methods are compared with the some existing method. It overcomes all such issues in the images. In spite of more advanced methods, optimization using proposed method segmentation is still very common and in active use. This is partly due to its simple implementation, but also to its direct applicability to general non-convex functional. In future more advanced optimization techniques can be applied on segmentation of images. In case of a diseases like retinal detachment, Diabetic Retinopathy, Glaucoma, a standard eye examination is performed to detect changes in size or shape of the eye, The detection of object boundary will be useful for the doctors to locate any object clearly, the doctor may required to observe the veins of the retina very closely to find out any crack in veins. Proposed method helps in accurate locating the boundary and minutely outlines the fine and thin veins and side by side giving faster convergence.

REFERENCES

Andersson, T., Gunnar, L., Lenz, R., & Magnus, B. (2013). Modified Gradient Search for Level Set Based Image Segmentation. *IEEE Transactions on Image Processing*, 22(2), 621–630. doi:10.1109/TIP.2012.2220148 PMID:23014748

Andersson, T., Gunnar, L., Reiner, L., & Magnus, B. (2013). Modified Gradient Search for Level Set Based Image Segmentation. *IEEE Transactions on Image Processing*, 22(2), 621–630. doi:10.1109/TIP.2012.2220148 PMID:23014748

Birgit, M., & Stefan, P. (2012). Comparing Active Contours For The Segmentation of Biomedical Images. *9th IEEE International Symposium on Biomedical Imaging (ISBI)*, 736-739.

Bresson, X., Esedoglu, S., Vandergheynst, P., Thiran, J. P., & Osher, S. (2007). Fast global minimization of the active contour/snake model. *Journal of Mathematical Imaging and Vision*, 28(2), 151–167. doi:10.100710851-007-0002-0

Caselles, V., Kimmel, R., & Sapiro, G. (1995). *Geodesic active contours. Proc. IEEE Int. Conf. Comput. Vis.*

Chan, T. F., Esedoglu, S., & Nikolova, M. (2006). Algorithms for finding global minimizers of image segmentation and denoising models. *SIAM Journal on Applied Mathematics*, 66(5), 1632–1648. doi:10.1137/040615286

Chan, T. F., & Vese, L. A. (2001). Active contours without edges. *IEEE Transactions on Image Processing*, 10(2), 266–277. doi:10.1109/83.902291 PMID:18249617

Charpiat, G., Keriven, R., Pons, J.-P., & Faugeras, O. (2005). Designing spatially coherent minimizing flows for variational problems based on active contours. Proc. IEEE Int. Conf. Comput. Vis., (2), 1403–1408.

Cohen, L. D. (1991). On active contour models and balloons. *CVGIP. Image Understanding*, *53*(2), 211–218. doi:10.1016/1049-9660(91)90028-N

Dubey, S. R., Singh, S. K., & Singh, R. K. (2015). Local diagonal extrema pattern: A new and efficient feature descriptor for CT image retrieval. *IEEE Signal Processing Letters*, *22*(9), 1215–1219. doi:10.1109/LSP.2015.2392623

Felipe, J. C., Traina, A. J. M., & Traina, C. Jr. (2003). Retrieval by content of medical images using texture for tissue identification. *Proc. IEEE 16th Symp. Comput.-Based Med. Syst.*, 175–180. 10.1109/CBMS.2003.1212785

Gonzalez, R. C., Woods, R. E., & Eddins, S. L. (2004). *Digital Image Processing Using MATLAB*. Pearson Education.

Grady, L. (2011). Random Walks for Image Segmentation. *IEEE Transactions on Pattern Analysis and Machine Intelligence*, *28*(11), 1768–1783. doi:10.1109/TPAMI.2006.233 PMID:17063682

Heydarian, M. N., Michael, D., Kamath, M. V., Colm, B., & Poehlman, W. F. S. (2009). Optimizing the Level Set Algorithm for Detecting Object Edges in MR and CT Images. *IEEE Transactions on Nuclear Science*, *56*(1), 156–167. doi:10.1109/TNS.2008.2010517

Kass, M., Witkin, A., & Terzopoulos, D. (1988). Snakes: Active contour models. *International Journal of Computer Vision*, *1*(4), 321–331. doi:10.1007/BF00133570

Kass, M., Witkin, A., & Terzopoulos, D. (1988). Snakes:Active Contour Models. *International Journal of Computer Vision*, *1*(4), 321–331. doi:10.1007/BF00133570

Kearfott, R. B. (1996). *Rigorous Global Search: Continuous Problems (Nonconvex Optimization and Its Applications), 13*. Dordrecht, The Netherlands: Kluwer. doi:10.1007/978-1-4757-2495-0

Kichenassamy, S., Kumar, A., Olver, P., Tannenbaum, A., & Yezzi, A. (1995). Gradient flows and geometric active contour models. *Proc. Int. Conf. Comp. Vis.*, 810–815. 10.1109/ICCV.1995.466855

Kimmel, R. (2003). Fast edge integration. In *Geometric Level Set Methods in Imaging, Vision and Graphics*. New York: Springer-Verlag. doi:10.1007/0-387-21810-6_4

Kirkpatrick, S., Gelatt, C. D., & Vecchi, M. P. (1983). Optimization by simulated annealing. *Science*, *220*(4598), 671–680. doi:10.1126cience.220.4598.671 PMID:17813860

Li, C., Huang, R., Ding, Z., Chris, G. J., Dimitris, N., & John, G. C. (2011). A Level Set Method for Image Segmentation in the Presence of Intensity Inhomogeneities With Application to MRI. *IEEE Transactions on Image Processing*, *20*(7), 2007–2016. doi:10.1109/TIP.2011.2146190 PMID:21518662

Malladi, R., Sethian, J. A., & Vemuri, B. C. (1995). Shape modeling with front propagation: A level set approach. *IEEE Transactions on Pattern Analysis and Machine Intelligence*, *17*(2), 158–175. doi:10.1109/34.368173

Marian, B. (2007). Active Contours and their Utilization at Image Segmentation. *5th Slovakian-Hungarian Joint Symposium on Applied Machine Intelligence and Informatics*, 313-317.

McInerney, T., & Terzopoulos, D. (2000). T-snakes: Topology adaptive snakes. *Medical Image Analysis, 4*(2), 73–91. doi:10.1016/S1361-8415(00)00008-6 PMID:10972323

Metropolis, N., Rosenbluth, A. W., Rosenbluth, M. N., Teller, A. H., & Teller, E. (1953). Equation of state calculations by fast computing machines. *The Journal of Chemical Physics, 21*(6), 1087–1092. doi:10.1063/1.1699114

Mohammadreza, H., Noseworthy, M., Kamath, D., Markad, V., Boylan, C., & Poehlman, W. F. S. (2009). Optimizing the Level Set Algorithm for Detecting Object Edges in MR and CT Images. *IEEE Transactions on Nuclear Science, 56*(1), 156–167. doi:10.1109/TNS.2008.2010517

Moorthi, M. S., Gambhir, R. K, Misra, I., & Ramakrishnan, R. (2011). Adaptive stochastic gradient descent optimization in multi temporal satellite image registration. *IEEE Recent Advances in Intelligent Computational Systems (RAICS),* 373-377.

Morse, P. M., & Feshbach, H. (1993). The variational integral and the Euler equations. Proc. Meth. Theor. Phys., 1, 276–280.

Mumford, D., & Shah, J. (1989). Optimal approximation by piecewise smooth functions and associated variational problems. *Communications on Pure and Applied Mathematics, 42*(5), 577–685. doi:10.1002/cpa.3160420503

Murala, S., Maheshwari, R. P., & Balasubramanian, R. (2012). Directional binary wavelet patterns for biomedical image indexing and retrieval. *Journal of Medical Systems, 36*(5), 2865–2879. doi:10.100710916-011-9764-4 PMID:21822675

Murala, S., & Wu, J. Q. M. (2013). Local ternary co-occurrence patterns: A new feature descriptor for MRI and CT image retrieval. *Neurocomputing, 119,* 399–412. doi:10.1016/j.neucom.2013.03.018

Nguyen, T., Nhat, A., Jianfei, C., Zhang, J., & Zheng, J. (2012). Constrained Active Contours for Boundary Refinement in Interactive Image Segmentation. *IEEE International Symposium on Circuits and Systems,* 870- 873.

Nocedal, J., & Wright, S. J. (2006). *Numerical Optimization* (2nd ed.). New York: Springer-Verlag.

Osher, S., & Fedkiw, R. (2002). *Level Set Methods and Dynamic Implicit Surfaces.* New York: Springer-Verlag.

Paragios, N., & Deriche, R. (2000). Geodesic active contours and level sets for the detection and tracking of moving objects. *IEEE Transactions on Pattern Analysis and Machine Intelligence, 22*(3), 266–280. doi:10.1109/34.841758

Paragios, N., & Deriche, R. (2002). Geodesic active regions: A new framework to deal with frame partition problems in computer vision. *Journal of Visual Communication and Image Representation, 13*(1-2), 249–268. doi:10.1006/jvci.2001.0475

Patil, D. D., & Deore, S. G. (2013). Medical Image Segmentation: A Review. *IJCSMC, 2*(1), 22–27.

Quellec, G., Lamard, M., Cazuguel, G., Cochener, B., & Roux, C. (2010). Wavelet optimization for content-based image retrieval in medical databases. *J. Med. Image Anal, 14*(2), 227–241. doi:10.1016/j.media.2009.11.004 PMID:20007020

Riedmiller, M., & Braun, H. (1993). A direct adaptive method for faster backpropagation learning: The RPROP algorithm. *Proc. IEEE Int. Conf. Neural Networks, 1*, 586–591.

Rumelhart, D. E., Hinton, G. E., & Williams, R. J. (1986). Learning Internal Representations Error Propagation. Cambridge, MA: MIT Press.

Sakhre, V., Singh, U. P., & Jain, S. (2016). FCPN Approach for Uncertain Nonlinear Dynamical System with Unknown Disturbance. *International Journal of Fuzzy Systems (Springer), 5*. doi:10.100740815-016-0145

Singh, U. P., & Jain, S. (2016). Modified Chaotic Bat Algorithm-Based Counter Propagation Neural Network for Uncertain Nonlinear Discrete Time System. *International Journal of Computational Intelligence and Applications, 15*(3), 1650016. doi:10.1142/S1469026816500164

Singh, U. P., Saxena, K., & Jain, S. (2011). Semi-Supervised Method of Multiple Object Segmentation with Region Labeling and Flood Fill. *Signal and Image Processing International Journal (Toronto, Ont.), 2*(3), 175–193.

Singh, U. P., Saxena, K., & Jain, S. (2011). Unsupervised Method of Object Retrieval with Region Labeling and Flood Fill" *International Journal of Advanced Computer Science and Applications. Special Issue on Artificial Intelligence, 1*, 41–50.

Singh, U. P., Saxena, K., & Jain, S. (2011). A Review: Different Types of Similarity Measures. *Pioneer Journal of Computer Science and Engineering Technology, 2*(1), 43–63.

Souleymane, B. A., Gao, X., & Wang, B. (2013). A Fast and Robust Level Set Method for Image Segmentation Using Fuzzy Clustering and Lattice Boltzmann Method. *IEEE Transactions on Cybernetics, 43*(3), 910–920. doi:10.1109/TSMCB.2012.2218233 PMID:23076068

Srivastava, P., & Singh, U. P. (2014). Noise Removal Using First Order Median Filter. *IEEE International Conference CSIBIG-2014.* 10.1109/CSIBIG.2014.7057004

Sun, X., Kashima, H., Matsuzaki, T., & Naonori, U. (2010). Averaged Stochastic Gradient Descent with Feedback: An Accurate, Robust, and Fast Training Method. *IEEE International Conference on Data Mining*, 1067-1072. 10.1109/ICDM.2010.26

Sundaramoorthi, G., Yezzi, A., & Mennucci, A. (2007). Sobolev active contours. *International Journal of Computer Vision, 73*(3), 345–366. doi:10.100711263-006-0635-2

Traina, A., Castanon, C., & Traina, C., Jr. (2003). Multiwavemed: A system for medical image retrieval through wavelets transformations. *Proc. IEEE16th Symp. Comput.-Based Med. Syst.*, 150–155.

Wang, G., Pan, Z., Xu, J., Zhang, Z., Liu, C., & Ding, J. Y. (2011). Active Contour Model for Images Corrupted by Multiplicative Noise with Rayleigh Distribution. *IEEE 5th International Conference on Cybernetics and Intelligent Systems (CIS)*, 124-127.

Xu, N., Ahuia, N., & Bansal, R. (2007). Object segmentation using graph cuts based active contours. *Computer Vision and Image Understanding*, *107*(3), 210–224. doi:10.1016/j.cviu.2006.11.004

Yi, F. (2012). Image segmentation: A survey of graph-cut methods. *Inkyu Moon, Systems and Informatics (ICSAI), IEEE International Conference*, 1936-1941.

Zakeri, F. S., Behnam, H., & Ahmadinejad, N. (2012). Classification of benign and malignant breast masses based on shape and texture features in sonography images. *Journal of Medical Systems*, *36*(3), 1621–1627. doi:10.100710916-010-9624-7 PMID:21082222

Zhao, W., Kang, L., & Irwin, G. W. (2013). A New Gradient Descent Approach for Local Learning of Fuzzy Neural Models. *IEEE Transactions on Fuzzy Systems*, *21*(1), 30–44. doi:10.1109/TFUZZ.2012.2200900

Chapter 12
An Intelligent–Based Wavelet Classifier for Accurate Prediction of Breast Cancer

Anandakumar Haldorai
Anna University, India & Sri Eshwar College of Engineering, India

Arulmurugan Ramu
Bannari Amman Institute of Technology, India

ABSTRACT

The detection of cancer in the breast is done using mammograms (x-ray images). The authors propose a CAD framework for distinguishing little changes in mammogram which may demonstrate malignancies which are too little to be felt either by the lady herself or by a radiologist. In this chapter, they build up a framework for analysis, visualization, and prediction of cancer in breast tissue by utilizing Intelligent based wavelet classifier. Intelligent-based wavelet classifier is a new approach constructed using texture value and wavelet neural network. The proposed framework is applied to the genuine clinical database of 160 mammograms gathered from mammogram screening focuses. The execution of the CAD framework is examined utilizing ROC curve. This will help the specialists in determination of the breast tissues either cancerous or noncancerous in an accurate way.

INTRODUCTION

Breast cancer is presently a standout the most well-known sicknesses among ladies in the both developed and developing nations. In the real situation, one out of 500 ladies will get breast cancer sooner or later in her life (Ramón González, Moreno, Fernández, Izquierdo, Borrás, & Gispert, 2005). It's recorded that 23% cancer cases and 14% lead to death. It is evaluated that more than 1.6 million new instances of breast cancer disease happened among ladies worldwide in 2010 (Jemal, Bray, Forman, O'Brien, Ferlay, Center, & Parkin, 2012). In 2011, about 1.7 million individuals were risked having breast malignancy; in that 527 new USA patients of breast cancer were analyzed every day and 110 individuals were die

DOI: 10.4018/978-1-5225-5246-8.ch012

in every day. Early detection stays vital for survival, especially in low and moderate nations where the sicknesses are analyzed in late stages and assets are extremely constrained. One demonstrated method for diminishing mortality from bosom tumor is the screening of asymptotic ladies by mammography.

Mammography is the best screening method that utilizations low amount X-ray beams to make a picture of the breast to discover breast tumor. The screened Images are shown in Figure 1. Mammography has been successful in screening asymptomatic ladies. The Cancer Society prescribes that all ladies who completed 40 years should go screening mammography once in a year. Thick breast tissue can look white or light dots on a mammogram. This can make mammograms harder to decipher in younger ladies, who have a tendency to have denser breast shown in Figure 2.

Figure 1. Mammogram of the breast

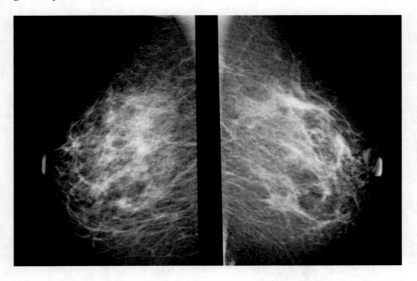

Figure 2. a) Fatty and b) Dense tissue

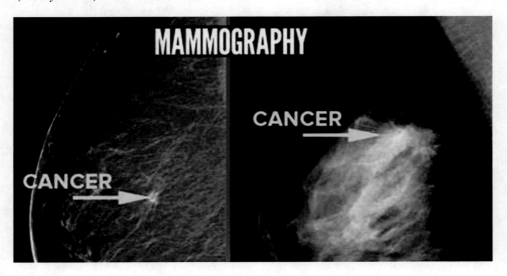

Because of the thickness of the breasts radiologists may miss up to 30% of malignant tissue that cause cancer. Fortunately, even well trained radiologists may felt difficulties in diagnosing mammograms. Two capable markers of malignancy that are generally utilized as a part of assessing mammograms .There are masses and micro calcifications. The first method diagnosing breast using masses in computerized mammography is more complex. This done by using feature selection and ensemble methods. Later technique is calcification in which complexity lesser than mass analysis. CAD (Computer Aided Diagnosis) of Micro calcifications in Digital Mammograms was used to support Early Diagnosis of Breast cancer.

In order to support the radiologists in finding accurate cancer tissue, Computer Aided Diagnosis is used. Computer aided design can discover tumors that are invisible to radiologist. After CAD analysis as shown in Figure 3, radiologist will do a visual check of those abnormalities and able to separate cancer tissues from genuine one.

RELATED WORKS

The second leading cause of death for women in the world is Breast cancer. It represents about 22% of new cancer cases. As per the World Health Organization report, breast cancer causes 450,000 deaths worldwide every year. Although the incidence of breast cancer all over the world has increased over the past decade, mortality rate has declined among women of all ages. It is due to the widespread adoption of the technique of mammography screening, and the significant improvements made in breast cancer

Figure 3. Identification of calcifications area in breast through CAD

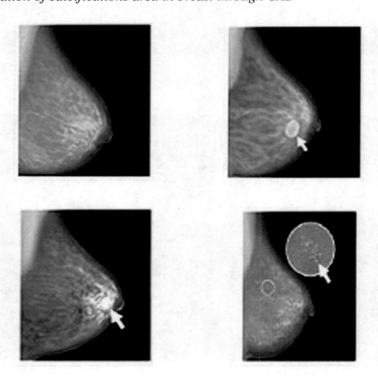

treatment has paved the way for the reduction of mortality rates (Anandakumar & Umamaheswari, 2017). Mammography has been proved as the best method of screening which has reduced the mortality rates by 30-70%. Computer Aided Diagnosis (CAD) systems can aid the diagnosis of the disease by increasing the sensitivity to abnormalities when compared to the double checking that would be performed by the radiologists. These systems have proved to be cost-effective and efficient and also they are available commercially.

An investigation of different Medical image processing and Computer Aided Diagnosis (CAD) approaches are utilized for the recognition of breast cancer. Early detection of breast cancer is vital as it can expand the rate of analysis, cure and survival of ladies is increased. In 2006, Yuehui Chen Forouzanfar et al (2011) explored the issue of computer aided based recognition and division of cell cores in substantial scale histological pictures. Optimum Laplacian of Gaussian Assimilator (OLGA) was the proposed technique to recognize the general number of cells and after that the harmful cells was sectioned by utilizing a PCA and histogram-examination based strategies. A separate Computer Aided Detection (CAD) for breast cancer can enhance the discovery rate from 4.7% to 19.5% with radiologists.

Preprocessing steps are important for the radiologists as they provide a better environment to perceive even small abnormalities. The diagnostic features in mammograms like masses and micro-calcifications might be small and have low contrast which couldn't be detected easily in the real time without a CAD system (Kolb, Lichy & Newhouse, 2002). Histogram equalization method focuses on maximizing the entropy i.e. obtaining a lot of information by equalizing the histogram of the mammographic image as possible. The next method, Contrast stretching utilizes all the possible values by improving an image through stretching of all the intensity values. Convolution masking enhancement method focuses on adding a highly filtered and scaled image to the original image itself. Local enhancement techniques improve the local contrast by using the properties of the neighborhood region like local mean and local standard deviation, suppress them and increase the contrast of the region of interest. Region based enhancements methods like the Adaptive Neighborhood contrast enhancement algorithm (ANCE) works by taking each pixel in the region as the seed pixel in the procedure of region growing which in turn identifies the pixels which are similar and connected to the seed pixel (Luo & Cheng, 2010)..Based on the performance comparisons made between the various preprocessing techniques, The ANCE algorithm was found to give a better performance. Table 1 describes various NN architecture that used for Medical Image Processing.

Table 1. Medical image processing using neural network system

S.No	Neural Network types	Image Type	Output
1	Cellular NN	X-ray	Boundary Detection
2	Genetic Algorithm and Convolution Neural Network	X-ray	Detect shadows of nodular
3	Hybrid Neural Digital CAD	X-ray	Classify 3-15 mm size nodules
4	ANN Feed Forward network	X-ray	Increase sensitivity & accuracy
5	Artificial CNN & application	X-ray	Identified False Positive & increase sensitivity
6	CNN	X-ray	Decrease False & Increase True Positive
7	Two - level CNN	X-ray	Highly reduced False Positive
8	NN Ensembles	X-ray	Highly reduced False Positive

Segmentation plays a vital role in the cancer detection since the outline of the lesion when identified properly creates a faithful description to its characteristics. The classification should be aimed at increasing the detection of true negatives and decreasing that of the false positives. The Segmentation methods include the Region based segmentation, Contour based segmentation, Clustering based segmentation methods. Region based segmentation divides the given input image into various homogeneous and spatially connected regions. They are divided into regions that are distinct and uniform with certain set of properties lie texture, color etc (Cheng, Shi, Min, Hu, Cai, & Du, 2006). The Contour based segmentation methods concentrate on the boundaries of the various regions which is used to distinct the regions from one another one such method is the Watershed segmentation method. Clustering based methods are employed to group the pixels of same properties which have higher intra cluster similarity than the inter cluster similarity. From the study made, the Contour based methods were found to produce faster results and produced results with good sensitivity and specificity.

Considering the histogram in the mammogram, base on data hypothesis which have more data for classifications of tissue in images (Fu, Lee, Wong, Yeh, Wang, & Wu, 2005). It is normally difficult to recognize benign from malignant due to variance in breast appearances. The human breast changes significantly in the piece, and mammographic appearances differing form complex patterns. To identify accurate malignant, ROC (Receiver Operating Characteristic) for classifiers used by considering sensitivity and specificity. CAD has effectively uncovered breast masses and micro calcifications on screening mammography for revealing cancer using Sensitivity of Commercial CAD Systems for Detecting Architectural Distortion (Buseman, Mouchawar, Calonge & Byers, 2003). Mammograms extracted feature was used for screening and taken prior to the detection of a malignant mass for early discovery of breast cancer.

Feature extraction is the next important step in image processing for breast cancer detection. This step involves the extraction of features that could describe the objects qualitatively and quantitatively. It describes the low level image with low-level information into high level information which could better describe the shapes and structures in the image analytically. Classification is the last step in breast cancer detection which could be done is two ways either supervised or unsupervised. The unsupervised method like K-means classification works with the specified number of classes (K) which is set by the user. It calculates the intra-class distance and reattached cluster centers based on the distance values. The drawback is the necessity to determine the number of classes in advance. Also the method was found to be sensitive to initial data distribution. Another unsupervised classification method is the Self Organizing Map(SOM) which is a Neural Network based method which projects the high dimensional data in two-dimensional space and is efficient in recognizing a certain set of input (Arulmurugan, Sabarmathi & Anandakumar, 2017).

Supervised classification method could be adopted if the user has got enough information regarding the classes. The classification model has to be provided with a training set of samples for each of the classes and then the model is tested against the test set data. Linear Discriminant Analysis (LDA) is used to separate the images into classes based on the construction decision obtained by optimizing the error criterion. This method is suitable only for linearly separable data which is not possible always (Yaffe, 2010). The Artificial Neural Network (ANN) is based on the perceptron theory consists of the input layer with descriptors and the output layer that indicates the classification result and a number of hidden layers. It would be helpful to model a large number of highly complex non-linear systems but the major drawback is the choice of hidden layers and neurons in each layer of the system.

Adaptive Resonance Neural Network (ARNN) (Anandakumar & Umamaheswari, 2017) is an unsupervised learning method employed to coach the neurons. The authors have used Wisconsin database, with 600 samples trained the network.This proposed work has Recall of 75%, Accuracy 82.64% and precision rate 79%. Ciatto, et al (2003) utilized factual elements from WBCD. The feature extraction is trained by utilizing Radial Basis Function(RBF), Probabilistic Neural Networks (PNN), Generalized Regression Neural Networks (GRNN) and Multi-Layer Perception (MLP). MATLAB 6.0 Neural Network Toolbox, Classification rate were 96.18% for RBF, 97.0% for PNN, 98.8% for GRNN and 95.74% for MLP. Chen, Wang, and Yang (2006) proposed Statistical features from breast images applied with Support Vector Apparatus (SVM) and other machine learning methods like LDA, NDA, PCA and ANN.

SVM was able to accomplish bigger allocation accurateness for early detection of breast cancer. Rangayyan and Leo Desautels (2007) developed an ANN, ANFIS combined with Linear discriminate models (LDA) and PCA for finding of cancer tissues in breast. The target area and shape of affected tissues is classified. A plan for investigating mammograms by utilizing a multi-resolution portrayal using Gabor wavelets is introduced by Zimmerman, Pizer, Staab, Perry, McCartney, and Brenton (1988). The technique is utilized to recognize asymmetry in the fibro-glandular plates of left and right mammograms with a specific end goal to analyze breast tissues malignancy. In their work a word reference of Gabor channels is utilized and the channel reactions for various scales and introduction are investigated by utilizing the Karhunen–Loéve change, which is connected to choose the main parts of the channel reactions.

The neural systems and fuzzy system for finding benign (non-cancerous) and malign (cancerous) tumors is introduced (Morrow, Paranjape, Rangayyan, & Desautels, 1992). The pictures were segmented and highlighted as rugosity vectors, which are then prepared and gone for defuzzification rules for positioning. The high level of rugosity is used from the two classes specimens utilized for testing. A more comparable way to deal with our own is one by Cao, Hao, and Xia (2009), which tries to group mammograms into non-cancerous, cancerous, and inside the last two classes between sorts of lesions, for example, radial, circumscribed, and microcalcifications. A multiresolution portrayal of every mammogram is figured by utilizing Haar, Daubechies, and a shiftable change. The grouping is endeavored by utilizing a metric proposed by Cao, Hao, and Xia (2009). A few outcomes are given indicating better classification rates.

The wavelet domain has great confinement property in frequency level as well in time dimensions. Numerous analysts have utilized the wavelet to identify and categories the various regular and irregular parts of signals presented feed forward systems made out of wavelets. The discrete wavelet is utilized along with feed forward neural system for analyze of various data. WNN-based (Anandakumar & Umamaheswari, 2017) is an effective model for recognition pattern in non-linear form. The following Table 2 summary of literature survey on cancer diagnosis.

PROPOSED METHODOLOGY

This paper shows the utilization of Wavelet based neural network for the detection of breast cancer tissues. Feature extraction techniques used for handling Mammograms based on image processing methods. Figure 4 demonstrates the essential phases of cancer identification in Breast.

The proposed system consists of 3 steps. The initial step includes image-preprocessing techniques for image enhancement and the region of interest of mammogram is separated. The second step car-

Table 2. Existing methodology of various NN algorithms for cancer diagnosis

Authors	Methodology	Algorithms	Outcome
Ramón González, J., Moreno, V., Fernández, E., Izquierdo, Á., Borrás, J., & Gispert, R. (2005)	ANN	Hierarchical Radial Basis Function	Detection of Breast cancer using hierarchical RBF gives accuracy of 97.09%.
Jemal, A., Bray, F., Forman, D., O'Brien, M., Ferlay, J., Center, M., & Parkin, D. M. (2012)	ANN	Adaptive Resonance Theory	Detection of cancer using ART with accuracy 82.64%.
Forouzanfar, M. H., Foreman, K. J., Delossantos, A. M., Lozano, R., Lopez, A. D., Murray, C. J. L., & Naghavi, M. (2011)	ANN	Back propagation Neural network Algorithm	Classification of malignant or benign for Breast cancer achieved the accuracy rate of 94.11% and 100%
Kolb, T. M., Lichy, J., & Newhouse, J. H. (2002)	CAD System and Probabilistic NN	Competitive Learning Algorithm	Brain Tumor Detection accuracy rate is 100%.
Luo, S.-T., & Cheng, B.-W. (2010)	ANN	Back propagation Neural network Algorithm	Detection of lung cancer with accuracy of 96.6%.
Yaffe, M. J. (2010)	Image processing and ANN	Multilayer Perceptron Training Algorithm	Classification of breast cancer in mammographic images of accuracy rate is 95.49%.
Rangayyan, R. M., Ayres, F. J., & Leo Desautels, J. E. (2007)	ANN	Back propagation Neural network Algorithm	Classification and detection Breast cancer using ANN with accuracy of 94%

Figure 4. Intelligent wavelet based ANN

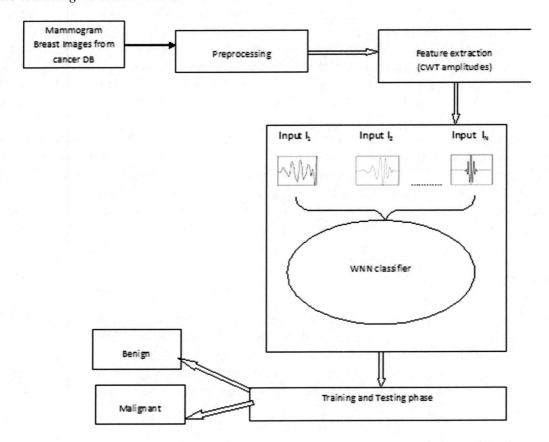

ried out through features extraction by removing textures from mammograms. In last step the Wavelet based Neural Network is utilized to classify the mammogram as noncancerous (benign) or a cancerous (malignant) are predicted.

The image acquisition for a mammogram is finished by compacting the breasts of the patient between two acrylic plates for a couple of moments when the X-beam is radiated. A mammogram is a obtained with gray levels, demonstrating the various contrast levels and differentiation inside the breast which shows typical tissue, vessels, distinctive masses of calcification, and commotion shown in Figure 5.

Intelligent systems have constructed using a wavelet-based neural network that learns in an environment even during vulnerability condition and predicts better output. Our WNN is a feed forward neural system which consists of an input layer in which takes wavelet as input, followed by hidden layer that contains wavelet as function and an output layer consists of linear function that comprises the sum of weighted previous layer (hidden) output which is shown in Figure 6. The back propagation is used to train based on error correction in order to reduce Mean Square Error (MSE) which has less error rate than feed forward neural network.

In the Wavelet Neural Network Classifier structure,

ω_i – Weights of input and hidden layer

ω_j – Weights of hidden and output layer

$X_1, X_2 \ldots \ldots X_N$ -Input parameters

Y-Output vectors

$$\Psi(X) = \psi\left(\frac{x - b_k}{a_k}\right) \tag{1}$$

Figure 5. Intensified mammogram image of left and right breast

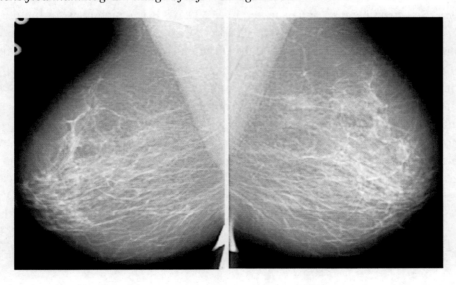

In above equation (1), $\Psi(x)$ – Wavelet function

a_k – Dilation parameter of kth hidden neuron

b_k – Translation parameter of kth hidden neuron

There are many wavelet functions such as the Morlet wavelet, the Haar wavelet, and the Shannon wavelet are considered in our research. The mathematical expressions of these wavelet functions are given below in Equation (2) (3) (4)

Morlet wavelet: $\psi(X) = \cos(1.75X).e^{-X^2/2}$ (2)

Haar wavelet: $\psi(X) = \begin{cases} +1, & 0 \leq X < \dfrac{1}{2} \\ -1, & \dfrac{1}{2} \leq X < 1 \\ 0, & otherwise \end{cases}$ (3)

Shannon wavelet: $\psi(X) = \dfrac{\sin(\pi \dfrac{X}{2})}{\dfrac{\pi X}{2}} . \cos\left(\dfrac{3\pi X}{2}\right)$ (4)

Mammograms are collected from Clinical DB in which consists of 50 different patients. The proposed framework has been planned and executed in MATLAB 8.1, which goes for building up a CAD framework for breast cancer tissue recognition. The preprocessing of the clinical images is executed for collected sample (Figure 6) datasets, and the region of interest is identified as shown in Figure 7. After completion of preprocess of the mammograms, texture features of kernel are extracted from every pixel of the ROI clinical image. The preparation dataset contains 1023 sets of input–output different training patterns. Then training of WNN is carried out based on wavelet function. The classification performance is checked with number of neurons used in hidden layer of WNN.

Table 4 shows the performance of different classifiers in terms of neurons count. The maximum efficiency is given at when 120 neurons are used during training. The maximum accuracy is achieved by WNN is 86.26%. The zone under the ROC curve is a measure of how well a parameter can recognize two analytic classes such as normal /abnormal tissues). The entry performance of CAD systems has been measured and revealed in the form of classification accuracy in which correctness of the diagnostic decisions is considered. The ROC curve defined by using sensitivity (True Positive rate) + specificity (False positive rate). There are potential outcomes for a computerized classifier to miss certain varia-

Figure 6. Structure of the Wavelet neural network classifier

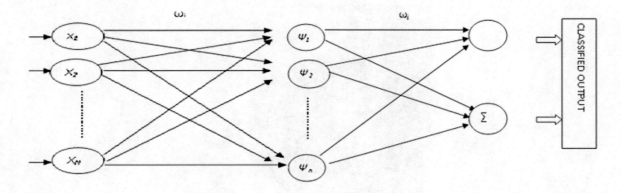

Table 3. Algorithm for WNN Training

Step 1: To set the WNN parameters.
Step 2: Assign Input parameters and target value for training
Step 3: Calculate the WNN function for output determination using Equation (5)

$$\gamma = \sum_K \omega_j \psi \left(\frac{\sum_i \omega_i X_i - b_k}{a_k} \right) \tag{5}$$

Step 4: Analyze the output value with the target and figure out the sum of square of error
Step 5: If the target value of sum of square of error is not obtained at the nth epoch, identify the difference between the target value and the output obtained (E) based on the learning rate and the momentum
Step 6: Repeat steps 1-5 till convergence is accomplished

Figure 7. Cancerous mammogram

Figure 8. ROI of a mammogram

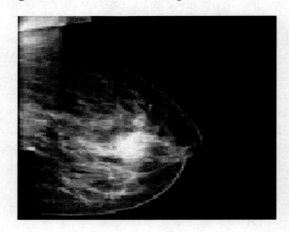

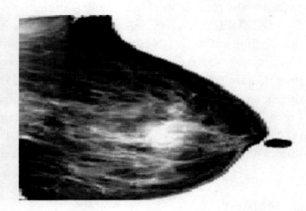

Figure 9. Classified region of cancerous in mammogram

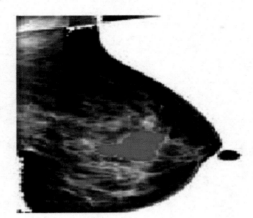

Table 4. Performance of various classifiers

No. of neurons in hidden layer	Classification accuracy%		
	FFBNN	**RBF NN**	**WNN**
40	71.089	70.124	79.70
60	72.01	74.67	80.46
80	73.57	78.34	81.54
100	76.39	78.97	83.20
120	**77.64**	**81.28**	**86.267**
150	76.276	80.82	84.87

tions from the norm and may miss anticipate the normal tissues as malignant tissue, this is known as the misclassification rate. To avoid this misclassification rate, investigation was made for Texture elements to decide the reasonable discriminate features.

ROC of different classifiers is shown in Figure 10. The outcome from various classifiers emphasizes the capability of the WNN algorithm can be utilized for better breast cancer tissue classifier. The classifier concentrates the experimentation on attempting to enhance the classification rate by focusing on beginning neural-arrange settings. Thus, by utilizing advanced parameter settings for wavelet neural systems the characterization exactness is enhanced radically. A high order rate was accomplished for the ideally tuned wavelet neural systems. The improved wavelet neural system classifier is the most superior than other classifiers. The WNN approach creates a sensitivity of 93.17% with a specificity of 92.21%. The misclassification rate is observed to be 0.07 which is less when compared with well know other classifiers.

SUMMARY

The WNN joins the elements of time–frequency contents from the wavelet domain and of self-learning from the neural system. It makes to a classify complicated patterns more accurately. The novel approach

Figure 10. ROC for classifiers

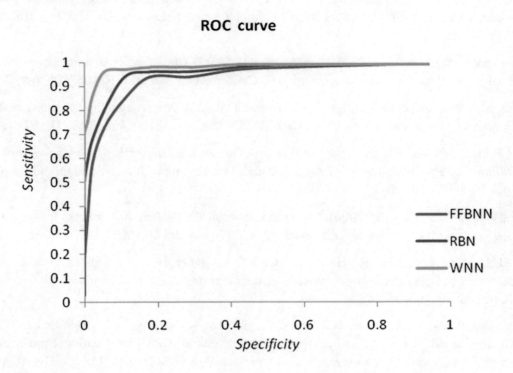

introduced in this paper exhibited that the WNN classifier delivers a good accuracy rate which related CAD supported investigation of computerized mammograms for early detection of breast cancer diagnosis. The calculation formed here characterizes mammograms into noncancerous and cancerous. Initially, the ROI of the mammograms is picked then texture components are removed and trained with WNN for Classification. The advantage of WNN based classifiers is utilizing the properties of both wavelet and neural system give great accuracy and specificity by decreasing the false positives and false negatives rate. The results obtained through WNN based feed forward back propagation network gives better accuracy and Minimum error rate when compare with other neural networks like feed forward neural network, RBF.

REFERENCES

Anandakumar, H., & Umamaheswari, K. (2017a). Supervised machine learning techniques in cognitive radio networks during cooperative spectrum handovers. *Cluster Computing, 20*(2), 1505–1515. doi:10.100710586-017-0798-3

Anandakumar, H., & Umamaheswari, K. (2017b). An Efficient Optimized Handover in Cognitive Radio Networks using Cooperative Spectrum Sensing. *Intelligent Automation & Soft Computing,* 1–8. doi:10 .1080/10798587.2017.1364931

Anandakumar, H, & Umamaheswari, K. (2017c). A bio-inspired swarm intelligence technique for social aware cognitive radio handovers. *Computers & Electrical Engineering*. doi:10.1016/j.compeleceng.2017.09.016

Arulmurugan, R., Sabarmathi, K. R., & Anandakumar, H. (2017). Classification of sentence level sentiment analysis using cloud machine learning techniques. *Cluster Computing*. doi:10.100710586-017-1200-1

Buseman, S., Mouchawar, J., Calonge, N., & Byers, T. (2003). Mammography screening matters for young women with breast carcinoma. *Cancer, 97*(2), 352–358. doi:10.1002/cncr.11050 PMID:12518359

Cao, Y., Hao, X., & Xia, S. (2009). *An improved region-growing algorithm for mammographic mass segmentation. MIPPR 2009: Medical Imaging*. Parallel Processing of Images, and Optimization Techniques. doi:10.1117/12.833044

Chen, Y., Wang, Y., & Yang, B. (2006). Evolving Hierarchical RBF Neural Networks for Breast Cancer Detection. *Lecture Notes in Computer Science, 4234*, 137–144. doi:10.1007/11893295_16

Cheng, H. D., Shi, X. J., Min, R., Hu, L. M., Cai, X. P., & Du, H. N. (2006). Approaches for automated detection and classification of masses in mammograms. *Pattern Recognition, 39*(4), 646–668. doi:10.1016/j.patcog.2005.07.006

Ciatto, S., Del Turco, M. R., Risso, G., Catarzi, S., Bonardi, R., Viterbo, V., ... Indovina, P. L. (2003). Comparison of standard reading and computer aided detection (CAD) on a national proficiency test of screening mammography. *European Journal of Radiology, 45*(2), 135–138. doi:10.1016/S0720-048X(02)00011-6 PMID:12536093

Forouzanfar, M. H., Foreman, K. J., Delossantos, A. M., Lozano, R., Lopez, A. D., Murray, C. J. L., & Naghavi, M. (2011). Breast and cervical cancer in 187 countries between 1980 and 2010: A systematic analysis. *Lancet, 378*(9801), 1461–1484. doi:10.1016/S0140-6736(11)61351-2 PMID:21924486

Fu, J. C., Lee, S. K., Wong, S. T. C., Yeh, J. Y., Wang, A. H., & Wu, H. K. (2005). Image segmentation feature selection and pattern classification for mammographic microcalcifications. *Computerized Medical Imaging and Graphics, 29*(6), 419–429. doi:10.1016/j.compmedimag.2005.03.002 PMID:16002263

Jemal, A., Bray, F., Forman, D., O'Brien, M., Ferlay, J., Center, M., & Parkin, D. M. (2012). Cancer burden in Africa and opportunities for prevention. *Cancer, 118*(18), 4372–4384. doi:10.1002/cncr.27410 PMID:22252462

Kolb, T. M., Lichy, J., & Newhouse, J. H. (2002). Comparison of the Performance of Screening Mammography, Physical Examination, and Breast US and Evaluation of Factors that Influence Them: An Analysis of 27,825 Patient Evaluations. *Radiology, 225*(1), 165–175. doi:10.1148/radiol.2251011667 PMID:12355001

Luo, S.-T., & Cheng, B.-W. (2010). Diagnosing Breast Masses in Digital Mammography Using Feature Selection and Ensemble Methods. *Journal of Medical Systems, 36*(2), 569–577. doi:10.100710916-010-9518-8 PMID:20703679

Morrow, W. M., Paranjape, R. B., Rangayyan, R. M., & Desautels, J. E. L. (1992). Region-based contrast enhancement of mammograms. *IEEE Transactions on Medical Imaging, 11*(3), 392–406. doi:10.1109/42.158944 PMID:18222882

Ramón González, J., Moreno, V., Fernández, E., Izquierdo, Á., Borrás, J., & Gispert, R. (2005). Probabilidad de desarrollar y morir por cáncer en Cataluña en el período 1998-2001. *Medicina Clínica, 124*(11), 411–414. doi:10.1157/13072840 PMID:15799846

Rangayyan, R. M., Ayres, F. J., & Leo Desautels, J. E. (2007). A review of computer-aided diagnosis of breast cancer: Toward the detection of subtle signs. *Journal of the Franklin Institute, 344*(3-4), 312–348. doi:10.1016/j.jfranklin.2006.09.003

Yaffe, M. J. (2010). Basic Physics of Digital Mammography. *Medical Radiology*, 1–11. doi:10.1007/978-3-540-78450-0_1

Zimmerman, J. B., Pizer, S. M., Staab, E. V., Perry, J. R., McCartney, W., & Brenton, B. C. (1988). An evaluation of the effectiveness of adaptive histogram equalization for contrast enhancement. *IEEE Transactions on Medical Imaging, 7*(4), 304–312. doi:10.1109/42.14513 PMID:18230483

Chapter 13

Improving the Classification Accuracy of Multidimensional Overlapping Objects Based on Neuro–Fuzzy Analysis of Generalized Patterns

Sergey Viktorovich Gorbachev
National Research Tomsk State University, Russia

Tatyana Viktorovna Abramova
National research Tomsk state University, Russia

ABSTRACT

To improve the classification accuracy of multidimensional overlapping objects, a new hybrid neuro-fuzzy FCNN-SOM-FMLP network, combining the fuzzy cell neural network of Kohonen (FCNN-SOM) and the fuzzy multilayer perceptron (FMLP), and the algorithms for its training are proposed. This combination allows for clustering of generalized intersecting patterns (the extensional approach) and training the classification network basing on the identification of integrated pattern characteristics in the isolated clusters (intentional approach). The new FCNN-SOM-FMLP architecture features a high degree of self-organization of neurons, an ability to manage selectively individual neuronal connections (to solve the problem of "dead" neurons), the high flexibility, and the ease of implementation. The experimental results show the temporal efficiency of algorithms of self-organization and training and the improvement of the separating properties of the network in the case of overlapping clusters. Calculated technological and economic generalized values of countries.

DOI: 10.4018/978-1-5225-5246-8.ch013

INTRODUCTION

The recognition is called the problem of constructing and applying formal operations on numeric or symbolic representations of objects, in real or ideal world, the outcomes of decisions of the objects reflect the relationship of equivalence between them. The relations of equivalence express the membership of evaluated objects to any of the classes, considered as independent semantic units.

The classes of equivalence can be defined by a researcher while constructing recognition algorithms who uses his own substantive views or uses an external information about the similarities and differences of objects in the context of the problem being solved. In this case the term "pattern recognition with a teacher" is used (Kohonen, 2008). Otherwise, when the automated system solves the classification problem without engaging external teaching information, the automatic classification or "pattern recognition without a teacher" is spoken about.

A problem of clustering (the classification without a teacher) is quite common in many applications connected with data mining. The traditional approach to the solution of these tasks assumes that each observation can belong to only one cluster. In this case, the most widely used are Kohonen neural networks (Kohonen, 2008), which have a single-layer architecture with lateral connections and which are trained on the basis of "winner takes all" (WTA) or "winner takes more" (WTM). The more natural situation is the situation when the processed feature vector with different levels of conditioning (probability, possibility) can belong to multiple classes. This situation is the subject of fuzzy cluster analysis, which developed a self-learning hybrid neuro-fuzzy model (Gorbachev & Syryamkin, 2014), which is a generalization of the Kohonen neural network and have, due to the use of special algorithms for the adjustment of their semantic weights, more functional opportunities. Thus, there was a modification of Kohonen network introduced in Vuorimaa (1994a, 1994b) based on fuzzy rules. This network has shown its effectiveness in a number of tasks associated with recognition, however, the numerical complexity hinders its practical use. In Lutsenko (1996), a Kohonen network with fuzzy inference trained on the basis of the combination of the Kohonen and Grossberg's rules was proposed. The main disadvantage of this design is the dependence of the results from the choice of free parameters of the training procedure.

In Anikin and Karmanov (2014) the possibility of training of the Kohonen's artificial neural network by cellular automaton (CNN-SOM) was proved, which can greatly enhance the quality and speed of training, however, the issues of separating properties of CNN-SOM in the case of overlapping clusters are not resolved.

In this paper we introduce a new two-layer Kohonen cellular neural network (FCNN-SOM), which is the adaptive modification of the FKSN (Bezdek, Tsao & Pal, 1992) and the further development of the composition, considered in Anikin and Karmanov (2014) and the algorithms for its training.

On the basis of combining FCNN-SOM and fuzzy perceptron (FMLP) we describe a new hybrid neuro-fuzzy method of patterns recognition based on, according to the classification by D. Pospelov (1990), two ways of representing knowledge – intensional and extensional in this paper.

Note that most algorithms of pattern recognition require the involvement of very considerable computing power, which can be achieved only with high-performance computer equipment. Therefore, an urgent task is to build such a compact network architecture.

LITERATURE REVIEW

Various authors (Barabash, Vasiliev, Gorelik, Skripkin, Duda, Hart, Kuzin, Peregudov, Tarasenko, Temnikov, Tu, Gonzalez, Winston, Fu, Tsypkin, etc.) give different classification methods of pattern recognition. Some authors distinguish between parametric, nonparametric and heuristic methods, others isolate group of methods, based on historical schools and streams in this area. For example, in the work of V.A. Duke (1994), in which an academic overview of recognition methods is given the following typology is used:

- Methods based on the principle of separation;
- Statistical methods;
- Methods based on "potential functions";
- Methods of computing ratings (voting);
- Methods based on propositional calculus, in particular on the unit of the algebra of logic.

The basis of this classification is the difference in formal methods of pattern recognition and, therefore, the consideration of the heuristic approach to the recognition is omitted, which has received the full and adequate development in expert systems. The heuristic approach is based on the knowledge difficult to formalize and the researcher's intuition. The researcher decides which information and how the system should use it to achieve the desired effect of recognition.

Such a typology of recognition methods with varying degrees of detail is found in many works on recognition. At the same time well-known typologies do not take into account one very significant characteristic that reflects the specificity of the method for representing the domain knowledge with the help of any formal algorithm of an image recognition.

D. A. Pospelov in 1990 distinguishes two main ways of representing knowledge:

- Intensional, in the form of diagrams of relationships between the attributes (characteristics).
- Extensional, with specific facts (objects, examples).

Intensional representation captures patterns and connections that explain the structure of the data. In the context of diagnostic tasks such fixation is to define operations on the attributes (characteristics) of objects, leading to the desired diagnostic result. Intensional representations are implemented by operations on attribute values and are not intended to operate on particular information with facts (objects).

Inversely, the extensional representation of the knowledge is associated with the description and fixation the particular objects of the subject area and implemented in operations, the elements of which are objects as a whole system.

You can draw an analogy between intensional and extensional knowledge and the mechanisms underlying the activities of the left and right hemispheres of the human brain. If the right hemisphere is characterized by the prototype of a holistic representation of the world, the left hemisphere deals with patterns that reflect the relationship between the attributes of this world.

Based on the above-described two fundamental ways of representing knowledge Lutsenko (1996, 2002) has suggested the following classification of methods of pattern recognition:

- Intensional methods based on operations characteristics;
- Extensional techniques based on operations with objects.

It should be stressed that the existence of these two (and only two) groups of methods of recognition (operating with characteristics, and operating with objects) is deeply regular. From this point of view, neither one of these methods, taken separately from the other, provides an adequate reflection of the subject area. According to the author, between these methods there is a relation of complementarity in the sense of Bohr (1961), so a promising recognition system needs to provide an implementation of both methods but not just one of them.

Thus, it is possible to draw the following conclusions.

1. The basis of classification of pattern-recognition methods is built on fundamental laws underlying the human method of cognition in general, which puts her in a very special (privileged) position compared to the other classifications, which seem more lightweight and artificial.
2. An overview of recognition methods reveals the following contradiction. Currently, a number of different methods of pattern recognition and classification on the grounds is theoretically developed and described in the literature. However, the software implementation of most methods is missing and it is highly regular, it might be even said to be "predefined" by characteristics of the recognition methods themselves. This is evidenced by the fact that such systems receive little coverage in the literature and other sources of information.
3. Consequently, the question of the practical applicability of certain theoretical methods of pattern recognition, which are to solve practical problems in real (i.e. quite large) dimensions of the data and on the real modern computers remains insufficiently developed.

The above-mentioned fact can be understood if it is recalled that the complexity of the mathematical models exponentially increases the complexity of software implementation of the system and to the same extent reduces the chances that the system will practically work. This means that you can really implement in market only those software systems which are based on rather simple and transparent mathematical models. Therefore, the developer interested in the replication of his/her software, considers the choice of the mathematical model not only from a scientific point of view, but as a pragmatist, given the capabilities of the software implementation. He believes that the model should be as simple as possible, and thus be realized with less cost and more efficiently, and work (be practically effective).

In this regard, the task of implementing the mechanism of generalization of objects descriptions belonging to one class in the recognition systems is particularly relevant, i.e. the mechanism of formation of compact generalized images. It is obvious that the mechanism of generalization would "squeeze" any in the dimension of the training sample to the pre-known by the dimension of the basis of generalized images. It will also set and solve a number of tasks that cannot be even formulated in these recognition methods, as the method of comparison with the prototype, the method of k nearest neighbors and the algorithm of calculating estimates.

That are the tasks of:

- Determining the information contribution of the signs in the information portrait of a generalized image;
- Cluster-constructive analysis of generalized images;

- Determining the semantic load of the attribute;
- Cluster semantic-structural analysis of the signs;
- Meaningful comparison of the generalized images of the classes with each other and the signs with each other (the cognitive chart, including the chart Merlin).

In practice, the original data are often difficult to formalize, often have an inhomogeneous structure with deliberately overlapping classes of images. Another problem is the incompleteness of the training samples and its strong noise. In the discriminant analysis in cases of uncertainty about the response on image belonging to the class of images, the answer can be obtained in the form of a probability of belonging to each of the image classes of images. However, the above-described features of the data in many cases do not allow to construct an adequate probabilistic and statistical models which motivates the creation of empirical methods and approaches, and during their development methods and models from the field of soft computing become convenient. A significant scientific contribution to the theory and practice of creation of diagnostic test systems is built on fuzzy logic and neural networks, introduced by domestic and foreign scientists: Zadeh, Pospelov, Yu, Bortsov, Wasserman, Hassoun, Rotshtein, Gostev, Galushkin, Kruglov, Rutkowski, Pilinsky, Omatu etc.

Methods of fuzzy logic and neural network technology currently relate to the perspective of adaptive technologies of information processing and solving problems of pattern recognition and prediction, allowing to create high quality intelligent systems in conditions of crossing objects analysis (Gorbachev, 2000, 2001; Gorbachev & Syryamkin, 2014). The feature of the "fuzzy" knowledge representation, as well as the possibility of using the required number of input and output variables allow, in combination with neural network technology, not only to improve the recognition accuracy, but also to deduce logically transparent rules for the interpretation of the result.

As a tool for the implementation of generalized patterns in this chapter we propose to modify the fuzzy Kohonen self-organizing maps (FKSN) as an extensional method of unsupervised learning. This method integrates FCM model (Bezdek, Tsao & Pal, 1992) and Kohonen network (Kohonen, 2008). FKCN improved the error convergence as well as reduced labeling errors problem on FCM. The output results of clustering in the data of the generalized overlapping patterns can be used for building compact classifier based on the fuzzy multilayer perceptron (FMLP) as intensional training method with teacher.

Despite the advantages of FKCN, known algorithms for the adjustment of synaptic weights of neurons in the SOM have common disadvantages which is the presence of heuristic parameters and procedures for solving the problem of "dead" neurons which increases the training time. They are:

- «Winner Takes All» (WTA);
- «Conscience Winner Takes All» (CWTA);
- «Winner Takes Most» (WTM);
- «Time Adaptive Self-Organizing Map» (TASOM) (Gorbachev & Syryamkin, 2014).

In Anikin and Karamov (2014) the possibility of learning of Kohonen's self-organizing maps by cellular automaton was proved (cellular neural networks (CNN) were introduced by Chua and Yang (1988a, 1988b; Wu & Yang, 2003) and became effectively used in computational models of image processing) that can significantly improve the quality and speed of learning, however, the issues of dividing the network properties in the case of overlapping clusters are not resolved.

Thus, there might be a situation while processing real-world data when one object belongs to different classes at the same time and these classes mutually intersect (overlap). Conventional SOMs do not take into consideration this occasion, but this problem can be considered with the help of fuzzy clustering techniques (Hoeppner et al., 1999; Xu & Wunsch, 2009).

The well-known and most commonly used fuzzy clustering algorithms can't be called fuzzy in the full sense, because their results are significantly defined by the value of a special parameter (also known as a fuzzifier β) which is chosen empirically. The case when β belongs to an interval from 1 to ∞ corresponds to a transition from crisp borders ($\beta \to 1$), which are obtained with the help of the K-means procedure, to their complete blurriness ($\beta \to \infty$), when all observations belong to all clusters with the same membership level. We should note that the case $\beta=2$ corresponds to the fuzzy C-means procedure (FCM) by Bezdek, Tsao, and Pal (1992).

The remainder of this chapter is organized as follows: the "Methodology" section contains a new architecture of hybrid fuzzy neural network FCNN-SOM-FMLP for recognition of overlapping patterns. It integrates fuzzy cellular neural network Kohonen (FCNN-SOM) and fuzzy multilayer perceptron (FMLP). Next, we describe their structural, functional characteristics and learning algorithms (sections «Extensional approach» and «Intensional approach»). In the section «Solutions and recommendations» there are comparative results of clustering and classification of the test data using CNN and FCNN-SOM, and the dependence of the parameters of FMLP on the learning rate is investigated. In the section «Experimental results» we describe the neuro-fuzzy model of world technical and economic portrait based on FCNN-SOM. Conclusions and prospects for future research are given in the final section.

METHODOLOGY

To improve the classification accuracy of the multidimensional overlapping of objects the author of this paper Gorbachev has developed a hybrid fuzzy neural network FCNN-SOM-FMLP (Figure 1) including a fuzzy cellular neural network of Kohonen (FCNN-SOM) and fuzzy classification multilayer perceptron (FMLP). FCNN-SOM-FMLP allows to hold the cluster partitioning of the generalized overlapping images (extensional approach) and to train a network with fuzzy classification based on the identification of integral characteristics of images into the selected clusters (intensional approach).

Extensional Approach

Phase One: Self-Organization

Within the extensional approach, we propose to perform a segmentation into clusters of certain classes of patterns by Kohonen self-organizing maps (SOM) (Kohonen, 2008), thus it was solved the problem of the separating properties in the case of overlapping clusters. This will allow to improve recognition quality.

SOM has a simple architecture including zero receptor layer and only one layer of Kohonen neurons which are adaptive linear adder such as rectangular grid on the plane (Figure 2). Each j-th neuron ($j=1,...,m$) is characterized by an n-dimensional vector of synaptic weights $W_j=(w_{j1}, w_{j2}, ..., w_{jn})^T$.

The input vectors $x(k) = (x_1(k), ..., x_n(k))^T$, where k is the number of the example in the training set, are sequentially distributed from the receptive (zero) layer to all the neurons N_j of the Kohonen layer, in addition their synaptic weights $w_{ji}(k)$ define centroids m of overlapping clusters.

Figure 1. The architecture of hybrid fuzzy neural network based on fuzzy cellular Kohonen neural network (FCNN-SOM) and fuzzy multi-layer perceptron (FMLP)

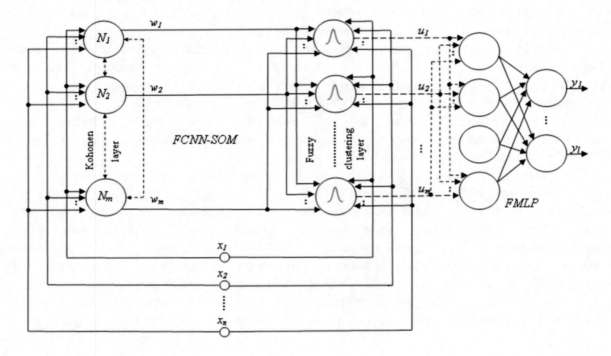

Figure 2. The model of Kohonen self-organizing networks

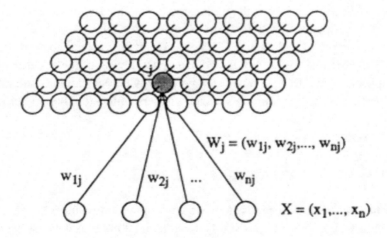

The basis for the self-organization of neural networks is the observed regularity that the global ordering of the network becomes possible as a result of self-organizing operations, independently of each other conducted in various local segments of the network. In accordance with the submitted signals, neurons are activated. Finally one neuron becomes active in the network (or in a group). The output neuron that won the competition is called the winner neuron.

Neurons in the course of the competitive process, due to changes in the values of the synaptic weights, are selectively tuned to different input vectors or classes of input vectors. In the learning process there is a tendency to increase the values of the weights, because of which a peculiar positive feedback is created: more powerful exciting impulses - higher values of weights - greater activity of neurons.

In this case, there is a natural stratification of neurons into different groups, individual neurons or their groups cooperate with each other and they are activated in response to excitation created by specific training vectors, suppressing other neurons by their activity. One can speak as about cooperation between neurons within a group, and about competition between neurons within a group and between different groups.

Among the mechanisms of self-organization, there are two main classes: self-organization based on the associative Hebb's rule, and the mechanism of neuron competition based on the generalized Kohonen rule. In the future, we will consider the mechanism of neuron competition.

The formation of self-organizing networks begins with the initialization of the synaptic weights of the network. Usually, the synaptic weights are assigned small values which are generated by the random number generator. During this initialization, the network initially does not have any order of signs of the input vectors. After the initialization of the network, three basic processes are implemented (Kohonen, 2008):

1. **Competition**: For each input vector, network neurons calculate the relative values of the discriminant function.
2. **Cooperation**: The winning neuron determines the topological neighborhood of a group of neurons, providing a basis for cooperation between them.
3. **Synaptic Adaptation**: Correction of synaptic weights of excited neurons allows us to increase their eigenvalues of discriminant functions with respect to input vectors. The correction is made in such a way that the output signal of the winner neuron is increased in case of the subsequent application of similar input vectors.

Thus, the basis of the SOM training procedure is the competition between neurons based on the value of the activation function in response to the incoming signal.

Assume that the inputs and synaptic weights are pre-normalized, and the Euclidean measure is used as the distance:

$$d(x, w_i) = \left\| x - w_i \right\| = \sqrt{\sum_{j=1}^{N}(x_j - w_{ij})^2} \; .$$

Then using the Euclidean measure, partitioning the space into zones of neuron dominance is equivalent to splitting into Voronoi domains. If we use another measure (scalar product, measure relative to the norm of L1 (Manhattan) or a measure relative to the norm of L∞), another division of neuron influence areas is formed.

With normalized input learning vectors, the weight vectors that strive for them are normalized automatically. It should be noted that when the weight vector is normalized, the Euclidean measure and the scalar product are equivalent to each other, since:

$$\left\|x - w_i\right\|^2 = \left\|x\right\|^2 + \left\|w_i\right\|^2 - 2x^T w_i$$

So, $\min\left\|x - w_i\right\|^2 = \max(x^T w_i)$ at $\left\|w_i\right\| = const$.

The winner neuron is determined with the minimum distance to the presented input vector:

$$D(x(k), w^*_j(k)) = \min_j \left\|x(k) - w_j(k)\right\|^2,$$

or for normalized vectors that is the same:

$$D(x(k), w^*_j(k)) = \max_j x^T(k) w_j(k) = \max_j \cos(x(k), w_j(k)).$$

It is obvious that $-1 \leq \cos(x(k), w_j(k)) \leq 1$ и $0 \leq \left\|x(k) - w_j(k)\right\|^2 \leq 4$.

A topological neighborhood $S_w(t)$ is formed around the winning neuron with a certain energy which decreases with time. The neuron-winner and all the neurons lying within his neighborhood are subjected to adaptation, during which their weight vectors change in the direction of the vector x according to the Kohonen rule:

$$w_i(t+1) = w_i(t) + \eta_i(t)(x - w_i(t))$$

for $i \in S_w(t)$, where:

$\eta_i(t)$ - coefficient of training of the i-th neuron on the neighborhood $S_w(t)$ at the t-th time.

The value $\eta_i(t)$ decreases with increasing of distance between the i-th neuron and the winner.

Weights of neurons that are outside the neighborhood of $S_w(t)$ do not change. The size of the neighborhood and the training coefficients of neurons are functions whose values decrease with time. In Borisov, Kruglov, and Fedulov (2012) it is proved that adaptation according to the Kohonen rule is equivalent to the gradient method of training, based on the minimization of the objective function:

$$E(w) = \frac{1}{2} S_i(x(t))\left[x_j(t) - w_{ij}(t)\right]^2,$$

and $S_i(x(t))$ is a function of the definition of the neighborhood, which varies during the learning process.

After the presentation of two different vectors x_1 and x_2, two network neurons are activated, whose weights are closest to the coordinates of the corresponding vectors. These weights, denoted w_1 and w_2, can be displayed in space as two points. Approximation of the vectors x_1 and x_2 causes a corresponding change in the arrangement of the vectors w_1 and w_2.

In the limit, the equality $w_1 = w_2$ is satisfied if and only if x_1 and x_2 coincide or are practically indistinguishable from each other. The network in which these conditions are met is called a topographic map or a Kohonen map.

Note that the tuning of the synaptic weights of the winner neuron can also occur in other algorithms: according to the rule «Winner Takes All» (WTA) or with modified learning algorithms, giving better results than the WTA algorithm, for example, «Conscience Winner Takes All» (CWTA), «Winner Takes Most» (WTM) or «Time Adaptive Self-Organizing Map» (TASOM) [21].

A common drawback of these algorithms SOM is the presence of heuristic parameters and procedures for solution of the problem of "dead" neurons increase the training time, with the impossibility of overlapping clusters separation. When the network weights are initialized randomly, some of the neurons may be in the region of space in which there is no data or their number is negligible. These neurons have little chance of winning and adapting their scales, so they remain dead. Thus, the input data will be interpreted by a smaller number of neurons, and the error in the interpretation of the data will increase. Therefore, an important problem is the activation of all neurons in the network, which can be done if the algorithm of training provides for the calculation of the number of victories of each neuron, and the training process is organized so as to give a chance to less active neurons to win.

Phase Two: Additional Terms and Restrictions

We require that the desired self-organizing of neuro-fuzzy network was possible under the following conditions:

1. High degree of self-organization of neurons;
2. An ability of selectively control of individual connections between neurons to solve the problem of "dead" neurons;
3. High flexibility, simplicity of realization and temporal efficiency of the algorithm;
4. Raising of the dividing network properties in the case of overlapping clusters with output of the membership degree of the signal to each cluster.

Phase Three: The Architecture of Fuzzy Cellular Neural Networks of Kohonen

Cellular neural networks (CNN) were introduced by Chua and Yang (1988a, 1988b) and became effectively used in computational models of image processing. In Anikin and Karamov (2014) it proved the possibility of learning of Kohonen's neural nets by cellular automaton (CA) that can significantly improve the quality and speed of learning, however, it had not resolved the issues dividing the network properties in the case of overlapping clusters.

Author of this paper S.Gorbachev proposed a fuzzy cellular architecture of the Kohonen neural network (FCNN-SOM) which contains 3 layers (Figure 1):

1. Input (receptor) layer;
2. The layer of Kohonen neurons with lateral connections, which is trained by CA to identify centroids of overlapping clusters;
3. Additional (output) layer of fuzzy clustering (Figure 1) calculating the degree of membership of current vector to each cluster.

Consider the work of the FCNN-SOM in stages.

Phase Four: The Learning Algorithm of fuzzy Cellular Neural Networks of Kohonen

Source data – sample of observations, formed from N n-dimensional signs vectors $x(k)$, $k=1,....,N$.

The goal of learning – division of learning sample data into m clusters with some levels of membership $u_j(k)$ of k-th signs vector to the j-th cluster $(j=1,....m)$.

Step 1: Data pre-processing

Input data is centered and standardized for all ordinate so that all observations belonged to hypercube $[-1;1]^n$. Redefinition of the vector components is performed in accordance with the formula:

$$x_{i,new} = \frac{x_i}{\sqrt{\sum_{i=1}^{N} x_i^2}}.$$

Centering can be done by two ways:

1. Relative to the average, calculated by the formula:

$$m_i(k) = m_i(k-1) + \frac{1}{k}(x_i(k) - m_i(k-1)). \tag{1}$$

2. Relative to the median to make the centering procedure of the robust properties (protection against abnormal observations) by the recurrent formula:

$$me_i(k) = me_i(k-1) + \eta_m \, sign(x_i(k) - me_i(k-1)), \, i = 1, 2, \ldots, n,$$

where η_m is the parameter of the search step selected in accordance with the conditions of stochastic approximation of Dvoretzky (1956).

Step 2: Initialization of the initial state of neural network

Initialization of the initial state of neural network is self-adaptive deployment of network neurons with the formation of an ordered self-organizing Kohonen maps. The main idea of this method is described in Anikin and Karamov (2014) and consists in the gradual retraction of inactive neurons in the normalized hypercube space of the training samples by the active neurons.

Step 3: Training of the Kohonen layer by Moore's cellular automation on simply or multiply SOM (Anikin & Karamov, 2014).

Step 4 (new): Network training by algorithm of Bezdek's fuzzy clustering instead of the WTA algorithm, when the power of lateral connections in the Kohonen layer is disabled.

Among the known algorithms of fuzzy clustering, the most reasonable from a mathematical point of view, we noted the approach based on target functions (Bodyanksy & Rudenko, 2004) and solves the problem of optimization under certain assumptions, for example, a probabilistic algorithm based on minimizing the following criterion (objective function):

$$E(u_j, w_j) = \sum_{k=1}^{N} \sum_{j=1}^{m} u_j^{\beta}(k) \left\| x(k) - w_j \right\|^2 \tag{2}$$

with conditions:

$$\sum_{j=1}^{m} u_j(k) = 1,\ 0 \le \sum_{k=1}^{N} u_j(k) \le N,\ u_j(k) \in [0,1], \tag{3}$$

where $\beta \ge 0$ is a parameter of fuzzyfication (fuzzifier), which determines the fuzziness of borderlines between clusters, $k=1,...,N;$

$u_j(k)$ is the level of membership of k-th feature vector to a j-th cluster $(j=1,....m)$.

The result of clustering is a *(N x m)* – matrix $U = \{u_j(k)\}$, called matrix of fuzzy partitioning. The elements of the matrix U can be considered as the probability of the hypotheses of membership of vectors given to specific clusters. Entering of objective Lagrangian's function:

$$L(u_j(k), w_j, \lambda(k)) = \sum_{k=1}^{N} \sum_{j=1}^{m} u_j^{\beta}(k) \left\| x(k) - w_j \right\|^2 + \sum_{k=1}^{N} \lambda(k) (\sum_{j=1}^{m} u_j(k) - 1),$$

where $\lambda(k)$ – undetermined Lagrange's multiplier, and solving the system of equations of Karush–Kun–Tucker:

$$\begin{cases} \dfrac{\partial L(u_j(k), w_j, \lambda(k))}{\partial u_j(k)} = 0, \\ \nabla_{w_j} L(u_j(k), w_j, \lambda(k)) = 0, \\ \dfrac{\partial L(u_j(k), w_j, \lambda(k))}{\lambda(k)} = 0, \end{cases}$$

We get the required solution in the form:

$$u_j(k) = \frac{(\|x(k) - w_j\|^2)^{\frac{1}{1-\beta}}}{\sum\limits_{l=1}^{m} (\|x(k) - w_l\|^2)^{\frac{1}{1-\beta}}}, \; w_j = \frac{\sum\limits_{k=1}^{N} u_j^\beta(k) x(k)}{\sum\limits_{k=1}^{N} u_j^\beta(k)}, \lambda(k) = -((\sum\limits_{l=1}^{m} \beta \|x(k) - w_l\|^2)^{\frac{1}{1-\beta}})^{1-\beta},$$

coinciding at $\beta \to 1$ with algorithm of Hard K-Means (HKM) (Dawod, Hasan & Daood, 2017) and at $\beta = 2$ with the algorithm of fuzzy C-means of Bezdek (FCM) (Bezdek, Tsao & Pal, 1992):

$$u_j(k) = \frac{\|x(k) - w_j\|^{-2}}{\sum\limits_{l=1}^{m} \|x(k) - w_l\|^{-2}}, \; w_j = \frac{\sum\limits_{k=1}^{N} u_j^2(k) x(k)}{\sum\limits_{k=1}^{N} u_j^2(k)}. \tag{4}$$

We rewrite the expression (4) in the form:

$$u_j(k) = \frac{1}{1 + \|x(k) - w_j(k)\|^2 \sum\limits_{\substack{l=1 \\ l \neq j}}^{m} \|x(k) - w_l(k)\|^{-2}} = \frac{1}{1 + \dfrac{\|x(k) - w_j(k)\|^2}{\sigma_j^2(k)}}. \tag{5}$$

We get expression which specifies the bell-shaped membership function with the center in point $w_j(k)$ and with setting:

$$0 \leq \sigma_j^2 = \frac{1}{\sum\limits_{\substack{l=1 \\ l \neq j}}^{m} \|x(k) - w_l(k)\|^{-2}} \leq \frac{4}{m-1}, \tag{6}$$

where m is the number of clusters.

Bell-shaped membership function is characterized by smoothness, symmetry and simplicity of the writing and this is the most used to describe fuzzy sets (Figure 3).

Thus, the proposed method not only calculates the parameters of the centers and width, but unlike (Karayiannis & Pai, 1996; Wu & Yang, 2003) automatically solves the question about the type of membership function used for data fuzzification. Assumes that the whole sample which is subject to clustering, is pre-defined and cannot change during processing.

Intensional Approach

Within the intensional approach, we solved the task of developing a neuro-fuzzy classifier that uses as input the results of the fuzzy clustering obtained in the previous stage of the pattern recognition, and capable of fuzzy separating of the overlapping classes.

Figure 3. Curve of the bell-shaped membership functions

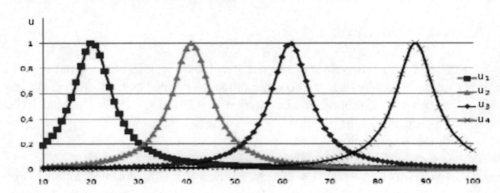

For the first time, the features of neural fuzzy networks of this type were described in Keller and Hunt (1985). Keller and Hunt had proposed the concept of fuzzy recognition with a perceptron. Various options are available for such a network, when either strategy of teaching or its individual parameters which significantly affect the quality of education is modified. Later the idea of introducing fuzziness to the structure of neural networks was developed by Pal and Mitra (n.d.) while creating a fuzzy version of the multilayer perceptron used for classification of patterns, providing the possibility of processing of vague and imprecise information.

Consider the case of linear indivisibility of object classes (Figure 4) when separate classes are overlapping, and the samples (examples of the training sample), lying in the zone of overlap, lead to the unstable behavior of the training algorithm of the classical perceptron (Borisov, Kruglov & Fedulov, 2012).

Figure 4. An example of linear indivisibility of the two classes

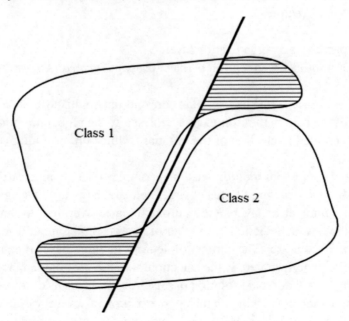

The training set consists of N examples of the following:

$(x_1(k),\ldots, x_n(k); u_1(k),\ldots, u_m(k)), k=1,\ldots,N,$

where $x(k)= \{ x_1(k),\ldots, x_n(k) \}$ - the values of the vector of input variables $x_1,\ldots, x_n$ in the k-th sample;

$u_1(k),\ldots,u_m(k)$ are the corresponding membership functions defined by the formula (5) as measure of a fuzzy partition of the space of inputs into m clusters with relation to these vectors and indicating the degree of membership of each of these vectors to each of the clusters;

N is the total number of examples in the training set.

This should be provided in the formula (3).

Input vector $x(k) = \{ x_1(k),\ldots, x_n(k)\}$, $k = 1, \ldots, N$ is given to the input of the Kohonen layer (Figure 1), where the vector of the distances from this vector to each of the neurons of the Kohonen layer is formed. Next, this vector goes to the input of the fuzzy self-organizing layer, whose output vector is formed, composed of grades of membership, calculated in accordance with expression (5), (6) under the limitation (3). After that, the vector of membership degrees goes to an input of multilayer perceptron. The outputs of the fuzzy multilayer perceptron are treated as the degree of membership of the presented object to the appropriate class.

There is a fuzzy operator for the formation of the input variables membership level to specific for them clusters in accordance with formula (5), (6) in the model of fuzzy multilayer perceptron.

In this fuzzy neural network the method of back propagation of error is realized as the learning algorithm.

Training the network takes place in three steps.

Step 1: The Kohonen layer is trained.

As a result of training the weights vectors of neurons in this layer with minimum error display the data distribution of training vectors.

Step 2: The learning of fuzzy self-organization layer.
Step 3: The training of multilayer perceptron by back-propagation errors algorithm.

The learning process proceeds much faster than conventional multi-layer perceptron learning, due to the good localization of the data in the Kohonen layer. Usually the global minimum of error function is achieved. However, the issue of selection of the optimal architecture of multilayer perceptron requires more detailed studies.

In the processing and analysis of multidimensional complex data, using an artificial neural network, above all, it has to design the structure of the network adequate to the task. Designing a neural network, one must decide on the number of layers and neurons in each layer, and to determine the necessary connections between the layers. Selection of number of neurons in the input layer is determined by the dimensionality of the input vector x. The number of neurons in output layer is equal to the dimension of the reference vector d. A major problem is the selection of number of hidden layers and the number of neurons in each of them. The theoretical solution of this problem in terms of the conditions of adequacy was proposed by mathematicians working on the approximation of several variables functions. It should be noted that the neural network acts as a universal approximator of the training data (x,d) (Gorbachev

& Syryamkin, 2014). Determining of the minimum number of hidden layers in the network is based on the properties of approximating functions. The possibility of such generalization comes from A.N. Kolmogorov's theorems and from theorem of universal approximation, which can be considered as a natural extension of the Weierstrass theorem.

Let N be the number of input nodes of a multilayer perceptron, and K is the number of output neurons of the network. Then the theorem of universal approximation is formulated in the following way.

Let $\varphi(.)$ be a bounded, not constant monotonically increasing continuous function.

Let I_N be an N – dimensional unit hypercube $[0,1]^N$.

Let the space of continuous functions on I_N is denoted by $C(I_N)$.

Then for any function $\varphi(.)$ and $\varepsilon > 0$ there is an integer K and a set of real constants w_i, w_0 and w_{ij}, where $i=1,...,K, j=1,..,N$ that

$$F(x_1,...,x_N) = \sum_{i=1}^{K} w_i \varphi(\sum_{j=1}^{N} w_{ij} x_j + w_0) \tag{7}$$

is an implementation of the approximation of the function $f(.)$, which is:

$$\left|F(x_1,...,x_N) - f(x_1,...,x_N)\right| < \varepsilon \tag{8}$$

for all $x_1,...,x_N$, belonging to the input space.

The theorem of universal approximation is directly applicable to a multilayer perceptron.

First, in the model of multilayer perceptron limited, a monotonically increasing sigmoidal functions are used as functions of the activation which satisfies the conditions imposed by the theorem on the function.

Secondly, the formula (7) describes the output signal of the following network:

The network contains N input nodes and one hidden layer consisting of M neurons. The inputs are designated $x_1,...,x_N$.

Hidden neuron i has synaptic weights w_{i1}, ..., w_{iN} and w_{i0} is the weight of the threshold element.

The network output is a linear combination of output signals of the hidden neurons, weighted synaptic weights of the output neurons – w_1, ..., w_K.

Thus, the theorem states that a multilayer perceptron with one hidden layer is sufficient to construct a uniform approximation accuracy ε for any training set, represented by a set of inputs $x_1,...,x_N$ and the expected outputs $d=f(x_1,...,x_N)$.

Nevertheless, it does not follow from the theorem that one hidden layer is optimal in terms of learning time, ease of implementation, and, more importantly, quality of generalization. The theorem on universal approximation provides the necessary mathematical basis for proving the applicability of direct propagation networks with one hidden layer for solving approximation problems. However, it does not provide a method for constructing a multilayer perceptron having such properties. In addition, the universal approximation theorem assumes that the approximable continuous function is known, and a hidden layer of unlimited size can be used to approximate it. In practice, these assumptions face a number of difficulties.

The problem of a multilayer perceptron with one hidden layer is that neurons can interact with each other at the global level. With two hidden layers, the approximation process becomes more manageable. In particular, we can state the following.

1. Local characteristics are extracted in the first hidden layer, that is, some neurons of the first hidden layer can be used to divide the input space into generalized areas, and the other layer neurons should be trained in local characteristics characterizing these areas.
2. Global attributes are extracted in the second hidden layer. In particular, the neuron of the second hidden layer "generalizes" the output signals of the neurons of the first hidden layer related to a particular area of the input space. Thus, it learns the global characteristics of this area, and in other areas its output signal is zero.

In practical implementations of networks, networks with one hidden layer are most often used, more rarely with two hidden ones, and the number of neurons in the layer can vary (usually from N to $3N$) (Gorbachev & Syryamin, 2014).

We deduce an estimate of the optimum parameters of the multilayer perceptron architecture.

One of the most important properties of a neural network is the ability to generalize the knowledge obtained. A network trained on a set of input vectors generates the expected results by submitting test data related to the same set, but not directly involved in the learning process, to its input. As part of the training data, you can select a specific subset of the control data used to determine the accuracy of training the network. At the same time, the training data should not contain unique data whose properties differ from the expected values.

The ability of a network to recognize data from a test subset characterizes its ability to generalize knowledge. There is a trade-off between accuracy and the generalizing ability of the network, which can be optimized by choosing the number of hidden neurons for a given network. The number of hidden neurons, on the one hand, should be sufficient to solve the task posed, and on the other - should not be too large to provide the necessary generalizing ability. There is no easy way to determine the required number of hidden network elements. A number of contradictory requirements are superimposed on the number of weight coefficients of the network.

First, you need to have enough data to train the network with the selected number of weights. If the aim of the training was only the memorization of training samples, then their number could be equal to the number of weights. However, such a network will not have the generalization property, and can only restore data. The number of weights is partly due to the number of input and output elements and, consequently, the method of encoding input and output data.

Secondly, the network must be trained on an excessive set of data in order to have the generalization property. In this case, the weights will not be adapted to individual samples, but to their statistically averaged populations. Network training is conducted by minimizing the objective function $E(w)$, determined only on a subset of training data, which ensures sufficient correspondence of the network output signals to the expected values from the training sample. The true goal of the training is to select the architecture and network parameters that will provide a minimum error in recognizing a test subset of data that is not involved in training. The criterion for the correctness of the final results is the generalization error calculated from the test sample. From a statistical point of view, the error in the generalization of E depends on the level of error in learning H and on the confidence interval and is characterized by the ratio:

$$E \leq H + \varepsilon,$$

where $\varepsilon = \left(\dfrac{P}{h}, H \right)$ is the confidence interval;

P is the volume of the training sample;

h is a measure of Vapnik-Chervonenkis.

Measure Vapnik-Chervonenkis (*VC*-measurement) reflects the level of complexity of the network and is closely related to the number of contained in it weights. The greater the number of different weights, the greater the complexity of the network and, correspondingly, the value of the *VC*-measurement. The exact method for determining this measure is unknown, but it is possible to determine the upper and lower limits of this measure in the form of the formula:

$$2 \left[\frac{M}{2} \right] N \le h \le 2W(1 + \lg L), \tag{9}$$

where M is the number of neurons in the hidden layer;

N is the dimension of the input vector;

W is the total number of network weights;

L is the total number of neurons in the network.

It follows from formula (9) that the lower bound of the range is approximately equal to the number of weights connecting the input and output layers, while the upper boundary exceeds twice the total number of all network weights.

As an approximate value of the *VC*-measurement, the total number of weights of the neural network can be used. Thus, the generalization error is affected by the ratio of the number of training samples to the number of network weights. A small amount of training subset with a fixed number of weights causes a good adaptation of the network to its elements, but does not enhance the ability to generalize, since in the process of learning, there is a relative excess of the number of parameters chosen over the number of pairs of actual and expected network output signals. These parameters adapt with excessive and uncontrolled accuracy to the values of particular samples, and not to the ranges that these samples should represent. In fact, the approximation problem is replaced in this case by the problem of approximate interpolation. As a result, all kinds of irregularities in training data and noise can be perceived as essential properties of the process.

SOLUTIONS AND RECOMMENDATIONS

On the basis of experimental data, there are the following recommendations for choosing the number of hidden neurons of the multilayer perceptron.

1. You should not choose the number of hidden neurons more than twice number of input elements.

2. The number of training data must be at least $\frac{1}{\varepsilon}$ times more than the number of weights in the network, where ε - the error of the learning error.

3. It is necessary to identify the characteristics of the neural network, because in this case it is needed less hidden neurons than the inputs. If there is information that the dimensionality of the data can be reduced, then it should be used a smaller number of hidden neurons.

4. During the training on non-structural inputs, it is necessary that the number of hidden neurons was greater than the number of inputs. If the dataset does not have common properties, you should use more hidden neurons.

5. There is a mutually exclusive relationship between generalizing properties (fewer neurons) and accuracy (more neurons), which is specific for each application.

6. A larger network requires more time for training.

Also, there are practical recommendations for modifying the algorithms for network design.

1. If the learning error is small and the test error is high, therefore, the network contains too many weighting factors.

2. If both the learning error and the testing error are large, therefore, the weighting coefficients are too small.

3. If all weights are very large, therefore, weights are too few.

4. Adding weights is not a panacea - if you know that weighting factors are enough, you should consider other causes of errors, such as insufficient training data.

5. You should not add too many weighting factors to avoid exceeding the limits set earlier.

6. And, finally, the initial weighting factors should be random and small in size (for example, between *+1* and *-1*).

The experimental study were holded in stages on a well-known example of the classification of iris flowers (Fisher problem), where there are three classes of iris flower: Setosa (class 1), Versicolor (class 2), and Virginica (class 3). For each iris flower measured 4 independent parameters: the length and width of sepal, the length and width of petal.

Step 1: Normalized four-dimensional training sample data contained 50 specimens of iris flowers of classes 1, 2 and 3, and the samples of class 1 were linearly separable from the samples of classes 2 and 3.

Step 2: The initial coordinates of the neurons that are set while initializing the network:

neuron 0 - (-0.55, 0.08, -0.78, -0.83),

neuron 3 - (0.20, -0.30, 0.20, 0.5),

neuron 15 – (0.15, -0.30, 0.50, 0.68),

the other neurons were placed on hypersphere of initial conditions in coordinates (0, 0, 9.33, 3.60). Note that the coordinates of the neurons 0, 3, 15 are selected coincident with the coordinates of one of the training samples of classes 1, 2 and 3 respectively, which is necessary for successful activation of all neurons of the network in deployment phase.

Step 3: The Kohonen map was trained by 3-connected cellular automaton (Figure 5) with the following parameters:

number of runs – 30;

ages expand network – 5;

epochs of interaction – 25.

The results of clustering of the iris by the cellular neural network of Kohonen (CNN-SOM) are shown in Figure 6.

Figure 5. The structure of the 3-connected learning cellular automaton

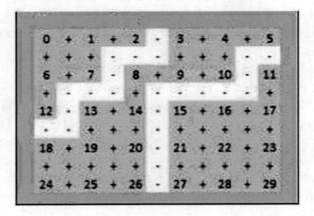

Figure 6. Iris flower clustering by the cellular neural network of Kohonen (CNN-SOM)

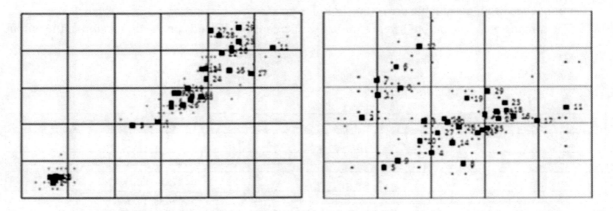

The dividing of neurons into clusters is shown in Table 1.

Additional cluster 2/3 neurons form a network, located on the border between linearly inseparable clusters 2 and 3. For a more accurate separation of clusters 2 and 3, holded additional stage fuzzy clustering (step 4).

Step 4: The lateral connections in the Kohonen layer are disabled, and centroids calculated in the previous stage $w_j(k)$ was applied to the layer of membership degrees calculation. Network is additionally trained by the algorithm of Bezdek fuzzy clustering with the following parameters:

the number of clusters - 3;

maximum number of iterations - 100;

the minimum value of improvement of the objective function during one iteration - 0.000001.

A graphical illustration of the initial classification of Iris data and results of fuzzy clustering by FCNN-SOM is shown in Figure 7.

The goal of experimental researches was the determination of effectiveness of proposed fuzzy neural networks in the process of clustering of generalized patterns and subsequent fuzzy classification. The dependence of the parameters of fuzzy multi-layer perceptron was researched (volume training set, the learning step of the network, the function of fuzzification and the number of neurons in the hidden layer) from the learning rate. As a result we can make the following conclusions:

1. The training sample of larger dimension does not improve the quality of training the neural network, but only causes its insusceptibility to redundant data.
2. Fast learning network increases the risk of deviation from the solution. Low values of the learning step eliminates this problem, leading to slowing down the process of network training.
3. Learning of fuzzy multi-layer perceptron with bell-shaped function is fairly effective and predictable.
4. Fuzzy multilayer perceptron naturally leads itself to all stages of training.
5. The number of neurons in the fuzzy layer is determined by the number of clusters.
6. The number of hidden layers of multilayer perceptron and the number of neurons in these layers is custom, although usually to restore the data with the required accuracy just one layer is enough.
7. With the increase of neurons number in the hidden layer the fuzzy multilayer perceptron trained up to a specified acceptable error threshold faster.
8. The dimension of the output layer of multilayer perceptron depends on the dimension of the output vector.

Table 1. Dividing of neurons into clusters

Cluster	A neurons of Cluster
1	0, 1, 2, 6, 7, 12
2	3, 4, 5, 10, 18, 19, 20, 24, 26
3	11, 15, 16, 17, 21, 22, 23, 27, 28, 29
4	8, 9, 13, 14, 25

Figure 7. The comparative results of clustering on the dataset "Iris":
1. The original data and the classification of irises;
2. Results of fuzzy clustering by FCNN-SOM

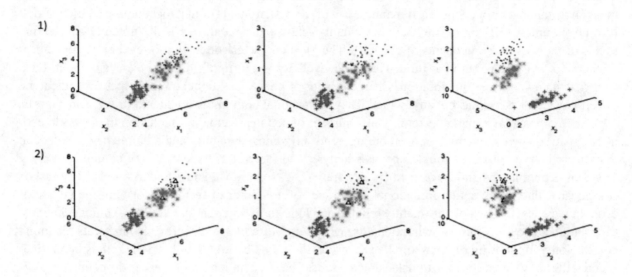

EXPERIMENTAL RESULTS

In this section we describe the methodology of multicriterial neural-fuzzy network analysis of global technical and economic development (TED) for a set of quantitative and qualitative indicators, which characterizes the modern technological order, examines issues of technological and social measurement of the transition process to the 6th technological order. For a fuzzy separation of overlapping clusters, we use a new hybrid architecture – Kohonen fuzzy cellular neural nets (FCNN-SOM). The modified neural-fuzzy network model of the trajectory of global technical and economic development, distinguished by a fairly simple but powerful strategy for improving clustering accuracy interpretability, with the assessment of the level of TED, the characteristics of the TED of individual countries and for predicting future values of the multidimensional process, is based on it. Intercountry comparison of model characteristics on the etalon and national TED trajectories allows to get predictive estimates not only of speed, but also of the level of technical and economic development of each country. Experimental results we have implemented show the effectiveness of the new architecture and clustering algorithms.

Methodological Approaches to the Study of the Economic Cycle Phases

The relevance of research topic is due to the fact that the problem of long-term fluctuations in economic dynamics and methods of global modeling of these processes occupied one of the central places in global studies of Russian and foreign scientists in the 20th century and especially attract the attention of modern scientists in this transition period from the 5th to the 6th technological order. In the last decade, based on the scientific schools developing the work of N.D. Kondratiev and J.Schumpeter, a new paradigm of economic science is being formed, the representatives of which have merged into the international research network GLOBELIX.

Cyclicity is the universal form of the movement of national economies and world economy as a single thing. It expresses the uneven of functioning of various elements of the national economy, the replacement of revolutionary and evolutionary stages of its development, economic progress. Finally, cyclicality is the most important factor of economic dynamics, one of the determinants of macroeconomic equilibrium. It is often extremely difficult to single out individual cycles because of the difficult, mutually intersecting trends of the various components of cyclicity. The most characteristic feature of cyclicity - movement - occurs not in a circle, but in a spiral. Therefore, cyclicity is a form of progressive development. Each cycle has its own phases, its duration. Characteristics of phases are unique in their specific indicators. Specific cycle or phase has not any twines. They are original both in historical and in regional aspects.

The emergence of a market economy in a number of countries and their inclusion to the world economic space dispelled the myth of overcoming trends in cyclical dynamics and required new intellectual interdisciplinary approaches to retrospective analysis and forecast of large cycles of conjuncture (long waves of economic dynamics) opened by Kondratieff, Yakovets, Yu, and Abalkin (2002). The task is complicated due to the action in national economies of a number of factors deforming the course of economic cycles, the lack of sufficiently reliable and long-term time series. Because of unique features, each national economy has its own rational trajectory of future fuel and energy resources. Its planning, possible only in the form of approximate scenarios, should be based on global TED trends taking into account the above-mentioned national characteristics. The most important of these is the country's position in the intercountry hierarchy of TED. To conduct such an assessment, the model of the etalon fuel-energy trajectory, which sets a common reference frame and scale common to all countries, is relevant and serves as a basis for measuring the technical development of national economies.

Thus, in our opinion, the correct assessment of the technical development of the national economy, its position in the world technical and economic development is related to finding of adequate method of measuring the level and rates of TED relative to the etalon trajectory.

Due to the patterns of reproduction of social capital, the life cycle of the technological order in a market economy is reflected in the specific form of the Long Wave (LW) of the economic conjuncture. The so-called Long waves, or Kondratieff waves, are the subject of study of a special direction of economic research - analysis of long-term processes of social reproduction. In modern periodization, there are 5 long waves (Figure 8).

In the empirical studies of the Long Wave, a fundamental one-pointedness of the technological changes taking place in different countries, the similarity of national TED trajectories and also the tendency to synchronize macroeconomic fluctuations and technological changes, was established.

In particular, the same shape of fuel and energy resources trajectories in countries with both market and directively managed economies had been identified in the structure of energy consumption, in metallurgy and in the extractive industry, in the dynamics of transport infrastructure and in other sectors of the economy. The unidirectional nature of energy resources in different countries, as well as the formation of a single rhythm of the world economic system, is due to the establishment of a global market and the rapid expansion of international economic ties since the industrial revolution. The experience of macroeconomic research tells not only about the possibility, but also about the fruitfulness of using cross-country comparisons to obtain both qualitative and fairly accurate quantitative conclusions, including the forecast character.

Many researchers note that global technological changes are generated by the countries leading in the life cycle of the corresponding technological orders (Glazyev & Kharitonov, 2009). Although the technological shifts that make up the content of the life cycle of each technological order take place

Figure 8. Modern periodization of Kondratieff long waves

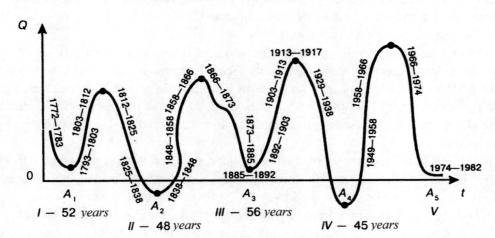

on the scale of the world market, the economic structure of the leading countries most fully projects the structure of the corresponding TUs, and the dynamics of their TED projects the evolution of these technological orders. Therefore, the trajectory of the actual TED of the leading countries of the corresponding technological order can be considered as a etalon trajectory of TED.

There are several types of economic cycles known as "waves." They are difficult to distinguish because of the multiplicity of their indicators, because of the temporary blurring of the boundaries between them. So-called "long waves" (cycles) have a length of 40-60 years. The development of the theory of long waves was begun in 1847, when the Englishman H. Clark drew attention to the 54-year gap between the crises of 1793 and 1847. He suggested that it was not by chance that the gap was objectively conditioned. A significant contribution to the development of the theory of long waves was made by his compatriot V. Jevons, who first drew statistics on price fluctuations to explain a phenomenon new to science.

K. Marks made a significant contribution to the theory of cyclicity. He paid all the attention to the study of short waves, which in the economic literature received the name "periodic cycles," or "periodic crises of overproduction." Each cycle, according to Marks, consists of four phases: crisis, depression, revival, recovery, - which completely agrees with the theory of cyclicity (Kondratiev, Yakovets, Yu, and Abalkin, 2002).

The mention of long-term fluctuations can be found in the studies of M. Tugan-Baranovsky. The theory of cyclicity was reflected in the works of the Russian scientist A. Gelfand (Parvus). He made an attempt to prove that cyclicity is immanent to capitalism. The original statistical treatment of the material is contained in the works of Dutch scientists J. Gelderen and S. Wolf. The novelty of their studies was that they considered technical progress as a factor of cyclicity, and also analyzed the terms of the functioning of the transport infrastructure.

The understanding of the cyclical nature of the development of the economy became especially widespread at the end of the 19th and the beginning of the 20th centuries, when scientists of many countries paid attention to the dynamics of certain economic indicators. This gave grounds for classifying the theories of economic cycles, which was most fully presented by U. Mitchell in his work "Economic cycles". The American economist distinguishes the following theories of economic cycles:

1. Theories that reduce economic cycles to natural-physical processes. These theories explained the cyclicity of economic life by cycles of solar radiation, the change in the position of Venus relative to the Earth, meteorological conditions.

2. Theories that reduce economic cycles to psychological causes which create either a favorable or unfavorable environment for economic activity. According to some economists, fluctuations in the mass sentiments of people precede fluctuations in wholesale prices, influence decision-making in the economic sphere. The basis of these theories is a fact noted in public life, indicating the periodicity of the change in society of motivational structures, creative activity of the population, social moods.

   Cyclic changes in the socio-psychological variable, encompassing the "degree of activity" of the population, its enterprising, "optimistic outlook" and other individual and socio-psychological aspirations of people, determine long-term cycles of economic development.

3. Theories that reduce economic cycles to institutional processes. The essence of cyclicity, from the standpoint of these theories, is that economic cycles arise from changes in economic institutions. The greatest influence on the formation of the cyclical nature of economic development is provided by the functioning of existing economic institutions.

4. Other theories proceed from the assertion that cycles arise because of the imbalance in the processes of total production and consumption of goods. Favorable trade and industrial conditions lead to a rapid growth of industrial equipment, later to an increase in output and, ultimately, to a fall in the marginal prices of demand for consumer goods. A consequence of this is depression, during which the growth in the number of industrial equipment and products is interrupted. Finally, the marginal prices of demand for consumer goods rise again, and a new period of recovery begins.

The most profound development of the concept of economic cycles is primarily connected with the works of the national economist Kondratieff, Yakovets, Yu, and Abalkin (2002). He put forward a hypothesis about the mechanism of long cycles in the economy ("large cycles of conjuncture" in his terminology), linking them not only with the price dynamics, but also with the process of capital accumulation, the growth rates of production and the dynamics of innovation, with the constant evolution of the national economy. The motion of long-term oscillations according to Kondratieff proceeds according to the following principle. Before the start of a large cycle, a sufficient amount of free funds accumulates - the growth of bank reserves, which allows creditors to reduce the interest rate. The percentage of long-term premises is low. During the previous period of the decline, a significant amount of technical novelties (inventions) accumulated. Under these conditions, capital investment in large facilities begins to increase, which causes serious changes in the conditions of production (technical opportunities for generating profits are generated), while production becomes profitable, and then, respectively, the upswing of a large cycle of economic conjuncture.

The main modern theories of long waves:

1. Innovative theory (J. Schumpeter). Its essence is that there are people who want to get entrepreneurial profit. They invest in new technologies and industries, followed by followers. This is a period of recovery. Gradually, the market is saturated, profit is reduced, and people withdraw their funds from production - this is a recession.

2. The theory of overaccumulation in the capital sector (D. Forrester). The capital sector, which produces the means of production, provides machines and equipment not only for industries that produce consumer goods, but also for themselves. The growth of consumption causes an even faster growth of the means of production, that is, the accelerator acts between the two branches. The magnitude of this accelerator in real life is much greater than that required for the equilibrium motion. All these factors contribute to overaccumulation in the capital sector. Orders first increase sharply, and then abruptly contract. This is sufficient for the appearance of long-term oscillations.

3. Theories related to labor (K. Freeman). This group of theories is based on consideration of the theory of long waves from the point of view of the laws of the labor force. Mechanism: the introduction of new technologies brings to life new industries. In the early stages of the application of pioneer technologies, the demand for labor is limited. This is due to the fact that the volumes of new production are not yet large and require not a mass, but a particularly skilled labor. Gradually, production increases, demand for labor begins to increase. This growth continues to saturate demand for both labor and related goods. In parallel, wages are rising and costs are increasing. There is a need for labor-saving innovations. There is an outflow of labor, a decline in wages, and general demand, that is, a decline in the economy.

4. Price theories (U.W. Rostou). In the theories examined, the prices of goods either were not considered at all, or played the role of indicators of the processes taking place in the sphere of production. However, the pricing process and the price dynamics are directly related to the explanation of the long-term cycle and its turning points. Changes in the demand and supply of raw materials and food products, and, consequently, the prices for them, affect the innovation activity that determines the sequence of the leading industries and itself depends on them.

In the structure of the cycle, the higher and the lower points of activity and the phases of recession and ascent lie between them. The total cycle time is measured by the time between two neighboring higher or two adjacent lower activity points. Accordingly, the duration of a decline is the time between the highest and the next lowest activity points, and the rise is the opposite. The National Bureau of Economic Research stated that in the development of the US economy from 1854 to 1991, there were 31 cycles. The average time between the two highest points was 53 months, of which 18 months accounted for the recession and 35 months - on the rise.

In more detailed analysis, the economic cycle is divided into four phases (Figure 9).

Figure 9. Modern periodization of Kondratieff Long Waves

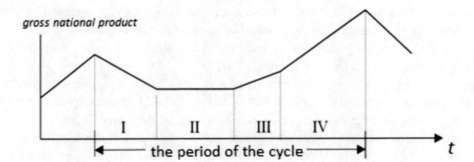

Phase One: The Crisis Phase (Recession)

The main manifestation of the crisis is a fall in production volumes and a reduction in the size of gross national product. Accordingly, the production capacities of enterprises are not fully loaded, the profit is falling, the share price is falling, the employment of the population is falling, the level of wages is falling, the living standard of the population is falling, and poverty is increasing. As a result, the aggregate demand decreases, in response to this, production is further reduced and, accordingly, the supply. In general, this phase is characterized by an excess of the aggregate supply of aggregate demand. To ensure macroeconomic balance, it becomes necessary to reduce production.

Over time, the crisis can last from several months to several years, as it was during the Great Crisis of 1929-1933.

Phase Two: The Phase of Depression

This phase is characterized by the fact that after the liquidation during the crisis of commodity stocks, the production decline ceases, but there is still no growth. Accordingly, employment is at a low level, but unemployment has already stopped, stabilized, albeit at a low level, wages and profits of enterprises, their business activity is not high. Depression can last from a few months to several years. For example, the depression that began in 1933 after the Great Crisis lasted until 1938, that is, practically until the war itself.

Phase Three: The Phase of Recovery

The name of the phase speaks for itself. It is characterized by a revival of the economy, some gross national product growth is occurring, the demand for labor, on loan capital is increasing. The most important thing is that the investment activity of enterprises is intensified. Usually this phase does not last long, it quickly passes into the next phase.

Phase Four: The Lifting Phase

This phase is also called a boom, since it is characterized by fairly rapid economic growth. There is an increase in employment, unemployment is resolving, and sometimes in some industries there is a shortage of labor. The wages are rising, the aggregate demand is growing, the volume of sales is growing, the profit of enterprises is increasing. The population and enterprises have free money, their offer on money markets increases, so the interest rate does not increase, and sometimes it starts to decline. Comparatively inexpensive is credit. The share price of many enterprises has a tendency to grow.

The problems of the theory of economic cycles cause the application of complex dynamic models using differential equations (Gorbachev & Syryamkin, 2015).

To characterize the economic situation, a number of economic indicators are used (gross national product, unemployment rate, personal income, industrial output, price level and many others). Depending on how the value of economic parameters varies during the cycle, they are divided into pro-cyclical, countercyclical, and acyclic. The procyclical parameters in the ascent phase increase, and in the cycle phase they decrease (loading of production capacities, aggregates of the money supply, the general level of prices, corporate profits, etc.).

Countercyclical parameters are indicators whose value decreases during the recession, and decreases during the ascent (unemployment rate, number of bankruptcies, stocks of finished products, etc.).

Acyclic parameters are called whose dynamics do not coincide with the phases of the economic cycle (for example, the volume of exports).

In addition, there are three types of parameters on the basis of the synchronization on the classification of the National Bureau of Economic Research USA - forward-looking, and the corresponding delayed. Leaders reach a maximum or a minimum before approaching the peak or the lowest point (these are changes in stocks, money supply, etc.). The laggards reach a maximum or a minimum after a peak or a low point (the number of unemployed, the specific costs of wages, etc.). The coinciding parameters change in accordance with the fluctuations in economic activity (gross national product, inflation, industrial production, etc.).

Currently, statistics and economists are not able to give accurate forecasts of the economic situation, but can only determine its general trend. First, it is difficult to take into account all the factors, especially during the period of economic instability and political turmoil. Secondly, the international environment has a significant impact on the national economy. Thirdly, even correctly determining the trend, it is difficult to predict the exact dates of the passage of phases and change the economic policy in time. Finally, the actions of entrepreneurs can exacerbate undesirable deviations in the conjuncture.

Technological and Social Dimension of TED

Prior to the results of the comparative analysis of TED, two factors should be distinguished. On the one hand, the objects and territories of states, regardless of their size and role in overall economic development, are not self-sufficient economic entities and, despite the existence of internal trends and interrelations, can not plan their development based only on their own dynamics and proportions. On the other hand, although the countries united by the international division of labor are developing along the general lines of technical and economic evolution, they differ significantly in terms of the absolute level of TED indicators (measured in relative units - per inhabitant or unit of national income), even if they are on the same level TED. This is explained by historical, scientific, educational, cultural, psychological, natural and climatic and other features of each country, which are reflected in its economic structure (Gorbachev & Syryamkin, 2015). Therefore, in order to construct an adequate model of the fuel-energy trajectory in the group of parameters studied, we introduced a qualitative growth component-the index of productivity of primary resources, which is measured as the ratio of gross national product to the value of primary raw materials consumed by the economy (Gorbachev & Syryamkin, 2015). Primary raw material resources are a set of such primary organic and inorganic resources that are massively used both for consumption of the population and for further processing in the process of material production (food, construction materials, fuel and energy resources).

Leading countries that have the lowest energy and material intensity for the main types of resources, nevertheless consume *1.5-2.5* times more primary raw materials per capita than less developed countries such as Russia, Brazil, India and China.

Productivity as an indicator of the effectiveness of resource use reflects the progress of science and technology. Even in the period of recession (1991-1998), Russia was experiencing quite intensive processes to improve the quality of products and services (Figure 10).

This was reflected in the fact that the productivity of primary resources increased by an average of 2.3% per year. Taking into account the fact that during this period the dynamics of the quality compo-

Figure 10. Dynamics of Russia's gross national product in 1990-2003 to the level of 1990

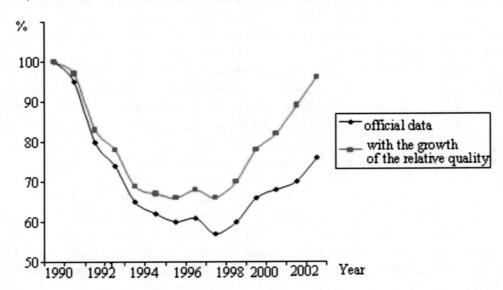

nent of growth for the USA decreased substantially (to 0.95% per annum compared to 2.3% a year on average over the previous 30 years), the index of improving the proportions of exchange for the Russian economy was 1.016.

Since 1998, during the recovery period, the dynamics of the quality component of growth for Russia has increased to almost 4% per year. However, as the qualitative growth component for the US also increased during this period (up to 2.4% per year), the index of change in the proportions of the exchange changed insignificantly - to 1.017.

Therefore, the gap in the economic development of Russia and the US can be completely overcome if the growth of productivity (science and technology) in Russia is outstripping growth. When modeling the TED trajectory, it is necessary to take into account that innovations reveal and define the essence of the technical process at the present stage of history. Selected quantitative and qualitative indicators of technical and economic development we supplemented with indicators of the country's innovative potential, divided into 4 groups:

1. Indicators characterizing the financial component of the innovation potential (the share of investment relative to gross national product, the share of investments in their total volume, etc.);
2. Indicators that characterize the material component of the innovation sphere (the number of organizations associated with scientific activity, the value of their fixed assets, the specific weight of scientific organizations).
3. Indicators characterizing the personnel component of the innovation potential (the number of workers associated with innovation, their average salary, average age, their specific gravity).
4. Indicators characterizing the resulting component of the innovation potential as a factor of economic growth and showing its ability to produce an effect (sales volumes, costs and profits associated with innovation, the number of created, exported and imported technologies, filed patent applications and issued patents, their specific weight).

Neuro-Fuzzy Model of World Technical and Economic Portrait

As a TED trajectory, a multidimensional time series is modeled, which is a collection of several one-dimensional time series, each of which describes the change in time of any of the listed characteristics characterizing the object of researches (Figure 11).

For each year t, a particular country is represented by a point in the multidimensional space of quantitative and qualitative characteristics.

In our opinion, statistical processing of data for the description of the TED trajectory can not be recognized as a reliable and adequate tool for solving such weakly structured tasks. It does not allow you to establish the cause-effect relationships of the parameters of the predicted system as a whole. In addition, the construction for each country of its generalized TED curve by linear contraction of the input vector space and their intercountry comparative analysis is not entirely incorrect due to, firstly, the "fluid" nonequilibrium nature of technical and economic development, with waves of falling and take-off (waves Kondratieff); And secondly, which is very important - the input parameters for trajectory construction, in our opinion, should not be rigidly specified - they depend both on the national system of accounts in each country, and on historical, cultural-psychological, natural-climatic and other features of the country at the time of observation t, while the significance of the same parameters for the construction of the model will be different for different technological structures and phases of cycles.

To improve the modeling quality, in Gorbachev and Syryamkin (2015) we proposed a complex neural network analysis of quantitative and qualitative indicators, which in the training process are ranked by weight coefficients by the level of significance for solving the problem. Based on the available data

Figure 11. One-dimensional time series by countries
(indicator - percentage of expenditure on R & D in gross national product dynamics)

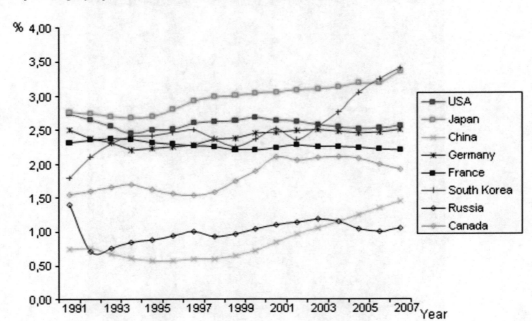

samples, a time series of Kohonen SOM was constructed, reflecting the dynamics of global technical and economic development (Figure 12).

This model makes it possible to simplify a multidimensional structure, it can be considered one of the methods of projecting a multidimensional space into a space with a lower dimension.

Figure 13 shows a neural network model of the world technical and economic portrait reflecting the current hierarchy of countries in 2010.

Each country in terms of its TED level in the current year is displayed by a specific cell on the map. Cells with the same coordinates contain countries with a close state of TED. The further on the map the coordinates of the countries, the more their technical and economic portrait differs from each other.

Based on the results of the training, four clusters of countries with the similar levels of TED relative to the reference value were identified (Table 2).

Thus, network neurons that are located on the boundaries between linearly inseparable, intersecting clusters form additional clusters 1/2, 2/3 and 3/4. For more accurate separation of clusters, we used FCNN-SOM - Figure 14, Table 3 and Table 4 shows the results of fuzzy clustering.

Each country in the i-th year of observation is characterized by a set of parameters (Y_i, A_i, B_i, C_i), where:

Y_i - level of fuel and energy resources of the country in the i-th year;

A_i – the actual distance (the number of years elapsed since the reference level of the TED parameter corresponded to the level of the country in question in the i-th year of observation);

Figure 12. The model of the TED trajectory as a time series of Kohonen SOM in the multidimensional feature space

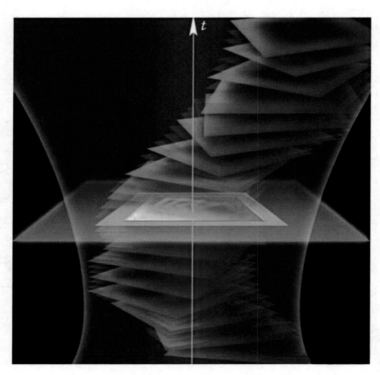

Figure 13. SOM-model of the world technical and economic portrait in 2010

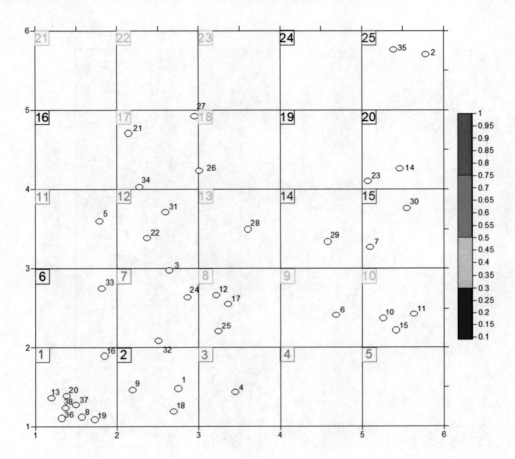

Table 2. Separation of neurons from clusters corresponding to groups of countries

Cluster	Cluster neurons	Group of countries	Color on the map
1	1	Leaders of TED	Red
2	3,4,5,7,11,12	Developed countries	Orange
3	8,9,10,13,17,18,21,22,23	Countries with a moderate level of TED	Yellow
4	14,15,25	Developing countries	Green
1/2	2,6	?	Black
2/3	16	?	Black
3/4	19,20,24	?	Black

Figure 14. Modified neuro-fuzzy model of world technical and economic portrait in 2010 based on FCNN-SOM

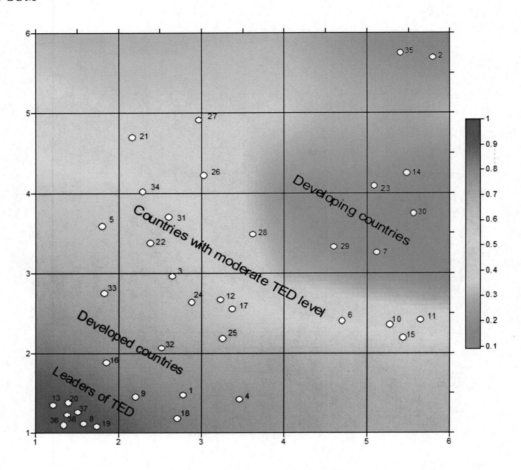

Table 3. The list of countries in Figure 14

1	2	3	4	5	6	7	8	9	10	11	12	13	14	15	16	17	18	19
Belgium	Bulgaria	Brazil	Switzerland	China	Cyprus	Greece	Germany	Denmark	Estonia	Spain	Finland	France	Croatia	Hungary	Ireland	India	Iceland	Italy

Table 4. The list of countries in Figure 14 (continued)

20	21	22	23	24	25	26	27	28	29	30	31	32	33	34	35	36	37	38
Japan	Lithuania	Luxembourg	Latvia	Malta	Netherlands	Norway	Poland	Portugal	Romania	Serbia	Russia	Sweden	Slovenia	Slovakia	Turkey	U.K.	USA	Canada

B_i – the prospective distance (the number of years that will be required by a given country, starting from the i-th year, to reach the standard level of technical development in the i-th year of observation);

C_i – conditional distance (the number of years that this country needs to enter the reference trajectory).

This set of parameters is used to calculate the level of TED, the characteristics of the individual country's fuel and energy resources and to predict future values of the multidimensional process. Their comparison on the reference and national TED trajectories makes it possible to obtain a reliable estimate not only of the speed, but also of the level of the technical and economic development of each country.

Based on the results of the modified neuro-fuzzy clustering of data, the countries under study are divided into 4 main categories according to the level of their TED (Table 5), which takes the value from *1* for the reference level of TED to *0.1* for the minimum level of development. For each country, the growth rate of TED for the five-year period is also calculated. For each five-year period, the calculation is based on the output values of FCNN-SOM, reflecting the change in the level of TED by multidimensional characteristics for this period.

The results of calculations for the parameter "actual distance" are presented in Table 6.

SUMMARY

On the basis of many domestic and international scientific research, a methodology for multicriteria neural network analysis of global technical and economic development has been generated for a set of

Table 5. Country categories, distinguished by the level and rate of TED by results neuro-fuzzy modeling (2005-2010)

Group	Leaders of growth (> 4%)	Countries with an average growth rate (2 – 4%)	Countries with low growth rate (1 – 2%)
Leaders of TED	Canada	USA, UK, Italy, France, Germany	Japan
Developed countries	Ireland, Denmark, Sweden, Switzerland	Iceland, Slovenia	Belgium, Luxembourg, Netherlands
Countries with moderate levels of TED	India, Brazil, China, Russia, Cyprus, Estonia	Hungary, Lithuania, Poland, Portugal, Finland, Slovakia	Norway, Spain, Malta
Developing countries	Turkey, Bulgaria, Romania	Greece, Latvia	Croatia, Serbia

Table 6. Country categories identified by the "actual distance" parameter based on the results of neuro-fuzzy modeling (2010)

The actual length	Country
< 10 years	Switzerland, Finland, Germany, Denmark, Sweden, UK
10 – 20 years	Russia, Czech Republic, Greece, Malta, Portugal, Hungary, Lithuania, Bulgaria, Poland, Slovakia, Italy, Norway, Spain
> 20 years	Romania, Latvia, Turkey, Croatia

quantitative and qualitative indicators, including the technological and social dimension of TED. Based on it, a flexible neural-fuzzy network model of the trajectory of global technical and economic development is constructed in the form of a dynamic series of fuzzy clustering Kohonen cellular maps that are distinguished by a fairly simple but powerful strategy for increasing the clustering accuracy without compromising interpretability with an estimate of the level of fuel and energy resources to predict future values of a multidimensional process. Their comparison on the etalon and national TED trajectories makes it possible to obtain a reliable estimate not only of the speed, but also of the level of the technical and economic development of each country.

To build a predictive model on a neural network, there is no requirement for stationarity of the process. Neural networks, being a universal tool, are able to identify with the necessary accuracy nonlinear regularities and interrelations between the components of multidimensional random processes. Using fuzzy clustering allows for a more accurate separation of intersecting clusters.

FUTURE RESEARCH DIRECTIONS

Prospects of future studies involve the development of an efficient fuzzy neural networks based on different principles: the introduction of fuzziness in the structure and on the basis of modification of teaching strategies.

CONCLUSION

The scientific novelty of the developed hybrid neural fuzzy network FCNN-SOM-FMLP is in a good structural and functional combining through the layer of fuzzy clustering of advantages of cellular neural self-organization (high degree of self-organization of neurons, the ability to control selectively individual connections between neurons to solve the problem of "dead" neurons) and multilayer perceptron, while mathematically proved and the question of the type and parameters of membership functions is automatically solved – the successful combination of the advantages of the bell-shaped membership functions of the fuzzy self-organizing layer outputs (smoothness, symmetry) and sigmoid activation functions of neurons in the perceptron hidden layer allows using a gradient training algorithm to adjust the synaptic weights of the network with a given accuracy.

Practical value consists of high flexibility, simplicity and time efficiency of the method. High speed of training and universal approximating properties of the proposed network will be particularly useful during processing multidimensional functions of a vector argument.

Listed below the main results obtained in this chapter are.

1. The classification problem of the multidimensional overlapping of objects reduces to a fuzzy modification of the pattern recognition tasks.
2. Basing on the promising developments in the field of cellular self-organizing neural networks and fuzzy clustering procedures, the author proposed a hybrid fuzzy neural network for pattern recognition and algorithms for training, characterized by the high degree of neurons self-organization, the absence of heuristic parameters of training, the ability to control selectively individual connections

between neurons to solve the problem of "dead" neurons, the high convergence rate and improvement of the separation properties of the network in the case of overlapping clusters and classes.

3. The proposed FCNN-SOM can be effectively used not only for multidimensional clustering semi-structured data in the form of generalized patterns, but also for automatic configuration of the parameters and the type of membership functions (fuzzification) in adaptive fuzzy inference systems.

4. The network can operate in the mode of exact and fuzzy clustering, depending on the nature of the data processed.

5. To improve the accuracy of the intersecting features classification the fuzzy multilayer perceptron is proposed based on the introduction of fuzziness in the structure of a classic perceptron and the use of the results of fuzzy clustering FCNN-SOM as input.

6. The research is conducted and the recommendations for the optimal parameters of the multilayer perceptron architecture are formed.

7. The proposed recognition methods are based on the fundamental regularities typical for the human method of cognition. If the right hemisphere is characterized by the prototype of a holistic representation of the world, the left hemisphere deals with patterns that reflect the relationship between the attributes of this world. Therefore, the prospective detection system must provide an implementation of both methods but not just any one of them, as due to the formation of generalized patterns the independence of the recognition time from the volume of training sample is achieved. It is known that the existence of this dependence leads to an almost unacceptable cost of computer time to recognize via such methods as the method of k nearest neighbors, the algorithm for computing the estimates in such volume of training samples when it is possible to talk about sufficient statistics.

In conclusion, note that the hybrid neuro-fuzzy networks have a great potential in terms of creation of intellectual systems of analysis, control and decision support in the case of processing multidimensional semi-structured data describing complex objects. Computer simulation demonstrates the effectiveness of the proposed approach for the decision of tasks of recognition of overlapping patterns in a semi-structured and noisy data.

ACKNOWLEDGMENT

The studies were performed according to the program of increasing the competitiveness of National research Tomsk state University, with the financial support of RFBR (grant number 16-29-12858).

REFERENCES

Anikin, V. I., & Karmanov, A. A. (2014). The training of the artificial neural network Kohonen's self-organizing cellular automaton. *Información Tecnológica, 11*, 73–80.

Bezdek, J. C. (1981). *Pattern Recognition with Fuzzy Objective Function Algorithms*. New York: Plenum Press. doi:10.1007/978-1-4757-0450-1

Bezdek, J. C., Tsao, E. C.-K., & Pal, N. R. (1992). Fuzzy Kohonen Clustering Networks. *IEEE Transactions on Fuzzy Systems*, 1035–1043.

Bodyanskiy, Ye., Gorshkov, Ye., Kolodyaznhiy, V., & Stephan, A. (2005). Combined learning algorithm for a selforginizing map with fuzzy inference. *Proceedings of Computational intelligence, theory and applications: International Conference 8th Fuzzy Days in Dortmund*, *33*, 641-650.

Bodyansky, E. V., & Rudenko, O. G. (2004). *Artificial neural networks: architectures, learning, applications*. Kharkov, Ukraine: TELETECH.

Bohr, N. (1961). *Atomic physics and human knowledge*. Moscow, Russia: Mir.

Borisov, V. V., Kruglov, V. V., & Fedulov, A. S. (2012). *Fuzzy models and networks*. Moscow, Russia: Telecom.

Chua, L. O., & Yang, L. (1988a). Cellular neural networks. Theory. IEEE Transactions on Circuits and Systems, 10, 1257-1272. doi:10.1109/ISCAS.1988.15089

Chua, L. O., & Yang, L. (1988b). Cellular neural networks. Applications. IEEE Transactions on Circuits and Systems, 10, 1273– 1290. doi:10.1109/ISCAS.1988.15089

Dawod, M., Hasan, M., & Daood, A. (2017). Experimental Study: Comparison of clustering algorithms. *Int. Journal of Engineering Research and Application*, *7*(8), 23–34.

Duke, V. A. (1994). *Computer psychodiagnostics*. Saint Petersburg, Russia: Brotherhood.

Dvoretzky, A. (1956). On stochastic approximation. In *Proc. 3-rd Berkley Symp. Math. Statistics and Probability* (pp.39-55). Academic Press.

Glazyev, S., & Kharitonov, V. (2009). *Nanotechnology as a key factor in the new technological order in the economy*. Moscow: Twent.

Gorbachev, S. V. (2000). Intelligent mapping system ",Informeo": the experience of using neuroinformation technologies. In *Proceedings of VIII all-Russian seminar "Neuroinformatics and its applications"* (pp. 146-148). Krasnoyarsk, Russia: Publishing house Krasnoyarsk state University.

Gorbachev, S. V. (2001). Building neural network control system to solve the problem of the identification of geological bodies 3-D. In *Proceedings of the IX all-Russian seminar "Neuroinformatics and its applications"*, (pp.113-114). Krasnoyarsk, Russia: Publishing house Krasnoyarsk state University.

Gorbachev, S.V., & Syryamkin, V.I. (2014). *Neuro-fuzzy techniques in intelligent systems of processing and analysis of multidimensional information*. Tomsk, Russia: Publishing house Tomsk state University.

Gorbachev, S. V., & Syryamkin, V. I. (2015). Cognitive neural network modeling of the trajectory of global technical and economic development. In *Proceedings of International Conference on Cognitive Computing and Information Processing CCIP-2015* (pp.341–346). NOIDA.

Gorban, A. N. (1990). *Training of neural networks*. Moscow, Russia: Paragraf.

Hoeppner, F., Klawonn, F., Kruse, R., & Runkler, T. (1999). *Fuzzy Clustering Analysis: Methods for Classification, Data Analysis and Image Recognition*. Chichester, UK: John Wiley & Sons.

Karayiannis, N. B., & Pai, P. I. (1996). Fuzzy algorithm for learning vector quantization. *IEEE Transactions on Neural Networks*, 5(5), 1196–1211. doi:10.1109/72.536314 PMID:18263514

Keller, J. M., & Hunt, D. J. (1985). Incorporating fuzzy membership function into the perceptron algorithm. IEEE Transactions on Pattern Analysis and Machine Intelligence, 7, 693-699. doi:10.1109/TPAMI.1985.4767725

Kohonen, T. (2008). *Self-organizing maps.* Moscow, Russia: BINOM. Knowledge laboratory.

Kondratiev, N. D., Yakovets, Yu. V., & Abalkin, L. I. (2002). *Large cycles of conjuncture and theory of foresight: Selected works.* Moscow: Economy.

Lutsenko, E. V. (1996). *Theoretical bases and technology of adaptive semantic analysis to support decision-making.* Krasnodar, Russia: CUI MVD RF.

Lutsenko, E.V. (2002). *Automated system-cognitive analysis in the management of active objects.* Krasnodar, Russia: KubSAU.

Mitra, S., & Pal, S. K. Fuzzy multi-layer perceptron, inferencing and rule generation. IEEE Transactions on Neural Networks, 6, 51-63. doi:10.1109/72.363450

Pospelov, D.A. (1990). *Artificial intelligence. Reference. Book 2. Models and methods.* Moscow, Russia: Radio and communication.

Vuorimaa, P. (1994). Fuzzy self-organizing map. *Fuzzy Sets and Systems, 66*(2), 223–231. doi:10.1016/0165-0114(94)90312-3

Vuorimaa, P. (1994). Use of the fuzzy self-orginizing map in pattern self-recognition. In *Proc. 3-rd IEEE Int. Conf. Fuzzy Systems «FUZZ-IEEE'94»* (pp. 798–801). Orlando, FL: IEEE.

Wu, K.L., & Yang, M.S. (2003). A fuzzy-soft learning vector quantization. *Neurocomputing is, 55*, 681-697.

Xu, R., & Wunsch, D. C. (2009). Clustering. In *IEEE Press Series on Computational Intelligence* (pp. 842–751). Hoboken, NJ: John Wiley & Sons.

KEY TERMS AND DEFINITIONS

Artificial Neural Network: The mathematical model, representing the system of connected and interacting simple processors (artificial neurons) according to the principle of the organization and the functioning of biological neural networks.

Cellular Automaton: A discrete model studied in mathematics, theory of computation, physics, theoretical biology and microstructure modeling. It consists of a regular grid of cells, each of which can be in one of a finite number of states, such as 1 and 0.

Fuzzification (Introduction Fuzziness): Matching the numerical value of the input variable of the fuzzy inference system and value of membership function corresponding term of a linguistic variable.

Fuzzy Logic: The branch of mathematics that is the generalization of classical logic and set theory, based on the concept of fuzzy sets as an object with a function element to the set that accepts any value in the interval [0, 1], not just 0 or 1.

Fuzzy Neural Network: The system of artificial intelligence that combines the methods of artificial neural networks and fuzzy logic.

Perceptron: The mathematical or computer model of information perception by the brain, proposed by Frank Rosenblatt in 1957 and first implemented in the form of an electronic machine "Mark-1" in 1960. The perceptron was one of the first models of neural networks, and "Mark-1" is the world's first neurocomputer.

Self-Organizing Map Kohonen: A neural network with unsupervised learning that performs the task of visualization and clustering.

Chapter 14
Multimodal Semantics and Affective Computing from Multimedia Content

Rajiv Ratn Shah
Indraprastha Institute of Information Technology Delhi, India

Debanjan Mahata
Infosys Limited, USA

Vishal Choudhary
Singapore University of Technology and Design, Singapore

Rajiv Bajpai
Nanyang Technological University, Singapore

ABSTRACT

Advancements in technologies and increasing popularities of social media websites have enabled people to view, create, and share user-generated content (UGC) on the web. This results in a huge amount of UGC (e.g., photos, videos, and texts) on the web. Since such content depicts ideas, opinions, and interests of users, it requires analyzing the content efficiently to provide personalized services to users. Thus, it necessitates determining semantics and sentiments information from UGC. Such information help in decision making, learning, and recommendations. Since this chapter is based on the intuition that semantics and sentiment information are exhibited by different representations of data, the effectiveness of multimodal techniques is shown in semantics and affective computing. This chapter describes several significant multimedia analytics problems such as multimedia summarization, tag-relevance computation, multimedia recommendation, and facilitating e-learning and their solutions.

DOI: 10.4018/978-1-5225-5246-8.ch014

INTRODUCTION

The advent of the social media websites, advancements in smartphones, and affordable network infrastructures have enabled anyone with an Internet connection and a smartphone to easily express their ideas, opinions, and content (*e.g.*, photos, videos, and texts) with millions of other people around the world. Thus, the amount of user-generated content (UGC) on websites has increased rapidly in recent years. Emotions and sentiments play a crucial role in our everyday lives. They aid decision-making, learning, communication, and situation awareness in human-centric environments. Over the past two decades, researchers in artificial intelligence have been attempting to endow machines with cognitive capabilities to recognize, infer, interpret and express emotions and sentiments. All such efforts can be attributed to affective computing, an interdisciplinary field spanning computer science, psychology, social sciences and cognitive science. Sentiment analysis and emotion recognition also become a new trend in social media, avidly helping users understand opinions being expressed on different platforms. Moreover, it is evident from an interesting recent trend is that the most social media websites such as Flickr, YouTube, and Twitter create opportunities for users to generate content, instead of creating content by themselves. Since many users spend their significant time on such social media websites, companies are interested in sensing users' behaviors to provide personalized services and recommendations. Moreover, semantics and affective information computed from UGC are very useful in providing an efficient search, retrieval, and recommendation. For instance, they are useful in several significant social media analytics problems such as tag recommendation and ranking for photos, music recommendation for photos and videos, and recommending items to users based on their behaviors on social media websites. Thus, to benefit users and companies from an automatic semantics and affective understanding of UGC, this chapter focuses on developing efficient algorithms for semantics and affective computing.

Despite knowledge structures derived from the semantics and sentiment computing of user-generated content are beneficial for both users and companies in an efficient search, retrieval, and recommendation, it is difficult to get correct semantics and sentiment information. It is because real-world UGC is complex, and extracting the semantics and affective information from only content is very difficult. Since suitable concepts for sentiment and sentiment analysis are exhibited by different modalities, it is important to exploit the multimodal information of UGC (Shah, 2016c; Shah, 2016e; Shah and Zimmermann, 2017). For an efficient semantics computing, they leveraged both content and contextual information of user-generated content. Due to the increasing popularity of social media websites and advancements in technology, it is possible now to collect a significant amount of important contextual information (e.g., spatial, temporal, preference, and opinion information). Similarly, for an efficient affective computing, they exploited textual modality with information from other modalities such as audio and visual. Earlier contributions on the semantics and affective computing either work in unimodal setting or leverage limited information from other modalities. For instance, most work in semantics and sentiment computing do not leverage many of the contextual, audio, visual, gaze, and other information together. This chapter describes many multimodal techniques that augment knowledge structures for an efficient semantics and sentiment understanding.

In this chapter, to show the effectiveness of multimodal techniques in semantics and affective computing, several significant multimedia analytics problems are solved exploiting multimodal information. For instance, knowledge structures extracted from multiple modalities are useful in applications related to multimedia summarization (Shah et al., 2015a; Shah et al., 2016a), tag ranking and recommendation (Shah et al., 2016d; Shah et al., 2016f), preference-aware multimedia recommendation (Shah et al.,

2014a; Shah et al., 2014c), and multimedia-based e-learning (Shah et al., 2014b; Shah et al., 2015b). It is very challenging to address these problems efficiently due to the following reasons: (i) difficulty in capturing the semantics of UGC, (ii) the existence of noisy metadata, (iii) difficulty in handling big datasets, (iv) difficulty in learning user preferences, and (v) the insufficient accessibility and searchability of video content. However, the above-mentioned work confirm that exploiting the multimedia content (e.g., visual content) and associated contextual information (e.g., geo-, temporal, and other sensory data) helped in providing efficient solutions for these problems. These multimodal techniques are based on an intuition that different knowledge structures are represented by different sources or representation of data. Thus, multimodal information is useful to overcome above-mentioned challenges. Figure 1 shows the framework of the proposed multimodal semantics and affective computing approach.

First, for a better semantics understanding of an event from a large collection of photos, this chapter first presents the EventBuilder system (Shah et al., 2015a) that enables people to automatically generate an event summary in real-time. It exploited Wikipedia as the event background knowledge to obtain more contextual information about the event. This information was very useful in an effective event detection. Next, we solve an optimization problem to produce text summaries for the event. Subsequently, the EventSensor system (Shah et al., 2016a) is presented that aims to address affect understanding and produces a multimedia summary for a given mood. It extracted concepts and mood tags from the visual content and textual metadata of user-generated content and exploited them in supporting several significant multimedia analytics problems such as a musical multimedia summary. EventSensor supports sentiment-based event summarization by leveraging EventBuilder as its semantics engine component. Furthermore, this chapter focus on semantics and sentiment understanding from videos since they have a significant impact on different areas of a society (e.g., enjoyment and education).

Since many outdoor UGVs lack a certain appeal because their soundtracks consist mostly of ambient background noise, this chapter presents a solution to make UGVs more attractive by recommending a matching soundtrack for a UGV by exploiting content and contextual information (Shah et al., 2014a; Shah et al., 2014c). In particular, first, it predicts scene moods from a real-world video dataset. Users collected this dataset from their daily outdoor activities. Second, it performs heuristic rankings to fuse the predicted confidence scores of multiple models, and third, it customizes the video soundtrack recommendation functionality to make it compatible with mobile devices. Furthermore, this chapter describes the problem of knowledge structure extraction from educational UGVs to facilitate e-learning. Specifically, it discusses the solution for topic-wise segmentation of lecture videos (Shah et al., 2014b; Shah et al., 2015b). To extract the structural knowledge of a multi-topic lecture video and thus make it easily accessible, it is very desirable to divide each video into shorter clips by performing an automatic topic-wise video segmentation. However, the accessibility and searchability of most lecture video content are still insufficient due to the unscripted and spontaneous speech of speakers. This chapter presents the ATLAS and TRACE systems to perform the temporal segmentation of lecture videos automatically. In these studies, authors constructed models from visual, transcript, and Wikipedia features to perform such topic-wise segmentations of lecture videos. Moreover, they investigated the late fusion of video segmentation results derived from state-of-the-art methods by exploiting the multimodal information of lecture videos. Experimental results showed that their proposed methods outperform their state of the art.

Next, this chapter focuses on computing tag relevance for photos on social media such as Flickr. Since many search engines are still text-based for efficiently searching and indexing photos, tags (i.e., keywords or phrases) are very important. Social media platforms such as Flickr and Facebook enable users to annotate photos with tags or descriptive keywords. Such keywords help in making multimedia

Figure 1. The framework of multimodal semantics and affective computing

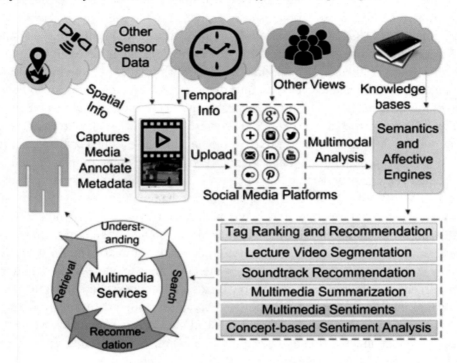

content easily understandable, searchable, and discoverable. However, due to the manual, ambiguous, and personalized nature of user tagging, many tags of a photo are in a random order and even irrelevant to the visual content. Furthermore, manual annotation is cumbersome and very time-consuming for most users. Thus, it is difficult to search and retrieve relevant photos. To this end, this chapter discusses the computation of relevance scores to predict and rank tags of photos. Specifically, this chapter presents systems for tag recommendation and ranking. First, it introduces PROMPT, a tag recommendation system, which recommends personalized tags for a given photo leveraging personal and social contexts. Next, it presents CRAFT, a tag ranking system, which is based on voting from photo neighbors derived from multimodal information. In the proposed tag recommendation and ranking approaches in the chapter, authors leverage multimodal information of photos. Experimental results confirm the effectiveness of their multimodal approaches on these problems.

RELATED WORK

This section first provides a detailed literature survey for different multimedia analytics problems that are addressed in this chapter. Next, it describes some knowledge bases that are used by different approaches described in this chapter. Specifically, this section first presents a literature review for the following multimedia analytics problems: (i) multimodal event detection and summarization, (ii) soundtrack recommendation for user-generated videos, (iii) lecture video segmentation, and (iv) tag relevance computation is presented. Finally, it describes different knowledge bases that are used to address above-mentioned problems.

The area of event modeling, detection, and understanding from multimedia content observes significant work (Scherp & Mezaris, 2014) over the past few years. Earlier methods (Zaharieva et al., 2013) leveraged multimodal information to detect events automatically from a large collection of multimedia content such as Flickr. Another work (Fabro et al., 2012) presented an algorithm that summarizes real-life events based on community-contributed multimedia content using photos from Flickr and videos from YouTube. Furthermore, a unified workflow of event detection, tracking, and summarization of microblog data (e.g., Twitter) is presented by Long et al., 2011. They selected topical words from the microblog data exploiting its characteristics for event detection. Wang & Kankanhalli, 2015 proposed a novel multi-layer tweeting cameras framework leveraging visual sensors to tweet semantic concepts for event detection. Researchers also focus on the area of sentiment analysis that attempts to determine the sentiments details of multimedia content based on the concepts exhibited from their visual content and metadata (Cambria et al., 2015). This chapter presents both semantics and sentiments-based event detection and summarization.

Despite significant efforts that have focused on music recommendation techniques (Schedl & Schnitzer, 2014) in recent years, researchers have paid little attention to music recommendation for sets of images or UGVs. Moreover, Hanjalic et al., 2005 recognized emotions from videos but the field of video soundtrack recommendation for UGVs is largely unexplored. Rahmani et al., 2010 proposed context-aware movie recommendation techniques based on background information such as users' preferences, movie reviews, actors and directors of the movie, and others. Furthermore, Chen et al., 2012 proposed an approach by leveraging a tripartite graph (user, video, query) to recommend personalized videos. Research work (Snoek et al., 2015) confirm that late fusion techniques perform well for semantic video analysis. Schedl & Schnitzer, 2014 proposed hybrid music-recommendation algorithms that combine information of the music content and the context of music and user, to build a music retrieval system. A recent work by Lin et al., 2016 presented an emotional temporal course representation and deep similarity matching for automatic music video generation.

Due to advancements in technologies, the number of digital lecture videos on the web has increased rapidly. It makes distance learning very easy but traditional video retrieval based on a feature extraction cannot be efficiently applied to e-learning applications due to the unstructured and linear features of lecture videos. Manual segmentation and indexing of lecture videos can be a probable solution. However, considering the rapid growth in the number of videos, the manual approach is not feasible. Speech transcripts are more personalized as compared to normal documents but it is more difficult to segments speech transcripts compared to normal documents. Earlier work (Haubold & Kender, 2005; Lin et al., 2005; Yamamoto et al., 2003) attempted to segment videos automatically by exploiting visual, audio, and linguistic features. Most of state of arts on the lecture video segmentation are based on exploiting only one modality (e.g., text, visual content, or speech). For instance, Bhatt et al., 2013 used to perform the segmentation of lecture videos based on the different events such as slide transitions, visibility of speaker only, and visibility of both speaker and slide but they only used visual content.

A significant work has been done to compute the tag relevance of photos. Li et al., 2009 proposed a neighbor-voting algorithm that determines tag ranking of photos by accumulating votes from visual neighbors of an input photo. Rae et al., 2010 proposed an extendable framework that can recommend additional tags to partially annotated images using a combination of different personalized and collective contexts. Anderson et al., 2008 presented a tag prediction system for Flickr photos, which combines both linguistic and visual features of a photo. In another work (Nwana & Chen, 2016), authors proposed a novel way of measuring tag preferences, and also proposed a new personalized tagging objective function that explicitly considers a user's preferred tag orderings using a (partially) greedy algorithm. Furthermore, Wu et al., 2009 proposed a multi-modality recommendation based on both tag and visual correlation, and formulated the tag recommendation as a learning problem. Each modality is used to generate a ranking feature, and Rankboost algorithm is applied to learn an optimal combination of these ranking features from different modalities. In another popular work (Liu et al., 2009), authors proposed a tag-ranking scheme, aiming to rank tags associated with a given photo according to their relevance to the photo content automatically. They estimated initial relevance scores for the tags based on probability density estimation, and then performed a random walk over a tag similarity graph to refine the relevance scores. In a recent work (Rawat & Kankanhalli, 2016), authors exploited user context for recommending tags of photos. Furthermore, Moxley et al., 2009 explored the ability to learn tag semantics by mining geo-referenced photos, and categorizing tags as places, landmarks, and visual descriptors automatically. Earlier work (Zhuang et al., 2011; Xiao et al., 2012) leveraged both textual and visual content to computing tag relevance for photos. In a recent work (Zhang et al., 2015), authors proposed a framework to learn the relation between a geo-tagged photo and tags within different Points of Interests (POI). Furthermore, Wang et al., 2015 proposed a user tag-ranking scheme in the micro-blogging website Sina Weibo based on the relations between users.

This chapter describes different knowledge bases and APIs that are used to solve several significant multimedia analytics problems. First, it presents a semantics parser since a natural language text consists of words and phrases (keywords) and it is required to extract useful information (i.e., keywords) from texts for a better semantics and sentiment analysis. Poria et al., 2015 presented a parser that derives keywords (i.e., multi-word concepts) from a given text. For instance, for a given text, "India is a great country with diverse cultures and languages.", the parser produces the following concepts: country_with_language_and_culture, great_country, country, and diverse_culture. Next, it presents WordNet, a well-known lexical database of English (Miller, 1995). It groups nouns, verbs, adjectives, and adverbs into sets of cognitive synonyms, called synsets. Each synset represents a distinct concept. Thus, it groups words together based on their meanings. Moreover, WordNet labels the semantic relations among words. For instance, auto, automobile, machine, and motorcar are the synsets for the word "car". Subsequently, it describes the SenticNet knowledge base, presented a knowledge base with affective labels (Poria et al., 2013). They refer this knowledge base as SenticNet-3, with approximately 30000 common and common-sense concepts such as party, accident_happen, and food (Cambria et al., 2014a). They also provided an API that provides semantics and sentiment information for such concepts (Cambria et al., 2014b). For a given concept, this API provides the following sentiment information: pleasantness, attention, sensitivity, and aptitude (Cambria et al., 2012). Moreover, as the part of semantics information, this API provides five semantically related concepts from SenticNet-3 for the given concepts. Poria et al., 2014 presented another knowledge base, named EmoSenticNet, that maps concepts of SenticNet-3 to six affective labels. The affective labels were anger, disgust, fear, joy, sadness, and surprise. For an efficient sentiment analysis, SenticNet knowledge base and WordNet are automatically merged (Poria et al., 2012a; Poria et al., 2012b). Finally, it describes the Foursquare API that provides a list of geo-categories such as Park, Hotel, and Beach for a given GPS point. Such geo-categories are very useful in determining the semantics and sentiment information for locations in different user-generated multimedia content. For instance, many texts (e.g., tweets and Facebook posts), photos, and videos on social media websites are embedded with locations. Geo-categories for such locations help in understanding semantics (e.g., scenes in photos and videos) and sentiments (e.g., emotions, since many times location types indicate the mood of the environment). Foursquare provides three levels of hierarchies for geo-categories including ten high-level categories (e.g., restaurant) that are divided into approximately 1300 low-level categories (e.g., Indian restaurant, Chinese restaurant, and Italian restaurant) further.

PROBLEMS AND SOLUTIONS

This chapter presents a survey of several significant problems related to social media that are benefitted by the multimodal information of multimedia content. It shows that multimodal information of user-generated content is very much useful in solving these problems. For instance, first, it has described problems on social media that deal with information from different modalities such as texts (e.g., tags), photos, videos, audio, and context. It has also emphasized the uses several existing knowledge bases such as WordNet and SenticNet-3 to address these problems efficiently. Specifically, this section provides details of problems and solutions for soundtrack recommendation, lecture videos segmentation, event summarization, and tag relevance computation as follows.

Multimodal Event Detection and Summarization

The growth and popularity of social media are due to the advancements in technologies and affordable network infrastructures. These results in a huge amount of photos and videos are accumulated on social media websites. Since such photos and videos exhibit users' behaviors and preferences, it is very useful for companies to analyze content on social media to provide different services. Social media giants such as Facebook, Google, Yahoo, and others spend much on building models and algorithms that derive useful information from such content to provide personalized services. For instance, Google Cloud Vision API able to derive semantic and sentiment concepts from photos. This helps in understanding real-world photos and videos that are complex and noisy. However, deriving semantics and affective information from only content is not feasible because suitable concepts may be exhibited in different representations. Since semantics and sentics knowledge structures are very useful in multimedia search, retrieval, and recommendation, researchers analyze the content from multiple modalities for a better understanding. To this end, this section first presents a multimedia summarization system, called Event-Builder. It deals with semantics understanding and automatically generates a multimedia summary for a given event in real-time by exploiting different social media such as Wikipedia and Flickr. This section also presents a system to address the affective understanding from social media content, called EventSensor. It produces a sentiment-based multimedia summary for a given mood. It extracts concepts and sentiments (emotional/mood tags) from visual content and textual metadata of user-generated content (social media content). EventSensor exploits such knowledge structures in building several significant multimedia-related services such as a musical multimedia summary. EventBuilder and EventSensor together build a novel system that provides both semantics and sentiment services from social media content.

Figure 2 depicts the framework of the EventBuilder system. EventBuilder consists of two component. First, an event detection component. Second, an online processing component that leverages results from the event detection component. Thus, EventBuilder provides a multimedia summary for a given event in the following two steps. First, it performs an offline event detection. Multimodal information is useful in determining complete knowledge structures since different modalities represent different aspect

Figure 2. The framework of EventBuilder (Shah et al., 2015a)

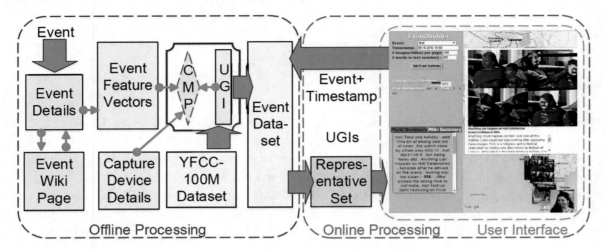

social media content. Thus, the proposed approaches described in this chapter leverage both content and contextual information of social media data. Specifically, in EventBuilder, authors extract knowledge structures from the following information: (i) names of events, (ii) spatial information, (iii) temporal information, (iv) keywords of events, and (v) device characteristics that captured the photos and videos. Next, they compute similarities between photos and events based on these five criteria. Finally, users get the overall similarity score of a photo/video for a given event by fusing the similarity scores based on the above-mentioned five criterion. Experimental results indicate that similarity based on names of events is the most salient and the similarity based on the characteristics of devices are the least important in determining the overall relevance score of a photo/video for a given event. The relevance scores of photos and videos used in offline event detection (see the left block of the Figure 2). Next, it generates an online event summary for the event (see the right block of the Figure 2). The online event summary consists of two sections. First, the visualization of photos and videos with high relevance scores for events is presented on the Google map. Second, text summaries for events from the textual descriptions of photos and videos is produced by solving an optimization problem. Both objective and subjective evaluations are performed to evaluate the proposed multimedia summarization system. Experimental results confirm that EventBuilder outperforms baselines. The YFCC100M dataset from the Flickr is used for the experiment. YFCC100M consists of 100 million photos and videos from Flickr. This dataset provides much metadata information such as user tags, visual tags (automatically derived tags from the visual content), spatial information, and temporal information. Photos and videos in this dataset are from top cities such as Tokyo, New York, London, and Hong Kong. In the evaluation, we consider the following seven events in our evaluation: (i) Olympics Games, (ii) Hanami, (iii) Holi, (iv) Occupy Movement, (v) Batkid, (vi) Byron Bay Bluesfest, and (vii) Eyjafjallajkull Eruption. The detailed information of the EventBuilder is provided in (Shah et al., 2015a; Shah et al., 2016a).

Figure 3 depicts the framework of the EventSensor system. It uses EventBuilder as a semantics engine. EventSensor consists of two components. The first component is a GUI client and the second component is a backend server. The GUI client accepts users' inputs (e.g., mood tags, timestamps, and dates) and displays the affective multimedia summarization to users. The client communicates with the backend component to get results for given inputs. The semantics engine of EventSensor leverages multimodal

Figure 3. The framework of EventSensor (Shah et al., 2016a)

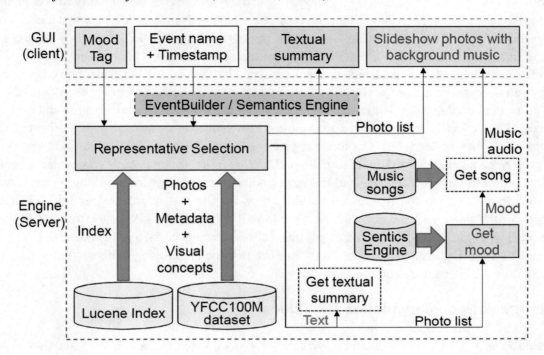

information of photos and videos to get the representative media for given events or queries. Next, the Sentics engine (i.e., affective or sentiment engine) determines mood tags for each photo in the representative set. Finally, EventSensor selects the soundtrack for the most occurred mood tags for photos and plays a slideshow of photos with a background soundtrack. The produced musical soundtrack enhances the viewing experience of multimedia summaries for given events or queries.

Figure 4 shows the framework of the affective (sentics) engine in the EventSensor system. It is useful in providing sentiment-based multimedia-related services to users from photos and videos accumulated on social media websites. In the proposed affective engine (Shah et al., 2016a), authors exploited information from both multimedia content and contextual information. They leveraged multimodal information since

Figure 4. The framework of affective computing in EventSensor (Shah et al., 2016a)

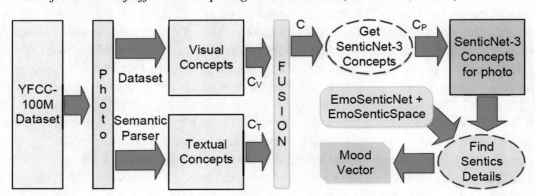

determining emotions from photos is very subjecting and relying only on one modality suffers prediction accuracies. Specifically, first, they determined concepts (keyword phrases) from content and contextual information of photos and videos using a semantics parser (Poria et al., 2015). Next, they fused concepts derived from different modalities. Since such keywords create an endless pool of concepts and it is not feasible to consider all such possible concepts produced by the semantics parser. Thus, they mapped all derived concepts to a fixed set of 30,000 common and common-sense keywords of SenticNet-3, a well-known knowledge base. SenticNet-3 contains semantics and affective information and bridges the conceptual and affective gap. Authors also exploited EmoSenticNet knowledge base (Poria et al., 2014) that maps concepts of SenticNet-3 to six emotional tags (anger, disgust, joy, sad, surprise, and fear). In this way, they constructed a six-dimensional mood vectors from the content and contextual information of all photos and videos. They selected the most dominant mood tags from all photos and videos in the representative sets to construct a musical slideshow. For the evaluation, they used the YFCC100M dataset. For the soundtrack dataset, they used the ISMIR'04 dataset of 729 songs from the ADVISOR system (Shah et al., 2016a) for generating a musical multimedia summary. This dataset is annotated with the 20 most frequent. Evaluation results confirm that the proposed systems outperform baselines (see, Shah et al., 2016a, for details).

Soundtrack Recommendation for Videos

The number of videos on social media is increasing rapidly due to the ubiquitous availability of smartphones and affordable network infrastructures. It is now very convenient for users to capture videos anywhere, anytime, and share them online on social media websites. However, often many such videos are captured at outdoor locations. Since many outdoor user-generated videos (UGVs) consists mostly of ambient background noise, they lack appeal in viewing and sharing. Since many such videos are captured at outdoor locations, we have much contextual and sensor information that can be useful in enhancing the viewing and sharing experience of these videos. Thus, aimed at making user-generated videos more attractive, researchers present the ADVISOR system. Figure 5 depicts the system framework of the ADVISOR system. It consists of the following two components: (i) a smartphone application and (ii) a backend server. The proposed smartphone application captures continuous sensor information such as GPS, compass, and other mobile sensors in conjunction with video recording. The steps to get the soundtrack recommendation of outdoor UGVs are as follows. First, a user captures a sensor-rich video through our smartphone application. The user requests for the recommended soundtrack by clicking the get recommendation button in the app. This button uploads sensor information (metadata) and a few keyframes to the backend server. The backend server processes the uploaded information and predicts mood tags for the video through offline SVM^{hmm} models. Such SVM^{hmm} models are constructed from geographic, visual, and audio features, and are trained to mood tags for videos. Multimodal information from different sources provides different types of video characteristics that are useful in predicting mood tags for videos more accurately. For instance, geographic contextual information (i.e., geo-categories such as Beach, Hotel, Lake, Plaza and others derived from Foursquare) captured by geo-sensors (GPS and compass), can serve as an important dimension to represent valuable semantic information of multimedia data while video frame content is often used in scene understanding. Thus, offline SVM^{hmm} models are constructed leveraging both geographical information and multimedia content. Next, when the backend system predicts mood tags for the videos using the proposed SVM^{hmm} models then the system retrieves a list of soundtracks corresponding to the predicted mood tags using the soundtrack retrieval compo-

Figure 5. The framework of our ADVISOR system (Shah et al., 2014a)

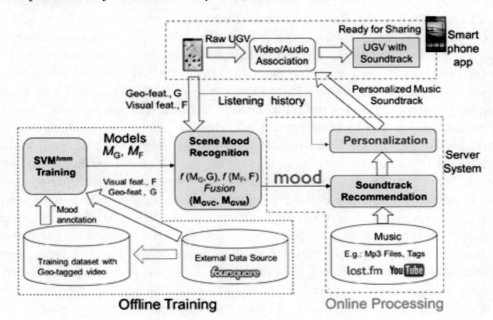

nent. Finally, the system provides the personalized soundtracks for videos by computing the correlation between the listening history of users and soundtracks retrieved by the soundtrack retrieval component.

Shah et al., 2014a investigated several machine learning models leveraging multimodal information to find the best performing mood prediction model for videos. Specifically, we consider outdoor videos in our study since we want to investigate the importance of geographical contextual information in improving the viewing experience of videos. Thus, in order to provide personalized, we leverage video capture location (i.e., GPS information) and online listening histories (i.e., a list of most frequent songs) as user-centric preference-aware activities. Figure 6 shows the framework of computing affective labels for sensor-rich videos leveraging several proposed SVM^{hmm} models and selecting matching soundtracks automatically. Specifically, this consists of two components. Left side in the Figure 6 depicts a music

Figure 6. The framework of multimodal affective computing in ADVISOR (Shah et al., 2014a)

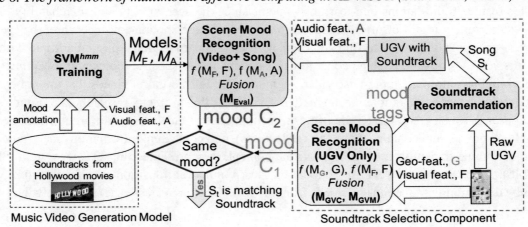

video generate model component that consists of offline SVM^{hmm} models constructed by leveraging visual and audio features of Hollywood movies. 402 video soundtracks (1 min each from the middle of the clip) from Hollywood movies are used from all main genres such as action, comedy, romance, war, horror, and others. Since such video soundtracks are produced by professions and their genres, lyrics, and context are known, emotions (mood tags) elicited by these soundtracks are easy to determine. Authors used the 20 most frequent mood tags from a well-known music website, called Last.fm. These mood tags are divided into four clusters further. For the evaluation of soundtrack selection accuracy, such Hollywood movie soundtracks are annotated with affective labels. The full details of this work are described in the earlier work (Shah et al., 2014a). This work describes that we trained two types of learning models, first, where we used four mood clusters as ground truths, and second, where they used 20 mood tags as ground truth for videos. The reasons for using two types of learning models is to improve the mood tags prediction accuracies. Since increasing the number of classes suffers the prediction accuracy, they perform the prediction in two steps. First, they predict mood clusters. Next, they only consider mood tags from the predicted mood clusters. Experimental results show that the model based on the fusion of geo and visual features gives the best prediction results. Thus, for automatically attaching a soundtrack for an outdoor user-generated video, they first predict the mood tags using the fusion model and next attach soundtracks from the predicted mood tags to the video one by one. Since the model constructed from the model constructed from the fusion of visual and audio features of Hollywood movies predicts mood tags for a music video, they predict mood tags for the video after attaching soundtracks using the music video generation model. Based on the heuristics that if the mood tags predicted by two models are same then they treat the attached soundtrack as a matching soundtrack for the video. Full details of models and experiments are provided in the earlier work (Shah et al., 2014a).

Lecture Video Segmentation

In the modern era, education is also much influenced by the advancements in technologies. Now, teachers use multimedia content to enhance the learning of students and facilitate others who could not attend classes due to some reasons. Thus, there is a true globalization in the modern education system where anyone can learn from video recordings of lectures delivered by experts despite they are miles away. This results in the increasing popularity of the e-learning systems. For instance, many websites as Coursera and MIT Open Course Ware. However, due to the ubiquitous availability of devices (smartphones and cameras) and affordable network infrastructures, a huge amount of lecture videos is accumulated on the web. This results in limitations in e-learning systems since the accessibility and searchability of most lecture video content is still insufficient due to the unscripted and spontaneous speech of the speakers. Moreover, since it is often easy to find a particular video and hard to find a particular topic within the video, it is very desirable to enable people to navigate and access specific topics within lecture videos by performing an automatic topic-wise video segmentation. Furthermore, videos that are not captured in good qualities make this problem even harder. To address this problem, researchers present a multimodal approach (Shah et al., 2015b) that finds transition cues in videos from different modalities such as visual content, textual content (transcripts of lectures), and contextual information (see Figure 7). In order to determine transition cues from the visual content, they presented the ATLAS system (Shah et al., 2014b). ATLAS consists a SVM^{hmm} model that learn temporal transition cues from lecture videos content by determining transitions in videos from the following three classes: (i) when only the speaker

Figure 7. The framework of multimodal lecture video segmentation (Shah et al., 2015b)

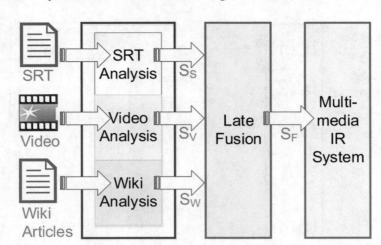

is visible in the video, (ii) when only the slide is visible in the video, and (iii) when both the speaker and slides are visible in the video. Subsequently, considering that contextual information is very useful in determining knowledge structures, they present the TRACE system to automatically perform lecture video segmentation. It is based on a linguistic approach that also exploits Wikipedia texts.

TRACE has the following two main contributions. First, it extracts linguistic-based Wikipedia feature from the contextual information of the video (say, Wikipedia page for the video topic) to segment lecture videos efficiently. Second, it investigates the late fusion of video segmentation results derived from state-of-the-art algorithms that only leverage either transcripts or visual content. Specifically for the late fusion, we combine confidence scores produced by the models constructed from visual, transcriptional, and Wikipedia features. We used videos from VideoLectures.NET and NPTEL for experiments. Full details of experiments are provided in our earlier work (Shah et al., 2014b; Shah et al., 2015b) where the proposed algorithms in the ATLAS and TRACE systems are compared with state-of-the-art algorithms. Figure 8 depicts the framework of computing segment boundaries from lecture videos leveraging the proposed Wikipedia features. The proposed method in TRACE is as follows. First, it creates feature vectors for every Wikipedia blocks and SRT blocks based on noun phrases in the entire Wikipedia texts. There is one block for each Wikipedia topic and 120 words in one SRT block. Next, it computes the similarity between a Wikipedia block and an SRT block using cosine similarity. Finally, the SRT block that has both the maximum cosine similarity and is above a similarity threshold is considered as a segment boundary corresponding to the Wikipedia block. Experimental results confirm that our proposed model outperforms baselines. The proposed approach of leveraging a crowdsourced knowledge base such as Wikipedia in lecture video segmentation work is the first to attempt to segment lecture videos as per the best of our information. Usually, the duration of lecture videos ranges from several minutes to a few hours. Thus, it takes much computing resources and time to extract the visual and audio features from lecture videos. However, the proposed TRACE system is based on a linguistic approach (i.e., text processing). Thus, it does not require the much resources and time to compute visual and audio features from lecture videos. This makes TRACE scalable and fast. Figure 9 depicts segment boundaries derived from different modalities for a sample video.

Figure 8. The framework of computing lecture video segmentation using Wikipedia (Shah et al., 2015b)

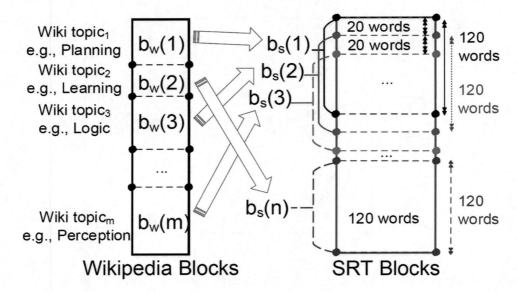

Figure 9. Lecture video segmentation results for a sample lecture video (Shah et al., 2015b)

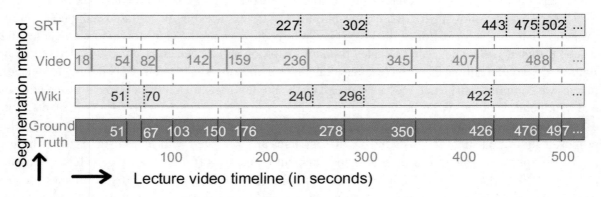

Tag Relevance Computation

Despite a huge amount of multimedia content (both photos and videos) are present on the web, the most of the search engines are text-based. Often search engines represent multimedia content as a bag-of-concepts and index them through keywords (concepts). Moreover, due to a rapid growth of content on the web, it is not feasible to annotate the content manually. This requires an annotation system that automatically annotates keywords (also known as tags) for photos and videos. Furthermore, for an efficient searching and retrieval of multimedia content, it is helpful to rank the annotated tags for photos and videos. To this end, this chapter presents two systems. First, the PROMPT system, that predicts personalized tags for a given photo leveraging personal and social contexts. Second, the CRAFT system, that ranks tags of a given photo based on voting from photo neighbors derived from multimodal information. Figure 10 shows the framework of the CRAFT system. CRAFT determines photo neighbors leveraging multimodal

Figure 10. A multimodal framework of computing tag ranking in CRAFT (Shah et al., 2016d)

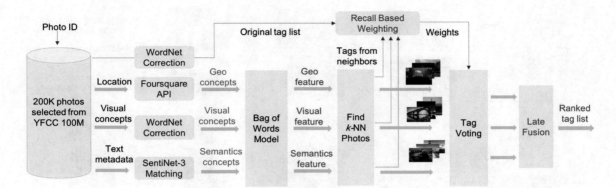

information such as geo, visual, and semantics concepts derived from spatial information, visual content, and textual metadata, respectively. Shah et al., 2016d leveraged the proposed high-level features instead traditional low-level features to rank tags of photos. They evaluated the approach on 200K photos from the YFCC100M dataset, a collection of 100 million photos and videos. They determined geo concepts using Foursquare API that provides a list of geo categories such as *Park, Hotel, Office,* and *Beach* for a given GPS point. Visual concepts are provided as the part of the YFCC100M dataset. Visual tags are automatically generated tags from the visual content of the photos and videos using deep learning models. Finally, semantics concepts are common and common-sense tags from SenticNet-3 that are derived from mapping concepts that are extracted using Semantics parser to SenticNet-3. Leveraging the proposed high-level features, they determine k-nearest neighbors from the dataset and perform tag voting from the neighboring photos. Finally, they perform the late fusion to get the ranked list of tags for photos.

Experimental results confirm that the proposed tag ranking model outperform state-of-the-art models. Full details of CRAFT is provided in the earlier work (Shah et al., 2016d). Figure 11 depicts the working of CRAFT system through a representative seed photo. That is, authors determine neighbors of seed photos from different modalities such as visual, geographical, and textual information. Next, we perform voting on the tags of the photo by the tags of the neighboring photos. Figure 12 shows the original and ranked tags for a few representative photos from the YFCC100M dataset. These photos are chosen randomly. It is evident from results that ranked tags significantly improve the understanding of photos. Voting from neighboring photos also helps in removing non-relevant and noisy tags.

In order to address tag relevance problem, researchers present a tag recommendation system (Shah et al., 2016f) in addition to the tag ranking system because often photos are not tagged with any keywords. Thus, prior to ranking photos, it is good to get a list of recommended tags that can be further ranked based on relevancy. For predicting a list of tags for photos, we present the PROMPT system. Figure 13 shows the framework of our tag recommendation system. It recommends personalized tags for a given photo leveraging personal and social contexts. Specifically, first, it determines a group of users who have similar tagging behavior as the user of the photo, which is very useful in predicting personalized tags. Next, it finds candidate tags from visual content, textual metadata, and tags of neighboring photos, and recommends the five most suitable tags. They initialize scores of the candidate tags using asymmetric tag co-occurrence probabilities and normalized scores of tags after neighbor voting and later perform random walk to promote the tags that have many close neighbors and weaken isolated tags. Finally, we

Figure 11. A representative framework of the CRAFT system using a seed photo (Shah et al., 2016d)

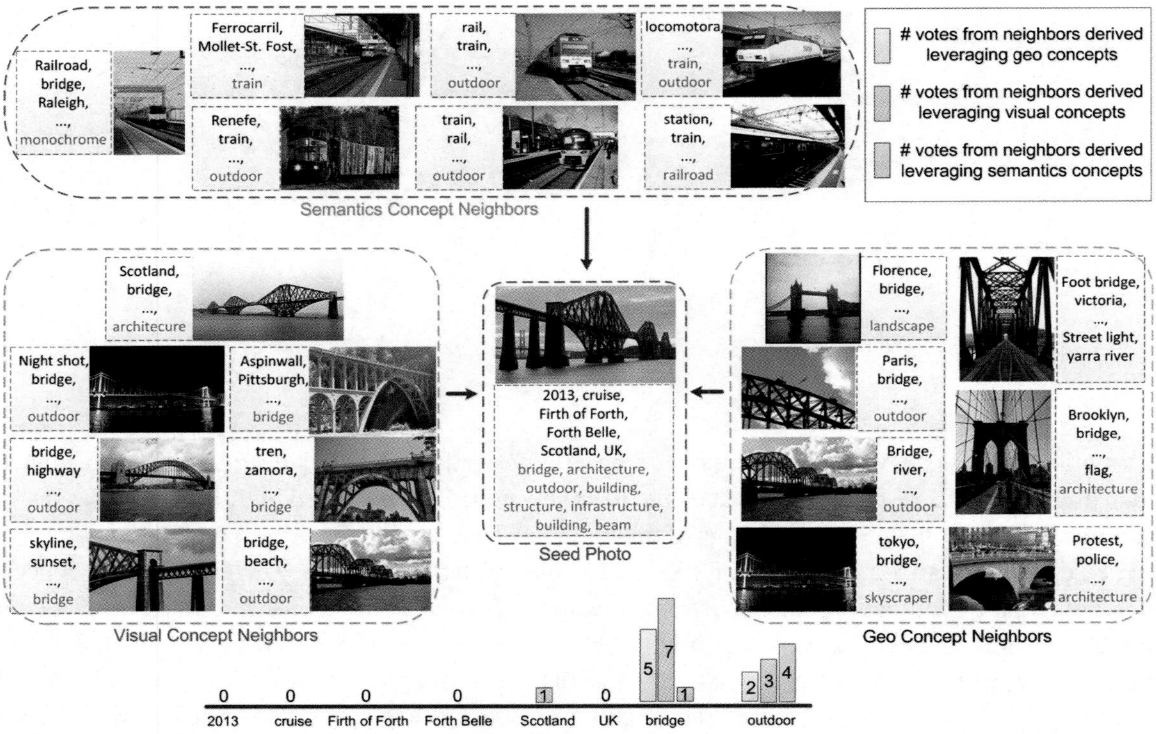

Figure 12. Examples of ranked tags for Flickr photos (Shah et al., 2016d)

Figure 13. The framework of tag recommendation system in PROMPT (Shah et al., 2016f)

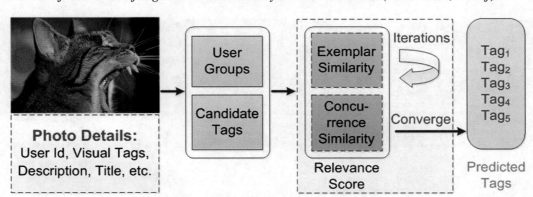

recommend top five user tags to the given photo. Figure 14 depicts the working of the PROMPT system through a representative seed photo. Full details of our approach are described in the earlier work (Shah et al., 2016f). Figure 15 shows the original tags and recommend tags for a few randomly chosen photos from the YFCC100M dataset. Since recommending tags from an endless pool is a NP-hard problem. Thus, for the tag recommendation task, they consider a specific subset of the most frequent 1,540 user tags from the YFCC100M dataset from Flickr. Experimental results confirm that the tag recommendation approach performs well.

FUTURE RESEARCH DIRECTIONS

An event is an activity that takes place in some location at some time and involves some entities (e.g., person, building, and scenery). People often capture these activities through texts (e.g., tweets, blogs,

Figure 14. A representative framework of the PROMPT system using a seed photo (Shah et al., 2016f)

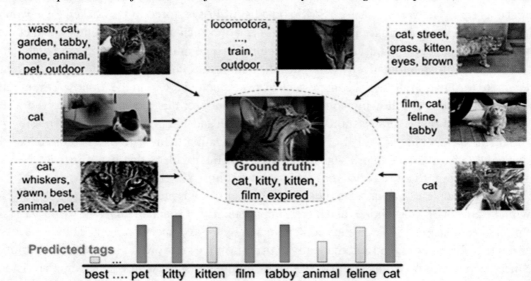

Figure 15. Examples of recommended tags for Flickr photos (Shah et al., 2016f)

and posts), photos, and videos. Moreover, due to affordable network infrastructure and increasing popularity of social media websites, people often share such content on different websites such as Flickr, Facebook, and Twitter. Such content depicts the behaviors of users on the web, which is very useful in providing personalized search, retrieval, and recommendation. Thus, we would like to discover event-specific informative content from social media to facilitate event analysis (Mahata et al., 2015; Mahata and Agarwal, 2012). Mahata and Talburt, 2014 proposed a framework for collecting and managing entity identity information from social media. Since the characteristics of different events are different, in the future we would like to discover event-specific information from different perspectives. This research direction is also inspired by the work of Singh et al., 2010 that present the mining the blogosphere from a socio-political perspective. Moreover, we would like to exploit deep learning techniques to derive useful knowledge structures from the multimedia content since deep neural networks (DNN) have yielded immense success in the areas of computer vision, natural language processing, and speech processing. Thus, DNN-based new text and image representations should be very useful in the analysis of problems (e.g., events) that involves multimedia content.

In the future, we would also like to build SMS (Short Message Service) or MMS (Multimedia Message Service) based event retrieval services. We are inspired by the SMS based FAQ (Frequently Asked Questions) systems (Shaikh et al., 2013a; Shaikh et al., 2013b) to build the SMS/MMS based event retrieval systems. Similar to SMS based FAQ retrieval that retrieves a list of FAQs based on computing similarities scores between the given SMS and a list of FAQs stored in the backend, we would like to retrieve a list of events leveraging multimodal information such as location, content, and contextual information. For instance, say, a user captures a picture at some music concert and send that picture to some event provider that automatically computes the similarities between characteristics of events and the given photo (or other multimedia content such as tweets and videos). In the proposed event retrieval system, there would be the following components: (i) an analyzer that analyzes the received SMS and MMS, (ii) a controller that leverages multimodal information and computes similarities, and (iii) recommender that finally recommends a list of events after correlating them with users' preferences. In the future, we would also like to explore sensor-rich user-generated videos that benefit society such as in news videos uploading (Shah et al., 2016b) and map matching (Yin et al., 2016).

User-generated content such as texts (posts), photos, and videos are ubiquitously available on social media with the advent of smartphones and increasing popularity of social media. Due to this vast amount of content, it is not feasible to search such content manually for any query or event. Thus, it necessitates that such content should be tagged automatically with descriptive keywords or link with some knowledge bases. Since deep neural networks (DNN) have shown immense success in NLP, computer vision, and recommendation, we would like to use DNN technologies. A recent study (Zheng et al., 2017) confirms that DNN technologies are very useful in improving recommendation. Thus, we would like to build a general DNN-based framework that should be able to support all kind of recommendation problems. Furthermore, in the future, we would like to fuse information from multiple modalities efficiently to derive useful knowledge structures.

CONCLUSION

This chapter presented a study on multimodal semantics and affective computing from multimedia content. It discussed several research problems such as: (i) helping in event understanding by proving event summarization, (ii) making user-generated videos more attractive by adding matching soundtracks, (iii) enhancing e-learning by lecture videos segmentation, and (vi) facilitating searching and retrieval by computing tag relevance for photos on social media. Experiments described in the chapter confirm that multimodal information is very useful in deriving knowledge structures from different sources of user-generated multimedia content. Researchers show that multimodal information is useful since different knowledge structures are represented by the different representations of the user-generated multimedia content. Specifically, they emphasized that contextual information in addition to content information is of great use in an efficient semantics and sentiment understanding from the user-generated multimedia. Moreover, this chapter proposed several interesting problems to readers as future research directions.

ACKNOWLEDGMENT

This research is supported by the National Research Foundation, Prime Minister's Office, Singapore under its International Research Centres in Singapore Funding Initiative.

REFERENCES

Anderson, A., Ranghunathan, K., & Vogel, A. (2008). Tagez: Flickr tag recommendation. *Proceedings of the Association for the Advancement of Artificial Intelligence*.

Bhatt, C. A., Popescu-Belis, A., Habibi, M., Ingram, S., Masneri, S., McInnes, F., ... Schreer, O. (2013). Multi-factor segmentation for topic visualization and recommendation: the MUST-VIS system. In *Proceedings of the 21st ACM international conference on Multimedia* (pp. 365-368). ACM.

Cambria, E., Livingstone, A., & Hussain, A. (2012). The hourglass of emotions. *Cognitive behavioural systems*, 144-157.

Cambria, E., Olsher, D., & Rajagopal, D. (2014a). SenticNet 3: a common and common-sense knowledge base for cognition-driven sentiment analysis. *Twenty-eighth AAAI conference on artificial intelligence*.

Cambria, E., Poria, S., Bisio, F., Bajpai, R., & Chaturvedi, I. (2015). The CLSA Model: A Novel Framework for Concept-Level Sentiment Analysis. In *Proceedings of the CICLing* (vol. 2, pp. 3-22). Academic Press. 10.1007/978-3-319-18117-2_1

Cambria, E., Poria, S., Gelbukh, A., & Kwok, K. (2014b). *Sentic API: a common-sense based API for concept-level sentiment analysis.* Academic Press.

Chen, B., Wang, J., Huang, Q., & Mei, T. (2012). Personalized video recommendation through tripartite graph propagation. In *Proceedings of the 20th ACM international conference on Multimedia* (pp. 1133-1136). ACM.

Del Fabro, M., Sobe, A., & Böszörmenyi, L. (2012). Summarization of real-life events based on community-contributed content. In *Proceedings of the Fourth International Conferences on Advances in Multimedia* (pp. 119-126). Academic Press.

Hanjalic, A., & Xu, L. Q. (2005). Affective video content representation and modeling. *Proceedings of the IEEE Transactions on Multimedia, 7*(1), 143–154. doi:10.1109/TMM.2004.840618

Haubold, A., & Kender, J. R. (2005). Augmented segmentation and visualization for presentation videos. In *Proceedings of the 13th annual ACM international conference on Multimedia* (pp. 51–60). ACM; doi:10.1145/1869652.1869662.

Li, X., Snoek, C. G., & Worring, M. (2009). Learning social tag relevance by neighbor voting. *Proceedings of the IEEE Transactions on Multimedia, 11*(7), 1310–1322. doi:10.1109/TMM.2009.2030598

Lin, J. C., Wei, W. L., & Wang, H. M. (2016). DEMV-matchmaker: emotional temporal course representation and deep similarity matching for automatic music video generation. In *Proceedings of the International Conference on Acoustics, Speech and Signal Processing* (pp. 2772-2776). IEEE. 10.1109/ICASSP.2016.7472182

Lin, M., Chau, M., Cao, J., & Nunamaker, J. F. Jr. (2005). Automated video segmentation for lecture videos: A linguistics-based approach. *Proceedings of the International Journal of Technology and Human Interaction, 1*(2), 27–45. doi:10.4018/jthi.2005040102

Liu, D., Hua, X. S., Yang, L., Wang, M., & Zhang, H. J. (2009). Tag ranking. In *Proceedings of the 18th international conference on World Wide Web* (pp. 351-360). ACM. 10.1145/1526709.1526757

Long, R., Wang, H., Chen, Y., Jin, O., & Yu, Y. (2011). Towards Effective Event Detection, Tracking and Summarization on Microblog Data. In *Proceedings of the Web-Age Information Management* (pp. 652-663). Academic Press. 10.1007/978-3-642-23535-1_55

Mahata, D., & Agarwal, N. (2012). What does everybody know? Identifying event-specific sources from social media. In *Computational Aspects of Social Networks (CASoN), 2012 Fourth International Conference on* (pp. 63-68). IEEE. 10.1109/CASoN.2012.6412379

Mahata, D., & Talburt, J. (2014). A Framework for Collecting and Managing Entity Identity Information from Social Media. In *19th MIT International Conference on Information Quality* (pp. 216-233). Academic Press.

Mahata, D., Talburt, J. R., & Singh, V. K. (2015). From Chirps to Whistles: Discovering Event-specific Informative Content from Twitter. In *Proceedings of the ACM Web Science Conference* (p. 17). ACM. 10.1145/2786451.2786476

Miller, G. A. (1995). WordNet: A lexical database for English. *Communications of the ACM, 38*(11), 39–41. doi:10.1145/219717.219748

Moxley, E., Kleban, J., Xu, J., & Manjunath, B. S. (2009, June). Not all tags are created equal: Learning Flickr tag semantics for global annotation. In *Proceedings of the IEEE International Conference on Multimedia and Expo.* (pp. 1452-1455). IEEE. 10.1109/ICME.2009.5202776

Nwana, A. O., & Chen, T. (2016). Who ordered this?: Exploiting implicit user tag order preferences for personalized image tagging. In Proceedings of the International Conference on Multimedia & Expo Workshops, 2016 (pp. 1-6). IEEE. doi:10.1109/ICMEW.2016.7574753

Poria, S., Cambria, E., Gelbukh, A., Bisio, F., & Hussain, A. (2015). Sentiment data flow analysis by means of dynamic linguistic patterns. *IEEE Computational Intelligence Magazine, 10*(4), 26–36. doi:10.1109/MCI.2015.2471215

Poria, S., Gelbukh, A., Cambria, E., Hussain, A., & Huang, G. B. (2014). EmoSenticSpace: A novel framework for affective common-sense reasoning. *Knowledge-Based Systems, 69*, 108–123. doi:10.1016/j. knosys.2014.06.011

Poria, S., Gelbukh, A., Cambria, E., Yang, P., Hussain, A., & Durrani, T. (2012b). Merging SenticNet and WordNet-Affect emotion lists for sentiment analysis. In *Signal Processing (ICSP), 2012 IEEE 11th International Conference on* (Vol. 2, pp. 1251-1255). IEEE. doi:10.1145/3003421.3003426

Poria, S., Gelbukh, A., Hussain, A., Howard, N., Das, D., & Bandyopadhyay, S. (2013). Enhanced SenticNet with affective labels for concept-based opinion mining. *IEEE Intelligent Systems, 28*(2), 31–38. doi:10.1109/MIS.2013.4

Poria, S., Gelbukhs, A., Cambria, E., Das, D., & Bandyopadhyay, S. (2012a). Enriching SenticNet polarity scores through semi-supervised fuzzy clustering. In *Data Mining Workshops (ICDMW), 2012 IEEE 12th International Conference on* (pp. 709-716). IEEE.

Rae, A., Sigurbjörnsson, B., & van Zwol, R. (2010). Improving tag recommendation using social networks. In *Proceedings of the Adaptivity, Personalization and Fusion of Heterogeneous Information* (pp. 92-99). Academic Press.

Rahmani, H., Piccart, B., Fierens, D., & Blockeel, H. (2010). Three complementary approaches to context aware movie recommendation. In *Proceedings of the Workshop on Context-Aware Movie Recommendation* (pp. 57-60). ACM.

Rawat, Y. S., & Kankanhalli, M. S. (2016). ConTagNet: exploiting user context for image tag recommendation. In *Proceedings of the ACM on Multimedia Conference* (pp. 1102-1106). ACM. 10.1145/2964284.2984068

Schedl, M., & Schnitzer, D. (2014). Location-aware music artist recommendation. In *Proceedings of the International Conference on Multimedia Modeling* (pp. 205-213). Springer.

Scherp, A., & Mezaris, V. (2014). Survey on modeling and indexing events in multimedia. *Proceedings of the Multimedia Tools and Applications, 70*(1), 7–23. doi:10.100711042-013-1427-7

Shah, R., & Zimmermann, R. (2017). *Multimodal Analysis of User-Generated Multimedia Content.* Springer. doi:10.1007/978-3-319-61807-4

Shah, R. R. (2016c). Multimodal Analysis of User-Generated Content in Support of Social Media Applications. In *Proceedings of the 2016 ACM on International Conference on Multimedia Retrieval* (pp. 423-426). ACM. 10.1145/2911996.2912032

Shah, R. R. (2016e). Multimodal-based Multimedia Analysis, Retrieval, and Services in Support of Social Media Applications. In *Proceedings of the 2016 ACM on Multimedia Conference* (pp. 1425-1429). ACM. 10.1145/2964284.2971471

Shah, R. R., Hefeeda, M., Zimmermann, R., Harras, K., Hsu, C. H., & Yu, Y. (2016b). NEWSMAN: Uploading Videos over Adaptive Middleboxes to News Servers in Weak Network Infrastructures. In *International Conference on Multimedia Modeling* (pp. 100-113). Springer. 10.1007/978-3-319-27671-7_9

Shah, R. R., Samanta, A., Gupta, D., Yu, Y., Tang, S., & Zimmermann, R. (2016f). PROMPT: Personalized User Tag Recommendation for Social Media Photos Leveraging Personal and Social Contexts. In IEEE International Symposium on Multimedia (ISM), 2016 (pp. 486-492). IEEE. doi:10.1109/ISM.2016.0109

Shah, R. R., Shaikh, A. D., Yu, Y., Geng, W., Zimmermann, R., & Wu, G. (2015a). Eventbuilder: Real-time multimedia event summarization by visualizing social media. In Proceedings of the 23rd ACM international conference on Multimedia (pp. 185-188). ACM. doi:10.1145/2733373.2809932

Shah, R. R., Yu, Y., Shaikh, A. D., Tang, S., & Zimmermann, R. (2014b). ATLAS: automatic temporal segmentation and annotation of lecture videos based on modelling transition time. In Proceedings of the 22nd ACM international conference on Multimedia (pp. 209-212). ACM. doi:10.1145/2647868.2656407

Shah, R. R., Yu, Y., Shaikh, A. D., & Zimmermann, R. (2015b). TRACE: Linguistic-Based Approach for Automatic Lecture Video Segmentation Leveraging Wikipedia Texts. In IEEE International Symposium on Multimedia (ISM), 2015 (pp. 217-220). IEEE. doi:10.1109/ISM.2015.18

Shah, R. R., Yu, Y., Tang, S., Satoh, S. I., Verma, A., & Zimmermann, R. (2016d). Concept-Level Multimodal Ranking of Flickr Photo Tags via Recall Based Weighting. In *Proceedings of the 2016 ACM Workshop on Multimedia COMMONS* (pp. 19-26). ACM. 10.1145/2983554.2983555

Shah, R. R., Yu, Y., Verma, A., Tang, S., Shaikh, A. D., & Zimmermann, R. (2016a). Leveraging multimodal information for event summarization and concept-level sentiment analysis. *Knowledge-Based Systems*, *108*, 102–109. doi:10.1016/j.knosys.2016.05.022

Shah, R. R., Yu, Y., & Zimmermann, R. (2014a). Advisor: Personalized video soundtrack recommendation by late fusion with heuristic rankings. In *Proceedings of the 22nd ACM international conference on Multimedia* (pp. 607-616). ACM. 10.1145/2647868.2654919

Shah, R. R., Yu, Y., & Zimmermann, R. (2014c). User preference-aware music video generation based on modeling scene moods. In *Proceedings of the 5th ACM Multimedia Systems Conference* (pp. 156-159). ACM. 10.1145/2557642.2579372

Shaikh, A. D., Jain, M., Rawat, M., Shah, R. R., & Kumar, M. (2013a). Improving accuracy of sms based faq retrieval system. In *Multilingual Information Access in South Asian Languages* (pp. 142–156). Berlin: Springer. doi:10.1007/978-3-642-40087-2_14

Shaikh, A. D., Shah, R. R., & Shaikh, R. (2013b). SMS based FAQ retrieval for Hindi, English and Malayalam. In *Post-Proceedings of the 4th and 5th Workshops of the Forum for Information Retrieval Evaluation* (p. 9). ACM.

Singh, V. K., Mahata, D., & Adhikari, R. (2010). Mining the blogosphere from a socio-political perspective. In *Proceedings of the International Conference on Computer Information Systems and Industrial Management Applications*, (pp. 365-370). IEEE. 10.1109/CISIM.2010.5643634

Snoek, C. G., Worring, M., & Smeulders, A. W. (2005). Early versus late fusion in semantic video analysis. In *Proceedings of the 13th annual ACM international conference on Multimedia* (pp. 399-402). ACM. 10.1145/1101149.1101236

Wang, X., Jia, Y., Chen, R., & Zhou, B. (2015). Ranking User Tags in Micro-Blogging Website. In *Proceedings of the 2nd International Conference on Information Science and Control Engineering*, (pp. 400-403). IEEE.

Wang, Y., & Kankanhalli, M. S. (2015, May). Tweeting cameras for event detection. In *Proceedings of the 24th International Conference on World Wide Web* (pp. 1231-1241). International World Wide Web Conferences Steering Committee. ACM. 10.1145/2736277.2741634

Wu, L., Yang, L., Yu, N., & Hua, X. S. (2009). Learning to tag. In *Proceedings of the 18th international conference on World Wide Web* (pp. 361-370). ACM. 10.1145/1526709.1526758

Xiao, J., Zhou, W., Li, X., Wang, M., & Tian, Q. (2012). Image tag re-ranking by coupled probability transition. In *Proceedings of the 20th ACM International Conference on Multimedia* (pp. 849-852). ACM. 10.1145/2393347.2396328

Yamamoto, N., Ogata, J., & Ariki, Y. (2003). Topic segmentation and retrieval system for lecture videos based on spontaneous speech recognition. *Proceedings of the INTERSPEECH*.

Yin, Y., Shah, R. R., & Zimmermann, R. (2016). A general feature-based map matching framework with trajectory simplification. In *Proceedings of the 7th ACM SIGSPATIAL International Workshop on GeoStreaming* (p. 7). ACM.

Zaharieva, M., Zeppelzauer, M., & Breiteneder, C. (2013). Automated social event detection in large photo collections. In *Proceedings of the Third ACM International Conference on Multimedia Retrieval* (pp. 167-174). ACM. 10.1145/2461466.2461495

Zhang, J., Wang, S., & Huang, Q. (2017). Location-based parallel tag completion for geo-tagged social image retrieval. *Proceedings of the ACM Transactions on Intelligent Systems and Technology*, 8(3), 38. 10.1145/3001593

Zheng, L., Noroozi, V., & Yu, P. S. (2017). Joint deep modeling of users and items using reviews for recommendation. In *Proceedings of the Tenth ACM International Conference on Web Search and Data Mining* (pp. 425-434). ACM. 10.1145/3018661.3018665

Zhuang, J., & Hoi, S. C. (2011). A two-view learning approach for image tag ranking. In *Proceedings of the fourth ACM international conference on Web search and data mining* (pp. 625-634). ACM. 10.1145/1935826.1935913

Compilation of References

Abdel-Maksoud, E., Elmogy, M., & Al-Awadi, R. (2015). Brain tumor segmentation based on a hybrid clustering technique. *Egyptian Informatics Journal, 16*(1), 71–81. doi:10.1016/j.eij.2015.01.003

Achanta, R., Hemami, S. S., Estrada, F. J., & Süsstrunk, S. (2009). Frequency-tuned salient region detection. In CVPR (pp. 1597-1604). IEEE Computer Society. doi:10.1109/CVPR.2009.5206596

Acharyya, M. a. (2001). Adaptive Basis Selection for Multitexture Segmentation by M-band wavelet packet frames. *International Conference on Image Processing, 2*, 622-625.

Acharyya, M. a. (2007). Image Segmentation using Wavelet Packet Frames and Neuro Fuzzy Tools. Vol 5, no 4. *International Journal of Computational Cognition, 5*(4), 27–43.

Acharyya, M., & Kundu, M. K. (2001). An Adaptive Approach to Unsupervised Texture Segmentation Using M-Band Wavelet. *Signal Processing, 81*(7), 1337–1356. doi:10.1016/S0165-1684(00)00278-4

Acharyya, M., & Kundu, M. K. (2008). Extraction of noise Tolerant, Gray-scale Transform and Rotation Invariant Features for Texture Segmentation using Wavelet Frames. *Multiresolution and Information Processing., 6*(3), 391–417. doi:10.1142/S0219691308002252

Agrawal, S., Panda, R., Bhuyan, S., & Panigrahi, B. K. (2013). Tsallis entropy based optimal multilevel thresholding using cuckoo search algorithm. *Swarm and Evolutionary Computation, 11*, 16–30. doi:10.1016/j.swevo.2013.02.001

Aguilar, G., Sanchez, G., Toscano, K., Nakano, M., & Perez, H. (2007). Multimodal biometric system using fingerprint. *Intellectuality Advancement System. International Conference on*, 145–150.

Aissaoui, A., Martinet, J., & Djeraba, C. (2012, September). 3D face reconstruction in a binocular passive stereoscopic system using face properties. In *Image Processing (ICIP), 2012 19th IEEE International Conference on* (pp. 1789-1792). IEEE.

Aja-Fern'andez, S., Jos'eEst'epar, R.S., Alberola-L'opez, C., Westin, C. F. (2006). Image Quality Assessment based on Local Variance. *28th IEEE EMBS Annual International Conference*, 4815-4818. 10.1109/IEMBS.2006.259516

Ali, M. R. (2004). Realization of the Contrast Limited Adaptive Histogram Equalization (CLAHE) for Real-Time Image Enhancement. *Journal of VLSI Signal Processing Systems for Signal, Image and Video Technology, 38*, 35-44.

Alonso-Fernandez, F., Fierrez, J., Ramos, D., & Gonzalez-Rodriguez, J. (2010). Quality-based conditional processing in multibiometrics: Application to sensor interoperability. *IEEE Transactions on Systems, Man, and Cybernetics. Part A, Systems and Humans, 40*(6), 1168–1179. doi:10.1109/TSMCA.2010.2047498

Al-Rababah & Al-Marghirani. (2016). Implementation of Novel Medical Image Compression Using Artificial Intelligence. IJACSA, 7(5).

American Academy of Dermatology. (n.d.). Retrieved from https://www.aad.org/media/stats/conditions/skin-cancer

AMIPCI. (2016). *Estudio Comercio Electrónico en México 2016*. Retrieved from: https://amipci.org.mx/images/Estudio_Ecommerce_AMIPCI_2016_by_comScore_Publica2.pdf

Amjoun, R., & Straßer, W. (2009). Single-rate near lossless compression of animated geometry. *Computer Aided Design*, *41*(10), 10. doi:10.1016/j.cad.2009.02.013

Anandakumar, H., & Umamaheswari, K. (2017a). Supervised machine learning techniques in cognitive radio networks during cooperative spectrum handovers. *Cluster Computing, 20*(2), 1505–1515. doi:10.100710586-017-0798-3

Anandakumar, H., & Umamaheswari, K. (2017b). An Efficient Optimized Handover in Cognitive Radio Networks using Cooperative Spectrum Sensing. *Intelligent Automation & Soft Computing,* 1–8. doi:10.1080/10798587.2017.1364931

Anandakumar, H, & Umamaheswari, K. (2017c). A bio-inspired swarm intelligence technique for social aware cognitive radio handovers. *Computers & Electrical Engineering*. doi:10.1016/j.compeleceng.2017.09.016

Anderson, A., Ranghunathan, K., & Vogel, A. (2008). Tagez: Flickr tag recommendation. *Proceedings of the Association for the Advancement of Artificial Intelligence*.

Andersson, T., Gunnar, L., Lenz, R., & Magnus, B. (2013). Modified Gradient Search for Level Set Based Image Segmentation. *IEEE Transactions on Image Processing*, *22*(2), 621–630. doi:10.1109/TIP.2012.2220148 PMID:23014748

Anikin, V. I., & Karmanov, A. A. (2014). The training of the artificial neural network Kohonen's self-organizing cellular automaton. *Información Tecnológica*, *11*, 73–80.

Anil, K. (2004). An Introduction to Biometric Recognition. *IEEE Transactions on Circuits and Systems for Video Technology*, *14*(1), 4–20. doi:10.1109/TCSVT.2003.818349

Argo, J. J., Dahl, D. W., & Morales, A. C. (2006). Consumer contamination: How consumers react to products touched by others. *Journal of Marketing*, *70*(2), 81–94. doi:10.1509/jmkg.70.2.81

Argo, J. J., Dahl, D. W., & Morales, A. C. (2008). Positive consumer contagion: Responses to attractive others in retail context. *JMR, Journal of Marketing Research*, *45*(6), 690–701. doi:10.1509/jmkr.45.6.690

Arulmurugan, R., Sabarmathi, K. R., & Anandakumar, H. (2017). Classification of sentence level sentiment analysis using cloud machine learning techniques. *Cluster Computing*. doi:10.100710586-017-1200-1

Ashwini, K., & Vincent, D. R. (2017). Trust in e-commerce. *Imperial Journal of Interdisciplinary Research*, *3*(5), 1637–1639.

Aspert, N., Cruz, D. S., & Ebrahimi, T. (2002). MESH: measuring errors between surfaces using the Hausdorff distance. In ICME (pp. 705-708). IEEE Computer Society.

Balaji, M. S., Raghavan, S., & Jha, S. (2011). Role of tactile and visual inputs in product evaluation: A multisensory perspective. *Asia Pacific Journal of Marketing and Logistics*, *23*(4), 513–530. doi:10.1108/13555851111165066

Balan, N. S., Kumar, A. S., Raja, N. S. M., & Rajinikanth, V. (2016). Optimal multilevel image thresholding to improve the visibility of plasmodium sp. in blood smear images. *Advances in Intelligent Systems and Computing*, *397*, 563–571. doi:10.1007/978-81-322-2671-0_54

Bauer, S., Wiest, R., Nolte, L. P., & Reyes, M. (2013). A survey of MRI-based medical image analysis for brain tumor studies. *Physics in Medicine and Biology*, *58*(13), 97–129. doi:10.1088/0031-9155/58/13/R97 PMID:23743802

Bazeille, S., Quidu, I., & Jaulin, L. (2012). Color-based underwater object recognition using water light attenuation. *Intelligent Service Robotics, 5*(2), 109–118. doi:10.100711370-012-0105-3

Beeler, T., Hahn, F., Bradley, D., Bickel, B., Beardsley, P., Gotsman, C., ... Gross, M. (2011, August). High-quality passive facial performance capture using anchor frames. *ACM Transactions on Graphics, 30*(4), 75. doi:10.1145/2010324.1964970

Berman, D., Treibitz, & Avidan, S. (2016). Non-local Image Dehazing. *CVPR*, 27-30.

Besbes, F., Trichili, H., & Solaiman, B. (2008). Multimodal biometric system based on fingerprint identification and iris recognition. *Information and Communication Technologies: From Theory to Applications, 2008. ICTTA 2008. 3rd IEEE International Conference on*, 1–5. 10.1109/ICTTA.2008.4530129

Bezdek, J. C. (1981). *Pattern Recognition with Fuzzy Objective Function Algorithms*. New York: Plenum Press. doi:10.1007/978-1-4757-0450-1

Bezdek, J. C., Tsao, E. C.-K., & Pal, N. R. (1992). Fuzzy Kohonen Clustering Networks. *IEEE Transactions on Fuzzy Systems*, 1035–1043.

Bhadouria, V. S., Ghoshal, D., & Siddiqi, A. H. (2014). A new approach for high density saturated impulse noise removal using decision-based coupled window median filter. *Signal, Image and Video Processing, 8*(1), 71–84. doi:10.100711760-013-0487-5

Bhandari, A. K., Kumar, A., & Singh, G. K. (2015). Modified artificial bee colony based computationally efficient multilevel thresholding for satellite image segmentation using Kapur's, Otsu and Tsallis functions. *Expert Systems with Applications, 42*(3), 1573–1601. doi:10.1016/j.eswa.2014.09.049

Bhattacharjee, A., Saggi, M., Balasubramaniam, R., Tayal, A., & Kumar, A. (2009). Decison theory based multimodal biometric authentication system using wavelet transform. *Machine Learning and Cybernetics, 2009 IEEE International Conference on, 4*, 2336–2342. 10.1109/ICMLC.2009.5212174

Bhatt, C. A., Popescu-Belis, A., Habibi, M., Ingram, S., Masneri, S., McInnes, F., ... Schreer, O. (2013). Multi-factor segmentation for topic visualization and recommendation: the MUST-VIS system. In *Proceedings of the 21st ACM international conference on Multimedia* (pp. 365-368). ACM.

Bhotika, R., Fleet, D. J., & Kutulakos, K. N. (2002, May). A probabilistic theory of occupancy and emptiness. In *European conference on computer vision* (pp. 112-130). Springer. 10.1007/3-540-47977-5_8

Bhuiyan, A. H., Azad, I., & Uddin, K. (2013). Image Processing for Skin Cancer Features Extraction. *International Journal of Scientific & Engineering Research, Vol, 4*, 1–6.

Bian, Z., & Tong, R. (2011). Feature-preserving mesh denoising based on vertices classification. *Computer Aided Geometric Design, 28*(1), 50–64. doi:10.1016/j.cagd.2010.10.001

Birgit, M., & Stefan, P. (2012). Comparing Active Contours For The Segmentation of Biomedical Images. *9th IEEE International Symposium on Biomedical Imaging (ISBI)*, 736-739.

Bodyanskiy, Ye., Gorshkov, Ye., Kolodyaznhiy, V., & Stephan, A. (2005). Combined learning algorithm for a selforginizing map with fuzzy inference. *Proceedings of Computational intelligence, theory and applications: International Conference 8th Fuzzy Days in Dortmund, 33*, 641-650.

Bodyansky, E. V., & Rudenko, O. G. (2004). *Artificial neural networks: architectures, learning, applications*. Kharkov, Ukraine: TELETECH.

Bohr, N. (1961). *Atomic physics and human knowledge*. Moscow, Russia: Mir.

Bolin, M. R., & Meyer, G. W. (1998). A Perceptually Based Adaptive Sampling Algorithm. In S. Cunningham, W. Bransford & M. F. Cohen (Eds.), SIGGRAPH (pp. 299-309). ACM. doi:10.1145/280814.280924

Bonfort, T., & Sturm, P. (2003, October). Voxel carving for specular surfaces. In *9th IEEE International Conference on Computer Vision (ICCV'03)* (Vol. 1, pp. 691-696). IEEE Computer Society.

Borisov, V. V., Kruglov, V. V., & Fedulov, A. S. (2012). *Fuzzy models and networks*. Moscow, Russia: Telecom.

Borsdorf, A., Raupach, R., Flohr, T., & Hornegger, J. (2008). Wavelet based noise reduction in CT-images using correlation analysis. *IEEE Transactions on Medical Imaging*, 27(12), 1685–1703. doi:10.1109/TMI.2008.923983 PMID:19033085

Boulos, F., Parrein, B., Le Callet, P., & Hands, D. (2009). Perceptual effects of packet loss on H.264/AVC encoded videos. VPQM workshop.

Boykov, Y., & Funka-Lea, G. (2006). Graph Cuts and Efficient N-D Image Segmentation. *International Journal of Computer Vision*, 70(2), 109–131. doi:10.100711263-006-7934-5

Bradley, A. P., & Stentiford, F. W. M. (2002). JPEG 2000 and region of interest coding. Digital Image Computing: Techniques and Applications (DICTA'02), 303-308

Brain Tumor Database (BraTS-MICCAI). (n.d.). Retrieved from http://hal.inria.fr/hal-00935640

Brenner. (2007). Computed Tomography an Increasing Source of Radiation Exposure. *The New England Journal of Medicine*.

Bresson, X., Esedoḡlu, S., Vandergheynst, P., Thiran, J. P., & Osher, S. (2007). Fast global minimization of the active contour/snake model. *Journal of Mathematical Imaging and Vision*, 28(2), 151–167. doi:10.100710851-007-0002-0

Broadhurst, A., Drummond, T. W., & Cipolla, R. (2001). A probabilistic framework for space carving. In *Computer Vision, 2001. ICCV 2001. Proceedings. Eighth IEEE International Conference on* (Vol. 1, pp. 388-393). IEEE. 10.1109/ICCV.2001.937544

Bryman, A. (1984). The debate about quantitative and qualitative research: A question of method or epistemology? *The British Journal of Sociology*, 35(1), 75–92. doi:10.2307/590553

Buades, A., Coll, B., & Morel, J.-M. (2005). A Non-Local Algorithm for Image Denoising. *Proceedings of the 2005 IEEE Computer Society Conference on Computer Vision and Pattern Recognition (CVPR'05)*, 2, 60–65. 10.1109/CVPR.2005.38

Buchsbaum, G. (1980). An analytical derivation of visual nonlinearity. *IEEE Transactions on Biomedical Engineering*, 27(5), 237–242. doi:10.1109/TBME.1980.326628 PMID:7380439

Bulbul, A., Çapin, T. K., Lavoué, G., & Preda, M. (2011). Assessing Visual Quality of 3-D Polygonal Models. *IEEE Signal Processing Magazine*, 28(6), 80–90. doi:10.1109/MSP.2011.942466

Buseman, S., Mouchawar, J., Calonge, N., & Byers, T. (2003). Mammography screening matters for young women with breast carcinoma. *Cancer*, 97(2), 352–358. doi:10.1002/cncr.11050 PMID:12518359

Cambria, E., Livingstone, A., & Hussain, A. (2012). The hourglass of emotions. *Cognitive behavioural systems*, 144-157.

Cambria, E., Poria, S., Bisio, F., Bajpai, R., & Chaturvedi, I. (2015). The CLSA Model: A Novel Framework for Concept-Level Sentiment Analysis. In *Proceedings of the CICLing* (vol. 2, pp. 3-22). Academic Press. 10.1007/978-3-319-18117-2_1

Cambria, E., Olsher, D., & Rajagopal, D. (2014a). SenticNet 3: a common and common-sense knowledge base for cognition-driven sentiment analysis. *Twenty-eighth AAAI conference on artificial intelligence*.

Cambria, E., Poria, S., Gelbukh, A., & Kwok, K. (2014b). *Sentic API: a common-sense based API for concept-level sentiment analysis*. Academic Press.

Cao, C., Bradley, D., Zhou, K., & Beeler, T. (2015). Real-time high-fidelity facial performance capture. *ACM Transactions on Graphics, 34*(4), 46. doi:10.1145/2766943

Cao, Y., Hao, X., & Xia, S. (2009). *An improved region-growing algorithm for mammographic mass segmentation. MIPPR 2009: Medical Imaging.* Parallel Processing of Images, and Optimization Techniques. doi:10.1117/12.833044

Caselles, V., Kimmel, R., & Sapiro, G. (1995). *Geodesic active contours. Proc. IEEE Int. Conf. Comput. Vis.*

Centers for Disease Control and Prevention. (2017). Retrieved from http://www.cdc.gov/cancer/skin/statistics/race.htm

Chack, S., & Sharma, P. (2015). An improved region based active contour model for medical image segmentation. *International Journal of Signal Processing. Image Processing and Pattern Recognition, 8*(1), 115–124. doi:10.14257/ijsip.2015.8.1.12

Chaddad, A., & Tanougast, C. (2016). Quantitative evaluation of robust skull stripping and tumor detection applied to axial MR images. *Brain Informatics, 3*(1), 53–61. doi:10.100740708-016-0033-7 PMID:27747598

Chang, C. I., Du, Y., Wang, J., Guo, S. M., & Thouin, P. D. (2006): Survey and comparative analysis of entropy and relative entropy thresholding techniques. *IEE Proceedings - Vision, Image and Signal Processing, 153*, 837-850. 10.1049/ip-vis:20050032

Chang, C. I., Chen, K., Wang, J., & Althouse, M. J. G. (1994). A Relative Entropy-Based approach to Image thresholding. *Pattern Recognition, Vol, 27*(9), 1275–1289. doi:10.1016/0031-3203(94)90011-6

Chan, T. F., Esedoglu, S., & Nikolova, M. (2006). Algorithms for finding global minimizers of image segmentation and denoising models. *SIAM Journal on Applied Mathematics, 66*(5), 1632–1648. doi:10.1137/040615286

Chan, T. F., & Vese, L. A. (2001). Active contours without edges. *IEEE Transactions on Image Processing, 10*(2), 266–277. doi:10.1109/83.902291 PMID:18249617

Charpiat, G., Keriven, R., Pons, J.-P., & Faugeras, O. (2005). Designing spatially coherent minimizing flows for variational problems based on active contours. Proc. IEEE Int. Conf. Comput. Vis., (2), 1403–1408.

Chen, H. C., & Wang, S. J. Visible colour difference-based quantitative evaluation of colour segmentation. *IEE Proceedings - Vision, Image and Signal Processing, 153*, 598-609. 10.1049/ip-vis:20045221

Chen, Q., & Medioni, G. (1999). A volumetric stereo matching method: Application to image-based modeling. In *Computer Vision and Pattern Recognition, 1999. IEEE Computer Society Conference on.* (Vol. 1, pp. 29-34). IEEE.

Chen. (1994). Subband analysis and synthesis of volumetric medical images using wavelet. *Visual Communication and Image Processing, 2306*(3), 1544–1555.

Chen, B., Wang, J., Huang, Q., & Mei, T. (2012). Personalized video recommendation through tripartite graph propagation. In *Proceedings of the 20th ACM international conference on Multimedia* (pp. 1133-1136). ACM.

Cheng, H. D., Shi, X. J., Min, R., Hu, L. M., Cai, X. P., & Du, H. N. (2006). Approaches for automated detection and classification of masses in mammograms. *Pattern Recognition, 39*(4), 646–668. doi:10.1016/j.patcog.2005.07.006

Chen, T., & Wu, H. R. (2001). Adaptive impulse detection using center-weighted median filters. *IEEE Signal Processing Letters, 8*(1), 1–3. doi:10.1109/97.889633

Chen, X., Zeng, X., Koehl, L., Tao, X., & Boulenguez-Phippen, J. (2014). Optimization of human perception on virtual garments by modeling the relation between fabric properties and sensory descriptors using intelligent techniques. In *International Conference on Information Processing and Management of Uncertainty in Knowledge-Based Systems* (pp. 606-615). Springer. 10.1007/978-3-319-08855-6_61

Chen, Y., Wang, Y., & Yang, B. (2006). Evolving Hierarchical RBF Neural Networks for Breast Cancer Detection. *Lecture Notes in Computer Science, 4234*, 137–144. doi:10.1007/11893295_16

Cherabier, I., Hane, C., Oswald, M. R., & Pollefeys, M. (2016, October). Multi-label semantic 3d reconstruction using voxel blocks. In *3D Vision (3DV), 2016 Fourth International Conference on* (pp. 601-610). IEEE.

Cheraghian, A., Faez, K., Dastmalchi, H., & Oskuie, F. B. (2011). An efficient multimodal face recognition method robust to pose variation. *Computers & Informatics (ISCI), 2011 IEEE Symposium on*, 431–435. 10.1109/ISCI.2011.5958954

Chien, C. H., & Aggarwal, J. K. (1984). A volume/surface representation. In *Proceedings of the International Conference on Pattern Recognition* (pp. 817-820). Academic Press.

Chien, C. H., & Aggarwal, J. K. (1986). Volume/surface octrees for the representation of three-dimensional objects. *Computer Vision Graphics and Image Processing, 36*(1), 100–113. doi:10.1016/S0734-189X(86)80031-7

Chien, C. L., & Tseng, D. C. (2011). Colour image enhancement with exact HIS colour model. Int. *J. of Innovative Computing, Information and Control, 7*, 6691–6710.

Choi, S., Zhou, Q. Y., & Koltun, V. (2015). Robust reconstruction of indoor scenes. In *Proceedings of the IEEE Conference on Computer Vision and Pattern Recognition* (pp. 5556-5565). IEEE.

Cho, J.-W., Prost, R., & Jung, H.-Y. (2007). An Oblivious Watermarking for 3-D Polygonal Meshes Using Distribution of Vertex Norms. *IEEE Transactions on Signal Processing, 55*(1), 142–155. doi:10.1109/TSP.2006.882111

Cho, S. S., & Workman, J. J. (2011). Gender, fashion innovativeness and opinion leadership, and need for touch: Effects on multi-channel choice and touch/non-touch preference in clothing shopping. *Journal of Fashion Marketing and Management, 15*(3), 363–382. doi:10.1108/13612021111151941

Chua, L. O., & Yang, L. (1988a). Cellular neural networks. Theory. IEEE Transactions on Circuits and Systems, 10, 1257-1272. doi:10.1109/ISCAS.1988.15089

Ciatto, S., Del Turco, M. R., Risso, G., Catarzi, S., Bonardi, R., Viterbo, V., ... Indovina, P. L. (2003). Comparison of standard reading and computer aided detection (CAD) on a national proficiency test of screening mammography. *European Journal of Radiology, 45*(2), 135–138. doi:10.1016/S0720-048X(02)00011-6 PMID:12536093

Cignoni, P., Rocchini, C., & Scopigno, R. (1998). Metro: Measuring Error on Simplified Surfaces. *Computer Graphics Forum, 17*(2), 167–174. doi:10.1111/1467-8659.00236

Citrin, A., Stem, D. E. Jr, Spangenberg, E. R., & Clark, M. J. (2003). Consumer need for tactile input: An internet retailing challenge. *Journal of Business Research, 56*(11), 915–922. doi:10.1016/S0148-2963(01)00278-8

Cohen, L. D. (1991). On active contour models and balloons. *CVGIP. Image Understanding, 53*(2), 211–218. doi:10.1016/1049-9660(91)90028-N

Collins, R. T. (1996, June). A space-sweep approach to true multi-image matching. In *Computer Vision and Pattern Recognition, 1996. Proceedings CVPR'96, 1996 IEEE Computer Society Conference on* (pp. 358-363). IEEE. 10.1109/CVPR.1996.517097

Conti, V., Milici, G., Ribino, P., Sorbello, F., & Vitabile, S. (2007). Fuzzy fusion in multimodal biometric systems. *Springer International Conference on Knowledge-Based and Intelligent Information and Engineering Systems*, 108–115.

Coren, S., Ward, L. M., & Enns, J. T. (2003). *Sensation and Perception.* Wiley & Son.

Corsini, M., Larabi, C., Lavoué, G., Petrík, O., Vása, L., & Wang, K. (2012). Perceptual Metrics for Static and Dynamic Triangle Meshes. In M.-P. Cani & F. Ganovelli (Eds.), Eurographics (STARs) (pp. 135-157). Eurographics Association.

Corsini, M., Gelasca, E. D., Ebrahimi, T., & Barni, M. (2007). Watermarked 3-D Mesh Quality Assessment. *IEEE Transactions on Multimedia, 9*(2), 247–256. doi:10.1109/TMM.2006.886261

Corsini, M., Larabi, M. C., Lavoué, G., Petřík, O., Váša, L., & Wang, K. (2013, February). Perceptual Metrics for Static and Dynamic Triangle Meshes. *Computer Graphics Forum, 32*(1), 1. doi:10.1111/cgf.12001

Creswell, J. W. (2007). *Qualitative inquiry & research design: Choosing among five approaches.* Thousand Oaks, CA: Sage.

Culbertson, W. B., Malzbender, T., & Slabaugh, G. (1999, September). Generalized voxel coloring. In *International Workshop on Vision Algorithms* (pp. 100-115). Springer.

Das, D., Roy, S., & Chaudhuri, S. S. (2016). Dehazing Technique based on Dark Channel Prior model with Sky Masking and its quantitative analysis. *IEEE Explore*, 207-210.

Das, T. K. (2016). Intelligent techniques in decision making: A survey. *Indian Journal of Science and Technology, 9*(12). doi:10.17485/ijst/2016/v9i12/86063

Datta, S. K., Hore, M., & Roy, S. (2016a). Objective Evaluation of Dehazed Image by DCP. *NCECERS2016-mainak.*

Datta, S. K., Hore, M., & Roy, S. (2016b). Mathematical Modelling of Image Formation through Atmosphere. *NS-AMTM2016.*

Dawod, M., Hasan, M., & Daood, A. (2017). Experimental Study: Comparison of clustering algorithms. *Int. Journal of Engineering Research and Application, 7*(8), 23–34.

de González, A. B., Mahesh, M., Kim, K. P., Bhargavan, M., Lewis, R., Mettler, F., & Land, C. (2009). Projected cancer risks from computed tomographic scans performed in the United States in 2007. *Archives of Internal Medicine, 169*(22), 2071–2077. doi:10.1001/archinternmed.2009.440 PMID:20008689

Del Fabro, M., Sobe, A., & Böszörmenyi, L. (2012). Summarization of real-life events based on community-contributed content. In *Proceedings of the Fourth International Conferences on Advances in Multimedia* (pp. 119-126). Academic Press.

Demirci, S. (2007). *Virtual touch: An experimental study on the effects of online sense of touch on consumer behavior.* Maastricht University.

Deubel, H., Schneider, W. X., & Bridgeman, B. (1996). Postsaccadic target blanking prevents saccadic suppression of image displacement. *Vision Research, 36*(7), 985–996. doi:10.1016/0042-6989(95)00203-0 PMID:8736258

Dhanachandra, N., Manglem, K., & Chanu, Y. J. (2015). Image segmentation using *K-means* clustering algorithm and subtractive clustering algorithm. *Procedia Computer Science, 54*, 764–771. doi:10.1016/j.procs.2015.06.090

Dhawan. (2011). A Review of Image Compression and Comparison of its Algorithms. *IJECT, 2*(1).

Digne, J., Chaine, R., & Valette, S. (2014). Self-similarity for accurate compression of point sampled surfaces. *Computer Graphics Forum, 33*(2), 155–164. doi:10.1111/cgf.12305

Dou, M., Fuchs, H., & Frahm, J. M. (2013, October). Scanning and tracking dynamic objects with commodity depth cameras. In *Mixed and Augmented Reality (ISMAR), 2013 IEEE International Symposium on* (pp. 99-106). IEEE.

Doukas, C., & Maglogiannis, I. (2007). Region of interest coding techniques for medical image compression. *IEEE Engineering in Medicine and Biology Magazine, 25*(5). PMID:17941320

Dou, M., Taylor, J., Fuchs, H., Fitzgibbon, A., & Izadi, S. (2015). 3d scanning deformable objects with a single rgbd sensor. In *Proceedings of the IEEE Conference on Computer Vision and Pattern Recognition* (pp. 493-501). IEEE. 10.1109/CVPR.2015.7298647

Drouin, M. A., Trudeau, M., & Roy, S. (2005, June). Geo-consistency for wide multi-camera stereo. In *Computer Vision and Pattern Recognition, 2005. CVPR 2005. IEEE Computer Society Conference* on (Vol. 1, pp. 351-358). IEEE. 10.1109/CVPR.2005.168

Dubey, S. R., Singh, S. K., & Singh, R. K. (2015). Local diagonal extrema pattern: A new and efficient feature descriptor for CT image retrieval. *IEEE Signal Processing Letters, 22*(9), 1215–1219. doi:10.1109/LSP.2015.2392623

Duke, V. A. (1994). *Computer psychodiagnostics*. Saint Petersburg, Russia: Brotherhood.

Dutagaci, H., Cheung, C. P., & Godil, A. (2011). Evaluation of 3D Interest Point Detection Techniques. In H. Laga, T. Schreck, A. Ferreira, A. Godil, I. Pratikakis & R. C. Veltkamp (Eds.), 3DOR (pp. 57-64). Eurographics Association.

Du, Y., Chang, C. I., & Thouin, P. D. (2004). Unsupervised approach to colour video thresholding. *Optical Engineering, 43*(2), 282–289. doi:10.1117/1.1637364

Dvoretzky, A. (1956). On stochastic approximation. In *Proc. 3-rd Berkley Symp. Math. Statistics and Probability* (pp.39-55). Academic Press.

Ehman, E. C., Guimarães, L. S., Fidler, J. L., Takahashi, N., Ramirez-Giraldo, J. C., Yu, L., & Harmsen, W. S. (2012). Noise reduction to decrease radiation dose and improve conspicuity of hepatic lesions at contrast-enhanced 80-kV hepatic CT using projection space denoising. *AJR. American Journal of Roentgenology, 198*(2), 405–411. doi:10.2214/AJR.11.6987 PMID:22268185

Ehman, E. C., Yu, L., Manduca, A., Hara, A. K., Shiung, M. M., Jondal, D., & McCollough, C. H. (2014). Methods for clinical evaluation of noise reduction techniques in abdominopelvic CT. *Radiographics, 34*(4), 849–862. doi:10.1148/rg.344135128 PMID:25019428

Eisenhardt, K. M. (1989). Building theories from case studies research. *Academy of Management Review, 14*(4), 532–550.

Eisert, P., Steinbach, E., & Girod, B. (1999, March). Multi-hypothesis, volumetric reconstruction of 3-D objects from multiple calibrated camera views. In *Acoustics, Speech, and Signal Processing, 1999. Proceedings., 1999 IEEE International Conference* on (Vol. 6, pp. 3509-3512). IEEE.

Elaiyaraja, G., & Kumaratharan, N. (2015). Enhancing Medical Images by New Fuzzy Membership Function Median Based Noise Detection and Filtering Technique. *Journal of Electrical Engineering & Technology, 10*(5), 2197–2204. doi:10.5370/JEET.2015.10.5.2197

Elder, D. E. (1994). Skin cancer Melanoma and other specific non melanoma skin cancers. *Cancer, 75*(1), 245-256.

Endres, F., Hess, J., Engelhard, N., Sturm, J., Cremers, D., & Burgard, W. (2012, May). An evaluation of the RGB-D SLAM system. In *Robotics and Automation (ICRA), 2012 IEEE International Conference on* (pp. 1691-1696). IEEE. 10.1109/ICRA.2012.6225199

Engelke, U., Pepion, R., Le Callet, P., & Zepernick, H. (2010). Linkingdistortion perception and visual saliency in h.264/AVC codedvideo containing packet loss. *Proc. SPIE*.

Esakkirajan, S., Veerakumar, T., Subramanyam, A. N., & PremChand, C. H. (2011). Removal of high density salt and pepper noise through modified decision based unsymmetric trimmed median filter. *IEEE Signal Processing Letters, 18*(5), 287–290. doi:10.1109/LSP.2011.2122333

Esteban, C. H., & Schmitt, F. (2004). Silhouette and stereo fusion for 3D object modeling. *Computer Vision and Image Understanding, 96*(3), 367–392. doi:10.1016/j.cviu.2004.03.016

Fakhri, T., Kai, W. & Jean-Marc, C. (2014). A curvature-tensor-basedperceptual quality metric for 3d triangular meshes. *Machine Graphics and Vision*, 1-25.

Fattal, R. (2008). Single Image Dehazing. *ACM Transactions on Graphics, 27*(72), 1–9. doi:10.1145/1360612.1360671

Faugeras, O., & Keriven, R. (2002). Variational principles, surface evolution, PDE's, level set methods and the stereo problem. IEEE.

Felipe, J. C., Traina, A. J. M., & Traina, C. Jr. (2003). Retrieval by content of medical images using texture for tissue identification. *Proc. IEEE 16th Symp. Comput.-Based Med. Syst.*, 175–180. 10.1109/CBMS.2003.1212785

Findlay, J. M. (2004). Eye scanning in visual search. In J. Henderson & F. Ferreira (Eds.), *The interface oflanguage, vision and action: eye movements and the visual world* (pp. 135–159). Psychology press.

Folkes, V. S. (1988). Recent attribution research in consumer behavior: A review and new directions. *The Journal of Consumer Research, 14*(4), 548–565. doi:10.1086/209135

Folkes, V., & Matta, S. (2004). The effect of package shape on consumers' judgments of product volume: Attention as a mental contaminant. *The Journal of Consumer Research, 31*(2), 390–401. doi:10.1086/422117

Forouzanfar, M. H., Foreman, K. J., Delossantos, A. M., Lozano, R., Lopez, A. D., Murray, C. J. L., & Naghavi, M. (2011). Breast and cervical cancer in 187 countries between 1980 and 2010: A systematic analysis. *Lancet, 378*(9801), 1461–1484. doi:10.1016/S0140-6736(11)61351-2 PMID:21924486

Fromherz, T., & Bichsel, M. (1995). Shape from multiple cues: Integrating local brightness information. In *Proceedings of the Fourth International Conference for Young Computer Scientists, ICYCS* (*Vol. 95*, pp. 855-862). Academic Press.

Fromherz, T., & Bichsel, M. (1994, August). Shape from contours as initial step in shape from multiple cues. In *Proceedings-SPIE the International Society for Optical Engineering* (pp. 249–249). SPIE International Society for Optical.

Fu, J. C., Lee, S. K., Wong, S. T. C., Yeh, J. Y., Wang, A. H., & Wu, H. K. (2005). Image segmentation feature selection and pattern classification for mammographic microcalcifications. *Computerized Medical Imaging and Graphics, 29*(6), 419–429. doi:10.1016/j.compmedimag.2005.03.002 PMID:16002263

Gal, R., & Cohen-or, D. (2006). Salient geometric features for partial shape matching andsimilarity. *ACM Transactions on Graphics, 25*(1), 130–150. doi:10.1145/1122501.1122507

Gamassi, M., Piuri, V., Sana, D., & Scotti, F. (2004). A high-level optimum design methodology for multimodal biometric systems. *Computational Intelligence for Homeland Security and Personal Safety, 2004. CIHSPS 2004. Proceedings of the 2004 IEEE International Conference on*, 117–124. 10.1109/CIHSPS.2004.1360221

Ganster, H., Pinz, A., Rohrer, R., Wildling, E., Binder, M., & Kittler, H. (2001). Automated Melanoma Recognition. *IEEE Transactions on Medical Imaging, 20*(3), 233–239. doi:10.1109/42.918473 PMID:11341712

García, B., & Brunet, P. (1998, January). 3D reconstruction with projective octrees and epipolar geometry. In *Computer Vision, 1998. Sixth International Conference* on (pp. 1067-1072). IEEE.

Garcia, U. L. (2009). Automatic Image Segmentation by Dynamic Region Growth and Multiresolution Merging. *IEEE Transactions on Image Processing, 18*(10), 2275–2288. doi:10.1109/TIP.2009.2025555 PMID:19535323

Gargallo, P., & Sturm, P. (2005, June). Bayesian 3D modeling from images using multiple depth maps. In *Computer Vision and Pattern Recognition, 2005. CVPR 2005. IEEE Computer Society Conference* on (Vol. 2, pp. 885-891). IEEE.

Gargouri, N., Ben Ayed, A. D. M., & Masmoudi, D. S. (2011). A new human identification based on fusion fingerprints and faces biometrics using lbp and gwn descriptors. Systems, Signals and Devices (SSD), 2011 8th International Multi-Conference on, 1–7.

Garland, M., & Heckbert, P. S. (1997). Surface simplification using quadric error metrics. In G. S. Owen, T. Whitted & B. Mones-Hattal (Eds.), SIGGRAPH (pp. 209-216). ACM. doi:10.1145/258734.258849

Garrido, P., Valgaerts, L., Wu, C., & Theobalt, C. (2013). Reconstructing detailed dynamic face geometry from monocular video. *ACM Transactions on Graphics, 32*(6), 158–1. doi:10.1145/2508363.2508380

Gelasca, E. D., Ebrahimi, T., Corsini, M., & Barni, M. (2005). Objective evaluation of the perceptual quality of 3D watermarking. *IEEE International Conference On Image Processing*, 241-244.

George, A. (2008). Multi-modal biometrics human verification using LDA and DFB. *International Journal of Biometrics and Bioinformatics, 2*(4), 1–10.

Gijsbertse. (2015). *Three-Dimensional Ultrasound Strain Imaging of Skeletal Muscles*. IEEE.

Glazyev, S., & Kharitonov, V. (2009). *Nanotechnology as a key factor in the new technological order in the economy*. Moscow: Twent.

Gonzalez, R. C., & Woods, R. E. (2008). *Digital Image Processing* (3rd ed.). Pearson.

Gonzalez, R. C., Woods, R. E., & Eddins, S. L. (2004). *Digital Image Processing Using MATLAB*. Pearson Education.

Gorbachev, S. V. (2000). Intelligent mapping system ", Informeo": the experience of using neuroinformation technologies. In *Proceedings of VIII all-Russian seminar "Neuroinformatics and its applications"* (pp. 146-148). Krasnoyarsk, Russia: Publishing house Krasnoyarsk state University.

Gorbachev, S. V. (2001). Building neural network control system to solve the problem of the identification of geological bodies 3-D. In *Proceedings of the IX all-Russian seminar "Neuroinformatics and its applications"*, (pp.113-114). Krasnoyarsk, Russia: Publishing house Krasnoyarsk state University.

Gorbachev, S.V., & Syryamkin, V.I. (2014). *Neuro-fuzzy techniques in intelligent systems of processing and analysis of multidimensional information*. Tomsk, Russia: Publishing house Tomsk state University.

Gorbachev, S. V., & Syryamkin, V. I. (2015). Cognitive neural network modeling of the trajectory of global technical and economic development. In *Proceedings of International Conference on Cognitive Computing and Information Processing CCIP-2015* (pp.341–346). NOIDA.

Gorban, A. N. (1990). *Training of neural networks*. Moscow, Russia: Paragraf.

Gortler, S. J., Grzeszczuk, R., Szeliski, R., & Cohen, M. F. (1996, August). The lumigraph. In *Proceedings of the 23rd annual conference on Computer graphics and interactive techniques* (pp. 43-54). ACM.

Gotlieb, C. C., & Kreyszig, H. E. (1990). Texture descriptor Based on Co-occurrence Matrix. *Computer Vision, Graphics, and Image Processing, 51*, 71-86.

Govindan & Saniie. (2014). Processing algorithms for three-dimensional data compression of ultrasonic radio frequency signals. *IET Signal Processing.* doi:10.1049/iet-spr.2014.0186

Grady, L. (2011). Random Walks for Image Segmentation. *IEEE Transactions on Pattern Analysis and Machine Intelligence, 28*(11), 1768–1783. doi:10.1109/TPAMI.2006.233 PMID:17063682

Greess, H., Wolf, H., Baum, U., Lell, M., Pirkl, M., Kalender, W., & Bautz, W. A. (2000). Dose reduction in computed tomography by attenuation-based on-line modulation of tube current: Evaluation of six anatomical regions. *European Radiology, 10*(2), 391–394. doi:10.1007003300050062 PMID:10663775

Grgic, S., Grgic, M., & Mrak, M. (2004). Reliability of objective picture quality measures. *Journal of Electrical Engineering, 55*(1-2), 3–10.

Grohmann, B., Spangenberg, E. R., & Sprott, D. E. (2007). The influence of tactile input on the evaluation of retail product offerings. *Journal of Retailing, 83*(2), 237–245. doi:10.1016/j.jretai.2006.09.001

Guéguen, N., & Jacob, C. (2006). The effect of tactile stimulation on the purchasing behavior of consumers: An experimental study in a natural setting. *International Journal of Management, 23*(1), 24–33.

Guo, J., Vidal, V., Cheng, I., Basu, A., Baskurt, A. & Lavoué, G. (2017). Subjective and Objective Visual Quality Assessment of Textured 3D Meshes. *TAP, 14*, 11:1-11:20.

Gupta. (2014). ROI Based Medical Image Compression for Telemedicine Using IWT & SPIHT. *International Journal of Advance Research in Computer Science and Management Studies, 2*(11).

Guy, G., & Medioni, G. G. (1997). Inference of Surfaces, 3D Curves, and Junctions From Sparse, Noisy, 3D Data. *IEEE Transactions on Pattern Analysis and Machine Intelligence, 19*(11), 1265–1277. doi:10.1109/34.632985

Hai, Y., Li, L., & Gu, J. (2015). Image Enhancement Based on Contrast Limited Adaptive Histogram Equalization for 3D Images of Stereoscopic Endoscopy. *2015 IEEE International Conference on Information and Automation,* 668-672 10.1109/ICInfA.2015.7279370

Hall, E. (1979). *Computer Image Processing and Recognition.* New York: Academic Press.

Hane, C., Zach, C., Cohen, A., Angst, R., & Pollefeys, M. (2013). Joint 3D scene reconstruction and class segmentation. In *Proceedings of the IEEE Conference on Computer Vision and Pattern Recognition* (pp. 97-104). IEEE. 10.1109/CVPR.2013.20

Hane, C., Zach, C., Cohen, A., & Pollefeys, M. (2017). Dense semantic 3d reconstruction. *IEEE Transactions on Pattern Analysis and Machine Intelligence, 39*(9), 1730–1743. doi:10.1109/TPAMI.2016.2613051 PMID:28113966

Hanjalic, A., & Xu, L. Q. (2005). Affective video content representation and modeling. *Proceedings of the IEEE Transactions on Multimedia, 7*(1), 143–154. doi:10.1109/TMM.2004.840618

Han, K., Wong, K. Y. K., & Liu, M. (2015). A fixed viewpoint approach for dense reconstruction of transparent objects. In *Proceedings of the IEEE Conference on Computer Vision and Pattern Recognition* (pp. 4001-4008). IEEE. 10.1109/CVPR.2015.7299026

Hanmandlu, M., Kumar, A., Madasu, V. K., & Yarlagadda, P. (2008). Fusion of hand based biometrics using particle swarm optimization. *Information Technology: New Generations, 2008. ITNG 2008. Fifth IEEE International Conference on,* 783–788. 10.1109/ITNG.2008.252

Haralick, R. M., Shanmugam, K., & Dinstein, I. (1973). Textural features for image classification. *Trans. on systems man and cybernetics, 3,* 610–621.

Hariprasath, S., & Prabakar, T. N. (2012). Multimodal biometric recognition using iris feature extraction and palmprint features. *Advances in Engineering, Scienceand Management (ICAESM), 2012 International Conference on*, 174–179.

Haubold, A., & Kender, J. R. (2005). Augmented segmentation and visualization for presentation videos. In *Proceedings of the 13th annual ACM international conference on Multimedia* (pp. 51–60). ACM; doi:10.1145/1869652.1869662.

Hautiere, N., Tarel, J. P., Aubert, D., & Doumont, E. (2011). Blind contrast enhancement assessment by gradient rationing at visible edges. *Image Analysis & Stereology*, 1–9.

Heenaye, M., & Khan, M. (2012). A multimodal hand vein biometric based on score level fusion. *Procedia Engineering*, *41*, 897–903. doi:10.1016/j.proeng.2012.07.260

He, K., Sun, J., & Tang, X. (2009). Single image haze removal using dark channel prior. *IEEE Conference on Computer Vision and Pattern Recognition*, 1956- 1963.

Henderson, J. M. (2003). Human gaze control during real-world scene perception. *Trends in Cognitive Sciences*, *7*(11), 498–504. doi:10.1016/j.tics.2003.09.006 PMID:14585447

Henderson, J., Williams, C., & Falk, R. (2005). Eye movements are functional during face learning. *Memory & Cognition*, *133*(1), 98–106. doi:10.3758/BF03195300 PMID:15915796

Herbort, S., Grumpe, A., & Wöhler, C. (2011, September). Reconstruction of non-Lambertian surfaces by fusion of shape from shading and active range scanning. In *Image Processing (ICIP), 2011 18th IEEE International Conference on* (pp. 17-20). IEEE. 10.1109/ICIP.2011.6115812

Heydarian, M. N., Michael, D., Kamath, M. V., Colm, B., & Poehlman, W. F. S. (2009). Optimizing the Level Set Algorithm for Detecting Object Edges in MR and CT Images. *IEEE Transactions on Nuclear Science*, *56*(1), 156–167. doi:10.1109/TNS.2008.2010517

Hoegg, J., & Alba, J. W. (2007). Taste perception: More than meets the tongue. *The Journal of Consumer Research*, *33*(4), 490–498. doi:10.1086/510222

Hoeppner, F., Klawonn, F., Kruse, R., & Runkler, T. (1999). *Fuzzy Clustering Analysis: Methods for Classification, Data Analysis and Image Recognition*. Chichester, UK: John Wiley & Sons.

Hoffman, J. E., & Subramaniam, B. (1995). The role of visual attention in saccadic eye movements. *Perception & Psychophysics*, *57*(6), 787–795. doi:10.3758/BF03206794 PMID:7651803

Hore, M., Datta, S. K., & Roy, S. (2016). Subjective & Objective Evaluation of Dehazed Image by DCP. *IC2C2SE*.

Hornik, J. (1992a). Effects of physical contact on customers' shopping time and behavior. *Marketing Letters*, *3*(1), 49–55. doi:10.1007/BF00994080

Hornik, J. (1992b). Tactile stimulation and consumer response. *The Journal of Consumer Research*, *19*(3), 449–458. doi:10.1086/209314

Houhou, N., Thiran, J.P. & Bresson, X. (2009). Fast texture segmentation based on semi-local region descriptor and active contour. *Numerical Mathematics: Theory, Methods and Applications*, *2*, 445-468.

Hou, X., & Zhang, L. (2007). *Saliency Detection: A Spectral Residual Approach*. CVPR. IEEE Computer Society.

Howard, J. (2002). *Seeing in depth*. Toronto: University of Toronto Press.

Hsieh, J., Nett, B., Yu, Z., Sauer, K., Thibault, J. B., & Bouman, C. A. (2013). Recent advances in CT image reconstruction. *Current Radiology Reports*, *1*(1), 39–51. doi:10.100740134-012-0003-7

Huang, T., Yang, G. J. T. G. Y., & Tang, G. (1979). A fast two-dimensional median filtering algorithm. *IEEE Transactions on Acoustics, Speech, and Signal Processing, 27*(1), 13–18. doi:10.1109/TASSP.1979.1163188

Human-eye blog. (n.d.). *Eye colour.* Retrieved from http://the--human-eye.blogspot.com/

Hwang, H., & Haddad, R. A. (1995). Adaptive median filters: New algorithms and results. *IEEE Transactions on Image Processing, 4*(4), 499–502. doi:10.1109/83.370679 PMID:18289998

Innmann, M., Zollhöfer, M., Nießner, M., Theobalt, C., & Stamminger, M. (2016, October). VolumeDeform: Real-time volumetric non-rigid reconstruction. In *European Conference on Computer Vision* (pp. 362-379). Springer International Publishing.

Instituto Nacional de Estadística y Geografía (INEGI). (n.d.). Retrieved from: http://cuentame.inegi.org.mx/monografias/informacion/nl/poblacion/

Isidoro, J., & Sclaroff, S. (2003, October). *Stochastic Refinement of the Visual Hull to Satisfy Photometric and Silhouette Consistency Constraints* (Vol. 1335). ICCV. doi:10.1109/ICCV.2003.1238645

ISLES. (2015). Retrieved from www.isles-challenge.org

ITK-SNAP. (n.d.). Retrieved from http://www.itksnap.org/pmwiki/pmwiki.php

Itti, L., Koch, E. N., & Niebur, E. (1998). A model of saliency-based visual attention for rapid science analysis. *IEEE Transactions on Pattern Analysis and Machine Intelligence, 20*(11), 1254–1259. doi:10.1109/34.730558

ITU-RBT.500-11. (2002). *Méthodologie d'évaluation subjective de la qualité des images de télévision.* Technical Report. International Telecommunication Union.

ITU-T Recommendation P.910. (2008). *Subjective video quality assessment methods for multimedia applications.* International Telecommunication Union.

Izadi, S., Kim, D., Hilliges, O., Molyneaux, D., Newcombe, R., Kohli, P., ... Fitzgibbon, A. (2011, October). KinectFusion: real-time 3D reconstruction and interaction using a moving depth camera. In *Proceedings of the 24th annual ACM symposium on User interface software and technology* (pp. 559-568). ACM. 10.1145/2047196.2047270

Jae-kyun, A. (2013). Efficient Fine-Granular Scalable Coding of 3D Mesh Sequences. *IEEE Transactions on Multimedia, 15*, 3.

Jahanbin, S., Choi, H., & Bovik, A. C. (2011). Passive multimodal 2-d+ 3-d face recognition using gabor features and landmark distances. *IEEE Transactions on Information Forensics and Security, 6*(4), 1287–1304. doi:10.1109/TIFS.2011.2162585

Jain, A., Nandakumar, K., & Ross, A. (2005). Score normalization in multimodal biometric systems. *Pattern Recognition, 38*(12), 2270–2285. doi:10.1016/j.patcog.2005.01.012

Jeguirim, S. E. G., Adolphe, D. C., Sahnoun, M., Douib, A. B., Schacher, L. M., & Cheikhrouhou, M. (2012). Intelligent techniques for modeling the relationships between sensory attributes and instrumental measurements of knitted fabrics. *Journal of Engineered Fabrics & Fibers, 7*(3), 88–97.

Jemal, A., Bray, F., Forman, D., O'Brien, M., Ferlay, J., Center, M., & Parkin, D. M. (2012). Cancer burden in Africa and opportunities for prevention. *Cancer, 118*(18), 4372–4384. doi:10.1002/cncr.27410 PMID:22252462

Jeni, L. A., Cohn, J. F., & Kanade, T. (2015, May). Dense 3D face alignment from 2D videos in real-time. In *Automatic Face and Gesture Recognition (FG), 2015 11th IEEE International Conference and Workshops on* (Vol. 1, pp. 1-8). IEEE.

Jeyanthi & Suganyadevi. (2016). A Survey on medical images and compression techniques. *International Journal of Advances in Science Engineering and Technology, 4*(2).

Jiang, Z., & Benbasat, I. (2007). The effects of presentation formats and task complexity on online consumers' product understanding. *Management Information Systems Quarterly, 31*(3), 475–500. doi:10.2307/25148804

Jia, S., Zhang, C., Li, X., & Zhou, Y. (2014). Mesh resizing based on hierarchical saliency detection. *Graphical Models, 76*(5), 355–362. doi:10.1016/j.gmod.2014.03.012

Jin, H. (2003, October). Tales of shape and radiance in multiview stereo. In *Computer Vision, 2003. Proceedings. Ninth IEEE International Conference on* (pp. 974-981). IEEE.

Jin, H., Soatto, S., & Yezzi, A. J. (2003, June). Multi-view stereo beyond lambert. In *Computer Vision and Pattern Recognition, 2003. Proceedings. 2003 IEEE Computer Society Conference on* (Vol. 1, pp. I-I). IEEE.

Jin, S. (2011). The impact of 3D virtual haptics in marketing. *Psychology and Marketing, 28*(3), 240–255. doi:10.1002/mar.20390

Johnson, A. E., & Hebert, M. (1999). Using Spin Images for Efficient Object Recognition in Cluttered 3DScenes. IEEE Transactions on Pattern Analysis and Machine Intelligence, 433-449.

Joseph, C. E. (1997). Unifying the derivations for the Akaike and corrected Akaike information criteria. *Statistics and Probability Letters, 33*(2), 201–208. doi:10.1016/S0167-7152(96)00128-9

Kabatek, M. a. (2009). An underwater target detection system for electro-optical imagery data. *OCEANS MTS/IEEE.*

Kabir, Y., Dojat, M., Scherrer, B., Forbes, F., & Garbay, C. (2007). Multimodal MRI segmentation of ischemic stroke lesions. *29th Ann Intern Conf IEEE Eng Med Biol Soc EMBC.* 10.1109/IEMBS.2007.4352610

Kalender, W. A., Wolf, H., Suess, C., Gies, M., Greess, H., & Bautz, W. A. (1999). Dose reduction in CT by on-line tube current control: Principles and validation on phantoms and cadavers. *European Radiology, 9*(2), 323–328. doi:10.1007003300050674 PMID:10101657

Kamalanand, K., & Jawahar, P. M. (2012). Coupled jumping frogs/particle swarm optimization for estimating the parameters of three dimensional HIV model. *BMC Infectious Diseases, 12*(1), 82. doi:10.1186/1471-2334-12-S1-P82 PMID:22471518

Kamalanand, K., & Jawahar, P. M. (2015). Prediction of Human Immunodeficiency Virus-1 Viral Load from CD4 Cell Count Using Artificial Neural Networks. *Journal of Medical Imaging and Health Informatics, 5*(3), 641–646. doi:10.1166/jmihi.2015.1430

Kanchana, R., & Menaka, R. (2015). Computer reinforced analysis for ischemic stroke recognition: A review. *Indian Journal of Science and Technology, 8*(35), 81006. doi:10.17485/ijst/2015/v8i35/81006

Kang, S. B., Szeliski, R., & Chai, J. (2001). Handling occlusions in dense multi-view stereo. *In Computer Vision and Pattern Recognition, 2001. CVPR 2001. Proceedings of the 2001 IEEE Computer Society Conference on* (Vol. 1, pp. I-I). IEEE.

Kang, C. C., & Wang, W. J. (2009). Fuzzy reasoning-based directional median filter design. *Signal Processing, 89*(3), 344–351. doi:10.1016/j.sigpro.2008.09.003

Kanungo, T., Mount, D. M., Netanyahu, N. S., Piatko, C. D., Silverman, R., & Wu, A. Y. (2002). An efficient k-means clustering algorithm: Analysis and implementation. *IEEE Transactions on Pattern Analysis and Machine Intelligence, 24*(7), 881–892. doi:10.1109/TPAMI.2002.1017616

Kapur, J. N., Sahoo, P. K., & Wong, A. K. C. (1985). A New Method for Gray-Level Picture Thresholding Using the Entropy of the Histogram. *Computer Vision, Graphics and Image Processing, Vol, 29*(3), 273–285. doi:10.1016/0734-189X(85)90125-2

Karayiannis, N. B., & Pai, P. I. (1996). Fuzzy algorithm for learning vector quantization. *IEEE Transactions on Neural Networks, 5*(5), 1196–1211. doi:10.1109/72.536314 PMID:18263514

Karni, Z., & Gotsman, C. (2000). *Spectral Compression of Mesh Geometry*. EuroCG, 27-30. doi:10.1145/344779.344924

Kartik, P., Vara Prasad, R. V. S. S., & Mahadeva Prasanna, S. R. (2008). Noise robust multimodal biometric person authentication system using face, speech and signature features. *India Conference, 2008. INDICON 2008. Annual IEEE, 1*, 23–27. 10.1109/INDCON.2008.4768795

Kass, M., Witkin, A., & Terzopoulos, D. (1988). Snakes: Active contour models. *International Journal of Computer Vision, 1*(4), 321–331. doi:10.1007/BF00133570

Kearfott, R. B. (1996). *Rigorous Global Search: Continuous Problems (Nonconvex Optimization and Its Applications), 13*. Dordrecht, The Netherlands: Kluwer. doi:10.1007/978-1-4757-2495-0

Keller, J. M., & Hunt, D. J. (1985). Incorporating fuzzy membership function into the perceptron algorithm. IEEE Transactions on Pattern Analysis and Machine Intelligence, 7, 693-699. doi:10.1109/TPAMI.1985.4767725

Kemelmacher-Shlizerman, I., & Seitz, S. M. (2011, November). Face reconstruction in the wild. In *Computer Vision (ICCV), 2011 IEEE International Conference on* (pp. 1746-1753). IEEE. 10.1109/ICCV.2011.6126439

Khoshelham, K. (2011, August). Accuracy analysis of kinect depth data. In ISPRS workshop laser scanning (Vol. 38, No. 5, p. W12). Academic Press.

Kichenassamy, S., Kumar, A., Olver, P., Tannenbaum, A., & Yezzi, A. (1995). Gradient flows and geometric active contour models. *Proc. Int. Conf. Comp. Vis.*, 810–815. 10.1109/ICCV.1995.466855

Kimmel, R. (2003). Fast edge integration. In *Geometric Level Set Methods in Imaging, Vision and Graphics*. New York: Springer-Verlag. doi:10.1007/0-387-21810-6_4

Kim, Y., Varshney, A., Jacobs, D. W., & Guimbretière, F. (2010). Mesh saliency and human eye fixations. *Transactions on Applied Perception, 7*(2), 1–13. doi:10.1145/1670671.1670676

Kirkpatrick, S., Gelatt, C. D., & Vecchi, M. P. (1983). Optimization by simulated annealing. *Science, 220*(4598), 671–680. doi:10.1126cience.220.4598.671 PMID:17813860

Kisku, D. R., Rattani, A., Gupta, P., & Sing, J. K. (2009). Biometric sensor image fusion for identity verification: A case study with wavelet-based fusion rules graph matching. *Technologies for Homeland Security, 2009. HST'09. IEEE Conference on*, 433–439. 10.1109/THS.2009.5168069

Kittler, J., & Illingworth, J. (1986). Minimum error thresholding. *Pattern Recognition, Vol, 19*(1), 41–47. doi:10.1016/0031-3203(86)90030-0

Klatzky, R. L., Lederman, S. J., & Matula, D. E. (1993). Haptic exploration in the presence of vision. *Journal of Experimental Psychology. Human Perception and Performance, 19*(4), 726–743. doi:10.1037/0096-1523.19.4.726 PMID:8409856

Koch, C., & Poggio, T. (1999). Predicting the visual world: Silence is golden. *Nature Neuroscience, 2*(1), 9–10. doi:10.1038/4511 PMID:10195172

Kohonen, T. (2008). *Self-organizing maps*. Moscow, Russia: BINOM. Knowledge laboratory.

Kolb, T. M., Lichy, J., & Newhouse, J. H. (2002). Comparison of the Performance of Screening Mammography, Physical Examination, and Breast US and Evaluation of Factors that Influence Them: An Analysis of 27,825 Patient Evaluations. *Radiology*, 225(1), 165–175. doi:10.1148/radiol.2251011667 PMID:12355001

Kolmogorov, V., & Zabih, R. (2002). Multi-camera scene reconstruction via graph cuts. *Computer Vision—ECCV 2002*, 8-40.

Kondratiev, N. D., Yakovets, Yu. V., & Abalkin, L. I. (2002). *Large cycles of conjuncture and theory of foresight: Selected works*. Moscow: Economy.

Kopf A.W., Salopek T.G., Slade J., Marghoob A.A., & Bart R.S. (1994). Techniques of cutaneous examination for the detection of skin cancer. *Cancer, 75*(2), 684–690.

Ko, S. J., & Lee, Y. H. (1991). Center weighted median filters and their applications to image enhancement. *IEEE Transactions on Circuits and Systems, 38*(9), 984–993. doi:10.1109/31.83870

Koschmieder, H. (1924). Theorie der horizontalensichtweite. *Beitr.Phys. Freien Atm., 12*, 171–181.

Kowler, E., Anderson, E., Dosher, B., & Blaser, E. (1995). The role of visual attention in the programming of saccades. *Vision Research, 35*(13), 1897–1916. doi:10.1016/0042-6989(94)00279-U PMID:7660596

Krishna, A., Elder, R. S., & Caldara, C. (2010). Feminine to smell but masculine to touch? Multisensory congruence and its effect on the aesthetic experience. *Journal of Consumer Psychology, 20*(4), 410–418. doi:10.1016/j.jcps.2010.06.010

Krishna, A., Lwin, M. O., & Morrin, M. (2009). Product scent and memory. *The Journal of Consumer Research, 37*(1), 57–67. doi:10.1086/649909

Krishna, A., & Morrin, M. (2008). Does touch affect taste? The perceptual transfer of product container haptic cues. *The Journal of Consumer Research, 34*(6), 807–818. doi:10.1086/523286

Krishneswari, K., & Arumugam, A. (2013). An improved genetic optimized neural network of multimodal biometrics. *Journal of Scientific and Industrial Research, 73*(1), 23–30.

Kullback, S. (1968). *Information theory and statics*. Dover.

Kumar, A., Hanmandlu, M., & Vasikarla, S. (2012). Rank level integration of face based biometrics. *Information Technology: New Generations (ITNG), 2012 Ninth IEEE International Conference on*, 36–4. 10.1109/ITNG.2012.14

Kumar, A., Kabra, G., Mussada, E. K., Dash, M. K., & Rana, P. S. (2017). Combined artificial bee colony algorithm and machine learning techniques for prediction of online consumer repurchase intention. *Neural Computing & Applications*, 1–14.

Kumar, A., & Kwong, C. (2013). Towards contactless, low-cost and accurate 3-D fingerprint identification. *Proceedings of the IEEE Conference on ComputerVision and Pattern Recognition*, 3438–3443. 10.1109/CVPR.2013.441

Kundu, M. a. (1986). Thresholding for edge detection by human psychovisual phenomenon. *Pattern Recognition Letter*, 433-441.

Kundu, M., & Acharyya, M. (2003). M-band Wavelets:Application to Texture Segmentation for real Life Image Analysis. *International Journal of Wavelets, Multresolution, and Information Processing, 1*(1), 115–119. doi:10.1142/S0219691303000074

Kutulakos, K. N. (2000, June). Approximate N-view stereo. In *European Conference on Computer Vision* (pp. 67-83). Springer.

Kutulakos, K. N., & Seitz, S. M. (2000). A theory of shape by space carving. *International Journal of Computer Vision, 38*(3), 199–218. doi:10.1023/A:1008191222954

La Riviere, P. J., & Billmire, D. M. (2005). Reduction of noise-induced streak artifacts in X-ray computed tomography through spline-based penalized-likelihood sinogram smoothing. *IEEE Transactions on Medical Imaging, 24*(1), 105–111. doi:10.1109/TMI.2004.838324 PMID:15638189

Ladický, L., Sturgess, P., Russell, C., Sengupta, S., Bastanlar, Y., Clocksin, W., & Torr, P. H. (2012). Joint optimization for object class segmentation and dense stereo reconstruction. *International Journal of Computer Vision*, 1–12.

Lakshmi, V.S., Tebby, S.G., Shriranjani, D., & Rajinikanth, V. (2016). Chaotic cuckoo search and Kapur/Tsallis approach in segmentation of T.cruzi from blood smear images. *Int. J. Comp. Sci. Infor. Sec., 14*, 51-56.

Lange, K., & Carson, R. (1984). EM reconstruction algorithms for emission and transmission tomography. *Journal of Computer Assisted Tomography, 8*(2), 306–316. PMID:6608535

Laurentini, A. (1994). The visual hull concept for silhouette-based image understanding. *IEEE Transactions on Pattern Analysis and Machine Intelligence, 16*(2), 150–162. doi:10.1109/34.273735

Lavoué, G. (2009). A local roughness measure for 3D meshes and its application to visual masking. *ACM Transactions on Applied Perception, 21*, 1-23.

Lavoué, G., Drelie Gelasca, E., Dupont, F., Baskurt, A., & Ebrahimi, T. (2006).Perceptually driven 3D distance metrics with application to watermarking. *Proceedings of SPIE, Applications of Digital Image Processing, 6312*, 63120L-63120L12.

Lavoué, G. (2011). A Multiscale Metric for 3D Mesh Visual Quality Assessment. *Computer Graphics Forum, 30*(5), 1427–1437. doi:10.1111/j.1467-8659.2011.02017.x

Lavoué, G., & Corsini, M. (2010). A Comparison of Perceptually-Based Metrics for Objective Evaluation of Geometry Processing. *IEEE Transactions on Multimedia, 12*(7), 636–649. doi:10.1109/TMM.2010.2060475

Lee, J., Moghaddam, B., Pfister, H., & Machiraju, R. (2004). Finding Optimal Views for 3D Face Shape Modeling. In FGR (pp. 31-36). IEEE Computer Society.

Lee, S. K., Lo, C. S., Wang, C. M., Chung, P. C., Chang, C. I, Yang, C. W., Hsu, P. C. (2000). A computer-aided design mammography screening system for detection and classification of micro calcifications. *Int. J. Med Inform.,60*, 29-57.

Lee, C. H., Varshney, A., & Jacobs, D. W. (2005). Mesh saliency. *ACM Transactions on Graphics, 24*(3), 659–666. doi:10.1145/1073204.1073244

Le, T., Chartrand, R., & Asaki, T. J. (2007). A variational approach to reconstructing images corrupted by Poisson noise. *Journal of Mathematical Imaging and Vision, 27*(3), 257–263. doi:10.100710851-007-0652-y

Li, X. (2013). *Research on the technologies of underwater image segmentation and object location based on monlcular vision* (Master's thesis). Harbin Engineering University.

Li, C. (2011). A level set method for image segmentation in the presence of intensity inhomogeneitics with application to MRI. *IEEE Transactions on Image Processing, 20*(7), 2007–2016. doi:10.1109/TIP.2011.2146190 PMID:21518662

Li, H., Vouga, E., Gudym, A., Luo, L., Barron, J. T., & Gusev, G. (2013). 3D self-portraits. *ACM Transactions on Graphics, 32*(6), 187. doi:10.1145/2508363.2508407

Lin, C. Y., Liaw, S. Y., Chen, C. C., Pai, M. Y., & Chen, Y. M. (2017). A computer-based approach for analyzing consumer demands in electronic word-of-mouth. *Electronic Markets, 27*(3), 225–242. doi:10.100712525-017-0262-5

Ling, H., & Okada, K. (2006). Diffusion Distance for Histogram Comparison. In IEEE CVPR (pp. 246--253). IEEE.

Lin, J. C., Wei, W. L., & Wang, H. M. (2016). DEMV-matchmaker: emotional temporal course representation and deep similarity matching for automatic music video generation. In *Proceedings of the International Conference on Acoustics, Speech and Signal Processing* (pp. 2772-2776). IEEE. 10.1109/ICASSP.2016.7472182

Lin, M., Chau, M., Cao, J., & Nunamaker, J. F. Jr. (2005). Automated video segmentation for lecture videos: A linguistics-based approach. *Proceedings of the International Journal of Technology and Human Interaction, 1*(2), 27–45. doi:10.4018/jthi.2005040102

Lin, P. H., Chen, B. H., Cheng, F. C., & Huang, S. C. (2016). A Morphological Mean Filter for Impulse Noise Removal. *Journal of Display Technology, 12*(4), 344–350.

Lin, T. C. (2007). A new adaptive center weighted median filter for suppressing impulsive noise in images. *Information Sciences, 177*(4), 1073–1087. doi:10.1016/j.ins.2006.07.030

Li, T., Li, X., Wang, J., Wen, J., Lu, H., Hsieh, J., & Liang, Z. (2004). Nonlinear sinogram smoothing for low-dose X-ray CT. *IEEE Transactions on Nuclear Science, 51*(5), 2505–2513. doi:10.1109/TNS.2004.834824

Liu, T., Xu, H., Jin, W., Liu, Z., Zhao, Y. & Tian, W. (2014). Medical image segmentation based on a hybrid region-based active contour mode. *Computational and Mathematical Methods in Medicin.* doi:.10.1155/2014/890725

Liu, Y., & Pearlman, W. A. (2006). Resolution Scalable Coding and Region of Interest Access with Three-Dimensional SBHP Algorithm. *Third International symposium on 3D Data Processing.* 10.1109/3DPVT.2006.120

Liu, D., Chen, X., & Yang, Y. H. (2014). Frequency-based 3d reconstruction of transparent and specular objects. In *Proceedings of the IEEE Conference on Computer Vision and Pattern Recognition* (pp. 660-667). IEEE. 10.1109/CVPR.2014.90

Liu, D., Hua, X. S., Yang, L., Wang, M., & Zhang, H. J. (2009). Tag ranking. In *Proceedings of the 18th international conference on World Wide Web* (pp. 351-360). ACM. 10.1145/1526709.1526757

Liu, G. H., & Yang, J. Y. (2008). Image retrieval based on the texton co-occurrence matrix. *Pattern Recognition, Vol, 41*(12), 3521–3527. doi:10.1016/j.patcog.2008.06.010

Liu, M., Hartley, R., & Salzmann, M. (2013). Mirror surface reconstruction from a single image. In *Proceedings of the IEEE Conference on Computer Vision and Pattern Recognition* (pp. 129-136). IEEE. 10.1109/CVPR.2013.24

Liu, X. a. (2016). Saliency segmentation and foreground extraction of underwater image based on localization. *Oceans.*

Liu, Z. (2014). A Novel Saliency Detection Framework. *IEEE Transactions on Image Processing, 23*(5), 1937–1952. doi:10.1109/TIP.2014.2307434 PMID:24710397

Liu, Z. a. (2005). Underwater acoustic image segmentation based on deformable template. *IEEE International Conference on Mechatronics and Automation, 4,* 1802-1806.

Liversedge, S. P., & Findlay, J. M. (2000). Saccadic eyemovements and cognition. *Trends in Cognitive Sciences, 4*(1), 6–14. doi:10.1016/S1364-6613(99)01418-7 PMID:10637617

Li, X., Snoek, C. G., & Worring, M. (2009). Learning social tag relevance by neighbor voting. *Proceedings of the IEEE Transactions on Multimedia, 11*(7), 1310–1322. doi:10.1109/TMM.2009.2030598

Long, R., Wang, H., Chen, Y., Jin, O., & Yu, Y. (2011). Towards Effective Event Detection, Tracking and Summarization on Microblog Data. In *Proceedings of the Web-Age Information Management* (pp. 652-663). Academic Press. 10.1007/978-3-642-23535-1_55

Lu, H., Kot, A. C., & Shi, Y. Q. (2004). Distance-reciprocal distortion measure for binary document images. *IEEE Signal Processing Letters*, *11*(2), 228–231. doi:10.1109/LSP.2003.821748

Luisier, F., Blu, T., & Unser, M. (2011). Image denoising in mixed Poisson–Gaussian noise. *IEEE Transactions on Image Processing*, *20*(3), 696–708. doi:10.1109/TIP.2010.2073477 PMID:20840902

Luong, Q. T., & Faugeras, O. D. (1996). The fundamental matrix: Theory, algorithms, and stability analysis. *International Journal of Computer Vision*, *17*(1), 43–75. doi:10.1007/BF00127818

Luo, S.-T., & Cheng, B.-W. (2010). Diagnosing Breast Masses in Digital Mammography Using Feature Selection and Ensemble Methods. *Journal of Medical Systems*, *36*(2), 569–577. doi:10.100710916-010-9518-8 PMID:20703679

Lutsenko, E.V. (2002). *Automated system-cognitive analysis in the management of active objects.* Krasnodar, Russia: KubSAU.

Lutsenko, E. V. (1996). *Theoretical bases and technology of adaptive semantic analysis to support decision-making.* Krasnodar, Russia: CUI MVD RF.

Lynn, M., Le, J., & Sherwyn, D. S. (1998). Reach out and touch your customers. *Cornell Hospitality Quarterly*, *39*(3), 60–65. doi:10.1177/001088049803900312

Maglo, A. (2013). 3D mesh compression: survey, comparisons and emerging trends. ACM Computing Surveys, 9(4).

Mahata, D., & Agarwal, N. (2012). What does everybody know? Identifying event-specific sources from social media. In *Computational Aspects of Social Networks (CASoN), 2012 Fourth International Conference on* (pp. 63-68). IEEE. 10.1109/CASoN.2012.6412379

Mahata, D., & Talburt, J. (2014). A Framework for Collecting and Managing Entity Identity Information from Social Media. In *19th MIT International Conference on Information Quality* (pp. 216-233). Academic Press.

Mahata, D., Talburt, J. R., & Singh, V. K. (2015). From Chirps to Whistles: Discovering Event-specific Informative Content from Twitter. In *Proceedings of the ACM Web Science Conference* (p. 17). ACM. 10.1145/2786451.2786476

Mahesh, P. K., & Shanmukha Swamy, M. N. (2010). A biometric identification system based on the fusion of palmprint and speech signal. *Signal and Image Processing (ICSIP), 2010 IEEE International Conference on*, 186–190. 10.1109/ICSIP.2010.5697466

Maier, Menze, B. H., von der Gablentz, J., Häni, L., Heinrich, M. P., Liebrand, M., ... Reyes, M. (2017). ISLES 2015 - A public evaluation benchmark for ischemic stroke lesion segmentation from multispectral MRI. *Medical Image Analysis*, *35*, 250–269. doi:10.1016/j.media.2016.07.009 PMID:27475911

Maier, O., Schröder, C., Forkert, N. D., Martinetz, T., & Handels, H. (2015). Classifiers for ischemic stroke lesion segmentation: A comparison study. *PLoS One*, *10*(12), e0145118. doi:10.1371/journal.pone.0145118 PMID:26672989

Maier, O., Wilms, M., Von der Gablentz, J., Krämer, U. M., Münte, T. F., & Handels, H. (2015). Extra tree forests for sub-acute ischemic stroke lesion segmentation in MR sequences. *Journal of Neuroscience Methods*, *240*, 89–100. doi:10.1016/j.jneumeth.2014.11.011 PMID:25448384

Malladi, R., Sethian, J. A., & Vemuri, B. C. (1995). Shape modeling with front propagation: A level set approach. *IEEE Transactions on Pattern Analysis and Machine Intelligence*, *17*(2), 158–175. doi:10.1109/34.368173

Mao, J. (2015). *Study of Image Dehazing with the self-adjustment of the Haze Degree* (Ph.D. Thesis). Division of Production and Information Systems Engineering, Muroran Institute of Technology.

Marian, B. (2007). Active Contours and their Utilization at Image Segmentation. *5th Slovakian-Hungarian Joint Symposium on Applied Machine Intelligence and Informatics,* 313-317.

Martin, W. N., & Aggarwal, J. K. (1983, February). Volumetric Descriptions of Objects from Multiple Views. *IEEE Transactions on Pattern Analysis and Machine Intelligence, 5*(2), 150–158. doi:10.1109/TPAMI.1983.4767367 PMID:21869096

Massone, L., Morasso, P., & Zaccaria, R. (1985, January). Shape from occluding contours. In *1984 Cambridge Symposium* (pp. 114-120). International Society for Optics and Photonics. 10.1117/12.946170

Mattila, A. S., & Wirtz, J. (2001). Congruency of scent and music as a driver of in-store evaluations and behavior. *Journal of Retailing, 77*(2), 273–289. doi:10.1016/S0022-4359(01)00042-2

Maximo, A., Patro, R., Varshney, A., & Farias, R. C. (2011). A robust and rotationally invariant local surface descriptor with applications to non-local mesh processing. *Graphical Models, 73*(5), 231–242. doi:10.1016/j.gmod.2011.05.002

McInerney, T., & Terzopoulos, D. (2000). T-snakes: Topology adaptive snakes. *Medical Image Analysis, 4*(2), 73–91. doi:10.1016/S1361-8415(00)00008-6 PMID:10972323

Meganez, G., & Thiran, J. P. (2002, September). Lossy to lossless object based coding of 3D MRI Data. *IEEE Transactions on Image Processing, 11*(9).

Meher, S. K., & Singhawat, B. (2014). An improved recursive and adaptive median filter for high density impulse noise. *AEÜ. International Journal of Electronics and Communications, 68*(12), 1173–11. doi:10.1016/j.aeue.2014.06.006

Metropolis, N., Rosenbluth, A. W., Rosenbluth, M. N., Teller, A. H., & Teller, E. (1953). Equation of state calculations by fast computing machines. *The Journal of Chemical Physics, 21*(6), 1087–1092. doi:10.1063/1.1699114

Miller, G. A. (1995). WordNet: A lexical database for English. *Communications of the ACM, 38*(11), 39–41. doi:10.1145/219717.219748

Mitchell, D. J., Kahn, B. E., & Knasko, S. C. (1995). There's something in the air: Effects of congruent or incongruent ambient odor on consumer decision making. *The Journal of Consumer Research, 22*(2), 229–238. doi:10.1086/209447

Mitra, S., & Pal, S. K. Fuzzy multi-layer perceptron, inferencing and rule generation. IEEE Transactions on Neural Networks, 6, 51-63. doi:10.1109/72.363450

Mitra, J., Bourgeat, P., Fripp, J., Ghose, S., Rose, S., Salvado, O., ... Carey, L. (2014). Lesion segmentation from multimodal MRI using random forest following ischemic stroke. *NeuroImage, 98*, 324–335. doi:10.1016/j.neuroimage.2014.04.056 PMID:24793830

Moezzi, S., Katkere, A., Kuramura, D. Y., & Jain, R. (1996). Reality modeling and visualization from multiple video sequences. *IEEE Computer Graphics and Applications, 16*(6), 58–63. doi:10.1109/38.544073

Moezzi, S., Tai, L. C., & Gerard, P. (1997). Virtual view generation for 3D digital video. *IEEE MultiMedia, 4*(1), 18–26. doi:10.1109/93.580392

Moghaddam, R. F., & Cheriet, M. (2010). A multi-scale framework for adaptive binarization of degraded document images. *Pattern Recognition, 43*(6), 2186–2198. doi:10.1016/j.patcog.2009.12.024

Monwar, M. M., & Gavrilova, M. L. (2009). Multimodal biometric system using rank-level fusion approach. *IEEE Transactions on Systems, Man, and Cybernetics. Part B, Cybernetics, 39*(4), 867–878. doi:10.1109/TSMCB.2008.2009071 PMID:19336340

Moorthi, M. S., Gambhir, R. K, Misra, I., & Ramakrishnan, R. (2011). Adaptive stochastic gradient descent optimization in multi temporal satellite image registration. *IEEE Recent Advances in Intelligent Computational Systems (RAICS),* 373-377.

Morrow, W. M., Paranjape, R. B., Rangayyan, R. M., & Desautels, J. E. L. (1992). Region-based contrast enhancement of mammograms. *IEEE Transactions on Medical Imaging, 11*(3), 392–406. doi:10.1109/42.158944 PMID:18222882

Morse, P. M., & Feshbach, H. (1993). The variational integral and the Euler equations. Proc. Meth. Theor. Phys., 1, 276–280.

Mostafa, A., Hassanien, A. E., & Hefny, H. A. (2017). Grey wolf optimization-based segmentation approach for abdomen CT liver images. Handbook of Research on Machine Learning Innovations and Trends, 562-581. doi:10.4018/978-1-5225-2229-4.ch024

Moxley, E., Kleban, J., Xu, J., & Manjunath, B. S. (2009, June). Not all tags are created equal: Learning Flickr tag semantics for global annotation. In *Proceedings of the IEEE International Conference on Multimedia and Expo.* (pp. 1452-1455). IEEE. 10.1109/ICME.2009.5202776

Mumford, D., & Shah, J. (1989). Optimal approximation by piecewise smooth functions and associated variational problems. *Communications on Pure and Applied Mathematics, 42*(5), 577–685. doi:10.1002/cpa.3160420503

Murakami, T., & Takahashi, K. (2011). Fast and accurate biometric identification using score level indexing and fusion. *Biometrics (IJCB), 2011 IEEE International Joint Conference on*, 1–8. 10.1109/IJCB.2011.6117591

Murala, S., Maheshwari, R. P., & Balasubramanian, R. (2012). Directional binary wavelet patterns for biomedical image indexing and retrieval. *Journal of Medical Systems, 36*(5), 2865–2879. doi:10.100710916-011-9764-4 PMID:21822675

Murala, S., & Wu, J. Q. M. (2013). Local ternary co-occurrence patterns: A new feature descriptor for MRI and CT image retrieval. *Neurocomputing, 119*, 399–412. doi:10.1016/j.neucom.2013.03.018

Muratov, O., Slynko, Y., Chernov, V., Lyubimtseva, M., Shamsuarov, A., & Bucha, V. (2016). 3DCapture: 3D Reconstruction for a Smartphone. In *Proceedings of the IEEE Conference on Computer Vision and Pattern Recognition Workshops* (pp. 75-82). IEEE.

Mythili, C., & Kavitha, V. (2011). Efficient technique for color image noise reduction. *The Research Bulletin of Jordan ACM, 2*(3), 41–44.

Nachbar, F., Stolz, W., Merkle, T., Cognetta A.B., Vogt T., Landthaler, M., Bilck, P., Braun-Falco, O., & Plewig, G. (1994). The ABCD rule of dermatoscopy: High Prospective value in the diagnosis of doubtful melanocytic skin lesion. *Journal of the American Academy of Dermatology, 30*, 551-559.

Naik, S. K., & Murthy, C.A. (n.d.). Hue Preserving Colour Image Enhancement without Gamut Problem. *IEEE Transactions on Image Processing, 12*, 1591-1598.

Naik, A., Satapathy, S. C., Ashour, A. S., & Dey, N. (2016). Social group optimization for global optimization of multimodal functions and data clustering problems. *Neural Computing & Applications.* doi:10.100700521-016-2686-9

Newcombe, R. A., Izadi, S., Hilliges, O., Molyneaux, D., Kim, D., Davison, A. J., . . . Fitzgibbon, A. (2011, October). KinectFusion: Real-time dense surface mapping and tracking. In *Mixed and augmented reality (ISMAR), 2011 10th IEEE international symposium on* (pp. 127-136). IEEE.

Nguyen, T., Nhat, A., Jianfei, C., Zhang, J., & Zheng, J. (2012). Constrained Active Contours for Boundary Refinement in Interactive Image Segmentation. *IEEE International Symposium on Circuits and Systems*, 870- 873.

Nocedal, J., & Wright, S. J. (2006). *Numerical Optimization* (2nd ed.). New York: Springer-Verlag.

Nouri, A., Charrier, C., & Lézoray, O. (2016a). *Cartes de saillance et évaluation de la qualité des maillages 3D* (Doctoral dissertation). Retrieved from HAL ARCHIVES OUVERTES. (Accession No. tel-01418334)

Nouri, A., Charrier, C., & Lezoray, O. (2016b). Full-reference saliency-based 3D mesh quality assessment index. In ICIP (pp. 1007-1011). Academic Press.

Nouri, A., Charrier, C., & Lezoray, O. (2017a). *Greyc 3D colored Mesh Database*. Technical report. Retrieved from https://nouri.users.greyc.fr/ColoredMeshDatabase.html

Nouri, A., Charrier, C., & Lezoray, O. (2017b). 3D Blind mesh quality assessment index. *Proc. of IS&T Electronic Imaging. Three-Dimensional Image Processing, Measurement (3DIPM), and Applications*, 9-26.

Nouri, A., Charrier, C., & Lézoray, O. (2015). Multi-scale mesh saliency with local adaptive patches for viewpoint selection. *Signal Processing Image Communication*, *38*, 151–166. doi:10.1016/j.image.2015.08.002

Nouri, A., Charrier, C., & Lézoray, O. (2015b). Multi-scale saliency of 3D colored meshes. *International Conference on Image Processing (IEEE)*, 2820-2824.

Nwana, A. O., & Chen, T. (2016). Who ordered this?: Exploiting implicit user tag order preferences for personalized image tagging. In Proceedings of the International Conference on Multimedia & Expo Workshops, 2016 (pp. 1-6). IEEE. doi:10.1109/ICMEW.2016.7574753

Oguchi, K., Sone, S., Kiyono, K., Takashima, S., Maruyama, Y., Hasegawa, M., & Feng, L. (2000). Optimal tube current for lung cancer screening with low-dose spiral CT. *Acta Radiologica*, *41*(4), 352–356. doi:10.1080/028418500127345451 PMID:10937757

Ojala, T., Matti, P. A., & Harwood, D. (1996). A comparative study of texture measure with classification based on feature distribution. *Pattern Recognition*, *29*(1), 51–59. doi:10.1016/0031-3203(95)00067-4

Oliver, K. a. (2010). Image feature detection and matching. *Progress in Biomedical Optics and Imaging*, *7*, 7678–7690.

Ondrúška, P., Kohli, P., & Izadi, S. (2015). Mobilefusion: Real-time volumetric surface reconstruction and dense tracking on mobile phones. *IEEE Transactions on Visualization and Computer Graphics*, *21*(11), 1251–1258. doi:10.1109/TVCG.2015.2459902 PMID:26439826

Osher, S., & Fedkiw, R. (2002). *Level Set Methods and Dynamic Implicit Surfaces*. New York: Springer-Verlag.

Otsu, N. (1979). A Threshold Selection Method from Gray-Level Histograms. *IEEE Transactions on Systems, Man, and Cybernetics*, *9*(1), 62–66. doi:10.1109/TSMC.1979.4310076

Padmavathi, G. A. (2010). Non linear Image segmentation using fuzzy c means clustering method with thresholding for underwater images. *International Journal of Computer Science Issues*, *7*, 35–50.

Pal, S. K., & Pal, N. R. (1989). Object Background segmentation using a new definition Entropy. *IEEE Proceedings*, *136*, 284-295. 10.1049/ip-e.1989.0039

Palani, T. K., Parvathavarthini, B., & Chitra, K. (2016). Segmentation of brain regions by integrating meta heuristic multilevel threshold with Markov random field. *Current Medical Imaging Reviews*, *12*(1), 4–12. doi:10.2174/1573394 711666150827203434

Palani, T., & Parvathavarthini, B. (2017). Multichannel interictal spike activity detection using time–frequency entropy measure. *Australasian Physical & Engineering Sciences in Medicine*, *40*(2), 413–425. doi:10.100713246-017-0550-6 PMID:28409335

Pal, N. R., & Pal, S. K. (1989). Entropic thresholding. *Signal Processing*, *16*(2), 97–108. doi:10.1016/0165-1684(89)90090-X

Pal, N. R., & Pal, S. K. (1991). Entropy: A New Definition and its Applications. *IEEE Transactions on Systems, Man, and Cybernetics*, *21*(5), 1260–1270. doi:10.1109/21.120079

Panchal & Singh. (2013). Multimodal biometric system. *International Journal of Advanced Research in Computer Science and Software Engineering, 3*(5), 1360–1363.

Paragios, N., & Deriche, R. (2000). Geodesic active contours and level sets for the detection and tracking of moving objects. *IEEE Transactions on Pattern Analysis and Machine Intelligence, 22*(3), 266–280. doi:10.1109/34.841758

Paragios, N., & Deriche, R. (2002). Geodesic active regions: A new framework to deal with frame partition problems in computer vision. *Journal of Visual Communication and Image Representation, 13*(1-2), 249–268. doi:10.1006/jvci.2001.0475

Parkhurst, D., Law, K., & Niebur, E. (2002). Modeling the role of salience in the allocation of overt visual attention. *Vision Research, 42*(1), 107–123. doi:10.1016/S0042-6989(01)00250-4 PMID:11804636

Patil, D. D., & Deore, S. G. (2013). Medical Image Segmentation: A Review. *IJCSMC, 2*(1), 22–27.

Peck, J., & Childers, T. L. (2003a). To have and to hold: The influence of haptic information on product judgments. *Journal of Marketing, 67*(2), 35–48. doi:10.1509/jmkg.67.2.35.18612

Peck, J., & Childers, T. L. (2003b). Individual differences in haptic information processing: The 'need for touch' scale. *The Journal of Consumer Research, 30*(3), 430–442. doi:10.1086/378619

Peck, J., & Johnson, J. (2011). Autotelic need for touch, haptics, and persuasion: The role of involvement. *Psychology and Marketing, 28*(3), 222–239. doi:10.1002/mar.20389

Peck, J., & Shu, S. B. (2009). The effect of mere touch on perceived ownership. *The Journal of Consumer Research, 36*(3), 434–447. doi:10.1086/598614

Peck, J., & Wiggins, J. (2006). It just feels good: Customers' affective response to touch and its influence on persuasion. *Journal of Marketing, 70*(4), 56–69. doi:10.1509/jmkg.70.4.56

Peng, W., Xu, C., & Feng, Z. (2016). 3D face modeling based on structure optimization and surface reconstruction with B-Spline. *Neurocomputing, 179*, 228–237. doi:10.1016/j.neucom.2015.11.090

Pentland, A. P. (1990). Automatic extraction of deformable part models. *International Journal of Computer Vision, 4*(2), 107–126. doi:10.1007/BF00127812

Pitas, I., & Venetsanopoulos, A. N. (1992). Order Statistics in Digital Signal Processing. *Proceedings of the IEEE, 80*(12), 1893–1921. doi:10.1109/5.192071

Pons, J. P., Keriven, R., & Faugeras, O. (2005, June). Modelling dynamic scenes by registering multi-view image sequences. In *Computer Vision and Pattern Recognition, 2005. CVPR 2005. IEEE Computer Society Conference* on (Vol. 2, pp. 822-827). IEEE. 10.1109/CVPR.2005.227

Poria, S., Gelbukh, A., Cambria, E., Yang, P., Hussain, A., & Durrani, T. (2012b). Merging SenticNet and WordNet-Affect emotion lists for sentiment analysis. In *Signal Processing (ICSP), 2012 IEEE 11th International Conference on* (Vol. 2, pp. 1251-1255). IEEE. doi:10.1145/3003421.3003426

Poria, S., Gelbukhs, A., Cambria, E., Das, D., & Bandyopadhyay, S. (2012a). Enriching SenticNet polarity scores through semi-supervised fuzzy clustering. In *Data Mining Workshops (ICDMW), 2012 IEEE 12th International Conference on* (pp. 709-716). IEEE.

Poria, S., Cambria, E., Gelbukh, A., Bisio, F., & Hussain, A. (2015). Sentiment data flow analysis by means of dynamic linguistic patterns. *IEEE Computational Intelligence Magazine, 10*(4), 26–36. doi:10.1109/MCI.2015.2471215

Poria, S., Gelbukh, A., Cambria, E., Hussain, A., & Huang, G. B. (2014). EmoSenticSpace: A novel framework for affective common-sense reasoning. *Knowledge-Based Systems*, *69*, 108–123. doi:10.1016/j.knosys.2014.06.011

Poria, S., Gelbukh, A., Hussain, A., Howard, N., Das, D., & Bandyopadhyay, S. (2013). Enhanced SenticNet with affective labels for concept-based opinion mining. *IEEE Intelligent Systems*, *28*(2), 31–38. doi:10.1109/MIS.2013.4

Pospelov, D.A. (1990). *Artificial intelligence. Reference. Book 2. Models and methods.* Moscow, Russia: Radio and communication.

Potmesil, M. (1987). Generating octree models of 3D objects from their silhouettes in a sequence of images. *Computer Vision Graphics and Image Processing*, *40*(1), 1–29. doi:10.1016/0734-189X(87)90053-3

Pour Yazdanpanah, A., Faez, K., & Amirfattahi, R. (2010). Multimodal biometric system using face, ear and gait biometrics. *Information SciencesSignal Processing and their Applications (ISSPA), 2010 10th IEEE International Conference on*, 251–254. 10.1109/ISSPA.2010.5605477

Prasad, B. (2003). Intelligent techniques for e-commerce. *Journal of Electronic Commerce Research*, *4*(2), 65–71.

Prisacariu, V. A., Kahler, O., Murray, D. W., & Reid, I. D. (2013, October). Simultaneous 3D tracking and reconstruction on a mobile phone. In *Mixed and Augmented Reality (ISMAR), 2013 IEEE International Symposium on* (pp. 89-98). IEEE.

Pun, T. (1981). Entropic Thresholding, A New Approach. *Computer Graphics and image processing*, *16*, 201-239.

Qian, X., Wang, J., Guo, S., & Li, Q. (2013). An active contour model for medical image segmentation with application to brain CT image. *Medical Physics*, *40*(2), 021911. doi:10.1118/1.4774359 PMID:23387759

Quellec, G., Lamard, M., Cazuguel, G., Cochener, B., & Roux, C. (2010). Wavelet optimization for content-based image retrieval in medical databases. *J. Med. Image Anal*, *14*(2), 227–241. doi:10.1016/j.media.2009.11.004 PMID:20007020

Radhika, V., & Padmavati, G. (2010). Performance of various order statistics filters in impulse and mixed noise removal for RS images. *Signal and Image Processing: An International Journal*, *1*(2), 13–20. doi:10.5121ipij.2010.1202

Rae, A., Sigurbjörnsson, B., & van Zwol, R. (2010). Improving tag recommendation using social networks. In *Proceedings of the Adaptivity, Personalization and Fusion of Heterogeneous Information* (pp. 92-99). Academic Press.

Rahmani, H., Piccart, B., Fierens, D., & Blockeel, H. (2010). Three complementary approaches to context aware movie recommendation. In *Proceedings of the Workshop on Context-Aware Movie Recommendation* (pp. 57-60). ACM.

Rai, R. A. (2012). Underwater Image Segmentation using CLAHE Enhancement and Thresholding. *International Journal of Emerging Technology and Advanced Engineering*, *2*, 118–123.

Raja, N. S. M., Rajinikanth, V., & Latha, K. (2014). Otsu based optimal multilevel image thresholding using firefly algorithm. Modelling and Simulation in Engineering.

Rajinikanth, V., & Couceiro, M. S. (2015). RGB histogram based color image segmentation using firefly algorithm. *Procedia Computer Science*, *46*, 1449–1457. doi:10.1016/j.procs.2015.02.064

Rajinikanth, V., Raja, N. S. M., & Latha, K. (2014). Optimal multilevel image thresholding: An analysis with PSO and BFO algorithms. *Australian Journal of Basic and Applied Sciences*, *8*, 443–454.

Rajinikanth, V., Satapathy, S. C., Fernandes, S. L., & Nachiappan, S. (2017). Entropy based segmentation of tumor from brain MR images–A study with teaching learning based optimization. *Pattern Recognition Letters*, *94*, 87–94. doi:10.1016/j.patrec.2017.05.028

Rajini, N. H., & Bhavani, R. (2013). Computer aided detection of ischemic stroke using segmentation and texture features. *Measurement*, *46*(6), 1865–1874. doi:10.1016/j.measurement.2013.01.010

Ramón González, J., Moreno, V., Fernández, E., Izquierdo, Á., Borrás, J., & Gispert, R. (2005). Probabilidad de desarrollar y morir por cáncer en Cataluña en el período 1998-2001. *Medicina Clínica*, *124*(11), 411–414. doi:10.1157/13072840 PMID:15799846

Rangayyan, R. M., Ayres, F. J., & Leo Desautels, J. E. (2007). A review of computer-aided diagnosis of breast cancer: Toward the detection of subtle signs. *Journal of the Franklin Institute*, *344*(3-4), 312–348. doi:10.1016/j.jfranklin.2006.09.003

Ravichandran, D. (2016). *Performance Analysis of Three-Dimensional Medical Image Compression Based on Discrete Wavelet Transform*. IEEE doi:10.1109/VSMM.2016.7863176

Rawat, Y. S., & Kankanhalli, M. S. (2016). ConTagNet: exploiting user context for image tag recommendation. In *Proceedings of the ACM on Multimedia Conference* (pp. 1102-1106). ACM. 10.1145/2964284.2984068

Ribaric, S., & Fratric, I. (2006). Experimental evaluation of matching-score normalization techniques on different multimodal biometric systems. *Electrotechnical Conference, 2006. MELECON 2006. IEEE Mediterranean*, 498–501. 10.1109/MELCON.2006.1653147

Riedmiller, M., & Braun, H. (1993). A direct adaptive method for faster backpropagation learning: The RPROP algorithm. *Proc. IEEE Int. Conf. Neural Networks*, *1*, 586–591.

Rizzolatti, G., Riggio, L., & Sheliga, B. M. (1994). Space and selectiveattention. In C. Ulmità & M. Moscovitch (Eds.), *Attention and performance* (pp. 231–265). Cambridge, MA: MIT Press.

Roerdink, J. B. T. M., & Meijster, A. (2001). The watershed transform: Definitions, algorithms and parallelization strategies. *Fundamenta Informaticae*, *41*, 187–228.

Rogowitz, B. E., & Rushmeier, H. E. (2001). Are image quality metrics adequate to evaluate the quality of geometric objects? In B. E. Rogowitz & T. N. Pappas (Eds.), Human Vision and Electronic Imaging (pp. 340-348). SPIE.

Rose, G., Khoo, H., & Straub, D. W. (1999). Current technological impediments to business-to-consumer electronic commerce. *Communications of the AIS*, *1*(16), 1–74.

Roth, J., Tong, Y., & Liu, X. (2015). Unconstrained 3D face reconstruction. In *Proceedings of the IEEE Conference on Computer Vision and Pattern Recognition* (pp. 2606-2615). Academic Press.

Roth, J., Tong, Y., & Liu, X. (2016). Adaptive 3D face reconstruction from unconstrained photo collections. In *Proceedings of the IEEE Conference on Computer Vision and Pattern Recognition* (pp. 4197-4206). IEEE. 10.1109/CVPR.2016.455

Roy, D., Banerjee, S., Roy, S., & Chaudhuri, S. S. (2016). Removal of the Artifacts Present in the Existing Dehazing Techniques. *IC2C2SE*.

Roy, S., & Chaudhuri, S. S. (2016). Development of Real Time Visibility Enrichment Algorithms. *NCECERS*, 32.

Roy, S., & Chaudhuri, S. S. (2016). Modelling and control of sky pixels in visibility improvement through CSA. *IC2C2SE*.

Roy, A., Singha, J., Devi, S. S., & Laskar, R. H. (2016). Impulse noise removal using SVM classification based fuzzy filter from gray scale images. *Signal Processing*, *128*, 262–273. doi:10.1016/j.sigpro.2016.04.007

Roy, S., & Chaudhuri, S. S. (2016). Modeling of Ill-Posed Inverse Problem. *International Journal of Modern Education and Computer Science*, *12*, 46–55. doi:10.5815/ijmecs.2016.12.07

Rumelhart, D. E., Hinton, G. E., & Williams, R. J. (1986). Learning Internal Representations Error Propagation. Cambridge, MA: MIT Press.

Rusinkiewicz, S. (2004). Estimating Curvatures and Their Derivatives on Triangle Meshes. In 3DPVT (pp. 486-493). IEEE Computer Society.

Russell, C., Kohli, P., & Torr, P. H. (2009, September). Associative hierarchical crfs for object class image segmentation. In *Computer Vision, 2009 IEEE 12th International Conference on* (pp. 739-746). IEEE.

Sabbagh, M. (2016). Accelerating Cardiac MRI Compressed Sensing Image Reconstruction using Graphics Processing Units. Northeastern University.

Saferstein, R. (2007). *An Introduction to Forensic Science*. Pearson Education.

Saha, S., & Dr. Gupta, R. (2014). An Automated Skin Lesion Diagnosis by using Image Processing Techniques. *International Journal on Recent and Innovation Trends in Computing and Communication, 2*, 1081–1085.

Saito, H., & Kanade, T. (1999). Shape reconstruction in projective grid space from large number of images. In *Computer Vision and Pattern Recognition, 1999. IEEE Computer Society Conference* on. (Vol. 2, pp. 49-54). IEEE. 10.1109/CVPR.1999.784607

Sakhre, V., Singh, U. P., & Jain, S. (2016). FCPN Approach for Uncertain Nonlinear Dynamical System with Unknown Disturbance. *International Journal of Fuzzy Systems (Springer), 5*. doi:10.100740815-016-0145

Salunke, S. (2014). Survey on Skin lesion segmentation and classification. *International journal of image processing and data visualization, 1*, 1-5.

Sang, E. (2005.). Underwater acoustic image segmentation based on deformable template. *Chinese Journal of Acoustics*, 164–171.

Sasi, N. M., Jayasree, V. K. (2013). Contrast Limited Adaptive Histogram Equalization for Qualitative Enhancement of Myocardial Perfusion Images. *Engineering, 5*, 326-331.

Satapathy, S., & Naik, A. (2016). Social group optimization (SGO): A new population evolutionary optimization technique. *Complex & Intelligent Systems, 2*(3), 173–203. doi:10.100740747-016-0022-8

Sathya, P. D., & Kayalvizhi, R. (2010). Optimum multilevel image thresholding based on Tsallis Eetropy method with bacterial foraging algorithm. *International Journal of Computer Science Issues, 7*(5), 336–343.

Savinov, N., Ladicky, L., Hane, C., & Pollefeys, M. (2015). Discrete optimization of ray potentials for semantic 3d reconstruction. In *Proceedings of the IEEE Conference on Computer Vision and Pattern Recognition* (pp. 5511-5518). IEEE. 10.1109/CVPR.2015.7299190

Saxena, P., & Kumar, R. S. (in press). A Locally Adaptive Edge Preserving Filter for Denoising of Low Dose CT using Multi-level Fuzzy Reasoning Concept. *International Journal of Biomedical Engineering and Technology*.

Schedl, M., & Schnitzer, D. (2014). Location-aware music artist recommendation. In *Proceedings of the International Conference on Multimedia Modeling* (pp. 205-213). Springer.

Scherp, A., & Mezaris, V. (2014). Survey on modeling and indexing events in multimedia. *Proceedings of the Multimedia Tools and Applications, 70*(1), 7–23. doi:10.100711042-013-1427-7

Schettini, R., & Corchs, S. (2010). Underwater image Processing:state of the art of image restoration and image enhancement methods. *EURASIP Journal on Advances in Signal Processing, 2010*(1), 1–14. doi:10.1155/2010/746052

Schöps, T., Sattler, T., Häne, C., & Pollefeys, M. (2015, October). 3D modeling on the go: Interactive 3D reconstruction of large-scale scenes on mobile devices. In *3D Vision (3DV), 2015 International Conference on* (pp. 291-299). IEEE.

Segundo, M. P., Silva, L., & Bellon, O. R. P. (2012, September). Improving 3d face reconstruction from a single image using half-frontal face poses. In *Image Processing (ICIP), 2012 19th IEEE International Conference on* (pp. 1797-1800). IEEE.

Seitz, S. M., & Dyer, C. R. (1995, June). Complete scene structure from four point correspondences. In *Computer Vision, 1995. Proceedings., Fifth International Conference* on (pp. 330-337). IEEE. 10.1109/ICCV.1995.466921

Seitz, S. M., Curless, B., Diebel, J., Scharstein, D., & Szeliski, R. (2006, June). A comparison and evaluation of multi-view stereo reconstruction algorithms. In *Computer vision and pattern recognition, 2006 IEEE Computer Society Conference on* (Vol. 1, pp. 519-528). IEEE. 10.1109/CVPR.2006.19

Senapati, R. K. (2016). Volumetric medical image compression using 3D listless embedded block partitioning. *SpringerPlus*. PMID:28053830

Shah, R. R., Samanta, A., Gupta, D., Yu, Y., Tang, S., & Zimmermann, R. (2016f). PROMPT: Personalized User Tag Recommendation for Social Media Photos Leveraging Personal and Social Contexts. In IEEE International Symposium on Multimedia (ISM), 2016 (pp. 486-492). IEEE. doi:10.1109/ISM.2016.0109

Shah, R. R., Shaikh, A. D., Yu, Y., Geng, W., Zimmermann, R., & Wu, G. (2015a). Eventbuilder: Real-time multimedia event summarization by visualizing social media. In Proceedings of the 23rd ACM international conference on Multimedia (pp. 185-188). ACM. doi:10.1145/2733373.2809932

Shah, R. R., Yu, Y., Shaikh, A. D., & Zimmermann, R. (2015b). TRACE: Linguistic-Based Approach for Automatic Lecture Video Segmentation Leveraging Wikipedia Texts. In IEEE International Symposium on Multimedia (ISM), 2015 (pp. 217-220). IEEE. doi:10.1109/ISM.2015.18

Shah, R. R., Yu, Y., Shaikh, A. D., Tang, S., & Zimmermann, R. (2014b). ATLAS: automatic temporal segmentation and annotation of lecture videos based on modelling transition time. In Proceedings of the 22nd ACM international conference on Multimedia (pp. 209-212). ACM. doi:10.1145/2647868.2656407

Shah, R. R. (2016c). Multimodal Analysis of User-Generated Content in Support of Social Media Applications. In *Proceedings of the 2016 ACM on International Conference on Multimedia Retrieval* (pp. 423-426). ACM. 10.1145/2911996.2912032

Shah, R. R. (2016e). Multimodal-based Multimedia Analysis, Retrieval, and Services in Support of Social Media Applications. In *Proceedings of the 2016 ACM on Multimedia Conference* (pp. 1425-1429). ACM. 10.1145/2964284.2971471

Shah, R. R., Hefeeda, M., Zimmermann, R., Harras, K., Hsu, C. H., & Yu, Y. (2016b). NEWSMAN: Uploading Videos over Adaptive Middleboxes to News Servers in Weak Network Infrastructures. In *International Conference on Multimedia Modeling* (pp. 100-113). Springer. 10.1007/978-3-319-27671-7_9

Shah, R. R., Yu, Y., Tang, S., Satoh, S. I., Verma, A., & Zimmermann, R. (2016d). Concept-Level Multimodal Ranking of Flickr Photo Tags via Recall Based Weighting. In *Proceedings of the 2016 ACM Workshop on Multimedia COMMONS* (pp. 19-26). ACM. 10.1145/2983554.2983555

Shah, R. R., Yu, Y., Verma, A., Tang, S., Shaikh, A. D., & Zimmermann, R. (2016a). Leveraging multimodal information for event summarization and concept-level sentiment analysis. *Knowledge-Based Systems*, *108*, 102–109. doi:10.1016/j.knosys.2016.05.022

Shah, R. R., Yu, Y., & Zimmermann, R. (2014a). Advisor: Personalized video soundtrack recommendation by late fusion with heuristic rankings. In *Proceedings of the 22nd ACM international conference on Multimedia* (pp. 607-616). ACM. 10.1145/2647868.2654919

Shah, R. R., Yu, Y., & Zimmermann, R. (2014c). User preference-aware music video generation based on modeling scene moods. In *Proceedings of the 5th ACM Multimedia Systems Conference* (pp. 156-159). ACM. 10.1145/2557642.2579372

Shah, R., & Zimmermann, R. (2017). *Multimodal Analysis of User-Generated Multimedia Content*. Springer. doi:10.1007/978-3-319-61807-4

Shahrbabaki, S. T. (2015). *Contribution de la couleur dans l'attention visuelle et un modèle de saillance visuelle* (Doctoral dissertation). Retrieved from HAL ARCHIVES OUVERTES. (Accession No. tel-01241487)

Shaikh, A. D., Shah, R. R., & Shaikh, R. (2013b). SMS based FAQ retrieval for Hindi, English and Malayalam. In *Post-Proceedings of the 4th and 5th Workshops of the Forum for Information Retrieval Evaluation* (p. 9). ACM.

Shaikh, A. D., Jain, M., Rawat, M., Shah, R. R., & Kumar, M. (2013a). Improving accuracy of sms based faq retrieval system. In *Multilingual Information Access in South Asian Languages* (pp. 142–156). Berlin: Springer. doi:10.1007/978-3-642-40087-2_14

Shannon, C. E. (1948). A mathematical theory of communication. *The Bell System Technical Journal*, *27*(3), 379–423. doi:10.1002/j.1538-7305.1948.tb01338.x

Shannon, C. E., & Weaver, W. (2001). The Mathematical Theory of Communication. *ACM SIGMOBILE Mobile Computing and Communications Review*, *5*(1), 3–55. doi:10.1145/584091.584093

Shanthakumar, P., & Kumar, P. G. (2015). Computer aided brain tumor detection system using watershed segmentation techniques. *International Journal of Imaging Systems and Technology*, *25*(4), 297–301. doi:10.1002/ima.22147

Shilane, P., & Funkhouser, T. (2007). Distinctive regions of 3D surfaces. *ACM Transactions on Graphics*, *26*, 7. Retrieved from http://doi.acm.org/10.1145/1243980.1243981

Shneier, M. O., Kent, E., & Mansbach, P. (1984, July). Representing workspace and model knowledge for a robot with mobile sensors. *7th International Conference on Pattern Recognition*.

Shreya, A. (2016). A Survey on DICOM Image Compression and Decompression Techniques. *International Journal of Computer Engineering and Applications*, *ICCSTAR-2016*(Special Issue).

Shukla & Mishra. (2010). A hybrid model of multimodal biometrics system using fingerprint and face as traits. *IJCSES*, *1*(2).

Shyu, M. S., & Leou, J. J. (1998). A genetic algorithm approach to colour image enhancements. *Pattern Recognition*, *31*, 881–890.

Silva, S., Santos, B. S., Ferreira, C., & Madeira, J. (2009). A perceptual data repository for polygonal meshes. *Second International Conference in Visualisation*, 207-212. 10.1109/VIZ.2009.41

Simari, P. D., Picciau, G., & Floriani, L. D. (2014). Fast and Scalable Mesh Superfacets. *Computer Graphics Forum*, *33*(7), 181–190. doi:10.1111/cgf.12486

Singh & Sharma. (2012). Hybrid Image Compression Using DWT, DCT & Huffman Encoding Techniques. *International Journal of Emerging Technology and Advanced Engineering*, *2*(10).

Singh, M., & Mehrotra, M. (2016). Bridging the Gap Between Users and Recommender Systems: A Change in Perspective to User Profiling. *International Journal of Intelligent Systems Technologies and Applications*, 379.

Singh, S. A. (2005). Segmentation of underwater objects using CLAHE enhancement and thresholding with 3-class fuzzy cmeans clustering. *IEEE International Conference on Mechatronics and Automation*, *2*, 1802-1806.

Singh, U. P., & Jain, S. (2016). Modified Chaotic Bat Algorithm-Based Counter Propagation Neural Network for Uncertain Nonlinear Discrete Time System. *International Journal of Computational Intelligence and Applications*, *15*(3), 1650016. doi:10.1142/S1469026816500164

Singh, U. P., Saxena, K., & Jain, S. (2011). A Review: Different Types of Similarity Measures. *Pioneer Journal of Computer Science and Engineering Technology*, *2*(1), 43–63.

Singh, U. P., Saxena, K., & Jain, S. (2011). Semi-Supervised Method of Multiple Object Segmentation with Region Labeling and Flood Fill. *Signal and Image Processing International Journal (Toronto, Ont.)*, *2*(3), 175–193.

Singh, U. P., Saxena, K., & Jain, S. (2011). Unsupervised Method of Object Retrieval with Region Labeling and Flood Fill" *International Journal of Advanced Computer Science and Applications. Special Issue on Artificial Intelligence*, *1*, 41–50.

Singh, V. K., Mahata, D., & Adhikari, R. (2010). Mining the blogosphere from a socio-political perspective. In *Proceedings of the International Conference on Computer Information Systems and Industrial Management Applications*, (pp. 365-370). IEEE. 10.1109/CISIM.2010.5643634

Sinha, S. N., & Pollefeys, M. (2005, October). Multi-view reconstruction using photo-consistency and exact silhouette constraints: A maximum-flow formulation. In *Computer Vision, 2005. ICCV 2005. Tenth IEEE International Conference on* (Vol. 1, pp. 349-356). IEEE. 10.1109/ICCV.2005.159

Sipser, M. (2013). *Introduction to the theory of computation* (3rd ed.). Cengage Learning.

Slabaugh, G. G., Culbertson, W. B., Malzbender, T., Stevens, M. R., & Schafer, R. W. (2004). Methods for volumetric reconstruction of visual scenes. *International Journal of Computer Vision*, *57*(3), 179–199. doi:10.1023/B:VISI.0000013093.45070.3b

Slabaugh, G., Schafer, R., Malzbender, T., & Culbertson, B. (2001). A survey of methods for volumetric scene reconstruction from photographs. In *Volume Graphics 2001* (pp. 81–100). Vienna: Springer. doi:10.1007/978-3-7091-6756-4_6

Slavcheva, M., Baust, M., Cremers, D., & Ilic, S. (2017). KillingFusion: Non-rigid 3D Reconstruction without Correspondences. In *IEEE Conference on Computer Vision and Pattern Recognition (CVPR)* (p. 19). IEEE.

Smith, A., & Anderson, M. (2016). *Online shopping and e-commerce*. Pew Research Center. Retrieved from http://www.pewinternet.org/2016/12/19/online-shopping-and-purchasing-preferences/

Smith, D. E., Gier, J. A., & Willis, F. N. (1982). Interpersonal touch and compliance with a marketing request. *Basic and Applied Social Psychology*, *3*(1), 35–38. doi:10.120715324834basp0301_3

Smith, J. K. (1983). Quantitative versus qualitative research: An attempt to clarify the issue. *Educational Researcher*, *12*(6), 6–13. doi:10.3102/0013189X012003006

Snoek, C. G., Worring, M., & Smeulders, A. W. (2005). Early versus late fusion in semantic video analysis. In *Proceedings of the 13th annual ACM international conference on Multimedia* (pp. 399-402). ACM. 10.1145/1101149.1101236

Sober, A. J., Fitzpatrick, T. B., & Mihm, M. C. (1979). Early recognition of cutaneous melanoma. *JAMA*, *242*(25), 2795–2799. doi:10.1001/jama.1979.03300250051033 PMID:501893

Song, R., Liu, Y., Martin, R. R. & Rosin, P. L. (2014). Mesh saliency via spectral processing. *ACM Trans. Graph.*, *33*, 6:1-6:17.

Song, R., Liu, Y., Zhao, Y., Martin, R. R., & Rosin, P. L. (2012). Conditional random field-based mesh saliency. In ICIP (p./pp. 637-640). IEEE. doi:10.1109/ICIP.2012.6466940

Sorkine, O., Cohen-Or, D., & Toledo, S. (2003). High-Pass Quantization for Mesh Encoding. In L. Kobbelt, P. Schröder & H. Hoppe (Eds.), *Symposium on Geometry Processing* (pp. 42-51). Eurographics Association.

Souleymane, B. A., Gao, X., & Wang, B. (2013). A Fast and Robust Level Set Method for Image Segmentation Using Fuzzy Clustering and Lattice Boltzmann Method. *IEEE Transactions on Cybernetics*, *43*(3), 910–920. doi:10.1109/TSMCB.2012.2218233 PMID:23076068

Spangenberg, E. R., Crowley, A. E., & Henderson, P. W. (1996). Improving the store environment: Do olfactory cues affect evaluations and behaviors? *Journal of Marketing*, *60*(2), 67–80. doi:10.2307/1251931

Spiggle, S. (1994). Analysis and interpretation of qualitative data in consumer research. *The Journal of Consumer Research*, *21*(3), 491–503. doi:10.1086/209413

Sridevi. (2012). A Survey on Various Compression Methods for Medical Images. *I. J. Intelligent Systems and Applications*, *3*, 13-19.

Srikanth, R., & Ramakrishnan, A. G. (2005). Contextual encoding in uniform and adaptive mesh-based lossless compression of MR images. IEEE Trans. Med. Imag., 24(9).

Srikanth, R., & Ramakrishnan, A. G. (2005). *Context based Interframe coding of MR Images. MILE labs*. Department of Electrical Engineering, Indian Institute of Science.

Srinivasan, K. S., & Ebenezer, D. (2007). A new fast and efficient decision-based algorithm for removal of high-density impulse noises. *IEEE Signal Processing Letters*, *14*(3), 189–192. doi:10.1109/LSP.2006.884018

Srivastava, P., & Singh, U. P. (2014). Noise Removal Using First Order Median Filter. *IEEE International Conference CSIBIG-2014*. 10.1109/CSIBIG.2014.7057004

Srivastava, S. K., & Ahuja, N. (1990). Octree generation from object silhouettes in perspective views. *Computer Vision Graphics and Image Processing*, *49*(1), 68–84. doi:10.1016/0734-189X(90)90163-P

Steffen, P., Heller, P. N., Gopinath, R. A., & Burrus, C. S. (1993). Theory of regular m-band bases. *IEEE Transactions on Signal Processing*, *41*(12), 3497–3510. doi:10.1109/78.258088

Strickland, R. N., Kim, C. S., & McDonnel, W. F. (1987). Digital colour image enhancement based on saturation component. *Optical Engineering (Redondo Beach, Calif.)*, *26*(7), 609–616. doi:10.1117/12.7974125

Subbarayudu, V. C., & Prasad, M. V. N. K. (2008). Multimodal biometric system. *Emerging Trends in Engineering and Technology-2008 (ICETET '08)IEEE. International conference on*, 635–640. 10.1109/ICETET.2008.93

Sundaramoorthi, G., Yezzi, A., & Mennucci, A. (2007). Sobolev active contours. *International Journal of Computer Vision*, *73*(3), 345–366. doi:10.100711263-006-0635-2

Sun, X., Kashima, H., Matsuzaki, T., & Naonori, U. (2010). Averaged Stochastic Gradient Descent with Feedback: An Accurate, Robust, and Fast Training Method. *IEEE International Conference on Data Mining*, 1067-1072. 10.1109/ICDM.2010.26

Suwajanakorn, S., Kemelmacher-Shlizerman, I., & Seitz, S. M. (2014, September). Total moving face reconstruction. In *European Conference on Computer Vision* (pp. 796-812). Springer.

Szeliski, R. (1993). Rapid octree construction from image sequences. *Computer Vision, Graphics, and Image Processing: Image Understanding*, *58*(1), 23-32.

Tal, A., Shtrom, E., & Leifman, G. (2012). Surface regions of interest for viewpoint selection. *IEEE Conference on Computer Vision and Pattern Recognition*, 414-421.

Tan, R. (2008). Visibility in Bad Weather from A Single Image. *IEEE Explore*, 1-8.

Tang, F. H., Ng, D. K. S., & Chow, D. H. K. (2011). An image feature approach for computer-aided detection of ischemic stroke. *Computers in Biology and Medicine*, *41*(7), 529–536. doi:10.1016/j.compbiomed.2011.05.001 PMID:21605853

Tanskanen, P., Kolev, K., Meier, L., Camposeco, F., Saurer, O., & Pollefeys, M. (2013). Live metric 3d reconstruction on mobile phones. In *Proceedings of the IEEE International Conference on Computer Vision* (pp. 65-72). IEEE. 10.1109/ICCV.2013.15

Tao, P., Cao, J., Li, S., Liu, X., & Liu, L. (2015). Mesh saliency via ranking unsalient patches in a descriptor space. *Computers & Graphics*, *46*, 264–274. doi:10.1016/j.cag.2014.09.023

Tarel, J. P., & Hautiere, N. (2009). Fast visibility restoration from a single color or gray level image. *IEEE 12th International conference on Computer Vision*, 2201 – 2208.

Tatler, B.W, Baddeley, R.J&Glichrist, I.D. (2005). Visual correlates of fixation selection: effects of scale and time. *Vision Research, 45*, 643-659.

Taylor, C. J. (2003, October). *Surface Reconstruction from Feature Based Stereo*. ICCV.

Terzopoulos, D., & Metaxas, D. (1990, December). Dynamic 3D models with local and global deformations: Deformable superquadrics. In *Computer Vision, 1990. Proceedings, Third International Conference* on (pp. 606-615). IEEE.

Thanaraj, P., Roshini, M., & Balasubramanian, P. (2016). Integration of multivariate empirical mode decomposition and independent component analysis for fetal ECG separation from abdominal signals. *Technology and Health Care*, *24*(6), 783–794. doi:10.3233/THC-161224 PMID:27315149

Toh, K. K. V., & Isa, N. A. M. (2010). Noise adaptive fuzzy switching median filter for salt-and-pepper noise reduction. *IEEE Signal Processing Letters*, *17*(3), 281–284. doi:10.1109/LSP.2009.2038769

Tong, J., Zhou, J., Liu, L., Pan, Z., & Yan, H. (2012). Scanning 3d full human bodies using kinects. *IEEE Transactions on Visualization and Computer Graphics*, *18*(4), 643–650. doi:10.1109/TVCG.2012.56 PMID:22402692

Toprak, A., & Güler, İ. (2006). Suppression of impulse noise in medical images with the use of fuzzy adaptive median filter. *Journal of Medical Systems*, *30*(6), 465–471. doi:10.100710916-006-9031-2 PMID:17233159

Traina, A., Castanon, C., & Traina, C., Jr. (2003). Multiwavemed: A system for medical image retrieval through wavelets transformations. *Proc. IEEE16th Symp. Comput.-Based Med. Syst.*, 150–155.

Treisman, A. M., & Gelade, G. (1980). A Feature-Integration Theory of Attention. *Cognitive Psychology*, *12*(1), 97–136. doi:10.1016/0010-0285(80)90005-5 PMID:7351125

Treuille, A., Hertzmann, A., & Seitz, S. M. (2004, May). Example-based stereo with general BRDFs. In *European Conference on Computer Vision* (pp. 457-469). Springer.

Treviño, T., & Morton, F. (2016). Online shopping in Mexico: Exploring the promising and challenging panorama. In C. M. Coria-Sánchez & J. T. Hyatt (Eds.), *Essays on Mexican Business Culture* (pp. 166–182). McFarland.

Tuba, M. (2014). Multilevel image thresholding by nature-inspired algorithms: A short review. *Computer Science Journal of Moldova*, *22*, 318–338.

Tyan, Y.S., Wu, M.C., Chin, C.L., Kuo, Y.L., Lee, M.S., & Chang, H.Y. (2014). Ischemic stroke detection system with a computer-aided diagnostic ability using an unsupervised feature perception enhancement method. *International Journal of Biomedical Imaging*. doi:.10.1155/2014/947539

Ueno, I., & Pearlman, W. (2003). Region of interest coding in volumetric images with shape-adaptive wavelet transform. *Proceedings of the Society for Photo-Instrumentation Engineers, 5022*, 1048. doi:10.1117/12.476709

Ukrit. (2011). A Survey on Lossless Compression for Medical Images. *International Journal of Computer Applications, 31*(8).

University of Michigan Health System. (n.d.). Retrieved from https://www.med.umich.edu/1libr/cancer/skin04.html

Usinskas, A., & Gleizniene, R. (2006). Ischemic stroke region recognition based on ray tracing. *Proceedings of International Baltic Electronics Conference.* 10.1109/BEC.2006.311103

Valgaerts, L., Wu, C., Bruhn, A., Seidel, H. P., & Theobalt, C. (2012). Lightweight binocular facial performance capture under uncontrolled lighting. *ACM Transactions on Graphics, 31*(6), 187–1. doi:10.1145/2366145.2366206

Vapnik, V. N. (1995). *The Nature of Statistical Learning Theory.* Springer. doi:10.1007/978-1-4757-2440-0

Vása, L., & Rus, J. (2012). Dihedral Angle Mesh Error: A fast perception correlated distortion measure for fixed connectivity triangle meshes. *Computer Graphics Forum, 31*(5), 1715–1724. doi:10.1111/j.1467-8659.2012.03176.x

Verma, N., & Singh, J. (2017). An Innovative Approach for E-Commerce Website Ranking. *International Journal of Advanced Research in Computer Science, 8*(4).

Vijaykumar, V. R., & Santhanamari, G. (2014). New decision-based trimmed median filter for high-density salt-and-pepper noise removal in images. *Journal of Electronic Imaging, 23*(3), 033011–033011. doi:10.1117/1.JEI.23.3.033011

Vision du futur. La rétine. (n.d.). Retrieved from http://lavisiondufutur.e-monsite.com/pages/l-oeil/la-retine.html

Vogiatzis, G., Torr, P. H., & Cipolla, R. (2005, June). Multi-view stereo via volumetric graph-cuts. In *Computer Vision and Pattern Recognition, 2005. CVPR 2005. IEEE Computer Society Conference on* (Vol. 2, pp. 391-398). IEEE. 10.1109/CVPR.2005.238

Vogiatzis, G., Torr, P., Seitz, S. M., & Cipolla, R. (2004). *Reconstructing relief surfaces.* BMVC. doi:10.5244/C.18.14

Vuorimaa, P. (1994). Use of the fuzzy self-orginizing map in pattern self-recognition. In *Proc. 3-rd IEEE Int. Conf. Fuzzy Systems «FUZZ-IEEE'94»* (pp. 798–801). Orlando, FL: IEEE.

Vuorimaa, P. (1994). Fuzzy self-organizing map. *Fuzzy Sets and Systems, 66*(2), 223–231. doi:10.1016/0165-0114(94)90312-3

Wang, G., Pan, Z., Xu, J., Zhang, Z., Liu, C., & Ding, J. Y. (2011). Active Contour Model for Images Corrupted by Multiplicative Noise with Rayleigh Distribution. *IEEE 5th International Conference on Cybernetics and Intelligent Systems (CIS)*, 124-127.

Wang, Y., & Kankanhalli, M. S. (2015, May). Tweeting cameras for event detection. In *Proceedings of the 24th International Conference on World Wide Web* (pp. 1231-1241). International World Wide Web Conferences Steering Committee. ACM. 10.1145/2736277.2741634

Wang, G., Li, D., Pan, W., & Zang, Z. (2010). Modified switching median filter for impulse noise removal. *Signal Processing, 90*(12), 3213–3218. doi:10.1016/j.sigpro.2010.05.026

Wang, H. a. (2013). Saliency-Based Adaptive Object Extraction for Color Underwater Images. *Proceedings of the 2nd International Conference on Computer Science and Electronics Engineering (ICCSEE 2013)*, 2651-2655. 10.2991/iccsee.2013.661

Wang, J., Li, T., Lu, H., & Liang, Z. (2006). Penalized weighted least-squares approach to sinogram noise reduction and image reconstruction for low-dose X-ray computed tomography. *IEEE Transactions on Medical Imaging, 25*(10), 1272–1283. doi:10.1109/TMI.2006.882141 PMID:17024831

Wang, K., Lavoué, G., Denis, F., & Baskurt, A. (2011). Robust and blind mesh watermarking based on volume moments. *Computers & Graphics, 35*(1), 1–19. doi:10.1016/j.cag.2010.09.010

Wang, K., Torkhani, F., & Montanvert, A. (2012). A fast roughness-based approach to the assessment of 3D mesh visual quality. *Computers & Graphics, 36*(7), 808–818. doi:10.1016/j.cag.2012.06.004

Wang, Q., Chen, X., Wei, M., & Miao, Z. (2016). Simultaneous encryption and compression of medical images based on optimized tensor compressed sensing with 3D Lorenz. *Biomedical Engineering Online, 15*(1), 118. doi:10.118612938-016-0239-1 PMID:27814721

Wang, X., Jia, Y., Chen, R., & Zhou, B. (2015). Ranking User Tags in Micro-Blogging Website. In *Proceedings of the 2nd International Conference on Information Science and Control Engineering*, (pp. 400-403). IEEE.

Wang, Z., & Bovik, A. C. (2006). *Modern Image Quality Assessment*. Morgan & Claypool Publishers.

Wang, Z., & Bovik, A. C. (2011). Reduced- and No-Reference Image Quality Assessment. *IEEE Signal Processing Magazine, 28*(6), 29–40. doi:10.1109/MSP.2011.942471

Wang, Z., Bovik, A. C., Sheikh, H. R., & Simoncelli, E. P. (2004). Image quality assessment: From error visibilitytostructural similarity. *IEEE Transactions on Image Processing, 13*(4), 600–612. doi:10.1109/TIP.2003.819861 PMID:15376593

Wansink, B., & Van Ittersum, K. (2003). Bottoms up! The influence of elongation on pouring and consumption volume. *The Journal of Consumer Research, 30*(3), 455–463. doi:10.1086/378621

Wick, M. M., Sober, A. J., Fitzpatrick, T. B., Mihm, M. C., Kopf, A. W., Clark, W. H., & Blois, M. S. (1980). Clinical characteristics of early cutaneous melanoma Cancer. *Cancer, 45*(1), 2684–2706. doi:10.1002/1097-0142(19800515)45:10<2684::AID-CNCR2820451033>3.0.CO;2-2 PMID:7379001

Widdel, H. (1984). Operational problems in analyzing eye movements. *Theoretical and applied aspects of eye movement research, 22*, 21-29.

Wolfe, J. M., Alvarez, G. A., & Horowitz, T. S. (2000). Attention is fast but volition is slow. *Nature, 406*(6797), 691. doi:10.1038/35021132 PMID:10963584

Wolfe, J. M., Cave, K. R., & Franzel, S. L. (1989). Guided research: An alternative to the feature integration model for visual research. *Journal of Experimental Psychology. Human Perception and Performance, 15*(3), 419–433. doi:10.1037/0096-1523.15.3.419 PMID:2527952

Wolfe, J. M., Palmer, E. M., & Horowitz, T. S. (2010). Reaction time distributions constrain models of visual research. *Vision Research, 50*(14), 1304–1311. doi:10.1016/j.visres.2009.11.002 PMID:19895828

Workman, J. E., & Caldwell, L. F. (2007). Centrality of visual product aesthetics, tactile and uniqueness needs of fashion consumers. *International Journal of Consumer Studies, 31*(6), 589–596. doi:10.1111/j.1470-6431.2007.00613.x

WSO. (n.d.). Retrieved from http://www.world-stroke.org/

Wu, K.L., & Yang, M.S. (2003). A fuzzy-soft learning vector quantization. *Neurocomputing is, 55*, 681-697.

Wu, J., Shen, X., Zhu, W., & Liu, L. (2013). Mesh saliency with global rarity. *Graphical Models, 75*(5), 255–264. doi:10.1016/j.gmod.2013.05.002

Wu, L., Yang, L., Yu, N., & Hua, X. S. (2009). Learning to tag. In *Proceedings of the 18th international conference on World Wide Web* (pp. 361-370). ACM. 10.1145/1526709.1526758

Wu, X., Zhang, D., & Wang, K. (2006). Palm line extraction and matching for personal authentication. *IEEE Transactions on Systems, Man, and Cybernetics. Part A, Systems and Humans, 36*(5), 978–987. doi:10.1109/TSMCA.2006.871797

Xhang, X., & Brainard, D. H. (2004). Estimation of Saturated Pixel Values in Digital Colour Imaging. *Optical Society of America, 21*(12), 2301–2310. doi:10.1364/JOSAA.21.002301

Xiao, J., Zhou, W., Li, X., Wang, M., & Tian, Q. (2012). Image tag re-ranking by coupled probability transition. In *Proceedings of the 20th ACM International Conference on Multimedia* (pp. 849-852). ACM. 10.1145/2393347.2396328

Xu, L., Jackowskia, M., Goshtasbya, A., Roseman, D., Binesb, S., Yu, C., Dhawand, A., & Huntley, A. (1999). Segmentation of skin cancer images. *Image and Vision Computing, 17,* 65-74.

Xu, L., Jackowxki, M., Goshtasby, A., Roseman, D., Bines, S., Yu, C., Dhawan, A., & Huntley, A. (1999). Skin Images Segmentation. *Vis. Comput., 17,* 65-74.

Xu, X.-N., Mu, Z.-C., & Yuan, L. (2007). Feature-level fusion method based on KFDA for multimodal recognition fusing ear and profile face. *Wavelet Analysis and Pattern Recognition, 2007. ICWAPR'07. International Conference on, 3,* 1306–1310.

Xu, C., & Prince, J. L. (1998). Snakes, shapes, and gradient vector flow. *IEEE Transactions on Image Processing, 7*(3), 359–369. doi:10.1109/83.661186 PMID:18276256

Xu, N., Ahuia, N., & Bansal, R. (2007). Object segmentation using graph cuts based active contours. *Computer Vision and Image Understanding, 107*(3), 210–224. doi:10.1016/j.cviu.2006.11.004

Xu, R., & Wunsch, D. C. (2009). Clustering. In *IEEE Press Series on Computational Intelligence* (pp. 842–751). Hoboken, NJ: John Wiley & Sons.

Yaffe, M. J. (2010). Basic Physics of Digital Mammography. *Medical Radiology,* 1–11. doi:10.1007/978-3-540-78450-0_1

Yahiaoui, A. F. Z., & Bessaid, Y. (2016). Segmentation of ischemic stroke area from CT brain images. *International Symposium on Signal, Image, Video and Communications (ISIVC).* 10.1109/ISIVC.2016.7893954

Yamamoto, N., Ogata, J., & Ariki, Y. (2003). Topic segmentation and retrieval system for lecture videos based on spontaneous speech recognition. *Proceedings of the INTERSPEECH.*

Yan, C. (2010). Study on underwater image segmentation technique. *International Conference on E-Health Networking,* 135-137.

Yang, F., & Baofeng, M. A. (2007). Two models multimodal biometric fusion based on fingerprint, palm-print and hand-geometry. *Bioinformatics and Biomedical Engineering (ICBBE), Wuhan. 1st International Conference on,* 498–501. doi:10.1109/ICIAS.2007.4658364

Yang, F., & Ma, B. (2007). A new mixed-mode biometrics informationvfusion based-on fingerprint, hand-geometry and palmprint. *Image and Graphics, 2007. ICIG 2007. Fourth IEEE International Conference on,* 689–693.

Yang, G(2007*Study on segmentation and recognition algorithms for underwater images based on fractal theory* (Master's thesis). Huazhong.

Yang, R. (2003, October). Dealing with textureless regions and specular highlights-a progressive space carving scheme using a novel photo-consistency measure. In *Computer Vision, 2003. Proceedings. Ninth IEEE International Conference on* (pp. 576-584). IEEE.

Yang, C., Chen, J., Su, N., & Su, G. (2014). Improving 3D face details based on normal map of hetero-source images. In *Proceedings of the IEEE Conference on Computer Vision and Pattern Recognition Workshops* (pp. 9-14). IEEE. 10.1109/CVPRW.2014.7

Yarbus, A. L. (2002). *Eye movements and vision.* Plenum Press.

Yee, Y. H., Pattanaik, S. N., & Greenberg, D. P. (2001). Spatiotemporal sensitivity and visual attention for efficient rendering of dynamic environments. *ACM Transactions on Graphics, 20*(1), 39–65. doi:10.1145/383745.383748

Yi, F. (2012). Image segmentation: A survey of graph-cut methods. *Inkyu Moon, Systems and Informatics (ICSAI), IEEE International Conference*, 1936-1941.

Yim, C., & Bovik, A. C. (2011). Quality Assessment of Deblocked Images. *IEEE Transactions on Image Processing, 20*(1), 88–98. doi:10.1109/TIP.2010.2061859 PMID:20682474

Yin, Y., Shah, R. R., & Zimmermann, R. (2016). A general feature-based map matching framework with trajectory simplification. In *Proceedings of the 7th ACM SIGSPATIAL International Workshop on GeoStreaming* (p. 7). ACM.

Yousefi, S., Qin, J., Zhi, Z., & Wang, R. K. (2013). Uniform enhancement of optical micro-angiography images using Rayleigh contrast-limited adaptive histogram equalization. *Quant Imaging Med Surg, 3*, 5–17. PMID:23482880

Yu, X. (2005). *Study on segmentation and recognition algorithms for underwater images based on fuzzy theory* (Master's thesis). Huazhong University of Science and Technology.

Yuko, A., Nakanishi, J., & JeffreyWestern, B. (2007). Advancing the state of-the-art in transportation security identification and verification technologies: Biometric and multibiometric systems. In *Intelligent Transportation Systems Conference, 2007. ITSC 2007.* IEEE.

Yushkevich, P. A., Piven, J., Hazlett, H. C., Smith, R. G., Ho, S., Gee, J. C., & Gerig, G. (2006). User-guided 3D active contour segmentation of anatomical structures: Significantly improved efficiency and reliability. *NeuroImage, 31*(3), 1116–1128. doi:10.1016/j.neuroimage.2006.01.015 PMID:16545965

Yu, T., Xu, N., & Ahuja, N. (2004). Shape and view independent reflectance map from multiple views. *Computer Vision-ECCV, 2004,* 24–29.

Zach, C., Hane, C., & Pollefeys, M. (2014). What is optimized in convex relaxations for multilabel problems: Connecting discrete and continuously inspired map inference. *IEEE Transactions on Pattern Analysis and Machine Intelligence, 36*(1), 157–170. doi:10.1109/TPAMI.2013.105 PMID:24231873

Zaharieva, M., Zeppelzauer, M., & Breiteneder, C. (2013). Automated social event detection in large photo collections. In *Proceedings of the Third ACM International Conference on Multimedia Retrieval* (pp. 167-174). ACM. 10.1145/2461466.2461495

Zakeri, F. S., Behnam, H., & Ahmadinejad, N. (2012). Classification of benign and malignant breast masses based on shape and texture features in sonography images. *Journal of Medical Systems, 36*(3), 1621–1627. doi:10.100710916-010-9624-7 PMID:21082222

Zeng, G., Paris, S., Quan, L., & Sillion, F. (2005, October). Progressive surface reconstruction from images using a local prior. In *Computer Vision, 2005. ICCV 2005. Tenth IEEE International Conference on* (Vol. 2, pp. 1230-1237). IEEE. 10.1109/ICCV.2005.196

Zeng, M., Zheng, J., Cheng, X., & Liu, X. (2013). Templateless quasi-rigid shape modeling with implicit loop-closure. In *Proceedings of the IEEE Conference on Computer Vision and Pattern Recognition* (pp. 145-152). IEEE. 10.1109/CVPR.2013.26

Zhang, J., Wang, S., & Huang, Q. (2017). Location-based parallel tag completion for geo-tagged social image retrieval. *Proceedings of the ACM Transactions on Intelligent Systems and Technology, 8*(3), 38. 10.1145/3001593

Zhang, L., & Seitz, S. (2001). Image-based multiresolution shape recovery by surface deformation. In *Proceedings-SPIE the International Society for Optical Engineering* (Vol. 4309, pp. 51–61). SPIE International Society for Optical.

Zhang, X., Zhan, Y., Ding, M., Hou, W., & Yin, Z. (2013). Decision-based non-local means filter for removing impulse noise from digital images. *Signal Processing, 93*(2), 517–524. doi:10.1016/j.sigpro.2012.08.022

Zhang, Y., Brady, M., & Smith, S. (2001). Segmentation of brain MR images through a hidden Markov random field model and the expectation maximization algorithm. *IEEE Transactions on Medical Imaging, 20*(1), 45–57. doi:10.1109/42.906424 PMID:11293691

Zhao, Y., & Liu, Y. (2012). Patch based saliency detection method for 3D surface simplification. In ICPR (p./pp. 845-848). IEEE Computer Society.

Zhao, Y., Liu, Y., & Zeng, Z. (2013). Using Region-Based Saliency for 3D Interest Points Detection. In R. C. Wilson, E. R. Hancock, A. G. Bors & W. A. P. Smith (Eds.), CAIP (vol. 2, pp. 108-116). Springer.

Zhao, Y., Liu, Y., Song, R., & Zhang, M. (2012). Extended non-local means filter for surface saliency detection. In ICIP (p./pp. 633-636). IEEE. doi:10.1109/ICIP.2012.6466939

Zhao, W., Kang, L., & Irwin, G. W. (2013). A New Gradient Descent Approach for Local Learning of Fuzzy Neural Models. *IEEE Transactions on Fuzzy Systems, 21*(1), 30–44. doi:10.1109/TFUZZ.2012.2200900

Zheng, Y., & Elmaghraby, A. (2011). A brief survey on multispectral face recognition and multimodal score fusion. *Signal Processing and Information Technology (ISSPIT), 2011 IEEE International Symposium on*, 543–550. 10.1109/ISSPIT.2011.6151622

Zheng, H. a. (2015). Underwater image segmentation via dark channel prior and multiscale hierarchical decomposition. *Oceans*.

Zheng, L., Noroozi, V., & Yu, P. S. (2017). Joint deep modeling of users and items using reviews for recommendation. In *Proceedings of the Tenth ACM International Conference on Web Search and Data Mining* (pp. 425-434). ACM. 10.1145/3018661.3018665

Zhou, S., Wang, J., Zhang, S., Liang, Y., & Gong, Y. (2016). Active contour model based on local and global intensity information for medical image segmentation. *Neurocomputing, 186*, 107–118. doi:10.1016/j.neucom.2015.12.073

Zhuang, J., & Hoi, S. C. (2011). A two-view learning approach for image tag ranking. In *Proceedings of the fourth ACM international conference on Web search and data mining* (pp. 625-634). ACM. 10.1145/1935826.1935913

Zhu, Q., Zhao, J., Du, Z., & Zhang, Y. (2010). Quantitative analysis of discrete 3D geometrical detail levels based on perceptual metric. *Computers & Graphics, 34*(1), 55–65. doi:10.1016/j.cag.2009.10.004

Zhu, X., Lei, Z., Yan, J., Yi, D., & Li, S. Z. (2015). High-fidelity pose and expression normalization for face recognition in the wild. In *Proceedings of the IEEE Conference on Computer Vision and Pattern Recognition* (pp. 787-796). IEEE.

Zhu, Y., Zhao, M., Zhao, Y., Li, H., & Zhang, P. (2012). Noise reduction with low dose CT data based on a modified ROF model. *Optics Express, 20*(16), 17987–18004. doi:10.1364/OE.20.017987 PMID:23038347

Zimmerman, J. B., Pizer, S. M., Staab, E. V., Perry, J. R., McCartney, W., & Brenton, B. C. (1988). An evaluation of the effectiveness of adaptive histogram equalization for contrast enhancement. *IEEE Transactions on Medical Imaging, 7*(4), 304–312. doi:10.1109/42.14513 PMID:18230483

Compilation of References

Zitnick, C. L., Kang, S. B., Uyttendaele, M., Winder, S., & Szeliski, R. (2004, August). High-quality video view interpolation using a layered representation. *ACM Transactions on Graphics*, *23*(3), 600–608. doi:10.1145/1015706.1015766

Zudiema, P. (1983). A mechanistic approach to approach to threshold behavour of visual system. *IEEE Transactions on Systems, Man, and Cybernetics*, *13*(5), 923–934. doi:10.1109/TSMC.1983.6313088

Zuo, X., Du, C., Wang, S., Zheng, J., & Yang, R. (2015). Interactive visual hull refinement for specular and transparent object surface reconstruction. In *Proceedings of the IEEE International Conference on Computer Vision* (pp. 2237-2245). IEEE. 10.1109/ICCV.2015.258

About the Contributors

Tatyana Abramova is a PhD student of National research Tomsk state University. Area of scientific interest: neural networks, fuzzy logic, cognitive technologies. Author of more than 30 educational-methodical and scientific works, textbooks and monographs.

Rajiv Bajpai has received B.E Electronics from Jiwaji University Gwalior in 2007, India. Then he joined a telecommunication Company in India in which he worked as Network Engineer from 2007-2009. In 2009 he was awarded with MIUR Fellowship in 'Web and Multimedia Technology' and worked with TNT Lab in Genoa. In 2013 he was awarded his Ph.D. from DITEN, University of Genoa, Italy following the completion of HEAP Project, which included internship in KTH Stockholm. Rajiv has specialized in the field of Hardware Architecture with focus on Machine Learning in Multithreading in multicore architectures; his PhD work is based on the development process for current and future multi-core and multi-threaded architectures. He would like to extend his research in the field of Machine learning, Big Data analysis in multicore and multithreaded architecture system with respect to theory and practical aspects of application. In 2013-14, he also worked with Standard Chartered Bank Singapore in the field of Predictive analytics? Machine Learning and Big Data analysis. Today Dr. Bajpai is Research Scientist at Temasek Lab and conduct his research on Artificial intelligence, NLP and data mining. He is Guest Editor of many other top-tier AI journals, e.g., IEEE CIM and IEEE Intelligent Systems, Cycling, etc.

Christophe Charrier received the M.Sc. degree from the Nantes University of Science and Technology, Nantes, France, in 1993, and the Ph.D. degree from the University Jean Monnet, Sainttienne, France, in 1998. He has been an Associate Professor with the Communications, Networks and Services Department, Cherbourg Institute of Technology, Cherbourg, France, since 2001. From 1998 to 2001, he was a Research Assistant with the Laboratory of Radio Communications and Signal Processing, Laval University, Quebec, QC, Canada. In 2008, he was a Visiting Scholar with the Laboratory for Image and Video Engineering, University of Texas, Austin. From 2009 to 2011, he was an Invited Professor with the Computer Department, University of Sherbrooke, Sherbrooke, QC, Canada. His current research interests include digital image and video coding, processing, quality assessment, and computational vision.

Sheli Sinha Chaudhuri is Professor at ETCE Department of Jaduvpur University. She completed her B-Tech, M-Tech, and PhD at Jaduvpur University. She has a vast teaching experience of fourteen years. She has large number of papers in International and national level journals as well as conferences. Currently research scholars are pursuing PhD under her guidance. She is the member of IEEE and IEI.

Vishal Choudhary received his B.Tech. from Rajasthan Technical University, India in 2011. He received his M.Tech. in IIIT Bhubaneshwar, India in 2013. Currently, he is also working as a research engineer at the Singapore University of Technology and Design (SUTD). Prior joining SUTD, he has worked with FunLAB Chang Gung University, Taiwan and eCO Lab School of Computing NUS, Singapore as a research assistant. His research interests include the multimodal analysis of user-generated multimedia content in the support of social media applications, embedded computing, and multimedia applications.

Sanjoy Das completed his B.E. from Regional Engineering College, Durgapur, M.E. from Bengal Engineering College (Deemed Univ.), and Howrah, Ph.D. from Bengal Engineering and Science University, Shibpur. Currently he is working as Associate Professor in Dept. of Engineering and Technological Studies, University of Kalyani. His research interests are Tribology and Optimization Techniques.

Nilanjan Dey, PhD., is an Asst. Professor in the Department of Information Technology in Techno India College of Technology, Rajarhat, Kolkata, India. He holds an honorary position of Visiting Scientist at Global Biomedical Technologies Inc., CA, USA and Research Scientist of Laboratory of Applied Mathematical Modeling in Human Physiology, Territorial Organization Of- Sgientifig And Engineering Unions, BULGARIA, "Honorary Research Scientist" of Laboratory of Graph and Bioinformatics Algorithms (LGBA) - National Dong Hwa University, Taiwan. Associate Researcher of Laboratoire RIADI, University of Manouba, TUNISIA. He is the Editor-in-Chief of International Journal of Ambient Computing and Intelligence (IGI Global), US, Editor-in-Chief (co) of International Journal of Synthetic Emotion (IGI Global), US, International Journal of Rough Sets and Data Analysis (IGI Global), US, International Journal of Natural Computing Research (IGI Global), US, Series Editor of Advances in Geospatial Technologies (AGT) Book Series, (IGI Global), US, Associate editor of IEEE ACCESS, International Journal of Information Technology, Springer, Executive Editor of International Journal of Image Mining (IJIM), Inderscience, Regional Editor-Asia of International Journal of Intelligent Engineering Informatics (IJIEI), Inderscience and Associated Editor of International Journal of Service Science, Management, Engineering, and Technology, IGI Global. His research interests include: Medical Imaging, Soft computing, Data mining, Machine learning, Rough set, Mathematical Modeling and Computer Simulation, Modeling of Biomedical Systems, Robotics and Systems, Information Hiding, Security, Computer Aided Diagnosis, Atherosclerosis. He has 15 books and 250 international conferences and journal papers. He is a life member of IE, UACEE, ISOC, etc.

Krishna Gopal Dhal completed his B.Tech and M. Tech from Kalyani Government Engineering College. Currently he is working as Assistant Professor in the department of Computer Sc. & Application, Midnapore College (Autonomous). His research interests are image Processing and Nature inspired optimisation Algorithms.

Soumyadip Dhar is currently an Assistant Professor Dept. of IT, RCCIIT.

Deepika Dubey was born on 10 September 1988 in Gwalior Madhya Pradesh India. she has completed his schooling from Kendrya Vidhyala No.1 Gwalior. She has completed her Bachelor of Engineering and Master of Engineering from RGPV University, Bhopal, India. At present, she is perusing Ph.D. from Uttrakhand Technical University, Dehradun, India. Her area of interest are Image Processing, Computer Vision, and networking.

Rimon Elias received the M.C.S. and Ph.D. degrees in computer science from the University of Ottawa, Ottawa, ON, Canada, in 1999 and 2004, respectively. He is the author of "Modeling of Environments" published by Lambert Academic Publishing, "Digital Media: A Problem-solving Approach for Computer Graphics" published by Springer and of several book chapters, encyclopedia, journal, and conference papers. His interests embrace different image-related fields including computer vision, image processing, computer graphics, and visualization.

Siddesh G. K. is an Associate Professor in JSS Academy of Technical Education Bangalore, obtained his Bachelors and Masters Degree in Electronics and Communication Engineering from Bangalore University and Manipal Academy of Higher Education, Karnataka respectively. He also obtained his doctoral degree from Visvesvaraya Technological University Belgaum, Karnataka, India. He has 20 international journal publications/international conference publication to his credit. His research area and area of specialization includes Wireless communication, Computer Networks, Image and Data compression and Processing.

Mohamed Gabr received the M.C.S. in computer science from the German University in Cairo, Cairo, Egypt, in 2013. He is a Faculty Member in the department of Computer Science & Engineering, faculty of Media Engineering and Technology, German University in Cairo, Cairo, Egypt. His research interests are in computer vision and image processing with applications to image-based modeling.

Sergey Gorbachev is a senior researcher of international laboratory "Computer Vision Systems" of National research Tomsk state University. Area of scientific interest: data mining, management of complex objects, forecasting, foresight, neural networks, fuzzy logic, cognitive technologies. Author of more than 100 educational-methodical and scientific works, textbooks and monographs, 17 inventions and certificates in the field of cutting-edge interdisciplinary research in neuro-fuzzy economics, psychology, technical and medical diagnostics, robotics, exploration.

Anandakumar H., Associate Professor, Department of Computer Science and Engineering, Sri Eshwar College of Engineering,, Coimbatore, Tamilnadu, India has completed his Master's in Software Engineering from PSG College of Technology, Coimbatore. Currently he is pursuing his PhD in Information and Communication Engineering from PSG College of Technology under, Anna University, Chennai. He has published more than 35 papers in international journals. His research areas include Cognitive Radio Networks, Mobile Communications and Networking Protocols.

Shashidhara H. R. is working as Assistant Professor in the Department of Electronics and Communication Engineering, JSS Academy of Technical Education, Begaluru and obtained his doctoral degree in VLSI and Image processing from Visvesvaraya Technological University, Belgaum, India. He obtained his M. Tech degree in VLSI Design and Embedded System from Visvesvaraya Technological University in the year 2008 and Bachelor of Engineering in Electronics and Communication from Mangalore University in the year 2001. His major area of research On-Chip and ASIC implementation of Image processing techniques, TLM architecture and Verification Methodologies, Network on chip design and implementation, Biometric and Image processing. He is Life member of IETE.

R. Sukesh Kumar, PhD, is a Professor in Department of Electronics and Communication Engineering at Birla Institute of Technology in Mesra, Ranchi, in India. His main area of research includes Medical Imaging, CBIR, Image Watermarking.

Olivier Lézoray, received the M.Sc. and doctoral degrees in computer science from University of Normandie, France, in 1996 and 2000, respectively. From 1999 to 2000, he was an assistant professor in the Computer Science Department at the same university. From 2000 to 2009, he was an associate professor at the Cherbourg Institute of Technology in the Communication Networks and Services Department. Since 2010, he has been a full professor at the Cherbourg Institute of Technology. His research is focused on color image segmentation and filtering (graph-based variational and morphological methods) and machine-learning techniques for image mining (neural networks and support vector machines).

Hong Lin holds a Ph.D. in Computer Science. His graduate work includes theoretical and empirical studies of parallel programming models and implementations. Dr. Lin has worked on large-scale computational biology at Purdue University, active networks at the National Research Council Canada, and network security at Nokia, Inc. Dr. Lin joined UHD at 2001 and he is currently a professor in computer science. He has worked on parallel computing, multi-agent systems, and affective computing since he joined UHD. He established the Grid Computing Lab at UHD through an NSF MRI grant. He has been a Scholars Academy mentor, an REU faculty mentor, and a CAHSI faculty mentor. He is a senior member of ACM. A faculty member at University of Houston-Downtown since 2001.

Debanjan Mahata is a Research Scientist at Infosys Limited in Palo Alto, California. He received his B.Sc and M.Sc in Computer Science from Banaras Hindu University, India in 2008 and 2010, respectively. He received his PhD from University of Arkansas at Little Rock, USA in 2015. His research interest includes identifying event-specific informative content from user generated data in social media channels, applying deep learning techniques to natural language processing tasks like phrase embeddings, keyword extraction, text summarization and semantic similarity between text documents. He has received Outstanding Publication Award and Outstanding PhD Graduate award from University of Arkansas at Little Rock in the year 2015. He is involved in reviewing research articles from many international conferences and journals.

Mahmoud Mahmood is an assistant professor in Cairo University.

Flor Morton is currently an Associate Research Professor at Universidad de Monterrey. She holds a Ph.D. in Management Sciences from EGADE Business School, Tecnológico de Monterrey and graduated with honors of a Major in Marketing from the same University. She has collaborated as a marketing consultant in diverse projects for national and international companies. Her research interests focus on sensory marketing and digital technologies.

Anass Nouri received both the M.Sc. degree in intelligent systems and imaging from the IBN TOFAIL-University, Kenitra, Morocco and the M.Sc. degree in telecommunications and image processing from the University of Poitiers, France in 2013. In 2016, he obtained the Ph.D. degree in computer science from the University of Caen Normandie. He was an assistant professor in the computer science department at the High School of Engineering of Caen (ENSICAEN). Currently, he is a postdoctoral researcher at the Institut du Thorax-INSERM at the University of Nantes. His current research interests include 3D mesh processing, visual saliency of 3D meshes/2D digital images, quality assessment of 3D meshes/2D digital images, 2D/3D medical imaging and computational vision.

Soujanya Poria received his BEng in Computer Science from Jadavpur University, India in 2013. He then joined Nanyang Technological University as a research engineer in the School of Electrical and Electronics Engineering, and later in 2015, he joined NTU Temasek Labs, where he is conducting research on sentiment analysis in multiple domains and different modalities. Since February 2014, Soujanya has also started his PhD studies at the University of Stirling (Computing Science and Mathematics). His research areas include natural language processing, opinion mining, cognitive science and multimodal sentiment analysis. In 2013, Soujanya received the best undergraduate thesis and researcher award from Jadavpur University. He was awarded Gold Plated Silver medal from the University and Tata Consultancy Service for his final year project during his undergraduate course. He is also a fellow of the Brain Sciences Foundation and a program committee member of SENTIRE, the IEEE ICDM workshop series on sentiment analysis.

Arulmurugan R. received his PhD. degrees in Information and Communication Engineering from Anna University, Chennai, Tamil Nadu, India. He is currently working as Assistant Professor in the Department of Information Technology, Bannari Amman Institute of Technology, Sathyamangalam, Tamil Nadu. His research interests include Digital Image Processing, Biomedical Image Processing Computer vision, pattern recognition, and machine learning.

Swarnajit Ray completed his BTech from the Narula Institute of Technology and MTech from the Kalyani Government Engineering College, West Bengal, India. Currently, he is working as a Software Engineer in JBMatrix Technology Pvt. Ltd., India. His research interests are Digital image processing and Medical Imaging.

Hiranmoy Roy is currently Assistant Professor Dept. of IT, RCCIIT.

Sangita Roy is an Assistant Professor at ECE Department of Narula Institute of Technology under WBUT. She has a teaching experience of more than eighteen years. She was in Bells Controls Limited (instrumentation industry) for two years and West Bengal State Centre, IEI (Kolkata) in administration for two years. She completed her Diploma (ETCE), A.M.I.E (ECE) and M-Tech (Comm. Egg.). Currently perusing her PhD under Dr. Sheli Sinha Chaudhuri at ETCE Department of Jaduvpur University since 2012. She is the member of IEI, IETE, FOSET, ISOC, and IEEE ComSoc. She has published Journals as well as conference papers. Research interest included Data Mining, Machine learning and soft computing applications. Editorial board member of several reputed journals. Published more than 110 research papers in various reputed journals and conference proceedings. Senior member of IEEE and Life member of CSI. Edited more than forty conference proceedings from Springer LNCS, AISC, LNEE, SIST.

Priyank Saxena, ME, is an assistant professor at the Department of Electronics and Communication Engineering, Birla Institute of Technology, Ranchi. He received his Master of Engineering degree in 2007. His area of interest includes Medical Imaging, Image watermarking, Computer Networking.

Mandira Sen completed her B.Tech from Academy of Technology and M.Tech from Kalyani Government Engineering College, West Bengal, India. Her research interests are Digital image processing and medical imaging.

Rajiv Ratn Shah received his B.Sc. with honors in Mathematics from Banaras Hindu University, India in 2005. He received his M.Tech. in Computer Technology and Applications from Delhi Technological University, India in 2010. Prior joining Indraprastha Institute of Information Technology Delhi (IIIT Delhi) as an assistant professor, Dr Shah has received his PhD in Computer Science from the National University of Singapore. Currently, he is also working as a research fellow in living analytics research centre (LARC) at the Singapore Management University. His research interests include the multimodal analysis of user-generated multimedia content in the support of social media applications, multimodal event detection and recommendation, and multimedia analysis, search, and retrieval. Dr Shah is the recipient of several awards, including the prestigious European Research Consortium for Informatics and Mathematics (ERCIM) Fellowship and runner-up in the Grand Challenge competition of ACM International Conference on Multimedia. He is involved in reviewing of many top-tier international conferences and journals.

Uday Singh was born on February 6, 1979 in Sultanpur, U.P., India. Dr. Singh graduated in Mathematics from Dr. Ram Manohar Lohiya University Sultanpur, U.P. in 1998. He obtained his first M.Sc. degree in Mathematics & Statistics (Gold Medalist) in 2000, from Dr. Ram Manohar Lohiya University Faizabad, U.P. and Second M.Sc. degree in Mathematics & Computing from Indian Institute of Technology, Guwahati. He later received his Doctorate Degree in Computer Science from Barkatullah University, Bhopal, in 2013. He is currently working as an Assistant Professor in the Department of Applied Mathematics, Madhav Institute of Technology & Science, Gwalior, India. Dr. Singh has published/presented about 56 research papers in International/National Journals and at Conferences, 08 Book Chapters on Evolutionary Computation, Soft Computing, Image Processing, etc. His areas of research include Nature Inspired Metaheuristic Algorithm, Soft Computing, and Image Processing etc. He has also qualified from CSIR (NET). He is a life member of the Computer Society of India and IAENG.

Rajinikanth V., PhD., is Professor in the Department of Electronics and Instrumentation Engineering in St. Joseph's College of Engineering, Chennai, Tamilnadu, India. His research interests include: Medical Imaging, Soft computing, Controller design, Mathematical Modeling and Computer Simulation. He has 50 international conferences and journal papers.

Index

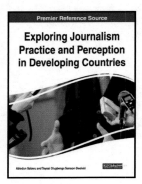

Ensure Quality Research is Introduced to the Academic Community

Become an IGI Global Reviewer for Authored Book Projects

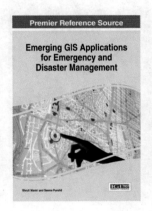
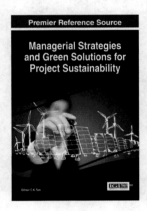

The overall success of an authored book project is dependent on quality and timely reviews.

In this competitive age of scholarly publishing, constructive and timely feedback significantly expedites the turnaround time of manuscripts from submission to acceptance, allowing the publication and discovery of forward-thinking research at a much more expeditious rate. Several IGI Global authored book projects are currently seeking highly qualified experts in the field to fill vacancies on their respective editorial review boards:

Applications may be sent to:
development@igi-global.com

Applicants must have a doctorate (or an equivalent degree) as well as publishing and reviewing experience. Reviewers are asked to write reviews in a timely, collegial, and constructive manner. All reviewers will begin their role on an ad-hoc basis for a period of one year, and upon successful completion of this term can be considered for full editorial review board status, with the potential for a subsequent promotion to Associate Editor.

If you have a colleague that may be interested in this opportunity, we encourage you to share this information with them.

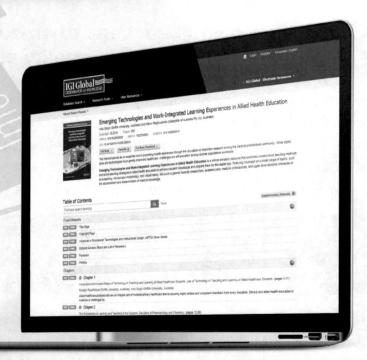

Printed in the United States
By Bookmasters